From the BEAST *to the* BLONDE

Under the sign 'Mother Goose Tales', an old servant spins by the hearth, telling her fairy tales to the children of the family. The frontispiece to Charles Perrault's collection Histoires ou contes du temps passé *of 1697, might have been inspired by his own family.*

From the BEAST *to the* BLONDE

ON FAIRY TALES AND THEIR TELLERS

246

MARINA WARNER

FARRAR, STRAUS AND GIROUX
NEW YORK

Copyright © 1994 by Marina Warner
All rights reserved
Printed in the United States of America
Originally published in 1994 by Chatto & Windus
First American edition, 1995

Library of Congress Cataloging-in-Publication Data
Warner, Marina.
From the beast to the blonde:
on fairy tales and their tellers /
Marina Warner.
p.   cm.
Includes bibliographical references and index.
1. Fairy tales—History and criticism.
2. Women—Folklore.
3. Feminist literary criticism.
I. Title.
GR550.W38   1995   398.2—dc20   94-33640   CIP

Acknowledgements

Icould not have begun to tell the story I have put down here without the help of numerous friends and colleagues. I began the research as a Visiting Scholar at the Getty Center for the History of Art and the Humanities in 1987–8, where I was given precious time to write as well as access to superb bibliographical support: to all the staff there, my profound thanks, especially to John Walsh, Kurt Forster, Herb Hymans, Thomas Kren, Marcia Reed and the researchers, Amy Morris and Lori Repetti. My colleagues there and in the wider circle of Los Angeles that year were an inspiration: Caroline Walker Bynum, Ruth Mellinkoff, David Kunzle, Svetlana Alpers, Daniel Selden, Ellen Kemp, Wolfgang Kemp, Martin Lowry, Carl Schorske, Charles Dill, Conrad Rudolph created a community of argument and knowledge which sharpened my wits and gave me many new ways of looking at material. The first ideas for the book were written as a series of eight public lectures on fairy tales as Tinbergen Professor at Erasmus University, Rotterdam (1989–90); in the Netherlands, Rudolf Dekker, Lotte van de Pol, and Jan van Herwaarden were true friends, and also helped with excellent advice and numerous references. Gerard Rooijakhers shared with me his wide knowledge of catchpenny prints and popular illustration. In 1993, I was made a Visiting Fellow of The British Film Institute, where I continued very enjoyable research into the theme, as explored in film. To Colin MacCabe and Duncan Petrie, special thanks.

At different stages in my quest, the path was marked by Peter Dronke, Mariët Westermann, Terence Cave, Malcolm Jones, Ruth Padel, David Constantine, Jack Zipes, Ruth Bottigheimer, and my debt to them is very deep. Peter Dronke also read part of the finished typescript and saved me from many horrors; Terence Cave read the final draft and gave me the benefit of his perception and learning. I am profoundly grateful to them both. Susannah Clapp put inspiring and fascinating books my way for review: for this, much thanks. So too have Alan Hollinghurst, Jan Dalley, Lyndsay Duguid, Blake Morrison. Many libraries and librarians helped me: Tessa Chester of the Renier Collection, Clive Hurst of the Bodleian's Special Collections, the staff of the Osborne Collection, Toronto, of the Pierpont Morgan Library in New York, of the Clark Collection in Los Angeles, of the Victoria and Albert Museum, the London Library, the Warburg Institute and, of course, the British Library. Various lectures I gave often prompted some extremely acute and rich responses, so my thanks are due to all who invited me and came to hear and comment.

Iona Opie, Dubravka Ugrešić, A. D. Deyermond, Lisa Appignanesi, John Dickson, John Forrester, Elaine Showalter, Roy Porter, Patricia Morison, Joanna Innes, Jacqueline Simpson, Arnold Smeets, Roy Judge, Diane Purkiss, Valerie Yule, Mathilde van Dijk, Robert Smith, Scott Mandelbrote, Dimphena Groffen, David Scrase, Hermione Lee, Roy Foster, Laura Mulvey, Paul Taylor, Birté Carlé, Ben Haggarty, Jennifer Chandler, Naomi Lewis, Ella Westland, Joseph Farrell, Susan Rubin Suleiman, Roger Cardinal, Julia O'Faolain and Lauro Martines, Janet Nelson, Roger Malbert, Jet Bakels, Anneke Mulder-Bakker, Norman F. Cantor, Henri Colomer, Richard Wentworth, Kathleen Davis, W. A. Jackson, Joan Aiken, Isabel Cardigos, Margaret Meek, Nicholas Tucker all gave me vital information and insights at different stages. Misri De, Ben Ramos, Linda Weston, Daniel Welldon, James Forrester, Anne Francis gave me support in different ways, and I thank them all and hope that they do not object too strongly to the results.

Special acknowledgements are due, for the quotations I have used from their poetry, to Eavan Boland, 'What we Lost …' from *Outside History*, Carcanet Press; Olga Broumas, 'Cinderella' from *Beginning with O*, Yale University Press; Liz Lochhead, 'Men Talk' from *True Confessions and New Clichés*, and 'The Storyteller' from *Dreaming Frankenstein*, Polygon; and Ruth Padel, 'Reading Snow White' from *Summer Snow*, Hutchinson.

At my publishers, I was given every encouragement and great friendship throughout; the appearance of this book results from the work and care of Peggy Sadler, Anna Pinter and Pippa Lewis. The support I was shown by Carmen Callil gave me the energy and conviction I needed; the editing and criticism of Alison Samuel have been tonic and invaluable. To Jonathan Burnham and Frances Coady, too, much thanks, for encouragement throughout. Gill Coleridge has battled spiritedly on my behalf, and I am very grateful indeed to her. As the book has taken me several years, there were more helpers on the way (those kindly spirits who appear in misfortune to grant a boon) and they scattered so much more flour, a bounty of crumbs for me to follow down new tracks. John Dewe Mathews never abandoned me: a rare patience and understanding, and the book would not have been made without him. To them all, salaams, and more than three wishes, if it could be.

Marina Warner
Kentish Town, 1994

For Ruth Padel, in friendship
With Gwen in mind

Contents

The author, Giovanni Boccaccio, is depicted seated outside the circle of storytellers, eavesdropping as they take turns to while away their time of voluntary exile from plague-stricken Florence. This fifteenth-century frontispiece to The Decameron sustains the narrative convention that male authors often acted as mouthpieces for women's firsthand experience.

Introduction

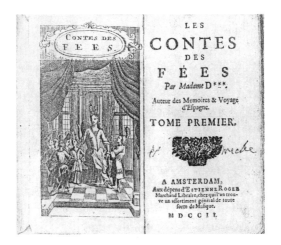

In her first anthology of fairy tales, Angela Carter included a story from Kenya: while a poor man's wife in the village thrives, the Sultana in the palace grows thinner and scrappier by the minute. The Sultan summons the poor man and demands to know the secret of his wife's happiness. 'Very simple,' he replies. 'I feed her meat of the tongue.' The Sultan sends out for all the tongues money can buy – ox tongues and lambs' tongues and larks' tongues; still his sad Sultana withers away. He orders his litter, makes her change places with the poor man's wife; she immediately starts to thrive, becoming the picture of health, plumper, rosier, gayer. Meanwhile, in the palace, her replacement languishes, and soon has become as scrawny and miserable as the former queen.

For the tongue meats that the poor man feeds the women are not material, of course. They are fairy tales, stories, jokes, songs; he nourishes them on talk, he wraps them in language; he banishes melancholy by refusing silence. Storytelling makes women thrive – and not exclusively women, the Kenyan fable implies, but other sorts of people, too, even sultans.

When I was young and highly robust, I still felt great hunger for fairy tales; they

Madame D ***, otherwise Marie-Catherine le Jumel de Barneville, Baronne d'Aulnoy, was one of the leading enthusiasts in the new literary fashion for telling fairy stories, orally in salons as well as on the page, in Paris at the end of the seventeenth century. (Frontispiece to one of several collections she wrote, Contes des fées, *Amsterdam, 1702.)*

seemed to offer the possibility of change, far beyond the boundaries of their improbable plots or fantastically illustrated pages. The metamorphoses promised more of the same, not only in fairy land, but in this world, and this instability of appearances, these sudden swerves of destiny, created the first sustaining excitement of such stories. Like romance, to which fairy tales bear a strong affinity, they could 'remake the world in the image of desire'. That this is a blissful dream which need not be dismissed as totally foolish is central to the argument of this book.

I decided, for this study, to start with the collection which inaugurated the fairy tale as a literary form for children: Charles Perrault's *Histoires ou contes du temps passé*, or *Contes de ma Mère l'Oye*, of 1697. The book, published in Paris, contains 'The Sleeping Beauty', 'Red Riding Hood', 'Bluebeard', 'Puss in Boots', 'Cinderella, or the Little Glass Slipper', and 'Tom Thumb' – some of the best known and best loved fairy tales in the world. This small volume is the stone I cast, and I then followed the wave patterns it made as the Perrault tales set ripples in motion which crossed stories by his contemporaries and friends, as well as later tales, from the Grimm Brothers' *Die Kinder- und Hausmärchen* (Children's and Household Tales, 1812–57) and Hans Christian Andersen's collection of 1837–74. Charting from the Perrault epicentre, as it were, meant I was focussing on fairy tales with family dramas at their heart, rather than the jests and riddles, animal fables and proverbial cautionary tales also often described under the catch-all name of fairy tale.

I began investigating the meanings of the tales themselves, but I soon found that it was essential to look at the context in which they were told, at who was telling them, to whom, and why. In the eyes of posterity, Charles Perrault (1628–1703) has become the most famous pioneer teller of fairy tales. But he was greatly outnumbered, and in some instances also preceded, by women aficionadas of *contes de fées* whose work has now faded from view. *Le Cabinet des fées* (The Fairy Library), a series of forty-one volumes which published hundreds of the tales of the seventeenth and eighteenth centuries, the heyday of the genre as a literary form, includes more than twenty authors; of these over half are women. Marie-Catherine, Baronne d'Aulnoy, has a volume of stories to herself, and several more tales in subsequent volumes, while some of the men contribute only a single tale, as in the case of the philosopher Jean-Jacques Rousseau and his story, '*La Reine fantasque*'. The pattern of female authorship is repeated in a companion sequence of volumes, entitled *Voyages imaginaires, songes, visions et romans cabalistiques*. Fantastic journeys are mixed up with magic-realist novels and fairy tales by

D'Aulnoy and other women contemporaries, like Henriette-Julie de Castelnau, Comtesse de Murat.

These editions solicited an adult audience; the older generation were being eased into taking pleasure in make-believe, in pretending they had become child-like again and had returned to the pleasures of their youth through tales of magic and enchantment and the homespun wisdom of the hearth. In 1714, the court tutor the Abbé Fénelon, writing to a friend, said that the most serious men today enjoy 'fables – even those which are like fairy tales … We willingly become children again.'

When I was a child, the escapism implied by such wishful thinking made liking fairy tales slightly shameful; with their pinnacled castles and rose-wreathed princesses, their enchanted sleeps and dashing princes showing a leg, they were also definitely girly, and though the accusation was never spoken aloud in my hearing, the taste for them revealed lack of intellectual – and possibly moral – fibre. Boys might surrender to the pleasures fairy tales offered before they were

Charles Perrault was a distinguished scholar, courtier, poet and polemicist. The glass slipper and the pumpkin coach appear in print for the first time in his 'Cinderella'; he also published several of the best known fairy tales, such as 'The Sleeping Beauty in the Wood', 'Red Riding Hood', 'Tom Thumb' and 'Puss in Boots'. (Eighteenth century, after François Tortebat's portrait.)

CHARLES PERRAULT

Né à Paris en 1637. Mort en 1703.

taught otherwise, but they soon sternly put them away, like skipping and doll's houses, and would scoff from their superior world of electric trains and airforce yarns. Fairy tales offered gratifications that were already, at the age of eleven, considered feminine: dreams of love as well as the sweets of quick and capital revenge; they became part of the same private world of growing up female as the treasure drawer in which I hoarded special pictures and tokens or the diary which came with a key.

I was given collections to read – two or three of the Andrew Lang coloured Fairy Books, French anthologies, Hans Christian Andersen – but I was expected to grow out of them, I could tell. 'Fond and amorous Romances and fabulous Histories of Giants ... imprint false Notions, and irregular Conceits, and fill the Heads of Children with vain, silly and idle imaginations,' protested one author of an improving paraphrase of Genesis in 1690. His plaint goes on echoing: Rousseau recommended banning fairy tales from his model pupil Emile's curriculum. Children were already quite imaginative enough, in his view, and there should be no surrender to their love of fantasy and excitement. Even John Updike commented, as recently as 1988, on the wonderful, rich, vibrant collection of Italian folk tales made by the fabulist Italo Calvino, 'their inner glint, their old life, is escapism. They were the television and pornography of their day, the life-lightening trash of preliterate peoples ...' Fairy tales were tarnished too for different, feminist reasons: critics in the 1970s found Cinderella's story an oppressor's script for female domestication – the prince's castle as a girl's ultimate goal. As the Ugly Sisters sing in one Victorian pantomime:

> We'll work ourselves, and never have another kitchen-maid,
> We have been idle all our lives – we'll try another way
> And be industrious instead – it really seems to pay.

But fairy tales survived, irrepressibly, and I have become even more drawn to them as I have grown older, because they began to represent childhood, that vividness of experience in the midst of inexperience, the capacity for daydreaming and wonder. I have since discovered that there is nothing in the least childlike about fairy tales, and this, together with the suspect whiff of femininity hanging around them, attracted me to study them.

The Russian structuralist Vladimir Propp preferred to use the term 'wonder tale', from the German *Wundermärchen*, to embrace both fairy tales and folk tales. But I have continued to use 'fairy tale' in this book because I am concentrating on

Marie-Jeanne L'Héritier de Villandon hotly defended 'the old wives' tale' against its detractors, wrote spirited stories herself, and influenced her older cousin Charles Perrault in the recovery of fairy tales as a legitimate branch of French literature. (Early eighteenth century.)

stories that have always been called by that term, even when they do not feature any fairy characters: in Perrault's 'Red Riding Hood' the wolf talks, and in 'Bluebeard' the bloodstained key is *'fée'* (magic), but there are no winged messengers from the other world, above or below; Marie-Jeanne L'Héritier's 'The Subtle Princess' (*'L'Adroite Princesse, ou Les aventures de Finette'*) shows the heroine's cunning escape from a cruel predator, by using her wits, although the narrative moves through a landscape stocked with such wonders as doorless towers where maidens are kept prisoner, glass distaffs which shatter by magic, and barrels lined with knives.

Shape-shifting is one of fairy tale's dominant and characteristic wonders: hands are cut off, found and reattached, babies' throats are slit, but they are later restored to life, a rusty lamp turns into an all-powerful talisman, a humble pestle and mortar becomes the winged vehicle of the fairy enchantress Baba Yaga, the beggar changes into the powerful enchantress and the slattern in the filthy donkeyskin into a golden-haired princess. More so than the presence of fairies, the moral function, the imagined antiquity and oral anonymity of the ultimate source, and the happy ending (though all these factors help towards a definition of the genre), metamorphosis defines the fairy tale.

The marvels and prodigies, the seven-league boots and enchanted mirrors, the talking animals, the heroes and heroines changed into frogs or bears or cats, the golden eggs and everflowing supplies of porridge, the stars on the brow of the good sister and the donkeytail sprouting on the brow of the bad – all the wonders that create the atmosphere of fairy tale disrupt the apprehensible world in order to open spaces for dreaming alternatives. The verb 'to wonder' communicates the receptive state of marvelling as well as the active desire to know, to inquire, and as such it defines very well at least two characteristics of the traditional fairy tale: pleasure in the fantastic, curiosity about the real. The dimension of wonder creates a huge theatre of possibility in the stories: anything can happen. This very boundlessness serves the moral purpose of the tales, which is precisely to teach where boundaries lie. The dreaming gives pleasure in its own right, but it also represents a practical dimension to the imagination, an aspect of the faculty of thought, and can unlock social and public possibilities.

Paradoxically, the remoteness of their traditional setting – the palace, the forest, the distant and nameless kingdom, the anonymity and lack of particularity of their cast of characters, the kings and queens and princesses with names like Beauty or the Fair with the Golden Hair – which could not belong to anybody in the social and historical milieu of the tellers or the receivers of the tale – all this underpins the stories' ability to grapple with reality. As Wallace Stevens believed, it helps us to see the actual world to visualize a fantastic one. Fairy tales typically use the story of something in the remote past to look towards the future, their conclusions, their 'happy endings' do not always bring about total closure, but make promises, prophecies. Despite all their supernatural elements, these are not tales of the uncanny either; they do not leave open prickly possibilities, or enter unnegotiated areas of the unknown, as in fantasy or surrealist literature or ghost stories, like *The Turn of the Screw* and some of M. R. James's inventions, and even at times the short stories of Raymond Carver. For 'The Sleeping Beauty' and 'Cinderella' and 'Donkeyskin' come to an orderly resolution, and the characters, one is left imagining, return to ordinary life. On the whole fairy tales are not passive or active; their mood is optative – announcing what might be. Imagining the fate that lies ahead and ways of dealing with it (if adverse – as in 'Hansel and Gretel' and 'Donkeyskin'), or achieving it (if favourable – as in 'Puss in Boots'), is the stuff of Mother Goose tales. The genre is characterized by 'heroic optimism', as if to say, 'one day, we might be happy, even if it won't last'.

The prodigies are introduced to serve this concealed but ever-present vision-ariness of the tale, and serve it well by disguising the stories' harshly realistic core: the magic entertainment helps the story look like a mere bubble of nonsense from the superstitious mind of ordinary, negligible folk. The enchantments also uni-versalize the narrative setting, encipher concerns, beliefs and desires in brilliant, seductive images that are themselves a form of camouflage, making it possible to utter harsh truths, to say what you dare. The disregard for logic, all those fairytale non-sequiturs and improbable reversals, rarely encompasses the emotional con-flicts themselves: hatred, jealousy, kindness, cherishing retain an intense integrity throughout. The double vision of the tales, on the one hand charting perennial drives and terrors, both conscious and unconscious, and on the other mapping actual, volatile experience, gives the genre its fascination and power to satisfy. At the same time, uncovering the context of the tales, their relation to society and history, can yield more of a happy resolution than the story itself delivers with its challenge to fate: 'They lived happily ever after' consoles us, but gives scant help compared to 'Listen, this is how it was before, but things could change – and they might.'

But trying to do this, to place fairy tales in relation to society and history, is hampered from the start by the difficulty of composing any kind of firm chron-ology or origin. The collector of stories may find a silent princess or an enchanted ass in a new, earlier manuscript, but these examples do not mean the older version is the ancestor of the other. One theory, diffusionism, holds that stories are passed on across borders, from distant origins – often Eastern: India is, for instance, invoked as the source of a seminal collection of seventy tales, the *Panchatantra* (The Five Books), which was put together around the sixth century AD, and attributed to Bidpai (or Pilpay), a legendary Brahmin sage. Jean de La Fontaine, wandering along the quais in Paris in the 1660s, came across a volume by Bidpai; he bought it, and the tales he read there became one of the founding inspirations of his own Fables, commonly assumed to represent the apogee of Gallic urbanity. Elements of Greek romance, Roman moralities, Arabian nights, animal fables, medieval jests, pious saints' lives jostle and unite with unbuttoned lack of inhibi-tion in the fairy tale. The nature of the genre is promiscuous and omnivorous and anarchically heterogeneous, absorbing high and low elements, tragic and comic tones into its often simple, rondo-like structure of narrative. Motifs and plotlines are nomadic, travelling the world and the millennia, turning up on parchment in medieval Persia, in an oral form in the Pyrenees, in a ballad sung in the Highlands, in a fairy story in the Caribbean.

An opposing theory – of archetypes – proposes that the structures of the imagination and the common experiences of human society inspire narrative solutions that resemble one another even when there can have been no contact or exchange: there are tales of animal metamorphosis in the legends of the Algonquin and other Native American peoples, which seem to echo – or vice versa – Asian and European fairytale transformations. But there are problems of vagueness with these comparisons; when it comes to details of narratives and particular plot features (splinters of flax which cause a beauty to fall into an enchanted sleep; invisible attendants and dishes which appear of their own accord in a magic castle), a literary source usually lies at the story's origin. Exchanges between voice and text then continually take place, adding, enriching, adapting, changing, in ceaseless permutation of motifs and pattern. The Hellenistic tale of 'Cupid and Psyche' provides powerful evidence of the dependency of the genre on texts: until a manuscript of the second-century metaphysical romance *The Golden Ass*, in which it appears, was rediscovered, perhaps by Boccaccio, this pair of star-crossed lovers do not leave a trace in medieval narrative. Similarly, the story of another famous couple of lovers, *Aucassin et Nicolette*, becomes the stuff of fairy tale again only after the one surviving manuscript is recovered in 1715. A version, the story '*Etoilette*' (Starlight), attributed to the Comtesse de Murat, then appears almost simultaneously (see Chapter Eleven).

Remarkable, exhaustive efforts have been made, notably by the folklorists of the Scandinavian school, Antti Aarne and Stith Thompson, to tabulate and classify systematically story types and motifs within the stories. But this taxonomy provides a list of ingredients and recipes with no evocation of their taste or the pleasure of the final dish, nor sense of how or why it was eaten. However universally distributed, stories spring up in different places dressed in different moods, with different twists, and regional details and contexts which give the satisfaction of particular recognition to their audiences.

Because complex characters are rare, and the distribution of villainy and virtue is not muddied by ambiguity, Red Riding Hood or Snow White have become rich symbols for psychoanalysts to gloss. But the thrust towards universal significance has obscured the genre's equal powers to illuminate experiences embedded in social and material conditions. These are subject to change over time and ultimately more capable of redress than the universal lessons of greed, lust and cruelty which fairy tales give us; in one sense, the historical interpretation of fairy tale holds out more hope to the listener or the reader than the psychoanalytic or mystical approaches, because it reveals how human behaviour is embedded in material circumstance, in the laws of dowry, land tenure, feudal obedience, domestic hierarchies and marital dispositions, and that when these pass and change, behaviour may change with them.

Theorists today prefer to visualize models of fairy tales' dissemination by borrowing metaphors from science: wave theory offers an image of a stone thrown in a pond, radiating in rings outwards where they might meet other ripples and join in chevron patterns with other stones cast in other seas of story. Robert Irwin, in his 1994 companion to *The Arabian Nights*, offers an image from genetics, of a 'selfish word-string' which, like a selfish gene, continues to reproduce itself in different host bodies: the ragamuffin who becomes a beautiful princess, the simpleton who kills a giant, the monster who turns into a radiant bridegroom might present such selfishly unappeasable and indestructible word-strings. Yet another way to think of fairy tales is to imagine them as a language of the imagination, with a vocabulary of images and a syntax of plots.

But even when the teller is known and the circumstances of the telling are clear, fairy tales are still rebarbative as historical documents: the transmission problems make them resemble an archaeological site that has been plundered by tomb robbers, who have turned the strata upside down and inside out and thrown it all back again in any old order. Evidence of conditions from past social and economic arrangements co-exist in the tale with the narrator's innovations: Angela Carter's Beauty is lost to the Beast at cards, a modern variation on the ancient memory, locked into the plot of 'Beauty and the Beast', that daughters were given in marriage by their fathers without being consulted on the matter. The matter of fairy tale reflects such lived experience, with a slant towards the tribulations of women, and especially young women of marriageable age; the telling of the stories, assuming the presence of a Mother Goose, either as a historical source, or a fantasy of origin, gains credibility as a witness's record of lives lived, of characters known, and shapes expectations in a certain direction. Fairy tale offers a case where the very contempt for women opened an opportunity for them to exercise their wit and communicate their ideas: women's care for children, the prevailing disregard for both groups, and their presumed identity with the simple folk, the common people, handed them fairy tales as a different kind of nursery, where they might set their own seedlings and plant out their own flowers. Charting the circumstances of their making and remaking, analysing the politics and history embedded in the tales, does not mean trampling, I hope, on the sheer exuberance of their entertainment, or crushing the transcendent pleasures they so often give. For these are stories with staying power, as their antiquity shows, because the meanings they generate are themselves magical shape-shifters, dancing to the needs of their audience.

The first half of the book looks at storytelling, at its practitioners and images, in art, legend and history, from the prophesying enchantress who lures knights errant into her false paradise to the jolly old beldame, Mother Goose, and her masqueraders in the real world. The rich and fluctuating perceptions of women's relation to fancy and fairy tale became, as my work progressed, the absolutely necessary ground on which the familiar figures like Cinderella and her wicked stepmother stepped into place. Prejudices against women, especially old women and their chatter, belong in the history of fairy tale's changing status, for the pejorative image of the gossip was sweetened by influences from the tradition of the Sibyls and the cult of Saint Anne, until the archetypal crone by the hearth could emerge as a mouthpiece of homespun wisdom. I found that I was discovering a kind of fairytale origin for the figure of Mother Goose herself, as I followed the tracks left by the Queen of Sheba, taking me into Islamic as well as Christian territory. It turned out she had left a strangely shaped print – of either a hoof or a webbed foot – which led me on, deeper into the layered character of the traditional narrator. The interconnections of storytelling with heterodox forms of knowledge, with illicit science and riddles – the juggling tricks of the Devil – emerge, only to be themselves domesticated, contained by the context of the children's nursery. Once this imagined voice was established as legitimate for certain purposes – the instruction of the young – writers co-opted it as their own, using it as a mask for their own thoughts, their own mocking games and even sedition – from the élite *salonnière* in the old régime to Angela Carter in our time.

The second half of the book, The Tales, takes up a handful of the most familiar fairy tales themselves and, in the light of the tellers' position and interests, examines the painful rivalry and hatred between women in tales like 'Cinderella' and 'The Sleeping Beauty' and the possible reasons for this virulence in such loved stories. Somewhat like the pardon letters which criminals wrote from prison in the sixteenth century, in which they tried to move the king to a reprieve by describing their plight when they had murdered their wife, husband, or child, so the violence in fairy tales about family strife can often be read as offering a plea of extenuating circumstances. The fairy tale's relationship to romance gives the question of love pride of place among its concerns, and four chapters follow which take up the portrait of marriage – or, more particularly, of men and marriage: I look at the fears of young women through the tales of forced union with an ogre like Bluebeard. 'Beauty and the Beast' tells, in its many diverse variations, a different story, of a bridegroom redeemed from monstrousness; the changes to this fairy tale probably reveal, more clearly than in any other, the interweaving of social custom and law with fantasy narratives. It also encloses a microcosmic history of re-evaluated relations between humanity and animals, and different answers to the questions, who is the beast, who is the brute?

There follows an analysis of 'Donkeyskin', the fairy tale about a father who wants to marry his daughter, which tackles the meanings of incest as reflected in fairy tales. Once widely told, now almost suppressed, this peculiar story sympathetically dramatizes an early phase in the establishment of adolescent autonomy. The heroine disguises herself in a filthy donkeyskin to hide away after her father's proposal, but at the climactic moment her golden hair reveals her worth.

The blondeness of the fairytale beauty is one of the most potent and recurrent symbols within the genre, and I try to restore even this predominant, quasi-mystical image of light and vitality to its historical and social context. Some of the counterparts of 'Donkeyskin' take refuge from violation or unfair accusations in silence: so in the last chapter the issue of voice returns, for fairy tales give women a place from which to speak, but they sometimes speak of speechlessness as a weapon of last resort. The book, beginning with gossip as a woman's derided instrument of self-assertion, closes with muteness, as another stratagem of influence.

The happy endings of fairy tales are only the beginning of the larger story, and any study which attempts to encompass it wholly must stumble and fall before any kind of ending can be made: the story of storytelling is a tale that will never be done. As one traditional closing formula implies, the story is made by both together: 'This is my story, I've told it, and in your hands I leave it.'

From the BEAST *to the* BLONDE

PART ONE
The Tellers

The old woman sighed sympathetically. 'My pretty dear,' she said, 'you must be cheerful and stop worrying about dreams. The dreams that come in daylight are not to be trusted, everyone knows that, and even night-dreams go by contraries ... Now let me tell you a fairy tale or two to make you feel a little better.'

Apuleius

There are indeed many wonders, and with regard to the stories people tell one another, it may be that such tales go beyond the true account and, embellished with iridescent lies, beguile them.

Pindar

VLTIMA CVMÆI VENIT IAM
CARMINIS AETAS MAGNVS
ABINTEGRO SAECLORVM
NASCITVR ORDO IAM RE
DIT ET VIRGO REDEVNT
SATVRNIA REGNA IAM
NOVA PROGENIES CÆLO
DEMITTITVR ALTO

SIBYLLA CVMANA CVIVS MEMINIT VIRGILIVS ECLOG IV

The Sibyl of Cumae was something of a trickster as well as a seer: when Tarquin of Rome would not pay her price for the Sibylline books, she burned three, and then three more. He paid, rather than see the remaining books in her hand join the pyre at her feet. (Giovanni di Stefano, 1482, pavement, Duomo of Siena.)

Chapter 1

In the Cave of the Enchantress

For me your love is only pain
I've opened up my eyes
And seen in you, my lady fair,
The devil in disguise.

The Tannhäuser Ballad

When it looked as if Christianity was taking hold in her native Campania in southern Italy, the Sibyl left her labyrinth of caves in Cumae below the temple of Apollo. She had pronounced her oracles there for hundreds of years, but she was now taking to the hills, to make one of the last stands of paganism on the highest ridge of the Apennines, still called the Monti Sibillini in her honour.

She had shown Aeneas the way down to the pagan underworld in Virgil's epic; she had sold the volumes of Sibylline leaves, her oracles written on palms, to the last king of Rome, Tarquin the Proud, and had proved that she was worldly-wise as well as deep: when he would not pay the price she asked for the nine books, she burned three, and when he still would not pay, she burned another three, and so he found himself outmanoeuvred and had to pay the full price for the last remaining three volumes rather than risk their total destruction. But, with the new faith gaining ground, the oracles' author was obliged to run, to conceal herself in a cave, and practise her forbidden arts there, under the rose. One of these was making up stories, passing on information; giving a picture of what the future might hold for her hearers. In some accounts, she had even invented the first alphabet in the West – but there are one or two other contenders for this title.

The 'Grotta della Sibilla' in the Umbrian mountains is first mentioned in medieval not classical legend: it appears in the chivalric romance *Guerino il Meschino*, written by Andrea da Barberino (also called Andrea dei Magnabotti) in 1391 and subsequently read by the literati, as well as told and retold by professional storytellers, the *cantastorie*. Its eponymous hero, Guerino the Wretch, soon became a byword for Italian cunning and fearlessness: he is an orphan hunting for his parents in the company of an innkeeper's son; in the course of their wanderings, the two youths reach a mountain pass near Norcia in Umbria, where they meet the Devil. The Devil wants Guerino's soul – what else? – and tempts him with news of a great *fata*, a fairy, an enchantress, called Sibilla, who lives near by, in a subterranean kingdom where every delight will be his. Guerino takes up the new quest eagerly, though he is warned what might lie in store for him when he comes across Macco, a victim of the fairy, at the mouth of the cave; changed by the enchantress into a terrible snake, he has been left there, ordered to keep guard.

The Christian origin of this legend demanded that the two great enemies of the faith in Barberino's day – Jews and heathens – be represented in some sort of conspiracy together. By giving the fairy's victim the name Macco, the author was demonstrating his orthodoxy. For 'Malco' was the Wandering Jew of legend, and the serpentine shape would then reflect the anti-semitism of such Christian legends, just as the fantasies of female magic emanate from the religion's prejudices against all daughters of Eve, 'the Devil's gateway'. In the story, Guerino immediately tramples the snaky Macco underfoot, and passes blithely on. Inside the cave, he finds the *fata*: 'so great was her charm that she would have deceived any human being, and with her sweet words and her lovely greetings, there was courtesy in her beyond measure ...' In her subterranean kingdom, trees flower and fruit at the same time, and there is no pain or age or sorrow. She offers to discover the identity of Guerino's lost father if only the hero will yield to her charms, and these are considerable: 'when he was in bed, she laid herself down by his side and showed him her beautiful, white flesh, and her breasts indeed seemed to be made of ivory ...' He learns from the fairies in her entourage that she is the learned Cumaean Sibyl, and that she will live until the crack of doom. According to a divergent variation on the legend, she had fled to her present refuge because, after prophesying the birth of the Saviour from a virgin, she had expected to be chosen herself for the task. 'She [had been] so virginal ... she thought God would descend into her when he went and took flesh.' To her disgust, the lot had fallen upon Mary instead.

Guerino, a type of folkloric trickster, and a wily survivor, manages to keep his virtue and resist the *fata*, in spite of all the enchanted blandishments and treats with which he is regaled in the cave. Her 'paradise' offers a life of endless feasting, music, fashionable dress, no pain, no hunger, no poverty, no ageing. But he rejects her, and he becomes glad of his strength of mind, for he soon discovers that on Saturdays Sibilla turns into a monster, and her beautiful attendant ladies into other horrible creatures. He learns it when he peeps and sees their deformed

The highest peaks in the Apennines were associated with the defeat of paganism, but seekers after unorthodox wisdom continued to climb to the Sibyl's 'paradise' and join her in her bower of bliss. Antoine de La Sale mapped the hazards of the journey he made in 1420.

nether limbs under their skirts. So he turns on his lover, and rejects her and her fairy kingdom in fury. She protests at this cruelty, invoking the name of Aeneas, recalling how much more courteously she was treated by that great founding father of civilization, a man who surpassed even Guerino in accomplishments, as he had instituted the Roman empire. But Guerino will not be swayed; he is a pattern of Christian virtue, and he manages to make his escape – he goes to Rome and is absolved of his misspent year in the Sibyl's company.

A few years later, in 1420, Antoine de La Sale, tutor to Giovanni di Calabria, the son of Louis III, King of Sicily and Count of Anjou, decided to look into the legend of this Sibyl; he travelled from Norcia, across the wide dry bed of a glacial lake called the Piano Grande, crossed the ridge of the Sibillini beneath the 2500-metre peak of the Monte Vettore, and climbed up to the site of the cave from a shepherd's village on the other side called Montemonaco. He mapped the route he took, and added drawings of the landmarks to the account he produced, '*Le Paradis de la Reine Sibille*', one of the miscellaneous ingredients in his entertaining *La Salade* of 1437–42 (a pun on his name, adopted 'because in a salad one puts many good herbs'). '*Le Paradis*' follows some exempla in the art of good government and passages from Roman history, but it represents a complete change of

'A beautiful woman above, a serpent writhing below': Mélusine taking her Saturday bath is one of many snaky or otherwise monstrous enchantresses of legend, whose human lovers discover their magical deception just in time. (Frontispiece to F. Nodot, Mélusine Paris, 1697.)

register, as Antoine is writing a form of travel autobiography, about a journey he had made himself twenty years before. He mentions local flora, for instance, used in cooking and medicine, but he continually shrugs off responsibility by referring to his sources: 'the old chatter of the common people'. He was gathering local accounts about those who had made the long, difficult journey to the Sibyl's lake in the crater on one peak, and to the Sibyl's cave on the other, to dedicate their *grimoires*, or books of spells, and consult the enchantress in her grotto, and he warns that permission to visit it has to be given by the villagers and their lords because storms rose and damaged the harvest when pagan necromancers, intent on improving their diabolical arts, made the pilgrimage to the grotto. The villagers would capture such visitors and deal with them summarily – a bad priest and his companion had been torn to pieces, La Sale reports, and thrown into the lake quite recently. He himself did not dare journey any further than the opening of the cave, but he dwells stirringly on the perils en route – the narrowness of the path, the dizziness he felt, the rampart of stone 'three lances high' which had to be crossed by one of two tracks you had to dismount to negotiate. 'And I assure you that the better of these two pathways is enough to put fear into the heart of some-one who would not be afeared of any mortal fear …' Antoine de La Sale did not stint on the storyteller's hyperbole, though it may be true that the summit is indeed so high that on a clear day the sea is visible on both sides of Italy – the Sibyl's refuge was situated on a magic apex.

La Sale found the entrance, shaped like 'a pointed shield', and crawled through it on all fours to enter a small square chamber, lit by a hole above, with seats carved into the rock on all sides. He did not dare scramble in deeper, but remained content to describe what his informants told him: the corridor running deep into the mountain, which led to polished doors of metal, opening on to the inner labyrinth, the doors of crystal that followed, the great wind 'very horrid and marvellous' which howled up from the lower regions, the narrow bridge over a torrent after that, and the two dragons breathing fire at the end. The names of lost knights, who had ventured in and never returned, were carved in the rocks on either side of the grotto's mouth. The writer in La Sale inspired him to copy them down, and he added his own.

Antoine de La Sale stands as a precursor of a Rider Haggard hero or an Indiana Jones, the type of intrepid explorer relying on hearsay to advance into dread, unknown adventures. He was accompanied by a local doctor and other inhabitants of Montemonaco, and on the mountain they heard 'a loud voice crying as if it were the cry of a peacock which seemed very far away'. The others told him it was the voice of the Sibyl's paradise, but, La Sale adds scathingly, 'as for myself, I don't believe a word of it'. It was the neighing of the horses, he asserted, which they had left below, before the last leg of the climb.

The early humanist tradition, of which La Sale forms a part, gave the legend of the Sibyl of the Apennines the character of a secular romance, and as such it becomes enriched and entangled with folklore about fairy seductresses: the winged siren Mélusine from the French medieval romance, the deceiving Lamia and the witch Alcina in the chivalrous cycle of Roland stories also turn into monsters unbeknownst to the heroes until it is – almost – too late. These tales have multiple forebears, in classical mythology (the *Odyssey* – Calypso, Circe) as well as Celtic faery lore, for the Sibyl's secret paradise resembles in many ways the kingdom of Tir-na-nog, the isle of perpetual youth in Irish myth. The tale of Guerino the Wretch becomes, in La Sale's telling, a jaunty love story, about a German knight who finally reaches the Sibyl's kingdom across all those perils inside the mountain and enters there a garden of earthly delights, thronged with beautiful young men and women in exquisite clothes, drinking and dancing and dallying with grace, and speaking every language with ease, and passing on instantly all their accomplishments, so that after only nine days any new arrival finds his tongue loosed as well. But then, alas, peeping at his beloved at midnight one Friday, when, as is her custom, she has shut herself away, this knight discovers, like the worthy and chaste Guerino, that she is really an illusion, and 'all her ladies in the state of snakes and serpents all together'. The Sibyl's paradise is nothing but a trick of the Devil, its sweets poison.

The German knight realizes that he must set himself free, and at last, after 330 days – the final term beyond which all escape is impossible (La Sale's hero does not cut short his time of bliss) – he manages to leave the accursed mountain, and travel to Rome to see the pope and obtain his forgiveness for his great season in Hell. But in this version, the pope refuses, and the knight goes back to rejoin his lady the Sibyl – having usefully told his story to the world outside – to live in bliss for ever more (except on Saturdays).

Clive Bell, in a sprightly nursery rendition of 1923, thought the story preached excellent epicureanism, just the message that was needed:

> ... tons of may-be bliss don't measure
> One ounce of certain, solid pleasure.

And he concludes, addressing the errant knight:

> In my opinion, you did well
> To live for love, though love is hell.

Antoine de La Sale's princely pupil was only ten years old when *La Salade* was written for him, to celebrate his recent marriage – the arranged unions so central to fairy tale's concerns. La Sale himself, born around 1388, a Provençal by birth, had taken up writing late in life after decades as a soldier and a courtier in the Angevin household; he was in his fifties when he was tossing his *Salade*, a ripe age for the period. He tells his young charge that he has set the story down 'to laugh and pass the time, and I am sending it to you so that … one day … you might go there to amuse yourself, and I promise you that the queen and all those ladies will give you a great welcome and feast you in very great joy'. In the fifteenth century, men had a different idea about the education of young princes than we might expect.

La Sale tells tales with relish – and a touch of mischief. In the case of the story of the Sibyl, he wants to have it both ways, and so he too makes several bows to orthodoxy, delivering himself finally of a ringing palinode in which he denounces the woman and all her works, accusing her of being a false prophet, even in terms of classical legend; Christ's death had brought all pagan devilry to an end. Significantly, he does not relate the Sibyl's prophecy of Christ's birth from a virgin: the idea that the pagan and the Christian could overlap in truth-telling in this way perhaps struck too risky a note.

The legends Antoine de La Sale collected appeared in different forms elsewhere: Fazio degli Uberti (*d.* 1367) had written a poem about Simon Magus, in which the wizard travels to the area to dedicate his *grimoire* to the pagan oracle; Aeneas Sylvius Piccolomini (*d.* 1464), who became Pope Pius II, first identified Sibilla with the goddess of love, Venus herself. This was an appropriate move, perhaps, for him to make, as he had enshrined a Roman sculpture of the Three Graces in the centre of his private chapel in the Duomo of Siena. The reputation of the Sibylline peak combined erotic fantasy and pagan magic in a witch's brew, and it exercised a potent fascination, as a story and as a place. The poet Leandro Alberti, writing in 1550, mentioned that he had been told the story by women when he was a child: it was circulating in high and low forms, literary and oral, learned and popular. Around the same time, the Inquisition obtained a confession of witchcraft from Zuan delle Piatte, who described a journey to the Sibyl's mountain, where he renounced his faith and met 'Donna Venus' and many of her victims, sleeping an enchanted sleep in the cave. Among them was Tannhäuser, and indeed, the legend is principally known to modern audiences through Wagner's interpretation. Inspired by broadsheet *Lieder* accounts of the German knight's attempt to enter the earthly paradise ('I've … seen in you, my lady fair, a devil in disguise!'), Wagner used the variant name, the Venusberg, for the mountain stronghold of diabolical passion, reinterpreting it in *Tannhäuser* to convey his own torments about love and lust.

The cave can no longer be entered; a combination of circumstances has destroyed access to the chthonic world of the legends. In 1497, Rome was already threatening excommunication to any profane pilgrims to the area, and in the early

The Sibyl of Cumae's ruses were not successful with Apollo, god of prophecy. When he fell in love with her, she asked for a long life; he granted her wish, but as she still spurned him, he did not remind her to ask for eternal youth as well. (Salvator Rosa, River Landscape with Apollo and the Cumaean Sibyl, *c. 1655, detail.)*

seventeenth century, it seems, the authorities had ordered that it be filled up to prevent the growing number of pilgrims, and sentries posted at the approaches. They were coming, it was said, in great numbers to dedicate their *grimoires,* consult the Sibyl and increase their powers. In 1898, a mountaineering journal reported that the grotto had been dynamited to prevent wizards from escaping. The word for an inhabitant of Norcia – *norcino* or *nursino* – actually became synonymous in Italian with 'necromancer', and still is.

In Ovid, the Cumaean Sibyl tells Aeneas that Phoebus Apollo had fallen in love with her and offered her anything she wanted if she would only sleep with him – she then asked for as many 'birthdays as there were grains of dust' in a heap she scooped together in her hands. But she had forgotten to ask for eternal youth as well. Apollo had reminded her, but she still 'scorned him'. When she meets Aeneas, she tells him she will 'shrink from her present fine stature into a tiny creature ... shrivelled with age', and that, eventually, her outer form will disintegrate altogether. Then she concludes, 'But still, the fates will leave me my voice, and by my voice I shall be known.'

In the *Satyricon* by Petronius, written more than a thousand years before La Sale's account, Trimalchio claims that he has seen the Sibyl herself in her cave, so shrivelled with age that she was no bigger than a bat; she was hanging in a bottle, he says, from the roof, moaning that the only thing she wanted was to die. But another traveller reports that he had seen her tomb, at Delphi, inscribed with the epitaph:

> I Sibylla, Phoibos's wise woman,
> am hidden under a stone monument:
> I was a speaking virgin but voiceless
> in this manacle by the strength of fate.
> I lie close to the Nymphs and to Hermes:
> I have not lost my sovereignty.

These words capture the paradox of the Sibyl of myth: she is exiled, even abandoned, her voice is muffled, even muted. Yet from inside the 'manacle' of the monument, she goes on speaking.

The voiceless who voice their 'sovereignty' against the odds are by no means always female. But the blocked-up cave is unblocked in the imaginary world of her story, by the memory of her presence inside, the fantasy of her magic and knowledge. The cave represents a pleasure dome, a dream of longliving gaiety and delight – and it is the creation of a figure who is both a teller of tales (the Sibyl, the prophet), and the protagonist of the multiple legends she inspires. The negative value attached to her kingdom never quite convinces: it remains at the same time a garden of earthly delights, a paradise indeed, which its visitors, its reporters, serve. In this sense, the Cumaean Sibilla, taking refuge in the mountains, bodies forth the sheer value of entertainment, as Antoine de La Sale was well aware. That his cautions would fall on deaf ears, he also knew. Fairy tales often claim the moral ground, but their spellbinding power lies with the enchantresses and giants, the magic, the wonders, the mishaps and the good fortune they relate.

Stories often described as fairy tales, be they told in the Caribbean, Scotland or France, can flow with the irrepressible energy of interdicted narrative and opinion among groups of people who have been muffled in the dominant, learned milieux. The Sibyl, as the figure of a storyteller, bridges divisions in history as well as hierarchies of class. She offers the suggestion that sympathies can cross from different places and languages, different peoples of varied status. She also represents an imagined cultural survival from one era of belief to another: Sibilla exists as a Christian fantasy about a pagan presence from the past, and as such she fulfils a certain function in thinking about forbidden, forgotten, buried, even secret matters.

'By my voice I shall be known': it is no bad epitaph for a storyteller.

CHAPTER 2

The Old Wives' Tale: Gossips I

Women
Rabbit rabbit rabbit women
Tattle and titter
Women prattle
Women waffle and witter

Men Talk. Men Talk …

Women gossip Women giggle
Women niggle-niggle-niggle
Men Talk …

Liz Lochhead

In *The Old Wives' Tale*, a play by George Peele of around 1590, Xantippa, who is fair of face but evil-tongued, goes to the well to draw up the water of life, and finds a severed head rising from the water instead. It chants to her:

Faire maiden, white and red
Stroke me smoothe and combe my head,
And thou shalt have some cockell bread.

But she is not called Xantippa after Socrates' proverbial shrew of a wife without good reason; she believes that words count: 'A woman without a tongue/Is as a souldier without his weapon … '. She wields her weapon, and as she lays into the wheedling head with her curses, she breaks her jug over it. A bolt of lightning, a clap of thunder, and a monster husband appears to claim her. As he is deaf as a post, her tongue will struggle against him in vain.

Her sister Celanta follows her to the well; she is foul of face, but sweet-natured, and so she responds kindly when the head comes up and asks her:

Gently dippe but not too deepe,
For feare thou make the goulden beard to weep.
Faire maide, white and redde,
Combe me smoothe, and stroke my head;
And every haire a sheave shall be,
And every sheave a goulden tree.

She takes up the invitation without flinching, does as she is told, combs the head smooth and strokes it, and finds corn and gold fall into her lap. When a husband appears to carry her off in turn, he turns out to be blind, so is said to be able to put up with a fright for a wife.

George Peele included the folk tale known as 'Three Heads in a Well' in a blithe farrago of a play in which he mixed all kinds of materials – classical myth, nonsense verse, fairy stories, literary allusions, pantomimic double entendres (as above) and local superstitions. When he called his comedy *The Old Wives' Tale*, he provided possibly the earliest instance of the phrase used in a title. In the framing plot, an old 'Gammer' unfolds the story. Gammer meant Granny, the pair of Gaffer, and both words carried strong connotations of chattiness; a certain Dame Chat, indeed, another garrulous old character, also appears in another farcical fairytale play of the time, *Gammer Gurton's Needle* by William Stevenson. These

Opposite Eloquence – and gold – are the rewards for special kindnesses: when the heroine does not flinch at grooming three heads in a well, gold and jewels fall from their hair and her lips. (H. J. Ford's illustration to 'Bushy Bride', Andrew Lang's variation, 1890.)

are the Old Wives of the Tales as recounted by their parodists.

Peele's play marks a moment in England when such a tale or tales turn into drama, when oral fairy tales become fixed in print as popular entertainment. The flavour of his drama, its combination of the magical, fantastic and patently ridiculous, catches the precarious value of the old wives' tale, poised between wisdom and folly. Similarly, in France, at the end of the seventeenth century, when the literary fairy tale emerges in print for the first time, commentators connected old women with fantastic tale-telling; the Abbé Fénelon, for instance, imagines Achilles saying to Homer, 'The *Odyssey*'s just a heap of old wives' tales.' Both the English poet's and the French priest's concern with women's tongues point to an issue that beats at the heart of the fairytale genre and its development as a moralizing and socializing instrument in the lives of girls – and boys.

Plato in the *Gorgias* referred disparagingly to the kind of tale – *mythos graos*, the old wives' tale – told by nurses to amuse and frighten children. This is possibly the earliest reference to the genre. When the boys and girls of Athens were about to embark for Crete, to be sacrificed to the Minotaur, old women are described coming down to the port to tell them stories, to distract them from their grief. In *The Golden Ass*, Charite, a young bride, is captured by bandits, forcibly separated from her husband and thrown into a cave; there, a disreputable old woman, drunken and white-haired, tells her the story of Psyche's troubles before she reaches happiness and marriage with Cupid: 'The old woman sighed sympathetically. "My pretty dear," she said, " … let me tell you a fairy tale or two to make you feel a little better." ' The picture of another's ordeals will console Charite and distract her from her own distress. William Adlington published his exuberant translation of 'sondrie pleasaunt and delectable Tales, with an excellent Narration of the Marriage of Cupide and Psiches …' in 1566; it is most improbable that a writer like George Peele would not have known this earliest recognizable predecessor of 'Cinderella' and 'Beauty and the Beast'.

In Latin, the phrase Apuleius uses is literally 'an old wives' tale' (*anilis fabula*); the type of comic romance to which 'Cupid and Psyche' belongs was termed 'Milesian', after Aristides of Miletus, who had compiled a collection of such stories in the second century AD; these were translated into Latin, but are now known only through later retellings. The connection of old women's speech and the consolatory, erotic, often fanciful fable appears deeply intertwined in language itself, and with women's speaking roles, as the etymology of 'fairy' illuminates.

The word 'fairy' in the Romance languages indicates a meaning of the wonder or fairy tale, for it goes back to a Latin feminine word, *fata*, a rare variant of *fatum*

Like the fates who spin the future, fairies see the life to come; their words are magic, their spells are binding: the fairies' prophecies at the princess's christening are fulfilled when she pricks her finger on a spindle and falls into a thousand-year sleep. (Arthur Rackham, 'The Sleeping Beauty', 1920.)

(fate) which refers to a goddess of destiny. The fairies resemble goddesses of this kind, for they too know the course of fate. *Fatum*, literally, that which is spoken, the past participle of the verb *fari*, to speak, gives French *fée*, Italian *fata*, Spanish *hada*, all meaning 'fairy', and enclosing connotations of fate; fairies share with Sibyls knowledge of the future and the past, and in the stories which feature them, both types of figure foretell events to come, and give warnings.

Isidore of Seville (*d*. 636), in the *Etymologies*, gives a famous, sceptical definition of the pagan idea of fate and the Fates: 'They say that fate is whatever the gods declare, whatever Jupiter declares. Thus they say that fate derives from *fando*, that is, from speaking ... The fiction is that there are three Fates, who spin a woollen thread on a distaff, on a spindle, and with their fingers, on account of the threefold nature of time: the past, which is already spun and wound onto the spindle; the present, which is drawn between the spinner's fingers; and the future, which lies in the wool twined on the distaff, and which must still be drawn out by the fingers of the spinner onto the spindle, as the present is drawn to the past.' These classical Fates metamorphose into the fairies of the stories, where they continue their fateful and prophetic roles. But fairy tales themselves also fulfil this function, quite apart from the fairies who may or may not make an appearance: 'Bluebeard' or 'Beauty and the Beast' act to caution listeners, as well as light their path to the future.

Although they do not have the same root, 'fairy' has come under strong semantic influence from 'fay' and 'fair', both of which may be derived ultimately from

The storyteller of imagination inherits the fates' role, spinning possible versions of the future: in the second-century novel The Golden Ass, *a disreputable old woman tries to console the weeping bride Charite, kidnapped by bandits on her wedding day, by telling her a love story with a happy ending. (Agostino Veneziano, after Michel Coxie, c. 1530.)*

the Middle English *'feyen'*, Anglo-Saxon *'fegan'*, meaning to agree, to fit, to suit, to join, to unite, to bind. Thus the desirable has the power to inspire – even compel – agreement, as well as to bind. Binding is one of the properties of decrees, and of spells. Interestingly, this root also gives 'fee', as in payment, for transferrals of money too arise from agreed bonds, as a response to a desire, a need.

Although the ultimate origin, in time and place, of a fairy tale can never really be pinned down, we do sometimes know the teller of an old tale in one particular variation, we can sometimes identify the circle of listeners at a certain time and place. The collectors of the nineteenth century occasionally recorded the name of their sources when they took down the story, though they were not as interested in them as historians would be now. One salient aspect of the transmission of fairy tales has not been looked at closely: the female character of the storyteller.

Italo Calvino, in his 1956 collection of Italian *Fiabe*, or Tales, the Italian answer to the Grimms, drew attention to this aspect of the tradition, noticing that several of the nineteenth-century folklore anthologies he drew on and adapted cited female sources. Agatuzza Messia, the nurse of the Sicilian scholar and collector of tales Giuseppe Pitré, became a seamstress, and, later, a quilt-maker in a section of Palermo: 'A mother, grandmother, and great-grandmother, as a little girl, she heard stories from her grandmother, whose own mother had told them having herself heard countless stories from one of her grandfathers. She had a good memory so never forgot them.' The *Kalevala*, the national poem of Finland, was collected from different oral sources and reshaped by Elias Lönnrot in the mid-nineteenth century in the form in which it is read today; Sibelius, who would compose many pieces inspired by the *Kalevala*'s heroes and heroines, heard the epic in part direct from Larin Paraske, a woman bard, who held eleven thousand lines of such folk material in her head. Karel Čapek, the utopian Czech writer most famous for his satire *RUR* (which introduced the concept of Robots), wrote an acute essay about fairy tale in 1931, in which he decided:

> A fairy story cannot be defined by its motif and subject-matter, but by its origin and function … A true folk fairy tale does not originate in being taken down by the collector of folklore but in being told by a grandmother to her grand-children, or by one member of the Yoruba tribe to other members of the Yoruba tribe, or by a professional storyteller to his audience in an Arab coffee-house. A real fairy tale, a fairy tale in its true function, is a tale within a circle of listeners …

He himself remembered his mother and his grandmother telling him stories – they were both millers' daughters, as if they had stepped out of a fairy tale. The *traditio* does literally pass on, as the word suggests, between the generations, and the predominant pattern reveals older women of a lower status handing on the material to younger people, who include boys, sometimes, if not often, of higher position and expectations, like future ethnographers and writers of tales.

So although male writers and collectors have dominated the production and dissemination of popular wonder tales, they often pass on women's stories from intimate or domestic milieux; their tale-spinners often figure as so many Scheherazades, using narrative to bring about a resolution of satisfaction and jus-tice. Marguerite de Navarre, in the *Heptaméron*, gives the stories to ten speakers, five of whom are women: they too, like the narrator of *The Arabian Nights*, put their own case, veiled in entertaining and occasionally licentious fantasy. Boccaccio, and his admirer and emulator (to some degree) Chaucer, voiced the stories of women, and some contain folk material which makes a strong showing in later fairy stories; the Venetian Giovan Francesco Straparola (the 'Babbler') reported the stories told by a circle of ladies in his entertaining and sometimes scabrous fantasies, filled with fairytale motifs and improbabilities, called *Le piacevoli notti* (The Pleasant Nights), published in 1550; the Neapolitan Giambattista Basile, in *Lo cunto de li cunti* (The Tale of Tales), also known as *Il Pentamerone* (The Pentameron), published posthumously in 1634–6, featured a group of wizened and misshapen old crones as his sources.

The women who inaugurated the fashion for the written fairy tale, in Paris at the end of the seventeenth century, consistently claimed they had heard the stories they were retelling from nurses and servants. Mme de Sévigné, writing to her daughter, revealingly reported a metaphor borrowed from the kitchen to describe the new enthusiasm: *'cela s'appelle les [contes] mitonner. Elle nous mitonna donc, et nous parla d'une île verte, où l'on élevait une princesse plus belle que le jour'* (it's called simmering them [tales]; so she simmered for us, and talked to us about a green isle where a princess grew up who was more beautiful than the day).

Charles Perrault's collection of 1697 bore the alternative title of *Contes de ma Mère l'Oye* (Mother Goose Tales); in an earlier preface, to the tale 'Peau d'Ane' (Donkeyskin), Perrault also placed his work in the tradition of Milesian bawdy, like the tale of 'Cupid and Psyche', but he added that he was passing on 'an entirely made up story and an old wives' tale', such as had been told to children since time immemorial by their nurses. While referring to a written canon, he thus disengaged himself from its élite character to invoke old women, grandmothers and governesses as his true predecessors. He was quick to add, however, that unlike the moral of 'Cupid and Psyche' (*'impénétrable'*), his own was patently clear, which made it far superior to its classical predecessors:

> These Milesian fables are so puerile that it is doing them rather an honour to set up against them our own Donkeyskin tales and Mother Goose tales, or [they are]so filled with dirt, like *The Golden Ass* of Lucian or Apuleius … that they do not merit that we should pay them attention.

Perrault may have had his tongue in his cheek when he protested that 'Donkeyskin', a tale of father–daughter incest, was morally impeccable. But a contemporary pedant, the Abbé de Villiers, took his argument at face value, and rounded in outrage on Perrault and the writers of fairy tales, penning a pamphlet against the genre, 'As a preventive measure against bad taste.' There he lumped women and children together as the perpetrators of the new fad: 'Ignorant and foolish, they have filled the world with so many collections, so many little stories, and in short with these reams of fairy tales which have been the death of us for the last year or so.' The diminutive form of the nouns (*sornettes, bagatelles, historiettes*) recurs in the rhetoric of detractors and supporters alike; the former branding fairy stories as infantile, the latter praising them as childlike. This tension between opposing perceptions of the child informs the development of the tales and continues to do so.

Villiers sets up an imaginary debate between a fashionable Parisian and a sensible visitor from the provinces. The provincial calls them *sottises imprimées* (follies in print) and compares them derogatorily to fables, scorning them as 'Tales to make you fall asleep on your feet, that nurses have made up to entertain children'. The Parisian counters that nurses have to be highly skilled to tell them. To which the provincial retorts that if such tales ever contained a coherent moral purpose, they would not be considered in the first place 'the lot of ignorant folk and women'. The battle was joined, over the value of fairy tales; their female origin was not really contested.

Villiers's Parisian was putting forward the views of poets and literati like Mlle Marie-Jeanne L'Héritier de Villandon (p. xv) (1664–1734), a cousin and close friend of Perrault, who defended the form with fighting spirit precisely because it conveyed the ancient, pure wisdom of the people from the fountainhead – old women, nurses, governesses. In her preface to the story *'Marmoisan, ou l'innocente tromperie'* (Marmoisan, or the innocent trick) of 1696, she declared herself a partisan of women and their stories, remembering: 'A hundred times and more, my governess, instead of animal fables, would draw for me the moral features of this surprising story ... Why yes, once heard, such tales are far more striking than the exploits of a monkey and a wolf. I took an extreme pleasure in them – as does every child.'

L'Héritier could never rid her praise of its defensive tone ('the moral features'), and for good reason. The phrase 'old wives' tale' was superficially pejorative when Apuleius used it on the lips of his hoary-headed crone of a storyteller; it remained so, in the very act of authenticating the folk wisdom of the stories by stressing the wise old women who had carried on the tradition. It is still, in English, an ambiguous phrase: an old wives' tale means a piece of nonsense, a tissue of error, an ancient act of deception, of self and others, idle talk. As Marlowe writes in *Dr Faustus*, 'Tush, these are trifles and mere old wives' tales'. On a par with trifles, 'mere old wives' tales' carry connotations of error, of false counsel, ignorance, prejudice and fallacious nostrums – against heartbreak as well as headache; similarly 'fairy tale', as a derogatory term, implies fantasy, escapism, invention, the unreliable consolations of romance.

But the idealistic impulse is also driven by dreams; alternative ways of sifting right and wrong require different guides, ones perhaps discredited or neglected. Women from very different social strata have been remarkably active in the fields of folklore and children's literature since the nineteenth century. The Grimm Brothers' most inspiring and prolific sources were women, from families of

The veillées, *or evening gatherings for gossip, news, and stories, were part of artisan as well as agricultural working life, in cities as well as the country. Emile Fréchon took this photograph of a woman and her audience, in a series on the Pas de Calais, around 1900, and called it 'Narration'.*

friends and close relations, like the Wilds – Wilhelm married Dortchen, the youngest of four daughters of Dorothea Wild, who possessed a rich store of traditional tales, and she provided thirty-six for the collection. Dorothea, the Grimms' sister, married Ludwig Hassenpflug, and his three sisters passed on forty-one of the tales. From the Romantic literary circle of the artistic aristocratic von Haxthausens (who contributed collectively no fewer than sixty-six of the Grimms' tales) Annette von Droste-Hülshoff, the poet, and her sister Jenny were among the women who eagerly took part in telling the brothers the stories they had heard as children and more recently from their local area of Westphalia. Oscar Wilde's father, a doctor in Merrion Square, Dublin, in the mid-nineteenth century, used to ask for stories as his fee from his poorer patients: his wife Speranza Wilde then collected them. Many of these were told to him by women, and in turn influenced their son's innovatory fairy tales, like 'The Selfish Giant' and 'The Happy Prince'. At the end of the century, the omnivorous Scottish folklorist Andrew Lang relied on his wife Leonora Alleyne, as well as a team of women editors, transcribers and paraphrasers, to produce the many volumes of fairy stories and folk tales from around the world, in the immensely popular *Red, Yellow, Green, Blue, Rose Fairy Books*, which he began publishing in 1890. The writer Simone Schwarz-Bart stitched her memories of Creole stories from her Martinique childhood into her poetic, adventurous, linguistically hybrid fictions. The grandmother Reine Sans Nom (Queen-With-No-Name) in *Pluie et vent sur Télumée Miracle* (1972) embodies survival and history, and keeps the memory of slave culture, and of Africa before that. With the help of her friend, a sorceress, she passes on lore, fables, fairy tales, ghost stories to her granddaughter. As Simone Schwarz-Bart once said in an interview, 'The tale is, in large part, our capital. I was nourished on tales. It is our bible … I don't have a technique, but I know. I'm familiar. I've heard.

The proverbial wise woman narrator was placed on the outskirts of the village, on the edge of the woods, and, according to the tradition of children's literature, she is very old while her listeners are young. (Tom Pouce, Paris, 1825.)

I've been nourished … when an old person dies, a whole library disappears.'

It would be absurd to argue that storytelling was an exclusively female activity – it varies from country to country, from one people to another, and from place to place within the same country, among the same people – but it is worth trying to puzzle out in what different ways the patterns of fairytale romancing might be drawn when women are the tellers.

The pedagogical function of the wonder story deepens the sympathy between the social category women occupy and fairy tale. Fairy tales exchange knowledge between an older voice of experience and a younger audience, they present pictures of perils and possibilities that lie ahead, they use terror to set limits on choice and offer consolation to the wronged, they draw social outlines around boys and girls, fathers and mothers, the rich and the poor, the rulers and the ruled, they point out the evildoers and garland the virtuous, they stand up to adversity with dreams of vengeance, power and vindication.

The *veillées* were the hearthside sessions of early modern society, where early social observers, like Bonaventure des Périers and Noël du Fail in the sixteenth century, describe the telling of some of today's most familiar fables and tales, like 'Donkeyskin' and 'Cinderella'. These gatherings offered men and women an

Monotonous tasks that are never done, like so much routine household work, provoked retaliation, in the form of dreams, gossip, stories, fairy tales. (Geertruid Roghman, Woman Spinning, *Dutch, mid-seventeenth century.)*

opportunity to talk – to preach – which was forbidden them in other situations, the pulpit, the forum, and frowned on and feared in the spinning rooms and by the wellside. Taking place after daylight hours, they still do not exactly anticipate the leisure uses of television or radio today – work continued, in the form of spinning, especially, and other domestic tasks: one folklore historian recalled hearing the women in her childhood tell stories to the rhythm of the stones cracking walnuts as they shelled them for bottling and pickling. As Walter Benjamin wrote in his essay on 'The Storyteller':

[The storyteller's] nesting places – the activities that are intimately associated with boredom – are already extinct in the cities and are declining in the country as well. With this the gift for listening is lost and the community of listeners disappears …

Benjamin never once imagines that his storytellers might be women, even though he identifies so clearly and so eloquently the connection between routine repetitive work and narrative – storytelling is itself 'an artisan form of communication', he writes. And later, again, it is 'rooted in the people … a milieu of craftsmen'. He divides storytellers into stay-at-homes and rovers – tradesmen and agriculturalists, like the tailors and the shoemakers who appear in the stories, on the one hand; on the other, the seamen who travel far afield adventuring, like the questing type of hero. He neglects the figure of the spinster, the older woman with her distaff, who may be working in town and country, in one place or on the move, at market, or on a pilgrimage to Canterbury, and who has become a generic icon of narrative from the frontispiece of fairytale collections from Charles Perrault's onwards. The Scottish poet Liz Lochhead, who has drawn on much fairytale imagery in her work, has written:

> No one could say the stories were useless
> for as the tongue clacked
> five or forty fingers stitched
> corn was grated from the husk
> patchwork was pieced
> or the darning was done …
>
> And at first light …
> the stories dissolved in the whorl of the ear
> but they
> hung themselves upside down
> in the sleeping heads of the children
> till they flew again
> into the storyteller's night.

Spinning a tale, weaving a plot: the metaphors illuminate the relation; while the structure of fairy stories, with their repetitions, reprises, elaboration and minutiae, replicates the thread and fabric of one of women's principal labours – the making of textiles from the wool or the flax to the finished bolt of cloth.

Fairy tales are stories which, in the earliest mentions of their existence, include that circle of listeners, the audience; as they point to possible destinies, possible happy outcomes, they successfully involve their hearers or readers in identifying with the protagonists, their misfortunes, their triumphs. Schematic characterization leaves a gap into which the listener may step. Who has not tried on the glass slipper? Or offered it for trying? The relation between the authentic, artisan source and the tale recorded in book form for children and adults is not simple; we are not hearing the spinsters and the knitters in the sun whom Orsino remembers chanting in *Twelfth Night*, unmediated. But the quality of the mediation is of great interest. From the mid-seventeenth century, the nurses, governesses, family domestics, working women living in or near the great house or castle in town and country existed in a different relation to the élite men and women who may have once been in their charge, as children. The future Marquise de la Tour du Pin recalled in her memoirs how her nurse was her mainstay and that, when she turned eleven and a governess was appointed instead, 'I used to escape whenever I could and try to find her [the nurse], or to meet her about the house.' Another noblewoman, Victorine de Chastenay, also wrote that her own mother alarmed her and dominated her, and that she took refuge with her nurse and her nurse's family. The rapports created in *ancien régime* childhood shape the matter of the stories, and the cultural model which places the literati's texts on the one side of a divide, and popular tales on the other, can and should be redrawn: fairy tales act as an airy suspension bridge, swinging slightly under different breezes of opinion and economy, between the learned, literary and print culture in which famous fairy tales have come down to us, and the oral, illiterate, people's culture of the *veillée*; and on this bridge the traffic moves in both directions.

Women writers like Marie-Jeanne L'Héritier and Marie-Catherine d'Aulnoy mediated anonymous narratives, the popular, vernacular culture they had inherited through fairy tale, in spite of the aristocratic frippery their stories make at a first impression. Indeed, they offer rare and rich testimony to a sophisticated chronicle of wrongs and ways to evade or right them, when they recall stories they had heard as children or picked up later and retell them in a spirit of protest, of polite or not so polite revolt. These tales are wrapped in fantasy and unreality, which no doubt helped them entertain their audiences – in the courtly salon as well as at the village hearth – but they also serve the stories' greater purpose, to reveal possibilities, to map out a different way and a new perception of love, marriage, women's skills, thus advocating a means of escaping imposed limits and prescribed destiny. The fairy tale looks at the ogre like Bluebeard or the Beast of 'Beauty and the Beast' in order to disenchant him; while romancing reality, it is a medium deeply concerned with undoing prejudice. Women of different social positions have collaborated in storytelling to achieve true recognition for their subjects: the process is still going on.

For a long time, authenticity was an issue – the scientific folklorist, in the nineteenth and early twentieth century, sought to catch the accent of the common people; and authenticity was equated with the pristine, the autochthonous, the tale pure and unadulterated by élite ideas; the enterprise was closely associated with romantic nationalism, as in the case of the Grimms. Oral purity is, however, a quest doomed to failure; the material of fairy tale weaves in and out of printed texts, the Greek romances, *The Arabian Nights*, *Tristan* cycle or *matière de Bretagne*, the novels in verse of Chrétien de Troyes, *Mélusine*, saints' lives, and so forth – language conducts from mouth to page and back again, and orature, or, in the West, oral literature, has not existed in isolation since Homeric times. The evangelists knew they had to write down Christ's teachings, in order to continue the process of passing them on by word of mouth, for preachers to use. But the sacred appeal of oral transmission remains crucial. The memory or the fancy of the story's origin inspires the simulation of a storyteller's voice in the literary text, and this performance modifies the narrative, it solicits the audience.

The pretence at anonymity, even in a signed work, like D'Aulnoy's '*La Chatte blanche*' (The White Cat) or '*Serpentin vert*' (The Great Green Worm) or the Grimm Brothers' 'Juniper Tree', confers the authority of traditional wisdom accumulated over the past and acknowledged and shared by many on account of its truthfulness and capacity to teach and be useful.

Fairy tale is essentially a moralizing form, often in deep disguise and often running against the grain of commonplace ethics: Benjamin uses the generic term, 'the storyteller', in order to lift his writers into fantasy figures on a priestly level: 'He [the storyteller] has counsel,' writes Benjamin, in messianic mode. 'Not for a few situations, as the proverb does, but for many, like the sage.' And he concludes, 'The storyteller is the figure in which the righteous man encounters himself.' For the élite writers, who lie behind so many of the famous fairy tales as they have come down to children today, the figure of fairytale storyteller, embodied in the righteous old serving woman, was the figure through whom they could encounter their own enhanced value (Benjamin's 'righteousness'), a field where they could struggle for their ideas and vision.

The orality of the genre remains a central claim even in the most artificial and elaborate literary versions, of the French, or the Victorians or later inventions; it is often carried in the texts through which fairy tales have circulated in writing for three hundred years by the postulation of a narrator, a grandmotherly or nanny type, called Gammer Gurton or Aunty Molesworth or Mother Hubbard as well as Mother Goose or some such cosy name, and by the consequent style, which imitates speech, with chatty asides, apparently spontaneous exclamations, direct appeals to the imaginary circle round the hearth, rambling descriptions, gossipy parentheses, and other bedside or laplike mannerisms that create an illusion of collusive intimacies, of home, of the bedtime story, the winter's tale.

The old wives' tale might be stuff and nonsense, but it too could yield a harvest in corn and gold, if you stroked it smooth and combed it through. Just as history belongs to the victors and words change their meanings with a change of power, stories depend on the tellers and those to whom they are told who might later tell them again. 'Never trust the artist. Trust the tale,' D. H. Lawrence's famous dictum, fails to notice how intertwined the teller and the tale always are.

The old wives' tongues are wagging RIGHT as they pass on lonelyhearts lore in a bawdy parody of sententious manuals, Les Evangiles des quenouilles, or The Gospel of Distaves (Bruges, c. 1475); the patron saint of trouble and strife, dubbed Aelwaer, or All-True ABOVE also makes mock of pious conventions, and rides on an ass like the Virgin Mary fleeing into Egypt, holds a squealing piglet under one arm instead of a baby, while a magpie perches on her head instead of the dove of the Holy Ghost. (Cornelis Antonisz., Amsterdam, c. 1550.)

Word of Mouth: Gossips II

Patient as an old master
I love to study the faces
of pious, spiteful old women.

The mortality of their lips,
and the immortality of the power
that pressed those lips together.

Olga Sedakova

A French print of 1660 depicts '*Le Médecin céphalique*', or Skull Doctor, hard at work at an unusual task: with the help of a hammer and anvil, he is forging new heads for women brought to him by their menfolk – husbands, chiefly – in order to make them into properly docile wives. In jocular style, the inscription relates how the doctor learned the secrets of his trade in Madagascar – a suitably remote, orientalist provenance, with overtones of head-hunting and -shrinking – and then goes on to itemize the women's offences: they are shrewish, loud-mouthed, devilish, angry, mad, haggard, bad, annoying, obstinate. On one side, where French couples are arriving, the inscription above reads:

Great man, through your care almost all our wives
Are now well behaved and give us peace …

And it goes on to say that Frenchmen cannot offer adequate thanks for the great feats the doctor has performed, except to honour his name – Lustucru – for ever more. Lustucru derives from *L'eusses-tu cru?* (Would you have believed it?).

On the opposite side, foreign husbands add their voices to the praises of Lustucru: men from Germany, Switzerland and Sweden, as well as Spaniards, Dutchmen and Armenians, beg the great doctor to visit their countries now and effect the same transformation on their women. Superannuated, severed heads fill the shelves of Lustucru's surgery, or hang from the ceiling; outside, more heads are impaled to advertise his remedy. The shop sign shows a headless woman (*'Une femme sans tête'*) with the legend, 'Everything about her is good', while in the

'I will make you good,' declares the doctor Lustucru, as he hammers out a wife's head on the anvil. 'Husbands, rejoice!' says his assistant, while another woman, with mouth open, waits her turn. The sign outside the smithy, 'A La Bonne Femme', shows a headless woman. This popular eighteenth-century woodcut from Normandy, takes up a satire against bluestockings, feminists, scolds, and other opinionated women of almost a hundred years before.

centre, on the anvil, the inscription reads, '*Touche fort sur la bouche. Elle a meschante langue*' (Strike hard on the mouth: she has a wicked tongue).

The print of this burlesque smithy is one of several variations; in another (p 28), Lustucru is saying, as he hammers, '*Je te rendrai bonne*' (I will make you good) while an onlooker exclaims, '*Maris, réjouissez-vous!*' (Husbands, rejoice!). There are also Italian and German versions extant; prints continue to appear into the eighteenth century. It was the brainchild – the cephalic offspring, indeed – of a certain *curé*, and was inspired by the controversy over the bluestockings of the Paris salons, writers and poets like Madeleine de Scudéry, whom Molière satirized in his famous plays *Les Précieuses ridicules* of 1659 and *Les Femmes savantes* of a few years later; it belongs to a prolonged and intense satirical conflict provoked by the intellectual ambitions of seventeenth-century aristocratic women. Their ideas and their way of life challenged the conventions of the time: from their position of influence as hostesses in Parisian society, they criticized arranged marriages and the dynastic and social market in wives, and sought instead to cultivate equal, companionable relations between men and women, exchanging ideas in an atmosphere of literary and artistic sophistication. The Querelle des Femmes, in this phase, was fierce, but not always bitter. For instance, a gallant, male partisan of the *Précieuses*, the poet Baudeau de Somaize, composed an elegy, '*La Mort de Lustucru: lapidé par les femmes*' (The Death of Lustucru: Stoned by Women) which was recited in the course of one of his comedies, *Véritables Précieuses* (The Authentic Précieuses), in 1660. It was his learned retaliation against the great number of burlesque sketches in which Lustucru figured as the champion of hen-pecked husbands, a hero among men.

The last decades of the seventeenth century saw an early outbreak of feminist argument, and the right of women to voice their opinions was at the centre of the struggle. Christian tradition held the virtues of silence, obedience and discretion as especially, even essentially, feminine, but this view spread far wider than the circle of the devout. The Silent Woman was an accepted ideal. That cliché about the sex, 'Silence is golden', can be found foreshadowed in the pages of Aristotle: 'silence is a woman's glory', he writes in the *Politics*, adding, 'but this is not equally the glory of man'.

The First Epistle to Timothy, attributed to Saint Paul, contains the famous injunction, 'Let the woman learn in silence with all subjection' (2: 11). The letter then continues, 'But I suffer not a woman to teach, nor to usurp authority over the man, but to be in silence' (2: 12). The author gives his reasons, moving in a characteristically Pauline way to an allegorical exegesis of the Fall: that Adam was made first, to symbolize his precedence over Eve, and that Eve, the pattern of all women to come, sinned through speech, by tempting Adam to eat with her words. So speech must be denied her daughters. The prejudice against women's talk has scriptural legitimacy.

The epistle later lists the varieties of improper speech in which women will so frequently indulge, and it proscribes at least five of them: above all, Timothy must not listen to 'profane and old wives' fables' (4: 7). Even younger widows, too, warns Paul, are 'not only idle, but tattlers also and busybodies, speaking things which they ought not' (5: 13). He fears gossip as well, and observes that young widows' behaviour will give rise to talk unless they remarry. By contrast, he exhorts his disciple to be 'an example of the believers, in word, in conversation ...' (4: 12), and at the end to avoid 'profane and vain babblings' (6: 20).

The translators of the King James Authorized Version, working in the period 1604–11 – that is, just subsequent to George Peele's play *The Old Wives' Tale* – had no difficulty with English words for these different types of condemned speech; and in this matter, at least, Catholics and Protestants were in agreement: garrulousness was a woman's vice, and silence – which was not even considered an appropriate virtue in the male – one of the chief ornaments a good woman should cultivate. It is a commonplace that what counts as articulateness in a man becomes stridency in a woman, that a man's conviction is a woman's shrillness, a man's fluency a woman's drivel. The speaking woman also refuses subjection, and turns herself from a passive object of desire into a conspiring and conscious stimulation: even fair speech becomes untrustworthy on a woman's lips. The *mulier blandiens* or *mulier meretrix* of Ecclesiasticus (25: 17–36) and Proverbs (6: 24–6) comes in for much vituperation; the biblical text 'A man's spite is preferable to a woman's kindness' (Ecclus. 42: 14) provoked much nodding of pious heads, as well as pamphlet and chapbook confirmation.

The interdiction on female speech tolls down the years, one of those insistent refrains of misogyny that has acquired independent life, regardless of context, of the times, or the speaker's own circumstances. The French poet, historian and polemicist Christine de Pizan (*d.* 1430), who complained about the portrayal of women in the writings of predecessors like Jean de Meung in his *Roman de la rose*, noticed this poverty of invention in the abuse, the way such writings perpetuated the stale conceits of classical invective. The early middle ages had seen comparative tolerance towards women's communications, but by the fifteenth century reaction invoking the Church Fathers and classical authorities had set in. As Howard Bloch points out, in his study *Medieval Misogyny*, 'Misogyny is a way of speaking about, as distinct from doing something to, women'; such speech acts can sometimes seem as indestructible as those plastic containers which drift over vast distances, bobbing unaffected by on the various currents and deeps of changing individual experience. A packet of popular 'wheat wafers' called Miller's Damsel, currently on sale in English supermarkets, gives this explanation for its name:

> Our company name is derived from a three-tongued rod used in the milling process, which rotates and vibrates the hopper and enables wheat to be fed into the millstones. Over the years this rod has been referred to affectionately as a Miller's Damsel because 'it has three chattering tongues' and our symbol is a representation of it.

Nobody would suggest that this brand of biscuit will inspire in consumers a sudden fresh conviction in women's propensity to chatter in the world around them, any more than it will conjure up millers and damsels; but the example does illustrate the clinging character of certain ideas – which contain a reflection of reality, of experience perhaps, of imagination for certain.

The seduction of women's talk reflected the seduction of their bodies; it was considered as dangerous to Christian men, and condemned as improper *per se*. Female folly had brought about the Fall, so must be quelled. In the Vulgate, Jerome used *seducta* for Eve's transgression: the serpent led her astray, and she then 'seduces' Adam, too. The connotations of the verb are already sexual. Women's words are mixed up with women's wiles – beauty and expression go hand in hand, as Paul implies when he also lays down that women should dress modestly, without show of jewels or elaborate coiffures (1 Tim. 2: 9). Eve sinned by mouth: she bit into the apple of knowledge, she spoke to the serpent and to Adam, and she was in consequence cursed with desire, to kiss and be kissed ('Thy desire shall be to thy husband' (Gen. 3: 16)).

When the Knight of La Tour Landry composed a manual for his daughters' behaviour in the fourteenth century, he enumerated the nine follies of Eve: 'And know ye that the sin of our first mother Eve came by evil and shrewd acquaintance by cause she held parlement with the serpent which as the History saith had a face right fair like the face of a woman. And spake right meekly.' The chapter and verse of Eve's folly continues to concentrate on her speaking: to the serpent in the first place, to Adam about the fruit, to God when she tried to excuse herself. 'Therefore my fair daughters,' the Knight admonishes, 'herein may you take good example, that if one require you of folly or of any thing that toucheth your hon-our and worship you may well cover and hide it saying that you shall speak thereof to your lord.' The virtue of Prudence, portrayed as a good housewife, wears a padlock on her mouth. Sixteenth-century morality tales likewise painted the portraits of the Wise Man and the Wise Woman (p. 34), the latter declaring through lips firmly under lock and key:

> Everyone look at me because I am a wise woman …
> A golden padlock I wear on my mouth at all times
> so that no villainous words shall escape from my mouth
> but I say nothing without deliberation
> and a wise woman should always act thus …
> do not tell tales on others' actions, I say to you roundly …

By contrast, the foolish prattler was a standard, and often bitter, subject of jest. A figure from the topsy-turvy world of carnival, the Dutch saint Aelwaer – Saint All-True – was envisaged by the artist Cornelis Antonisz. in a broadsheet of around 1550 which brazenly parodies holy pictures (p. 26). Sister to other mock patrons of such sinners as sluggards (Sinte Luyaert; Sainte Fainéante), spend-thrifts (Sint Reijnuut), and prattlers (Sainte Babille), Aelwaer was paid tribute in a lengthy but not entirely ill-tempered ballad which targeted many men who marched under her banner:

> On Saint All-True's head sits a bird
> Called a magpie, who always chatters,
> Just so is a quarrelsome man who never shuts up
> Who never has anything good to say …

She was made patron saint of all quarrellers, rioters, troublemakers, revellers, musicians and other rowdy crew of Flanders and of Amsterdam in particular. She wears a screeching magpie on her head, carries a squealing pig under her arm, and holds up a fighting and no doubt caterwauling cat in her other hand. This comic epitome of the fighting, nagging, scolding, malicious, prattling, tongue-wagging busybody rides upon an ass: a blasphemous parody of the Virgin – of Dürer's *Flight into Egypt* in particular – with a piglet replacing the baby, and the magpie the Holy Ghost. Interestingly, the anonymous verses celebrate her powers and the chorus calls all to join in worship of the Great, the Holy Aelwaer, presiding genius of all uproar, for at the end of the day the gravity of such noise, says the anonymous author, has been much exaggerated.

Gossip was perceived to be a leading element in women's folly, and in the sex's propensity to foment riot. Yet the changes in meaning of the word 'gossip', however pejoratively weighted, illuminate the influential part of women in communicating through informal and unofficial networks, in contributing to varieties of storytelling, and in passing on their experience in narrative.

II

In 1014, the word 'gossip' was used in English for a baptismal sponsor, godmother or -father; by 1362, it denoted a 'friend' and applied almost exclusively to female friends invited by a woman to the christening of her child. A 'gossiping' is an old word for a christening feast. Jan Steen's high-spirited painting known also by that title, in the Wallace Collection in London (Pl. 3), shows a kitchen bustling with friends and helpers; the confined mother lies in bed in an alcove, looking very weak, while two women keep by her side; around the table, by the chimney, more women are heating water, gesturing to each other, engaged in conversation as they focus on the newborn child. From 1590 to the 1660s, when such festivities were set to become ever more popular and lavish sources of social bonding, among Catholics and Protestants alike, the word 'gossip' had gone into free fall, and came to mean 'a person, mostly a woman, especially one who delights in idle talk; a newsmonger, a tattler'.

The words *compadre* and *comare* or *commare* reveal a similar shift in meaning in Italian: originally a co-father or co-mother, the masculine variant retained its meaning of godfather (Marlon Brando continued the custom in the film). The feminine version meanwhile shifted to refer to a midwife. In modern Italian, *commare* means a gossip or crony, one of the grackle women dressed in black who can still be seen sitting out in the street passing the time of day with her friends in the traditional daily *chiacchiere* or gossip. The word's connection to midwives has become obsolete, but was current before the seventeenth century and the (male) professionalization of the skill. Scipione Mercurio's early treatise on childbirth was entitled *La commare o' raccoglitrice*, and was published in 1595, with a dedication in verse to the 'learned daughter of a wise man' whom everyone honours for her skills. In French, *commère* followed the same downward path: originally a godmother, it too came to mean a gossip-monger, a telltale; the English 'Cummer', now obsolete, also meant godmother, intimate friend and gossip, as well as midwife and wise woman until the last century.

The Wise Woman, a paragon compounded of classical and biblical morality, wears a padlock on her lips to signify obedience and discretion, and declares that she would rather die, like Lucretia, than dishonour her husband. Her key signifies good housekeeping, the mirror recalls the transience of worldly pleasures, the snakes at her waist warn of evil backbiting and quarrelling, the jug represents her charity to those in need, and her horses' hooves stand here for sure-footedness in the treacherous ways of temptation; she exhorts all wives to follow her example. (Anton Woensam, c. 1525.)

There are several strands in this web of associations around women as gossips which, pulled together, enhance the emblematic figure of the storyteller. Women dominated the domestic webs of information and power; the neighbourhood, the village, the well, the washing place, the shops, the stalls, the street were their arena of influence, not only the household. To some extent, in some societies, women still do so, and their roles as unofficial carers, voluntary fund-raisers, parish helpers often make women newsbearers and informal fixers in the modern city as well as the medieval, and in London as well as Naples.

The control of fertility and mortality, through skills like midwifery, and the direction of attitudes and alliances and interests through gossip exist in close relation to each other in the unofficial networks of the social body; informal speech and exchanges are 'a catalyst of the social process', which can produce harmony and conflict, which can divide and bind: 'Gossip is a powerful social instrument', writes the anthropologist Robert Paine, 'for any person who learns to manage it and can thereby direct or canalize its catalytic effect.'

Gossipy gatherings of women together were the focus of much male anxiety about women's tongues in Reformation as well as Catholic Europe: when the Knight of La Tour Landry's instruction manual was published in Augsburg in 1498, the woodcuts illustrating it pictured women in church incited to chatter by the Devil; the following page showed a group of them gossiping during Mass

Sinful women prattle during Mass and keep the devils busy: one chews on a parchment to stretch it so that the devil scribe will have enough room for all the wicked tittle-tattle he overhears. (From Der Ritter von Turn, Augsburg, 1498.)

(above). One devil is sitting in the corner with pen and inkwell, taking down what they are saying, while another is busy stretching the parchment with his monstrous mandibles because, as the Knight wrote, it was too short to contain all the talk. Tellingly, the Knight included men among the chatterers in church in his text, but the illustrator shows only women so engaged. His men are depicted at prayer.

Typical meeting places for women alone, like public laundries and spinning rooms, were feared to give rise to slander and intrigue and secret liaisons. Of all the professions, official and unofficial, those which allowed women to pass between worlds out of the control of native or marital family seemed to pose the greatest threat to apparent due order. Prostitutes, midwives and wetnurses occupied no fixed point in the structure of society, as they physically moved between worlds: in a 1508 edition of *The Hours of Simon Vostre*, one of the earliest printed prayerbooks in Europe, a dance of death depicts the Reaper gathering up one woman after another to the grave. He dances off with a queen, a duchess, a regent, a knight's lady, an abbess, a prioress, a damoiselle, a market vendor, a theologian – *théologienne!* – all the way down the moral and social scale to the witch, the bigot and the fool – *la sote* (p. 352). All are wearing headgear or hairstyles appropriate to their walk in life, and of all the older women, only the *nourrice* (wetnurse) has her hair escaping, untidily, from under her headcloth – this unkemptness betokening the essential disarray of her role, neither virginal (symbolized by long maiden hair) nor matronly (hair hidden beneath a wimple) nor cloistered (veiled), but passing between those states, as a 'mother' to other women's children, perhaps unattached herself, a messenger bringing news, gossip, from another place.

One of the earliest secular books of tales attributed to women, *Les Evangiles des quenouilles* – or *The Gospel of Distaves*, as it was known in the translation printed by Wynkyn de Worde – first appeared around 1475 in French, in Bruges, and it relates a typical session – or so it claims – of women's gossiping and consultation. Numerous references in other works, from sermons to plays, attest the wide diffusion of this book; there was a copy in the library of the château at Chantilly, and Colbert, the great statesman and financier of the early part of Louis XIV's reign, owned another. Colbert was Charles Perrault's patron and friend, so that the *Evangiles* were known in the circle of the first writers of fairy tales as literature.

The book belongs, generally speaking, to the tradition of gossiping and eavesdropping, of which tale-telling is a branch – Straparola, the author of *Le piacevoli notti*, when summoned before the Inquisition for indecency, defended himself by pleading that he had only taken down the stories he had heard from the lips of the lady storytellers.

The pretext is a common one, and disingenuous, as we shall see in the case of the *Evangiles des quenouilles*, where the writer informs us, from the start, that he has been called in as a mere scribe to record the wit and wisdom of the gathering, exchanged over a series of six days, a traditional hexameron (p. 27). The questions are practical, and frequently erotic; the group of matrons – of old wives – give remedies for impotence, wife-beating, unwanted babies, they interpret dreams and omens and weather portents, they recommend love potions, they give advice about handling animals, they foretell the future – all tasks intimately connected with natural processes. This was of course the domain of midwives, layers-out – and witches – and the target concern of a hellfire preacher like the Franciscan Olivier Maillard, who inventoried current superstitions. He naturally denounced sorcerers, who made pacts with the Devil, but he also attacked the practices described in *Les Evangiles*: *carminatores* (charmers) who use verbal spells to heal, diviners who prognosticate, chiromancers who interpret bodily signs, and interpreters of dreams, all fell to the lash of his tongue.

The friar was in deadly earnest, but in *Les Evangiles* the author has his tongue in his cheek. The whole proceedings are presented in facetious, mock-scholarly style, with Question and Answer in the schoolmen's favourite manner of *disputatio*, and glosses offered by the attendant ladies. The woodcuts included in the first edition of *Les Evangiles* depict the participants telling the points of their arguments on their left hand with the index finger of their right, in the classical style of the rhetor, while the youthful scribe sits at work to the side with pen and scroll. Apart from the off-colour character of the remarks, the participants are given burlesque, dirty-minded names – Sebille des Mares (Sybil of the Swamps), Ysabel de la Creste Rouge (Isabella Red Crest) – or downright bawdy – Belote la Cornue, Perrette du Trou-Punais, Noir Trou (Big Horned Bella, Little Perry Stink-Hole, Black Hole), and so forth; the artist represents some in full matronly veils and coifs, their younger companions in décolletage and the fashionable steeple wimples of the late fifteenth century. Though it is indisputable that the book contains lore in circulation as seriously intended remedies and methods of redress, it passes it mockingly as lewdness and superstition and guys the purveyors as whores and bawds, beldames and trots. The distaff, the symbol of women's domestic industry, also carried dubious connotations, on account of its shape, and it was frequently positioned by artists at a suggestive angle. It is also featured as a recurrent double entendre in the solution to obscene popular riddles – for instance, 'I am one span long, delicate, round and white …' (p. 137).

When one of the distaff-wielding beldames, Transie d'Amour (Transported by Love), hears from the group that the loss of a shoe means that a lover or husband will go astray, she comments that this must be correct, as she lost her garter in the street a few days ago and has not seen her lover Joliet – Little Pretty One – since. The text does not fail to tell us that she is sixty-seven years old – a stereotypical figure from the *danse macabre* of the crone inflamed with lust. Cuckoldry fans the jokes, at the expense of women who instigate chaos and of men who allow it, just as in Steen's christening feast a guest is already surreptitiously making the sign of the horned beast over the baby's head, an apotropaic gesture, perhaps, against the humiliation inevitably threatening his future in this unruly society dominated by the deceits and scandalous appetites of women (Pl. 3).

Les Evangiles des quenouilles sends out conflicting messages, but it clearly parodies a type of circulating medieval text which had on occasions been written by a woman: the mirror of conduct, or, in other words, 'life, a user's manual'. Christine de Pizan, for instance, earnestly composed deeply felt variations on this didactic genre, and when she was invited, by a nobleman, to compose a poem about an unhappy love affair, she took the opportunity to combine a long verse romance with personal, stinging comments on the problem of passion for women. Like a beldame in the circle of the *Evangiles des quenouilles*, she doled out advice in the risky area of sex. But unlike them, she was sceptical of love's promises. *The Book of the Duke of True Lovers* was probably written between 1403 and 1405, and in it Christine creates, as the mouthpiece of her practical discourse against romance, an older woman with the emblematically lofty name of Sebille de Monthault, Dame de la Tour. This Sibylline figure interrupts the lovers' poetic duet to warn that their adultery is folly and will bring them misery and shame.

Not a message for gallant ears, and indeed a dynamic part of Pizan's continuing campaign against medieval perceptions of women's primary erotic role, for good or ill. The letter Sebille writes the lovers reappears as an example of the good advice a chaperone might send her mistress in Christine's *The Treasure of the City of Ladies* of 1405, and it takes up a theme already present in yet another urgently phrased document, the earlier *Debate of Two Lovers*: thraldom to love, she points out there, very rarely truly happens, in spite of romance literature's obsession with its power. 'That's a very common *conte*', she writes dismissively, 'a tale told to women', and 'she who believes it in the end is not considered very wise'.

Bearing in mind Christine's Sibylline rejection of prejudice and fraudulence in traditional courtly romance and her level-headed warnings against its harmfulness, the claim that the parodic old women in *Les Evangiles des quenouilles* are peddling ancient, typical female wisdom looks collusive with that precise fraudulence. Attributing to women themselves the kind of salacious advice that corroborates adultery conveniently portrays women inciting and perpetuating the conditions which make them – as well as men – suffer. The male scribe, the male author, by picturing such erotic conspiracies among women alone, exculpates his own kind from responsibility for current fantasies about the opposite sex. But it is also clear, both from Christine's strictures and from the *Evangiles*' author's asides, that storytelling and spindle chatter were agreed to gather together women of different classes, and to disseminate dangerous attitudes to love and the governance of men.

In the *Evangiles* the female 'secrets' on which he eavesdrops transgress as well in refusing a rational perception of the universe – as Christine implies with her reproaches against mother-wit. At the end, the self-styled scribe evades involvement altogether, and issues a warning that what is written in these Gospels demonstrates the frailty of those who give way to gossip when they find themselves together.

In France and England, in the two centuries following the publication of the *Evangiles*, the theme of women's gossip and its dangerous powers grew in intensity. In the seventeenth century, broadsheets denounced women's rattling tongues. They were associated with curses and spells, with the vices of nagging and tale-bearing; there even exist, from the same century that saw the development of Mother Goose tales, branks or scold's bridles – contraptions like dog muzzles designed to gag women who had been charged and found guilty of blasphemy and defamation. In England, in 1624, a law against cursing was passed, and its targets were not only men who swore, but women who could conjure. Victims identified as witches in league with the Devil by inquisitors and prickers were often only poor old folk who might use swearing and vituperation to retaliate against maltreatment or neglect in default of other means of defence. The classical and medieval topoi of unruly wives and matrimonial pains survived sturdily in the culture of print and gained a more sinister social and legal footing.

In France, the unruliness of women's wagging tongues was illustrated in a print of around 1560 called '*Le Caquet des femmes*', in which the women are shown brawling among themselves as well as provoking fights between men as a consequence of their chatter. An early seventeenth-century English broadsheet – 'Tittle Tattle; or the several Branches of Gossiping' – similarly depicts the feared sites where women's tongues will wag, where they find themselves alone and able to communicate without supervision (pp. 40–1). The first place is 'At the Childbed'. Women friends of the new mother – the gossips – are arriving to help with the birth. The 'Market' follows, then the bakehouse, the baths, church, and the river for laundry. The admonition concludes:

> Then Gossips all a Warning take,
> Pray cease your Tongue to rattle;
> Go Knit and Sew and Brew and Bake
> And leave off Tittle Tattle.

The word *caquet*, cackle, was used in the titles of a popular variety of book, collections of supposed female secrets: *Caquets des poissonnières* (1621–2) (Fishwives' Chatter), *Caquets des femmes du Faubourg Montmartre* (1622), and, the

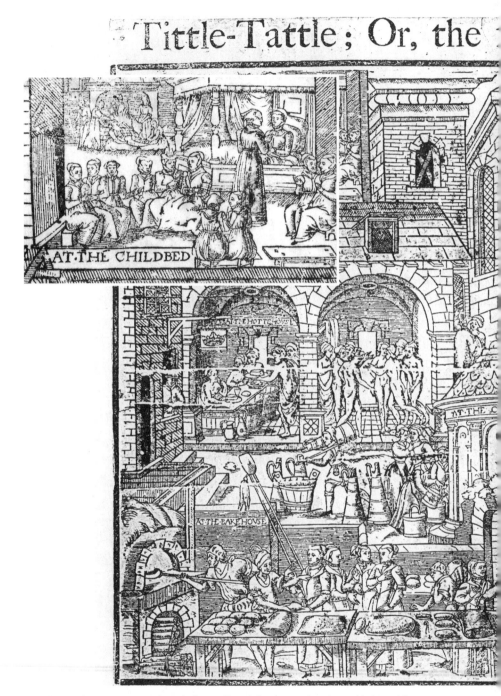

The places where women gathered alone offered dangerous freedom, this broadsheet warned, in the lively exchange of news and gossip. At the lying-in TOP LEFT, in the hothouse, and then at the baker's, the well (conduit), the alehouse, the river bank for the laundry, at the market, and in church they mark ordinary moments of a woman's work (and play). However

eral Branches of Gofsipping.

AT THE CHVRCH.

AT THE MARKET.

WACHERS AT THE RIVER

AT THE ALLE HOVS

fighting CENTRE *and other unruliness results. The author says: 'At Child-bed when the Gossips meet,/ Fine stories we are told;/ and if they get a Cup too much,/ Their Tongue, they cannot hold.' ('Tittle-Tattle, or the several Branches of Gossipping', English, c. 1603.)*

most successful, *Les Caquets de l'accouchée* (Chatter at the Lying-in), which first appeared in 1623 with several reprints (one appeared later in the same publisher's list of *Facéties*, or Jests, alongside *Les Evangiles des quenouilles*). As in *Les Evangiles des quenouilles*, this chatter at the childbed by the mother's friends and cronies was reportedly transcribed at her behest by *un secrétaire* over a period of eight days. The women are imagined to exchange complaints about men: for instance husbands do not work hard enough to provide their wives with luxuries. The mother-to-be is twenty-four and a half and already has borne seven children, but still her mind fixes on frivolities (of course). The text, in spite of its levity, includes sober reflections on the cost of dowries, and the difficulties poor women have in finding a husband who will accept them dowerless. On the whole, it jokes against women, focussing on their erotic adventures. It reports that a sick man was advised by his physician to smuggle himself in to listen, as what he would overhear would stir him up so much he would regain his health.

It would be absurd piety to suggest that the transformed meanings of the word 'gossip' and all its pejorative connotations do not spring from experience. But, as ever, it depends whose experience, where, and when. The gossip-mongering of the Roman *borgo* or inner-city neighbourhood can look rather different from a woman's point of view. Elisabetta Rasy, the contemporary Italian novelist, offers some pungent observations on the prejudice against the *chiacchiera*, the traditional chatter of women in the street in Italy; gossip carried knowledge of secrets, of intimate matters – including illicit information about sex, contraception and abortion which threatened the official organs of the Church, the law, and science. Gossip includes mother-wit, and mother-wit knows a thing or two that They don't know, or rather, that They don't want to be known. Or, again, that They fear they don't know. Rasy makes the connection between intimate talk and the control of women's flesh – its pleasures and its sufferings – which those locker-room-minded mischief-makers, the anonymous authors of *Les Evangiles des quenouilles* and *Les Caquets de l'accouchée*, were insinuating, but she makes it as a partisan of gossip, not its enemy.

In a tobacconist's shop in Jalisco province in Mexico, two postcards were recently on sale, both lurid caricatures: in one a bent old harridan hauls her shopping while two lounging men look on approvingly: she has a huge padlock through her lips (Pl. 14). In the other, a sharp-featured woman's eyes are popping in terror as a hairy fist pulls out her viper's tongue and prepares to cut it off with scissors (p. 50). These images correspond to cautionary children's literature of the late nineteenth century, in which a similar asymmetry between the value of men's and women's expression governs the laws of good behaviour. The wife of Monsieur Croquemitaine the bogeyman comes for little girls who show too much curiosity and shuts them up in a trunk. The practice of storytelling was adapted to curb the tales children themselves might tell.

III

Rhetoric and iconography which exhibit fear of gossips' influence have persisted in singling out the ageing woman as culprit. The high-spirited bawdy of *Les Evangiles des quenouilles* makes fun of old women's lusts; later, the accusation turns nastier, and by the seventeenth century the outward form of the garrulous crone was established as an allegory of unwifely transgressions, of disobedience, opinion, anger, outspokenness, and general lack of compliance with male desires and behests. Female old age represented a violation of teleology, and this carried implications beyond the physical state, into wider prescriptions of femininity.

The satire of Lustucru's smithy gave a new twist to a medieval theme: the recycling of wives when their husbands are tired of them. Lustucru works as doctor and smith at one time, but the texts return to the verb *repolir* – to repolish. This ingenious topos relates to the medieval burlesque image of *The Mill of Old Wives*, which also circulated in print form. In a nineteenth-century woodcut version from Denmark (below), undesirable crones approaching the mill (one is being wheeled by her husband): they are shown being fed into the mill, ground and

Early cosmetic surgery: halt and maimed, bald and toothless, crones are encouraged to try the magic of The Mill for Old Wives. Helped into the hopper and ground on the millstone, they emerge bright-eyed and bushy-tailed into the arms of gallant young husbands. (Danish, nineteenth century.)

whittled, until they re-emerge whole and young and vigorous and amorous – again. 'Their mouths', says the inscription, 'will be all the better for kissing now.' The turning of the millstone does the work of Lustucru's hammer; the women are worked and honed and polished. (Curiously, the men themselves have not suffered the effects of old age – an imperviousness which signals the unimportance of the issue in their case.)

The virtue of Obedience was traditionally represented by the iconic representation of Silence; the third of the Franciscan vows, Obedience puts a finger to her lips in the thirteenth-century fresco by the Maestro delle Vele in Assisi. When the object of desire raised her voice, her desirability decreased; speaking implied unruliness, disobedience. And the penalty for this – the quick, ready-to-hand expression of this undesirable lack of compliance – was the appearance of physical decay. Decrepitude enciphered ugliness, ugliness unloveliness, unloveliness unwomanliness, unwomanliness infertility: a state of being against nature. The association between a woman's body and her speech, between her face and figure and her tongue, lies at the heart of the public male quest for a desirable match. To look fair and speak fair are linked feminine virtues; to look foul and speak foul equally; the hag curses, the scold is ugly. The womb redeems the tongue; vulgarly speaking, a wombful excuses a mouthful. The First Epistle to Timothy makes the link explicit : motherhood redeems woman not merely from sexuality, but from her sinfulness as a speaking woman: 'A woman ought not to speak … Nevertheless she will be saved by childbearing' (1 Tim. 2: 15).

Consequently, the infertile woman, past the age of childbearing, transgresses the function and purpose of her sex, and like any transgressor against the God-given, natural order could serve to represent other pejorative and repugnant aberrations. As lewdness was a vice, and inappropriate lewdness, in a woman past her bloom, an even greater vice, the bedizened crone, or the hag who seeks to tempt love, emerges as an emblem of Sin itself, in allegories of vice in a wide variety of media, in secular and religious manuscript illumination, in sculpture, embroideries, tapestries, ivory, enamel work, as well as the major fine arts. This iconographic language remains stable, like its verbal counterpart – the word 'hag' has not shifted in meaning since it first was established in English usage in the sixteenth century; Shakespeare, in whose work it acts as a synonym for witches, also frequently associates the word with an evil tongue.

Although allegory is a learned language, it travels, and it combines with cultural *données* to convey shared, material attitudes. Uncovering its structural axioms can help dismantle those conventionally attributed meanings themselves. For instance, in René d'Anjou's early fifteenth-century romance, *Le Livre du cueur d'amours espris* (The Book of the Heart Smitten with Love), Jalousie, a female, lies in wait for the hero, the Knight of the Heart, and waylays him in the forest. The chivalric novel describes her in ferocious terms:

> A hunchbacked dwarf made all at cross purposes [*contrefaicte*] in face and body ... hair ... like the pelt of an old boar ... eyes ... like fiery coals ... nose ... large and twisted ... mouth long and wide to her ears ... yellow teeth, ears hanging down more than a palm's length ... dugs big and soft and hanging on her belly ... her feet broad and webbed like a swan's ...

Jealousy is represented with unkempt hair and pelts of beasts (as well as withered dugs and splay feet) as she waylays the page Ardent Desire, in the foreground and the Knight of the Heart, visored behind him. (René d'Anjou, Livre du cueur d'amours espris, French, fifteenth century.)

The key word here is '*contrefaicte*' – counterfeit, or 'made against', implying that her physical condition flouted nature's laws and purposes. More particularly, Jalousie represents, in the romance, wicked counsel or speech, for she has captured and gagged the helpful and beautiful youth called Bel Acueil (Fair Welcome) who was to lead the lovers through the forest; and with her long, wide mouth she utters dreadful curses on them to impede their progress.

A female personification – Justice or Charity, for instance – embodies meaning in its absolute and ideal ontological fullness, but does not pretend to represent the virtue's active human agent (the good judge, the almsgiver). By contrast, allegories of the vices usually perform their wicked deeds themselves. They communicate meaning by anecdote and example: in the choir at Chartres, Gula (Greed) prepares to eat a large pork pie, while on the South Portal, Luxuria (Lust) is represented as a lewd embrace between the Devil and a lady. The vices cannot belong

When it comes to images of hags, the conventions of allegory merge with the assumptions of moralizing: a classic representation of Vanity, as a wrinkled old flirt, with mirror, fripperies, and roses doomed to fade, is renamed for publication in print as 'The Old Procuress at the Toilet Table' and passes for a portrait of a real life bawd. (Jeremias Falck, after Bernardo Strozzi, seventeenth century.)

in the universal world of fixed forms, without falling into the Manichaean heresy of granting equal power and existence to the realm of the Devil. So they must be made flesh, take on humanity; when that humanity is female, the sin and the sinner become one and the same, allegory flows into anecdotal or literal depiction, the figured idea acquires social, historical and material context, participating in a narrative of either imaginary or lived experience. In the area of sexuality and its linked sins – like Vanity – the ageing woman emerges as the most fittingly abhorrent image. A seventeenth-century *Allegory of Vanitas*, for instance, was drawn by Jeremias Falck after a painting by Bernardo Strozzi. When the engraving was published, it was given a different title, namely, *The Old Procuress at the Toilet Table* (above). This hesitancy, which fails to distinguish clearly between the social document – an image from a brothel – and the figuration of an abstract idea – Vanity – in the engraving reveals a crucial historical aspect of the representation of vice as an old woman.

Allegories of vice are often hard to see; they can wear a look of naturalistic documentation; the allegorical tradition mingles with and influences the conventions of the naturalistic mode of representation, and whereas idealization is easy to detect, vituperation can present itself in the guise of verisimilitude.

In seventeenth-century Dutch painting, the figure of the bawd, as painted by Strozzi, recurs as a conventional character. She is often toothless, chapfallen, and scraggy; in *The Procuress* by Dirck van Baburen, this kind of crone scratches the palm of her hand avariciously as a client embraces a smiling and voluptuous girl

(Pl. 5). Yet the confessions of prostitutes and their madams in seventeenth-century Amsterdam reveal that many of the bawds began their careers in their twenties – as soon as they could leave the activity of prostitution and run a girl or two themselves, they did so. In consequence, the average age of the bawds was between thirty and thirty-five, around ten years older than the young women working under their control. Even allowing for different life expectancy and health, the bawds in Strozzi's or Van Baburen's paintings could not be in their thirties: the tradition of allegorical vice has modified the artists' pictorial language and led them to the hag in order to convey the moral meanings they intended.

When the Dutch genre painters turned to scenes of urban life, the language available to them for communicating the identity of a procuress was particular and limited. It was provided by a medieval vocabulary of sensual sin, which provided hags as the principal characters in a cautionary tale about the ugliness and the penalties of lust.

Allegory has a long reach, deep into the most seemingly realistic ways of representation. The topos does not belong exclusively to the Judaeo-Christian tradition and its expression in Dutch Protestant culture. Since classical times, the hag has been reviled; and the hag who does not know herself to be a hag but primps and coquettes like a young woman came in for special abuse. Desire in a woman who cannot justify it by the grace of fecundity becomes excessive and unnatural; her lust *ipso facto* a mark of perverse insatiability. But the allegorical hag's sins are not bodied forth only by the impairments and disfigurements of age, the sagging breasts and scrawny genitals against which medieval poems like the pseudo-Ovidian *De Vetula*, for instance, inveigh. A constant tendency inspires the image of transgressions as sins of her mouth: especially the noisy evils of her tongue. The classical personification of Ira (Anger) resembles Invidia (Envy) in her railing, and both derive from the Greek daimon Eris, or Strife, in Homer. Similarly, the conventional allegory of Invidia, Envy, is associated with wrongful speech; Cesare Ripa, author of the influential handbook on symbolic representation, the *Iconologia*, recommends that she be represented raging, gnawing her own heart and crowned with a mane of hissing snakes.

The principal sin, however, with which the tongue is particularly connected is lust, for, since the days of Eve and the serpent, as we have seen, seduction lies in talk, and the tongue is seduction's tool. In medieval representations, the Devil at his work of temptation sometimes mirrors Eve's own face, but he also often has wrinkled female dugs – his perversion blazoned on his chest as breasts that have lost their true purpose of nursing. Consequently, the body of an infertile woman, when invoked in any way as a body, expresses perforce a perverted dimension of the natural, becomes transgressive in itself, open to derision as well as fear.

The mill of youth and the anvil of Lustucru stand as emblems that the old woman's voice was particularly disagreeable and disturbing, to male ears in particular: 'Strike hard on the mouth: she has a wicked tongue.'

IV

Both the linguistic link between godmothers and old gossips, and the social link between ageing women and secret, wicked powers, are crucial in the world of fairy tale; wresting control of that evil tongue occupied the energies of many of the pioneers of nursery tales.

Old women, either as godmothers or wicked fairies, dominate the channels of influence depicted within the tales, as Charles Perrault flippantly underlines in his moral to '*Cendrillon*', his famous Cinderella story, when he adds how important it is for a young person to have a well-placed godmother. Perrault was alluding to the worldly society of aristocratic Paris, but in his story he translated the powers of networking into traditional wise-woman magic to assist his heroine's social success – the rat coachman, the lizard footmen (advisedly picked because lizards bask in the sun all day and footmen were notoriously idle) and the pumpkin coach. Such metamorphoses, half a century before Perrault was writing, would have marked the fairy down for a most nefarious witch; indeed, Perrault appears almost to be punning on the fantasy of the witches' stew. Common fears circulated – especially about women who could destroy married bliss by casting spells which made the husband impotent: they were called *noueuses d'aiguillettes* because they were thought to achieve their ends by tying knots using little needles on images of their victims. But by 1697, Perrault and his audience could make light of any dangers from sorcery, while enjoying the fancy of such wonderful powers.

The practice of godparenting created bridges between different social islands: between the poor and the nobility, and vice versa. The disadvantaged might seek a sponsor among the powerful, but an aristocratic family, like the family of the Montaignes, would invite a beggar to hold the infant Michel, the future essayist, at the font at his baptism in 1533, to instil at an early age Christian principles of humility. This custom of infant sponsorship, or co-parenthood, came under pressure from reformers, but it survived, and was ritualized in continued exchanges of hospitality, gifts, and information, as new social alliances were forged at very different levels. The bond was considered so close and strong that it debarred co-sponsors from marrying each other, as if they stood in blood relationship. Gossips created family ties: they marked out the faultlines of allegiance and dissociation.

Gossip and fairy tales have in common a cavalier relation to accuracy; the truths they seek to pass on do not report events with the veracity of a witness in court. They are partial, tending to excess in both praise and blame; tale-bearing is a partisan activity. Though both forms of speech tend to be practised by the least advantaged members of society, they can achieve considerable, even dangerous, influence by such means. Defamation, scandal, hearsay, all aspects of gossip, reappear metamorphosed in fairy tale's plots, featuring wicked stepmothers, false brides, bloodsucking ogres, and predatory suitors. Children, of whatever rank, who play around the women gossiping are learning the rules of the group; fairy tales train them in attitudes and aspirations. This can be a conservative influence: the old can oppress the young with their prohibitions and prejudices as well as enlighten them. But the tale-bearing will in either case pass on vital information, about the values and beliefs of the community in which they are growing up, will instruct them in who is trusted and who is not, about what is considered praiseworthy and what is condemned, about alliances and enmities, hopes and dangers. Stories function in a similar manner: they chart the terrain. Some directions are urged, but the signposts are not entirely coercive. Gossip and narrative are sisters, both ways of keeping the mind alive when ordinary tasks call; the fictions of gossip – as well as the facts – act as compass roses, pointing to many possibilities.

The literary women who wrote fairy tales, the sophisticated milieu in which 'Cinderella', 'The Blue Bird', 'The Subtle Princess' and 'The Sleeping Beauty' were produced, mounted a critical attack on many prejudices and practices of their day, which confined and defamed women in their view and coarsened the minds and manners of all members of society. Paradoxically, gossip was one of the battlefields on which they engaged their enemies, one of the weapons they seized. The culture of the salons in the second half of the seventeenth century fostered the art of conversation as one of the foundation skills of civilization.

The Marquise de Rambouillet (née Catherine de Vivonne de Savelin, 1588–1665), found the court of Louis XIII rather too rustic for her taste, and started receiving at home instead. As a hostess, she made many innovations of a startling kind, which in themselves developed in form and style the custom of the lying-in. She invited her guests to attend her in her *chambre bleue*, her blue bedroom, and she refashioned the interior of the Hôtel de Rambouillet so that they approached this inner sanctum through a sweeping enfilade of rooms, until they reached their hostess. In this 'alternative court' the lady lay in bed, on her *lit de parade* (her show bed) in her *alcôve*, waiting to be amused and provoked, to be told stories, real and imaginary, to exchange news, to argue and theorize, speculate and plot. The Marquise de Rambouillet sat her favourite guests down to talk to her by her side in the *ruelle* – the 'alley' – which was the space between her bed and the wall. *Ruelles* became the word for such salons, which sprang up in imitation of hers in the city; those who attended were called *alcôvistes*, privy to the *alcôve*. This arrangement of social space, both public and private at the same time, was presided over by women and it lasted until the Revolution. The word 'salon' itself came into use only after the practice had died out.

Ruelles were the frames in which the most familiar fairy tales of the modern nursery were sown and carefully tended, as part of a conscious project to overturn prejudices and refashion conventional values and attitudes. Among these, some of the most lively and refreshing experiments focussed on the pursuits and powers of women, especially in private matters. Gossip was transformed in the *ruelles* into an art of cosmopolitan finesse; stories were elaborated to entertain and instruct; relationships were defined and refined through exchanges of intimate intensity but unbesmirched decorum. Madeleine de Scudéry, the most successful novelist of the day, devised the *Carte de Tendre*, or Map of [the land of] Tenderness, which charted the journey true lovers must take across a symbolic landscape of seas of enmity, lakes of indifference, wastelands of betrayal in order to discover tenderness, in its varied forms, loving friendship as well as ardent passion. If the *académies*, controlling the written word, were dominated by male authors and thinkers, then the *ruelles* were the sphere of women, where they presided over the spoken word and its uses. The grammarian Claude Favre de Vaugelas even conceded them this territory when, in his almost scriptural *Remarques sur la langue française* of 1647, he noted, 'in case of doubt about language, it is ordinarily best to consult women'. The *ruelle* was a space created by noblewomen in the image of the humbler, more chaotic gathering, the gossiping, and among its varied pastimes it strove to give new value to that traditionally despised pursuit and talent of women, old and young: to give tittle-tattle its due as an art of communication, as an aspect of storytelling.

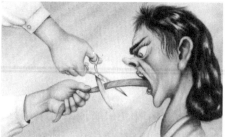

Strong measures for rattling tongues: Mexican postcard, c. 1985.

CHAPTER 4

Game Old Birds: Gossips III

Storks were descending in slow circles in the direction of the river, soon to hold their first parliament before flying off to warmer lands. Helena suddenly recalled the local superstition – if a young woman sees a stork in a meadow it means that she'll become pregnant soon. What has happened, she thought. What have I done? But she was in a state of sleepy bliss.

Tadeusz Konwicki

During the closing, valedictory session of *Les Evangiles des quenouilles*, one of the hags, Dame Berthe de Corne, tells the company that she is going to give away 'a marvellous secret few men know'. She then reveals, 'I tell you true: storks, which keep themselves in these parts in summer and in winter return to their own country near Mount Sinai, are creatures just like us.'

Another member of the company, *'vieille à merveille'* (wondrously ancient), with the cod name Dame Abreye l'Enflée (Dame Put-down Over-the-top), confirms this secret, relating that she had often heard how her uncle Claus from Bruges had been to the monastery of Saint Catherine in the Sinai and had become

The goose was sacred to the Goddess of Love, Aphrodite, who occasionally settled herself sidesaddle in the crux of the bird's neck and wing to travel through the air LEFT. (White ground cup attributed to the 'Pistoxenos Painter', c. 460 BC.) A millennium or two on, and 'Old Mother Goose when she wanted to wander, / Would fly through the air on a very fine gander.' (Arthur Rackham, 'Mother Goose', The Old Nursery Rhymes, 1913.)

separated from his companions. But then he had met a creature, and when he addressed her in Flemish, she had immediately answered him in his own language and showed him the way. She also told him that she was a stork in his own part of the world, and made her nest in Flanders on the roof of one of his neighbours. Then she gave him a ring which he recognized – it belonged to his wife Mal Cenglée (Badly Beaten). The stork returned the ring to him on condition that he forbade the members of his household to maltreat his wife any longer 'as they were in the habit of doing'. He agreed, and on his return kept his promise. And so, the old woman goes on to say, he died fat and happy – with a waistline of fourteen hands in breadth.

At this happy outcome, all the matrons laugh and put away their distaffs. The scribe then rounds off the whole book by describing how the ladies, suddenly conscious again of his presence, wished to reward him, and offered him his pick amongst them. But he declines, with a *'facétie joyeuse'* (a merry jest). His reintroduction of himself into the story, and his clearly underlined merit, protests too much, but his chastity does draw attention yet again to the off-colour character of the stork-ladies' solicitations.

Contes de la cigogne (Tales of the Stork) was an alternative French phrase for fairy tales. In 1694, the long awaited *Dictionnaire* of the Académie Française offered the following remarks by way of defining the word *conte*:

> *Le vulgaire appelle* conte au vieux loup. conte de vieille. conte de ma Mère l'Oye. conte de la cigogne, conte à la cicogne. conte de peau d'asne. conte à dormir debout. conte jaune, bleu, violet, conte borgne, *Des fables ridicules telles que sont celles dont les vieilles gens entretiennent et amusent les enfants.*

> [The common people call 'old wolf's tale', 'old wives' tale', 'Mother Goose tale', 'tale of the stork', 'tale in the stork style', 'donkeyskin tale', 'tale to fall asleep on your feet', 'yellow, blue, violet, one-eyed tale' all those ridiculous fables the like of which old people tell to entertain and amuse children ...]

The phrase *conte de la cigogne* could also be related to another early term for a folk tale, *conte de la quelongne* – an alternative spelling for *quenouille*, used by Martin Le Franc some time before 1461; this term creates a wonderfully rickety but possible morphological bridge for a medieval gossip to cross, from a distaff to a stork.

The dictionary intensified the gender distinctions of the term in a related entry under *oye*, goose: giving as an example, 'This nurse tells Mother Goose tales', and adding, in counterpoint, 'It is also said that "A man tells Mother Goose Tales", when he says things in which there is no semblance of reason.' What was speech proper to a nurse turned into fribbles on the lips of a man. When the preacher Olivier Maillard sententiously attacked *Les Evangiles des quenouilles*, he warned: 'All those things that will do nothing for the salvation of those to whom one speaks, are considered fables, those tales one makes up to while away the time, those tales of the stork, as people say.' Rabelais also uses the phrase to characterize popular narratives.

Christine de Pizan was stern, as we have seen, about the power of *contes* to present false dreams and foster illusions about love; the author of the *Evangiles* mocks the tattle of women while remaining agog about its supposed mysteries. The lubricious character of much of his material does not however succeed in concealing altogether certain harsh realities and the role of storytelling in resisting them. Readers of *Les Evangiles* might be expected to laugh at these old women with their foolish notions and their lascivious know-how, but they also communicate revealing material about women's areas of complaint, and stratagems of redress: the story of the stork with the wife's ring seems to threaten a husband that she will run away and refuse to come back unless things change at home. The old wife telling the tale is shown to be pressing her own case and the case of women who are like her under duress.

As if it were a folding ruler, the text attempts to collapse many different angles of view on to a single ribald level, yet through the voice of the male scribe transmitting his scorn and mockery, his fear and contempt for the old wife and her foolish husband who is so gullible, we can nevertheless also catch a woman's genuine plea for self-respect, and the respect of others; Mal Cenglée does not want to be badly beaten any more. Fairy lore and *contes* – the women are dubbed fairies as well as storks, one of them is even called Gombarde la Faée (Gombarda the Fairy) – can help women to defend themselves. Mother-wit can be wised up to a great deal – however foolish it may appear.

The knowledge conveyed is twofold, at least: about women's experience, and about men's perception of it, about women's defences and men's retaliation too. Mal Cenglée, the obliquely mocked object of this jest, yet establishes herself as an exemplary subject of such narratives: the badly beaten wife, in one way or the other, tells her story through the layered tragi-comedies of fairy tales. The author of the *Evangiles* might present the tale as the height of nonsense – whoever heard of a husband agreeing to such terms? – but his nonsense can still read as another man's – or woman's – good sense.

In folklore flourishing in countries where storks returned in the spring to nest on house chimneys, the bird became a symbol of birth; in the nineteenth century, children were told that storks fetched new babies from wells and marshes, and then delivered them to their human parents. (Ida Rentoul Outhwaite, 'A Mothers' Meeting', Melbourne, 1916.)

In classical mythology, which is particularly rich in bird metamorphoses, storks were believed to migrate to the Isles of the Blessed when they died, there to change into human form. The story in *Les Evangiles des quenouilles* only faintly echoes this belief, displacing in the manner of fairy tale the afterlife with the present time; and merging the comic figure of the story stork with the old wife, gossip, peddler of tall tales and foolish wisdom. Pierre Jannet, the bookseller–publisher who reissued *Les Evangiles* in 1815, added that the original was a manuscript in the collection of M. Armand Cigongne (sic), proof that the French can nudge and wink as well as any British panto dame. Both large birds familiar in the domestic setting who yet remain untamed, the goose and the stork became the imaginary authors of children's fairy stories.

II

The title *Contes de ma Mère l'Oye* first appears in print as a title of a collection of stories in 1697, in the frontispiece of Charles Perrault's *Contes du temps passé*; not on the title page, but in a panel hanging on the wall behind the engraved image of a crone telling stories to three children (p. ii). The same year, the *commedia dell'arte* players at the Hôtel de Bourgogne staged a burlesque romance called *Les Fées ou Les Contes de ma Mère l'Oye*, which was set in 'a cave of ogres' and featured Harlequin and Pierrot as well as all the stock figures of fairy tale: a weeping and about-to-be-ravished princess, her beloved prince, the ogre who wakes up at the scent of 'the fresh meat' of the prince and says that the princess can have a haunch if she loves him so. The script throws in seven-league boots, an old wife who tells a tall tale as well as lots of metamorphoses. The princess is originally imprisoned in an iron tower, but the ogre captures her with a magnet, 'And made her follow after him like a little spaniel.' It all ends happily, of course.

The company of Italian players was closed down by order of the king that same year; Louis had come under the pious influence of Madame de Maintenon and they had made fun of her. Their frivolity was deemed improper and they were banished.

Contes de ma Mère l'Oye were referred to before this date, but in passing in earlier literature, as in Loret's *La Muse historique* of 1650. The term was often coupled with the phrase *contes de Peau d'Ane*, or 'Donkeyskin tales', after the heroine of the fairy tale: Cyrano de Bergerac called the works of his fellow poet Scarron 'a pot pourri of Donkeyskin and Mother Goose tales', and Scarron himself imagined the young Astyanax in Troy being entertained by his grandmother Hecuba's tales, among which he also included 'Donkeyskin'. Mme de Sévigné, writing to the king's sister in 1656, told her the story of *la cane de Montfort*, a kind of precursor of Jemima Puddleduck. This was a ninny who forgot to say her prayers to Saint Nicholas, changed into a duck and so was ever afterwards obliged on his feast to leave her pond with her ducklings and offer them all up in expiation at the altar. Mme de Sévigné adds that this was not exactly a tale of Mother Goose:

> *Mais de la cane de Montfort,*
> *Qui, ma foi, lui ressemble fort.*

> [But of the duck of Montfort who,
> upon my soul, strongly resembles her.]

She thus projected the foolishness of the protagonist on to the type of story in which she figures, significantly transposing the character of the teller to the subject of the tale.

The terms for *contes* were interchangeable and their tone at best bantering, at worst contemptuous, and both the image of the goose and that of the stork prove on examination to be richly compacted of belief and fantasy. The goose serves as the emblematic beast par excellence of folly and, more particularly, of female noise, of women's chatter. The anonymous sixteenth-century lyric which begins 'The silver swan who living had no note ...' ends with the couplet:

Farewell all joys, O death come close mine eyes,
More geese than swans now live, more fools than wise.

The sinister Cesare Lombroso, in his pseudo-scientific *La Femme criminelle et la prostituée* of 1896, argued that women's foolish tongues were biologically determined, and he used traditional proverbs in Latin as well as modern languages to prove that their nature had been understood since time immemorial. But many of these sayings, from all over Europe, focus on geese as gossips' emblematic creatures: *'Deux femmes et une oie font une foire'* (Two women and a goose a fair make), or again, according to the fifteenth-century English proverb, 'Many women, many words; many geese, many turds.' La Fontaine, a contemporary of Perrault, tells in one of his *Fables*, *'Les Femmes et le secret'*, how a husband, as a test of his wife's discretion, cries out in the night that he has laid an egg; she immed-iately rushes to her neighbour and the egg grows four times the size, the neighbour runs on, and the egg increases to three in number, and so forth, until the whole town marvels that he has laid more than a hundred. The metaphor of laying a giant egg, used here for telling a whopper, animates the image of the storytelling goose who believes the tall tales she passes on.

Birds' language inspired a large body of stories in classical myth: the most popular form of metamorphosis, they were credited with the invention of many aspects of human culture, as well as hidden, lucid foreknowledge, both ominous and wonderful; what was apparently random, opaque and unreflecting could become transparent and eloquent. In one myth their tracks, writing a natural cuneiform in the sand, lay at the origin of the alphabet; Hermes, watching the flight of cranes in wedge formation, hit upon the idea of letters (in this, he becomes a rival pioneer to the Sibyl of Cumae); their twittering followed a code which seers like Tiresias could crack, and Odysseus was warned of danger by the cries of swallows and herons. Later, in Rome, state augurs interpreted the omens of wing and beak, liver and innards. Later still, in the *Narrenschiff* or *The Ship of Fools*, the German poet Sebastian Brant would inveigh against diviners who fancied they could read the future in the heavens and their portents – starry or avian. In German folklore, too, 'birds converse together', wrote the Grimm brothers, 'on the destinies of men, and foretell the future'. The noise of birds was occasionally easy to understand: 'the crane with his trumpe' gave warning of rain, and geese made excellent sentries, famously raising the alarm on the Capitol at the approach of the Gauls. But in spite of this august historical role, the goose was traditionally graded among the lower creatures, associated with low functions.

In French, the verb *cacarder* is used for the noise made by a goose; *caquet* or chatter, as we saw, means women's talk as well as the goose's cry. Not as onomatopoeic as the English 'honk', *cacarder* does catch the coprological side of infantile existence more than 'cackle'. However, the associations of the bird do not end there. Geese strike erotic not just scatological resonances: they were sacred to Isis as well as to Aphrodite, who uses them as her flying steeds, standing on an outstretched bird in a dish from Boeotia of the sixth century BC, and riding most gracefully sidesaddle on a particularly beautiful white ground kylix made around 460 BC (p. 51). (Though it must be said that it is not always possible, in the silence of monochrome artefacts, to tell geese and swans apart.) The goose was specifically sacred to Peitho, the nymph who personifies Persuasion and stands at Aphrodite's side in scenes of seduction – the embodiment of her sweet-talking tongue. In France *la petite-oie*, little goose, was used of fripperies of dress, and, by extension, of favours begged and received between lovers.

The overtones grew more explicit, too: 'goose' became a term for venereal disease in England in the sixteenth century. The folklore scholar Malcolm Jones suggests that the way geese waggle their short tails may have given rise to these connections, and cites the nickname of a prostitute like Johanna Culdoe (*Cul d'oie*: Goosebottom) from Paris, in 1292. A squat goose appears on the sign hanging above the brothel in Bosch's painting of *The Prodigal Son*, and Chester Kallman and W. H. Auden gave the brothel-keeper in their opera of *The Rake's Progress* the name Mother Goose. *Oies blanches* is still used in France for convent girls, ripe for picking; goosefeather beds are synonymous with luxury, and the prodigious infant Gargantua, after trying out every kind of material to wipe his bottom, concludes that there is nothing in the world as blissfully soft as gosling's down.

The sexual associations led inevitably to a connection with reproduction: the 'goose-month' was a term used for a woman's lying-in before the birth of a child. But the goose could also convey bliss under a more benign aspect: not only sex, but cosiness, the partner in the (goose-feather) bed who is a skilled homemaker too. In Normandy, fairies took the form of geese to turn a good deed (or a foul) on humans. Ducks carry similar associations in contemporary survivals: the Cockney endearment 'ducks', for instance. In rhyming slang 'goose and duck' means 'fuck'. Meanwhile the French *canard* (false trail, old rag) continues to net birds and tall tales together.

III

These associations grow even richer with regard to another of the larger non-passerine birds, the stork. The *Dictionnaire de l'Académie* attributed fairy tales to storks as well as geese; around a hundred and fifty years later, Hans Christian Andersen opened 'The Bog King's Daughter' (1858), one of his most complex and beautiful stories, with the words:

> The storks tell their young ones many stories and fairy tales ... [They] know two stories that are very ancient and very long: one of them is the story of Moses ... The other tale is not well known, possibly because it is a bit provincial. It is a fairy tale that has been told by stork mothers for a thousand years ... The first storks who told it had experienced it themselves ...

Children's publishers in Victorian England took up the image and illustrated the storytelling stork on the covers of their collections of fairy tales (p. 65).

The symbol of the stork flourishes within a myth of rich complexity, edifying and bawdy at once. The beldames of the *Evangiles des quenouilles* are really storks in disguise, because their particular areas of expertise – venery, parturition, the domestic hearth, curing – took the bird as totem. The bestiaries of the middle ages, following Aristotle and other classical sources after him, describe the stork caring for its parents in their old age – in Ovid's *Metamorphoses*, Antigone who looked after the blinded Oedipus is changed into a stork, and in Renaissance paintings the bird symbolizes filial piety. The beldames of *Les Evangiles* are claiming the high ground of fidelity, in itself a matter of intended merriment for the book's readers. But it is they who are also likely to have received the news of the crones' disguise as a scabrous reference.

In his encyclopedia, *On the Property of Things*, Bartholomaeus Anglicus (also called Bartholomew de Glanville) passed on a traditional Just-So story of the time:

> A stork is a water fowl and purgeth herself with her own bill, for when she feedeth herself with much meat she taketh sea water in her bill and putteth it in at her hinder hole and so into her guts, and that water neisschith [softens] hardness of hard meat and biteth the guts and putteth out superfluities.

Monkish teleological reason hunts for the divine plan behind such an exaggerated aspect of creation as the beak of a stork. The book was compiled in Paris in the mid-thirteenth century, but it appeared in print only around 1470, almost contemporaneously with *Les Evangiles*. The idea was not confined to one source. Polydore Vergil included a chapter about animals' contributions to knowledge in his compendium on inventions, published in 1546. He marvels at the sandpiper's benevolent picking of crocodiles' teeth, and moves on to the ibis:

> Likewise it was a bird in Egypt who demonstrated a similar thing. The name of this bird is an ibis, and it is almost the same as a stork, and is also the enemy of snakes and very harmful to them. This bird, with the hooked part of its beak, washes itself and washes again in that part where the dross of foodstuffs are expelled.

The ibis of Egypt, which was identified with the stork in more northerly climates, was credited with the invention of the clyster in medieval zoology; hence the bird was also connected to pollution, illness and tabooed, secret knowledge. (Andreas Alciatus, Emblemata, *1550).*

The passage concludes, 'From this doctors first learned the use of the clyster.'

The identifying implement of a midwife, or woman healer, in images of the seventeenth century, was the clyster or large syringe, which can be used, ibis- or stork-style, to deliver enemas before childbirth. A scene of such medical attention is carved on a misericord of 1531 in the church at Walcourt, Belgium, dedicated to Sainte Materne. The woodcarver may have been making a tongue-in-cheek pun on the church's patron saint (Saint Motherly). A seventeenth-century painting called *The Sick Lady*, attributed to Jan Steen, in the Boymans van Beuningen Museum, Rotterdam, shows a leering matron in veil and wimple approaching a fashionably dressed, ailing younger woman and flourishing a medical instrument of this type; the scene takes place in the patient's bedroom and, in spite of its air of

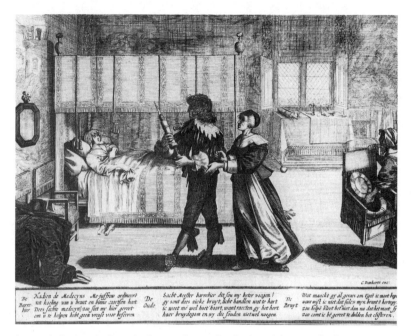

In a variation on the bawdy theme of remedies for lovesickness, a barber-apothecary approaches a patient. A clystering will cool the patient's 'fire', says the barber, but the old woman, with a restraining hand on his arm, wants to take over the operation. The 'bride' in the bed meanwhile calls out impatiently for treatment. (Cornelius Danckertsz, after Abraham Bosse, mid-seventeenth century.)

a genre report on reality, includes many bawdy clues: the scarlet stays of the patient, as well, of course, as the crude angle and size of the clyster itself. The joke here is simply coarse, an allusion to a basic remedy for love pangs. A print of Abraham Bosse published in 1633 shows an apothecary (male) armed with the same tool and sets innuendo aside in the caption:

J'ay la syringue en main, hastez-vous donc, Madame …
De prendre pour le mieux ce petit lavement
… l'outil que je tiens entrera doucement.

[I've the syringe in hand, so hurry, Madam, and accept this little purging to make you better … the tool I'm holding will go in gently …]

But the image carries in some cases a more unruly meaning. Women's access to contraception and abortion through informal channels of information were epitomized by clucking gatherings of women alone, as we saw in Chapter Three; this in turn implied infidelity. Steen's image, ostensibly a painting of illness, could also carry an illicit message, in a spirit of combined humour and blame. For this type of syringe could and can be used to douche the vagina. A print by Cornelius Danckertsz from 1660 (left), after the earlier Bosse image, shows the same scene, but includes some different suggestive verses in which the old woman takes over the handling of the clyster from the man, protesting, 'This would be more suitable for me ... I know how this should be done.' The topos was not confined to a popular taste for the seamy or to sturdy Dutch realism: no less graceful a painter than Watteau drew an energetically erotic scene known as *Le Remède*, showing a maid approaching a naked woman on a bed with a syringe.

Healers using such an instrument were either servicing women's desires by undoing their consequences, or giving them clandestine pleasures. When old women storytellers were dubbed with the name Mother Stork or Mère Cigogne, derogatory – dirty – innuendoes, connected to bodily functions of various unmentionable kinds, would also have sounded in contemporary ears.

The imagery of the clyster begins to be applied to male physicians around the beginning of the seventeenth century, it seems, when the medical profession was establishing control over the healing arts and even ousting women from

Doctors came to be nicknamed 'clysters' in England, and their costume in time of plague in Denmark RIGHT included a bird mask with a curved beak; the French fantasist Grandville punned with his brilliant wit on the connection, LEFT, in P. J Stahl, Scènes de la vie privée et publique des animaux *(Paris, 1842).*

practising their usual skills in obstetrics and gynaecology. Later, by analogy, physicians were actually nicknamed 'clysters' in English, and the same dubious message was passed. In Holland, plague doctors wore a remarkably carnival-like costume: a tall hood with a long, curved, beak mask which was filled with prophylactic herbs (p. 61, right); indeed, on the feast day of their patron saints, Cosmas and Damian, medical students in France would dress up as storks, and let loose with syringes, squirting passers by. Grandville's caricature, drawn in the mid-nineteenth century, recalls with more pointed and genial wit the legendary origin of the instrument (p. 61, left).

Obstetrical instruments adopted stork motifs: a knife for cutting the umbilical cord, made in England in 1870 from mother of pearl and steel, has a pivoted blade in the shape of a stork's beak. It is of course common lore that the stork brings babies: the *Hours of Catherine of Cleves*, illuminated around 1440 in Utrecht, includes a painting of a stork and a baby in a cradle in the marginal decorations to the image of the Judgement of Solomon. While the wise king calls for the baby to be cut in two in order to discover the true mother, the artist teases from the margins, with rather donnish wit, that the real mother is not human at all, but a stork (p. 64). The old wives of the *Evangiles des quenouilles* refer to this aspect of the bird's legend, too, reporting that storks always pay their tithe to God after they have 'made some little ones'. A richly painted manuscript of around the same date as *Les Evangiles* includes a stork bystander at the scene of Julius Caesar's birth – he is being delivered by caesarean section from the body of his dying mother.

The nineteenth-century love of euphemism spread the story more thoroughly through stories for children, especially in urban settings. Interestingly, the association of this waterfowl with midwifery was stronger then than now: children were told that a midwife had pulled the new baby up out of the household well. Gradually the stork eclipsed the figure of the woman, which has been all but totally forgotten, partly because the midwives' sphere of knowledge was declared definitely off-limits to the children. The stork took its place among the fantasy cast – Easter Bunny, Santa Claus, Tooth Fairy – who provided appropriately child-like explanations for events in the adult world as well as encoding a system of rewards and punishments. The bird also satisfied the new European tribalism of the times, as part of the dreamed-of authentic pagan past.

For Hans Andersen, storks not only bring babies, but their repertory consists of stories about the arrival of babies: Moses in the bulrushes, and the Marsh King's daughter herself, whom the stork family find lying in a waterlily. In an earlier tale, 'The Storks' (1838), Andersen imagined the primal scene: 'There is a pond where all the little children lie until the stork comes and gets them for delivery to their parents. There they lie dreaming far more pleasantly than they ever will later in their lives … '. On greetings cards and christening gifts today (which still can include scissors in the shape of the bird), a stork is often represented carrying the baby suspended from her beak in a shawl or a basket, and leaving it in the cradle. In this act of delivery, the stork is of course playing midwife, not mother, the woman with authoritative knowledge of the body's functions. The word is often feminine in gender in countries where the belief in the stork's powers circulates: in French (*cigogne*) or Italian (*cicogna*). In Dutch (*ooievaar*) the word is not gender marked, but in German, *Storch*, the word is masculine, with corresponding, revealing effects on the folklore of the bird's role in bringing babies about: it is associated more with conception than delivery, for it was common in Germany, until this generation, to answer children's questions about where babies came from by saying, 'A stork came and bit Mummy in the foot.'

This would seem a clear euphemism, as *Storch* is related to *stark,* meaning stiff or rigid, and to such cognates as stoke and stick and stock. The Grimms glossed the alternative archaic and poetic word for the bird, *odebero*, as a possible conjunction of *ot*, riches, and *od*, progeny – the bringer of gifts would be an appropriate etymology for the bird who delivers babies. This word is interchangeably used with 'stork' in nursery rhymes:

> *Adebar, du goder, bring mi'n lutjen Broder.*
> *Adebar, du bester, bring mi'n lutje Swester.*
>
> [Stork, good stork, bring me a little brother.
> Stork, best of storks, bring me a little sister.]

English, being a language largely lacking gender inflections, has adopted the German linguistic implications, and frequently understands the stork to be a male bird: it appears dressed in a doctor's suit on greetings cards, and in the latest novelty, two-foot-high plastic Dr Stork balloons bearing the news 'It's a boy!' (blue balloon) / 'It's a girl!'(pink balloon). These modern manifestations still connect with the symbol's distant origins, however, and sometimes in other, suggestive ways: the trading device of Régielinge, a French laundry offering a special nappy service, shows a stork bearing a bag of dirty linen in its beak – a survival of the bird's associations with process and pollution. In Britain, more salubriously, a leading adoption pressure group has called itself Stork.

Wise King Solomon suggests cutting the baby in half; the true mother pleads for the child's life. The illuminator of this fable about motherhood included a baby in a rocking cradle and a stork-like bird on the right. (The Hours of Catherine of Cleves, Utrecht, c. 1440.)

Historically, stork imagery, in art and literature and even clothing, frequently returns the searcher to the Netherlands, where the folklore about the bird still flourishes. In 1695 the stork's role was mentioned in a Dutch Harlequin play – and this is the decade which saw the publication of *contes de la cigogne* by both D'Aulnoy and Perrault in Amsterdam. The English poet John Heath-Stubbs has made the inspired suggestion that the beliefs about the stork migrated with the Dutch themselves, and that, like Santa Claus, they were naturalized in Western culture by the settlers of New York, whence they spread back to Europe far beyond their original territories, losing in the crossing all comic, even pornographic connotations and becoming happy ciphers with which to greet a new arrival. This would illuminate a coincidence in the largely forgotten lore about the bird, that the Dutch word for the bill-clattering noise they make (*klepperen*) corresponds to popular disparagement of women's talk (or babbling) as *clapperij* or *clapperatie*.

Mother Stork's part in storytelling moves along two axes: how she communicates (her clatter, her chatter) and what she talks about (her naughty claptrap). This folklore does not belong in the classical tradition of myth; it grew up at the childbeds, the lyings-in, the bedrooms and the nurseries of more recent history, and more northerly climates than Greece or Sicily. Storks were more common in continental Europe than they are today, though they can still be seen, sometimes. Migrating south in the winter, as *Les Evangiles des quenouilles* reports, they returned as heralds of the spring, of the rise of sap and the season of fertility, so that the mere sight of them, for instance, augured conception, as described in the recent novel *Bohin Manor* by the Polish writer Tadeusz Konwicki.

Storks can still be seen in parts of central and northern Europe, though they are now much less numerous than they were. Stately and poised in black and white livery, they graze in couples in the fields in summertime and take off with magnificent ease, controlling their flight with deep wing-beats, skimming the earth or rising high in the sky till they are lost to view.

Emblematic signs of the goose and stork, like the webbed foot or the long beak, recur in synecdoche to denote female sexual knowledge and power, as well as the implied deviancy which accompanies them; the sirens who lured men on to the reefs with their song were also bird-bodied and web-footed, in the classical tradition. These signs were attached to the stories and other materials in which such knowledge was transmitted and counterpoised to male strengths, both physical and social, the domain of fertility opposed to the male domain of sovereignty: *contes de ma Mère l'Oye, contes de la cigogne*. Waterfowl and large amphibious birds were connected to the most fundamental mystery of all: where do babies come from? And the question gave Mother Goose or Mother Stork the right to speak replies aloud and pass them on. The fine ladies writing fairy tales in the seventeenth and eighteenth centuries inherited the tradition, both as its agents and renewers, and as its objects: the misogyny which buoys *Les Evangiles des quenouilles* greeted the *salonnières'* fad for fairy tales, yet the targets of scorn found in the form's marginal and despised status a means to articulacy and a way of struggle.

In famous fairy tales, like 'Cinderella' or 'Beauty and the Beast', ascribed to the voice of Mother Goose, the narrator hides under the bird's vulgarity while at the same time transcending it by the act of narrative itself. Such a heterodox and ambiguous figure could not, however, have infiltrated the nursery and settled herself down by the fire if she had not combined with other figures, or been remoulded by another context. The cosy, well-behaved, even respectable nursery storyteller who emerges in the late seventeenth century entered mainstream culture with the help of contacts, of her own variety of godmothers: the Sibyls on one side and Jesus' grandmother, Saint Anne, on the other.

Mother storks can deliver stories, as well as babies.
(London, c 1911.)

S. Persica.

Verbum invisibile fit tangibile.
t'Onsienlik Woort sal getast worden.

The Sibyls, ten, or sometimes twelve in number, were imagined to have prophesied from every corner of the known earth; as the only group of female figures from paganism to survive in the Christian Pantheon they offered artists a rich opportunity for visual pleasure and invention. Here the Persian Sibyl in a magnificent turban (that heathen headgear) raises her index finger to point out the truth; 'She made the invisible Word tangible in words', says the caption, referring to her prophecy of Christ's coming. (Simon de Vries, early seventeenth century.)

CHAPTER 5

No Hideous Hum: Sibyls I

Meanwhile the prophetess ... ran furious riot in the cave ...

Virgil, *Aeneid* VI

Heraclitus, around 500 BC, described how the 'Sibyl with frenzied lips, utter-ing words mirthless, unembellished, unperfumed, penetrates through a thousand years with her voice'. His is the earliest source to mention such a prophetess; Pausanias, describing Delphi and its surroundings, later establishes the seer's monstrous aspects for the first time. He reports that the Lamia, the snake-woman so sumptuously imagined later by Keats, bore a daughter after coupling with Zeus: 'they say she was the first woman to sing oracles and was named Sibyl by the Libyans'. Here, in this enterprising travel writer's aside, we find an early trace of the later, wonderfully rich and suggestive legend about an oracular woman with some hidden, snaky nature, which later influences the fairy-tale cast of fairy queens, demon brides, wicked enchantresses and cursing god-mothers. Pausanias also records that in Alexandria, a Sibyl was reputed to have warned Hecuba, through the interpretation of a dream, that Troy would fall – 'that future which we know was to come true'. He quotes a snatch of a song she used to sing as she stood by her rock at Delphi which begins: 'I was born between man and goddess, / slaughterer of sea-monsters and immortal nymph ...'

The books of Sibylline prophecies which had survived the burning bargain driven by the Cumaean Sibyl with Tarquin were kept on the Capitol in Rome and guarded by a select number of the Republic's great and good; in times of crisis, they were opened at random to offer a diagnosis and maybe a remedy (more sac-rifices, more worship) until the temple of Capitoline Jupiter, which housed them, was itself burned down in 83 BC. Under the Empire, envoys were despatched to find more oracles, and this new harvest, under Augustus, was enshrined in the temple dedicated to Apollo, a more provident patron, perhaps, for prophecies, since the art was under his protection. There they were consulted, it would appear for the last time, in AD 363, half a century after the classical gods had been officially set aside by Rome, though the last Roman temple of the Sibyl's secrets was closed only in the fifth century (in spite of the legend of the Sibyl of Cumae's earlier flight). Though the books were lost (much to the disgust of early humanists) fragments continued to circulate, and quotations in secondary sources recorded the Sibyls' apocalyptic warnings and resonant denunciations, expressed with great determination, but indeterminately open to interpretation. These materials offered shelter – and a house style – to later Sibylline fortune-telling.

Early in the fourth century AD, Lactantius gave an account of the ten Sibyls in some detail in his book *The Divine Institutions*, citing Varro as his source. Lactantius is a crucial figure in the story of Sibylline imagery's dissemination: a classical rhetor, like Augustine, and born like him in the North African possessions of the pre-Christian empire, he first lost his professorship under the persecuting emperor Diocletian, and lived in poverty. With the conversion of Constantine, he was eventually restored and appointed tutor to the imperial family. Thus Lactantius, who himself spanned the worlds of the old faith and the new, was eager to demonstrate that the Sibyls acted as hyphens between the past and the present, that Christianity need not break altogether with the culture of its enemies. He offered semi-biographical sketches for the Sibyls, and by individualizing them, furnished a sequence of mnemonics for the later authors of the flourishing oracular literature which imitated the classical model. His descriptions helped to anchor the Sibyls' characters in the mind of his audience. He also quoted some remarkable examples of the Sibyls' prescience: 'He will satisfy five thousand from five loaves and a fish of the sea.' The Sibyl's Song, filled with eschatological prophecies, even created in the first letters of each line an acrostic 'JESUS SOTER', or Jesus Saviour:

> Judgement's sign: the earth shall drip with sweat;
> Everlastingly the King shall come from heaven, who
> Shall be present to judge bodies and the world.
> Unfaithful and faithful shall thus behold God
> Sublime among the saints, at time's utmost limit.

Such apparently irrefutable proofs of Sibylline powers allowed these prophets of antiquity a unique place in Christian thought. The medieval romances which feature the exiled Sibyl of Cumae demonized her when they associated her with sexuality and sensual enchantments of every kind. But in this the secular legends parted from an important strand of learned medieval Christian syncretism, which incorporated the Sibyls into the scheme of redemption – as gifted seers who had enjoyed foreknowledge of the Messiah, 'Christians before time'. The Emperor Constantine, in his Oration to the Council of Nicaea on Easter Day, 325, invoked various witnesses who had foreshadowed him in proclaiming the truth of Christ, and he included among them the Sibyl who, he declared, had prophesied the coming of the Saviour to Virgil in the Fourth Eclogue: 'I cannot but think the Sibyl blessed, whom the Saviour thus chose to unfold his gracious purposes for us.' The poem heralds the advent of 'the last age, sung of by the Cumaean Sibyl', and greets the birth of the boy child who will bring about a new beginning.

Another legend of the early Church, which was well established by the sixth century and retained its popularity in the middle ages, featured the Emperor Augustus meeting his local, Rome-based, prophetess, the Tiburtine Sibyl, on the Capitoline Hill, and hearing her proclaim, '*Ecce ara primogeniti Dei*' (Behold the altar of the firstborn son of God). The scene, as represented in many Italian and Northern European Renaissance paintings, shows the Virgin Mary (herself a type of seat or altar for the Christ child) floating in a blaze of glory in the heavens above the Sibyl and the emperor. The Capitol, in Republican times the site of the vault where the Sibylline leaves were guarded, was dedicated to S. Maria in Aracoeli in the early years of Christianity – it was already considered an ancient basilica in the sixth century and the legend may well provide a mythic aetiology for its foundation. This was the spot where Gibbon heard the monks chanting and was set to musing on the glory that was Rome – the Sibylline connection no doubt helped to inspire his own prophetic meditation on fatality and frailty in the passage from paganism to Christianity.

Developing from both the Athenian and Roman prophetic traditions, the *Oracula sibillina*, the collection of religious-political documents attributed to the prophetesses, circulated in eight books of Greek hexameters; believed now to have originated among Christian and Jewish circles from the mid-second century BC to around AD 300, they were transcribed in many languages, though a full Greek manuscript was not rediscovered in Western Europe until 1545, by a scholar, Xystus Betuleius, who found one in Augsburg; this was translated into Latin ten years later. The materials had proved very popular far afield: the Tiburtine Sibyl's prophecies exist in no fewer than a hundred and thirty manuscripts, thirty of them before 1200, in many languages which include Ethiopic and Arabic as well as Latin and Greek. So when later local legends ascribed the Cumaean Sibyl's flight to a fit of spite that Mary had been chosen to be the mother of the coming Redeemer instead of her, they were embroidering on exalted connections between paganism and Christianity, on beliefs that she, like her Tiburtine sister in prophecy, had indeed foreseen Christ's coming.

The Sibyls make an interesting, even unique showing in Christian mythology, since they are directly inherited from the pagan belief system, and were long assimilated to demonesses, witches and fairies. Yet no less a figure than Saint Augustine himself had quoted Sibylline prophecies with approval: 'She [the Erythraean Sibyl] seems to me to have been a citizen of the city of God.' Consequently, the Sibyls managed to win wholehearted endorsements from thinkers like Peter Abelard, and to be accepted as severe prophets of the coming, Christian salvation – or doom. The Franciscan poet Thomas of Celano took an apocalyptic view in the beautiful thirteenth-century sequence for the Mass of the Dead still sung today:

> *Dies irae, dies illa*
> *solvet saeclum in favilla,*
> *teste David cum sibylla.*

> [The day of wrath, that day will dissolve the world into ashes,
> as David and the Sibyl testify.]

Relics of paganism, the Sibyls constitute the only such group of female figures in Christian tradition; in spite of some Neoplatonist efforts in the fifteenth century, and again by some hermeticists in the seventeenth, to establish the classical gods as Christian angels in disguise or allegorical forerunners, classical divinities or heroes remained effectively in permanent exile from orthodoxy.

From the mid-fifteenth century onwards, the surviving fragments of the *Oracula sibillina* grew in popularity until, with the invention of printing, they reached a wide, secular readership as well. Translations and variations and attributions began being published in the vernacular, in illustrated books and booklets from Germany, Venice, St Gallen, predominantly for readers in Catholic communities; they inspired many works, like the beautiful sgraffito pavement of Siena Cathedral, created by several hands in 1482–3, which gives individualized portraits of Lactantius' ten Sibyls (p. 2). As the Old Testament prophets are to the Jews, so in the Renaissance, the Sibyls became to the Gentiles. Mantegna's grisaille painting *A Sibyl and a Prophet*, of around 1495, conveyed a characteristic humanist desire to reconcile ancient wisdom with biblical soteriology. The very imitation of antique bronze bas relief on the canvas enacts an analogous collapsing of the centuries that have elapsed: the once upon a time in which the seers exchanged knowledge can be remade in the present tense through mimesis. Michelangelo's Sistine ceiling probably gives the Sibyls their most celebrated and monumental interpretation, as the five he chose to portray take their places on the pendentives between their biblical counterparts, the prophets (Pl. 4). To the Church exegetes, these heathen seers came to represent the unredeemed world's foreknowledge of the Christian faith and, in consequence, stood for the universality of the scheme of salvation: all of history retroactively could be gathered under the mantle of the Holy Roman Church, for these female prophets from all points of the known world, named to gather in the furthest borders of the Roman and Greek empire, had prophesied aspects of the true, coming redemption. In France, they make an appearance in miracle plays, and sometimes are introduced to endorse arguments in praise of women.

The Sibyl, as a cross-cultural symbol, necessarily denies historical difference; her words, originating in the past, apply to the rolling present whenever it occurs; however, the perceived fact of her roots in that distant past adds weight to her message precisely because it is free of the historical context in which she uttered it; she was not fettered by her historical time and place but could transcend it with her visionary gifts. In their very identity as truth-tellers, the Sibyls of tradition cancel connections to history – this is crucial in their contribution to the composite character of the female narrator and inventor of future fictions. They speak their verses, or sing their messages, and though they are always communicating a prior, universal wisdom, they are seen as actively shaping it – their voices are the instruments of the knowledge they pass on in order to prepare for life ahead. As a sibylline poem declares:

> Many a song my own singings have uttered within myself;
> the songs which I write, those God knows …

In art the motifs were not confined to the high manner and high ceilings of Renaissance masters. The *Oracula sibillina* inspired a proliferating number of lowly engravings and woodcuts printed for distribution in vernacular series throughout Christendom, as recognizable as the familiar intercessors and mysteries of redemption. The Erythraean Sibyl, for instance, was depicted foreseeing Christ as the Man of Sorrows and his mocking at the hands of his jailers, in a crudely drawn print of 1473 from Germany (p. 72), redolent of the anti-semitism which became a feature of this material (see Chapter Eight).

The popular print series tend to follow Lactantius and portray ten Sibyls; Filippo Barbieri, in some widely circulated verses first published in Venice in 1481, follows Lactantius in listing them as the Persian, the Libyan, the Delphic, the Cimmerian, the Erythraean, the Samian, the Cumaean, the Hellespontine, the Phrygian and the Tiburtine, and then adds two – by name Europa and Agrippa – to match them to the twelve apostles.

The classical sources also specify the Sibyls' ages, not it seems with some arcane numerological intent, but to anchor them in real history as well as geography: some are said to be rather young – the Cumaean Sibyl, for example, is only

The printed material of sayings ascribed to the Sibyls often reflected current propaganda against non-Christians: the Erythraean Sibyl foresees Christ as the Man of Sorrows, and evokes the mocking of his gaolers. Her anachronistic fifteenth-century dress underlines the ugly contemporary message of the image. (Ulm, 1473.)

eighteen in Lactantius' account. The Delphic Sibyl, likewise, is young, aged twenty. These two youngest Sibyls were coincidentally the most famous *vates* of antiquity, attending powerful and popular shrines and directly serving the god of prophecy, Apollo, whose inspiration, writes Virgil, made the earth shake in the Sibyl's cave. It is not surprising that they take shape as the most fascinating temptresses in the subsequent folklore, as in the case of the Cumaean at Norcia.

The Cimmerian Sibyl, from the far north, was specified as twenty-four years old. All the rest are frequently portrayed in various stages of decrepitude; they are old women who reverse the classical and medieval misogynist trend relying on the crone to represent vice. In the case of the Sibyls, the processes of physical ageing, however faithfully rendered, are not assumed to be repugnant, or even pitiful, as they so commonly were in earlier didactic literature. Old age, in this tradition of Sibylline iconography, stands for wisdom. This antiquity figures forth their memory of deep time as well as their foreknowledge of the deep future. In the series of woodcuts printed around 1514 in Oppenheim, for instance, the Hellespontine Sibyl is evoked: 'An old woman wrapped in an ancient rustic dress, with an old veil tied about her head and wrapped around her throat to her shoulders, looking down at what she writes, just as Heraclitus wrote …' (p. 74).

Every Sibyl was ascribed a defining attribute which could also act as a mnemonic; it emphasized the approved message of the particular prophecy, allowing the receiver – especially among the illiterate – to understand the story behind the image. In the attractive series of woodcuts printed in St Gallen, Switzerland, in 1485, each Sibyl sits facing the fulfilment of her prophecy in the New Testament on the facing page. The Samian carries a wooden cradle of the type which would have been in use in St Gallen at the end of the fifteenth century, for her prophecy concerns the birth of Christ in a manger. The nativity accordingly appears opposite, in an early example of the cartoon-strip form of narrative, in which the speaker's text turns into pictures before the reader's eyes. The Hellespontine Sibyl usually enters the cycle later, and her message correspondingly takes up the story late in Jesus' life and passion. Her attribute is the cross, and her prophecy often focusses on the crucifixion: for example, *'Felix ille deus ligno qui pendet ab alto'* (Happy the god who shall hang from that beam on high).

But the iconography of the Sibyls varies, and their textually prescribed attributes cannot be wholly relied upon to identify them. Nor does an appearance of old age or youthfulness remain consistent – the northern Italians of the Quattrocento for instance resist depicting them as halt and wrinkled. The different oracular messages passed down in the verbal tradition are also frequently transposed from one to another. It seems the case that the printed materials distinguished the Sibyls by age, emblem, prophecy more scrupulously than do the single standing figures *in situ* by a major artist, as in the pavement of the Duomo of Siena. For such works, lessons take second place to aesthetics.

The Sibyls provided a teaching tool. In themselves, they represented the expansiveness of the divine plan, while their prophecies provided a topic for a preacher to expound. They are depicted raising an index finger to Heaven, or tapping a scroll or book like a schoolmistress teaching her pupils a new vocabulary. Both these gestures characterize other-worldly inspiration, male and female; it is the text which the Sibyl cites or explains which confers authority on her. God speaks through her, she is an unwitting medium, even, of the divine afflatus which proclaims Christianity before time.

Without this heavenly corroboration, a Sibyl would be nothing more than a

The Sibyls offered the spectrum of human experience, varying in age from young to very old; the Hellespontine, was often one of the most gnarled and vatic, and her message usually singles out the crucifixion. (Oppenheim, c. 1514.)

woman unlawfully possessed, exercising her powers of speech wantonly. By the sixteenth century and the era of the great witch hunts, the terror of old, prophetic women had contaminated the Sibyls, too; they were denounced as mouthpieces of the Devil, even if what they had said was true. Suspicion grew when the new humanist techniques of textual criticism at last showed that the *Oracula sibillina* were by no means as ancient as Augustine and others had believed. Sibylline imagery begins strikingly to resemble negative representations of women's talk, of old women and their ramblings. These prophetesses remained the most ancient participants in the business of remembering and recording; but change the text, and women's speech, especially crones' chatter, becomes a very dangerous thing, a lure, a false seduction.

II

John Milton, in his famous 'Hymn on the Morning of Christ's Nativity', alludes to the legend that all infidel seers were silenced by the coming of Christ:

The oracles are dumb,
No voice or hideous hum
   Runs through the archèd roof in words deceiving …
No nightly trance, or breathèd spell
Inspires the pale-eyed priest from the prophetic cell.

Walter Ralegh had also spoken of the silence that fell on Apollo's priests in each of their sanctuaries, and a sixteenth-century commentator on Spenser had written that at the Nativity, 'All oracles surceased and enchaunted spirits that were wont to delude people, thenceforth held their peace.' Milton, like Ralegh, refers in particular to the abandonment of Apollo's shrine at Delphi, where the oracles were attributed more commonly to the Pythoness, or Pythia, a *vates* or female voice, but also to a Sibyl.

The spectre of frenzied prophetesses, like Manto and Cassandra, has been invoked even in modern times as an argument for the exclusive male priesthood: fascination with the classical practice runs through the Catholic and Protestant attitudes to female inspiration – with varying results, from burning at the stake to sanctification. But the concern more surprisingly migrates from its native habitat of religious debate into the secular sphere, and this journey can be seen in the changing status of folklore. The history of fairy tales, as a form of literature, becomes entangled with changing attitudes to these female voices speaking with a claim to knowledge. The Cumaean Sibyl, surviving in the legend of the Apennines, hands us a magic key to enter the magic mountain of

The Hellespontine Sibyl prophesies that the cross will be put to shame, as the instrument of Christ's death. Artists sometimes resisted depicting the Sibyls as old: though the inscription says that she was fifty years of age, she wears her long hair loose like a young girl. (Paris, 1508.)

fairy tale in its social context. For among the oracles which were supposedly silenced at Christ's birth, we find the perceived prototypes of the crones of the nursery hearth, as well as the inspiration for many of the types of tales they told in the period when fairy tales become established as literature fit for children.

In his essay 'The Cessation of the Oracles', the literary historian Constantinos Patrides develops, with some skilled bibliographical sleuthing, an account of the disputes about the pagan prophetesses' survival, and he fingers the end of the seventeenth century as the moment when the sceptics begin to express their views, and belief in the miracle of the oracles' silencing starts to decline. The French philosopher Bernard Le Bovier de Fontenelle (1657–1757) published his essay '*L'Histoire des oracles*' in 1687; it mocked with ironic grace the notion that the Devil spoke through the pagan oracles, and, in consequence, that the seers had all been silenced overnight when Christ was born. This is a significant date, for it falls during the time the first written fairy tales were being produced, in France, and Fontenelle was a friend of La Fontaine, one of Perrault's chief inspirations, as well as of many writers in the circle which told stories as a pastime. Mme d'Aulnoy's first fairy tale, '*L'Ile de la félicité*' (The Isle of Happiness), appeared in a novel of 1690, *Histoire d'Hypolyte, Comte de Duglas*; Mlle L'Héritier's pioneering collections in the decade following; Perrault's Mother Goose tales were being written at the same time and published soon after. This does not mean that the profane was being reclaimed, but that it was no longer perceived in certain quarters as perilous. The Catholic view, that Sibyls were both privileged witnesses of salvation and beyond redemption as she-demons, enchantresses, began to lose ground, and the effect can be seen in particular among early liberal thinkers.

Fontenelle was putting a huge distance between himself and the witch hunters of the early part of the century. A cleric like Pierre de Lancre, for example, who in 1608 had been sent by royal command to cleanse the Labourd, in Basque country, reported the usual night-flyings, sabbath orgies, obscene rites of Christian belief in sorcery, and reported that women were much more prone to becoming possessed, owing to their weakness of character and their long tradition in the craft. He adduced as predecessors: 'those whom the Italians called Fairies, Nymphs, Sibyls, White Ladies, Ladies, Goodwomen …' In 1680, Mme de Sévigné reported that the Duchesse de Bouillon had paid a celebrated poisoner, abortionist and witch to conjure Sibyls to tell her future and give her love charms.

But this was the other side of the picture to Fontenelle's lucid vision. He found his inspiration in a diligent Latin work – in two volumes – by Antonius Van Dale, published in freethinking Amsterdam in 1683; but unlike the Dutch writer,

Fontenelle had a succinct wit, and the observant court, thoroughly reformed under the pastoral care of Mme de Maintenon and the Jesuits, did not like what he said or how he said it. Like La Fontaine, Fontenelle's trifling with Catholic pieties landed him in deep trouble, and he remained so, twenty years after the book's appearance; he was denounced as an atheist to Louis XIV by the king's confessor, and escaped being stripped of his pension and liberty only through the good offices of friends who still had some influence. It was dangerous to be tolerant. Fontenelle refused to reply to the Jesuit attacks, but wrote privately in a letter: 'I dislike all quarrelling. I'd rather the Devil had been a prophet, since the Jesuit father wishes it and believes it to be more orthodox.'

The battle was joined: for the Catholic clerisy, the in-betweenness of a fairy land where phenomena took place that were not the result of *maleficium*, where supernatural beings who were not of the party of the Devil were believed to exist, could not be tolerated. But the sharpness of this disagreement denotes the weakening, too, of the orthodox position. The rise of fairy tale as a printed genre of literature coincides with permission to accept that between Heaven and Hell and Purgatory there lies another kingdom, a realm of human fantasy, in which the traditional categories of good and evil clash and find resolution in ways that may differ from the doctrine of orthodox faith and, even, ethics. The fairy tale, thronged with devilish figures like witches and goblins, refused to take them seriously; this could present an enlightened attitude from one point of view, blasphemy and consequent damnation from another.

Fontenelle was not endorsing, in the manner of a last surviving just heathen, an alternative supernatural arrangement, but rather pointing to the human origin of the magic and miracles of the past. His scepticism embraced the scorn shown by his contemporaries at follies or credulity of all kinds, especially Catholic. Another learned Dutch scholar continued Van Dale's labours, with Casaubon-like omnivorousness, principally in order to refute Sibylline claims altogether. He poured furious scorn on almost all *prophetissae* and on those who credit them, up to and including more recent manifestations, like Joan of Arc, to whom he devotes several incensed pages. His views on 'these legends or fables' correspond to those of the Académie Française, who were at the same time compiling their French dictionary, with its disparaging definitions of the word *conte*. Their lexicography carried the contempt that the new scepticism felt about ancient lore. But this contempt also can be taken to imply the cessation of the fear which accompanies belief. Heterodox magic and prophecy no longer held any terrors for some French writers and thinkers of the time. Fairyland's phantasmagoria had become nonsense, foolish nonsense. And foolish nonsense could lead on to certain kinds of entertainment, full circle back to the realm of fancy and pleasure, the very place where the fairy queen presided. The fairies in fairy tales could be malignant and dangerous, or they could work powerful magic, but they were no longer understood to be emissaries of the devils who had lured witches; let alone metamorphoses of the Devil himself. The imps who had brought some women – and men – to the stake were mischievous, not diabolical; the talking animals the friendly helpers of folklore, not familiars from the coven.

Yet the whole story does not lie there, as levity can also act as a defensive measure against those same old creeds' command of allegiance. Those goose or stork or one-eyed fairy tales represent a variant position for the supernatural to occupy, and a delighting mockery greets this enduring reflex of the unenlightened, superstitious mind; only children need believe in fairies. At the same time, the idea that the pagan oracles did not have to be silenced in order for Christianity to prevail, and that they might have survived a while until they dwindled and simply faded, does permit the new domestication and publication of their products – the fantasies of fairyland – as took place from the 1690s and through the eighteenth century.

Fontenelle had written in his preface that he wanted women in particular, who did not know Latin, to be able to read his ideas, hence his French version of Van Dale. He knew the issue was of interest to women, though he could not have predicted that, far from rejecting the connection of the female sex with such credulity and heterodox inspiration, it would be claimed and reasserted with unexpected vigour by his contemporaries and their posterity.

In 1782, for instance, several of the fairy stories of Mme la Baronne d'Aulnoy were collected and published in English under the title 'Queen Mab: containing a select collection of Only the Best, most Instructive and Entertaining Tales of the Fairies'. The title went on, 'To which are added A Fairy Tale in the ancient (English) style ... and Queen Mab's Song'. This 'Fairy Tale in the ancient style' features Oberon and Robin Goodfellow and other figures of local faery lore; and tells a Scottish ballad tale about the magical cure of the despised protagonist, Edwin the hunchback – a typical fairy tale about the weak vindicated. The transmitter of this story, one Dr Parnell, ends by invoking a childhood memory – and this is where he makes a patent association of a most interesting kind. He writes:

> This Tale a Sibyl-Nurse a-read
> And softly stroak'd my youngling Head,

And, when the Tale was done,
Thus some are born, my Son (she cries)
With base Impediments to rise, –
    And some are born with none.

But virtue can itself advance
To what the fav'rite Fools of Chance
    By Fortune seem'd design'd ...

The immemorial storyteller, Mother Goose, or Mother Stork, or Mother Bunch, is a figure of fun, a foolish, ignorant old woman, a typical purveyor of old wives' tales. But she is also established, by the early eighteenth century, as a Sibyl-Nurse – who instils morality and knowledge of the world, and foresees the future of her charges and prepares them for it. The appended moral, transmitted by the wisdom of old age to the young, was ascribed to this figure, the Sibyl-Nurse, in order to justify the frequent violence, bawdy, and extravagant fantasy of fairytale material. Perrault, for example, insisted on his edifying intentions in his prefaces and added sprightly and often rather dubious morals to his conclusions. The tendency towards sententiousness grew, as the genre became more and more identified with the moral education of children.

The nexus which gathers together these different manifestations of the imaginary narrator does not exist merely at an associative, symbolic level – indeed, the symbolic cannot be sequestered at this distance anyway, but spreads through material culture. A figure like Mother Goose turns out to have a recorded, empirical history, to be compacted of many beliefs. Their shifts of shape over time have altered hers, as the earth changes under a delta to make new land masses.

The ambiguous tradition of the Sibyl shaped reception of the fairy tale whose source was perceived as an old wise woman or witch; the classical prophetesses' role in pagan lore positioned them to influence one of its popular survivals, in fairy tales. But they were not alone in helping to draw the sting of heterodoxy from the genre; the cult of Saint Anne, as it developed in France in the seventeenth century, combined with the Sibyls to give the crone narrator the kindly face of a favourite and familiar grandmother.

The education of Mary to her high calling was a favourite theme of devotional art: in a domestic setting, Saint Anne, the legendary mother of the Virgin, is shown teaching her daughter her letters from the scriptures in which Mary's destiny is written. (Bartolomé Esteban Murillo, The Virgin and Saint Anne, *c 1655.)*

CHAPTER 6

Saint Anne, Dear Nan: Sibyls II

Dormi dulcis, dormi bella
Caeli gaudium puella
Dormi, dormi blandula.

[*Sleep my sweet, sleep my pretty,*
Little girl who is heaven's joy
Sleep, sleep, my little shining child.]

Lullaby to the Infant Mary

A nne of Austria, Queen of France, attributed the late arrival of the future
Louis XIV to the intercession of her patron Saint Anne. She had travelled to
Apt to touch the relics of the mother of Mary, on one of many such pilgrimages
she undertook in her long struggle to conceive an heir to the throne. And in 1638,
after twenty-three years of a childless marriage to Louis XIII, she bore the
Dauphin.

Relics of the Saviour's grandmother – her arm and the shroud in which her
body had been buried – had been deposited there by Saint Auspicius, the town's
first bishop; he had saved them from desecration in their shrine at Marseilles,
where no less a figure than the resurrected Lazarus had brought them, after he
and Mary Magdalen arrived in the South of France from the Holy Land. The
shrine at Apt was hallowed by a miracle, ascribed to Easter Day, AD 776, during a
visit of the Emperor Charlemagne, when a young deaf-mute nobleman pointed
to some flagstones in the floor of the church. When they were lifted, the relics of
the saint, buried there for safe-keeping by Auspicius, were uncovered. The youth
then recovered his powers of speech. The inventory of the relics was carried out
in 1602, so the miracle would have been recorded at that time in full, marking the
beginning of the huge rise in Saint Anne's cult in France during the century. It is a
significant cure, since it concerns a young boy – at a time when historians tell us
children were of little consequence to society at large or their families; and, of

course, it describes a coming-to-language, the ending of silence and the beginning of talk for that child. Anne was seen above all as a patroness of childless women and grandmothers, but she was also an educator, who in numerous cult images teaches her daughter Mary to read (p. 80).

The image of Saint Anne, flourishing in a place and at a time when terror of witches was rife, when the deviancy of wise women was a commonplace belief, mitigates these suspicions and fears. Anne offers an alternative, inspiring, contrastingly humane image of aged female expertise, and although a certain degree of clerical taming is implied as well (here was a proper old woman, keeping herself busy in edifying ways), the permitted benevolence is unexpected, and consolatory. The positive value the old wise-woman storyteller achieved in seventeenth-century secular culture represents a change in itself from earlier abuse against old women, witches and the old wives' tale, and as this devotion emerged to full flower in France at the same time as the courtly and metropolitan appetite for fairy stories, it undoubtedly combined with it to loosen the hold of prejudice against female old age and its beliefs. Her cult drew safe borders around risky territory: the skills of crones in medicine, sympathy, traditional knowledge, warnings, prophecy, language, consolation and talk were acknowledged and disarmed; and the grandmother of Jesus nourished the image of the old Gammer goodwives and grannies of nursery literature.

Anne of Austria was enthusiastic at popularizing her miracle-working patron, as was her son later in her honour. After his birth, the queen endowed the Cathedral of St Anne in Apt in Provence with a reliquary chapel, and she acquired relics, including two of the saint's fingers, from all over the Christian world. Almost concurrently in Brittany, a peasant called Yves Nicolasic had a vision of Saint Anne in which she asked that a chapel that had stood in his fields and been dedicated to her be restored; two years later, in 1623, ploughing there, he dug up an ancient statue of a goddess suckling two infants – possibly the Roman Bona Dea – which was identified as a miraculous *Selbdritt*, or trinity of Anne, Mary and Jesus. The memory of the last duchess of independent Brittany, Anne de Bretagne (p. 89), who had died in 1514, fuelled veneration of the discovery: the statue was enshrined at Auray, Saint Anne was declared a patron saint of Brittany and became the focus of the great annual *pardon* pilgrimages which still take place in the province. The cult was also transported overseas, as part of French culture, to the new colonies of the French empire: Marie de l'Incarnation, a widow who had entered the Ursuline teaching order, founded a branch of it in Quebec in 1639; the French possession had been dedicated to Saint Anne, and yet more relics were despatched there in 1670 to stimulate devotion. Anne of Austria herself reputedly embroidered the chasuble which the votive statue of Sainte Anne de Beaupré still wears on special occasions.

Anne of Austria may have encouraged and enriched the cult of her patron saint, but she did not initiate it. The mother of Mary had been the focus of one of the most lively devotions of the middle ages. Though Saint Anne does not appear in the Gospels by name, her story circulated widely in one of the most popular apo cryphal books, the Protoevangelium of St James, which was first written in the second century, and repeated with flourishes in the influential *Golden Legend* by the Dominican Jacobus de Voragine of the thirteenth century. His account of the embrace of Anne and Joachim, Mary's mother and father, at the Golden Gate of Jerusalem became the emblematic moment of her conception: a sinless arrival, miraculously vouchsafed by God to a woman who had passed childbearing and had never had children before.

Anne's story echoes biblical tales of barrenness reversed by God as a special sign of his favour to the parents and a singular benediction on their late, longed-for offspring: the birth of John the Baptist to the aged and childless Elisabeth and Zacharias in the Gospel of St Luke; an account that itself is foreshadowed by the miraculous birth of Isaac to Sarah in her late age and of Samuel to Hannah in the Old Testament. Indeed the very name of Mary's mother was inspired – according to a train of association typical of the Apocrypha – by the character of Hannah, an exemplary mother, and of an exemplary child, a prophet who prefigures Jesus. Popular medieval handbooks like the *Speculum humanae salvationis* and the *Biblia pauperum*, which were illustrated to help the faithful to absorb the tenets and stories of their religion, organized the narrative of God's redemption in a sequence of answering typologies from the Old and New Testaments; the compilers drew on collections of legendary and fanciful tales, and their taste definitely tended to the wondrous and the entertaining. They picked the most vivid episodes, about the ravens who feed the prophet Elijah (1 Kgs. 17: 1–6), and the never failing pot of meal and cruse of oil belonging to the widow of Zarephath (1 Kgs. 17: 12–16), about the fatal vow of Jephthah that he will sacrifice the first thing he sees, and it turns out to be his own daughter (Jg. 11, 12) – an ancient myth, a motif of fairy tale, as in the story of Beauty and the Beast. They liked to create rhymes across time, revealing the relationship between the past and the present. So, on the same page, Hannah offers Samuel, Anne presents Mary, and Mary and Joseph take the child Jesus to the Temple, in a symmetrical arrangement of rituals which affirms the similarities between the different mothers and their prodigious offspring.

As an old woman in the tradition of the grieving barren mothers of the Old and New Testaments, Saint Anne's character also drew on another scriptural namesake, the aged seer Anna, who in the infancy Gospel of Luke prophesies at the presentation of Jesus in the Temple. 'A prophetess, the daughter of Phanuel, of the tribe of Aser: she was of a great age, and had lived with an husband seven years from her virginity; and she was a widow of about fourscore and four years …', this Anna lived in the Temple, fasting and praying night and day. 'And she coming in that instant gave thanks likewise unto the Lord, and spake of him to all them that looked for redemption in Jerusalem' (Luke 2: 36–8).

In scenes of the Presentation of Jesus in the Temple (right), the old prophetess Anna appears like an aged Sibyl, indicating with her finger, either pointing to heaven, as for instance in Pietro Cavallini's mosaic, made in the thirteenth century for S. Maria in Trastevere in Rome, or she holds a phylactery, quoting the words of the Gospel which identify her as a *'profetissa'*, in her left hand and

OppOSITE *Saint Anne appears here in the character of a sibyl, indicating the heavenly origin and spiritual meaning of her daughter's virgin motherhood, as Mary holds out her baby to bless his cousin.* (Leonardo da Vinci, The Virgin and Child with St Anne and John the Baptist. Cartoon, c. 1507–8.)

LEFT *At the presentation of Jesus at the temple, Simeon holds the baby in his arms, and the seer Anna recognizes Jesus as the Saviour; together they foreshadow the role of Christian godparents.* (Ambrogio Lorenzetti, The Presentation in the Temple, *first half fourteenth century.*)

indicates the future Saviour with her right, as in Giovanni di Paolo's panel for an altarpiece, painted in Siena in 1450–55. Like the pagan visionaries, she too stands outside the faith, as the artists suggest by placing her on the periphery of the presentation scene; but she has been granted foreknowledge.

The Jewish ritual observed by Jesus' earthly parents at the Temple in Jerusalem was taken in patristic exegesis to prefigure the Christian baptism of infants, and the two Gospel witnesses at Christ's presentation – Simeon on the one hand and Anna on the other – were allotted the role of precursors to Christian godparents. When Anna endorses Simeon's vision, of the future glory and the pain of Jesus' mission, she anticipates all those prophesying fairies of the tales who foresee the baby's fate: like the several godmothers at the christening of Sleeping Beauty.

Seepage is a feature of medieval lore, visual and verbal, and Anna the prophetess's role in Christ's infancy seeps into his grandmother Anne's; when she presents Mary as a child to the Temple, she too sees into her future. When the

Christ child is born, she assists at the lying-in, though she is not represented as the glowing grandmother, but rather heavy-browed with grief at the torments she foresees. The Italian painters of the High Renaissance thus interpreted Anna formally as a Sibyl: Leonardo, in the famous cartoon in the National Gallery, shows Anne sitting at Mary's shoulder, pointing straight up to Heaven with her left hand (p. 84); Caravaggio developed the theme with vivid, even histrionic imagination when he painted Jesus, aged about six, helping Mary crush the head of a snake under her heel, while Saint Anne stands by, hands clasped together as if in prayer at this proleptic action.

Saint Anne becomes sibylline in her teaching capacity, too. Her English, French, German and Lowland devotees particularly emphasize this aspect of her character. In the early Renaissance outpourings of the imagined sayings and exempla of this exemplary mother, she is portrayed as a matriarchal source of wisdom, the founder of a mighty dynasty of saints and the repository of a kind of tribal Christian wisdom. In Germany, where the cult of the Holy Kinship, the extended family of Jesus, grew to intense popularity, the Hebrew name Anna became linked with the Old German *Ana*, grandmother, itself a feminine form of

Opposite The role of grandparents in the family was increasingly emphasized in the nineteenth century: here, one old nan, under a picture of Tom Thumb, cosily gathers up her brood to read them a story. (Gustave Doré, Frontispiece, Les Contes de Charles Perrault, Paris, 1862.)

In medieval legend, Saint Anne was attributed three husbands and wondrous fecundity; she became the holy grandmother above of the Saviour's brethren. (The Holy Kinship, Geertgen tot Sint-Jans.)
Her cult often placed her in recognizable, contemporary domestic settings as in this devotional print left, in which she sits by the fire, while angels rock Mary's cradle. (Jerome Wierix, The Life of the Virgin Mary, Mother of God, Antwerp, early seventeenth century.)

Ano, grandfather or ancestor (modern German *Ahn*); they are in turn related to Greek *annis* (maternal or paternal) grandmother, and Latin *anūs*, old woman, married or unmarried. The affectionate English word 'Nan' for Grandma, echoes this etymology, while the extension of the usage to 'Nanny', for nurse, reflects the role grandmothers like Saint Anne have traditionally played.

The legends surrounding her became ever more extravagant, provoking the fury – and the shame – of reformers like Luther. Her votaries allotted Anne no less than two previous husbands and several other children before her marriage to Joachim and the birth of the incomparable Mary. She became a dynastic ancestor, a tribal elder in the saga of the Holy Family, the bearer of John the Evangelist, James the Great and the Less, Thaddeus, Barnabas, and other saints. This constituted an ingenious but far-fetched attempt on the part of the Catholic faithful to provide a genealogy for those 'brethren' of Jesus so awkwardly referred to in the Gospels; by providing Jesus with all these close cousins, no damage was done to belief in Mary's perpetual virginity (p. 87).

Daughters and heirs to noble houses were possibly called after Anne rather than her daughter because they were hoped to be greatly fruitful, too, to found unshakeable, prolific dynasties: Anne's liturgical titles included *Stirps beata* (Blessed Stock) and *Radix sancta* (Holy Root); her patronage implied fertility to a degree Mary's single conception could not. French queens and princesses in particular were prominent promoters of Anne's cult, after their parents had named them for the saint: as the founder of the Holy Family, she personified dynastic success, and as the tutor of the young Mary, she also represented female sagacity. The cultivated Anne de Bretagne, for example, daughter to the defeated Duke of Brittany, made three dynastic marriages, as if echoing her patron saint. First to the Holy Roman Emperor Maximilian I, then to Charles VIII of France, and after his death in 1498, she remained queen when she married his successor Louis XII. *Les Grandes Heures d'Anne de Bretagne*, painted by Jean Bourdichon between 1500 and 1508, contains an intense portrait of her at prayer. An aged Saint Anne, heavily swathed in veils, eyes turned to heaven, indicates the queen with her right hand as her spiritual daughter (right).

Meditations on Saint Anne's life and virtues, however expansive in their fantasy, stress her crucial moral role in raising the future Saviour and his mother. Both are represented as her children in this strand of piety, sometimes both even sitting on her lap. In 1496, Jan van Denemarken gave a eulogistic account of Saint Anne's teachings; it was published in the Netherlands and its frontispiece showed her holding a book on her lap, with her right hand raised in the gesture of exposition, while Mary and Jesus receive the benefits of her instruction. Johannes Trithenius, a writer in the circle of the Emperor Maximilian, composed his *De laudibus sanctissimae matris Annae*, as a commission for foreign merchants' use, in 1524, the same year as her feast became a first-class festival of the Church; his influential book both constituted a response to existing devotion to Saint Anne in

Anne's fertile example fitted her for special efficacy in fulfilling dynastic hopes, and she became a favourite royal patron saint; she indicates here her spiritual daughter, Anne of Brittany, Queen of France. (Jean Bourdichon, Les Grandes Heures d'Anne de Bretagne, 1500–1508.)

imperial and merchants' circles, but also diffused the theme of her authority. She was popular far beyond the clerical circles of her propagandists: the fantastic apocryphal life invented for her guaranteed the worth of marriage and abundant offspring.

Her cult also reached wide, urban diffusion among artisans and labourers, breaking through the Latin or scholarly boundaries of the liturgy and the cloister, partly because the propaganda in her praise either appeared in or was quickly rendered into the vernacular. The carpenters' confraternity attached to the Carmelites in Paris placed itself under Saint Anne's aegis, and called her the 'Tabernacle of God' – as if she were a kind of wooden ambry such as they might make themselves. In 1673, Louis XIV confirmed this confraternity's statutes; other associations of workmen also adopted Anne as their patron saint and issued holy pictures in support. Throughout her cult, however, her value is guaranteed by her child: she is always lesser than Mary, and serves her so that she may fulfil her destiny. This character of servant sometimes inspires the artist to differentiate the two women's clothing: Mary wears the finery of a nobleman's child, and Anne the sober tunic of a housekeeper (p. 80).

Usually, mother and daughter are reading from the Bible, which doubles as an oracle of Mary's future and a primer for her lessons. By contrast, Mary often shows letters to Jesus in a book of hours; Anne's recourse to the authority of scripture, like a Sibyl, provides assurance of her dependability as an instrument of God rather than an original narrator. In this respect, the literate Saint Anne acts as a counterweight to the illiterate storyteller – or at least proposes that a master narrative can be followed faithfully by an old woman: Anne acts as a wishful euphemism, countering prevailing prejudices.

Her role as a teacher in such images also offers iconic support for the idea of women's learning among themselves. *Les dévotes* – as the religious women of France were known – fastened on to Anne's part in raising Mary as a model young woman, in order to express their own desire for education. Paintings like Georges de la Tour's grave and beautiful image of a lesson by candlelight, from the first half of the seventeenth century, possibly represent lessons in literacy between generations as they took place. In a sixteenth-century sculpture by an anonymous artist in Apt, Saint Anne, busy teaching from the Bible, raises the index finger of her right hand in the classic gesture of the prophet and storyteller. This raised right arm and telling finger, traditional in classical scenes of *declamatio* or *adlocutio*, recurs again and again, in the frontispieces to printed collections of stories. Women still predominate today, interestingly, as teachers at stages when most of the work is still being done aloud, as in kindergartens and primary schools.

The title page of John Bulwer's *Chirologia*, a curious and fascinating volume on an aspect of rhetoric – hand gestures – which was published in 1644, compresses these circulating ideas about speaking in a manner which bears on the image of the woman narrator in the formative period of printed fairy tales (right). William Marshall, the artist, portrays two female figures standing opposite each other. On the left (and nothing is accidental), a plump *Natura loquens* (Eloquent Nature), with very long, unruly hair and many bare breasts in the pagan manner of Diana of the Ephesians, stands beneath an oak tree labelled 'Dodona' for Zeus' sacred grove. She appears to be leaping on to a small wheel of fortune with one foot, while one hand pours water into a well with the inscription '*Hinc latices*' (The waters flow from here). Her counterpart on the right, also pouring water into the well, is called Polyhymnia, muse of rhetoric, and she has both breasts covered and both feet firmly on the ground, and is declaring, '*Digitisque loquor Gestumque decoro*' (I speak with my fingers and I ornament gesture). In the book which follows, Bulwer produces a remarkably vivacious catalogue of all types of wave and clench, sign and gesture, from street to school and back again, and his title-page artist is putting the author's point that human communication is a poor, lame, incomplete thing without gesture. But the polarity expressed in the imagery is couched in a language lying at a deep, unconscious stratum of mid-seventeenth-century thinking: the Sibylline, however eloquent, is natural, wild, unkempt and highly risky; the social discipline of rhetoric, which includes all declamatory techniques like pose and gesture suitable for public performance, is necessary for human communication. Saint Anne, commonly found with her nose in a book, redeems the dubious status of natural female speech because she is represented as fully aware of the social proprieties of transmission, and understands how to relate with decorum. In short, here was a sage who was *sage* in the French sense of well-behaved; here was a Sibyl elder who knew how to behave.

While the imagery reinforcing Anne's stature as tribal ancestor and mentor continues to flourish in the sixteenth and seventeenth centuries, another existing aspect begins to develop even stronger popular devotion: 'the caring housewife

Natural Eloquence, long hair loose, bare-footed and many breasted, stands beside the oracular oak tree of Dodona, opposite Polyhymnia, the disciplined muse of rhetoric: two aspects of speech, personified in classical female form, combine in the cistern of expressiveness. (William Marshall, frontispiece, Chirologia, London, 1644.)

and gentle granny'. In woodcuts and engravings as well as on grand altarpieces and votive paintings, artists, often inspired by writers, interpret the story of Anne's life with powerful emotional involvement. This often personal commitment can be felt in particular in pictures of Mary's birth, which gave painters the pretext to portray the lying-in of their own contemporaries, of their own wives and perhaps even their own mothers (Pl. 2). Women friends – the godparents or gossips – are often shown arriving in the bedroom, while Saint Anne reaches out to hold her baby who has just been bathed by some helpers. In Francisco Zurbarán's magnificent version of around 1627, one can see how an artist could interpret – indeed remember – such a scene very differently, for here Saint Anne sits propped up and worn out in bed while two young women bring her food and drink. In the foreground, two midwives, both careful and loving portraits of old women, attend to the newborn. Contemporary costumes and medical practices are clearly depicted, including the use of stork-shaped instruments. The atmosphere of mutual help, practical and other, of a society's internal bonds, of the best aspects of gossiping, speaks in such images of the births of children in the past.

The cult of the grandmother saint rose on a new wave of Christian piety which focussed with intense, sentimental fervour on the ordinariness, the humbleness, the domestic familiarity of the Holy Family. In the seventeenth century Anne was enjoying the height of enthusiasm: biographies, eulogies, meditations poured from the minds of her devotees – symptoms of a religious craze spreading through Europe to Poland in the east and Spain in the south. No fewer than seven books of Saint Anne's praises were banned in the five years 1673–8, placed on the Index for excessive enthusiasm. At the same time as Anne the Regent of France identified herself with her patroness, her prodigious Dauphin, who succeeded to the throne at the age of five, was identified with the Christ child, and a cult of the Child Jesus at court, rooted in Carmelite mysticism, instilled the virtues of a childlike spiritual demeanour, of spontaneous devotion, and simple affective language of prayer.

Anne of Austria's passion for the Infant Christ was developed with renewed zest fifty years after her son's birth, in the newly pious atmosphere of his court in the 1680s. Under the influence of the mystic Mme Guyon and the Abbé Fénelon, imitation of a child's state again became the guiding principle of fervent devotions (right). The cult was termed *repuerascentia*, after a concept developed by Erasmus – 'growing childlike again'; while the disciples became as little children, following Christ's call, their spiritual advisors were cast in the role of nurses. The spiritual formation of the young person's soul became the template of the relation with

REPUERASCAT OPORTET, SERVARI QUISQUIS CUPIT   MATTHEI · 19 · 13

Christ's love of children and his injunctions to imitate them were highlighted during the mystical enthusiasm at court which coincided with the rediscovery of fairy tales. (After Pieter van Borcht, 'Whoever desires to serve must be a child again', seventeenth century.)

God, wisdom, all manner of higher things. Scenes from the New Testament which had hitherto seldom been selected by artists begin to recur in illustrated printed Bibles, or other educational and pious publications and pictures: the moment when Christ insists, 'Suffer the little children to come unto me ... for of such is the kingdom of God' (Mk 10: 14; Matt. 19: 13) inspires compositions which resemble the classic scene of nursery storytelling, with Christ cast as the fostering, loving teacher of the young, and his listeners as his adopted offspring (above). A confessor advised one of his spiritual charges:

> Speak as a daughter, speak as a good child ... If you can follow me in this, begin to become little. Tell daddy, and then you will call God your daddy, and not only My Lord; both titles belong to him. But the Apostle Paul tells us that the Spirit of God that is in us cries out, 'Abba, Pater,' which is a tender name that little children use to their father.

The family of God was intimate, human, Christian souls were Jesus' siblings, and his mother and grandmother were as mummy and granny to them as well.

The literary historian Yvan Loskoutoff, in a fine study of the exchanges between mysticism and literature in Louis XIV's court, points out that it was in the royal nursery that the king's grandson's fervent tutor Fénelon, who was appointed in 1689, inaugurated the use of fairy tales as moral exempla for the young, alongside more traditional lessons from the scriptures. Fénelon's stories were inspired by classical myth, by Aesop and La Fontaine, and they are, for the most part, rather flavourless, since they sedulously keep under control heterodox fancies about hobgoblins and fairies, luck and magic. But they do precede in date the great vogue of storytelling in the next decade, and, even more significantly, their context reveals the interconnections of fairy tale as a genre with piety and with education. For the benefit of the young Duke of Burgundy, the royal tutor focussed with apparent ingenuousness on the dangers of despotism, the evils of greed and ambition, the need to be content with one's given station in life, as well as the risks of eating too many sweets – on the Ile des Plaisirs, where mountains of jam swim in rivers of syrup, excessive gratification leads, perforce, to the calamity of rule by women.

When Fénelon's mentor, Mme Guyon, was disgraced in 1695, her enemies were provoked to particular scorn by the 'profane' reading materials found in the rooms of this self-styled living saint: the blue-wrapped volumes of popular stories, like *Don Quixote* and *La Belle Hélène* and Perrault's earliest tales, of '*Peau d'Ane*' and 'Patient Griselda', the ultimate type of suffering, childlike victim who surrenders herself wholly to the tutelage of authority, however brutal. But however much the moral of such fairy tales promoted self-abnegation, Mme Guyon's accusers found them frivolous, bawdy, and unworthy and herself tarred by implication. This conflict over the character of fairy tale mirrors the conflict about the origin of oracles, as we saw in Chapter Five, and it continues throughout its period of intense growth, and profoundly affects the perception of women involved in its production.

When the written fairy tale began to emerge at court, when the practice of telling such stories aloud caught the courtiers' imagination and began to be cultivated as an art of polite society, the cult of Saint Anne and the Christ child was flourishing simultaneously, and it shed its benign beams on the notion of storytelling. Just as the grandmotherly figure of Anne could provide a model of female teaching for the new orders of missionaries and nuns like the Ursulines, so she also offered an unimpeachable, unthreatening model for the storyteller posited by the writers of tales: the perception of grandmotherly wisdom, and of the older female generation's role in passing on knowledge to the young in the seventeenth-century cult colours the character of the archetypal narrator who begins to appear in text as well as illustration in printed volumes of fairy stories. Anne and Mary (and Jesus) also represented the communion of women and children from different social spheres and the possibilities their experience held out to more sophisticated minds. Cult and iconography responded, affirming an unexpected yearning for suppleness in social relations: the court tutor Fénelon accepted instruction from the inspired Mme Guyon; the Dauphin was considered greater than his mother. Old age and infancy, nobles and bourgeois and even nurses met on the territory of holy simplicity. A child's unadulterated vision is granted the crone, and this faculty of innocent insight produces the power of fantasy they share in common, and its product, the wonder tale.

The intimate meditations on the infancy of Mary by Jerome Wierix, one of the Dutch engraver family working in the sixteenth and seventeenth centuries, depict Saint Anne after her daughter's birth, in a contemporary Lowlands domestic setting, with lattice windows, potted plants on a runner laid on the sideboard, and the newborn baby lying in a wooden cradle, attended by angels, who are playing the lute and singing a lullaby while one rocks the crib (p. 87). As this choir of angels performs, Saint Anne, a bundled old woman in simple dress, sits by the hearth warming herself at a blazing fire. The gusts of smoke, curling out from under the chimneypiece, add another unforced touch of authenticity to this nativity scene, authorizing the resemblance to the role of women in the frontispiece of Perrault's *Contes du temps passé*, for instance (p. 86). The Wierix printshop disseminated imagery in small scale. Their domestic, sometimes sentimental holy pictures travelled along the missionary network of the Counter-Reformation Church: their original compositions became patternbooks for the faithful, and reworkings and variations can still be recognized in popular holy pictures, handed out at Mass today in Mexico as well as London.

The origin of fairy tale itself forms a fairy tale, and the search for the nature of the teller, for the character of Mother Goose itself, takes on the character of a fairytale quest. The image of Saint Anne, the good wise grandmother, exerted a benevolent influence on the related figures of women with occult or even forbidden knowledge. But deeper in the story chest of the European past, the Queen of Sheba, a legendary figure compounded of fantasy and scripture, seriousness and comedy, lies hidden; she mixes the fairy godmother and the fool, the enchantress and the houri, the wise woman and the witch, the Sibyl and the granny, and overlaps in a significant fashion with the proverbial storyteller of later nursery tradition.

A Moorish Queen of Sheba pays tribute to the wisest man in the world. The inscription says, 'In the gifts the queen secretly intimates her faith', for her acts in the Bible were compared to the later coming of the Three Kings, who recognized the truth of the Christian Saviour. (Nicholas of Verdun, altar, enamel, 1181.)

CHAPTER 7

The Magic of the Cross: The Queen of Sheba I

They felled us all.
We crashed to the ground, cruel Weird,
and they delved for us a deep pit.

The Lord's men heard of it,
His friends found me ...
it was they who girt me with gold and silver

'The Dream of the Rood'

The Queen of Sheba comes to see Solomon in the Bible (1 Kings 10: 1–13; 2 Chr. 9: 1–12); the description is famous, but scanty: she hears of his fame, and wishes to 'prove' him with 'hard questions'. For his part, he gives her 'all her desire' and answers all her questions; in response to this, she is winded ('breathless'), recognizes the truth of his god, Yahweh, and gives him handsome tribute, gold and spices – 'there came no more such abundance of spices as these which the queen of Sheba gave to king Solomon'.

From these biblical beginnings, the Queen of Sheba inspires a rich body of folklore, religious and secular, European and Asian, Christian and Muslim. She also embodies – as a seeker after wisdom, as a putter of hard questions, as a woman who learns and passes on what she has learned – the multiple roles of fairy tales and their tellers from the seventeenth century onwards. Moreover, she is marked by heterodoxy, a marginal woman, like the Sibyls, who never quite belongs in the fold, yet exercises power; this remains crucial to the pleasure, the excitement and the ambiguous status of the fairy tale as a genre. The fairy tale in which she herself moves may in itself provide a lost key to the last but most important meaning of the Mother Goose figure.

The suggestion that the king granted 'the queen of the south' all her desire inspired much speculative, amorous development later, including the birth of a son Menyelek (or Menelek), who founds the Ethiopian Christian Church. But the queen also functions, in Western Christian thought, as an official witness of the true God in Heaven, not only of bliss on earth: in the New Testament, Jesus invokes her as one of the just who will rise up to condemn unbelievers (Matt. 12: 42; Luke 11: 31), implicitly identifying himself with Solomon, and 'the queen of the south' with the Church, his beloved spouse.

Christian writers were consequently able to assimilate Sheba into the tradition of the Sibyls, a pagan with foreknowledge of the Redemption. As she remains anonymous in the Old Testament, she is often known by the name of her kingdom (like Cleopatra, sometimes called 'Egypt'). But various scholars offered evidence in support of her Sibylline character by giving her other names: Pausanias reported that there was a Jewish Sibyl called Sabbe, for instance, and the Byzantine scholar George Monachos strengthened the identification when he reported in his *Chronicle* that the Queen of Sheba's real name was Sibylla. A booklet filled with dire threats, published in Augsburg in 1515, names her on the title page as author: 'The thirteenth Sibyl / A Queen of Sheba who long ago gave [us] future events to be recognized'. The tiny six-page document then prophesied doom to the world through the actions of unbelievers and Jews and their monstrous progeny, the Antichrist. It incorporated, in particular, the warnings given by the Hellespontine Sibyl that Christ would hang from a high tree, and ascribed them to the Queen of Sheba. Other, similar anthologies of anti-semitic and apocalyptic fire and brimstone also feature the Queen of Sheba, in company with the twelve Sibyls, foreseeing the Crucifixion, and with it the end of the evils of the unbelievers, heathen and Jew.

The prophecies of death to the infidel, which strike contemporary ears as so offensive and despicable, were enmeshed in a web of Christian lore which grew throughout the middle ages. Beginning amid the earliest Christian communities in Syria, different authors developed a symbolic and fantastic tale to provide a mythological aetiology for the relics of the true cross, linking their discovery in the Holy Land with the original prohibited tree of knowledge in the Garden of Eden. This legend intersected with the rich literature of Sibylline oracles and introduced the Queen of Sheba into the story, as one of the prophets with an oblique part to play in the establishment of the Christian faith. Dozens of versions exist of this highly popular, picaresque legend, in English, French, German, Italian, Dutch, Russian, Bulgarian and Icelandic; the plot was itself constantly sprouting new branches and shooting new foliage as it recounted the adventures of the cross-tree, the instrument of God's plan of salvation from the beginning of time to Judgement Day, tracing the loss of the relic at the time of Christ's death to its rediscovery and subsequent dispersal. Splinters were enshrined all over the Christian world, and the cult inspired extraordinary works of metaphysical intensity, like the Anglo-Saxon poem 'The Dream of the Rood' in the eighth century. The legend was mentioned towards the end of the twelfth century by the encyclopedic Petrus Comestor (*d.* 1178). (He was given this nickname – Peter the Eater – because of his omnivorous mind.) But the story subsequently travelled far from scholastic circles, and was much relished, told, and illustrated in medieval and Renaissance materials, in a range of media and a variety of forms, from Books of Hours, to Piero della Francesca's fresco cycle in Arezzo, to Thomas Malory's *Le Morte d'Arthur*, written c. 1470, only a little after Piero was painting. In oral literature of all kinds as well – from plays to sermons – the Queen of Sheba plays a part in this story, and one which conveys the all-encompassing embrace of the catholic or universal Church on earth, which promises to enfold pagan and Jew, male and female, past and present, and make them all one in Christ Jesus.

But it is the *Legenda aurea*, or *Golden Legend*, compiled in the mid-thirteenth century by the proselytizing Dominican, Jacobus de Voragine, that became the most widely used source. This anthology related material about Jesus, Mary and the saints which was circulating in other forms, and arranged the stories as a day book following the liturgical year; many of the tales share the conventions of fairy tales, with grisly horrors and heavenly wonders, happy resolutions (of a sort) and not a shred of anxiety about the implausibility of the contents. The thesaurus was a tiebeam in the edifice of Christian culture; it would be difficult to overestimate the uses to which artists and sermon-writers put Jacobus' fantastic, spirited, violent and often bigoted work.

On 3 May, the feast day of the Invention, or Finding of the Holy Cross in Jerusalem, *The Golden Legend* relates how Adam's son, Seth, plucked a branch of the tree in the Garden of Eden and planted it in the mouth of his dead father (p. 101). (This feast, no longer of much consequence in the Catholic calendar, was such a holy day then that the Muslim rulers of the holy places agreed to allow Christian pilgrims to enter Jerusalem freely to worship for a space of twenty-four hours.) The branch grows – from the Old Adam who foreshadows the Second Adam, Christ – until one day, many centuries later, King Solomon orders the tree to be cut down for the building of the Temple. But the workmen find that the wood refuses to comply with their tools or their measurements, and so they throw it away, and it falls into the stream of Kidron, which flows below the

Temple mount, and becomes a footbridge for passers by.

It is at this point that the Queen of Sheba enters the story. As in the Bible, she is on her way to meet the famous and wise king Solomon; her own wisdom includes foreknowledge of the cross-tree. She recognizes there and then that the footbridge is made of the tree which will prove the future instrument of salvation – the same wood that will become the cross of the Crucifixion. She therefore draws back from desecrating it by setting her idolater's foot upon it, and wades the stream instead (p. 110), prophesying that this same piece of wood will bring about an end to the Kingdom of the Jews: 'And when the Queen of Sheba came to visit Solomon', translates Caxton, 'she worshipped this tree because she said that the Saviour of all the world should be hanged thereon, by whom the realm of the Jews shall be defaced and cease.'

Solomon, fearing for his future, has the bridge destroyed and the wood thrown away, into a pond. But it has miraculous powers of healing, and so the pool where it has been cast becomes the 'piscina [which] … has such virtue that the angels descended and moved the water, and the first sick man that descended into the water after the moving was made whole of whatsoever sickness he was sick of'. Here, Jacobus de Voragine is synthesizing folk materials with the Gospel accounts of the miracles at Bethesda in Jerusalem. The place was known to pilgrims: in 1483, when the Dominican friar Felix Faber visited the pool, he recalled, 'Solomon caused the wood which the Sibyl showed him, and whereon she prophesied that Christ should suffer, to be plunged into the depths of the cistern.' It is worth noting that, for this pilgrim, there was no doubt that the Sibyl and Sheba were one and the same figure.

When the time comes for Christ's death, the wooden beam rises from the bottom of the pool and floats there – 'and of this piece of timber made the Jews the cross of our Lord,' writes Jacobus.

Visual interpretations of the story are almost more important to understanding the narrative than any verbal account, as more people would have absorbed the story from wall paintings and prints produced by shrines in which relics of the true cross were venerated. The most notable and surprising interpreter of Jacobus' narrative scheme turns out to be Piero della Francesca.

In the chancel of the church of San Francesco in Arezzo, painted in 1452–66, Piero faithfully interpreted the tale as reported in the *The Golden Legend*, although the intellectual geometry of his style obscures the Christian triumphalism and prejudice of his source; his serene perspectives and controlled arrangement of the sequence belie the occasional cruelty and coarseness of the stories being told. Yet the same observation could also be put differently: that Piero's graphic calm, his poise and lucidity, match the message, the import, of the tale he tells. His fresco cycle tells the story of the triumph of the true cross; Sheba has a crucial role to play in its unfolding. Piero is setting to rights disorder and deformity, in the same way as the history of the Church has straightened the deviant and enlightened the darkness; he is rounding off jaggedness and incoherence. The Queen of Sheba is only one of a series of outsiders in the cycle who becomes an insider through the power of grace, working through the wood of the cross. The idea that Sheba was, like the Sibyls, an outsider who gained an insider's understanding is crucial to Piero's representation, as it is to the role of storytellers, who point out paths to inclusion, acceptance, success for their hearers. The Legend of the True Cross relates to fairy tale on account of its fantastic character, but even more because it shows a way to belong, and the fairy tale as a genre reveals the common values and desires of the group – in this case, the dominant Christian scheme of things. Like many other popular narratives, it diagnoses the beasts, the pariahs. But in this case, through the figures of salvation, like Sheba, it offers the promise of meta-morphosis, of becoming 'one of us'.

Piero interpreted Adam's death as a naked return to the naked earth, with an old and shrunken Eve beside him, and their sons and daughters around; Seth is seen in the background collecting the branch of the tree from an angel at the gates

Adam is dying, and Seth, his son, is given a branch of the tree of mercy by an angel in the Garden of Eden to plant in the mouth of his father: this was the opening episode of the popular Christian legend of the True Cross. (Piero della Francesca, The Death of Adam, *Arezzo, 1452–66)*

of Eden, and, again, planting the tree in the mouth of his shrouded father (p. 101). Below this scene, the Queen of Sheba makes her approach towards Jerusalem, and comes to the plank across the stream (Pl. 8). Granted her prophetic insight into the wood's future role as the instrument of salvation, Piero's queen kneels gravely in worship on the bank, her hands joined in prayer, her head slightly bowed, her mantle a cerulean blue that looks forward to the Madonna's livery, as does her fervent pose. The bridge can only be glimpsed in the corner, but the story was familiar to spectators, and did not need emphasis. In the adjoining fresco, Solomon and Sheba meet, they clasp right hands in the gesture of a pact between equals, but she bows her head while he remains upright.

A powerful votive polychrome wooden Crucifixion hangs in the centre of the chapel above the main altar, and behind it, on either side of the tall lancet window on the narrow end wall, Piero's programme continues to follow the fate of the cross after Christ's death, as it despatches one enemy after another, like a dragon slayer in objective shape.

After a vision of the cross, the emperor Constantine fights under its banner and wins a famous victory at the Milvian bridge over the rival emperor Maxentius in 312; he is instantly converted to Christianity and orders the Roman world to follow him. He then despatches his mother Helena to the Holy Land to find the relics of the true cross, the material form of the sign by which he now lives. Helena finds out where the cross has been hidden by forcing a confession from a Jew who knows the secret. Significantly, his name is Judas – Judas Cyriacus – and the empress mother has him dropped into a dry well and kept there until he capitulates. On the back wall, Judas is being winched up from the well; an unbeliever of the same persuasion as Solomon, he then reveals the burial place of the three crosses used to hang Christ and the two thieves. Queen Helena has the area excavated – the theme of the central tier of the lefthand wall of the chancel. The true cross, the one on which Christ died, is then proved – identified – by the miraculous cure of a youth over whose naked, afflicted body it is held in blessing.

Opposite the victory of Constantine, Piero then deploys, in a choreographed sweep across the breadth of the wall, another triumph: the battle in which in the seventh century the emperor Heraclius defeated Chosroes, King of the Persians, an idolater and deadly enemy of Christendom (pp. 104–5). In this mighty frieze, banners fly above the heads of the warriors and horses in the mêlée – it is an army 'terrible with banners'. Just to the left of centre, one flag displays an upright white cross on a scarlet field, the emblem of Christian chivalry and another epiphany of the Holy Rood, the protagonist of Piero's scheme. Beside it, another flag, lying aslant the horizontal, is emblazoned with the head of a Moor in profile on an escutcheon; the same head then reappears above, painted on the crest of a knight's heraldic helm three times larger. This flag is torn – for the Moor's head hints at Chosroes' infidel allegiance, though in 615, the date of the theft of the relics from Jerusalem, Islam itself was yet to be established. In the fresco on the opposite wall showing Constantine's victory, the same heraldic Moor's head appears among his enemy's ranks.

Piero was speaking to a contemporary audience in the rhetoric of the Crusades – a language they shared: such insignia were familiar among the coats of arms of crusaders, several hundred years after Maxentius' and Chosroes' reigns, and were adopted to recall their struggles with a later stripe of unbeliever, the Saracens; they emblazoned such trophies on their family escutcheons. Caxton, translating *The Golden Legend*, calls Chosroes and his men 'paynims' – a word which in English then implied Mohammedan or Saracen. His narrative, like Jacobus', was universalist in its reach, bringing enemies into contact with divine power; its principal dynamic, which often drives later spoken or written popular stories as well, is conversion: the conversion of its subjects from the unfamiliar to the familiar.

As Sheba is Queen of the South, Constantine Emperor of the West, so Chosroes rules the East and has dominion over heathens like the Moors of Islam. One by one, each incomer, each stranger, is represented succumbing to the inclusive powers of the Church, the outstretched arms of the cross, which annihilate what they cannot contain.

In the Song of Songs, attributed to Solomon, the beloved who speaks of her love to the king was traditionally identified with the queen. She says of herself, towards the beginning of the poem, 'I am black, but comely …' ('*Nigra sum sed formosa*') (Song of Solomon 1: 5). It is a telltale 'but', that '*sed*' in the Vulgate translation. It functions to mark openly an oxymoron, which was only implied in the original Hebrew, in which *V* means 'and' as well as 'but'. The Vulgate's '*sed*' betrays the Church's ambivalence about blackness, the colour-coded livery of the underworld, and its double power of dread and fascination.

In medieval European iconography, the biblical associations had inspired images of a Moorish Queen of Sheba: an enamel plaque on the altar of Nicholas of Verdun of 1181 (p. 96), a stained-glass window in the church of St Thomas at Strasbourg of around a hundred years later. By Piero's time, however, artists often only hint at the queen's race and geographical origins, by introducing a maid from Africa into her train, as in the Arezzo fresco where such a figure plays a background role, literally placed in the middle distance to one side and behind the

dominant group of gracious Quattrocento white patrician Tuscans, Sheba and her attendants (Pl. 8). The maid, signifying in this reticent manner the foreignness of Sheba's origins, wears a beehive-shaped African cap of bound reeds or quills or maybe even ivory – Piero likes millinery to indicate origin and this hat is exactly the kind of exotic curio that Renaissance connoisseurs would collect to ornament their cabinets. The Master of the *Hours of Catherine of Cleves* also includes a grace-ful portrait of a black lady-in-waiting on the other side of the stream behind the queen (p. 110). But sometimes the artists are not so evasive: a Bohemian manu-script illuminated before 1405 even attempts a reconciliation of history and Western ideals by later overpainting, giving the Queen blue-black face and hands – but she retains her flowing golden hair (Pl. 7).

Consistently, however, by some sleight of hand, the biblical placing of Sheba's kingdom in 'the south' is transformed into an elsewhere far away, marked by

One of the most popular Christian stories related the sufferings and the triumph of the relics of the cross on which Jesus died. Here, Heraclius, the seventh-century emperor of Byzantium, brings about a great victory over the pagan ruler of the Persians, Chosroes. When he refuses to convert, he is beheaded (far right); other symbols of the vanquished infidel, like the torn flag with a Moor's head, convey the story's message of conversion or exclusion. (Piero della Francesca, The Legend of the True Cross, *Arezzo, 1452–66.)*

difference from mainstream Christendom.

The topographical position of the land of Sheba was – and is – hazy. Saba, in south-west Arabia, became fabulously wealthy, but only long after Solomon's alleged reign; Seba, in the Bible, is identified with Cush, or Ethiopia. The Ethiopian Church have venerated the Queen of Sheba as their founding mother for centuries, finding of course nothing exotic in her blackness; the present-day religious movement of Rastafarians count her among their most important saints.

Archaeologists are digging today in the Yemen in what are considered the remains of the queen's realm, which stretched to include Sabaean settlements in the north of the Arabian peninsula. Josephus, the Jewish historian writing in the first century AD, interprets the queen's origins as African, and locates her realm in Egypt and Ethiopia. This version overlaps with the Ethiopian Church's view, though it places her territory further south and west.

The imaginary geography of Sheba can be mapped much more precisely than its historical position. From readings of the Bible itself, Sheba, or Saba, represents the far south, redolent of luxury and sensual pleasures. In the figure of the Queen of Sheba, the beckoning and voluptuous Orient becomes embodied; its imaginative territory in classical sources encompassed meridian and outlandish exoticism, sensuality, wonders, and luxuries. Herodotus' fanciful reports of the warm south continued to resonate: 'The most southerly country is Arabia,' he wrote:

> and Arabia is the only place that produces frankincense, myrrh, cassia, cinnamon, and the gum called ledanon [laudanum] … When they gather frankincense, they burn storax … to drive off the flying snakes … keep[ing] guard over all the trees which bear the frankincense … Still more surprising is the way of getting ledanon … Sweet-smelling substance though it is, it is found in a most malodorous place; sticking, namely, like glue in the beards of he-goats … It is used as an ingredient in many kinds of perfume …

In Arabia, fair rises from foul, rare perfumes from filthy billy-goats.

When the Queen of Sheba in the Bible brings from the south that great abundance of spices as well as gold as her gift to King Solomon, she stirs these associations, deeply rooted in antique myth of the Orient.

The transmission of the queen's story, in Western Christian iconography and folklore, thus places her sultry, heady southern domain in an easterly direction, marching with the original cradle of civilization in Mesopotamia, with the Garden of Eden. For the receivers of her story in the middle ages and Renaissance, this location of her possessions merges them with Islam's; they converge with the later religion's extensive dominions. Whether Arabian, or African, or from the hinterlands of presentday Iran and Iraq, she is identified with the Moors' sphere of influence, and her biblical encounter with Solomon encrypts proleptically the promise of a Moor's conversion to the future Christian faith, the return to the fold of a heathen potentate. On the same page of the *Hortus deliciarum*, the Abbess Herrad of Hohenburg's inspired spiritual encyclopedia, compiled in the twelfth century, the Queen of Sheba is placed next to the scene of the apostle Philip baptizing the Ethiopian eunuch (Acts 8: 27–39) – seldom represented in art before the encounter with the New World. The Queen of Sheba is a Muslim before time, and she becomes a Christian before time, just as Solomon is a precursor, one of the just who will be drawn from limbo at the Crucifixion; by the very fact of her difference, the Queen of Sheba plays a pivotal role in establishing conversion to orthodoxy.

In mathematics, in which Piero was an adept, the cross of course symbolizes addition: the sign of plus, of unity in sum. It appears in his paintings high in the sky above the throng in the battle of Chosroes and Heraclius, and once more, in the final lunette of the fresco cycle, above worshippers gathered from the four quarters to venerate the symbol of Christianity which has been restored to Jerusalem by the emperor Heraclius. Again they wear splendid hats to denote exoticism, and Piero conveys the new life they will enjoy now that they have entered the fold, by placing the raised cross-timber between the luxuriant foliage of two living green and silvery trees – are they olives, emblem of peace? – against a clear blue sky.

The formal plan of Piero's narrative proclaims divine providence's all-encompassing love, universal forgiveness, salvation; or, in other terms, its will to power, its catholic reach, its imperium. The whole sequence reduces and patterns time, in the same way as Piero's pictorial storytelling telescopes space; but it also selects homologies across the centuries in order to provide a rhyming structure to the disparate episodes.

The epiphany brought about by Sheba in the ancient world returns in the vision of Queen Helena under the new dispensation; in Piero's arrangement, the Queen of Sheba with her attendants kneeling by the bridge and Helena with her entourage praying reverently at the scene of the miracle wrought by the unearthed cross openly mirror each other on opposite walls of the chapel. The artist even used the same cartoon in reverse for the two compositions.

Saint Helena, the mother of the first Christian emperor, acts as cornerstone in the Church Militant's establishment on earth. The cross became Saint Helena's identifying attribute. Artists, interpreting the story of the finding of the relics, saw visionary representatives of the ancient pagan world – the Hellespontine Sibyl and the Queen of Sheba who foresaw the fate of the wood of the cross – thus recapitulated in another saint, Helena. The Sibyl predated the redemption, but Helena came afterwards: she was herself one of the saved, the saint who was mother to the first converted ruler, who brought the whole Roman empire with him into the Church. In printed holy pictures of Helena, she even wears the crown of the Holy Roman Emperor (p. 108).

Saint Helena, mother of the first Christian emperor, Constantine, unearthed the relics of the cross in Jerusalem; personification of the Church militant, she wears the crown of the Holy Roman Empire and carries the cross of Faith. Defeated pagan satyrs look on aghast. Virgil Solis, the artist, worked in Nuremberg, where the Emperor was crowned at that time, c. 1553.

The symmetry of this scheme reflects the scholastic taste for recapitulation and prefiguration, binding the Old Testament to the New in a series of typological formulae, leading from Sibyl to queen to saint. In the *Hortus deliciarum*, the Queen of Sheba already stood for the Church of the Gentiles, consecrated by Solomon, a forerunner of Christ, and prophet in the sister Church of the (converted) Jews. It is a reward for her role in the scheme of salvation that she takes her place beside biblical patriarchs, kings and prophets in the portals of the Romanesque and Gothic cathedrals and abbeys of France, at Chartres, Reims, St Nicolas of Amiens (now destroyed), Corbeil (now in the Louvre) and in the stained glass of Canterbury Cathedral.

By the time that influential manual of theological instruction, the *Speculum humanae salvationis*, or *Mirror of Human Salvation*, was first composed, in the first half of the fourteenth century, the Queen of Sheba as the proleptic figure of Christian conversion was established. Though the programme of such texts or of Piero's frescoes seems confusing and complex to today's viewer, they speak the lingua franca of their time; when Henry VIII was establishing himself as Supreme Head of the Christian Church in England, he was drawn by Hans Holbein as Solomon receiving the submission of the Queen of Sheba: the allusion to Rome's subordination was clear.

The Queen of Sheba plays her part in this inaugural legend of Catholic Christianity when she acquiesces to Solomon's superiority. In her proving of Solomon's wisdom, Sheba stands for Gentile or pagan wisdom, while he embodies Jewish faith and learning: both will be enfolded in the bosom of the Church later. By so doing, she takes her place in medieval tradition, as a future Christian granted a vision of the cross's destiny, like the Sibyls. The legend of the true cross is not the only place, however, where she can be found playing a pivotal part in the development of Christian mythology and stories.

Her condition as a heathen outside the fold, who receives enlightenment and abjures her native faith, is intertwined with her femaleness: she acts as the reciprocating Other who completes the male principle of wisdom, embodied by King Solomon; she symbolizes the carnal condition of woman in its fullest form – vitality, seductiveness, fertility and ... wisdom, too. This added element, Sheba's reputation for wisdom which matches Solomon's, her status as his peer and natural partner, gives a different, mixed flavour to the heathenness, the heat, the meridian, the Moorishness of her persona. It makes her an insider as well as an outsider, anticipating such ambiguously positioned characters as the Arabian *alemah*, the figure of the wise dancing girl, who recited poetry and was adept at all civilized pleasures, and whose greatest forebear was Scheherazade, who told stories to save her life.

The Queen of Sheba is saved within the story that enfolds her, and she develops into a source of wisdom for others. Her southernness – her outlandishness, in the literal sense that she comes from the periphery, far from the centre – also marks her character in Arabian folklore; and this quality of her difference, figured forth not by blackness but by other signs, relates in significant and fascinating ways to her later popular European manifestations, in fairy tale and nursery lore.

The erotic overtones of Solomon and Sheba's meeting in the Bible inspired painters of dowry chests: Sheba appears here as both queen and bride. (Anon., late fifteenth century.)

The Queen of Sheba, watched by two gracefully dressed ladies-in-waiting, wades the stream rather than set foot on the bridge made of the future cross; in the margins the illustrator introduces a market woman spinning, as a sly comment perhaps on the character of the story. (The Hours of Catherine of Cleves, Utrecht, c. 1440.)

CHAPTER 8

The Glass Paving and the Secret Foot: The Queen of Sheba II

Tell me, where all past years are,
Or who cleft the Devil's foot.

John Donne

In folk tales of the Middle East, Solomon hears, from his messenger the hoopoe, that a fabulously rich queen, called Bilqis, has come to the throne in the south. He becomes curious. She worships the sun, he is told, not Allah: she stands in relation to this Muslim Solomon as a pagan, just as she does to the Jewish proto-Christian king; and, just as Sheba in the Old Testament realizes the truth of King Solomon's God, so she does in the Koran. In a late version of the story, Solomon is so delighted with the hoopoe's report that he rewards his messenger with a feathered crest for her head and a gilded beetle for her lunch.

Solomon and the Queen of Sheba were celebrated in Islamic doctrine and scripture. The wise king is as vital a persona in the Muslims' holy book as he is in the Bible, and more of a wizard. Attended by djinns and magic animals, he can work wonders and enchantments greater than any other king, so, when he orders the queen to come to him 'submissively', and she is reluctant, he uses his prodigious powers of goety, or (black) magic, and performs various tricks to bring her to him. They include conjuring a stream across the floor of his courtyard that looks like water but is really made of mirror (Pl. 6). When the queen arrives, the Koran continues:

She was bidden to enter the palace; but when she saw it she thought it was a pool of water, and bared her legs. But Solomon said, 'It is a palace paved with glass.'

'Lord,' she said, 'I have sinned against my own soul. Now I submit with Solomon to Allah, Lord of the creation.'

This highly compressed encounter is indecipherable without additional information, without knowledge of the accompanying lore which attributed a peculiarity to the Queen of Sheba, a deformity located under her dress. Legends which predate the writing of the Koran spread the rumour that she had ass's hooves. In more genial variations, she simply suffers from hairy legs. Some of the stories tell how the stream cures her affliction – it miraculously turns to healing water. In other versions, doubtless popular in the bazaar, in which her problem is hairiness, Solomon comes to her rescue and, with the assistance of his djinns, invents a depilatory cream. The recipe is given in some texts: a drastic solution of lime and arsenic.

But in the Koran, her unwitting exposure of her legs brings about her recognition of the true god. Her false faith, her earlier worship of the sun, is somehow bodied forth in the cryptic allusion to her legs, revealed by Solomon's enchantments and then magicked away.

The story travelled. Brought back to Western Europe by crusaders and pilgrims, it was conflated with other stories in circulation; by the twelfth century, the queen's suspect nether parts had merged with the fancies of colder climates, about witches' and demonesses' and sorceresses' feet, and fantasies flourished which embroidered on her Koranic deformity: she was rumoured to be splay-, web- or bird-footed, or to have reptilian, dragon- or griffin-like limbs concealed under her clothes. The water which cured her deformity becomes transferred to her limbs, bequeathing to her marine extremities, suitable for wading.

The most packed, eloquent and powerful interpretation of the legend in Western Europe occurs in the upper portion of the fantastically patterned mosaic floor of the Cathedral of Otranto, in Puglia, itself the heel of Italy's boot. It is also the earliest of the surviving visual examples, as it was created in 1165 by the monk Pantaleone who signed and dated his remarkable work. He includes King Solomon and the Queen of Sheba in separate roundels side by side at the summit of one of the three great branching trees of life – trees of story – which cover the entire floor like a sumptuous prayer carpet. The queen, who is labelled 'Regina Austri' (Queen of the South), is richly arrayed and bejewelled in an oriental diapered and belted tunic and diadem (Pl. 9); she is seated on an ornamental stool and holds up one shoe in her right hand; it is studded with the same bright blue stones as the earring she wears. Her left foot is bare, and though the mosaic admittedly has been damaged over the intervening centuries, the foot is wedge-shaped like the ace of spades, and shows no divisions for the toes. (The feet of other figures, like Adam and Eve, in the same mosaic, possess carefully delineated digits.) In the margins of the roundels, where Pantaleone placed glosses and comments with the sly humour of the scriptorium (a donkey harpist, a fox cymbalist), there also appears, facing the queen, across Solomon, a tall, leggy, standing bird somewhat like a crane, a stork or an ostrich.

The two roundels are arranged next to two more which enhance their significance by analogy, in the manner of typological pendants. On the left, corresponding to the Queen of Sheba, a double-tailed mermaid, who wears similar earrings to Sheba's, presents herself face forward, split at the crotch in the style of a Celtic *sheila-na-gig*, holding up her two tails in each hand (Pl. 10); beside her, in the margins, an octopus undulates its several limbs in witty imitation. The complementary female symbolisms lightly deployed by the artist monk around the figure of the prophetic queen – bird/heathen, siren/octopus – are rooted in biblical and classical mythical metonymy. The mosaic floor of Otranto, with its images of the splay-footed queen, the snaky and tentacular undulations of the polyp, and the exhibitionist siren, anticipates Freud's identification of snaky-haired Medusa with the female genitals; Freud also analysed the symbolism of feet in sexual practice and imagery with relevant perceptiveness:

> The foot owes its preference as a fetish – or a part of it – to the circumstance that the inquisitive boy peered at the woman's genitals from below, from her legs up; fur and velvet – as has long been suspected – are a fixation of the sight of the pubic hair, which should have been followed by the longed-for sight of the female member.

The euphemistic as well as fetishistic substitution occurs very early: the seraphim of Isaiah have six wings, two to cover their faces, two to cover their feet and two for flying (Isa. 6: 2). But, as the Jerusalem Bible points out, 'feet' here stand for sexual organs. In the case of the angels, this raises all kinds of fundamental questions, of course.

But the monk Pantaleone at Otranto was also drawing directly on the Bible when he gave Sheba the tall, ostrich-like bird and the mermaid for companions. The scholars rendering the Bible into Greek from Hebrew, into Latin from Greek, stumbled when they came across the wondrous jumble of hybrid creatures of pagan and classical fantasy, as they tried to match them across cultures: the Greek Bible rendered as *seirenes* the Hebrew *thannim*, and Saint Jerome, who usually translated *thannim* as *dracones* (dragons), chose instead the word *struthio* (ostrich) to paint the desolation of Babylon after its overthrow:

But beasts of the desert will lie there,
and owls fill its houses.
Ostriches will make their home there
and satyrs have their dances there.
Hyenas will call to each other in its keeps,
jackals in the luxury of its palaces …

(Isa. 13: 21–2)

To a picture of wilderness reclaiming a city, the jackals and owls and beasts lend some authority. But satyrs and ostriches make an odd pairing in any sort of natural history, whereas sirens, as companions to satyrs, would figure, representing emblematically the horrible sweets of pagan hedonism (Babylon, indeed). The King James Bible skips altogether the problem of species at this passage – its Babylonian wasteland is simply peopled by 'doleful creatures'. But the earlier choice of the bird species ostrich for creatures making siren-like noises gives the oddest results: even in the magnificent text of the modern Jerusalem Bible, it is 'the wailing' of the ostrich that is sometimes heard (Mic. 1: 8). The adult male ostrich booms at a low pitch at night, and the young warble: neither a siren song nor a lament. Nor does the bird belong in the folklore of seduction (unless one counts ostrich-feather boas) or in the rituals of death. But ostriches, unlike most birds, have cloven feet, which lent them to biblical symbolism. Sirens, on the other hand, do call, even wail, while their fins and their tails or tail (legs anomalously joined) correspond to other amphibious creatures' webbed toes.

The ostrich of the Bible was once a siren; and these residual pagan enchantresses had been called 'sirens' in the translations of the Bible before Jerome's Vulgate, as Jerome knew. But when he justified his rendering, he was revealing: '"*Thunnim*" are called sirens, but we will interpret them as demons or certain monsters or certainly great dragons, which are crested and fly.' (Ostriches do not fit this description either.) Later, in the same commentary on Isaiah, he argued: 'beasts and dragons and ostriches and hairy and howling creatures and sirens [which] we understand are bestial forms of angels or demons …' When he gives a list of the names of devils, he includes, last but not least, the Hebrew word which he himself had rendered as 'ostrich' rather than 'siren'. Perhaps he felt the word 'siren' was itself too seductive, too freighted with the classical ambiguities, not clear-cut enough as a term of disparagement. Something more unambiguously repugnant was needed. The sirens' '*lamentabilis vox*' (lamentable voice) and '*venenata ora*' (poisoned lips), he knew led their hearers astray – and he defined the danger in a particularly revealing way. 'The foods of these demons are the songs of poets,' he warned in one letter. In another, he condemned music and singing at banquets, comparing the guests to sailors who throw themselves on the rocks at the sound of the sirens, because amid such carousing, 'it is difficult to keep one's modesty'.

The immodest, tempting, singing siren of the seas survived patristic disapproval – and one of her refuges was fairy tale, in which she appears as a character (see Chapter Twenty-three) and as a concealed force, the underlying voice of the narrative.

Sirens and mermaids, with biblical warranty, entered the bestiary of heterogeneous monsters on medieval capitals, ivory caskets, misericords, and mosaic floors, as one variation among so many of the demonic temptations in circulation. These are hiding places which themselves convey the sirens' lingering, latent seduction, corners where they could still be seen and heard – but askance. The mosaic floor at Otranto is only one of the works of art that celebrate the banned voice of the siren – assimilating her in the process to the splay-footed queen who tested the wisdom of Solomon with her questions.

II

In one recension of the medieval legend of the cross, made in the twelfth century, the manuscript specifies that the Queen of Sheba was an Ethiopian and had webbed feet. But this may well represent a suggestive scribal error by a German monk, who wrote 'pes anserinus' (goose-footed) instead of 'pes asininus' (ass-footed) because he was confusing the Arabic legend with the rich homegrown tradition of amphibian swan-maidens, goblins, and elves who had skin joining their toes. The queen's outsider status would also have invited this change to the more particularly hybrid, telltale outward sign.

Like many curious slips of the pen – or the tongue – the image caught the recipients' fancy and was much repeated: on the portal of Saint-Bénigne, in Dijon, the Queen of Sheba was carved with one webbed foot appearing beneath the hem of her dress, standing beside King Solomon in an elegant, tapered, twelfth-century sculpture. Saint-Bénigne was defaced in the Revolution, but a drawing from 1739 survives.

Feet are ascribed telltale marks of identity and origin, perhaps through the literal-minded wordplay of the imagination, since they are the lowest part of the body and in touch with the earth as opposed to the heavens. When Sheba refuses to set foot on the bridge made of the wood of the cross, she admits that her tread would defile it – quite apart from any stigmatizing malformation of her foot itself. In the medieval legend, she steps into the water of the stream instead, and is miraculously cured, like her Koranic counterpart Bilqis. A German poem, composed between 1347 and 1378 and existing in many different redactions and manuscripts, shows how the skeins of the two stories were twisted together in northern Europe. In this text, the fantasy about the Queen of Sheba's deformed foot reappears; and in the same poem, she is called Sibilla, as if Sibyl were her name, appropriate to her function, for the poem belongs to the corpus of German apocalyptic literature spoken by the Sibyls. Thus, a triple connection is developed to form a narrative composed of the biblical Queen of Sheba, the Muslim legend of her peculiarity, and the Western milleniarist tradition about the Sibyls, among whom she can be included. And this triple persona is caught in the web of stories about the true cross:

> At this time when this report rang out
> everywhere, reaching every land,
> there lived a woman, a prophetess,
> and she was indeed wise in understanding.
> She was called Sibilla,
> and God had granted her
> that she could see in the stars
> what was to happen in the world
> for many thousands of years ...
> The lady was beautiful and noble
> and had a foot that looked
> as if it were a goose's foot.
> She was deeply ashamed of it,
> yet with it she walked and stood
> as other people do on their feet.
> Sibilla ...
> wanted to find out the truth,
> so she came to King Solomon.
> That wise man caught sight of her
> – he'd heard reports about her too –
> and received her with great eagerness.
> He said, 'Welcome, exalted guest!'
> She thanked him duly and firmly.

He said, 'My lady, Why are you here?
I have never been so glad to see
any guest as to see you.'

'I shall tell you,' she said:
'I have been told so much about your building
and your wisdom and the grace of your court
and so many other things besides,
that I want to see the truth of it.'
The King said: 'I do not want to miss
your eating with me.' 'Gladly,' she said.

As she wanted to go to eat in the court,
it happened that she had to pass over
the gangway made of Adam's tree.
She remained there, standing silently,
till she had fully perceived the wood,
then waded through the water and the brook,
to honour and pay homage to the wood
that was laid across the water.
And because of that honour, through God's power
the goosefoot was formed
into a human foot, like the other –
Sibilla was filled with joy.

In this poem, Sibilla then makes certain characteristic apocalyptic prophecies –
five in all – about the Incarnation, the Crucifixion, the Day of Judgement and the
coming of the Antichrist.

The picturesqueness and piquancy of this tale of metamorphosis captivated
many interpreters in Western Europe. Although there were two translations of the
Koran made in the twelfth century, and the humanist Nicholas of Cusa was
studying it at the beginning of the fifteenth, the Koran would not have provided
the dominant source of the tale for the versions that circulated this motif of
Islamic and Christian legend for over five hundred years .

An anonymous fresco painter in Bohemia, around 1450 – that is a little earlier
than Piero's frescoes in Arezzo – depicted the story on a chapel wall at Kutna Hora
monastery church, near Prague, showing the queen with a griffon's left foot,

The story of the Queen of Sheba's suspect foot travelled from the east: it reached Bohemia, and was painted in the monastery of Kutna Hora LEFT around 1485–92, and was disseminated in prints, too, as in the woodcut of Solomon and Sheba RIGHT from Ulm, also of around 1492.

fording the stream rather than treading on the wood of the cross (above left). More frequently, the story surfaces in rather more ephemeral 'low' materials, in woodcuts and songs, like a print from Ulm of around 1492; it was clearly still persisting in this area of Germany a hundred and fifty years after the poem quoted above. The print shows the Queen of Sheba with a single, sizeable goose-foot peeping out from the hem of her dress, while she engages Solomon in deep debate (above right). The woodcut was printed on the title page of a collection of the Sibyl's sayings, as well as on a broadsheet with verses stressing God's mercy to those who repent and the pains of hellfire for those who do not.

Ulm, a prosperous and aspiring humanist city, was a crossroads for pilgrims between the West and the Holy Land and their different folklore; it was for instance the home of Felix Faber, the monk who recorded most compendiously of all medieval pilgrims his two journeys to see the holy places and who also retold the story of Sheba's recognizing the bridge. Several printshops sprang up in the city in the monk's lifetime, immediately after the development of printing, and published such literature as Aesop and Boccaccio in German translation. The city prided itself on its progressive humanism: Heinrich Steinhowel, the translator of these profane authors, was nevertheless rewarded, it is thought, by a portrait in the cathedral itself. Among the busts in the choir stalls which Jörg Syrlin carved from 1468 to 1470, he appears as the comic playwright Terence.

Terence is one of the busts portraying classical philosophers, from Pythagoras to Cicero, who form poppyhead finials on the stalls, while kings, prophets and other biblical heroes in bas-relief fill the ogive panels on the wall behind. This male pantheon balances the throng, on the opposite side of the choir, of their female counterparts: Sibyls for the finials, saints and heroines on the wall. Ninety-nine figures in all, and among them, some of the finest naturalistic fifteenth-century portraiture in the medium of wood carving: with the Tiburtine Sibyl, for instance, Jörg Syrlin achieves a remarkably lively study of female old age in his time, altogether free from the morbid brooding on decay and vanity and sin in the work of contemporaries like the Nuremberg sculptor Viet Stoss. The Phrygian Sibyl too is rendered with delicate psychological sympathy.

Jörg Syrlin strategically placed the Queen of Sheba in the gap between the

The Hellespontine Sibyl, whose prophecies focussed on the cross, displays a feathered buskin, as if to convey another pagan outsider's solidarity with Sheba. (Jean Guiramand, Cathedral of Saint-Sauveur, Aix-en-Provence, first quarter of sixteenth century.)

righthand choir stalls, against the wall over the door, overlooking the space where the Hellespontine Sibyl faces the Tiburtine – physically acting as a hyphen between the two antique seers, and holding the beam of the cross in her hand. This is a rare iconographic example of the pagan queen, inserted among her visionary colleagues in a schema of high cultural character, a surviving monumental expression of the parallels elaborated in commentaries on the Bible. Although Syrlin's meanings cannot be fully recovered, it is probable, given the publication of Sheba's Sybilline sayings in the city, that his contemporary audience would have grasped the reason for the queen's position in relation to the prophetesses.

A full book of sixty-four woodcuts called *Boec van der Houte* (The Book of the Rood), printed in the Netherlands by John Veldener in 1483, tells in Dutch rhyming couplets a different variation of the story of the wood of the cross, which follows the scheme found in Thomas Malory rather than *The Golden Legend*. It also includes a little-known episode: the torture of the Sibyl after she foretells the end of the kingdom of the Jews. This Sibyl has assimilated the character of the Hellespontine in particular, for she repeats her traditional prophecy almost verbatim: '*Dat Christus soulde hanghen in dat houte claer*'. (This Sibyl's traditional message

The bestial provided artists with the devilish imagery they needed: horns, fangs, claws, paws, talons, hooves, webbed digits, maws and jaws were mixed and matched. (Le Livre de la Vigne Nostre Seigneur, French, c. 1450–70.)

is '*Felix ille qui ligno pendet ab alto*' – the translator has chosen 'high' in the sense of exalted, '*claer*'.) Tied naked to the stake, the Sibyl places her best – webbed – foot forward. In the next woodcut the heroine refuses to set foot on the bridge and wades across instead. The poem then focusses on Helena, who, as in all the legends of the cross, finds the relics and brings about the conversion of Rome. The glissade in this volume from Sibyl to Queen of Sheba crucially strengthens the argument here, because within the specific narrative of the cross, the anomalous foot and the stream, it merges the wizened-crone type of Sibyl with the beautiful queen, and elides the difference in their positions in the social hierarchy.

Though the Devil's hoof is famously goatish and cloven, artists' fantasy did not stop there, and bird claws or webbed digits or hybrid varieties of both recur in illustrations of the tempter and his minions (left). In the medieval miracle play *Mary of Nimmegen*, for instance, the heroine's one-eyed devil suitor tells her:

> It's not in our power, we devils from hell
>   To incarnate ourselves ...
> Without some little defect here or there,
> Be it in the head or the hands or the feet.

Asymmetry often intensifies the presence of unofficial, even forbidden, knowledge: the Devil wears motley, his limbs are mismatched, and he limps, walking *pede claudo*, listing to the left. The theologian Fulgentius (*d.* 533) wrote that the bird-bodied sirens of classical myth have 'hen-like feet' because 'lust scatters all that it possesses'. The seductresses in medieval images of the temptation of Saint Anthony often have one bird-foot peeping from below the hems of their dresses, as in a painting of Saint Justina tempted by the Devil, for instance, by Friedrich Pacher, from the end of the fifteenth century (p. 122); in Sicily, in the latter half of the sixteenth century, women on trial for witchcraft confessed to night-flying with mysterious 'women from outside, who were beautifully dressed but had cats' paws or horses' hooves'. When the knightly hero is nearly deflected from his quest for true love by Jealousy, her foulness includes webbed feet, a recurrent sign of contrariness, and, in women, of deviancy (p. 45). These sinners might have inherited their dangerous talons from Judaic and Greek mythological harpies and she-monsters, like Lamia and Lilith (though these avatars tend to have both limbs misshapen). In Hellenistic magical belief, Hecate's foul offspring, the Empusae (literally, one-footed), were bloodsuckers, succubi and child-stealers, and had one foot of brass and the other an ass's hoof, but they could also disguise themselves

The devil could take cunning disguises; here he appears as a beautiful woman to tempt Saint Justina – but the bird talons under his dress betray him. (Friedrich Pacher, The Temptation of Saint Justina, *Austria, late fifteenth century.)*

as lovely girls to seduce victims. The tradition found its way into all levels of popular culture: a traditional children's game, called Old Witch, which resembles Grandmother's Footsteps, requires the catcher or 'It' to limp as s/he tries to catch the other players, in imitation of the old witch of the title.

The titillating side of the folk tale about the Queen of Sheba and King Solomon's magic trick hints through the metonymy of hairy legs or a misshapen foot at secrets hidden under women's dresses which men fear to see, but long all the same to know. In this allusion, it connects with the imagined avian metamorphoses of the beldames in such bawdy books as *Les Evangiles des quenouilles*, as another strand in the same DNA encoding female heterodoxy as bird-like. The image of the questionable foot arises from the fantasized illicit knowledge that women are supposed to possess, and from curiosity about tabooed domains, the very domains allotted to the old wives of the old wives' tale. The anonymous Master of the *Hours of Catherine of Cleves* included, in the ornamental margins of the miniature which shows the Queen of Sheba wading the stream, a vignette of an old market woman spinning as she sits in a tent with her produce laid out for sale on a board in front of her – a working woman, travelling and doing business independently, and networking as she does so, no doubt (p. 110).

The same fears were damagingly projected on to unbelievers of all kinds: anti-semitism demonized the physical appearance of Jews by fantasizing such defects as splay feet; Melanchthon and Luther issued a pamphlet in 1523 portraying Rome as a beast with one ass's hoof, one bird's claw, an ass's head, the torso of a naked woman and a cock crowing from her rump (p. 124); and when Edmund Spenser imagined the Catholic Church in *The Faerie Queene*, he drew on a similar phantasmagoric repertory of monstrous features. When Duessa, the witchlike daughter of Deceit and Shame, seduces the Knight, he realizes what she is only when he peeps at her bathing and

> Her neather partes misshapen, monstruous,
> Were hidd in water, that I could not see –
> But they did seeme more foule and hideous
> Then womans shape would beleeve to bee …

Later, the poet again specifies the bestial horror of her lower limbs:

> Her neather parts, the shame of all her kind,
> My chaster Muse for shame doth blush to write …
>   [But write he did]
> And eke her feete most monstrous were in sight;
> For one of them was like an Eagles claw
> With griping talaunts armd to greedy fight;
> The other like a beares uneven paw,
> More ugly shape yet never living creature saw.

The Faerie Queene, published during the reign of Henry VIII's Protestant daughter Elizabeth I, proclaimed the truth of the reformed Church against Rome, and the figure of Duessa, in counterpoise to valiant and virtuous Una, personifies the prostituted papacy, brimming with lies and luxury and lust. Luther and Spenser were turning back on the Church the very rhetoric it was accustomed to use to define its enemies.

A younger contemporary of the fairytale authors like L'Héritier and D'Aulnoy, the Breton-born writer Alain-René Lesage (*d.* 1747), wrote a highly successful comic and orientalizing wonder tale, *Le Diable boîteux* (The Limping Devil), which appeared in 1707. The devil Asmodeus is set free from a bottle, Arabian Nights style, and in return lifts the roofs off the houses of Madrid and shows his

A donkey head and cloven hoof, a rooster's claws and crowing beak help portray the monstrousness of Rome in a pamphlet by Luther and Melanchthon. ('The Papal Ass', Germany, 1523.)

rescuer everything going on inside. Lesage was able to paint a vivid and gaily satirical picture of contemporary Parisian society, and his device probably inspired Diderot's famous pornographic squib, *Les Bijoux indiscrets* (1748), in which all is revealed – but by means of a magic ring which has the power to make women's vulvae speak. The idea that the transgressive has access to the unknown and ineffable governs this repertoire of devices and images, and Mother Goose, unlikely as it may seem, belongs there, as an anomalous figure of forbidden knowledge. The Comtesse de Murat found Lesage's device so intriguing that she began a sequel to *Le Diable boîteux*, but did not complete it.

Though each and every type of beast or creature invoked, be it an ostrich or a stork or a goose or a bear or a snake, carries a set of particular associations, the exact form of the bestial nether limbs is mutable: webbed, clawed, gnarled, three-toed, five-toed, encurled, club-footed, not to forget cloven, the appendage itself partakes of polymorphous perversity within the range of the base, not-human possibilities (p. 120). Indeed, this very mutability informs the character of the heterodox and the dangerous. Bird, amphibian, lizard, serpent, the diabolical mutates into many guises, perhaps because a lingering Platonic correlation between beauty and form influences Christian images of the monstrous. Monstrousness shares in disorderliness's clumsiness, its defective classifications and harmonies, it enacts aberration by failing to remain consistent even with itself. A demon on a medieval cathedral can have the head of a ram, the tail of a donkey, the feet of an eagle, the bottom of a gryphon, the ears of a bat and the elbows of a rhinoceros, and so forth. Shifting and slippery forms in themselves convey that chaos which is evil, and, in the Judaeo-Christian tradition, sexuality offered the principal site of danger. When the Queen of Sheba's foot is restored to human shape, as related in one branch of the legend, it not only signifies her recognition of the true god, but announces the possible miraculous redemption of her femaleness.

III

In western and northern Europe, the goose-, the stork-, the bird-woman appear in a richly braided train of perverse associations, and these take us to the heart of medieval romance and the seed-bed of fairy tales. For the inherent tendency in the genre to topsy-turvy, to turning pauper to prince, bane to boon, affects the brandings and birthmarks and deformities of the protagonists as well: fairy tale chronicles conversions, too, in the form of transformations.

When the French fairytale writers in the salons of the seventeenth and eighteenth centuries traced the genre back to the troubadours of Provence, they were right in many ways: the medieval romances are the sources of many fairy tales. One of these, a pattern to which many later tales are cut, coincides in significant motifs with the legend of the Queen of Sheba.

In the mid-thirteenth century, the Brabançon minstrel Adenet le Roi composed a French verse romance about the mother of Charlemagne, Bertha, queen and wife of Pépin le Bref (Pippin the Short) in which he melded oriental romance, troubadour poetry and pseudo-historical record. He called his poem 'Berthe aus grant pié' (Big-Footed Bertha). The text does not expand on the reason for the name, just concentrates on the wealth of subsequent mishaps Berthe suffered until the triumphant appearance of the founder of the French royal line, her son Charles. But in other redactions and variations by minstrels all over Europe, the reason for her name was understood literally. In an early fifteenth-century codex, for instance, the writer tells us:

Ela oit li pe asa plus grant
Qe nulla autre dame soit de son courant.

[She had a foot indeed much larger than any other woman of her day.]

In folklore this misfortune inspired the sobriquet La Reine Pédauque (Queen Splayfoot), and in visual representations this was no Clementine-style aberration ('And her shoes were number nine') but a single webbed foot like that of a goose.

The historical Bertha (*d.* AD 783), daughter of the Count of Laon, gave birth to Charlemagne, the future Holy Roman Emperor, in 742. In French tradition, however, passed on in the romances, she was given a grander birth: Flor, the King of Hungary, for a father and Blancheflor, the daughter of the Byzantine emperor Heraclius, for a mother. Flor and Blancheflor were themselves characters in a jongleur romance of star-crossed love, while 'the daughter of the King of Hungary' becomes a stock figure of fairy tale, appearing as the wronged Constance in Chaucer's 'Man of Lawe's Tale', for example, as well as innumerable other stories. Physical deformity of some kind frequently brands the heroine-victim and brings about her – temporary – outcast state. But Bertha's romance family also fulfils another, more political function, confirming the holy and august character of the French royal house by connecting it to the established, ancient empire in the East and the selfsame ruler who had saved the relics of the cross from the infidel. Just to make sure of the family's credentials, Berthe was provided with a brother – Saint Martin of Tours, he who cut his cloak in half to give to a beggar.

Her romance coincides therefore with the Queen of Sheba's not only in the matter of her abnormality, but also in her typological position: as the Queen of Sheba stands to Solomon, Helena stands to Constantine, as we have seen; in turn, Helena, mother of the first Christian Roman emperor, finds a symbolic descendant in Bertha, the mother of Charlemagne. In 1165, the emperor Charlemagne was canonized as the 'powerful athlete of Christ', and was subsequently venerated as a saint himself throughout the middle ages, as one of the movers of Christian success in the West. In this light, the three queens make up a cluster, rhyming across time and place; all three helpmeets in the expansion of Christendom through their virtue and wisdom.

At a further, internally circumstantial level, Bertha belongs in the narrative later attributed to Mother Goose and Mother Stork. The romance Adenet interwove with French royal legend belongs to one of the most widespread and popular folk-story cycles in the world, about accused queens and wronged maidens, current since the fifth century at least. Adenet was alert to old sources of wonder tales: he also composed a versified '*Alexandre Le Grand*', using the fairytale material about the hero emperor from the fantastical Greek romance of the third century AD. The plight of the defamed or otherwise wronged wife was elaborated with variations in dozens of fairy tales, familiar for instance from Chaucer ('Patient Griselda'; 'The Man of Lawe's Tale') and Shakespeare (*The Winter's Tale*). The features of the wrongdoing vary, but in Adenet's poem, Berthe's maid Aliste, with the connivance of her wicked mother Margiste, treacherously takes the queen's rightful place in the king's bed, usurps her status as Pépin's queen and bride, and concocts all kinds of horrendous charges against her. Berthe suffers all in silence until the truth is revealed; she is reinstated and the false bride punished.

This plot provides the dominant frame story of Basile's firecracker of a collection of fairy tales, *Lo cunto de li cunti,* in the seventeenth century. His group of female storytellers exchange many tales of substituted brides and false queens, and at the end actually unmask a similar wicked usurper prospering in their midst. It is most famously developed in the body of modern fairy tales by the Grimm Brothers, in 'The Goose Girl': a servant takes the place of the true bride, who becomes a goose herd. Her mother gives her a magic horse Falada, who, even after the usurper has had his head cut off, continues to speak, even as a trophy mounted on the wall, and to tell the truth about his real mistress. For her own part, she is also able to perform magical tricks, and so is at last recognized and vindicated.

The transference, which accords the teller of the tale the characteristics of the protagonist, turning goose-footed and goose-herd heroines into taletelling mother geese, receives another scrap of supporting evidence from an Italian saying, which means once upon a time: '*Nel tempo over Berta filava* … ' (In the days when Bertha spun …); in the tradition that surrounds the old wives of the old wives' tale, they characteristically spin while they tell their tales of olden times. It is also axiomatic that they represent timeless folk memory reaching back through oral reminiscence to a time and a place out of time. Jacob Grimm writes that it was common to swear on Berthe's distaff, because the name Bertha belongs generically to the 'old grandmother or ancestress of the family'. He derives it from Teutonic roots meaning 'bright, light, white' (*peraht, berht, brecht*), writing that the abnormal foot of legend is a 'swan-maiden's foot, a mark of her higher nature'. He goes on to connect it with the splay foot of a woman who works a spinning wheel all day – again a return to the scene of storytelling – an association however which would postdate by some considerable interval the romance of 'Berthe aus grant pié,' as the spinning wheel reached Western Europe from the Middle East only some time in the fourteenth century.

In the story of the knight in the fairy kingdom who peeps at his beloved and finds that she has monstrous limbs, in the profusion of legends about women's hidden nether parts, furred, clawed or webbed, in Sheba's heterodox malformation as pictured by the spirited imagination of Pantaleone of Otranto, the fantasy and energy of curious imaginations – boys' and girls' – have faced the place of origin, the mother's genitals. Lacan argued that the phallus functioned as the dominant sign of symbolic language and that the vulva was bodied forth only by lack or absence; but it takes looking to see the obvious, the mutations and migrations performed by vernacular symbolism once on everybody's lips. The metonymy of bird feet for the secret, 'shameful' part of woman, that organ tempting men to sin, circulated in the common language of medieval and Renaissance Europe, attaching itself to figures as various as midwives, riddling queens, and nursery storytellers. It is even hinted at in the famous story of Cinderella, where she is proved by her foot – or does the love and recognition she wins from the prince heal her in the place where her innermost nature is marked? From a historical point of view, it is interesting that the earliest surviving tale of a wronged daughter dropping her shoe was set down in China in the ninth century when footbinding was practised (see Chapter Thirteen).

The stigma of the secret foot acknowledged the power of narrative to transmit knowledge, retaining the suspicion that stories and narrators could be highly unreliable; it represented an attempt to contain and subdue the heterodox; it accorded the tellers all the fascination that secrets hold, while it held out a promise that the act of narrative itself could enrol its makers and hearers back into the fold.

CHAPTER 9

On Riddles, Asses and the Wisdom of Fools: The Queen of Sheba III

And be these juggling fiends no more believ'd
That palter with us in a double sense …

Macbeth , V, vii

The hard questions the Queen of Sheba put to Solomon in the Bible are not given, but in the subsequent literature, they are consistently assumed to be riddles. Biblical commentators' cross-references direct the reader to other passages, where male heroes and prophets like Solomon distinguish themselves by setting or answering puzzles: to Samson who put the riddle of the lion's carcass that brought forth sweetness (Jg. 14: 12–18), to Daniel who interpreted the dreams and visions of Nebuchadnezzar (Dan. 1: 20).

The Book of Kings then goes on to say that the Queen of Sheba 'communed with him of all that was in her heart', and that Solomon reciprocated, sharing all his knowledge with her: 'And Solomon told her all her questions: there was not

'Know thyself': a fool in ass's ears is admonished by a stern nymph with a looking glass in an early example of instructive children's literature. (John Bewick, vignette in John Trusler, Proverbs Exemplified, *London, 1790.)*

any thing hid from the king, which he told her not.' Solomon, the wisest man on earth, trusts Sheba with all he knows and understands. No wonder she becomes 'breathless' when she hears him, and exclaims that reports of his wisdom have fallen short of the true dimensions of his brilliance and his munificence (1 Kgs. 10: 1–13).

But before she takes her leave of him, there is a further exchange: King Solomon gave the queen 'all her desire, whatsoever she asked ...' The passage continues, 'beside that which Solomon gave her of his royal bounty'. So his gifts included something more than material goods, and she is represented expressing desire: her body moves, her flesh breathes in a way that Solomon's does not. Though they are matched in wisdom (and in wealth, almost), and now share belief in the same God, their styles of articulating their meanings differ.

The distinction drawn between his 'bounty' and the fulfilment of other desires she may have expressed led hearers and readers of the Bible since the sixth century to imagine the passionate and fertile love of the king and queen. Medieval painters chose the subject, the meeting of Solomon and Sheba, for the decoration of sumptuous and festive *cassoni* or trousseau chests, clearly seeing their encounter as a form of bridal procession, with Sheba like a bride who comes to her groom's bed bringing with her a rich dowry (p. 109). The Ethiopians, as we saw, believed a child was born from their love. As a consequence of this suggestive enigmatic description in the Bible, Sheba's special province of expertise becomes sexuality, its distinctions, its rules; in a popular and important strand of her tradition, beyond the material in the Sibylline apocalyptic books, her hard questions, presented in the form of riddles, elucidated, slyly but clearly, tabooed or secret areas of knowledge.

When she is represented, as she so often is, pointing her index finger in the gesture of discrimination and instruction, she is seen to speak of sexual difference and correct moral judgements, as in a tapestry from Alsace of around 1475–1500, into which is woven one of the puzzles she puts to Solomon: how to tell the difference between boys and girls. Solomon scatters sweets on the ground and then points out that the boys scoop them up by the handful while the girls go down on their knees to gather them into their skirts one by one (right). 'There,' says Solomon in satisfaction. 'Kneeling shows the female sex.'

The encounter between Solomon and Sheba was thus recounted as a battle of the sexes as well as a battle of wits, and the challengers faced each other not only to determine the truth and errors of their gods, but the respective mettle of their minds. Middle Eastern beliefs about Solomon's wizardry travelled and grew,

The Queen of Sheba asks Solomon to tell the difference between girls and boys: he nonchalantly tosses balls among them and the boys catch them while the girls kneel to pick them up. 'Kneeling shows the female sex', declares this kingly paragon of wisdom in a tapestry from Alsace or Strasbourg, 'The Riddles of the Queen of Sheba' (c. 1475).

magical *grimoires* were frequently ascribed to his authorship from the thirteenth century onwards. By virtue of her contact with Solomon, Sheba could be accounted wise. However, just as kneeling showed the female sex, she is still rather less wise than the wise king, a messenger of his knowledge rather than an originator.

Alongside Christian legends of the cross, various materials imagined what the Queen of Sheba said and what she did in the course of her duel with Solomon. These texts illuminate again how in popular narratives, their shuttles flashing back and forth between oral warp and literary woof, the character of the teller encloses the tenor of the tale; how the teller enters and takes part in the story, becomes a protagonist; how Mother Goose herself exemplifies the type of the story she tells. The Cumaean Sibyl who knows hidden mysteries and can reveal them to mortals like Aeneas becomes confused with the dramatis personae of the stories about valiant knights who stray from the true path; she becomes the subject of a prophetic and cautionary narrative, she who used to be their inventor or narrator. Her journey gives us an insight into the relationship of the Sibylline queen with the evolution of the image of fairy storyteller.

For public repudiation turns to acceptance, and the excluded, derided figure of the pagan queen who attracts anti-semitic, anti-pagan, anti-Islam propaganda gains admittance to the fold, as in Piero's frescoes. And in consequence her heterodoxy, her difference, her whiff of marginal, secret wisdom returns, unrepressed, its poison drawn, its dangers passed, its owner tamed. Or so it is presented by the tale that she is reputed to tell – eventually.

The queen clearly knows beforehand some of the solutions to the riddles she asks and is merely trying Solomon's wit. For instance, on a related topic of forbidden sex, she asks: 'A woman said to her son, thy father is my father, and thy grandfather my husband; thou art my son, and I am thy sister.' Solomon answers, quick as a flash: 'Assuredly, it was the daughter of Lot who spake so to her son.' Both the daughters of Lot slept with their father after the destruction of Sodom and Gomorrah, when she and her sister feared there were no more people left on earth (see Chapter Nineteen).

Such family riddles are very old, and the history of their distribution remains hazy. They are examples of conundrums still enjoyed today, as in the rhyme, 'Brothers and sisters have I none, / But this man's father is my father's son.' (Answer: My son.) An eighth-century Syrian bishop and riddle-master included Lot's daughter's question in a collection of forty-two similar posers, and it reached England, making an appearance in the *Exeter Book of riddles*, a manuscript of around 1000. In a Midrash commentary on the Bible and the Book of Esther, composed in the fifteenth century by Yachya Ben Suleiman, several of the questions focus on questions of gender, on permitted erotic relations, and the mysteries of life. The transgression against the incest taboo preoccupies the Rabbi, for here too in her riddles the queen focusses on the marriage of Tamar to one of her own sons and the union of Lot and his daughters. She asks: 'Who are the three who went into a cave and came out five?' Again the answer comes: 'They are Lot, his two daughters and their two sons.'

The queen's puzzles also introduce the themes of pregnancy, childbirth, menstruation, and suckling: 'There is an enclosure with ten doors, when one is open, nine are shut; when nine are open, one is shut.' The answer to this is: 'The womb: the ten doors are the ten orifices of man [sic] – his eyes, ears, nostrils, mouth, the apertures for the discharge of the excreta and the urine, and the navel; when the child is in the embryonic state, the navel is open and the other orifices are closed, but when it issues [from the womb] the navel is closed and the others are opened.' In other collections, Sheba shows a lighter side; some of her riddles concern eye make-up and fast horses and other pleasures. But on the whole, her wisdom, in conjunction with Solomon's, concentrates on those mysteries of sex and the body – the suspect, alarming and magical territory commanded by midwives and matchmakers.

Examples of the queen's riddling can be found in rabbinical folklore, in secular theatre, in Christian poetry, in painting, as well as storytelling. The distinction between boys and girls even featured in a pioneering theme park in the Doolhof or Old Labyrinth in Amsterdam, opened during the first half of the seventeenth century. Automata of Solomon and Sheba surrounded by children performed the riddle in one of its versions. The contemporary guide book describes it:

> The queen has brought some of her most beautiful little pages and maids with her … all dressed in women's clothes, so that nobody could tell them [apart]. And the queen put the riddle to the king … [He] ordered at once a bowl of water, and commanded [this gaudy band] to wash their faces … The pages did not hesitate to rub their faces in a masculine fashion, while the girls, bothered by a virginal modesty, hardly dared to touch the water with their fingertips …

'All these above mentioned figures,' the guide concludes, 'make their movements with a delightful and artistic dexterity, and so do the four Roman pikemen and the dwarf.' The Labyrinth with its attractions remained until 1862, when all the figures were destroyed, except for David and Goliath.

The story of Sheba's riddle coursed through the cultural bloodstream and reached the capillaries of street entertainment; there, it was denounced as rubbish by the learned like the seventeenth-century Dutch scholar Servatius Gallaeius, who in his attack on the Sibyls, including Sheba, adduced the test of the children as an example of Solomon's and the queen's entirely non-Christian trickery.

II

Fairy tales similarly concern themselves with sexual distinctions, and with sexual transgression, with defining differences according to morals and mores. This interest forms part of the genre's larger engagement with the marvellous, for the marvellous is understood to be impossible. The realms of wonder and impossibility converge, and fairy tales function to conjure the first in order to delineate the second: magic paradoxically defines normality. Hence the recurrence, in such stories, of metamorphoses, disguises and above all the impossible tasks – the *adynata* – of folk narrative. These can take an active form: that the protagonist should fill a cribbled pail with four-leaved clovers, as in Marie-Catherine d'Aulnoy's 'Serpentin vert', or that the questor should come neither clothed nor naked, neither riding nor walking, neither bearing a gift nor not bearing one. This riddling demand, made in traditional tales in many different languages, was given to King Solomon and the trickster Marcolf in medieval texts, and to the poor peasant's clever daughter in the Russian fairy tale, collected in the nineteenth century. Verbal riddles do not always invite performed solutions, but Sheba's to Solomon do, and in her role in these stories she takes the place of the lowlife, cunning figure, like Marcolf, or the quickwitted peasant girl, as she tries to have the advantage over Solomon. This riddle is solved when the subject of the challenge rides on a goat (or a hare), with one shoe off and one shoe on, one leg on the ground, draped only in a net, and carrying a hare (or a quail) which springs to freedom as soon as he or she arrives.

The riddles posed by Sheba relate to the matter and the manner of many fairy tales, which dramatize 'witches' duels': in these the heroine or hero confounds the powers of fairy evil by surpassing them in verbal adroitness, in tricksterism. The Devil turns tricks, but those who elude him can outsmart him at his own game. In one of the highly popular ballad versions of 'The Elfin-Knight', for instance, a story which exists in different forms all over the world (the most famous being 'Rumpelstiltskin', hero of the Brothers Grimm's popular tale of that name), the heroine wrestles with the Elfin-Knight, who would snatch her away to the underworld as his bride, by using her verbal wit against his power. The Devil who has come for her in marriage sets her ten riddling questions, and she replies staunchly to all of them. He puts to her:

> O what is whiter than the milk
> Or what is softer than the silk?

To which she replies:

> Snow is whiter than the milk
> And love is softer than the silk.

When he asks:

> O, what is greener than the grass?
> And what is worse than woman was?

She gives the right answer again:

> O poison's greener than the grass
> And the devil's worse than e'er woman was.

With instant results:

> As sune as she the fiend did name,
> He flew away in a blazing flame.

Only God can remain the Unnameable: naming the Devil, knowing him for what he is, undoes his power. (Even Wittgenstein was moved to remark with regard to this type of fairy tale, 'Profound, profound.')

Turandot, Puccini's famous opera, is one of many works to take its inspiration from a fairy tale about a haughty princess who refuses to marry, ridding herself of all suitors by setting them impossible riddles – until her heart is touched by the kiss of the prince who gives the right solutions. Sheba's role, structurally, duplicates the adversary's in these tales – she sets the riddles and is answered; she is knowledgeable, taking the part of eliciting the right answers and the correct responses, while remaining morally ambiguous herself, like the Devil or the strong, cruel female protagonist; her testing of Solomon in the folk tales becomes a prelude to their love match, an early form of the blind-date interview.

Fairy tales likewise often seek to define, within a romantic contest, appropriate male and female conduct, to endorse the correct version and – usually – reward it with more than Solomon's bounty of sweets. Riddles, when they are included in a fairy tale, often reflect the incestuous relationship at the core of the plot, as in the cycle of Donkeyskin tales about a father who wants to marry his daughter (see Chapter Nineteen). Other stories dramatize trials of identity in which the heroine (usually) is concealed, as it were, in a riddle, and her sex is put to the proof, as in 'Marmoisan', by Marie-Jeanne L'Héritier, and 'Belle-belle, ou le Chevalier Fortuné' by Marie-Catherine d'Aulnoy. The high-spirited double cross-dressed tale of star-crossed lovers which Perrault may have written in collaboration with a notorious rake, the Abbé de Choisy, spoofs this basic convention of romance.

The literary form of the riddle, while still part of nursery lore in Britain, has more often than not split off from fairy tales themselves today. But in the early years of written wonder stories, riddles were embedded within them: Straparola's tales in *Le piacevoli notti* are punctuated with double entendres presented in riddle form. These were dropped from later, literary editions, but a scholar in Germany heard one about a 'churning-tub' which Straparola had included, from a twelve-year-old girl at the beginning of the century. Another set of verses described a distaff in merry terms ('Madam has me unceasingly, wishes me between her young fingers, or next to her thigh'), and was illustrated, in a Dutch edition of 1624, for instance, opposite a decorous engraving of a housewife alone at her spinning (p. 137).

Riddles are traditional, like tunes, and it is harder to date their origin, since their style remains fairly consistent. An eighteenth-century example asks:

> I am white and stiff it is well known
> > Likewise my Nose is red;
> Young ladies will as well as Joan,
> > Oft take me to their Bed.

'Answer: It is a candle.' This is the same kind of joke as the ones about distaffs and churning-tubs. In Italy today, a favourite children's riddle still goes: 'What goes in hard and comes out soft?' Again, the comedy lies in the second-guessing; the interrogator traps the listener into a dirty thought – a devilish trick. For the right answer is 'Macaroni'.

When printers first began directing their products at children, in the eighteenth century in Britain, they also included 'jest books', which told riddles. They are angled towards children, often in a jocular spirit; the frontispiece of *The Riddle Book, or Fireside Amusements*, for instance, shows a certain 'Miss Clever' who 'the prize from her visitors took / By unriddling riddles in this riddle book'. The recurrent ribaldry in the material shows the same temper as the equivocal, slightly comic tone of the legends about the wise queen's lower parts; her riddling, her secret knowledge, her suggestive sexuality ring in the same key as the foolish, naughty, comic, even scabrous old woman who is dubbed Mother Goose in children's literature later.

III

The animal most closely associated with merriment and folly is the ass; but, paradoxically, donkeys are also the beasts most endowed with powers of divination and wisdom in fairy and folklore. Indeed they rival geese in making fools of themselves and thus showing up the folly of others. The ass, whose hoof also appears to brand the body as marginal and dangerous, the outsider and the heathen, sets

The distaff's shape and role in women's work gave rise to ripe innuendoes, couched in merry riddles. (Anon. engraving, Enigmata sive emblemata amatoria *(Riddles, or Amorous Emblems) Leiden, 1624.)*

up such distinctions, and leads to another set of dynamic metaphors active in fairy tales. For in the same way as the genre exalts the little man (and woman) and shows up the mighty, defeats the giants and crowns the thumblings, so the stupidest of the beasts turns out to be the wisest according to the logic of the stories. This logic organizes the material of fairy tales internally, but its imagery, the costumes it assumes, are borrowed from elsewhere: and, as is the case so often, the topsy-turvy exemplar of the wise donkey can be found in the Old Testament and was passed on into secular folklore by medieval works like the *Speculum humanae salvationis* and the *Biblia pauperum*, in which Balaam and his ass, with the Queen of Sheba, are paired as unlikely but commendable prophets.

Monumental evidence exists of the pairing from an earlier date, which probably inspired the textual diffusion of the images: on both sides of the Portail Royal, the North door of Chartres Cathedral, elongated, solemn figures appear of Old Testament patriarchs and prophets. Carved around 1230, they occupy a place in the overarching scheme of the sculpture programme of the entire portal, connecting the time before the Redemption with the time after, prefiguring the New Covenant and the return of grace to the world. On the right side, one of the three lower statues is Solomon with Marcolf the jester crouched beneath his pedestal; next to him stands the Queen of Sheba, with her feet resting on a Moor; next to her Balaam with his ass.

What is the connection? Balaam enters the Bible as another magician and foreigner, like Solomon in the first case and Sheba in the second, to be granted a vision of the truth of the Jewish god and the coming Saviour. In the Book of Numbers, Balak, King of Moab, fears the Israelites who are settling in the valley of the Jordan 'because of their immense number' and asks Balaam, a powerful sorcerer, to come and pronounce a curse upon them: '"For this I know," he says, "the man you bless is blessed; the man you curse is accursed."' He sends money for the divination to Balaam by the hand of some Moabite elders, and Balaam responds that he will pray overnight to Yahweh. Yahweh warns him not to curse the Jews, and so Balaam refuses the king's request (Num. 22: 1–14).

A second embassy is sent to him by Balak, to change his mind, and this time Yahweh allows Balaam to go, but orders him to do 'nothing except what I tell you'. The wizard saddles his ass and on the way – this is the famous episode, for which he and his she-donkey have remained part of Christian storytelling – an angel with drawn sword bars the way forward. Balaam cannot see the angel, in spite of his spiritual powers. But his donkey can, and she runs away from the road. Balaam beats her until she returns to the path. The angel again bars the road, this time in a narrow place, so that Balaam grazes his foot as the donkey swerves to avoid the angel. Again she is beaten harshly for her refusal. A third time the angel stands in their way, and this time the donkey lies down, and Balaam takes a stick to her.

Then Yahweh opened the mouth of the donkey, who said to Balaam, 'What have I done to you? Why beat me three times like this?'

To which Balaam replies, 'Because you are playing the fool with me.' If he had a sword, he adds, he would kill the animal (Num. 22: 20–29). The tables are to be turned, of course, on a man who has not the wit to realize that a talking donkey is something out of the ordinary to be reckoned with. For after another bitter exchange, Yahweh vouchsafes the same vision to Balaam, and opens his eyes – the sentence echoes exactly the earlier miracle of the donkey's powers of speech – and he becomes able to see the angel with the sword barring the way. He falls on his face to worship; the angel tells him, again in a precise echo of Balaam's earlier threat to his ass, that he would have run Balaam through if the donkey had not stopped in time.

After this encounter, a chastened Balaam, newly alert to human folly, meets the King of Moab and showers blessings on Israel in a series of inspired oracles, spouting at some length and with enthusiasm, to the despair of Balak who had commissioned him rather to lay dreadful curses on the Israelites. Balaam's prophecies include, 'A star shall rise out of Jacob...' (Num. 24: 17) This was interpreted later to refer to the birth of Christ and connected to the portent which drew the wise men from the East to Bethlehem.

The miraculous donkey who speaks the truth when her master fails to see it represents the possibility that lowly creatures may prove wiser than their learned masters, that the meek shall inherit the earth – a fundamental Christian maxim that remains to be proved. Although the notes to the Jerusalem Bible comment that a she-donkey was considered a princely mount in biblical times, Balaam's talking ass was received as a symbol of humility, and entered the body of medieval ass-lore. The beast of burden acts as a totem of the most sublime of Christian virtues, humility, and is specially precious to God in consequence. The legend of Saint Anthony of Padua relates how scoffers about the real presence of Jesus in the host were taught a lesson by the saint: he presented a hungry donkey with a consecrated host and the beast knelt before it instead of wolfing it down (below).

The alliance between the prophets and Balaam's ass has been perpetuated by the sculpture programmes of twelfth- and thirteenth-century churches in

The donkey knows better than his master: according to the legend of St Anthony of Padua, while its owner insisted on denying the miracle of transubstantiation the animal knelt before the true host rather than eat it.(Taddeo Crivelli and Guglielmo Giraldi, The Gualenghi-d'Este Hours, *Ferrara, c. 1470.)*

The Fool, with his grotesque bauble, in his coxcomb with ass's ears, peeping through parted fingers, sees very well. (Anon. Dutch, Fool Laughing at Folly, *c. 1500.)*

Europe; but it was also made in a most significant fashion with regard to popular storytelling, in the more ephemeral form, liturgical drama – with lasting effects. The *Ordo prophetarum*, or Play of the Prophets, was performed at Matins at Christmas time; the earliest dramatic versions date from the eleventh century, but it was inspired by a sermon, which was written four or five hundred years before, and also chanted as a lesson at Christmas. Entitled 'Against Jews, Pagans and Arians', it was attributed to Augustine, whose august name added credibility to the sermon's bigotry. It upbraided all those who do not recognize the truth of Christ, by invoking the seers who did, in the usual unpleasant manner of the Sibylline oracles. The Jews are denounced by their own Old Testament prophets like Isaiah and Daniel and Moses, while famous pagans like the Sibyl join in the attack. Venerable old men and women from the New Testament who just pre-ceded Christ and were able to recognize him, like Simeon who was present at the Presentation of Christ in the Temple, then add their voices to the chorus.

This *Lectio*, or reading, was adapted in verse and set to music; the entry of each new prophet was greeted by a salvo of imprecations against those who had failed to acknowledge the true Saviour. In the thirteenth-century Laon version, the Sibyl preceded Simeon, 'in a woman's dress, bare-headed, garlanded with ivy and most like someone crazed'. She then sang her song, 'Judgement's Sign', with its prophetic acrostic, JESUS SOTER, as we saw in Chapter Five.

Bringing up the rear of this procession was Balaam, the fool turned wise, who was to be bearded, astride his ass, holding a palm frond and spurring on the animal. This was performed, not merely described: the manuscript provides that the 'puer sub asino' (the boy under the donkey) should now give the reason he cannot go forward, that he sees an angel standing in his way with a drawn sword.

Later versions of the Ordo prophetarum swelled the number of seers to as many as twenty-eight, and the ritual was sometimes performed after Christmas, on 1 January, the Circumcision, a feast which of its nature splices the Old Covenant with the New, since it presents Jesus accepting the law of the Jews while at the same time inaugurating a new era in which that law will no longer obtain. The similarity grows between this solemn Christmas rite and the carnivalesque Festum asinorum, or Feast of Donkeys, which was celebrated in other French churches like Rouen Cathedral in the same period. A King of Fools, riding an ass, was crowned while the congregation made merry. Karl Young, in his Drama of the Medieval Church, suggests that Balaam's ass was borrowed from the Feast of Fools, not vice versa, but does not really pursue the questions raised by introducing the magical ass with the power of speech into the presumably serious rite of the Ordo prophetarum. The Festum asinorum was rollicking and licentious in tone, in the tradition of the pagan Hilaria festival, and drew on classical associations with Dionysiac revelry – Silenus, Bacchus' lewd companion, was mounted on an ass who sometimes threw him, much to everyone's delight. Balaam's ass, impersonated by a puer, turned the solemnities upside down, made fools of the preceding prophets, including the Sibyl and her ilk, opened up the possibility of laughter. This too is the function of the grotesque, be it the bray of a wise ass in church, or the riddles of an ass-footed queen or a web-footed siren.

Donkeys were the jester's symbolic beast. The jester's cap bears ass's ears: in a splendidly lively, anonymous Dutch painting, A Fool Laughing, of around 1500, from the Wellesley Museum, his head-dress shows its origins in an asshide quite clearly (left); in Quentin Massys's Allegory of Folly of 1510, the fool's cap includes a crowing rooster and other emblems of rampant sex, as well as long, suggestively flaccid donkey ears.

The atmosphere of the thirteenth-century cathedral ritual cannot really be known; what can be uncovered are some illuminating connections between popular texts, like riddles and fairy tales, and medieval donkey-lore, and they deepen the relation between the genre and figures like women and geese, proverbially foolish creatures. In eighteenth-century riddle books, the riddles are sometimes put to an interlocutor labelled 'Balaam's Ass'. 'I answer,' the animal says, standing in as mouthpiece for the compiler, and then provides the solutions.

IV

Balaam's ass makes a mock of pomposity, and defends the right of the ignorant to knowledge. Talking animals in general could be considered a more reliable denominator of folklore than fairies themselves, especially the donkey, who features as hero, star and victim in hundreds of fables, by Aesop and Phaedrus as well as the comic romances and the Milesian farces. Charles Perrault, comparing the tone of his work favourably to the classics, was again having it both ways: enjoying the reproduction of classical levity and daring, and dressing it up as a moral apprenticeship to life for young people.

The wits of seventeenth-century Paris were indeed uneasy in their relations with the popular material which inspired the fairy tales they had espoused as an improving instrument of *civilité* in the *ruelles*. At the same time, however, they rel-

ished the tradition's naughtiness and the escape from the pompous euphemisms of the Académie Française that it offered. The donkey, like the goose, was a key actor in this comedy of wisdom and folly: the creature is the most popular hero – or heroine – of fable and fairy tale. Lucius in *The Golden Ass* is turned by mistake into a donkey by a witch, caught and put to work as a pack animal, and then witnesses all the events of the novel in that dumb, long-suffering shape, including the storytelling scene in which 'Cupid and Psyche' is related (p. 16).

Apuleius' romance draws its inspiration from the Greek comic genius Lucianus of Samosata, who had been translated into French and was still inspiring versions during the period fairy tales were beginning to be written down. Perrot d'Ablancourt, scholarly scourge of piety and platitude, translated a selection of Lucian's works, including his *Lucius, or the Ass*. The relationship between this bawdy tale, earlier, lost Greek texts, and Apuleius' much more elaborate romance *The Golden Ass* is complicated, and classicists are still reviewing it. The interest here lies however in the contents of *The Ass*, which closely resembles Apuleius' book; both books are of consequence in the formation of fairy tale.

In *The Ass*, Lucius the hero goes to stay in Thessaly, a province famous for the magic powers of its women, and asks the maidservant in the household to let him peep at his hostess while she casts her spells. As he watches, she smears an oint-

Opposite Lucius consults a renowned witch of Thessaly when he wants to fly like her; but she gives him the wrong ointment and he turns into a donkey. (Anon., engraving in Lucian, The Ass, *translated Perrot d'Ablancourt, Amsterdam, 1709.)*

Left Witchhunters' fantasies placed the donkey in the devil's crew; here three witches fly off to the Sabbath on their beast familiars. (Woodcut in Ulrich Molitor, De Lamiis et phitonicis mulieribus, (On Lamias and Witches), *Constance, 1489.)*

ment over her body and turns into a bird, sprouting feathers and flying out through the window. Lucius begs the maid to steal the same ointment for him, but she picks out the wrong box, and when he anoints himself he turns into an ass (p. 142). He then has to undergo terrible ordeals, until at last he is fed on roses – flowers sacred to Venus – the only food that can restore him to human shape.

The tone of *The Ass* is joyously lewd, and unremitting in its satire of human savagery and self-interest. After heroic sexual adventures with the maid, the hero enjoys even more strenuous entertainment with a woman who loves him precisely because he is an ass for obvious, pornographic reasons, and discards him when he is turned back into a man. Terrible tortures are plotted by the robbers; nobody behaves well: nothing is for the best in the worst of all possible worlds.

Perrot d'Ablancourt also translated, in 1658, Lucian's *True History*. This comic fiction is a natural predecessor of Baron Münchhausen's extravagant tales, and other, later hyperbolic raconteurs, down to Salman Rushdie and his novels today: the narrator vows to tell the truth and nothing but the truth and then proceeds to improvise the most farfetched and fantastical adventures. The hero's short romp includes a journey to the moon as well as a descent into the underworld, and brazenly parodies many of the most cherished epics of the classics – the wanderings of Odysseus, Thucydides' *The Peloponnesian War* – and sends them up in a truly postmodern spirit of pastiche, plagiarism and irreverence. In Hell, for instance, the voyaging hero becomes aware that 'Liars were especially tormented, and also those who had imposed on posterity with their fabulist writings, like Ctesias and Herodotus …' But this 'gave me some consolation. There's no vice of which I am less guilty.'

The exaggerations, marvels, dislocations of time and space, the supernatural forces and irrational sequence of events relate Perrot d'Ablancourt's work to the fairytale fashion in France which followed some thirty or so years later – the publication of his translation took place during its time of continuing popularity, in 1709. But Perrot's work is symptomatic of the interests of *littérateurs* exploring new registers of tone. His translation's ironic blitheness looks forward to Voltaire, and influences the literary fairy tale in its early printed form. The *True History*, for instance, even includes a pumpkin metamorphosis:

On the third day we were attacked by barbarians who navigated on great pumpkins six yards long, for, when they are dry, they hollow them out, using seeds instead of stones in the fighting and leaves instead of sails, with a reed for a mast.

Perrot d'Ablancourt's translation of Lucian was illustrated with engravings, including one showing the metamorphosis of the hero (p. 142). The juxtaposition of the conjuring sorceress with the man sprouting a donkey's head condenses vividly the underlying assumption that makes witches and donkeys natural allies (bedfellows): forbidden knowledge, specifically of an erotic character. The donkey belongs firmly in the bestiary of witchcraft: a woodcut from a tract on demonology printed in 1490 shows a witch with an ass's head riding on a broomstick with a devil beast pillion behind (p. 143). In one of Hans Baldung's ferocious drawings and engravings of witches at their covens, dated 1510, there appear the remains of a donkey: its skull lies in the foreground. The coven has probably distilled the famed potency of an ass for the potion the witch on the right flourishes against the curdled and bloody sky: an elixir of sexual enchantment, no doubt. The ass transgresses human society's norms by aggressive wantonness, and witches were suspected of the same polluting disregard of appropriate, moderate sexuality. In that most famous of fairy plays, Shakespeare's *A Midsummer Night's Dream*, Bottom the weaver, when 'translated into an ass', finds himself rapturously wooed by Titania, Queen of the Fairies, who has herself been cast under a spell by her husband after a domestic quarrel (see jacket). All is topsy-turvy as Oberon, with Puck his messenger, makes mischief. All is merry, too, and will be set to rights.

Lucius' misadventures as an ass had been passed on, with divergences and accretions, in Latin manuscripts of both Lucian's work and Apuleius'. Interestingly, Apuleius, who was born around AD 124 in that part of north Africa which is now Algeria, was accused by his wife's relatives of obtaining her love by witchcraft (she was rich, and a widow). He stood trial in Alexandria but was, it would appear, acquitted.

The lineaments and motifs of the story, if not its tone, went on shaping popular variations of 'Beauty and the Beast', long after *A Midsummer Night's Dream*, as we shall see in Chapter Seventeen. The Brothers Grimm edited and translated a version of *The Ass* in the early nineteenth century, when they were working on their folktale collection. They did not, however, include it in *Kinder- und Hausmärchen*, not just because it was bawdy, but because it was classical, and they were aiming at a purely German anthology.

Ludicrous compared to the other witch's familiar, the cat, associated with lubriciousness rather than seduction, the donkey also inspires pathos. The beast symbolizes Christ's humility and became the totem of Franciscan poverty, as Perrault himself discussed in his arguments against Cartesian views of animals. Descartes had argued that animals had no souls, and in consequence no consciousness, but were like machines. Perrault vigorously defended animals' powers of imaginative understanding by quoting Isaiah's messianic prophecy (Isa. 1: 3): 'The ox knoweth his owner, and the ass his master's crib'.

The braying of the beast could be used to convey anguish at its condition rather than brute ignorance: the anonymous lady who replied in high indignation to Richard de Fournival's thirteenth-century misogynist commentary on love, *Bestiaire d'amour*, wrote that he had provoked her so that she felt like the wild ass who cries out only when hunger makes him rage: 'O, by my faith, I should cry out indeed!' The ass could perform this empathetic role for a woman because it was the least of the beasts. To be a beast is to be dumb; to be a donkey is to be the dumbest beast of all: in French, *bête* means foolish, stupid as well as animal. But to be a donkey is also to possess a voice: a voice of a certain sort, like the cat and the rooster, the bray of an ass speaks for the passion of the creature without language: in numerous folk tales, as well as in bestiaries both ancient and medieval, the donkey is distinguished by the proud brutishness of its heehaw heehaw. In spite of the loudness and persistence of its cry, it is an animal that cannot communicate: the very intensity of the bray conveys that condition of powerlessness, of exile from human congress.

If lovers of stories could create a memory palace of narrative literature in order to remember what are its forms, its changes, its developments, the room that would represent fairy tales would lie between romance and fable, jokes and riddles, and its tenants would not only be the fairytale beauties, princes and princesses so often associated with the genre, but would include a donkey, a goose, a stranger queen with an anomalous foot, and an old woman, laughing. As the fairy tale became established as a literary form, directed at children, this last figure became, in the eighteenth and nineteenth centuries, the narrator's most important and visible mask, for male authors as well as female.

CHAPTER 10

Sweet Talk, Pleasant Laughter: Seduction I

There was an old woman tossed up in a basket,
Seventeen times as high as the moon;
Where she was going I couldn't but ask it,
For in her hand she carried a broom.
Old woman, old woman, old woman, quoth I,
Where are you going to up so high?
To brush the cobwebs off the sky!
May I go with you?
Aye, by-and-by.

Medea's nurse in Euripides' tragedy, or Juliet's in Shakespeare, eggs on the young to pleasure, to vice and folly; the old nurse or crone's connection with inflammatory, foolish advice, with artful persuasion and insider's erotic knowledge, led to their adoption as persuaders by a different variety of aspiring seducer: the storyteller. The effective seductiveness of the crone was so deeply implied that authors appropriated it for themselves to their own ends, or at least represented with some relish male impersonations of the storytelling old wife and

Mother Goose comes in many guises: John Inman takes up the traditional drag role in the pantomime, c. 1990.

her powers of persuasion. Vertumnus, god of autumn fruitfulness, fell in love with Pomona, goddess of summer fruitfulness, of orchards and gardens, but found that she was very zealous to keep her chastity; so he disguised himself as an old woman (Pl. 11). In this masquerade, as the first wolf in granny's clothing, the god of autumn softens Pomona; when he changes back into his 'undimmed manly radiance', she puts up no further resistance.

It is one of many stories of seduction which Ovid tells in the *Metamorphoses*, and he presents it as a true story, a little-known episode from the days of ancient Rome. The theme enters art in the seventeenth century: a sunny, pastoral version of this cross-dressed wooing was painted by the French artist Jean Ranc, around 1710–20 and another by Jan van Kessel in Holland (Pl. 11).

In *The Golden Ass*, in order to tell the story of Cupid and Psyche, the author, as we have seen, abandons his chief narrative voice, that of his hero Lucius, the eponymous ass, and assumes the voice of an old woman instead. Again, the book began to enjoy a new readership in the late sixteenth and seventeenth centuries, after it was censored (as often happens): it became a favourite subject of libertine reflection, when the works of Lucian, who had closely influenced the book, were condemned at the Council of Trent.

What men can do, women can also; impersonations of the old gossip, the knowing crone, adept at erotic arts and powerful with her magic and her secrets, do not end with the male scribe of *Les Evangiles des quenouilles*, with Apuleius' mouthpiece, or Vertumnus' seduction. Once the literary fairy tale began to be published and disseminated, the negative, pilloried figure of the crone proved a valuable mask, akin to the sorceress, which men and women could both assume when they wanted to find a mode of self-expression.

Il Pentamerone, or *Lo cunto de li cunti*, the cycle of fifty tales by the Neapolitan historian and belletrist Giambattista Basile, can lay claim to being the foundation stone of the modern literary fairy tale; published in 1634–6, it contains some of the earliest written versions of the most familiar stories – including 'Cinderella' and 'Sleeping Beauty'. Basile's tone throughout is extravagantly comic, often extremely bawdy, and this may come as a surprise to the twentieth-century reader, who no longer expects ribaldry to dominate the fairytale genre. The often seamy comedies Basile's female narrators tell are inextricably connected to their imagined voices, as well as arising as it were naturally from the 'delicate' matters the fairy tales deal with – erotic, transgressive, personal, intimate.

Basile's exuberant excesses unroll in a great cartwheel of narrative within a frame – the stories are told to a purpose, to unpack the riddle at the heart of the story. Significantly, this plot itself, which is accompanied by a sequence of jesting riddles, concerns the place and power of laughter.

The book opens with an introduction, in which appears a familiar figure from fairy tale: a heroine who cannot smile or laugh. Nothing Princess Zoza's doting father does can raise a titter out of her. He invites tumblers, jugglers, well-known comedians, performing monkeys, dancing dogs. No response, not a trace of a smile. Finally, her father orders a fountain of oil to be placed in the market square so that the huge crowds coming to market there will slip and slither and fall down – bringing merriment to all who watch them. An old woman comes to the fountain and begins collecting the oil with a sponge, filling a pitcher, when a young boy throws a stone and breaks it. She curses him roundly – her oaths cascade from Basile's exuberant fantasy for nine lines of demotic insults – very funny, very outrageous when spoken aloud. The boy retorts in kind, and this drives the old woman to such a pitch of fury that she lashes out to catch him – and slips. When she tumbles, her skirts fall over her head and she reveals what Basile calls 'la scena boschereccia' (the woodland or shrubby landscape) – this is a mock-pastoral, theatrical metaphor for the old woman's fanny.

The silent princess has never seen anything so funny in all her life and she begins laughing fit to burst. The old woman then curses her – sentencing her to fall hopelessly in love with a certain Prince of Camporotondo. When the princess summons her and asks for an explanation, the old woman tells her the prince is under an enchantment, buried in a tomb, and will only be revived if someone fills a jug with her tears in under three days. For such untoward laughter, the only absolution can be wrought by weeping.

The story then plunges into a multitude of complications, which tell how Zoza manages to fulfil this *adynaton*, or impossible task, only to lose her resuscitated Prince Taddeo to a base slave who steals the jar of tears and marries him instead. But Zoza, like a true fairytale heroine, is tenacious. With the help of several fairy godmothers, she perseveres, until at last she manages to smuggle in a magic doll to her beloved prince's household. The doll has been programmed to inspire in the usurping queen an insatiable craving – not for fruits or sweets or other toothsome delicacies – but for stories. The slave who had stolen Taddeo under false pretences is now pregnant, and if she does not hear stories, she will do herself and her future baby a great mischief.

To prevent this, Taddeo summons all the women of the district – and picks ten of the best storytellers from among them. They are each and every one an old hag, hunchbacked, cross-eyed, dribbling, and – limping. Comic crones, conforming to the type of gossip, old wife, witch and bawd; Basile's humour shows no mercy. Taddeo takes a seat beside his wicked wife under a baldaquin and invites the old women to eat, and then, over five days, to tell a story to relieve the desire of his wife in her delicate condition.

The book with its cycle of fifty stories unfolds, until the last tale is told by Zoza herself – and the usurping wife is unmasked, confesses her guilt, is summarily sentenced to be buried alive; and Zoza can now take her rightful place as the Prince of Camporotondo's true bride. This is where the framing narrative takes up the familiar folk theme, of the False or Substituted Bride, present in early medieval romances, like 'Berthe aus grant pié', and familiar from the Grimm Brothers' 'The Goose Girl'. Basile's overall architecture in his anthology thus begins with laughter as the catalyst of the action, when the old woman curses Zoza for laughing at her, and then moves through a dazzling sequence of stories, both romantic and grotesque, to arrive at the comic restoration of order.

The silent princess embodies the audience of fairy tale as well as taking part in the story itself, because the tale itself exists to excite responses, to bring life, to assert vulgar rude health against pale misery and defeat, to stir laughter or wonder or tears or hope. Fairy tales put an end to mutism; even when they are about dumbness and dumblings, they break the silence.

In Basile, Zoza's initial, fatal outburst of laughter was provoked by the sight of the old woman's genitals. This scene echoes the classical encounter between Demeter and the old woman, called Baubô or Iambe in the ancient sources, and recapitulates the grieving Demeter's response to Baubô's similar antics. But unlike Baubô, this old woman's exposure is involuntary, and she curses Zoza to quest, Psyche-like, through terrible trials for her true love.

In a bawdy Croatian version of a widespread folk tale, another princess cannot laugh, and it takes a younger brother, a 'Dummling', says the story, with a magic flute and the magnetism of the Pied Piper, to make her do so. The flute has been given to him by an old woman, to whom he was kind when his elder brothers spurned her. When he plays it, anything within earshot becomes stuck fast to him. So he appears before her window with three golden ducks, three greedy girls who wanted their feathers, a baker who smacked the girls' bare bottoms when the wind blew up their skirts, a trouserless naked monk who did the same, and a cock who pecked at the monk's bottom because it was still dirty. And when the princess sees this antic procession, she laughs for the first time in her life and marries the youth with the flute.

In the impassioned manifesto, *La Jeune née* (The Newly Born Woman) by

Hélène Cixous and Catherine Clément, the writers take up Freud's theories about laughter from a feminist perspective. Freud wrote:

> The ego refuses to be distressed by the provocations of reality, to let itself be compelled to suffer. It insists that it cannot be affected by the traumas of the external world; it shows, in fact, that such traumas are no more than occasions for it to gain pleasure … Humour is not resigned; it is rebellious. It signifies not only the triumph of the ego but also of the pleasure principle, which is able here to assert itself against the unkindness of the real circumstances.

Cixous and Clément reaffirm this, invoking laughter's power to explode prejudice, to confront fear, to destroy enemies, to resist oppression; and in the course of their enraptured battle cry, they place centre stage the figure of Baubô, the woman who made Demeter laugh in spite of herself, as prototype and model of women's potential for disruption and change.

Persephone, in the famous myth, had been abducted by Hades, Lord of Death, when she was playing with her friends in a springtime meadow in Sicily, and her mother Demeter's subsequent sorrow at her loss had blighted the earth, ending its eternal summer and bounty. But the grotesque crone Baubô, by telling her dirty jokes and even – perhaps – mooning, showing her bare bottom and genitals, like a fool who shows his bare rump, made the goddess forget to mourn for a moment, made her smile again, even laugh. In Clement of Alexandria's account, in the second century AD, Baubô offers water mixed with barley to the parched and grieving goddess; when Demeter refuses to be comforted by the drink, Baubô takes offence, and 'uncovers her secret parts and exhibits them to the goddess'. The goddess cannot help enjoying this, and agrees to drink – Clement calls this a shameful story and can barely contain his horrified disgust at this behaviour of the pagan gods. But he goes on to relate it to the Eleusinian mysteries, quoting a fifth-century BC hymn to Orpheus. This describes the sight Baubô reveals to the goddess in rather different terms: as the god Iacchus or Bacchus as a baby, the future presiding genius of merriment and wine, laughing and dancing there:

> This said, she drew aside her robes, and showed
> A sight of shame; child Iacchus was there,
> And laughing, plunged his hands below her breasts,
> Then smiled the goddess, in her heart she smiled,
> And drank the draught from out the glancing cup.

It is impossible to tell from the verse whether the child is present in the folds of her lifted clothes, or is a vision in her womb. But in either case, the enigmatic encounter between Demeter and Baubô combines licentiousness and laughter, through the release from melancholy of the goddess by means of Baubô's bodily display and gift of inebriating liquor.

The name Baubô was also used of the dildo, specifically for the leather dildo worn by comic actors in the satyr plays; hence when the old woman clowns, she alludes, through her very name, to the cathartic function of the bawdy, drunken Dionysiac comedies which concluded tragic trilogies. The actors were not however cross-dressed, as she is, but costumed to exaggerate sexual masquerade; her display of sexual organs, either her own, or the false stage attribute of the satyr's dildo, gains its comic force from its incongruity. Zoza in the Basile story laughs like Demeter when she sees the 'woodland scene', because it belongs to an ugly old woman. A beautiful young woman would not provoke the same degree of merriment – but desire, envy and maybe even fear. This incongruity lies at the heart of the grotesque, which is one of humour's manifestations; the inappropriate juxtaposition of elements is one of the principal dynamics of the joke.

Baubô's other name, in the Greek sources, is Iambe, the origin of 'iambus', the limping metre, one short syllable or stress followed by one long; the listing gait of the halt and the old, the ill-assorted and incongruous represented in sound – this is one of the reasons, inherited from pagan belief, for the imaginary misshapenness of the Devil and his agents.

Iambics were first used in lampoons, by the Greek satirists Archilochus and Hipponax from the mid-seventh to the mid-sixth century BC; Hipponax in his satires modifies an iambic trimeter to end in a spondee, thus creating the 'limping iambic' or scazon. Such syncopation implies a funny foot, and though Baubô/Iambe is not explicitly described as lame, her name and her age imply that she is. But the variations on this metre spread from these poets' work into so much high, tragic poetry that the rhythm's first freight of meaning has been covered over.

The iambic metre, however, is also one of the most ordinary speech rhythms in Greek and Latin. It is the beat to which common people commonly talked – and still do talk, in many languages, including English – the Bourgeois Gentilhomme may have been delighted to be talking in prose, but he was also likely to be talking in iambics. At least now and then.

Lameness returns as the mark of the outcast with secret resources; the limping, merrymaking crone persists as a stock figure of fun in medieval and Renaissance literature, appearing as both a joke and a joker, fooling and fooled.

The fool can speak out when the wise man stays mute, as *King Lear* shows: the Fool speaks in riddles, which encode a truth the king accepts as such when he will not resign himself to any honest declaration, of love or, later, hatred from his daughters or from anyone else. Mockery, playacting, riddling spring uncomfortable messages from the privy mind into the public domain with a freedom denied to those who speak or write in earnest; the puppet caricatures of television's *Spitting Image*, savaging figures from the Queen downwards with often deadly accuracy, the ferocious excesses of comedy series like *Yes, Minister* (catching the greed and ruthlessness of Thatcherite politicians in particular), are broadcast in Britain today even while self-censorship and political gagging of 'serious' criticism increase.

As long ago as the first century, Phaedrus (15 BC –AD 50) wrote in his collection of animal fables (which introduced the Aesopian genre to Rome):

Now I will briefly explain how the type of thing called fable was invented. The slave being liable to punishment for any offence, since he dared not say outright what he wished to say, projected his personal sentiments into fables, and eluded censure under the guise of jesting with made-up stories.

Phaedrus was himself born a slave, was freed and became the librarian of Augustus Caesar, so may have been especially alive to the issue of censored speech from both social vantage points.

The fool's cap marks fools out as different from the rest, belittles and segregates and demeans them. But at the same time it resembles the magic cap of invisibility from a fairy tale, because it frees the jester's tongue as if he were not there to be accused, or caught, or punished.

The fool fools because he makes no difference; it is not perhaps poetry that makes nothing happen, but jokes. Yet neither formula is quite right somehow: both shake out the mind, air it from a new window, lighten it, like laundry in the breeze. The revolutionary Russian philosopher Alexander Herzen commented: 'In church, in the palace, on parade, facing the department head, the police officer, the German administrator, nobody laughs. The serfs are deprived of the right to smile in the presence of the landowners.' (Wipe that smile off your face, says the bullying teacher.) Herzen concludes, 'Only equals may laugh.' So the laughter of the clown, the mockery of the fool, can be the expression of freedom, the gesture that abolishes hierarchy, that cancels authority and faces down fear.

Its release can lie in the way it abolishes hierarchy and authority. Riddle books in the eighteenth century, produced for children's amusement, and filled with concealed meanings, knew this function of laughter:

> Of Merry books this is the chief,
> 'Tis as a Purging Pill;
> To carry off all heavy Grief,
> And make you laugh your Fill.

But most riddling allusions, including the Fool's in *King Lear*, need glossing today; actors have increasingly stressed the physical sides of the part, performing as a draggle-tailed transvestite or as a circus acrobat, in order to put the character across. The double entendres tend to fall fast and thick on deaf ears among audiences today, unused to the dirty patter of medieval and Renaissance laughter.

II

Mother Goose becomes one of the vehicles for the survival of this folklore – as one of its personae as well as its mouthpiece. As an author, she enters English children's publishing in the late eighteenth century; not by any means associated exclusively with fairy tales, she is credited with every other kind of nursery entertainment: ditties, songs, traditional nursery rhymes, pantomime plots. A certain positivist tendency has led some researchers to hunt for real-life originals, and

RIGHT *Cackling and honking, Mother Goose acted as traditional mouthpiece for nonsense rhymes and ditties, children's stories and songs. (W. W. Denslow,* Mother Goose, *London, 1902.)*

OPPOSITE *At the blackboard, in fool's spectacles and granny bonnet, Mother Goose shows she can instruct the young as well as entertain them. (Chester Loomis,* Mother Goose Tales, *1888.)*

several candidates have been proposed: Mother Goose 'was not only a veritable personage', wrote one editor firmly, his tongue tucked away out of sight, 'but was born and resided many years in Boston, where many of her descendants may now be found ... This was the "Wealthy family of Goose" which is immortalized by Mr Bowditch in his book of Suffolk names ...' Another story maintained that a certain Mrs Vergoose, also living in Boston in the seventeenth century, drove her family mad with her incessant singing and reciting, until her son, a printer, collected her songs.

But there is not a trace of so early an edition of Mother Goose rhymes, which would predate by over a century the pioneering children's publisher John Newbery's *Mother Goose's Melody* of around 1765. Even the circumstances of Mrs Vergoose's story appear to be borrowed from traditional associations of women and talk: the antics of 'Mother Hubbard', for example, were first committed to paper in the now familiar verse form by Sarah Martin in 1805. She too was reckoned an irrepressibly garrulous old soul, cured by her venture into print. Besides, accepting a real-life character as the prototype of Mother Goose would mean setting aside the antiquity of the proverbial term, and all the condensed symbolism it contains, as we have seen.

Mother Goose took root in British folklore in the course of the late eighteenth and nineteenth centuries, as a comical witch figure compounded of many fancies and dreams, a fount of female wisdom, a repository of tradition, an instrument of children's entertainment, as well as a familiar butt of the material in which she starred. She has many relatives among other Baubôs of the nursery, who, like her, appeared between the covers of anthologies that actually bore her name:

> There was an old woman, and what do you think?
> She lived upon nothing but victuals and drink:
> Victuals and drink were the chief of her diet;
> And yet the old woman could never be quiet.

This nonsensical and ribald old woman, alongside Mother Hubbard, Old Dame Trot, Dame Wiggins of Lee and other characters of eighteenth-century nursery rhymes, shares in the illustrator's eyes Mother Goose's crone features, her chapfallen jaw, the toothless bight of chin and nose in profile, the Punch-like proboscis, the stick, the conical hat and the apron and petticoats (Pl. 13).

Burlesque witchcraft has continued a stock theme in children's literature this century. Willy Pogàny, in the 1920s, illustrated a little-known but wonderfully good-natured anonymous nonsense rhyme which had been published in London in 1805:

> There was an old woman who rode on a broom
>   With a high gee ho! gee humble;
> And she took her Tom cat behind for a groom,
>   With a bimble, bamble, bumble.
>
> They travelled along till they came to the sky
>   With a high gee ho! gee humble;
> But the journey so long made them very hungry
>   With a bimble, bamble, bumble.
>
> Says Tom, I can find nothing here to eat,
>   With a high gee ho! gee humble;
> So let us go back again, I entreat!
>   With a bimble, bamble, bumble.

But controlling children through bogeys, rather than lulling their terrors through merriment, inspires many famous tales in English in the nineteenth century. The earliest written version of 'Goldilocks', called 'The Three Bears' in a manuscript of 1831, does not feature the little girl of today but another witchy old woman, and in much less benign spirit than the characters of nursery rhymes. At first, she stoves in the chair she sits on and lands, legs flailing, on her bottom; her pranks in this story are at first intended to be funny but turn ambiguous. For the end appals: the bears 'drag forth the dame, half expiring with fear', maltreat her for a witch, throwing her on the fire to burn her, and then 'swimming' her in a pond where, like a reputed witch, she floats. As if this were not enough, they then 'chuck her aloft of St Paul's churchyard steeple'. The teller also illustrated her manuscript, which she was giving as a present to her nephew. The three bears' house is very large, gracious and well-appointed, and stands behind bayonet railings: the little nephew was learning about the social order. Violence in children's literature changes form, and its targets differ – but it never disappears.

The poet Robert Southey, who first published the story six years later, stressed the social message: 'a little old Woman came to the house. She could not have been a good, honest, old Woman ... She was an impudent, bad old Woman, and set about helping herself.' The story unequivocally takes the part of the bears when, at the end, the bad old woman jumps in terror out of the window: 'whether she broke her neck in the fall; or ran into the wood and was lost there; or found her way out of the wood, and ... was sent to the House of Correction for a vagrant as she was, I cannot tell. But the Three Bears never saw anything more of her.'

Southey's nasty children's story punishes an old woman in the attempt to contain or at least discipline beggars and vagrants – who had often been taken for witches. Later Victorian cheeriness can be seen to be extending a kind of amnesty of sorts, for most of the low-class, noisy, bawdy old nurses of nursery literature are pictured enjoying a special, easy, and safe relation with animals, their sorcery connotations recalled only in the highest spirits: bears, dogs, cats, monkeys and mice attend them as familiars in their cottages and kitchens. The rhymes frequently inspired illustrators to zestful, Rabelaisian mischief: the Dalziel Brothers created a richly waggish series of dogs capering and clowning for 'Old Mother Hubbard and her Dog' in the bumper compendium *Mother Goose's Nursery Rhymes and Fairy Tales* of 1892.

Like the absurd figure of the learned ass in popular comic lore, Mother Goose often dons spectacles; in her bird shape, with glasses perched on her beak, she presides before the blackboard in children's books like Chester Loomis's *Mother*

Goose Tales (p. 154).

Spectacles carry a double meaning: in medieval painting, the rabbi at Jesus' circumcision sometimes wears them, and Saint Anne, too, lays them down in the crease of her Bible (p. 87). But the learned can be fools, as in Swift's kingdom of Laputa, where the scholars all wear spectacles and see nothing. And fools, on the other hand, can be wise: Jan Steen's painting of 1671 shows King David returning in triumph to Jerusalem after his victory over Goliath; a jester is capering and beating a tambourine to the music-making of the crowd. He has a pair of pince-nez spectacles blazoned on his rump (right). In his novel *The Name of the Rose*, Umberto Eco threw these motley ingredients – the irreverent laughter and the wise fool's spectacles of the middle ages – into a witch's cauldron to produce his exuberant, cunning pastiche of scholasticism, sorcery and country house murder stories – a supreme work of contemporary folklore.

The British pantomime tradition has prolonged the life of the medieval diablerie, and Mother Goose, irreverently guying her betters, crossed over from the nursery and the riddle book to flourish on the boards. Significantly, Mother Goose is a drag role; like Widow Twankey or the Wicked Stepmother, she was played by a pantomime dame in the Christmas dramas and music-hall revues (p. 147). The earliest piece extant to pluck her from the pages of children's collections of tales or rhymes and put her on stage was called *Harlequin and Mother Goose; or, the Golden Egg*, and it blended, as the title suggests, *commedia dell'arte* stock characters with British comic fairytale motifs. Sex reversals pointed up the magic as well as the absurdity: the name of Pulcinella, Mister Punch's clownish ancestor from Italian masked comedy, ends in the feminine *a* which retains the memory of his travesty. Mother Goose triples the inversion: she is played by a man to look like a cross-dressed woman who herself looks like Pulcinella/Punch.

The pantomime was written by Thomas Dibdin, and opened at Drury Lane just after Christmas in 1806. With the help of a goose that lays golden eggs, the hero, Jack (who takes the Harlequin role), succeeds in winning the hand of the ogreish squire's lovely daughter (Columbine). Mother Goose is Jack's fairy godmother, and she provides him with the marvellous bird; she appears astride a gander as in the nursery rhyme ('Old Mother Goose/ When she wanted to wander / Would fly through the air / On a very fine gander') (p. 51); she may have even flown down on to the stage in a goose-shaped *machina*; she performs further wonders, whistling up a wind like a witch and – even more powerful than the weird sisters – raising the dead. In the impresario Joseph Grimaldi's production that year, Samuel Simmons played her as an ancient and mannish hag; in 1902, nearly

Glee of the weak at the defeat of the strong: the fool, spectacles blazoned on his bottom, dances at the feast of victory over Goliath, while a child urinates on the dead giant's head. (Jan Steen, David Returning Victorious, *detail, 1671.)*

a hundred years later, at the same theatre, the much loved music-hall performer Dan Leno wore periwig, jewels, ostrich feathers, frills and furbelows in a less gothic interpretation of the traditional figure of Mother Goose.

The transvestism of the pantomime part sharpens the comedy. But before the pantomime opened in London, Mother Goose was being annexed by less rambunctious voices, anxious to mitigate old women's wickedness, and to enrol her in education:

> I think I have now amused you with some very entertaining Tales, which shew you what has been done in Past Times. You know the Fairy days are now over and … it is your duty, in whatever station you are placed, to labour honestly and diligently for your support in life. No gifts are now bestowed upon us but what come from a Superior Cause. Consequently you cannot expect to grow good, rich, or opulent, without a proper use of those means which are most bounti-

fully given to all mankind. Study, therefore, to be useful, avoid censure and evil-speaking. Do good to all, and you may be assured that the best of gifts will fall to your share, namely, present as well as future happiness.

Mother Goose the wonderful and wonder-working crone was destined for a long career in pedagogy.

In the late seventeenth century and early eighteenth, the relation between official and unofficial culture in the sphere of folklore begins to undergo a transformation, in France and England: hitherto vulgar, and often unofficial, means of expression – the release of the belly laugh, the allure of the grotesque, the pleasure of fancy – are established at the centre of officially approved culture – but for young people. Mother Goose was annexed, occupied, and was to preside over the educationalist task of sweetening lessons in life by high jinks and hopeful romances; her double nature, her masquerade, was built into her role as a children's entertainer who is at heart bent on moral instruction.

In this the British incarnation of Mother Goose followed a parallel development to the role of *ma Mère l'Oye*, for in France, too, as we shall see, writers of fairy tales insisted loudly on their edifying intentions.

But the place of occupation can still be squatted, the invested city can always be re-invested; when the laughter of unequals has been muffled, it can erupt again. Mother Goose can take off her drag and turn out to be what she seems after all – a real woman, authentically vulgar, who speaks – and writes – in her own range of adopted voices.

Laugh that you may not weep: the Grimms Brothers' tales as sources of great merriment. (George Cruikshank's frontispiece to German Popular Tales, *volume one, 1823).*

CHAPTER 11

In the Kingdom of Fiction: Seduction II

Would you have me write novelles like the Countess of
D'Anois? And is it not better to tell a plain truth?

Lady Mary Wortley Montagu

The fairy tale which marks the beginning of the literary enthusiasm in Paris, Marie-Catherine d'Aulnoy's '*L'Ile de la félicité*' (The Isle of Happiness', of 1690, tells the story of Adolphe, Prince of Russia, who, one day, out hunting bears in a manly fashion, is overtaken by a storm. Taking shelter in a cave, he meets the little god Cupid, who tells him about a magic place of bliss: 'People have exhausted themselves trying to find it …' The prince pesters the god for more information and at last persuades Zephyr, the West Wind, to help him. Zephyr gives him a cloak which, worn with its green side out, will render the prince invisible to the monsters who guard access to the island. 'He [Zephyr] wanted to carry him on his wings, but he did not find this way comfortable …' So the wind picks him up in his arms instead and flies off until he reaches the island, and sets the prince down in a rose-scented, enchanted palace, with walls of precious stones and the best furniture from fairy cabinet-makers. Adolphe wanders on, past

Denunciations of arranged marriage were frequent but powerless: when his daughter refuses to marry the rich (and poxy) son-in-law her father has chosen, he has her literally tied to him. ('The Contagious Husband', Andreas Alciatus, Emblèmes, 1549.)

grottoes, honeysuckle arbours and musical fountains until he meets the princess, Felicity, seated on her throne, with adorable dallying nymphs and frolicking cupids all around her: 'The princess had never seen a human being, and so she was extremely surprised ... "Great princess," said [Adolphe], "I want to offer you my heart and devotion."'

So they live in bliss; meanwhile, time passes. Eventually, in spite of the perfection of his love, and the undiminished round of pleasures in her enchanted realm, the knight suddenly feels pangs of homesickness, and he asks how much time has passed since they have been together. The lady tells him to guess. Three months, he says. She exclaims in response, 'Why no! It's been three hundred years!'

He is appalled; what of his honour? his reputation in the world? his name? He wants to leave. 'You barbarian,' she cries, but his distress strikes him like a sickness, and he pines. She lets him go. He wanders back into the world above, where he finds across his path an overturned waggon, and an old man, pinned under its load. The prince, every inch a chivalrous knight, sees the old man's predicament, dismounts and gives him a hand. The old man seizes hold, jumps to his feet, vigorous and unharmed, and will not let go: his waggon is loaded with wings, and he says to Adolphe, 'Finally, ... Prince of Russia ... I've found you. I've used all the wings this waggon is carrying to cross the world in search of you ... nothing that lives can escape me.'

Not a fairytale happy ending, but a warning against the dream of eternal bliss. It is a story like Guerino il Meschino's or Tannhäuser's, and it is still being told – John Berger, the novelist and art critic, has recounted a version he heard in the Haute Savoie, in which Time's waggon is loaded with the shoes, not the wings, which he has worn out looking for the hero.

The *Dictionnaire de l'Académie* had sneered at the old wives' tale a century before *Le Cabinet des fées* first began appearing, but the writers of fairy tales, like Mme d'Aulnoy, retaliated, if not quite in kind, but with spirit. They would have recognized the description the *académiciens* gave, but they nevertheless aligned themselves with – and played to their subsequent identification with – *le vulgaire, les vieilles*, and the popular and oral transmission of fairytale material. They did, however, accord the genre a different value, and their act of identification, their placing of themselves in the old wives' traditional place, utterly transformed, in the manner of fairytale disenchantments, the status of the storyteller as well as the character and reception of the tales themselves.

Within the frame of one of her romances, *Don Gabriel Ponce de Léon*, Mme d'Aulnoy describes a storytelling scene in which the Duenna-governess and narrator cites as her immediate source '*une vieille esclave arabe*' ('an old Arab slave woman'). She adds that 'this slave knew a thousand fables from the famous Locman, so well known in the Orient, who it is thought was none other than Aesop, that character so naïve and childlike … many good minds consider them works which suit nurses and governesses more than people of good breeding …'

The naïve and childlike wisdom of the putative 'old Arab slave woman' derives immediately from Locman, who, it turns out, is the same person as Aesop – oriental and classical sources mingle and meld; this legacy of wisdom records the despotism of the fairies, and in some fairy tales (but not all) relates its undoing. These are tales of the fairies, but they do not celebrate them; to some degree they emanate from another sector of canny folk, powerless by comparison, victims of their powerful whims, their arbitrary enchantments. Mme d'Aulnoy, a glittering, cosmopolitan *mondaine*, nevertheless conveyed in her work her indebtedness as a writer to the low, enslaved, outsider figure of the most famous of the oral story-tellers, Aesop, who survives by tricksterism and fabrication.

In the fantasy biography by the Byzantine monk Planudes on which La Fontaine based his own sprightly account in the preface to the Fables, Aesop is a slave, and nature has made him 'misshapen and ugly of countenance, with barely a human face, to the extent of denying him almost altogether the use of speech'. But he has been given, inside, '*un très bel esprit*' (a very fine wit), and eventually, in the course of his adventures, he proves himself by many strokes of kindness and brilliance, and is rewarded not only by the loosening of his tongue, but by the freeing of his person from ownership. Aesop's own life follows the pattern of the Cinderella story.

With a difference, however: for it is through language, through native wit, that Aesop achieves liberty. La Fontaine identified himself openly with Aesop, who was one of his principal sources, of course, and the women writers of fiction and fable in the form of prose fairy tales grasped the same classical forebear for their own practice of homiletic humour.

When *grandes dames* fairytale writers found themselves prefigured by the male slave and the female servant in current mythology, they were not making common cause in a political sense: the sympathy was claimed through use of language, of sources, of voice. Fairy tale constituted in itself a genre of protest; at the level of content it could describe wrongs and imagine vindications and freedom; from the point of view of form, it was presented as modern, homegrown, comic fabulism, ironically suited to express the thoughts of an inferior group. The writers of fairy tale like Marie-Jeanne L'Héritier and Marie-Catherine d'Aulnoy are comic

Little is known of the life of Aesop, founding father of fables, but the surviving scraps of biography inscribe him in a fairy tale of his own: born a slave, dumb and ugly, he frees himself through his goodness and cleverness. (V.-F.-E. Biennoury, Aesop in the House of His Master Xanthus, *French, late nineteenth century.)*

writers in the broad sense: their tales end in reconciliation, vindication, partnership, the traditional happy outcome of the fairy tales, with the wronged child triumphant, the wicked punished, the poor made rich, the foundling identified as a princess, and so forth. Or, when they do not end happily, the mood is stoic, the author shrugs her shoulders with cool irony; dourness also aligns the late seventeenth-century fairy tale with the comic fantasist's mode. Their writings issue warnings about the future, and forestall hope about humankind with gallows humour.

Adopting the comic voice as a narrative tone constituted an acceptance of inferior status for their literary production; but in an ironical manner in itself. And

1 The fairy godmother as benign witch: gnarled and lame, with beaky nose, steeple hat, and pantomime-dame buckle shoes, she points a Sibylline finger as she reminds Cinderella of the midnight curfew. (Arthur Rackham, Cinderella, 1933.)

2 Saint Anne sits up in bed to receive her visitors, as the happy midwives prepare to bathe her newborn daughter, Mary; Domenico Ghirlandaio sets the scene as if among his contemporaries and family in fifteenth-century Florence TOP.

3 A 'gossipping' was an old word for a christening feast, as depicted in Jan Steen's bustling painting, at which family and friends – chiefly women – gathered to congratulate the mother and call down blessings on the baby, though the man in the doorway is making an ambiguous sign over its head. (Celebrating the Birth, 1664.)

4 The polarized meanings of female old age: the Cumaean Sibyl, wrinkled deep in time on Michelangelo's Sistine Chapel ceiling, is one of the wisest of all the prophets, who told Aeneas how to reach the underworld.

5 But the disfigurements of ageing were invoked as the penalties of sin, and crones also signified lewdness. Though historical brothel-keepers in Amsterdam were at most in their thirties, Dirck van Baburen portrayed 'The Old Procuress' as a hag. (Early seventeenth century.)

6 A master wizard, King Solomon summoned the Queen of Sheba to his court; he was curious about her because he had been told a rumour that she had hairy legs or ass's hoofs, and as she approached, he conjured a stream made of glass so that she would lift her skirts to ford it. The gratified king looks on with his djinns, hiding their smiles, in a sixteenth-century Persian illuminated manuscript. (Sultan Husayn Mirza, The Assembly of Lovers, 1552.)

7 *The beloved in the Song of Songs, who says of herself, 'Nigra sum sed formosa' (I am black but comely) was identified with the Queen of Sheba; different traditions placed her realm in Arabia or Ethiopia. In this manuscript, the artist has combined the conventional golden-haired maiden of the Christian heaven with the Biblical imagery. (From Conrad Kyeser,* Bellifortis, *Bohemia, before 1405.)*

8 In Piero della Francesca's fresco in Arezzo (1452–66), the Queen of Sheba on her way to visit Solomon refuses to set her pagan foot on a bridge made of the holy wood of the cross and kneels down to worship it TOP.

9 The popular medieval legend of the True Cross travelled, changing and growing, from the Middle East: the Queen of Sheba, with one shoe off, shows her anomalous foot on the mosaic pavement by the monk Pantaleone in the cathedral of Otranto, in southern Italy (1163–5).

10 Beside her, a mermaid, a classical figure of women's seduction, of fatal voices and the lure of sexuality, grasps her own unusual limbs in a witty, possibly apotropaic pun.

11 *The god of Autumn had no success with the lovely Pomona, who was determined to remain a virgin, until he hit upon the ruse of disguising himself as one of the honey-tongued nurses of myth and stories; in this persuasive shape, he found Pomona's qualms easy to overcome. (Jan van Kessel,* Vertumnus and Pomona, *mid-seventeenth century.)*

There was an old woman,
and what do you think?
She lived upon nothing
but victuals and drink:
Victuals and drink were
the chief of her diet;
And yet this old woman
could never be quiet.

12 The crone storyteller TOP casts a prophetic shadow against the screen as she keeps her mixed audience enthralled: Daniel Maclise, born in Ireland, worked very successfully in Victorian England, specializing in evocative, imaginary historical reconstruction. (A Winter Night's Tale, c.1867.)
13 The comic old woman – Mother Goose and her counterparts – also emerged then as a jolly figure of fun, mischievous and unruly, in this respect a child herself ABOVE. (W. W. Denslow, Mother Goose, 1902.)
14 A harsher, bullying undertone sometimes recurs, threatening to muzzle old women 'who could never be quiet' RIGHT. (Postcard, Chapala, Mexico, c. 1985.)

this oblique, comic position, from which the status quo could be challenged and injustices described if not corrected, was hallowed by the classical tradition of the fable, as perfected by La Fontaine. Although L'Héritier renounced association with the Aesopian tale, her colleagues did not, and the genre's features – didacticism, irony, and, not least, animal characters – intersect and overlap with the despised old wives' tale. But another node, of crucial importance with regard to women writers of fairy tale, connects the two forms: the imagined social origin of Aesop himself.

The storytellers grafted the Aesop of fable to an indigenous, homegrown – and female – figure of narrative tradition: the Story Stork, or Mother Goose, who shared with this imaginary Aesop a base social origin, credit for folk wisdom, and survival instincts. They responded to their situation with their own magic – lowborn, transformational, organic, and above all linguistic.

When the fables of the legendary Brahmin sage Pilpay were republished in French in 1697, the unnamed editor risked some pointed remarks in his Note to the Reader: after comparing the fables to Christ's parables, to the Talmud, to Lucian and Locman and Aesop, he concluded his panegyric of the genre:

> The greater number of monarchies in the Orient were despotic, and the subjects in consequence did not see themselves as free; as those peoples are ingenious, they found this way of being able to give advice, without risking their lives, to their kings, who treat them as slaves and do not give them the liberty to say what they think.

Between the start and the end of the sentence, a most interesting shift from the past tense to the present takes place, glidingly, unassumingly, and as it glides it travels not only across the years, but across the map as well, east to west.

This 'ingenious' use of the cryptic fable became distorted, however, by different uses to which such literature was soon put, especially as a children's readership was sought ever more keenly by English booksellers and printers in the early eighteenth century. The enthusiasm for the literary fairy tale crossed the Channel more swiftly then than many books from Europe today, and D'Aulnoy was one of the most successful authors, first for her *Memoirs* (see Chapter Seventeen), and then for her fairy tales. *Tales of the Fairies* appeared in 1699; other collections followed, in 1707 – two years after her death, and then again, in 1716 and 1721 and at repeated intervals through the century, predating the Perrault translation, first done by Robert Samber in 1729.

The huge enthusiasm for literary fairy tales just preceded and then overlapped with the reading public's appetite for Oriental tales, inspired or adapted from the *Arabian Nights*, which the French orientalist Antoine Galland translated – and in some cases made up, it seems – in his French edition of 1704–17. This too was quickly Englished, though in a garbled and anonymous version. Indeed bowdlerization was a problem for all writers, and D'Aulnoy was vulnerable, especially when the printer-publishers were aiming at parents' custom. Her stories lost ground before Perrault's dryer worldliness; the grotesque, even cruel undercurrent of brutality, ugliness, and murder beneath the frothy, rococo atmosphere of a *fête galante*, made pedagogues and publishers anxious. She can indeed write with a sadistic eye: of an ogre she says, he ate people 'like a monkey a chestnut', and in 'The White Cat', one of her most successful, mischievous tales of metamorphosis, the cat courtiers go hunting for baby eagles and other nestlings.

In some ways it could be said that D'Aulnoy's own bluff was called, with unexpected results. Though she was named in her first English publications 'that celebrated Wit of France, the Countess Danois [*sic*]', her assumed persona, the lowclass older woman, her very opposite in social class and age and privilege, soon threatened to eclipse her and subdue the peculiar, strong flavour of her fantasy. Later editions of her fairy tales forgot the 'Wit of France' and substituted Mother Bunch, and the stories' contents and tone were accordingly modified. D'Aulnoy, in age, position and thematic interest, resembles a Scheherazade telling stories for her life far more closely than a gnomic old granny type. But for purposes of pedagogy, the latter was more suitable, while the general, semi-affectionate scorn in which wonder tales of all kinds were held needed a figure like Mother Bunch to despise and respect at the same time; the siren Scheherazade offered a different, and far more difficult challenge to appropriation.

Two or three of D'Aulnoy's fairy tales have become classics and are still told and retold in children's collections – 'The Blue Bird', 'The White Cat', 'The Yellow Dwarf', 'The Hind in the Wood' – but they have often been heavily rewritten. Her sense of the grotesque and the satiric, her effervescence, her irony, her intoxicated pleasure in invention have been rubbed away in these versions. She can be comic as well as rococo, and the nursery editions which transmitted her, Georgian and Victorian, made her edifying by deadening her language, her tone, her chosen balance between the lyric and the mordant. For example, in French the heroine of '*L'Oiseau bleu*' gives the concise, magical summons: '*Oiseau bleu couleur du temps / Vole à moi promptement!*' (Blue bird, colour of time, Fly to me quickly!). In the English translation of 1721, this becomes :

Come, my pretty, gentle Bird
Whose livery is Blue,
Thy Constancy is true to me,
And mine is so to you.
Then hither to thy Princess fly
That on thee I may cast an eye.

D'Aulnoy's forthright attacks on arranged marriage – spoken from the heart – turn pious in her transmitters' mealy mouths.

Sans doute elle [Truitonne] ignorait qu'un pareil marriage
Devient un funeste esclavage
Si l'amour ne le forme pas …
A mon sens il vaut beaucoup mieux
Etre Oiseau Bleu, Corbeau, devenir Hibou même
Que d'éprouver la peine extrême
D'avoir ce qu'on hait toujours devant les yeux.
En ces sortes d'hymens notre siècle est fertile …

[Doubtless the Old Sow did not understand that that kind of marriage becomes deadly slavery if love doesn't shape it … In my view, it's much better to be a Blue Bird, a Crow, even become an Owl, rather than undergo the death sentence of always having what one hates before one's eyes. Our times are fertile ground for these kinds of unions …]

These hard-hitting concluding verses of 'The Blue Bird' are rendered as:

Rather than let the Hellish Truitonne
Be equal to him in his Bed or Throne
Would some kind Spirit now our Age direct
That Interest may not be the Guide …
Instead of Love Divine …
Our Smithfield Bargains then would cease,
And Wedlock throw her Chains aside …

In its own elaborate and artificial style, the literary fashion for fairy tale among women in late seventeenth- and early eighteenth-century France developed a latent aspect of the oral folk tradition to the point that it voiced open, partisan claims on their own behalf. Women's power in fairy tale is very marked, for good and evil, and much of it is verbal: riddling, casting spells, conjuring, hearing animals' speech and talking back to them, turning words into deeds according to the elementary laws of magic, and sometimes to comic effect. Women in fairy tale align themselves with the Odyssean party of wily speechmakers, with the Orphic mode of entrancement, with the Aesopian slave tradition of fabulism. Perceived with contempt as lesser, they adopted forcefully the despised *conte*.

For the writers of *contes* during the new fashion for the elaborate, literary fairy tale were of course by no means crones, neither goose-brained, nor ass-footed, nor one-eyed, nor were they common folk from anybody's point of view, but rather women (and men) like D'Aulnoy, of high status, the creators and frequenters of the *ruelles*, worldly, even influential, related to the independent women of the earlier generation, who had taken a leading role in the Fronde uprising of the nobles against the king, and then, after its defeat, developed the social ideals of *préciosité* as a polite revolt against the dominant culture. Fairy tales became part of this position of protest.

The *précieuses* had their male champions. Poets like Ménage, who had been equally lampooned by Molière, were enthusiastic devotees, more catholic than the pope in matters of feminism. Ménage had for instance published a biographical dictionary of women philosophers, which cited passages and references, and gave an entry to Hippo, the daughter of Chiron the centaur, as well as to Catherine of Siena and Héloïse. In collaboration with the epic poet Chapelain, Ménage mounted an attempt in the 1650s to include women in the Académie Française. But they failed, as we know, since Marguerite Yourcenar, a few years ago, became the first woman *académicienne*. When a woman poet, Catherine Bernard (1662–1712), actually won the prizes of the Académie on three occasions, she was ruled out of competition and debarred from collecting them – because she was a woman. Only exceptionally were daughters thought worth educating at all – by unusual fathers or guardians, as in the case of Madeleine de Scudéry, whose prolific romances of the mid-century, *Le Grand Cyrus* and *Clélie*, achieved such renown that, in spite of their length (ten volumes each and tens of thousands of pages), they were translated almost immediately into English.

The Abbé Fénelon, who began his pedagogic career in a hostel for fallen girls in Saint-Sulpice, pioneered the idea of female education in his very first book, but he could picture only a limited curriculum: polite manners, embroidery and the rudiments of scripture, reading and writing. He warned: 'Curb their spirit as much as you can to keep within commonly held confines, and teach them that their sex should have as delicate feelings of modesty about learning as the horror of vice inspires in them.'

Furthermore, the celibate ideal of the *précieuses* – to enjoy *tendresse* with men of equal intelligence and similar inclinations without the yoke of arranged marriages, their concomitant rejection of the economic basis of alliances, their argument for an end to the double standard which permitted male adultery but disgraced adulteresses – made them profoundly subversive, anomalous women within the social order of the *ancien régime*. The blunting of fairy tales as well as their infantilization, as they shed their context in pre-revolutionary society, has been one of the main changes to take place in their reception: the conservative romance of marriage and material comfort has usurped the fiery protest of a whole generation of French noblewomen against the serfdom of dynastic matrimony and mental inanition – and the two were bound together, as education was clearly unnecessary to the life of a *châtelaine*.

If arranged marriages were abolished, women would be free to express their own desires – and this would spell the end of male authority in the household. As a *réplique* to the misogynists, led by Boileau – an old enemy – Perrault republished an early poem, '*L'Apologie des femmes*', a rather touching hymn of praise to conjugal love, with a new preface. But Perrault, the champion of womankind, defender of old wives' wisdom, painting his paragon of a wife, invoked her perfect '*bouche enfantine*', her childlike mouth – ignorance as virtue.

When Perrault began writing fairy tales – the first man in France to do so, and certainly the first *académicien*, he was interleaving partisanship in the dispute about women with another bitter intellectual wrangle, the Querelle des Anciens et des Modernes. Defending fairy tales, he was not only defending women's tales but also promoting native 'modern' literature against the *Anciens*, who proclaimed the complete superiority of Greek and Latin over all things local, vernacular and of comparatively recent date. To the Moderns, the fairy tale was a living shoot of national culture; to the Ancients, the genre was a bastard child of the vulgar crowd. Perrault was wriggling a little, trying to have it both ways, when he called in the classical comic tradition as forebear, but in the literary politics of the time he was bravely and firmly with the Moderns. He even composed a magnificent album of encomia to the great men of the century: in his opinion, Virgil and Apelles would have to yield pride of place to Frenchmen like Racine and Poussin.

The femaleness of the genre became crucial in the argument for the aboriginal, homegrown, patriotic identity of fairy tales. Nothing can be more homegrown than mother's milk; and milk here can be taken to mean language. As we have seen, the *ruelles* ruled on the art of conversation, and the grammarian Vaugelas, in his *Remarques sur la langue française*, had written that 'in case of doubt about language, it is ordinarily best to consult women'. Vaugelas published his book in 1647; dislike of women arbiters in society had sharpened in academic circles in the capital since then.

But for different women fairytale writers in the circle in which Perrault moved, Mother Goose came to personify an imagined, primordial body of homegrown knowledge, which returned readers and listeners to their childhood and, through childhood, to their roots. They saw themselves as the guardians of language, its nurses, and its shapers.

II

Marie-Jeanne L'Héritier de Villandon began making up fairy tales in the 1690s, and published *Bigarrures ingénieuses* (Ingenious Medleys) in 1697 – the very title, with its allusion to cunning and to motley, announces her enterprise of taletelling, within the comic mode of tricksterism and fooling. She was born in 1664, the daughter of a poet, Nicolas L'Héritier, one of Louis XIV's many historiographers, and though she belongs in age to the younger generation, she was very close to Charles Perrault; their mothers, Françoise and Paquette Le Clerc, were either sisters or cousins. Though her family were impoverished after her father's early death (her mother may have taken in sewing to provide for her six children), Marie-Jeanne moved in high and learned circles in the capital. She became a fervent disciple of the older writer Madeleine de Scudéry, a frequenter of her *ruelle* or salon, and her great friend. She inherited the salon in 1702, after Mlle de Scudéry's death, and until 1711 continued there the earnest cultivation of a new civility. Marie-Jeanne L'Héritier wrote the eulogy after her friend's death, imagining a series of Petrarchan triumphs, almost entirely peopled by women – she did allow her own father, however, to attend the chariot of Clio. She also penned a triumph for another bluestocking friend, Antoinette Deshoulières, in which she described her apotheosis on Parnassus and the torments of her detractors: Boileau is condemned to be bitten by Cerberus as many times as he has insulted women, while Mme Deshoulières is gathered into the company of the Muses as the tenth.

But even as she cultivated this lofty, precious intellectual life, Marie-Jeanne L'Héritier was an outspoken partisan of the fairytale form, at the very time when it was being scorned by the dictionary of the Académie as a vulgar genre and a typical example of women's foolishness. She countered with a series of apologias, set as prefaces to her fairy tales, where she identified her sources as her governess and her nurse – whom she affectionately called '*ma mie*', which has no English equivalent except perhaps 'Nanny darling'. They had told her tales over and over again, by the side of the embers when she was a child. As L'Héritier was writing fairy tales before Perrault, possibly as early as 1692, it is likely that they exchanged ideas on the subject, and that the figure of Perrault's Mother Goose does not only conceal his handiwork and thinking, but also hers. In 1694, she added a madrigal as a comment on Perrault's first published story, '*Peau d'Ane*':

> *Le conte de 'Peau d'Ane' est ici raconté*
> *Avec tant de naïveté*
> *Qu'il ne m'a pas moins divertie*
> *Que quand auprès du feu ma Nourrice ou ma Mie*
> *Tenaient en le faisant mon esprit enchanté.*

[The tale of 'Donkeyskin' is told here with so much natural grace that it has entertained me no less than when, telling it beside the fire, my nurse or my darling nan held my spirit enthralled.]

The *gouvernante* acted as a hinge between the ranks of society; as a servant raised children in the nursery to prepare them to go 'downstairs', so the imaginary figure of the crone narrator was poised between high and low culture, a Mother Goose who has folded her wings. The post of governess indeed encompassed a broad range of ranks and birth: Mme de Maintenon, for instance, had taught her own *gouvernante* to read and write, but when she became in her turn governess to the royal bastards, she rose, spectacularly, to become the king's mistress, reformer and morganatic queen. Pleasure in stories could unite literate and respectable (upwardly mobile) *gouvernantes* with peasants who were appointed to mind the children: the *Bibliothèque Bleue*, where the romances of the middle ages were printed, was staple entertainment for women of different classes. The devout Mme Guyon was sneered at for reading them, as we saw, but as entertainment they were hotly defended by L'Héritier.

As her family had connections with Normandy, it has been suggested that the governess or nurse who told L'Héritier her tales was communicating Norman oral tradition. One commentator waxed lyrical at the thought: she 'had gathered honey from the lips of nurses and mothers, [she] had drunk from the source in the hollow of her hand'. However, it is clear that L'Héritier's immediate sources

The governess looks in at the game of her charges: this oblique relationship, often deeply affectionate, provided a vital conduit of information and stories. (After Sofonisba Anguissola, The Artist's Three Sisters and their Governess, Italian, 1555.)

are literary: Basile and the romances of chivalry, as in the case of her fellow writers, like Henriette-Julie de Murat and Marie-Catherine d'Aulnoy. But they are vernacular sources, popular, even low, ranging from the Milesian tales of Apuleius to the Italian Basile's collection which she shows signs of knowing at first hand. Moreover, the symbolic dimension of L'Héritier's retellings holds more interest than their putative geographical origin. She needs to declare that she is speaking for her old nurse, to claim that she is passing on the wisdom of employed staff, women of lower social status to herself, and she makes manifest her identification with her nurse in her chosen narrative form, the fairy tale: this is the most persuasive disguise she can assume for her chosen task of narrative seduction.

In two of Marie-Jeanne L'Héritier's fairy stories, '*Ricdin-Ricdon*', an early version of 'Rumpelstiltskin', and '*La Robe de sincérité*' (The Robe of Sincerity), a predecessor of 'The Emperor's New Clothes', the author evokes the world of medieval romance to provide the genre of the fairy tale with a noble pedigree. The tales are embedded in her novel *La Tour ténébreuse* (The Dark Tower), where they are told by no less a hero than Richard the Lion Heart in order to while away his captivity. His audience consists of the troubadour Blondel who has smuggled himself in in disguise, and who then commits the stories to memory to recount them later. This frame carefully sets up L'Héritier's theory of the national, Gallic matrix of the fairy tale, in the middle ages, among the troubadours and storytellers of Provence. She propounded it fully in the preface to her most famous fairy tale, 'L'Adroite Princesse, ou les aventures de Finette' (The Subtle Princess). She declares firmly that she wants neither prose nor verse, but instead a tale told anyhow, and as one speaks.

The genealogy from troubadour to nurse which L'Héritier puts forward differs from Perrault's; while he placed himself in line of descent from Latin fables and Milesian tales, she disclaims all kinship with such material (in spite of her manifest debt) and insists instead on their source in the national turf. The dedication of her first book of fairy tales, to her friend the Comtesse de Murat, stresses the national tradition and urges her to follow suit:

> L'antique Gaule vous en presse:
> Daignez-vous mettre dans leurs jours
> Les contes ingénus, quoique remplis d'adresse,
> Qu'ont inventé les Troubadours.

[Ancient Gaul expects it of you: deign to put in a favourable light the artless tales, yet so cunningly wrought, which the troubadours invented.]

Her plea won a warm and lasting response in the circles of fairytale writers: the story 'Etoilette' (Starlight), framed by the Comtesse de Murat's novel Les Lutins du Château de Kernosy, recognizably rings changes on the exquisite thirteenth-century chantefable, Aucassin et Nicolette, which had only just been rediscovered in a single manuscript and was published in 1752, in the Mercure de France, in a modern French version. 'Starlight', a bittersweet tale of lovelorn woe and final triumph, is recounted in the novel to the company by one of the guests in the manner of a troubadour, except that he relies on his own notebook; the scene represents vividly the early fairytale writers' methods of working back and forth from traditional material to variations in the contemporary, ornamental, ironical, and orientalizing style. The author could have known Aucassin et Nicolette from oral sources – or, which is more likely, the finding of this medieval romance, with its unsurpassed lyrical charm, was a source of tremendous excitement and instantly inspired in the ruelles homages in the form of retelling and variations. The discoverer, the antiquarian La Curne de Sainte-Palaye, probably circulated the news, and may have shown aficionados the manuscript itself.

L'Héritier was, however, keen to put some distance between her writings and the comic, bawdy and even indelicate character of so many medieval stories, and she went to some pains to explain her position: the language in which these ancient stories had been transmitted down the centuries had to be altered – had to be cleansed. For whereas, in the picture she paints of the genre's early days, bards travelled from castle to castle '*chez les personnes de qualité*' (calling on the quality) until no royal entertainment was complete without a troubadour, the passing on of narrative had since sunk down the social scale, and immoral characters and improper happenings and other unseemliness had befouled the tradition:

> These stories became filled with impurities as they passed through the mouth of the common people; in the same way as pure water becomes defiled with rubbish as it passes by a dirty culvert. If the people are simple, they are also coarse: they do not know what propriety is. Pass lightly over a licentious and scandalous event, and the tale they tell afterwards will be filled with every detail. One told these criminal deeds to a good purpose, to show that they were always punished, but the people, from whom we receive them, report them with no veil to cover them, and indeed have linked them so tightly to the matters they reveal that one is hard put to tell the same adventures and keep them under wraps.

The voice of experience sounds through this rather plaintive argument, in which poor L'Héritier, committed to believing in the virtuous simplicity and good faith and perfect manners of a pure French tradition, finds herself continually face to face with its vital and rude adulteration, and struggles to legitimize it again as courtly literature fit for retelling in the gracious company of the *ruelles*. L'Héritier's style could never be read as the voice of the people; she writes the flowery and learned prose of a *précieuse* from the aristocratic salons of the Sun King's Paris, directed at the entertainment of her coevals, the group of friends. The fairy tale is, in this sense, a game of charades.

Behind the mask of the nurse whose storytelling she quotes, the minstrelsy of a gracious and noble past still can be heard, she pleads. Her quandary as she both denies and confronts the character of the *gouvernante* (Mother Goose) takes us to a deeper ambivalence in the fairy tales that she and Perrault wrote, about magic and the people, about the grotesque and lowlife, about women's lore and men's, women's speech and men's, about truth-telling and fabrication.

In the fairy tale '*Ricdin-Ricdon*', L'Héritier's villain is called Songecreux (Idle Dreamer) and he is hand-in-glove with an evil goblin, the Ricdin-Ricdon of the title. Together they are trying to take over the Kingdom of Fiction, whose queen is called Riante Image (Smiling Image). Throughout, L'Héritier balances one kind of tale-spinning against another, good fiction against bad, until at last the spinning princess and her true love – and her mother – struggle free of the wicked Idle Dreamer and his wiles. However, what is intriguing is that L'Héritier adds, as an afterthought, that she knows she might also be guilty of dabbling in such dreams as Songecreux. Fairy tale must always be a fabrication, she acknowledges. There will always be those guilty of peddling empty dreams. 'I myself,' she reflects, 'talking here to you, I am perhaps foremost in the party of the Idle Dreamers, as I amuse myself rescuing from oblivion these ancient, foolish stories …'

But she evinces continual pleasure in seductive uses of language, as an aspect of feminine cunning. From the standpoint of an unmarried literary woman like herself, the principal issue at stake was intellectual rather than physical or material survival. L'Héritier's concern with language and storytelling, and women's access to narrative, both as tellers and receivers, was bound up with her self-esteem; she was also preoccupied with the relationship between magic and language that the idea of the magic spell expresses, and her stories about female triumphs against the odds, like 'The Subtle Princess', focus on fairy tale as an art akin to conjuring, on its potential benefits to heroines in their struggles. Utterance and freedom are linked, as verbal charms and spells are too in the very composition of the stories.

Whether her contact with the past store of tales be a servant or an educated woman, fairy tales originate in what L'Héritier calls *romans* – novels – or even, citing the Spanish term, *Romances*. Their authenticity is confirmed by direct contact with a speaking woman to whom they are second nature; their nobility on the other hand is guaranteed by their birth. The pattern of the legacy reappears: the near source is female and plebeian and ancient, but the origin is noble, French, male and youthful. Like a fairytale heroine, the story on the lips of Mother Goose is somehow in disguise, and is, under the simple, or even uncouth exterior, a radiant and well-born princess, like Cinderella, like Donkeyskin.

Marie-Jeanne L'Héritier recognized that her role in this transformation was to provide beautiful raiment. With a touch of defiance that looks forward to Romantic assertion of self, L'Héritier introduces one of the stories Richard the Lion Heart tells with an apology which, as apologies can be, is also a boast: 'It is therefore not King Richard, who is speaking, but me.'

Mother Goose conceals many ancestors beneath her skirts – kings, troubadours, poets – but her voice remains proudly that of the contemporary writer, masking and unmasking herself.

Within the tales themselves, however, L'Héritier's disguises are more dashing. Her salon name – Scudéry's had been 'Sapho' – was Télésille. Telesilla appears in Pausanias' description of the sanctuary of Aphrodite at Corinth, where her statue had been put up. She was a poet and songwriter and – even more significantly with regard to L'Héritier – she had defended Argos against the Spartans: after the massacre of many Argive men on the field and the treacherous murder of the remaining force which followed, Telesilla rallied the Argive women and led them into battle.

The desired passage into an exalted sphere of action, normally marked out as a male preserve, corresponds, in L'Héritier's tales as in other writings of her contemporaries, with the fairytale theme of metamorphosis: the heroines change their fates, move themselves by magical combinations of words or appearances, through verbal or visual deceptions. Unlike many of her contemporaries, L'Héritier does not introduce animal metamorphoses in her fairy tales, but like them, she does explore, as in the romances of chivalry, the flexibility offered by male disguise; her heroines prove themselves, like Telesilla, at traditional men's ordeals.

Counterfeit and masquerade lie at the core of many of L'Héritier's tales; they convey her own preoccupation with literary roleplaying. 'Marmoisan, ou l'innocente tromperie' (Marmoisan, or the innocent trick) is dedicated to Perrault's daughter, with a preface asking her to include it in the family's collection of tales. The story was not taken up by Perrault; but the reason is not known. It is a story of male disguise: the heroine goes to war in the place of her twin brother after he has been accidentally killed in a shameful erotic adventure – he falls off a ladder trying to enter a girl's bedroom without permission, and is run through by her father. In her brother's shape, Marmoisan distinguishes herself and heaps honour on her household; she struggles not to be revealed, though many traps are set for her by jealous courtiers who suspect her of being a girl, and by the prince who has fallen in love with her and longs for her to turn out not to be a boy. She maintains feminine decorum too, throughout, refusing to join in the rough ribaldry of the court at women's expense. In the end, she is wounded in the lists at a tourney, and her travesty uncovered – to rejoicing all round. L'Héritier discriminates within the category of maleness between virtues she affirms – courage, action, altruism – and characteristics she repulses: dirty talk among them. The virtues are not sex-specific, her story implies and claims, though the female objects of masculine attacks, both sexual and discursive, confer a more specifically male character on these faults. Social organization lies at the root of these evils.

In this, L'Héritier foreshadows the ironies of her fellow fairytale writer in 'Starlight', one of the stories interpolated, as we have seen, in a novel by Murat. There, Murat describes the topsy-turvy land of Quietlife Island: 'Not a sound was to be heard there; everyone spoke in whispers and walked on tiptoe. There were no quarrels, and hardly any wars. When it became absolutely impossible to avoid engaging in combat, only the ladies fought, throwing crab-apples from a distance. The men kept well away: they slept till midday, plied their spinning wheels, tied pretty bows, took the children for walks, and made their faces up with rouge and beauty spots.' When the manly hero, Izmir, finds himself in this company, he becomes enraged, and plunges into battle, laying about him with his sword until the dead and dying lie about, to the horror of the Quietlife Islanders. 'What on earth do you think you're doing?' cries the king. 'Stop for goodness's sake. You can't kill people like that without mercy. It would be a fine thing if you taught them to kill as well ...' This tale criticizes the male cult of military *gloire*, and unlike the medieval World Turned Upside Down, does not scoff at the inversion of norms, but holds it up in gentle, humorous reproach.

Murat's and L'Héritier's tales issue strong attacks on the feminine realm as traditionally prescribed, and this sets them against women who wield power by its rules; these collaborators are transmogrified into vicious fairies and wicked stepmothers and idle, addle-pated, babbling girls – but always in a spirit of challenging limits on women's expectations.

The recurrence of male imposture in women's fairy tales might arise simply from the device's splendid narrative possibilities; but there could be more to it. As a woman writer, L'Héritier identified with the travestied Marmoisan; she wanted to prove through her heroine that she could be a valiant knight and a completely feminine woman, who inspires love. Likewise, she could play a man's part in the world of letters and win approval and renown. Her fairy tales tend to validate the inferior category against the superior, the vernacular folk literature against the classics, oral tradition against book learning, the female against the male, by skilfully imitating the style of the dominant category, its learning and its refinement, by performing a successful masquerade.

In 'La Robe de sincérité', she adopts a central device, the titular motif of the story, to develop her defence of women and of fiction, in a world antagonistic to their skills, their arts, and their traditions, among which storytelling features prominently. She also uses it to press her concern about true and false love on the one hand, and to play again with the character of true and false art on the other; when truth is served at the conclusion, its witnesses are the pairs of lovers and their marriages: no fewer than four weddings are necessary to tie up the tale.

A Robe of Sincerity has the power, the wizard Misandre (advisedly named) claims at the beginning of the tale, to reveal to a married man whether his wife is faithful, to a brother his sister's chastity, to a son his mother's, and so forth: if the woman in quesion is pure, the pictures of virtuous women will be visible in light on the black cloth of the robe when she puts it on. If the embroidery remains invisible, she is guilty. The King of Crete, before whom Misandre has been demonstrating his magic tricks – 'the kind of thing you see at the St Germain fair', puts in L'Héritier condescendingly – instantly orders him to make such a robe. Herminie, the wizard's daughter, and her mother, start to weave it together, offering unheard protests to Misandre, who, as his name implies, is hell-bent on stirring up trouble at court. He succeeds: his erotic version of the Emperor's New Clothes drives every man crazy with suspicions about their wives and sisters.

L'Héritier shows her dark comic gifts when she describes the robe's mischief: the men in question all pretend of course that they can see the embroidery, and then rage with jealousy in secret afterwards. One court favourite, in a fit, mistakes a maid in the corridor at night for his wife and assumes she is stealing away to a secret assignation, manhandles her so that she spills the water she is carrying, which he then howls is his own blood; later, he gives chase in the dark to a dog, convinced that he has caught his wife and her lover *in flagrante*, and manages to crack his skull on the stairs. Giving an interesting glimpse into married life in those days, the author then describes how the innocent wife indignantly refuses to stay in the matrimonial bed and shuts herself up in her study to sleep in the armchair.

The theme of women's art resonates strongly throughout the tale, for Herminie, the weaver, also has a fairy godmother, a learned and rich widow, who paints portraits, and she becomes Herminie's patron and encourages her in her work (though she won't hear of her earning her living) until, in the way of romances, she is captured by pirates. Many different pictures featured in the story are wonder-working to different ends: at the conclusion, the many weddings are mirrored in the drawings Herminie has made, and her mother embroidered and woven, all on the theme of chaste, faithful women, like Penelope and Halcyone who could not bear to outlive her beloved husband.

L'Héritier is here taking up a thread in feminism which goes back to medieval ripostes to the *Roman de la rose* and Boccaccio. Above all, the narrator vindicates the robe itself, in a clever inversion: the instrument of deception and misery becomes a true instrument of discernment, distinguishing truth-tellers from liars, flatterers from honest folk, humble men from proud ones, since only the honest and virtuous spoke out that they saw nothing, that the robe was nothing but a trick. As in 'The Emperor's New Clothes', the famous version written by Hans Andersen in 1837, the fabricated artefact, itself an act of seduction and falsehood, turns out, like the scenes on Herminie's drawing and painting, to have genuine theurgic powers to tell true.

When her father the wizard is arrested for his deceit, Herminie throws herself on the mercy of the king and confesses that everything is her fault. This is a lie, gallantly told to save her father, but in one sense, as the author's alter ego, the artist did indeed make the robe: she sewed the stitches of the alliances, drew the design of the romance. The adulteries and other crimes men fantasize when they see nothing in the robe represent the slanders levelled at innocent women; Herminie's collaboration with her father reveals the web of conflicting allegiances in which women are trapped; her woven tales and pictures, like L'Héritier's own writings, stand for her protest – the different story, the women's version. Like Idle Dreams, the mischief-making robe provides a metaphor for the world of fancy and romance, the kingdom of fiction which can function as an instrument of greater honesty, too.

Devils are defeated when you guess their name, and so are unwanted suitors: Rumpelstiltskin tears himself in two. (George Cruikshank in Gammer Grethel's Fairy Tales, *London, nineteenth century.)*

'What big eyes you have!' Saucer-eyed herself in their shared bed, Little Red Riding Hood wonders at the change in her granny. (Gustave Doré, Les Contes de Charles Perrault, Paris, 1862.)

CHAPTER 12

Granny Bonnets, Wolves' Cover: Seduction III

– In bocca al lupo!
– E muoia il lupo!

['Into the jaws of the wolf!'
'Death to the wolf!']

Good luck sayings, Italy

For the famous fairy tale, '*Le Petit chaperon rouge*' (Little Red Riding Hood), Charles Perrault adapted a traditional story, in which a little girl takes food and drink to her grandmother and meets a wolf. It is likely that he set aside aspects which struck him as crude but which have survived in later retellings: in these, the wolf tricks the heroine into eating a piece of her granny's flesh and drinking some of her blood, but the little girl eventually manages to get away by refusing to get into bed, saying she has to pee. The wolf urges her to do it in the bed (!), but she refuses, so he ties her by a long cord to the bed post and lets her leave the cottage. Once in the woods, she manages to slip the knot and get away.

From the point of view of Mother Goose's symbolic identity and its connection to women's persuasive speech, Perrault's retelling continues an important aspect: the possibility of confusing wolf and granny. In Perrault's version, the wolf cannot be clearly distinguished from Red Riding Hood's beloved grandmother: that is the crucial collapse of roles in his story. (A children's glove puppet today neatly combines granny and wolf as a Janus-faced head under a single mob cap.)

The wolf is kin to the forest-dwelling witch, or crone; he offers us a male counterpart, a werewolf who swallows up grandmother and then granddaughter. In the witch-hunting fantasies of early modern Europe they are the kind of beings associated with marginal knowledge, who possess pagan secrets and are in turn possessed by them. Both dwell in the woods, both need food urgently (one because she is sick, the other because he has not eaten for three days), and the little girl cannot quite tell them apart. The climactic image of 'Red Riding Hood', the wolf's mouth, has led many commentators to note the emphasis on orality. This orality has been interpreted, by the Freudian Géza Róheim, as an allegory of a child's aggressive feelings towards the mother's breast. But the orality has not been interpreted as revealing another form of maternal nurturance: language or oral knowledge.

Perrault himself put on Granny's bonnet, as it were, when he hid behind the figure of an old nurse, telling stories to children of higher social rank than herself. On the title page and frontispiece of the *Contes du temps passé* (Tales of Olden Times), the author in fact doubled his disguise: Mother Goose was shown in the picture telling the stories, and Perrault's son, Pierre Darmancourt, was given as the author. The image might represent a memory of Perrault's own childhood, but even so, it offers an alter ego for Perrault himself which he uses as a cover: he was transmitting the voice of the storyteller, a compound of old woman and child.

Perrault's unhappy ending becomes very interesting indeed in this light, for his little girl is swallowed up into the body of the wolf along with her granny, and does not emerge again. There is a possible reading – among many possible readings – of this ending: like the children who grow up in traditional lore and language, Little Red Riding Hood is incorporated, the lineal and female descendant of the grandmother who has herself been devoured, and the wolf does not release either of them. The wolf to whom they are thus assimilated could represent the indigenous inhabitants of the countryside, hairy, wild, unkempt, untrammelled by imported acculturation, eating raw foods and meat, a native beast in the native landscape, where a specific age-old corpus of homegrown literature flourishes and is passed on. Such a counterpoint between the woods and the home Red Riding Hood leaves with her basket of prepared food – butter and cake – is suggested in the Perrault, and the theme was made explicit later in the interpretive literature. Certain German romantic patriots, for instance, commenting on the tale in the 1920s, allegorized the grandmother as ancient Aryan mother-right who must be regenerated by the granddaughter. On the other hand, accepting Red Riding Hood's death inside the animal as an allegory of national tradition clearly entails reading against the cautionary message of the story, and against the morality Perrault appended to the tale, in which he warns little girls against wolves.

In these final verses, Perrault distinguishes the hidden identity of the wolf:

Now, there are real wolves, with hairy pelts and enormous teeth; but also wolves who seem perfectly charming, sweet-natured and obliging, who pursue young girls in the street and pay them the most flattering attentions.

Unfortunately, these smooth-tongued, smooth-pelted wolves are the most dangerous beasts of all.

It is this wellspoken seducer, urbane, not rustic, who turns out to be Perrault's wolf, and who, eating up little girls and grandmothers, makes possible yet another twist in the significance of the story. For he overwhelms and absorbs them in the same way, one could say, as classical learning, metropolitan manners and other customs, alien rather than autochthonous, swallow up the homebred nursery culture of old women and their protégées, of Mother Goose and her young listeners.

It is not unusual in Perrault to find his *moralités* introducing an irony: here the wolf no longer stands for the savage wilderness, but for the deceptions of the city and the men who wield authority in it. He openly turns the usual identity of the wolf on its head and locates him near at hand, rather than far away and Other. It is almost as if Perrault could not bring himself to follow the convention of the happier ending, with Granny dead and Little Red Riding Hood cunningly escaped, because he wanted them to remain united, in the wolf's belly. Nor, apparently, did he want to introduce a huntsman, the figure of masculine civilization who restores them to life, as in the later Grimm version. But yet he could not stop at their ultimate and unregenerate incorporation into the wolf either, as he knew, deep down, this resolution did not represent the true facts of the matter. Tradition cannot be kept sealed off and apart; so at the last minute, in the moral, he switched the emphasis and turned the wolf from a forest creature into a polished and sweet-talking man, and by the way produced an allegory about the impossibility of separate female lore and language.

Perrault was also in two minds about the pristine, aboriginal source that L'Héritier proclaimed, for his jaunty tone consistently belies the earnestness with which he presses the claims of fairy tale to wisdom. His stories have been so romanticized in subsequent retellings that it comes as quite a revelation to find him cracking his typical jokes, at the expense of his material. When the Sleeping Beauty's death has been ordered by her cannibal mother-in-law (an episode usually left out these days), Perrault comments, 'she was over twenty years old, not counting the hundred years she had slept: her hide was a little tough, though lovely and white ...' Though Perrault often asserted the contrary in the quarrel with Boileau, the style of his Mother Goose tales betrays that he could not take the claims of native literature altogether seriously, that for him Mother Goose would always raise a laugh.

Speech is strong magic in fairy tales: the bad sister cursed the beggarwoman at the well and ends up spitting slugs and snails and puppy dog tails; roses and pearls fall from her good sister's lips. (The Arthur Rackham Fairy Book, London, 1933.)

Perrault was much less defensive about adopting the disguise of Mother Goose than his female colleagues; as Virginia Woolf pointed out, it is all very well to spurn Greek when you have been given the chance to study it, to reject tradition when you have been raised in it. But the Querelle des Anciens et des Modernes affected men and women writers differently. L'Héritier could not have composed a sonorous Latin ode or a canny epigram in Greek for the king's birthday even if she wanted to. She had to be a Modern, on the side of the mother tongue willy-nilly. No wolf was needed to dish up Mother Goose to hungry listeners: in some ways the most successful of accomplished L'Héritier's disguises was her conceal-ment of her true wolf nature. For it was she who came along and gobbled Grandmother, or Mother Goose, by making her clean and tidy and *sortable* – fit for polite society.

In L'Héritier's '*Les Enchantements de l'éloquence ou les effets de la douceur*' (The Enchantments of Eloquence or the effects of gentleness), a version of the story known to folklorists as 'Diamonds and Toads', the issue of women's talk is also central.

One day, when the heroine Blanche is drawing water at the well, a prince out hunting – inevitably – wounds her by mistake, but her soft answer enchants him, and he falls in love with her mild and unreproachful speech as much as with her beauty. Later, a fairy appears at the house in disguise as a poor old peasant woman to give Blanche a magic balm for her wound. Her fairy name is Dulcicula – little sweet, with its reminiscences of the *dolce stil novo* of the Italian troubadours. Blanche receives her kindly, even though – L'Héritier is careful to tell us – she does not swallow old wives' tales readily. Alix, the unkind and foul-mouthed step-sister, meanwhile flies off the handle in her fishwife way, and bawls her out in colourful idiom, calling her an old fool, a midwife and a beast in a single tirade. (L'Héritier unconsciously relishes the opportunity to foul her own mouth, it seems, by impersonating the profane Alix.) After this visit the fairy confers the gift of ever gentle speech on Blanche, and perpetual invective on Alix, thus locking them in their original personalities, rather than working any magical transformation. When another fairy, this time a brilliant court lady, radiant with jewels and silks, later appears by the fountain, she asks to drink. Blanche tilts the vessel to her lips; Alix visiting the fountain refuses with a stream of abuse. At this stage, diamonds and other jewels begin to spill from Blanche's mouth when she speaks, while Alix is condemned to spit toads and snakes and other ingredients of the witches' broth (left).

The complications and inconsistencies of L'Héritier's tale – why two fairies? would Alix really have been so rude to such a grand lady asking for a drink after she knew how Blanche had been rewarded? – can be unravelled if the author's partisan purposes are kept in mind. The first, seemingly redundant test – the offer of the peasant cure – is much more apt to her argument than the request for water at the well, because it exactly reflects her own belief in taking from the simple folk what is good with good sense, discrimination and unfailing courtesy. Alix is punished, at this stage, for being *grossière* (uncouth) with the poor. The fairy offering her remedy in the guise of a peasant with a possibly quack medicine is another Mother Goose, the source of pure water that does however need to be filtered. The second, resplendent fairy, called Eloquentia Nativa (Native Eloquence), meets L'Héritier's need to enter her own text as a new kind of speaking woman. There is no reason for the first fairy not to metamorphose into Eloquentia Nativa. But by keeping them distinct, the narrator can occupy the latter's place, and also continue her invitation to her friend Henriette-Julie de Murat, issued in her preface, to write with native eloquence of native things herself. Eloquentia Nativa is an awkward, Spenserian allegorical figure, in the midst of a lively story of virtue rewarded and vice punished, but she represents the issue of language in the present day for the tale's author; she embodies the potential gift of female eloquence, of speaking diamonds, not toads, for the modern receivers and disseminators of the tale, among whom L'Héritier counted herself. Mother Goose must learn to speak according to the principles of *civilité*, the aristocratic and *précieux* ideal of proper language, and L'Héritier continues to struggle to align this ideal with feminism. At one moment she pauses to issue another personal challenge, explicitly valuing women's eloquence over classical male oratory: 'I'd just as much like to say that pearls and rubies fell from Blanche's mouth ... as say that lightning flashes issued from that of Pericles'. As Marc Fumaroli has pointed out, the vindication of the heroine in fairy tales often expresses the teller's desire to vindicate the feminine, with which the genre was so closely identified.

This was not an issue for Perrault, and when he wrote his variation on the tale, 'Les Fées' (The Fairies), the good fairy's gifts remain purely monetary: jewels for the good sister, dust and ashes for the bad. It is doubly ironical, therefore, that Perrault imitated much more convincingly the bantering, old-womanly style of tale-telling associated with Mother Goose, while L'Héritier rejected false naïvety in favour of polish. For the feminine in L'Héritier's hands had to conform to certain high principles of the courtly *douceur* of her title: the toads were black magic, illusion, coarseness, unkindness, colloquial speech or orality, and the upstart bourgeoisie; the diamonds were theurgy, or white magic, truth-telling, refinement, kindness and written literature mediating peasant wisdom. The oral character of Mother Goose vanished into the courtly and scripted figure of Eloquentia Nativa, who is L'Héritier's ultimate source figure in a new travesty or disguise, all cleaned up and polished, *polie* – polite. This is the drift of fairy tales once they had reached print and entered the nursery. Make-believe children were to become bona fide innocents; Mother Goose must not talk dirty any more.

The Comtesse de Murat did follow her friend Marie-Jeanne L'Héritier's urgings, and wrote several fairy tales soon after. She dedicated her *Histoires sublimes et allégoriques* of 1699 to *Les Fées modernes* (Modern Fairies) and she anticipated the metamorphosis of Mother Goose with great clarity as she addressed them:

Oldentime fairies appear nothing but comedians next to you. Their occupations were lowly and childish, and the most significant effects their art brought about was to make people weep pearls and diamonds, blow emeralds out of their noses and spit rubies. Their entertainment was dancing by the light of the moon, turning themselves into crones and cats and monkeys and werewolves to terrorize children and weak minds. That is why all that remains today of their Exploits and Deeds are only Mother Goose Tales. They were almost always old, ugly, badly dressed and badly housed; and apart from Mélusine and half a dozen or so like her, all the rest of them were just beggarwomen …

Is there any irony in Murat's *envoi*? Or any regret? She certainly puts her finger on the identity of the fairies, the crones, the beggarwomen, the witches and the tale-tellers like Mother Goose. The campaign L'Héritier proclaimed through her tale 'The Enchantments of Eloquence', shows how a woman of independent mind had to manoeuvre between negative and positive images of her sex in order to continue what she was doing and argue for its value and acceptance. She had to sentence the foul-mouthed Alix to failure (she dies abandoned in the woods), eye the peasant's remedy with circumspection, rinse the stories she accepted in the purifying language of the court, disinfect Mother Goose of her associations with babbling and spells, and turn her into Eloquentia Nativa, the lifeless but direct precursor of the Sugar Plum Fairy, or even Tinkerbell. She championed the feminine, but in order to do so successfully she had to define its virtues very closely, and in some way betray the character of the very literature she was defending by repudiating the uncouth in favour of refinement, by consuming Granny and spitting her out again as diamonds and flowers.

Marie-Jeanne L'Héritier achieved some of the fame and standing she desired. She was the first woman elected to one of the prestigious and exclusive French academies, the Académie des Lanternistes of Toulouse, in 1696. She was also admitted, the following year, to the Ricovrati of Padua, who chose nine women for the nine Muses in their company (p. xv). But she is hardly read today, paradoxically because the highly refined and embroidered style she chose, the mannered and flowery eloquence she evolved in order to stave off criticisms about unsuitable material in improper hands, has dated and become tedious compared to the flashing and humorous concision of Perrault, who did not have to struggle so hard with the figure of popular, aboriginal female wisdom, as he could annexe Mother Goose without being confused with her.

It is a shame that L'Héritier is often so prolix and indeed so precious, that the flashes of feline wit and her moments of inventive cruelty are few and far between. Her predicament, poised between respectability and exclusion, mirrors that of the contemporary woman writer. The problem of Mother Goose's double tongue remains: is she truly a female storyteller, only now and then in drag, or does the drag constitute a claim on credence, advanced by men invoking something more authentic than themselves? If L'Héritier were as bawdy and comic and knowing as she describes her peasant sources, and as the British panto tradition has developed, she would have fed the prejudices that make old wives' tales suitable fare for no one but children and their lowclass minders. Or would she have been able to overcome that persistent tinge of contempt? It is a quest doomed to failure, both historically and psychologically, to try to occupy some imaginary primordial femaleness, an essentialist *hortus conclusus* where history and law and all the other factors in sexual politics have not gained entry. Furthermore, there is a distinction between a woman telling a story, and telling a story as a woman, though both run up against the difference their femaleness makes. Mother Goose does the latter; she may not have been a woman at all, but only a fantasy of nursery, of nurture, of female magic, of woman at the hearth. She vividly represents in Victorian culture and in our own the continuing mixed feelings both men and women experience about such a voice, such a practice. For a female writer, Mother Goose's presence is a comfort and a source of unease at one and the same time, holding up before us a long history of enchantment on the one hand, of ridicule on the other. Any writer who has identified herself with women's issues knows how she will trip up over mockery; yet laughter can be answered in kind, for it has its own retaliatory strength, as a goose knows when she cackles.

II

The German Romantics, in the late eighteenth and early nineteenth centuries, prized the products of the imagination, of fantasies and dreams, with unprecedented conviction, and they consequently accorded fairy tales the highest literary status they had ever achieved, even in the late seventeenth century. They identified the genre with the spontaneous, innocent, untutored mind – with children and with ordinary, unsophisticated people. Both were pure, not-adult – literally, unadulterated. The German mystical poet Novalis (1772–1801), who was one of the first thinkers to propose that fairy tales have the power to unlock mysteries of the spirit, wrote in his notebooks:

> A true fairy tale must also be a prophetic account of things – an ideal account – an absolutely necessary account. A true writer of fairy tales sees into the future. [They are] confessions of a true, a synthetic child – of an ideal child. (A child is a good deal cleverer and wiser than an adult – but the child must be an ironic child.)

Novalis, who had adopted his name to symbolize the new world that poetry and fantasy would bring about, realized that the new age of the child could not

Dorothea Viehmann, market saleswoman, daughter of an innkeeper and wife of a tailor, was one of the Grimm Brothers' chief sources; they liked to stress the Volk *character of their informants – she soon turns into a generic peasant, Gammer Grethel. (Ludwig Emil Grimm,* Children and Household Tales, *1819, copied, anon.,* Gammer Grethel's Fairy Tales, *London.) The historical woman gradually disappears. The first English translation of the Grimms, 1823, was illustrated by George Cruikshank; his storyteller was absorbed too into the image of the archetypal goody nurse of merry days of yore* OVERLEAF.

THE TRUE PORTRAIT
OF
GAMMER GRETHEL

depend on children themselves, but on people like himself assuming the persona of the child – ironical children. The old woman had been the preferred mask of the storyteller in the seventeenth century, but in the late eighteenth she ideally spoke as if she were still a child, from the memories of her infancy, which tallied, in the perspective of romanticism, with the childhood of the culture itself, before it became corrupt. Inside the wolf, child and crone are one.

Behind the old who tell the stories lurk the children they once were, listening, and with that fantasy there rises the memory of the storyteller the mother, grandmother or nurse who stood *in loco parentis*. She brings back the voice heard in childhood, its mixture of authority and cajolery, its irresistible formative view of

the world. The film theorist Kaja Silverman has called the maternal voice an 'acoustic mirror', which acts to reflect and mould the child's developing identity. In the context of seventeenth-century childrearing, this mirror was as often held up by nurses or grandmothers as by mothers, and not only in the circles of the aristocracy. The testimony of fairy tales as well as the imagined account of their origins reveals how intense the memory of this voice remained. There are reasons, psychological as well as social and literary, for the eclipse of the Scheherazade type of storyteller by the crone figure of Mother Goose, Mother Bunch, or Gammer Gurton.

Around 1811 Ludwig Emil Grimm, the artist brother of the family, drew a portrait of Dorothea Viehmann, one of the principal sources of the Brothers Grimm collection *Kinder- und Hausmärchen*. This portrait was engraved and published as a frontispiece in numerous popular editions; Frau Viehmann has become the most prominent of the many oral storytellers on whom the Grimms drew, and a kind of primal scene of folklore transmission, as conceived in the nineteenth century, featured her in her domestic setting, surrounded by her children and grandchildren as the two scholars listen attentively. The painter Ludwig Katzenstein in 1892 showed chickens pecking among the floorboards, the dresser laden with still lives, the curtains of the bed (in the kitchen) drawn aside, the door to the yard standing ajar: a Pieter de Hooch interior of perfect domestic husbandry.

The fairytale tradition held to an imaginary idea of the Grimms' methods. (Ludwig Katzenstein, Jakob and Wilhelm Grimm with the fairy-storyteller Dorothea Viehmann, *1892.)*

Dorothea Viehmann was not a peasant, but an innkeeper's daughter who later married a tailor, a smalltown dweller of the artisanal class, and worked at the quintessential storyteller's trade, itinerant marketing – of fruit, eggs and cheese. She told her stories to the daughters of the Huguenot pastor in Kassel, and came to the attention of the inspired, independent-minded circle of Romantic thinkers centred on the manor farm at Brakel, near Kassel, where the von Haxthausen family were landowners. There, in this German variation on the salons of Paris, the poets Clemens Brentano and Annette von Droste-Hülshoff (1797–1848) were also invited to stay and exchange ideas; Brentano became a pioneering writer of fairy tales himself, and Annette von Droste-Hülshoff was committed to the literature of the imagination and collected stories for the Grimms. It was she and her friends who 'discovered' Frau Viehmann and her repertory of fairy tales and recommended her to the Grimms. In Droste-Hülshoff's unfinished novel, *Ledwina*, a fiery autobiographical account of a daughter in rebellion against her brothers' world of conformism and unquestioned militarist hierarchy, it is strik-ing how passionately the heroine sympathizes, indeed identifies, with the family's old nurse, who has since retired to a poor cottage on their estate, continually taking the part of workers on the estate against the male authorities in the household.

The Grimm Brothers were building on the group's fervent interest in retriev-ing a vernacular, traditional, national literature, and had undertaken the patriotic task of recording local tales, in Low German dialects when the occasion arose, without the customary scholars' prejudice against the 'vulgar'. But they did not roam the countryside themselves, gleaning stories. Frau Viehmann travelled to Kassel, to visit the brothers in their study in the city. They also gathered tales from their own immediate family members, as well as from friends like Droste-Hülshoff, many of whom were in touch with French influences. Though the sto-ries are unquestionably traditional, they are not quite as homespun – or as rustically lowborn – as the brothers claimed.

Born in 1755, Dorothea Viehmann was fifty-five when she met them, and died soon afterwards, in 1815, poor and ill. Her tales – they include some of the most famous, like 'The Twelve Brothers', 'The Three Feathers', 'The Goose Girl', 'Mother Holle' – were recited to them over and over again so that they could take them down, as Wilhelm remembered in a preface: 'Among people who follow the old ways of life without change, attachment to inherited patterns is stronger than we, impatient for variety, can realize.' Later, however, the brothers reshaped their collection according to their requirements. But Dorothea Viehmann's presence in the frontispiece and the references continued to guarantee an illusion of direct, unmediated storytelling.

Ludwig Emil Grimm's portrait shows a thoughtful, even anxious woman, with permanently creased brow over high arched eyebrows, a gaze focussed on the horizon, a serious, closed, narrow mouth, beaky nose and hands folded over one another, holding a sprig of wild flowers (p. 189). She is wearing a regional bonnet over wispy grey hair, and there are other local touches in her kerchief and over-dress. The whole image betokens an identity rooted in a particular soil, where those wild flowers grow, while the pose and the gaze suggest a mind fixed on dis-tant times and events. Her expression confirms Wilhelm's express wish that the tales represented 'the reawakening of the long forgotten literature ... not only did we seek something of consolation in the past, our hope, naturally, was that this course of ours should contribute somewhat to the return of a better day'.

In fact, Dorothea Viehmann had been born Pierson, a French Huguenot (her father came from Metz), and her culture was much more mixed and rather less rootedly Hessian than the Grimm Brothers wanted to suggest. Like Perrault, who hid himself in the skirts of *ma Mère l'Oye*, the brothers put on the granny bonnet of Dorothea, icon and voice of the folk.

The connections and kinship of other Grimm informants have also been shown to be much more permeated with literary, French influence than the Romantic brothers wished, but until recent scholarship examined the tales, this aspect was neglected in favour of the mythical dream of autochthonous purity, which then becomes available to all who hear or read the stories.

In an English edition of fairy tales after Grimm, illustrated by George Cruikshank and introduced by Laurence Housman, the Emil Grimm portrait was redrawn for the frontispiece. The book's title is *Gammer Grethel's Fairy Tales*, and the caption to the picture says, 'The True Portrait of Gammer Grethel' – Gammer here being a word for old wife that had become itself archaic, giving off an authentic whiff of traditionalism (p. 189). 'For the true and unpolluted air of fairyland we have to go back to the old and artless tales of a day purer and simpler than our own,' writes Laurence Housman in the Introduction. 'Purer because so wholly unconcerned with any question of morals, simpler because so wholly unconscious of its simplicity.'

To this, wonder is indeed one possible response. Laurence Housman here shows one grownup's art of make-believe as he poses with such blatant disingenuousness as a child – an ironical child, not of the quality of Mme d'Aulnoy or Perrault or L'Héritier, but of their descendants. A child who is not a child, whose voice is always doubled, always deceitful, always masked, all the better to speak to you with, my dear, all the better to persuade you with.

III

In the twentieth century, traditional tales have paradoxically offered many imaginative writers a territory of freedom to express their rebellion; the granny bonnet, the wolf mask have offered a helpful disguise to some of the boldest spirits. Angela Carter's quest for eros, her perseverance in the attempt to ensnare its nature in her imagery, her language, her stories, drew her to fairy tales as a form, and before her death in 1992 she wrote some of the most original reworkings in contemporary literature in her collection *Fireworks* (1974) and *The Bloody Chamber* (1979); the posthumous *American Ghosts* (1993) contains a Cinderella story, told with the succinct lyrical poignancy of Carter at her most tender (see p. 205).

In the longer fiction, *The Magic Toyshop* (1967), *Nights at the Circus* (1984), and *Wise Children* (1991), Carter conjures gleefully with fairytale motifs: changelings and winged beings, muted heroines, beastly metamorphoses, arduous journeys and improbable encounters, magical rediscoveries and happy endings. Her recuperation of the form has had a widespread influence, palpable in the writings of contemporaries like Salman Rushdie, Robert Coover, and Margaret Atwood.

It is interesting, in the context of fairytale narrators' masquerades, that Carter was also deeply fascinated with female impersonation, as a literary device, as a social instrument of disruption, as an erotic provocation; with bravura, she made theatrical burlesque and music-hall travesties into a high style; her own prose was glitteringly, self-mockingly hybrid, contrived and slangy at once, mandarin and vulgar, romantic and cynical. These contradictions were conveyed through the figure of the cross-dressed male or female. As on the boards, cross-gender disguises provide a recurrent tease; from Shakespeare in his comedies and romances Carter borrowed the fantastic, perverse, bewildering entertainment of double drag – Rosalind and Viola dressed as boys played by boys cross-dressed as girls; she continually explored, in the personae of her protagonists, the imagination's own capacity for protean metamorphoses, which allows it to leap barriers of difference, or at least play with them till they seem to totter and fall. It is revealing that she enjoyed the fairytale motif of the witch's duel, when the heroine or hero seizes hold of the witch or evil fairy who has snatched away their beloved, and holds on and holds on; the witch shifts her shape, from one creature to another, but in vain, until dawn breaks and she has to let her victim go. Angela Carter understood both roles very well in her writing: mercurial slipperiness of identity, as well as the need to secure meanings.

The centrepiece of her novel *The Passion of New Eve* (1977) dramatizes, in a phantasmagoric, extreme Grand Guignol tableau, the wedding of Tristessa, the legendary screen goddess, who is really a man in disguise, and her longtime fan, the novel's New Eve and protagonist, who began life as a boy but has travelled a long way since then. In *Nights at the Circus*, seven years later, the American journalist and questing hero, Jack Walser, speculates at the very start that Fevvers, the winged giantess, might be a male in disguise.

Carter's treatment of travesty moves from pleasure in its dissembling wickedness and disruptiveness of convention in the early work, to exploring its function as a means of survival – and a specifically proletarian strategy of advancing, through the construction of self in image and language. In this, many of Carter's heroines – both in her writing and in life, like Fevvers, like the music-hall artistes the Chance sisters of *Wise Children*, like her idol Lulu/Louise Brooks – resemble the literary text of the kind she herself was writing: ornate, bejewelled, artificial,

Angela Carter knew the storyteller's time-honoured ruses, and played with the masks, the spells and the voices in her brilliant variations on fairy tales, The Bloody Chamber.

highly wrought prose playing hide-and-seek with the chatty, downmarket, vulgar unadorned personae of the characters underneath the greasepaint and the costumes. Her crucial insight is that women like the circus aerialiste Fevvers produce themselves as 'women', and that this is often the result of *force majeure*, of using what you have to get by. The fairytale transformations of Cinders into princess represent what a girl has to do to stay alive.

Angela Carter was a fantasist with a salty turn of mind, a dissident with a utopian vision of possibilities in the midst of disaster, who always sprang surprises and challenged the conventional response, as in her controversial essay of the late 1970s, *The Sadeian Woman*, which found in Sade a paradoxical champion of women's sexual liberation. In her novels of the 1960s and early 1970s (*Heroes and Villains*, *The Infernal Desire Machines of Dr Hoffman*), in the dazzling reworkings of *The Bloody Chamber*, and her last, full-stretch flights (*Nights at the Circus* and *Wise Children*), she developed Freud's polymorphous perversity with panache, and played with humour in a wide variety of keys, ranging from flamboyantly upfront ribaldry to the quietest, dryest, droll asides. She opened a recent anthology of fairy tales with Sermerssuaq, a character of contemporary Eskimo folklore, who was 'so powerful' that

> she could lift a kayak on the tips of three fingers. She could kill a seal merely by drumming on its head with her fists … Sometimes this Sermerssuaq would show off her clitoris. It was so big that the skin of a fox would not fully cover it. *Aja*, and she was the mother of nine children, too!

Carter was invited to moderate this passage, as its inclusion, especially in the heraldic position at the beginning of the book, would prevent teachers using the collection in schools. But she stood firm; she practised through her writing a constant stretching of the permitted, of the permissible. Taboo was her terrain, nothing was sacred (the title of a collection of journalism), and comedy was one of her ways of entering it. Not for her the humour of control, of convention, of censure. In one of the very last pieces she wrote, she celebrated the British pantomime tradition, its use of heavy innuendo and bawdy banter about sexual oppositions and its transvestite roles:

> The Dame bends over, whips up her crinolines; she has three pairs of knee-length bloomers … One pair is made out of the Union Jack … The second pair is quartered red and black, in memory of Utopia. The third and vastest pair of bloomers is scarlet, with a target on the seat, centred on the arsehole …

The Fool in Dutch painting deals in comic obscenity in this manner; fools can enter where angels fear to tread, and thumb their noses (show their bottoms) at convention and authority: tomfoolery includes iconoclasm, disrespect, subversion.

The Dame became one of Angela Carter's adopted voices (a woman speaking through a man disguised as a woman); this double drag scatters certainty about sexual identity, of course, it puts fixity to the question. But it was not always so, and in the broadening of her comedy one can decipher the risks and the difficulties she suffered as a writer. This transformation itself forms part of the larger shift that has taken place in recent times, which has made humour the weapon of the dispossessed, the marginal, the response of the victim who feels Punch's stick, not the manic joy of Mr Punch himself.

Her humour was of the unsettling variety, that made it necessary to examine one's own received ideas. It was so very impolite, with its particular idiosyncratic feminism, its blend of the irreverent and the gothic, its dazzling linguistic intricacy and relish for imagery. But it is this humour, its dark and even snaky stabs, that above all produced the shock and unease people felt at her work – which is of course what she – what Sermerssuaq, what the Panto Dame – intended.

The growing presence of humour in Carter's fiction signals her defiant hold on 'heroic optimism', the mood she singled out as characteristic of fairy tales, the principle which sustained the idea of a happy ending, whatever the odds. But heroic optimism shades into gallows humour. Although laughter breaks the silence and jesting can be provocative, disruptive, anarchic and unsettling, some laughter never unburdens itself from knowledge of its own pessimism; it remains intrinsically ironic.

In her later fiction, Carter used her own brand of carnivalesque comedy to mock the yearnings and delusions of eros, and she performed in *Wise Children,* a jesting burlesque on Shakespeare's *A Midsummer Night's Dream*, recasting this recension of 'Beauty and the Beast' as a full Hollywood spectacular, Cecil B. DeMille-cum-Busby Berkeley; like the Bard, a presiding presence in the book, Carter has fun at the Queen of the Fairies' expense, but she vividly takes the part of the rude mechanicals, too. *Wise Children* is another of Bottom's dreams: it literally looks at romance from the angle of those at rock bottom, the Chance sisters, and snatches victory from the jaws of defeat, as the donkey proves, against all expectations, that folly has its wisdom too.

It is uncomfortable to list to the iambic distych, to know you are identifying yourself as an outsider by what you say, that all the disguises in the wardrobe will never fix identity, all the voices in the repertory will not tell the complete story. Angela Carter was the most recent and most original of the goose-footed queens, of the riddling, scabrous dames, to put hard questions.

PART TWO
The Tales

O fellow, come, the song we had last night.
Mark it, Cesario, it is old and plain;
The spinsters and the knitters in the sun,
And the free maids that weave their thread with bones,
Do use to chaunt it: it is silly sooth,
And dallies with the innocence of love,
Like the old age.

Twelfth Night, II, iv

Each man
Is an approach to the vigilance
In which the litter of truths becomes
A whole, the day on which the last star
Has been counted, the genealogy
Of gods and men destroyed, the right
To know established as the right to be.
We shall have gone behind the symbols
To that which they symbolized, away
From the rumors of the speech-full domes,
To the chatter that is then the true legend,
Like glitter ascended into fire.

Wallace Stevens

As her sisters drive off, outcast and orphaned Cinderella wishes on the sapling growing from her mother's grave and finds herself clothed by magic in a dress and jewels and slippers, so that she can go to the ball. (Joseph Southall, Cinderella, 1893–5.)

CHAPTER 13

Absent Mothers: Cinderella

What happened to the mother
who looked at the snow? I don't say
(you don't know this grammar yet)
how mothers and stepmothers change,

looking, and being looked at.
It takes a long time …
Sinister twinkling animals,
Hollywood ikons, modern Greek style:

a basket of images, poison at work
in the woodland no Cretan child
ever sees. Closer to home
I've seen a loved girl turn feral.

These pages lurk in the mind,
speak of your sister,
her mother, and me. Perhaps,
already, of you.

Ruth Padel

The good mother often dies at the beginning of the story. Tales telling of her miraculous return to life, like Shakespeare's romances *Pericles* and *The Winter's Tale*, have not gained the currency or popularity of 'Cinderella' or 'Snow White' in which she is supplanted by a monster.

Figures of female evil stride through the best-loved, classic fairy tales: on this earth, wicked stepmothers, ugly sisters; from fairyland, bad fairies, witches, ogresses. In the most famous stories, monsters in female shape outnumber the giants and hobgoblins of 'Tom Thumb' or 'Puss-in-Boots' or 'Rumpelstiltskin', and certainly eclipse them in vividness and their lingering grip on the imagination: children are more thrilled than disgusted by the wolf who gobbles up Red Riding Hood, whereas they are repelled by the witch who fattens up Hansel to eat him. He exercises the beast's seductiveness, she is consigned to the flames of her oven to a loud sigh of relief, or even a hurrah.

All over the world, stories which centre on a heroine, on a young woman suffering a prolonged ordeal before her vindication and triumph, frequently focus on women as the agents of her suffering. The earliest extant version of 'Cinderella' to feature a lost slipper was written down around AD 850–60 in China; the story was taken down from a family servant by an official, and the way it is told reveals that the audience already knows it: this is by no means the *Ur*-text.

The Chinese Cinderella, Yeh-hsien, is 'intelligent, and good at making pottery on the wheel'. When her own mother dies, and is soon followed by her father, her father's co-wife begins to maltreat her, and to prefer her own daughter. A magic golden fish appears in a pond and befriends Yeh-hsien. When the wicked stepmother discovers this source of comfort for her hated stepdaughter, she kills it, eats it and hides the bones 'under the dung hill'. When Yeh-hsien, all unknowing, calls to the fish the next day as is her custom, an enchanter descends from the sky and tells her where to find the bones: 'Take [them] and hide them in your room. Whatever you want, you have only to pray to them for it … ' Yeh-hsien does so, and finds that she no longer suffers from hunger or thirst or cold – the fishbones care for her. On the day of the local festival, her stepmother and stepsister order her to stay behind, but she waits till they have left, and then, in a cloak of kingfisher feathers and gold shoes, she joins them at the festival. Her sister recognizes her, and it is when Yeh-hsien realizes this and runs away that she loses one of her gold shoes. It is picked up and sold to a local warlord: 'it was an inch too small even for the one among them that had the smallest foot. He ordered all the women in his kingdom to try it on. But there was not one that it fitted. It was as light as down and made no noise even when treading on stone.'

Yeh-hsien comes forward and, taking her fishbones with her, becomes 'chief wife' in the king's household. Her stepmother and sister are stoned to death. One of the few divergences from the later – much later – European tradition occurs here: the local people are sorry for the mother and sister and dub their grave 'The Tomb of the Distressed Women'; it becomes a fertility shrine, much visited by men: 'any girl they prayed for there, they got'.

The great antiquity of this story gives the reader today a dizzy feeling; in its essential structure and its lively details 'Cinderella' has been told for over a thousand years, passed on from voice to text and back again, over and over again until it reaches the decorous drawing rooms of the Parisian *précieuses* and finds its Western canonical form in Perrault's *'Cendrillon'*. The Chinese version exhibits many features of its social context. The tiny, precious golden shoe, a treasure among country people who would have gone barefoot or worn bark or straw pattens, also reverberates with the fetishism of bound feet: the T'ang dynasty, established in the sixth century, introduced this custom to China and it marked out highborn, valuable, desirable women. The strains between women in this Chinese Cinderella's family are knotted into the structure of polygamy. In China (and elsewhere), this type of marriage has inspired a huge body of literature about female rivalry – *Raise the Red Lantern*, the recent film directed by Zhang Yimou, dramatized the continuing tragic tensions in a warlord's palace between his wives in the 1920s, as each schemes to win their master's favours and he plays one against the other for his own pleasure.

In other settings, the lost shoe likewise denotes the wearer's beauty, and brutal imagery of deformation, cultural and literal, returns: in the Grimm Brothers' tale, the sisters hack off their toes, hack off their heels to fit the slipper, and birds warn the prince:

> Turn and peep, turn and peep,
> There's blood within the shoe.
> The shoe it is too small for her,
> The true bride waits for you.

In Aelian's brief, late second-century AD tale of Rhodope, her sandal is carried off by an eagle when she is bathing, and dropped at the feet of the Pharaoh in Memphis. He instantly vows he must possess the woman this delightful object fits; he searches the whole of Egypt to make her his wife. The ancient site in Naples, dedicated to the Madonna di Piedigrotta since the fourteenth century but known in pagan times, also enshrines a cult of a virgin's foot; some Neapolitans claim possession of Mary's own slipper – and very small it is, too. The symbolic erotic significance of the shoe has been thoroughly explored by Bruno Bettelheim in his influential study of fairy tales, *The Uses of Enchantment*; the substitution of body parts effected by the imagery relates to the webbed or otherwise odd foot of the storyteller, discussed earlier. The fairy tale proposes a perfect foot from knowledge of the imperfections of feet and what they stand for; it offers a remedy in itself for the problem. As the stream restores Sheba, so the recognition brought about by love in the flow of the narrative undoes the perception of ugliness. The story advocates small feet only at its most literal, patent level of meaning; like other variations in the cycle, it promises that what is hidden and not known can be beautiful, if beheld in the right spirit.

But Cinderella's goodness changes character; even her colouring reflects canons of virtue and standards of beauty according to circumstances: in China, pottery and intelligence, in contemporary England 'long golden hair, and eye-lashes that turn[ed] up like the petals of a daisy'. Above all, however, the Chinese imagery reveals itself in the choice of animal familiar, for fish occupy an exalted place in their mythological bestiary, which is taken up in their cuisine and their gardens – ornamented with carp of great price, with goggle eyes and swirling fins.

The animal helper, who embodies the dead mother in providing for her orphaned child, constitutes a structural node in the Cinderella story, but the crea-ture changes in later European versions until she takes the form of the fairy god-mother familiar today. In the Grimms' '*Aschenputtel*' of 1812, a hazel sapling grows up on the mother's grave, and her bones transform it into a powerful wishing tree, to work her daughter's revenge and triumph (p. 200). The tree shakes down the dresses of gold and the silken slippers this Cinderella wears to the ball, and shelters the doves, who act as her protectors: her father thinks she is hiding in the dovecote perched on its branches and he chops down the tree in his rage. It is the doves who sort the peas and the lentils her stepmother scatters, and who unmask

In perhaps the oldest illustration of Cinderella, she weeps by the hearth after her stepmother has tossed lentils and peas into the cinders and ordered her to sift them. (In Das irrige Schaf, *Nuremberg, early sixteenth century.)*

the false sisters with their song. At the end, they peck out the wicked sisters' eyes in punishment. No quarter is offered here, no posthumous shrine.

In 'Rashin Coatie', the appealing and lively Scottish version, published by Andrew Lang at the turn of the century, the dead mother returns in the form of a red calf, who offers the starving child food out of her ear; the stepsister spies on her, and the calf is killed; but it continues to protect her, giving her fine clothes and satin slippers, so she can go to church like the others and meet her young prince there. Variants on the tale from all over the world give the mother's ghost some kind of consoling and magical role in her daughter's ultimate escape from pain, and it was this aspect which drew Angela Carter. In her version, called 'Ashputtle', she creates a vision of dark, archaic grief in an uncanny short tale; the mother's ghost returns in the form of one animal after another to give back life to her child.

The little cat came by. The ghost of the mother went into the cat.

'Your hair wants doing,' said the cat. 'Lie down.'

The little cat unpicked her raggy lugs with its clever paws until the burned child's hair hung down nicely, but it had been so snagged and tangled that the claws were all pulled out before it was finished.

'Comb your own hair, next time,' said the cat. 'You've taken my strength away. I can't do it again.'

The same happens with a cow who gives this Cinders milk and a bird who gives her clothes; each time, the mother takes possession of the animal and is worn out by the task, until at last Ashputtle escapes – with a lover whom her evil stepmother had wanted.

'Now I can go to sleep,' said the ghost of the mother. 'Now everything is all right.'

II

In most of the more familiar retellings today of this classic and much-loved story of female wish-fulfilment, the heroine's mother no longer plays a part. In Basile's exuberantly fanciful 'La Gatta Cenerentola' (The Cinderella Cat), the heroine Zezolla first conspires with her governess to kill her wicked stepmother: she drops the lid of a trunk on her head while she is rummaging in it to find some rags for Zezolla to wear. All goes according to plan, and the governess duly marries Zezolla's father:

But after a very short time she completely forgot the kindness [Zezolla] had done her ... and she began to push forward six daughters of her own who had been kept secret till then ... And Zezolla from one day to the next was reduced to such a state that she went from the bedroom to the kitchen, from the canopy to the hearth, from splendid silks and gold to dish-clouts, from the sceptre to the spit ...

But the dirty and neglected hearth cat, living in the cinders, will find her feet: a fairy materializes in a date tree Zezolla's father has brought back for his daughter from his travels, and she casts the spells which transform her into the richly arrayed beauty who, appearing three times at the local festival, bedazzles all, including the prince.

Basile, by omitting any mention of graves or bones, severs the narrative link between the orphan's mother and the fairy enchantress – this disjunction returns in Perrault, and in all the best-known versions circulating today. Very occasionally, the original baptismal vow a godmother makes, that she will act *in loco parentis*, provides a motive: 'Up rose a Fairy! all at once, with wings and a wand, and it was her own god-mother who promised her dying mother to love her as her own child.' But on the whole, the absent mother no longer returns. 'Once upon a time there was a girl called Cinderella. She was very unhappy as she had no one who loved her' – this is the classic opening of the modern fairy tale, repeated again and again in the available editions. None of the Disney films suggest that the heroines' mothers return to help them – not even the crowd-pleasing calculations of the recent *Beauty and the Beast* could produce a natural mother for Beauty, but only a cosy teapot-cum-housekeeper in lieu.

Yet Cinderella is a child in mourning for her mother, as her name tells us; her penitential garb is ash, dirty and low as a donkeyskin or a coat of grasses, but more particularly the sign of loss, the symbol of mortality, which the priest uses to mark the foreheads of the faithful on Ash Wednesday, saying, 'Dust thou art, and to dust thou shalt return.' Basile only half explains her name – Gatta Cenerentola – when he says that she ends up sleeping in the ashes of the hearth like a cat; Perrault, likewise, when he writes that the kinder of the two stepsisters softens her nickname from Cucendron (Cinder-bottom; Cinder-fanny) to Cendrillon. But Perrault's withdrawn obscenity does preserve the hint at ritual pollution in ancient mourning customs, without apparently understanding it. The lays and romances of medieval literature are thronged with bereaved heroes and heroines who will not wash, or cut their hair or their beard, but hug the dirt to keep close to their lost loved one, to be outcast as they are in death, to keep their own personal Lent, wearing sackcloth and ashes. The knowing Basile writes that mourning lasts as short a moment as pain in the funny bone, but Cinderella, in her rags, in her sackcloth and ashes, is a daughter who continues to grieve.

It would be very simple-minded to pin the picture of female hatred and cruelty in the Cinderella cycle and fairy tales like 'Rapunzel', 'Snow White' and 'The Sleeping Beauty' on male authors and interpreters alone. They have contributed to it and confirmed it, from Charles Perrault's wittily awful sisters (not ugly but beautiful) and terrifying cannibal ogresses (in his 'Sleeping Beauty', see below) to the Grimm Brothers and their brilliantly successful spiritual heir Walt Disney, who made the cartoon films *Snow White and the Seven Dwarfs* (1937) and *Cinderella* (1950), which have done more than any other creation to naturalize female – maternal – malignancy in the imaginations of children worldwide.

Both films concentrate with exuberant glee on the towering, taloned, raven-haired wicked stepmother; all Disney's powers of invention failed to save the princes from featureless banality and his heroines from saccharin sentimentality. Authentic power lies with the bad women, and the plump cosy fairy godmother in *Cinderella* seems no match for them. Disney's vision has affected everybody's idea of fairy tales themselves: until writers and anthologists began looking again, passive hapless heroines and vigorous wicked older women seemed generic. Disney selected certain stories and stressed certain sides to them; the wise children, the cunning little vixens, the teeming population of the stories were drastically purged. The disequilibrium between good and evil in these films has influenced contemporary perception of fairy tale, as a form where sinister and gruesome forces are magnified and prevail throughout – until the very last moment, where, *ex machina*, right and goodness overcome them.

Visual artists have continued to bring relish to the task of portraying the wicked witches and evil stepmothers of the tales: Maurice Sendak and David Hockney have created memorably warty, hook-nosed, crouchback horrors in their illustrations to Grimm. Furthermore, father figures tend to be excused responsibility, as we shall see in more detail later (Chapter Twenty-one). The tales consistently fail to ask, why did Cinderella's father marry again so quickly, so unwisely? Or, why does he allow Cinderella's mistreatment at all?

Terror of the witch, so deliberately exorcized by Perrault's urbane wit, returns in malignant force through the imagination of pantomime, film, and children's books, not in the magic person of the fairy godmother, but in the vicious power of the evil stepmother.

The fairy godmother as witch: in steeple hat and pointy shoes, she tumbles down the chimney. (Arthur Rackham, Cinderella, *London, 1919.)*

Nevertheless, the misogyny of fairy tales engages women as participants, not just targets; the antagonisms and sufferings the stories recount connect to the world of female authority as well as experience. Also, as they so frequently claim to speak in a woman's voice (the storyteller, Mother Goose), it is worth pausing to examine the weight and implications of that claim before pointing the finger exclusively at Grimm or Disney or Cruikshank. Bengt Holbek observes that 'men and women often tell the same tales in characteristically different ways', and the scholar of German fairy tales Ruth Bottigheimer has recently studied the differences in narrators' approaches. Anthropologists, too, have proceeded along lines of inquiry into the differences. Reimar Schefold, working among the Mentawaians of Indonesia, was told a story by his assisant, Tengatiti: later, he was approached by a woman, 'a respected matron called Teuraggamimanai', who related the same tale in her version – it was her favourite, heard from her mother, and she wanted to give the Dutchman the chance to hear it in her, preferred, form. Schefold, who had not been told stories by women until that point, compared the two accounts and found there were significant differences of emphasis in a turbulent story of two rebellious sisters and their suitors. The woman narrator stressed co-operation in work and alliance brought by marriage, the man lineage and the acquisition of dowry; the woman's version enhanced the sisters' activity, courage, spirit, determination, their control of their dowries and labour. In Spain, in the 1980s, the American James Taggart studied storytelling in

Estremadura, and uncovered parallels and divergences between men's and women's ways with their versions of 'Cinderella', 'Snow White', 'Cupid and Psyche', and 'Beauty and the Beast'. The differences are often obvious, and their development stands to reason, but attention needs to be drawn to them with regard to our own fairy tales, which have been all too easily perceived as immemorially traditional, unchanging, and pure. The archetypal image of the timeless old crone of course serves this camouflaging atavism.

Instances and statistics of female storytelling are not however nearly as illuminating as internal evidence in the tales themselves. This yields a doubled aspect of femaleness: on the one hand the record of female experience in certain tales, and on the other the ascription of a female point of view, through the protagonist or the narrating voice. The male scribe of the literary monument of folklore, like Straparola or Lang or even Calvino, may be transmitting women's stories, as they claim. Or, like the male tragedian in the Greek amphitheatre who wears the mask of a woman to utter the speeches of Medea or Electra, these authors and scholars may be impersonating a woman. If they are inventing, rather than acknowledging a known female source, how does this ascription contribute to the impact of the tales? Even if an actual voice of a female narrator is not emerging muffled or distorted by the male mask she wears, what meanings does the fantasy of her original voice allow to flower within the stories?

The answer is composed of many strands: most obviously, storytellers the world over claim to know their material from an eye witness; the voice of the old nurse lends reliability to the tale, stamps it as authentic, rather than the concoction of the storyteller himself. More deeply, attributing to women testimony about women's wrongs and wrongdoing gives them added value: men might be expected to find women flighty, rapacious, self-seeking, cruel and lustful, but if women say such things about themselves, then the matter is settled. What some women say against others can be usefully turned against all of them.

The ravelled sleeve of these braided strands of male and female experience and wishes and fears can never be wholly combed out. If fairy tales are mere old wives' tales because they are told by women, is then what they say necessarily false, a mere trifle, including what they say about women? Or does the lowness of the genre, assumed on account of the lowness of its authors, permit a greater degree of truth-telling, as the jester's cap protects the fool from the consequences of his frank speech? Above all, if and when women are narrating, why are the female characters so cruel and the mother so often dead at the start of the story? Why have women continued to speak at all within this body of story which defames them so profoundly? Could they be speaking to a purpose? The poet Olga Broumas, in a poem which speaks in Cinderella's voice, grieves for the part she has played in this process:

> ... I am a woman in a state of siege,
> alone
>
> as one piece of laundry, strung on a windy clothesline a
> mile long. A woman co-opted by promises: the lure
> of a job, the ruse of a choice, a woman forced
> to bear witness, falsely
> against my kind ...

Fairy tales like 'Cinderella' bear witness against women. But there are possible reasons for the evidence they bring, be it true or false (and it is both), which mitigate the wrongs they describe, not entirely, but in part.

The absence of the mother from the tale is often declared at the start, without explanation, as if none were required; Beauty appears before us, in the opening paragraph of the earliest written version of 'Beauty and the Beast' with that title, in 1740 (see p. 290), as a daughter to her father, a sister to her six elders, a biblical seventh child, the cadette, the favourite: nothing is spoken about her father's wife. Later, it will turn out that Beauty is a foundling, and was left by the fairies, after her fairy mother was disgraced by union with a mortal – not the father Beauty knows, but another, higher in rank, more powerful.

This is the kind of romancing that earned fairy tale the scorn of the literati, both in the past and today. Fairy tales play to the child's hankering after nobler, richer, altogether better origins, the fantasy of being a prince or a princess in disguise, the Freudian 'family romance'. But this type of fantasy can also comfort bereaved children, who, however irrationally, feel themselves abandoned by their dead mothers, and even guilty for their disappearance. One English Cinderella story, called 'Tattercoats', perceptively focusses on this type of grief: the king figure mistreats his granddaughter 'because at her birth, his favourite daughter died'. In this case, her ragged, starving, neglected state reflects his excess of mourning and her anguished guilt, and neither of them can be healed of the wound – the story has an unhappy ending.

Paradoxically, the best possible intentions can also contribute to the absence of mothers from the tales. In the case of 'Schneewittchen' (Snow White), for instance, the Grimms altered the earlier versions they had taken down in which Snow White's own mother suffered murderous jealousy of her and persecuted her. The 1819 edition is the first to introduce a stepmother in her place; the manuscript and the editions of 1810 and 1812 place Snow White's natural mother at the pivot of the violent plot. But it was altered so that a mother should not be seen to torment a daughter. This is still the case in a version collected in the Armenian community in Detroit this century: having pursued her daughter with murderous rage, this mother finally dies of surprise when she hears from the moon that her daughter is still living and is more beautiful than her.

The Grimm Brothers worked on the *Kinder- und Hausmärchen* in draft after draft after the first edition of 1812, Wilhelm in particular infusing the new editions with his Christian fervour, emboldening the moral strokes of the plot, meting out penalties to the wicked and rewards to the just, to conform with prevailing Christian and social values. They also softened the harshness – especially in family dramas. They could not make it disappear altogether, but in 'Hansel and Gretel', for example, they added the father's miserable reluctance to an earlier version in which both parents had proposed the abandonment of their children, and turned the mother into a wicked stepmother. On the whole, they tended towards sparing the father's villainy, and substituting another wife for the natural mother, who had figured as the villain in the versions they had been told: they

Mothers, especially wicked stepmothers, abandon their children to the wolves. (The Babes in the Wood, *tableau, Madame Tussaud's, London, 1959.*)

felt obliged to deal less harshly with mothers than the female storytellers whose material they were setting down.

The disappearance here of the original mothers forms a response to the harshness of the material: in their romantic idealism, the Grimms literally could not bear a maternal presence to be equivocal, or dangerous, and preferred to banish her altogether. For them, the bad mother had to disappear in order for the ideal to survive and allow Mother to flourish as symbol of the eternal feminine, the motherland, and the family itself as the highest social desideratum.

Bruno Bettelheim has analysed this manoeuvre, using a Freudian principle of splitting, in *The Uses of Enchantment*. According to his analysis, the wicked stepmother acts as the Janus face of the good mother, who can thus be saved and cherished in fantasy and memory, split from the bad mother:

> While all young children sometimes need to split the image of their parent into its benevolent and threatening aspects to feel fully sheltered by the first, most cannot do it as cleverly and consciously as this girl [a case history] did. Most children cannot find their own solution to the impasse of Mother suddenly changing into 'a look-alike impostor'. Fairytales, which contain good fairies who suddenly appear and help the child find happiness despite this 'impostor' or 'stepmother', permit the child not to be destroyed by this 'impostor' ... These fantasies are helpful; they permit the child to feel really angry at the Martian pretender or the 'false parent' without guilt ... So the typical fairytale splitting of the mother into a good (usually dead) mother and an evil stepmother serves the child well. It is not only a means of preserving an internal all-good mother when the real mother is not all-good, but it also permits anger at this bad 'stepmother' without endangering the goodwill of the true mother who is viewed as a different person... The fantasy of the wicked stepmother not only preserves the good mother intact, it also prevents having to feel guilty about one's angry thoughts and wishes about her – a guilt which would seriously interfere with the good relation to Mother.

This theory is neat, satisfying and, as a convincing emotional stratagem, strikes home. It has consequently proved extremely persuasive: paediatricians have restored harsh fairy tales including the Grimms' to children's bookshelves, and endorsed the therapeutic powers of fictional cruelty and horror. The bad mother has become an inevitable, even required ingredient in fantasy, and hatred of her a legitimate, applauded stratagem of psychic survival. Bettelheim's theory has contributed to the continuing absence of good mothers from fairy tales in all kinds of media, and to a dangerous degree which itself mirrors current prejudices and reinforces them. His argument, and its tremendous diffusion and widespread acceptance, have effaced from memory the historical reasons for women's cruelty within the home and have made such behaviour seem natural, even intrinsic to the mother–child relationship. It has even helped to ratify the expectation of strife as healthy and the resulting hatred as therapeutic.

This archetypal approach leeches history out of fairy tale. Fairy or wonder tales, however farfetched the incidents they include, or fantastic the enchantments they concoct, take on the colour of the actual circumstances in which they are or were told. While certain structural elements remain, variant versions of the same story often reveal the particular conditions of the society which told it and retold it in this form. The absent mother can be read literally as exactly that: a feature of the family before our modern era, when death in childbirth was the most common cause of female mortality, and surviving orphans would find themselves brought up by their mother's successor (p. 262).

The chronicles of the Anglo-Saxon and Merovingian dynasties, before the establishment of primogeniture, are bespattered with the blood of possible heirs, done away with by consorts ambitious for their own progeny – the true wicked stepmothers of history, who become embedded in stories as eternal truths. Moreover, children whose fathers had died often stayed in the paternal house, to be raised by their grandparents or uncles and their wives. Their mothers were made to return to their natal homes, and to forge another, advantageous alliance for their own parents' future. Widows remarried less frequently than widowers. For example, in Tuscany in the fifteenth century almost all men widowed under the age of sixty took another wife and started another family. In France, 80 per cent of widowers remarried within the year in the seventeenth and eighteenth centuries. When a second wife entered the house, she often found herself and her children in competition – often for scarce resources – with the surviving offspring of the earlier marriage, who may well have appeared to threaten her own children's place in their father's affection too.

This antipathy seethes in the plots of many 'Cinderellas', sometimes offering an overt critique of social custom. Rossini's Cinderella opera, *La Cenerentola*, shows worldly-wise indignation at his heroine's plight – in her case, at the hands of her stepfather, Don Magnifico, who plots to make himself rich by marrying off his two other daughters, ignoring Cinderella. Tremendous buffoon he might be, but he treacherously pronounces Cinderella dead when he thinks it will help advance his own interests. And when she protests, he threatens her with violence. Dowries are the issue here, as they were in Italy in Rossini's time; sisters compete for the larger share and Don Magnifico does not want to cut his wherewithal three ways. As it was gradually amassed, such *corredo* (treasure) was stored in *cassoni*, which were often decorated with pictures of just such stories as 'Cinderella'.

The enmity of stepmothers towards children of earlier unions marks chronicles and stories from all over the world, from the ancient world to the present day; they exhibit the different strains and knots in different types of kinship systems and households, arising from patrilineage, dotal obligations, female exogamy, polygamy. One tale from Dahomey, written down in 1958, tells how a dead mother manages, from beyond the grave, to kill a wicked stepmother. The conclusion contains a threat and a boast, and conveys the full pathetic vulnerability of a motherless child far beyond polygamous households themselves:

> If a man has two wives and one dies leaving a child, you give that child to the second wife, and the second wife must look after the dead woman's child better than after her own children. And this is why one never mistreats orphans. For once you mistreat them, you die. You die the same day. You are not even sick. I know that myself, I am an orphan.

This story invokes the ghost of the dead mother as a tutelary spirit in the manner of the neglected versions of 'Cinderella'. But it also provides a precious and poignant clue to the function of stories for the narrator, not only for the audience, which can help to decipher the meanings of the most common fairy tales in which women are vilified. For the orphan from Dahomey is using the tale for his or her own protection; s/he is threatening with it any mother who maltreats a stepchild.

The underlying cautionary message of fairy tales like 'Cinderella' – 'You see what happens if you … ' – is almost always taken from the protagonist's point of view, because the prevalent view has seen fairy tales as unauthored and unanchored in specific circumstances. But another harvest of meanings can be gathered if the stories are analysed from the teller's vantage.

Psychoanalytical and historical interpreters of fairy tale usually enter stories like 'Cinderella', 'Snow White', or 'Beauty and the Beast' from the point of view of the protagonist, the orphaned daughter who has lost her real mother and is tormented by her stepmother, or her sisters, sometimes her stepsisters; the interpreters assume that the reader or listener naturally identifies with the heroine. Indeed, this is commonly the case. But that perception sometimes also assumes that because the narrator makes common cause with the protagonist, the narrator identifies with her too.

Fairy tales are not told in the first person of the protagonist, and though Cinderella or Snow White engages our first attention as well as the narrator's, the voice of the storyteller may be issuing elsewhere. Imagine the characteristic scene, the child listening to an older person telling this story, and the absent mother materializes in the person of the narrator herself. John Berger, the art critic and novelist, has observed :

> If you remember listening to stories as a child, you will remember the pleasure of hearing a story repeated many times, and you will remember that while you were listening you became three people. There is an incredible fusion: you became the story-teller, the protagonist and you remember yourself listening to the story...

Fusion perhaps does not quite convey the simultaneous occupation of different positions in relation to the tale, which a listener (or reader) can experience – including that of the storyteller. The audience is invited to take her part – or his – as well as identify with the mishaps and reversals in the protagonist's life.

This angle of perception can yield a different set of meanings; if the storyteller speaks as a real 'mother' herself – even if her mouthpiece, on the page, is a man, like Perrault or the Grimms – what sort of a mother is she? If we read the famous stories of child abandonment and suffering and subsequent salvation from the point of view of the putative teller, not the solicited audience of the child, we can cast a new light on the material and its bitter, internecine struggles between women.

If the storyteller is an old woman, the old wife of the old wives' tale, a nurse or a governess, she may be offering herself as a surrogate to the vanished mother in the story. Within the stories themselves, the narrator frequently accedes symbolically to the story in the person of the fairy godmother. Mother Goose enters the story to work wonders on behalf of her brood. Good fairies are frequently disguised as hideous and ragged crones in order to test the heroine's kindness, as in Perrault's 'Les Fées' (The Fairies), Marie-Jeanne L'Héritier's 'The Enchantments of Eloquence', some versions of 'Cinderella' (Pl. 1), and the Grimms' 'Frau Holle' (Mother Holle). In a single blast, the evil-tongued sister of L'Héritier's story calls the fairy in disguise 'une vieille folle' (an old fool), 'vermine de villageois' (village vermin), and connects her with procuresses and animals, particularly bitches – all

The fairy godmother, disguised as a blind beggar, prepares to change the rat, the mice and the pumpkin. (Chapbook, Cinderella, *London, c. 1820.)*

descriptions that were applied to the storyteller herself by fairy tale's detractors. Even when the fairy godmother is described in less disparaging terms, the perception of sympathy between storyteller and fairy need not be set aside; the claim reflects the wish-fulfilment of the storyteller herself as understood by her audience and disseminated through the printed versions of the tales: in 'Donkeyskin', the fairy helps the heroine to overcome the dangers her foolish/wicked mother has landed her in by her deathbed demand.

Illustrators unconsciously grasped the affinity between the teller who knows from the beginning the heroine's hidden virtue and the fairy godmother who brings about her happy recognition, and they disclosed it in their illustrations, even when little in the text openly proclaimed the identity, picturing the fairy godmother as bent, raddled, bespectacled and lame, the mirror image of the witchy storyteller who figured on the cover or the frontispiece (above). In George Cruikshank's original drawings for 'Cinderella', the fairy godmother is herself transformed and revealed to be a beautiful enchantress: the heroine's recognition reflected in her own.

If the narrator/good fairy is bidding to replace the mother whose death she announces in the story, if she is offering herself as the benevolent wonder-worker in the lives of the story's protagonists, she may be reproducing within the tale another historical circumstance in the lives of women beside the high rate of death in childbirth or the enforced abandonment of children on widowhood: she may be recording, in concealed form, the antagonism between mothers and the women their sons marry, between daughters-in-law and their husbands' mothers. The unhappy families of fairy tale typically suffer before a marriage takes place which rescues the heroine; but her situation was itself brought about by unions of one kind or another, so that when critics reproach fairy tale for the glib promise of its traditional ending – 'And they all lived happily ever after' – they overlook the knowledge of misery within marriage that the preceding story reveals in its every line. The conclusion of fairy tales works a charm against despair, the last spell the narrating fairy godmother casts for change in her subjects and her hearers' destinies.

The stories concentrate on unions made by law, on the reshaping of families from the biological order to the social: on mothers and sisters bestowed by legal arrangement, as well as the husbands. The plots characteristically strive to align such social fiats with the inclinations of the heart. In many variations on 'Beauty and the Beast' and 'Donkeyskin', the enemies of love are patriarchs; but in many fairy tales the tyrants are women and they struggle against their often younger rivals to retain the security that their husbands or their fathers afford them.

CHAPTER 14

Wicked Stepmothers: The Sleeping Beauty

This is the world we wanted.
All who would have seen us dead
are dead. I hear the witch's cry
Break in the moonlight through a sheet
of sugar: God rewards.
Her tongue shrivels into gas ...

Louise Glück

The word in French for stepmother is the same as the word for mother-in-law – *belle-mère*. Latin, Greek, Italian, German, have distinct words for the two relations, and both feature in their romances and fairy tales. In English usage, 'mother-in-law' meant stepmother until the mid-nineteenth century, while the term 'daughter-in-law' was used for stepdaughters as well. Although the term 'stepmother' was not used, it seems, for a husband's mother, there was clearly some confusion. The *Oxford English Dictionary* gives examples occurring from

Venus was the first – and maybe the worst – of tyrant mothers-in-law, and she had Psyche beaten for daring to sleep with her son. (The Master of the Die after Michel Coxie, c. 1530.)

Saint Bridget's visions (translated in 1516) to Thackeray, who, as late as 1848 in *Vanity Fair*, is still using the word in the sense of stepmother.

'Mother-in-law' is of course the *mot juste* for a stepmother: the new wife becomes the mother of the former wife's children by law, not by nature. It is still the custom for orphaned stepchildren to call the new wife of their father by whatever name they called their mothers, and in England today it is quite common for daughters-in-law to call their husband's mother Mum, or whatever diminutive is used in his family.

The mother who persecutes heroines like Cinderella or Snow White may conceal beneath her cruel features another familiar kind of adoptive mother, not the stepmother but the mother-in-law, and the time of ordeal through which the fairytale heroine passes may not represent the liminal interval between childhood and maturity, but another, more socially constituted proving ground or threshold: the beginning of marriage.

The absent mother may not have died in fact, though many did; she may have died symbolically, according to the laws of matrimony that substitute the biological mother in a young woman's life with another. Taking the story from one vantage point, and imagining that the storyteller is remembering her own life, and is speaking as a daughter-in-law, we can hear her venting all her antagonism against the older woman who as it were bewitched her and her potential allies, including the man she married: stories of the Beauty and the Beast group conjure a spouse to whom the young woman has been sacrificed at her father's wish, and then relate how an old and wicked fairy, usually with some kind of family hold on him – in Villeneuve's version, she is his foster mother and his mother's best friend – has cast the spell on him that makes him hideous and stupid, and unable to express his love to his bride until that spell is broken.

The weddings of fairy tale bring the traditional narratives to a satisfying open ending which allows the possibility of hope; but the story structure masks the fact that many stories picture the conditions of marriage during the course of their telling. It is clearly a late, conventional moral reflex on the part of Mother Goose to make *marriage* the issue between Beauty and the Beast: Beauty is living alone with the Beast from the moment she agrees to save her father by leaving home. The issue is not sex, but love, and the pledging of lifelong mutual attachment. Similarly, the Sleeping Beauty's enchanted sleep or Rapunzel's magic imprisonment may not represent the slow incubation of selfhood, of consciousness of the Other and eventual sexual fulfilment. Rather, it may stand for the dark time that can follow the first encounter between the older woman and her new daughter-in-law, the period when the young woman can do nothing, take charge of nothing, but suffer the sorcery and the authority – and perhaps the hostility – of the woman whose house she has entered, whose daughter she has become.

Perrault's '*La Belle au bois dormant*' (Sleeping Beauty) resembles, as many of his fairy tales do, a story in Giambattista Basile's collection of sixty years before, and both of them ring changes on a tale which appears in a vast Arthurian prose romance of the fourteenth century, *Perceforest*. *Perceforest* was first printed in 1528 and appeared in Italian as soon as three years later; it may have been known to Basile in this version. With regard to the familial conflicts represented in fairy tales, Basile and Perrault diverge, and are in turn reinterpreted by later retellings of 'Sleeping Beauty'; the changes are almost funny, they are so revealing of social prejudices and expectations.

In Basile, the saviour hero is already married to someone else at the start of the story; out hunting, he comes upon the sleeping beauty Talia, who has pricked her finger on a sliver of flax. When she will not wake up, however much he shouts, he 'plucked from her the fruits of love' (as Basile puts it), fathering two children on her in the act, twins called Sole and Luna. One of the babies, trying to nurse on the body of his comatose mother, sucks her finger instead of her breast, and so draws out the splinter of flax that has caused her to fall into her enchanted sleep. She wakes. The king, who had meanwhile forgotten about his little adventure, finds himself a year later riding in the same woods and it comes back to mind; he discovers his second family awake and flourishing. His wife suspects him, and she takes the steps that prefigure the manoeuvres of other ogresses, like Snow White's (step)mother: by a ruse, she summons the twins to court, then orders the cook 'to butcher them and turn them into various delicacies and sauces to give them to their vile father'. The cook, like the huntsman in 'Snow White', is too soft-hearted to kill the twins, and picks two goat's kids instead, which he serves 'in a hundred different dishes'; the king tucks in, exclaiming all the while with relish at the deliciousness of it all, while the queen grimly comments, 'Eat up, you're eating what's your very own.' To which he responds, in anger, 'I know very well I'm eating what's my own, because you have brought nothing to this house.' This taunt on the childlessness of their union does not excite Basile's pity for her; and is not intended to stir ours.

The queen is a Medea, a Lady Macbeth, a murderous and unnatural, unsexed anomaly, who then tricks Talia into coming to court to visit her, and berates her furiously, and will not listen when Talia protests she was fast asleep throughout the escapade and therefore blameless. A huge pyre is prepared for Talia's burning, but the queen, at her rival's entreaties, allows her to take off her clothes before-hand – partly, says Basile sourly, because she coveted her fine embroideries and jewels. Like Bluebeard's wife, Talia screams as she plays for time, taking off each garment one by one, until at the very last moment, as she is being dragged across to the cauldron now boiling on the fire, the king at last answers her yells for help. He asks for his children; his wife tells him that, like Titus Andronicus, he has eaten them. He instantly orders that she be thrown into the flames instead, along with her accomplices. But the cook pleads for his life, when it comes to his turn to die, by revealing the children he saved. The children, found again, are reunited with their father, who promotes the cook to gentleman of the bedchamber and marries Talia.

Basile's cheerful cynicism and often scabrous immoralism continues the tradi-tion of Boccaccio; though so much closer to Perrault in time, Basile is far distant from him in spirit. In Perrault's version of 'The Sleeping Beauty', the vengeful wife, who is herself destroyed by the fire she prepared for her rival, changes into the adventurous prince's mother, who, says Perrault baldly, 'était de race Ogresse' (was of the Ogre race) and, according to the tendency of ogres, liked eating the fresh meat of little children. The story follows the lines of Basile's version except that the queen mother specifies to the cook that she wants little Aurora dished up with a particular gourmet sauce – 'la sauce Robert'. A few days later, it is the little boy's turn. But in both cases, the tender-hearted cook has switched them, for a lamb and a kid respectively. The queen then expresses a desire to eat their mother, her daughter-in-law, as well. The once sleeping Beauty agrees meekly to her own death, as she imagines her children have preceded her. Again, the cook spares her, and serves a hind in her place; but a few days later the queen overhears one of the children crying in her hiding place, and, furious that they have escaped her, she orders a cauldron filled with toads and vipers and eels and snakes for her daughter-in-law, the babies, the steward and his wife and their servant into the bargain. The king arrives, in the nick of time, and his mother, enraged at being baulked, throws herself headfirst into the pot and 'was immediately devoured by the horrible creatures she had had put into it'. (As if the boiling water were not sufficient to kill her.) Perrault concludes, with his customary dryness: 'The king did not fail to be cross about it: she was his mother; but he soon consoled himself with his beautiful wife and children'.

Basile told of adultery; in his harsh tale, the first wife, in her infertility, commits a crime against the family. Perrault adapted the tale to speak of a more palatable crime: cannibalism seemed then much less scandalous than rape, adultery and bigamy, and more suited to the childish fantasy of the invoked audience. But Perrault's modified, still gruesome coda to the fairy tale no longer appears, after the eighteenth century, in children's editions. The story follows instead the Grimms' more romantic and innocuous account, '*Dornröschen*', (Little Briar Rose), and ends with the prince's famous saving kiss that wakes the sleeping beauty and leads to their wedding. Sometimes, for propriety's sake, the kiss is left out, too. The macabre excesses of Basile and Perrault were dismaying to the same Victorian editors who, aiming at children, also dropped Perrault's '*Peau d'Ane*'. The story's leading character, the terrible queen, migrated instead into the pages of the Grimms' 'Snow White' – as a wicked stepmother. It took Disney's film to make her face a familiar terror – her double face, for she appears twice over as an unsexed woman, endangering and destabilizing due order. First as the raven-haired queen ('Mirror, mirror on the wall … ') and then disguised as the old beggarwoman who gives Snow White the apple which chokes her. Basile's villain was a jealous wife, Perrault's a jealous mother-in-law; in our times, bad women come in the form of (step)mothers.

The doubling of negative female power has become very interesting to modern interpreters of fairy tales: in the recent English National Opera production of *Hansel and Gretel*, the opera by Engelbert Humperdinck, the witch doubled the part of the mother, following a Bettelheimian reading which envisaged the children's point of view and identified the mother who could abandon them with their persecutor in the woods.

Critics of both approaches – the Victorians' bowdlerizations, the twentieth century's appetite for maternal violence – are placed in a quandary by the matter of fairy tale when children are the presumed audience. The space and time of marriage and its problems – however farfetched – which were of crucial concern to the earlier, adult or mixed circle of listeners, have been pushed out of the narrative and replaced by courtship – the time before the wedding – as the generic theme of fairy tale.

Persinette, the heroine of a fairy tale of 1697 by Charlotte-Rose de La Force, is held captive in the tower by an old witch to whom she has been handed over, as in the Grimms' later version, the more famous 'Rapunzel'. (Persinette is called after the parsley from the witch's garden which her mother craves; Rapunzel after the rampion, another savoury herb, which her mother also desires so much that she promises the witch her baby in exchange.) Is Little Parsley-flower or Little

Rampion the victim of a rapacious and cruel foster mother, who wants to keep her for herself, or has the old woman been allowed to take the daughter away from her real mother, install her in her own house to do her bidding, and then rob her of her freedom and denied her lover access to her? This is what the story relates, and such a reading tallies with common experience in medieval and early modern society, when a daughter-in-law worked under the direction of her husband's mother, to whom she had been handed over often by family arrangement in tender youth, even childhood. The historian Janet Nelson gives a good Merovingian example, from the *Vita* of Rusticula: as a child, Rusticula was taken by her promised husband to his natal household, and brought up by his mother. This 'private arrangement' was effectively wardship, and underlined Rusticula's legal incapacity. In Shakespeare's *King John*, the conflict between France and England is patched up by bestowing Blanch on the Dauphin, but on the wedding day itself, the peace is shattered and the bride left centre stage, between her new husband, her father, her uncle the king and their competing claims on her allegiance. She cries out:

> The sun's o'ercast with blood; fair day, adieu!
> Which is the side that I must go withal?
> I am with both …
> They whirl asunder and dismember me …
> Whoever wins, on that side shall I lose …

Shakespeare's audience would have understood her feelings, and not only against a medieval backdrop. At the level of less exalted households, the conflicts in Basile's early collection of Italian fairy tales arise from the same divided loyalties; his stories seethe with married women's domestic turbulence.

The wicked stepmother who has become the stock figure of fairy tale makes her first literary appearance as a mother-in-law, in 'Cupid and Psyche' by Apuleius' , where Cupid's mother, the goddess Venus, orders her son to destroy Psyche, her rival in beauty. But instead Cupid falls in love with her. Though Apuleius does not say so in so many words, Cupid's mother's antagonism inspires his furtive behaviour: her envy of Psyche, his foreknowledge of her furious disapproval of his relations with her, require the clandestine, unseen lovemaking: his mother turns him into a mystery presence, which Psyche, goaded by her sisters, then suspects of monstrous, beastlike form. When Venus does discover the truth about their 'marriage', she blazes with fury, against Psyche for her unworthiness, against her son for his choice. The rhetoric is comic, the accents all too familiar:

> She found Cupid lying ill in bed … As she entered she bawled out at the top of her voice: 'Now is this decent behaviour? … A fine credit you are to your divine family … You trample your mother's orders underfoot … you have the impudence to sleep with the girl … at your age, you lecherous little beast! I suppose you thought I'd be delighted to have her for a daughter-in-law, eh?'

Venus pursues Psyche with her vengeance and, when the girl is eventually brought before her, she shrieks at her with hysterical rage, and orders the cruellest punishments: 'she flew at poor Psyche, tore her clothes to shreds, pulled out handfuls of her hair, then grabbed her by the shoulders and shook her until she nearly shook her head off …' (p. 218). She then sets her various impossible tasks – to sort lentils and millet wheat, barley, beans, poppy and vetch seeds, just as the wicked stepmother in medieval retellings and, later in Grimm, orders Aschenputtel as a condition of going to the ball (p. 204). And just as doves come to Aschenputtel's rescue, and peck the grain and seed into separate piles, much to the stepmother's astonishment, so Venus is horrified when she finds that Psyche has also managed the tasks.

Apuleius is jocular, trifling, wears his dislike of the vanity, snobbery and ruthlessness of Venus with a flourish, though at the concluding wedding feast, he relents enough to show the goddess relenting too: 'The music was so sweet that Venus came forward and performed a lively step-dance in time to it.'

In the fifteenth century, before the first extant variations on the tale were written down as fairy stories, 'Cupid and Psyche' was chosen by *cassone* painters as a fitting tale for the trousseau chests brides took to their new home; alongside other stories of wronged daughters and difficult unions, like the sufferings of Patient Griselda, the false witness of Potiphar's wife, or Paris' abduction of Helen of Troy, Psyche's troubles and eventual happiness could suitably furnish the room of a bride and help her keep in mind the pitfalls and the vindication of her predecessors in wedlock. Francesco di Giorgio (on a *cassone* panel in the Berenson Collection at I Tatti) chose the scene where Venus' vicious sidekick is dragging Psyche by her hair into the goddess's presence. 'Cinderella', 'Beauty and the Beast', 'Snow White' have directly inherited features from the plot of Apuleius' romance, as we have seen – Psyche's wicked sisters, the enchanted bounty in her mysterious husband's palace, and the prohibitions that hedge about her knowledge of his true nature. At a deeper level, they have also inherited the stories'

The steep stair, the plunging angle, the raked shadows, those eyebrows, that raven hair: the stepmother from Hollywood stalks her prey. (Walt Disney, Cinderella, © The Walt Disney Company.)

function, to tell the bride the worst, and shore her up in her marriage.

The more one knows fairy tales the less fantastical they appear; they can be vehicles of the grimmest realism, expressing hope against all the odds with gritted teeth. Like 'pardon tales', written to the king to win a reprieve from sentence of death, fairy tales sue for mercy.

The wicked stepmother makes a savage appearance as a mother-in-law in the *Vita* of Saint Godelive, patron saint of Bruges, a historical figure who, according to a certain Drogo, the priestly author of her *Vita*, was born around 1050 and married to the nobleman Berthulphe de Ghistelles. Hagiography and fairy tale are often intertwined, and Godelive's story develops along familiar lines. It relates how she gave away food and goods to the poor against her mean husband's wishes and behind his back, and how angels saved her from detection, replacing the supplies she had taken. Berthulphe's mother was furious at the match, and Berthulphe himself neglected his wife by his frequent absences and maltreated her when they were together, until finally mother and son conspired to murder her: she was held head down in a pond and throttled by their servants. She was then put back to bed to make out she had died in her sleep. Berthulphe remarried, but he later repented, made the pilgrimage to Jerusalem, and returned to become a monk. Godelive was canonized in 1084, very soon after her death, for miraculous cures had taken place: the blindness of one of her successor's children was suddenly lifted, and this was attributed to Godelive's intercession – a kind stepmother in this case working wonders beyond the grave and making amends for the wickedness of the rival mother in the story.

In one of Straparola's tales, yet another malignant mother-in-law substitutes three snapping curs in the childbed of her daughter-in-law for the beautiful triplets, with gold stars on their foreheads, to whom she has given birth. She orders their death, by drowning, and publicizes the disgrace of her hated daughter-in-law and her monstrous litter. Her plan is foiled, of course, though only after much suffering, and she herself is burned to death on a huge pyre built for her by her son. This is only one of dozens of fairy tales and other fictions which belong in the rich cycle of accused queens.

When a blind woman storyteller gave her account of the story set down by the Grimms as 'Das Mädchen ohne Hände' (The Maiden without Hands), at the turn of the century in Scandinavia, she included a poisoned letter written by the hapless heroine's mother-in-law denouncing her, in the usual fairytale terms, for giving birth to a dog; interestingly enough, a male storyteller at the same time attributed this wickedness to the Devil himself. The recent musical by Stephen Sondheim and James Lapine, *Into the Woods* (1988), assumes the possessiveness of a perverted mother-love between witch and captive in the Rapunzel story; a more historically based view would see that the old woman's desire for the baby girl corresponds to material needs for helping hands at home, and reflects the arranged transfer of girls to other families as prospective wives, or surrogate domestic servants. Her furious intervention between the girl and her suitor would then relate the conflicting, simultaneous fears of redundancy growing in a widowed woman whose son's marriage has made her insecure in what used to be her home, under her control. The vilification of older women in such interpretations belongs in a long tradition, as discussed in Chapters Two and Three; they bring to mind the medieval *fabliau*, in which a son-in-law performs a mock 'nutting' and pulls out from the body of his mother-in-law the bull's testicles which have made her so unfeminine.

Fairy stories relate the tensions between competitors for a young man's allegiance; they reflect the difficulty of women making common cause within existing matrimonial arrangements.

II

Hatred of the older woman, and intergenerational strife, may arise not only from rivalry, but from guilt, too, about the weak and the dependent. The portrait of the tyrant mother-in-law or stepmother may conceal her own vulnerability, may offer an excuse for her maltreatment.

Reversing the angle of approach, and coming at the matter of fairy stories from another vantage point, imagining that the teller speaks instead as an older woman, as herself a grandmother or a mother-in-law, we can then discover in the tales the

Authority at home inspires dreams of revenge: the old woman who plans to cook the children is drowned just in time. (David Hockney,' Fundevogel', Six Fairy Tales from the Brothers Grimm, London, 1970.)

fear she feels, the animus she harbours against her daughter-in-law or daughters-in-law: when the mother disappears, she may have been conjured away by the narrator herself, who despatches her child listeners' natural parent, replaces her with a monster, and then produces herself within the pages of the story, as if by enchantment, often in many different guises as a wonder-worker on their behalf, the good old fairy, the fairy godmother. Thus the older generation speaks to the younger in the fairy tale, prunes out the middle branch on the family tree as rotten or irrelevant, and thereby lays claim to the devotion, loyalty and obedience of the young over their mothers' heads. This structure underlies the classic Cinderella story; this ancient tussle has contributed to the misogyny in such tales.

A mother-in-law had good reason to fear her son's wife, when she often had to strive to maintain her position and assert her continuing rights to a livelihood in the patrilineal household. If she was widowed, her vulnerability became more acute. Christiane Klapisch-Zuber, the historian, uses the chilly phrase 'passing guests' when she describes the condition of wives in the households, both symbolic and geographic, which they had married into in fifteenth-century Florence.

The divergent claims on women of their paternal, natal home on the one hand and their later, marital households on the other would begin when they first left their parents and continue throughout their lives. These conflicting demands could greatly exacerbate women's insecurity, kindling much misery and hatred in consequence. Although the patterns of inheritance and household obviously vary – and in highly complex ways – at different times and in different places, the burden of evidence points to the relation between mothers-in-law and daughters-in-law as the acute lesion in the social body ('*la Tormenta*' is the name for mother-in-law in Spanish comedy). English wills of the seventeenth century show that widowed parents were customarily cared for in the household of their eldest child: the continuing right to shelter, to a place by the family hearth, to bed and board, was granted and observed. However, as *King Lear* reveals, even in the case of a powerful king the exercise of such a right could meet ferocious resistance and reprisals. Just as Cordelia is a fairytale heroine, a wronged youngest child, a forerunner of Cinderella, so Goneril and Regan are the wicked witches, ugly sisters; the unnatural women whom fairy tales indict.

But women lived longer than men, then as now, and there were more old female dependants needing bed and board, if not the hundred knights King Lear demands. In Florence, some widows who wished to return to the family of their birth, as they had a right to do, were forced to bring suits against their children in the marital household in order to wrest back the dowry which was also theirs by right and necessary to their survival outside. The Court of Chancery, established in England in the mid-fifteenth century, was set up to deal with abuses of widows' inheritance by heirs. Stepsons featured prominently among those who flouted their legal obligations. Chancery's attempts made matters worse, and widows' rights of inheritance were only effectively smoothed out by the Dower Act of 1833. The legal complexities are very great indeed, but in this respect England conformed more to Catholic, continental Europe than to another Protestant country, Holland, which offered unmarried and widowed women much greater independence.

Demographic change has affected the condition of old people. In a census taken in the small community of Eguilles, near Aix, in Provence, in 1741–70, and carefully analysed by David Troyansky in his book *Old Age in the Old Régime*, the figures show that many more widows survived and lived with their children – married and unmarried – than widowers, that half the marriage contracts notarized stipulated co-residence with the parents on one side or the other, and that the widowed mother of the husband – the mother-in-law in relation to the incoming wife – lived with her son and his wife in 25 per cent of cases. By contrast, the wife's parents lived with a married daughter only in 5 per cent of unions, the wife's mother on her own lived with the couple only in 16.7 per cent of the marriages. Thus a widowed woman had to get along with her daughter-in-law, and vice versa, rather more commonly than with her own daughter. Troyansky sums up: 'In the day-to-day fact of co-residence, the husband's family took precedence … Of 111 cases of co-residence [in the sample], 100, or 90 per cent, lived with the husband's parents and only 11 families (10 per cent) lived with the wife's [parents].' Almost a decade passed before the younger couple could expect to live on their own: the average length of time between their marriage and the death of (his) parents living with them was 9.8 years.

This interval could represent exactly that time of trial, of forged alliances, of varied struggles, which many fairy tales told by women across the generations record in code.

In France, after the Revolution, a widow did not retain her keys to the household or to the family's business. Thus dispossessed by her husband's death, she was often only grudgingly provided for by his legatees; co-residence declined as the population moved to the cities to work, and destitute and homeless old women became a feature of nineteenth-century society. At the same time, the rights of grandparents began to be considered: in 1867, for instance, an important law was passed in France allowing the mother's parents to visit children who had remained in their father's custody after a divorce. This sign that the grandparents' role in a child's upbringing was being recognized and valued coincides exactly with the publication of dozens of editions of *contes* in which an old woman is telling children tales by a fireside, both in France and England. Through the medium of children's literature, the old were shown to be entitled to continuing respect in society and a place in the family, and the fairy tales in which they play a part did not attempt to conceal the bitter conflicts within the romance of marriage that fairy tale spins.

Like gossip, fairy tales defame their objects in their attempt to establish – and extend – the speaker's influence.

III

The kind of woman who threatens society by her singleness and her dependency was not always a clinging mother, or a desperate or abusive widow. She could be a spinster, an unmarried mother, an old nurse or servant in a household – any woman who was unattached and ageing was vulnerable. In the centuries when the image of Mother Goose was being disseminated through numerous editions of fairytale collections, 'there was,' writes the historian Michelle Perrot, 'in a radical sense, no place for female solitude in the conceptual framework of the time'. She quotes Michelet: 'The woman who has neither home nor protection dies.' Yet there were many such, and they had to survive, however precariously. The census of 1851 in France showed that 12 per cent of women over fifty had never married, and 34 per cent were single; this ratio remained the same nearly fifty years later. The parish churches of England reveal, in the pious record of donations made to the 'oldest poor widows or single women living in the [said] ward', the chronic indigence of this social group in the same era: in 1824, in St Nicholas's church, King's Lynn, a bequest of £60 was made by Francis Boyce for the distribution of 4d. loaves on certain feast days to these needy women.

The old wives who spin their tales are almost always represented as unattached: spinsters, or widows. Mother Goose appears an anomalous crone, an unhusbanded female cut loose from the moorings of the patriarchal hearth; kin to the witch and the bawd. It is not difficult to see that such a storyteller may be speaking from a position of acute vulnerability, the kind that makes enemies in the heart of the family. In one of the most powerful scenes in *The Three Sisters*, Chekhov dramatized the old nurse Anfisa's plight when a new woman is brought into the family. Natasha, who marries the three sisters' brother, is the classic daughter-in-law head of household of fairytale nightmares, in that she does not feel she owes the family nurse anything – neither board nor lodging. Natasha comes in and adjusts her hair in the mirror, then notices that Anfisa is sitting by the fire. She turns on her 'coldly', say the stage directions, and bursts out, 'How dare you sit in my presence? Get up! Get out of here!' The old woman obeys, and Natasha then says to Olga, one of her sisters-in-law, 'I can't understand why you keep that old woman in the house.' Olga defends the old woman: 'Forgive me for saying it, but I can't understand how you …' But Natasha interrupts her. 'She's quite useless here. She's just a peasant woman, her right place is in the country … I don't like having useless people about.' In the end, Olga has to leave home, too, and she moves her old nurse in with her so that she will be looked after.

In fairy tales, such a useless old woman reappears in the form of the beggar whom the heroine meets by chance, and who turns out to be a powerful fairy in disguise. She has the secret power to reward virtuous sweet-talking girls (the Olgas of this world), who perform acts of kindness like giving her food and drink, and to punish the wicked mother and her unkind daughter (the Natashas) who scorn old women as useless. Again, paying attention to the internal structure of this story, one can assemble a picture of strain across three generations, in which the old struggle to survive and plead for the mercy of the young.

'*La Mère Cigogne*' (Mother Stork), for instance, a woodcut strip fairy tale from the *Imagerie Pellerin* at Epinal of around 1900 (pp. 232–3), reveals the full pathos of wishful thinking on the part of the old, as well as familiar moral instruction to the young to be good: 'Mother Stork had had from three dead husbands, over time, some thirty or more children, girls and boys.' But they have driven her out to beg for her wherewithal on the street. There a good fairy finds her who announces: 'May your sons who have wicked hearts change instantly into windmills!' No sooner said than done: the windmill–sons have to work on their mother's behalf, grinding flour for her bakery – as they should have in the first place. The worst offender of all becomes an ass, and provides her with the transport she was previously denied. She becomes rich, and distributes her cakes only to good little children. Eventually her own see the error of their ways, and all is forgiven. The story reproduces transparently an old woman's protest that she can be of use, directed past the next generation to the more sympathetic young who come after.

Such a *bande dessinée* literally tells an 'old wives' tale', full of threats, fear, and pathos. It provides a hinge between the instrumental use of literature to form the young, a process that has long been recognized, and the earlier annexation of narrative by speakers who were trying to help themselves.

The protagonist here, bearing one of the traditional names for a storyteller, talks about her indigence. Walter Crane, in 'My Mother' (1873), using the same Toy Book format as his illustrated 'Beauty and the Beast', turned to remind his readers of their future duties in characteristic Victorian fashion. Mother is pictured through the stages of life, first young and vigorous and playful ('Who dress'd my dolls in clothes so gay? My Mother'), then ageing and weakening, until she lies in bed dying: 'And when I see thee hang thy head, / 'Twill be my turn to watch thy bed.' If this book was read by a mother to her child, its injunction carried a special force.

The hostility shown towards the mother figure in modern fairytale interpretations narrows its sights too sharply; other women besides stepmothers, mothers-in-law and guardians were placed *in loco matris* and excited the powerful emotions pupillage always arouses. In '*Peau d'ours*' (Bearskin), one of the tales attributed to Henriette-Julie de Murat, Princess Hawthorn's godmother makes intermittent, dazzling appearances arrayed in jewels and flowers, but she trifles capriciously with her godchild, putting her to the test to discover the strength of her love, punishing the lovers for failing, or sometimes just for the pleasure of it, at whim, like her classical precursor the goddess of love. She refuses to help Hawthorn after her unwanted marriage to the predatory ogre Rhinoceros, for instance, because she

Cast out on the streets by her thankless children, Mother Stork cries, until a fairy appears, who takes her part and changes her wicked offspring into windmills and a pack ass to work on her behalf. ('La Mère Cigogne', Image d'Epinal, c. 1900.)

was not consulted by her father earlier. In this she resembles the fairies in Murat's tales in general, as well as her contemporaries': arbitrary, tyrannical, self-interested and untender, they have djinn-like powers of life and death over their charges' movements, prospects, wealth. These powers are defined as social and economic: when the father hands over the heroine to be brought up by a fairy, Murat writes, 'The power of the fairies does not extend to the qualities of the heart.' The fairies, not knowing gentleness or, in this particular story, constancy, cannot bestow it on their protégés. In some tales, fairies *in loco matris* have explicit designs on humans: in Villeneuve's '*La Belle et la bête*', the Beast has come to this pass because he turned down his guardian's propositions. Marie-Catherine d'Aulnoy's stories deal obsessively with these powerful, indeed fateful figures of female authority who are abusive of their position: Hidessa is plagued by Magotine's perverted desires, the Blue Bird is metamorphosed by another wicked fairy. In Murat's stories equally malign termagants bear self-explanatory names: Formidable, Danamo, Mordicante. Louise, Comtesse d'Auneuil, another aristocrat who put her hand to the writing of fairy stories, encapsulated the general antagonism against these designing females in the title of her one extant tale, '*La Tyrannie des*

fées détruite' (The Fairies' Tyranny Destroyed), which appeared in 1702. There, the lovers are kept apart, in hideous animal shapes, by the jealous fairy, Serpente.

All these older malevolent women stand in some degree of parental or guardian relation to the young on whom they prey and whose romances they attempt to spoil. Perrault's sprightly *moralité*, appended to his 'Cinderella', means more than might appear when he says that talent will never be enough for a young person's advancement in the world: a powerful godparent is required. Godmothers acted as co-maters: they stood *in loco parentis*. According to the laws of affinity in the early medieval Church, even god-siblings committed incest if they married, as their spiritual generation of the child into the Christian family made them true kin, even if there was no blood relation.

Fairy power in the stories borrows the clothes of the romance and mythological pantheon and assumes the kinship patterns of an earlier social organization in order to mirror female power within the extended kinship and patronage systems of the contemporary élite: the Vicomtesse of Kernosy, who wants to marry off her niece to cancel a debt, may love listening to fairy tales of an evening, but only because, in her overweening self-regard, she fails to see her own face in their looking glass.

Murat identified fairies with informal, aristocratic female power in the *ancien régime* very clearly. D'Aulnoy made the connection even more explicit when she dedicated one volume of her fairy tales, *Nouveaux Contes des fées,* to Madame, the sister-in-law of Louis XIV. She wrote: 'Here are Queens and Fairies, who having made the happiness of all who were most charming and most commendable in their own times, have come to seek at the court of your Royal Highness the most illustrious and delightful aspects of ours ...' Flattery, perhaps, a courtier's cunning, a smokescreen veiling the pullulating evil fairies of Mme d'Aulnoy's tales who hamper true lovers. Her good fairies often fail to command enough magic to withstand the enemy's evil machinations: at the end, the mermaid godmother in 'The Yellow Dwarf' cannot resuscitate the dead lovers, but only manages to turn them into intertwined palm trees. In the preamble to this same volume, D'Aulnoy describes walking with friends in the Parc de Saint Cloud, and sitting down by herself for a while. When her friends rejoin her, she describes how *'une jeune Nymphe'* with 'gracious and polite manners', who was able to remember the bygone days when Rhea ruled, had approached her there. Her friends press D'Aulnoy to tell them a story. The implication is that the nymph was a messenger, and D'Aulnoy will pass on what she said. But our storyteller confounds this expectation; she produces a notebook, and coquettes with the circle around her, saying that it contains tales which are treasures. Then she adds: 'All my friends the Fairies have been niggardly with their favours towards me hitherto, so I assure you that I am resolved to neglect them, as they have neglected me.' Distinguishing herself from classical nymphs on the one hand, and fairies on the other, she begins to read a tale from the book she has written herself. A tiny detail of nomenclature becomes significant, in this respect: Mme d'Aulnoy's first editions are entitled *Contes des fées* in the sense of 'about' not 'by' (Latin *de* not *a*). Tales *about* fairies, from a point of view that may take issue with the patronage of the fairies themselves. It is only in later editions and translations that the phrase 'tales of the fairies' takes root, and implies broad agreement between story and subject in an atmosphere of benign and happy 'fairytale' enchantments. Many early literary fairy tales tell stories of the fairies' undoing.

Echoing the prevalent abuses of wardship, Villeneuve also rings complicated changes on the theme of deviant motherhood within the social, rather than the natural or biological, family; in *'La Belle et la bête'*, Beauty, the heroine, was brought up in a foster home, discarded by her biological mother, like many other protagonists, when the fairies cast her out (the fairies figure as thinly disguised Versailles *mignons* and schemers) and compelled her to give up her child. For his part, the Beast has been raised by his mother's closest friend, and it is she who attempts to seduce him. In counterpoise to these wrongs, Villeneuve then multiplies different figures of female benevolence who make up for the false mothers' failings: sisters, godmothers, female friends abound in her elaborately constructed extended family, and at the end it is the maternal, sacrificial act of a fairy on behalf of her sister's child that brings about the completion of the story and the union of Beauty and the Beast. Improvised and entangled families of this sort were not uncommon in the *ancien régime*: Mme de Villeneuve herself lived under the protection of Crébillon *père*, and was writing at the same time as his son, the playwright Crébillon *fils*, was himself composing oriental fairy tales in a satirical, semi-licentious tone that became *à la mode* in the 1720s.

The proliferation of mother figures does not only reflect wishful thinking on the part of children, though fantasies of gratification and power over parents play their part; the aleatory mothers of Mme de Villeneuve's 'Beauty and the Beast' reflect the conditions of aristocratic and less than aristocratic life in early modern France. In Marie-Jeanne L'Héritier's apparently farfetched tales '*Ricdin-Ricdon*' and '*La Robe de sincérité*', the relations of wetnurses, foster parents, guardians, court patrons and godparents can be glimpsed as family networks interpenetrating and combining with the natural, biological family.

In English, French, and Italian, the very title 'mother' formerly designated many women who were not natural mothers, nor women acting directly in lieu of her, like a foster parent, but women who were occupied in some way with the care of other, often younger colleagues – sometimes including men: nuns on the one hand, like the celebrated Mère Arnault at the convent of Port Royal, brothel-keepers on the other, like the notorious real-life madam Ma Needham in Hogarth's *Progress of a Harlot*, who welcomes young Kate Hackabout to London. As with Mother Goose and Mother Stork, midwives and layers-out were granted maternal status. Until the mid-nineteenth century wetnurses were the regular object of sentimental idealization, in spite of the abuses which flourished (and the high death rate of the children). In the mid-eighteenth century, when the fairy tale was being domesticated for the nursery, Greuze was also painting uplifting scenes like *Le Retour au village*, showing a young man arriving rapturously to visit a nurse; surrounded by a multiplicity of offspring, like an allegory of Charity, she appears a paragon of natural bounty and health. Jonathan Swift, as a year-old baby, was farmed out to England for three years, and was taught to read from the Bible by his nurse and to 'spell', just as in *Gulliver's Travels* (1726) Gulliver is taught languages by his giant nurse, Glumdalclitch, and another servant, the sorrel nag. In the nineteenth century, George Sand passed her childhood, and laid the foundations of her fiction, in the company of her *vieille confidente*, her nurse. Freud was devastated by the disappearance of his nurse when he was two and a half. She was dismissed for stealing, and went to prison. In 1897, in the course of his self-analysis, Freud recalled her 'an ugly, elderly but clever woman, who told me a great deal about God Almighty and hell and instilled in me a high opinion of my own capacities …': Freud as Cinders, his nurse as the fairy godmother. Elsewhere, Freud added, 'she was my teacher in sexual matters and complained because I was so clumsy and unable to do anything': the secret enterprise of Mother Goose's narratives. If any of these maternal substitutes had told their nurslings stories, the mother might well have been absent; again the differences in rank between the wetnurse in the village and the mother in the town are reflected in so many fairy tales' frank assault on women with power over others and affection for others with less authority.

In French, bawds were also called mothers: *la mère maquerelle* in colloquial speech. 'Mother' was used in English as 'a term of address for an elderly woman of the lower class'. In usage, it also implies something subtly marginal, with a whiff of the comic, to do with taboo mysteries of the body and the associated matters of life and death. Mother Trot, for instance, as in 'Tell-troth's New Year Gift' of 1593, would be related to Old Dame Trot, of nursery-rhyme witchery, and both are popular descendants of Trotula, the author of the midwifery manual of the middle ages, who may or may not be a historical figure, but certainly gave her name to venereal and obstetric lore of all kinds. In North London until recently two pub names recalled two such characters, Mother Red Cap and Mother Shipton, the last a byword in witchcraft and prophecy who was first mentioned in a pamphlet of 1641 and went on to an illustrious afterlife as a pantomime dame. Both pubs have changed their names: the one to The End of the World, the other to The Fiddler's Elbow. The old names no longer held any meaning for their customers – a symptom of the historical forgettings that drain our culture, as well as a reflection of a deep shift in consciousness: the meanings of the word 'mother' are becoming more and more restricted to the biological mother in the nuclear family. Mothers cannot appoint themselves, or be assigned the role at will; they even need to be biologically proven by matching DNA. And with the coming of bottle-feeding, the practice of wetnursing has died out.

Oddly, this intense focus on the legitimacy of the maternal bloodline and the flesh bond of mother and child has implications in the reading of fairy tales. Our understanding of the stock villain, the wicked stepmother, has been dangerously attenuated and even misunderstood as a result. In the stories, she may not even be a stepmother, and the evil she does is not intrinsic to her nature, or to the strict maternal relation, or to her particular family position. It cannot and should not be extended to all women, for it arises from the insecurity of her interests in a social and legal context that can be changed, and remedied.

If the narrator's ambition to influence her audience, as a licit or illicit surrogate mother, if the storyteller's competition with a powerful woman in control of the household, emerge from the story, the targets of narrative hatred begin to fit in to the economy of family life. For although it does not appear clearly in the teller's interest to insist on the wickedness of women, as she might be tainted by association, the instrumental character of storytelling means that scaring children can be useful, too. Nannies use bogeymen to frighten children into obedience, and a woman storyteller might well displace the harsher aspects of her command on to another woman, a rival who can take the blame. But this is a social stratagem, not an ineluctable or Oedipal condition, and mothers or stepmothers today need not be inculpated *en masse*. As remarriage becomes more and more common, stepmothers find they are tackling a hard crust of bigotry set in the minds of their new children, and refreshed by endless returns of the wicked stepmother in the literature of childhood.

Fairy tale's historical realism has been obscured. One of the reasons may be the change in audience that took place through the nineteenth century, from the mixed age group who attended the *veillée* or the nursery reading of the tales, as in the seventeenth- and eighteenth- and early nineteenth-century evidence, towards an exclusively young audience who had the great enterprises like marriage still ahead of them. Furthermore, certain tales which star children have gained worldwide popularity ('Cinderella' and 'Jack and the Beanstalk'), while the range of the familiar problems dramatized in the stories reflects the youth of the dominant target audience of recent times. The increasing identification of fantasy with the child's mentality has also contributed to the youth of the protagonists.

Stories collected in Alaska in the 1960s often deal frankly with matters sunk deep beneath the surface of European fairy tales destined for children to hear. In one example, a mother-in-law, in the absence of her son, provides her daughter-in-law with food – seals she has hunted – and in return asks for the attentions of a wife – grooming, delousing, and sex, making love to her with the help of a penis of sealbone. When her husband returns from fishing and spies on them, he fetches his mother such a blow he kills her; his wife is disconsolate: '"You've killed my dear husband," she cried. And would not stop crying.'

This could be a concocted folk tale, and this brand of incest certainly remains undocumented further south. But its very anomalousness reveals how an alliance between a man's mother and his wife does not spring easily from the soil of Western, exogamous, patrilocal marriage, especially when the mother is widowed, and both women are competing for their material welfare and the man's attention. It is significant that when the Russian folklorist Vladimir Propp analysed the wonder tale, he broke the form down into seven spheres of action, to which correspond different functions of the dramatis personae: the villain, the hero, the donor, the helper, the princess and her father, the dispatcher and false hero.

When it came to the princess, Propp could not sever her function from her father's but treated them as belonging to a single sphere of action: 'The princess and her father cannot be exactly delineated from each other,' he wrote, thus disclosing, unwittingly, the strictly patriarchal character of the traditional marriage plots, the steps by which the narrative moves, the dynamic of the contract made according to her father's wish. Propp did not analyse the wonder tale's function from the point of view of a mother, did not probe the structure for the inverse rubbing of the father–daughter design: the mother–son. Mothers are distributed according to their part in the plot, as donors or villains, rather than their place in the system of family authority, like the father. Their disappearance from the foreground of his taxonomy replicates their silencing and absence from some of the stories themselves. Yet the tales' deeper, invisible structure can be differently anatomized, as a bid for authority on the part of women. Propp inadvertently reproduces the weight of male power in the wonder tale, and the consequent alliances which set women against women; the tension erupts within the stories as female dissension and strife.

The experiences these stories recount are remembered, lived experiences of women, not fairytale concoctions from the depths of the psyche; they are rooted in the social, legal and economic history of marriage and the family, and they have all the stark actuality of the real and the power real life has to bite into the psyche and etch its design: if you accept Mother Goose tales as the testimony of women, as old wives' tales, you can hear vibrating in them the tensions, the insecurity, jealousy and rage of both mothers-in-law against their daughters-in-law and vice versa, as well as the vulnerability of children from different marriages. Certainly, women strove against women because they wished to promote their own children's interests over those of another union's offspring; the economic dependence of wives and mothers on the male breadwinner exacerbated – and still does – the divisions that may first spring from preferences for a child of one's flesh. But another set of conditions set women against women, and the misogyny of fairy tales reflects them from a woman's point of view: rivalry for the prince's love. The effect of these stories is to flatter the male hero; the position of the man as saviour and provider in these testimonies of female conflict is assumed, repeated and reinforced – which may be the reason why such 'old wives' tales', once they moved from the spinning rooms and the nurseries on to the desks of collectors and folklorists, into the public forum of the printed page and the video screen, have found such success with mixed audiences of men and women, boys and girls, and have continued to flourish in the most popular and accessible and conventional media, like Disney cartoons.

When history falls away from a subject, we are left with Otherness, and all its power to compact enmity, recharge it and recirculate it. An archetype is a hollow thing, but a dangerous one, a figure or image which through usage has been uncoupled from the circumstances which brought it into being, and goes on spreading false consciousness. An analogy – a harmless one – occurs in metaphors of sunrise and sunset, familiar metaphors which fail to represent the movement of the sun or the relation of the planet to it.

In Greece, the women of the Thesmophoria rituals and the Eleusinian mysteries kept their disclosures to themselves, and forbade men access; they understood the risks involved in speaking of female matters. The open circulation of women's experiences in fairy tales has certainly given hostages to fortune, handed ammunition to the very figures – the princes – who often cause the fatal rivalry in the first place. Women were trapped on the fine reverse-barbed hooks of allegiances and interests, on which like trout they became more and more ensnared the more they attempted to pull away. It is revealing that one or two of the peasant or artisan sources to whom the Grimms were alerted were highly reluctant to share their stories with the keen scholars; these women may have felt abashed at the difference in education, social status, but they may also have felt uncomfortable with the idea of broadcasting their contents beyond predominantly female and worker-class circles. In one case, Wilhelm resorted to using the children of the manager of the Elizabeth Hospital (the poorhouse) in Marburg in which one storyteller was living to learn two of the tales she had previously refused to pass on to either his sister Lotte or himself. One of these was '*Aschenputtel*', the Grimms' version of 'Cinderella', which includes of course some of the bloodthirstiest moments of interfemale vengeance of all the famous tales.

A storyteller invites the audience to sympathize with the heroine; with Cinderella, with Beauty, with Snow White: she deals death – physical and moral – to the mother of the heroine; she effectively tells the audience that mothers abandon children to witches in return for the fruits she craves from their garden, as in

D'Aulnoy's 'The White Cat' or La Force's 'Persinette', that mothers order daughters to cut off their toes to please the prince, that they die and leave them to the mercies of the wicked. She is killing off the mother, replacing her, and can be aligned with the mother-in-law who talks to her grandchildren, and claims them for her own, overlooking, disparaging, undoing the work of her son's wife, their mother, and hoping she will not end in the poorhouse.

Yet, even as the voice of the fairy tale murders the mother who is her rival for the children, she remembers how she herself was maltreated: how she entered the house of another as an outsider and was reviled. One of the reasons for the fairy-tale prince's impeccable reputation is that, in a marriage where a bride enters the husband's family, he becomes her chief ally, and his love her mainstay against the interests of others. Many of the most famous and best-loved tales, like 'Bluebeard', and 'Beauty and the Beast', tell of the struggles the heroine undergoes in the quest to secure this love.

CHAPTER 15

Demon Lovers: Bluebeard I

'Loup off the steed,' says false Sir John,
'Your bridal bed you see;
For I have drowned seven young ladies,
The eight one you shall be.'

Scottish Ballad

Bluebeard is a bogey who fascinates: his very name stirs associations with sex, virility, male readiness and desire. His bloody chamber, which his latest wife opens with the key he has forbidden her to use, reveals the dead bodies of her many predecessors, and warns her of her impending doom: the fairy tale written by Perrault in 1697 thrills like a Hitchcock film before its time, it foreshadows thriving twentieth-century fantasies about serial killers and Jack the Rippers. Only it has a happy ending: the heroine's sister Anne calls for help from the top of the high tower of Bluebeard's castle as he is preparing to kill his latest bride, and their brothers gallop to the rescue and despatch the monster. In Georges Méliès's

The devil capers as the last of Bluebeard's wives cannot wash the key clean and learns, from the melancholy sight of her predecessors, the just fate of disobedience. (Georges Méliès directed and played the devil, Barbe Bleue, 1901.)

highspirited and comical film version of 1901, (p. 241) the brothers impale Bluebeard against the wall, where he continues to kick wildly; meanwhile, a friendly goblin appears in a puff of smoke, resurrects the deceased brides and then conjures up bridegrooms for every one of them so that the story climaxes with a multiple wedding.

Beardedness divided the men from the boys in the Olympic Games; in Saint Augustine's view 'the beard signifies strong men; [it] signifies young, vigorous, active, quick men'. Beards were also the mark of the goat, and given the goat's lustful and diabolical character, its kinship with satyrs and other classical embodiments of lust, like the god Pan, and the Devil himself (he actually wears a blue beard in the fourteenth-century stained glass at Fairford church, Gloucestershire (Pl. 21)), beards came increasingly to define the male in a priapic mode. Orderic Vitalis, for instance, in the twelfth century, complained of the influence of the East – of the Saracen – on Norman fashions: 'Now almost all our fellow countrymen are crazy and wear little beards, openly proclaiming by such a token that they revel in filthy lusts like stinking goats.' Beards were accorded much greater symbolic value in Islam than in Christianity: a strand of Mohammed's beard is still preserved in a reliquary in the Topkapi, Istanbul. Hair figures very rarely indeed, however, among the relics of Christian saints; the cultures' contrasting oaths point up the difference in value: Muslims swear by the Prophet's beard, Christians by the Saviour's wounds (though 'zounds' is not much found today beyond the pages of Regency romances).

Well out of fashion in the court of the Sun King, the beard of Perrault's villain betokened an outsider, a libertine, and a ruffian. The very word in French – *barbe* – looks as if it is related to *barbare*, barbarian, though the etymology remains fanciful. A mid-Victorian version took up the echo, calling Bluebeard a 'Barbe-hairy-un'. And it becomes the custom, beginning with the first woodcuts of the first edition, and continuing in the watercolours by Arthur Rackham and later artists, to portray Bluebeard as an Oriental, a Turk in pantaloons and turban, who rides an elephant, and grasps his wife by the hair when he prepares to behead her with his scimitar (p. 336–7). In later redactions of the story, she is sometimes called Fatima and he is given an absurd foreign name, like Abomélique, and the setting of his fabulous estate is sometimes specified: a retelling which Arthur Rackham illustrated takes place near Baghdad.

By the blueness of his protagonist's beard, Perrault intensifies the frightfulness of his appearance: Bluebeard is represented as a man against nature, either by dyeing his hair like a luxurious Oriental, or by producing such a monstrous growth without resorting to artifice. The colour blue, the colour of ambiguous depth, of the heavens and of the abyss at once, encodes the frightening character of Bluebeard, his house and his deeds, as surely as gold and white clothes the angels. The chamber he forbids his new wife becomes a blue chamber in some retellings: blue is the colour of the shadow side, the tint of the marvellous and the inexplicable, of desire, of knowledge, of the blueprint, the blue movie, of blue talk, of raw meat and rare steak (*un steak bleu*, in French), of melancholy, the rare and the unexpected (singing the blues, once in a blue moon, out of the blue, blue blood). The fairy tale itself was first known, in France, as a *conte bleu*, and appeared in familiar livery between the covers of the *Bibliothèque bleue*. Mme de Rambouillet received her *alcôvistes* in her blue bedroom. As William Gass has written, in his inspired essay 'On Being Blue', 'perhaps it is the blue of reality itself': and he goes on to quote a scientific manual: 'blue is the specific colour of orgone energy within and without the organism'. It is a polar tint: of origin and end, and in consequence adumbrates mortality, too: Derek Jarman, the late artist and film-maker, recently flooded a screen with indigo in order to meditate on his and his friends' death sentence from AIDS.

One of the many peculiar aspects of the familiar story of 'Bluebeard' is that the narrative concentrates on Fatima's act of disobedience, not on Bluebeard's mass murders. In this the tale resembles other favourites of the Victorian nursery, like 'Red Riding Hood', which admonishes the protagonist for stopping to pick flowers in the wood, and laying herself open to the wolf's wickedness; the wolf knows no better, but Red Riding Hood should have been better brought up. In 'Goldilocks', too, though the insatiably curious child escapes scot-free, there is a hint that she was lucky not to be skinned for the bears' supper and it would have been a good lesson to her if she had been (p. 303). Fairy tales are stories to frighten children, as well as delight them. In 'Bluebeard', the initial weight of the story swings the listener or reader's sympathies towards the husband who instructs his young wife, and presents his request for her obedience as reasonable, and the terror she experiences when she realizes her fate as a suitable punishment, a warning against trespass.

Perrault appears to side with Bluebeard and his strictures, but his tone remains tongue-in-cheek throughout. At the start, describing the house party Bluebeard lays on for his young fiancée and her friends, Perrault writes:

It was nothing but a continual round of parties, of walking, hunting, and fishing expeditions, dancing and banqueting and picnicking: no one went to bed, and the whole night was spent playing tricks on one another; in fact everything went so well, that the youngest began to find that the Master of the house no longer had such a very blue beard …

Perrault wants to have it both ways: he tells a rousing story of vindication and escape, but then appends two laddish remarks by way of a moral: that there are no longer any husbands as terrible as Bluebeard, and that, besides, between man and wife these days, 'Whatever the colour the beard might be, it's hard to tell who is master.'

Nevertheless, Perrault, in this story, as in the first tales he published – 'Griselda' and 'Donkeyskin' – dramatizes the abuse of male privilege and plucks his heroine from disaster and injustice at the end. 'Bluebeard' is a story, like 'Cinderella', in which the mighty are cast down. The overbearing husband, like the wicked step-mother and ugly sisters in 'Cinderella' and the incestuous father in 'Donkeyskin', is thwarted, to the joy and edification of all. 'Bluebeard' is a version of the Fall in which Eve is allowed to get away with it, in which no one for once heaps the blame on Pandora. Walter Crane, in his sumptuous full colour illustrations at the end of the last century, even shows the heroine against a wall painting of the Temptation in the Garden of Eden, making a direct analogy with Eve, and thus disclosing the inner structure of the fable: Bluebeard acts like God the Father, prohibiting knowledge – the forbidden chamber is the tree of the knowledge of good and evil – and Fatima is Eve, the woman who disobeys and, through curios-ity, endangers her life (right).

After Perrault, the story often comes with a subtitle, 'The Effect of Female Curiosity', – or, in case we should miss the point – 'the Fatal Effects of Curiosity', to bring it in line with cautionary tales about women's innate wickedness: with Pandora who opened the forbidden casket as well as Eve who ate of the forbidden fruit. The Grimms included a variant, *'Marienkind'*, (Mary's Child), one of the nastier morality tales in their book, in which the Virgin Mary herself, no less, plays the part of Bluebeard and savagely punishes the wayward girl who uses the forbidden key. In many illustrated tellings of the story, the key looms very large indeed, a gigantic forbidden fruit, so engorged and positioned that the allusion can hardly be missed. In Gustave Doré's engraving to Perrault, Bluebeard reveals the forbidden key – of gigantic proportions – to his wife with the leer of a pornog-rapher. The mid-nineteenth-century caricaturist Alfred Crowquill featured a key so monstrous in size that Bluebeard's young wife staggers under its weight like one of Beardsley's obscene marginalia. The heroine finds that she cannot rub

For a month after the wedding they
    lived and had good cheer,
And then said Bluebeard to his wife,
    " I 'll say good-bye, my dear :
" Indeed, it is but for six weeks that I
    shall be away,
" I beg that you'll invite your friends,
    and feast and dance and play :
" And all my property I 'll leave con-
    fided to your care :
" Here are the keys of all my chests,
    there's plenty and to spare.

*Eve stands behind, the first woman who was also afflicted with curiosity, as Bluebeard's wife
wonders why she should not use the key to enter the forbidden chamber. (Walter Crane,
Bluebeard, London, 1874.)*

away the stain of blood on the key rather in the same way as Adam and Eve try to
hide from God but cannot. And how the Victorian verses gloat on her unpleasant
newfound knowledge:

[She] looked within, and fainted straight the horrid sight to see,
For there upon the floor was blood, and on the walls were wives,
For Bluebeard first had married them, then cut their throats with knives.

Crowquill again provides a fearsome drawing of the hanged wives, tongues popping out, while his jocular collaborator F. W. N. Bayley compares them to the victims of famous modern murderers, like their contemporary Jack the Ripper, and exclaims:

Oh Fie! Oh Fie!
There they all were hanging up to dry!

Another, more disciplinarian author gloats: 'She found herself amidst the severed limbs and mutilated bodies of her husband's former wives', before going on to describe the message on the wall: 'The fate of broken promises and disobedient curiosity.' This Bluebeard manages – with his dying breath – to continue moulding his wife: 'I hope she will in future never break a promise, disobey those to whom she promises submission, nor give way to the impulse of improper and forbidden curiosity.'

Bluebeard the ogre husband plays two parts at least in his own story: the patriarch whose orders must be obeyed on the one hand, and on the other the serpent who seduces by exciting curiosity and desire and so brings death. As the witch-hunter Pierre de Lancre wrote in 1612, 'Satan is the true ape of God'. He mimics divine rewards and punishments in topsy-turvy, but, as Lancre added, 'Nevertheless, his imitation is imperfect.' In his double role in the fairy tale, he reflects a problem that is intrinsic to the morality tale: Erasmus pointed out that the Devil does God's work, testing sinners and proving saints. His beard is emblematic of his inherent contrariness, a patriarchal ornament, a devilish goatee. For Freudian commentators, like Bruno Bettelheim, the story of Bluebeard confronts the mystery of sexuality, and, by dramatizing so bloodily the terror of defloration, helps to assuage it.

As in the story of the Fall, the serpent may be at fault, but Eve is blameworthy too. In many of the later retellings of 'Bluebeard', the blue chamber is presented as the fitting penalty for his wives' previous wickedness in defying a husband's commands. Some storytellers, sensitive to the narrative inconsistency that Bluebeard's first wife cannot have been issued the same instruction (at that point there was as yet no forbidden knowledge, no bloody chamber), invent ingenious reasons for her murder, the start of the series. In 'The History of Bluebeard's Six Wives' by Sabilla Novello, illustrated by George Cruikshank, around 1875, the first victim is actually called Basbluella, or Bluestocking Ella, and is thereby already credited with knowledge both dangerous and unseemly in a woman. When a drunken Bluebeard reproaches her for her lack of merriment, she turns his beard blue in vengeance. It is often difficult to tell which side the authors are on, for an air of glee hangs around the telling, although Cruikshank himself was an earnest advocate of Temperance, and wrote a 'Cinderella' in which everyone at the ball is on the waggon, and at the wedding the fountains run with lemonade.

II

In Scottish and English ballads, fierce and eldritch tales are told of encounters with the underworld, and its demon denizens who prey on young women. The ballads have counterparts in literatures ranging from Tibetan to Dutch, and they go very far back; it is not my interest here to locate their place or point of origin, which scholars have tried to do, but to relate their narratives of sexual danger and escape to the fairy tales of Bluebeard which they resemble.

The Marian miracle play *Mary of Nimmegen*, or *Mariken van Nieumeghen*, which tells a version of this struggle in a form intended for popular entertainment, was published in the first quarter of the sixteenth century in Antwerp, in Dutch and

The lecherous Moonen (the devil in disguise) woos Mary of Nijmegen and wins her with his promises of an education – and riches. (Antwerp, c. 1518–9.)

English versions, as one of the series of chapbooks or *volksboeken* which disseminated folk tales and romances like the story of Alexander, or of Blancheflor, or the
Four Sons of Aymon, all material which flows into the fairytale tradition of the
seventeenth century onwards. The Devil here takes the form of the one-eyed
lecher Moonen; he seduces the protagonist into sex and marriage by promising
her power, in the Faustian tradition (p. 247). Mary's mind soon turns to riches
rather than learning, and he promises to shower her with jewels. When Mary has
duly surrendered to his irresistible charms, and set up house with him at the sign
of the Golden Tree, she entertains travellers and drinkers with her ballads:
'Nigromancy is a merry art ...', she explains before she sings.

Mariken 'has ado' with the fiend for seven years before she is saved by the
Virgin Mary; her rescue takes place at the performance of a miracle play, set in
Nijmegen, during which the representation of the Virgin Mary's mercy moves
her errant namesake to contrition then and there – again a demonstration of the
powers of persuasive speech, especially shaped by art. Thus *Mary of Nimmegen* tells
the story of one miracle play, within the frame of another. This story of a female
Faust is related to 'Bluebeard', because her story places a near-fatal union between
a virtuous maid and a fiend at its centre. Mary is saved, in this case – though she is
condemned to wear iron rings round her neck in penance for three years – but
Moonen, or the Devil inside him, will find another bride. The English version of
the play ends with the kind of moral fairy tales borrowed:

> Take all in gree, without grutching,
> This simple tale: 'twas writ for love,
> That we may win to heavenly glory above.

Ballads about the Elfin-Knight's wooing do not identify him directly as the
Devil, but only as a false suitor who kills the women he loves: in these songs, the
Lady Isabel, or May Colven, or Annie Miller – the heroine has many different
names – sees through her lover, tricks him with words and manages to turn the
tables on him and do him to death in the same way as he had planned to kill her.
In 'May Colven', for instance, he wins permission to marry her from her father
and rides off with her. They come to 'a lonesome part / A rock by the side of the
sea', where he orders her to dismount and prepare to die (see epigraph to this
chapter).

She replies by telling him to turn around so as not to see her take off her clothes,
and when he obliges, she seizes him and throws him into the sea in her stead.

In the Netherlands, a tragic medieval version of this ballad, called '*Heer Halewijn*', communicates an acute degree of terror about the consequences of sex: the bride disrobes herself to enter the sea, which is invoked as a bridal bed in which she will be drowned, like all her predecessors.

This movement from the pious to the secular, from the struggle with good and evil to the struggle with true and false love, describes the same pattern as the emergence of the individual as author of the tales: as theocentric narrative fades, named writers of tales stamp the traditional material from ballads, hagiography, folk tales with their unique experience and imagination and begin to express personal moral viewpoints in defiance of the established view. Perrault was indebted to popular hagiography, and wrote saints' lives himself, including a lengthy poem, '*Le Triomphe de Sainte Geneviève*', which tells a story that belongs in the accused queen–Snow White cycle. Interestingly, the vignette illustrating Bluebeard in the first edition of Perrault's *Contes* shows Bluebeard raising his scimitar above his hapless wife's head, like the executioner in any number of female martyrdoms familiar from religious iconography. Some scholars believe that Perrault himself made the original sketches, from which the printing blocks were drawn. His sly humour may therefore be parodying, at one level, the earnestness of edifying tales in which he himself had dabbled.

Marie-Jeanne L'Héritier's 'The Subtle Princess', which appeared in 1694, has frequently been attributed to Perrault and collected with Mother Goose tales (though Perrault would never have created such an Amazonian trickster for a heroine). Comparing her version with Perrault's famous 'Bluebeard', published three years later, reveals differences that offer sharp insights into ways of telling upbeat stories about a wicked husband. And as Perrault's version postdates his cousin's, his changes can be taken as emending hers, even teasing her for her treatment.

L'Héritier gives the heroine Finessa two elder sisters, with equally telltale names: Nonchalante and Babillarde – Lackadaisy and Loquatia in Gilbert Adair's recent translation. Lackadaisy is a lazybones who gets up 'at one in the afternoon … her hair dishevelled, her gown hanging loose and unfastened, her girdle missing … no one could prevail upon her to go other than in slippers: she found the wearing of shoes unutterably fatiguing'. Her sister Loquatia suffers from '*la démangeaison de parler*' (a frantic itch to talk); an example of the wrong kind of female prattler, a gossip, a telltale and – worse – a bore, she gets herself into trouble, too, coquetting with the young bloods at her father's court so familiarly they take advantage of her. With that priggishness that L'Héritier can sometimes show, she contrasts the elder sisters' worthlessness with Finessa the paragon's industry, intelligence, polished art of conversation and other endowments.

The three princesses are motherless (as usual), and the king their father has to leave them, so he consults a wise fairy, and on her advice locks them up in a castle on their own with three magic distaffs – that notorious and suspect emblem of womanhood – made of glass. Like the enchanted key Bluebeard gives his wife in the Perrault tale, the distaffs will reveal the young women's behaviour to him on his return: in Perrault, blood appears on the key after his most recent wife has opened the door to the chamber where her predecessors are hanging, and it cannot be rubbed off; in Finessa, the glass distaffs, emblems of the female and of virginity, will shatter if their owners' virtue fails.

The king their father has an enemy, and his son, a prince called Riche-en-Cautèle (Richcraft), acts in the story as Finessa's shadow side, her virtue a match for his evil assaults. Disguised as an old beggarwoman, Richcraft dupes Lackadaisy and Loquatia into letting him into the castle, though they have been forbidden all company whatsoever. Later, he reveals himself a prince, and first one sister, then the other, succumb to his flatteries and promises, marry him in turn, and suffer the immediate shattering of the magic distaffs. 'The world is full of such dupes,' comments the author.

Finessa naturally has her wits about her, and she realizes his falsehood. When her turn comes, she agrees to become his wife, promising to take him to 'a chamber in which there was a very soft and comfortable bed'. But when he tries to come near, she threatens him with an axe: 'Richcraft was not the bravest of young princes; and, seeing Finessa still with her axe, with which her fingers toyed as though it were light and airy as a fan', he desisted and 'went away to give her time to meditate'.

She quickly builds a bed on a flimsy scaffolding of branches over a castle sewer; when the evil Richcraft climbs in eagerly, he drops several hundred feet through the drainage system of the castle: filth to filth, the impure shatterer of glass distaffs broken himself in the sewers.

But he survives, and returns for vengeance. He leaves heaped baskets of juicy fruits within sight of the castle, and the sisters beg Finessa to go and fetch them some for they are subject to the cravings of pregnancy: both of them have instantly conceived. When she does so, she is captured by Richcraft, who heaps her with insults and then, showing her a barrel lined with knives, razors and hooked nails all around, declares he is going to roll her down in it from a great height. But as he leans over to gloat on the torments she is to suffer, Finessa 'deftly kicked him inside and started to roll the barrel down the mountain'

On his deathbed, this ogre makes his lovable younger brother Belavoir promise to marry Finessa and then stab her to death in bed on their wedding night. With a heavy heart, for he has fallen in love with Finessa's beauty, wit, and other points, this perfect younger brother of fairy tale prepares to kill her. But she has anticipated danger, with the help of a fairy, and has put a dummy in her bed instead, made of 'a bladder of sheep's blood, a bale of straw and the insides of a few of the animals they'd eaten that evening'. She watches her prince stab the dummy instead, then give himself up to lamentations at his deed. Then she reveals herself, and they all live happily ever after. Except her sisters, for Lackadaisy dies of vexation at the work she is given as a punishment, and Loquatia breaks her skull trying to escape the austere penitentiary where they have been placed. L'Héritier does not waste a moment's pity on them, nor tell us what happened to their two babies, except that they were smuggled by Finessa into their wicked father's death chamber where their presence proved so vocal, it hastened his end. (Perhaps the babies survived to become the foundling protagonists of another story.)

In Perrault's 'Bluebeard', the heroine arranges dowries for her sisters so that they can make good marriages with gentlemen of their choosing; L'Héritier shows much less interest in the worldly side of matters. Also, valiant intervention is not the only way for women to help themselves – and men; a critique of the conditions that set them against one another can emerge more quietly from depicting them without flamboyant gestures or even heroic action.

Words are also effective and binding in this fairy tale: language and magic make and unmake reality. The sisters break their father's command, they believe their seducer's sweet nothings, and come to grief; the good brother keeps his word and has to attempt Finessa's life against his better judgement. Finessa's simulacrum in the bed is only one of her performances, most of which are verbal. L'Héritier is funny when she describes Finessa passing herself off as a doctor to gain entry to Richcraft's bedroom with his babies: 'Finessa arrived ... tossing out the most obscure medical terms and signing the visitor's book in a wholly indecipherable hand ...' By contrast, Perrault's heroine is a helpless victim, very given to tears.

Pretences, ruses, riddles are the stuff of fiction, and in fairy tales they often become pivotal in the plot. L'Héritier made dramatic changes to her source, Basile's 'Sapia Liccarda', which features three brothers and ends in a triple wedding; the death of the false bridegroom, his fury at the appearance of the babies he has fathered, and the savagery of the traps and ordeals he dreams up for Finessa are all L'Héritier's inventions – or borrowings from other sources – and they betray her relish for drama. In Basile, for instance, the heroine makes her dummy of sweet pastry, and when her assailant stabs it, he is overcome with regret because of the sweet fragrance of the girl he has tried to kill. This is soft stuff compared to L'Héritier's gore. In the end, the dance Basile's Sapia Liccarda has led her suitor turns out to be a mere chivalric trial of his love. L'Héritier's sadism and her own implacable revenge on the wicked Richcraft reveal that she had far more at stake; and 'The Subtle Princess' is the most successful, pacey, controlled tale that she wrote.

After all the practical measures dreamed up by her protagonist, it is sobering to read one of the tales L'Héritier based on a *fait divers* from the *Gazette*, in her last collection of stories, *Caprices du destin*, of 1718. Some of these stories are taken from the past, wonder tales filled with magic and fantastic invention, but four are *modernes*, and she has changed the names to protect the identities of the characters. '*Le Jugement téméraire*' (The Bold Decision) is a tuppenny-ha'penny romance, rather tame and flat, and not a fairy tale at all. It would contain nothing of interest, except that it reveals the ordinary restrictions obtaining in a woman's life at that time and discloses the context in which someone like L'Héritier was making up her fantastic stories. For the temerity – the boldness – that the real-life heroine shows in her 'judgement' consists in deciding to travel alone in a public carriage to Paris when something has urgently called her to the capital and her own carriage is for some reason unavailable to her. A nobleman travelling in the same public vehicle imagines – what else would he think? – that she is a lady of easy virtue bent on adventure, '*une femme d'intrigue*', and behaves improperly. But when, in his mischievous lust, he continues, in Paris, to try and debauch her, he discovers her rank and status and has to stand by in shame when she turns the tables on him, receives him graciously and inspires his own son to fall virtuously in love with her and marry her.

No stirring deeds in the lists or bloody effigies in bed for this lady, just the complex tripping through the wires and snares of social prohibitions on women's movement and conduct.

Marie-Catherine d'Aulnoy showed more confidence, in her spin on the medieval tale of misalliance with the Devil or his agents. '*Le Nain jaune*' (The Yellow Dwarf), published as part of her novel *Don Fernand de Tolède* in 1698, features a haughty heroine, Toute-Belle, or All-Beautiful, so puffed up with her own perfections that she turns down twenty kings for husbands; her doting mother, on her way to consult the Fairy of the Desert about her delinquent daughter's future, comes across terrifying lions which threaten to eat her alive. She then discovers that she has lost the special cakes made of millet, sugar candy and crocodile eggs she had brought with her to pacify them. The Yellow Dwarf materializes from an orange tree where he lives; he has red hair, a fairy characteristic, inherited from the demons of Christian superstition, and he promises to guard her in return for marriage with her daughter. When later they all forget this promise, though Toute-Belle is wearing his ring of a single diabolical red hair on her finger, and she is about to wed after all one of her sighing swains (the King of the Golden Mines), the dwarf makes a tremendous entrance riding in on the wedding feast astride a great cat, seizes the bride and escapes; the Desert Fairy meanwhile takes a fancy to the groom and carries him off for her own. The tale ends with the murder of the king by the dwarf; and Toute-Belle expires instantly over his body. They are then turned into intertwined palm trees, like Ovid's faithful lovers Philemon and Baucis, by a kind-hearted mermaid who, as we have heard, is not quite powerful enough to bring them back to life.

The gloomy ending did not impede the story's attraction: it proved a popular subject for English pantomime in the early nineteenth century; but when Walter Crane retold it and illustrated it in 1875, he changed the morbid ending and gave the victory to the King of the Golden Mines. In another variation, he vanquishes the dwarf in the last scene, by cutting him in two with the enthusiastic assistance of the princess and a pair of magic scissors (p. 287).

D'Aulnoy and L'Héritier's contemporary, the writer Catherine Bernard, in a characteristically mordant passage of her 1696 romance, *Inès de Cordoue*, added a more cynical twist to the problem of the importunate and repellent suitor with her story '*Riquet à la Houppe*' (Ricky with the Tuft). Bernard draws on traditional topography when she describes her heroine's first encounter with her diabolical suitor: 'One day, when she was out walking by herself – a habit of hers – she saw a man hideous enough to be a monster emerge from the ground.' He offers her a bargain, promising her intelligence, which she conspicuously lacks, on condition she marries him after a year (p. 254). This is the conventional Faustian pact of the medieval morality play; so when Riquet's promised bride marries someone else, Riquet comes to claim her according to her promise. But then, against the grain of both saints' lives and fairy tales, Bernard simply allows her heroine two husbands. She lives bigamously, with her true love as well as the Devil to whom she so foolishly plighted herself. By a mischievous fairy's enchantment, these two men in her life look exactly alike, and she never could tell 'to whom she should address her lamentations for fear of mistaking the object of her hatred for the

The ill-favoured suitor tempts the beautiful but witless heroine with the gift of intelligence – in return for marriage. ('Ricky with the Tuft', Mother Goose Tales *, Amsterdam, 1754.)*

object of her love'. Catherine Bernard ends with a shrug: 'But perhaps she hardly lost anything there. In the long run lovers become husbands anyway.'

Charles Perrault's later tale, with the same title, is rather better known, as it appears in his famous collection, and it seems openly to rebut Catherine Bernard's jaundiced view with his own brand of romantic idealism. A queen near by has given birth to twin girls, one of whom is ugly and clever and eloquent, the other beautiful but vacuous. The beautiful girl bitterly regrets her stupidity, and is bemoaning her fate when she meets Riquet by chance. Perrault's Riquet is hideous, but exceptionally witty and fluent and charming withal; he promises her wit and wisdom if she will agree to marry him after a year. She tries to wriggle out of it, but he persuades her, telling her that if she will only love him, he will become the handsomest man in all the world. She agrees, and his transformation is wrought. Perrault draws the happy conclusion: 'This is not a fairy tale but the plain, unvarnished truth; every feature of the face of the one we love is beautiful, every word the beloved says is wise.' He forgets to acquaint us with the fate of the ugly, clever twin sister.

When fairy tales come to be seen as literature for children, and are expected to offer hope, not dash a reader's spirits, this conclusion appears far more suitable than Bernard's mutinousness. But Bernard was bitter about women's lack of freedom of movement; Perrault by contrast complacent; Bernard has been reprinted only through Jack Zipes's remarkable work in retrieving these writers, who have been so thoroughly eclipsed in later dissemination by Perrault.

The Grimm Brothers' variation, '*Fichters Vogel*' (Fitcher's Bird), was passed on to them by Dortchen Wild, wife of Wilhelm, and combined with another variation from another source. A wizard pretends to be a poor beggar, and spookily spirits away three sisters in succession to be his brides. When the first breaks the prohibition, she sees inside the forbidden chamber a 'large bloody basin … filled with dead people who had been chopped to pieces …'; in her alarm, she drops a magic egg the wizard has given her into the basin, and when she retrieves it, finds that the spots of blood on it will not wash away. After the death of her sisters, it falls to the youngest to outwit the ogre: she contrives a sinister effigy of herself, made of bones and flowers, and places it at the window as his bride; she meanwhile covers herself in honey and then slits open an eiderdown and rolls herself in it, and so, tarred and feathered, turns herself into the sinister 'Fitcher's bird' of the story's title in order to make her escape, for in this disguise the wizard lets her pass by without recognizing her.

The tale feels on the page like a rummage bag of scraps for the making of a patchwork quilt – there are bits from several different stories here; it echoes L'Héritier's 'Finessa' as well as Perrault's 'Bluebeard', but the effect is far murkier, for the bloody egg offers a queasy female symbol. The name Fitcher, interestingly enough, derives from the Icelandic *fitfugl*, meaning 'web-footed bird', so there may well be a buried memory here of those bird-women who rule narrative enchantments, and of the power of the story to effect the safety of its characters.

Again, a comparison with Italo Calvino's recent recension reveals the porousness of stories to their tellers' temper and beliefs. The Grimms' tale is eerie, volatile and curiously unfocused socially and politically; Calvino's is bright with energetic rebellion and peasant cunning. Calvino mingled, as was his method, different elements of the tale as he found it in three anthologies edited by ethnographers in the nineteenth century; they had taken down the tales from traditional *cantastorie*. The basic structure and title of the story '*Il naso d'argento*' (Silver Nose) came from Piedmont, while enlivening material and details were gathered from two of Calvino's richest sources, the Venetian Domenico Giuseppe Bernoni, who published booklets of tales from 1873 to 1893, and Carolina Coronedi Berti from Bologna, who published in 1874. On the orature taken down by these editors, Calvino comments: 'Though the names of the storytellers are not given, one is often conscious of a feminine presence, who tends at times to be sentimental, at others to be dashing.' Calvino's tale springs back to the tale's antecedents, among trickster folklore and miracle stories.

Instead of a blue beard, his villain has a silver nose. The eldest of three daughters of a poor washerwoman sighs that she would sell her soul to the Devil if she could only leave home and put an end to all this laundry. Soon afterwards, a tall dark stranger with the silver nose appears and asks for one of her girls to work for him. The eldest leaps at the chance; they set off together, eventually reaching a magnificent palace; he gives her keys to every room, but forbids her access to one. He also fastens a rose in her hair – surreptitiously.

She disobeys his injunction, and opens the door: flames and smoke explode from inside and she sees damned souls burning in Hell. When Silver Nose returns, the rose he pinned in her hair bears telltale scorchmarks and he knows she has disobeyed him; so he tosses her into the flames to join her predecessors.

The same thing then takes place with the second daughter. Silver Nose pins a carnation in her hair, and again it is singed and gives her away. For a third time, Silver Nose returns to the washerwoman, who fetches for him the youngest girl, Lucia. But 'she was the most cunning of them all'. She too opens the door, but she has left behind the 'jasmine blossom' that would have given her away in a jar of water in her room. One by one, Lucia retrieves her sisters from hellfire, bundles each one into a laundry bag and asks Silver Nose to take the washing back to her mother. In this way, unwittingly, he delivers the revived sisters home. Finally, Lucia makes a rag doll, puts it in the marital bed in her stead and hides herself in another bag of laundry, which again the Devil hauls off to be washed. So Lucia contrives to be rescued by her Devil bridegroom, and as she has also taken care to carry off a great deal of his money in the laundry bag with her, she and her family 'were now able to live in comfort and happiness'.

This Italian Devil is very interesting: he is presented 'in his customary aristocratic attire', a boss who demands sexual services along with good housekeeping, and his metal appendage could mask a nose wasted from syphilis.

Though 'Silver Nose' follows a similar narrative to nursery 'Bluebeards', it does not resemble in tone and message the horrid sermons which Perrault's version spawned, tut-tutting about female curiosity and unwifely behaviour. It represents, within the Bluebeard cycle, an alternative, triumphant, gleeful approach, mostly vanished from the nursery shelves. 'Silver Nose' descends from a version in which quickwitted female doubledealing overcomes the tyrant; by contrast, Perrault's 'Bluebeard' and the familiar stories based on it bring the heroine's brothers to the rescue in the nick of time, and resolve the matter with the death of Bluebeard at their hands.

But the horror that terrifies the wives in marriage is not always the ogre's direct responsibility – their fear may arise from another cause, which happily, for historical reasons, has been eclipsed by much more prominent phantom of the serial killer.

Satyr, Puck, Robin Goodfellow, the devil of folklore comes in many heathen shapes. 'Are not you he / That frights the maidens of the villagery?' asks a fairy in A Midsummer Night's Dream. 'I am that merry wanderer of the night', he replies. (Anon. ballad woodcut, Robin Goodfellow, seventeenth century.) ABOVE Bluebeard, on his return home, finds the enchanted key suspiciously bloodstained. (Alfred Crowquill in F. W. N Bayley, Blue Beard, London, 1844.)

Saint Margaret was swallowed by a dragon, but he spewed her up safe and sound; her delivery from the gaping maw made her the special patron of childbirth. (Raphael, Saint Margaret, c. 1520.)

CHAPTER 16

The Ogre's Appetite: Bluebeard II

The husband who comes secretly gliding into your bed at night is an enormous snake, with widely gaping jaws, a body that could coil around you a dozen times and a neck swollen with deadly poison. Remember what Apollo's oracle said: that you were destined to marry a savage wild beast … he won't pamper you much longer … when your nine months are nearly up he will eat you alive; apparently his favourite food is a woman far gone in pregnancy.

Apuleius

Saint Margaret of Antioch, one of the most popular saints of the middle ages, resisted the unwanted attentions of the Roman prefect Olybrius, seeing him off with the words, 'Thou shameless hound and insatiable lion! Thou hast power over my flesh, but Christ reserveth my soul.' Thrown into prison for this contumely, she is assaulted there by the Devil. He first appears as a dragon, and swallows her alive. But the power of her holiness proves too strong for his digestion: he regurgitates her safe and sound (left). He then makes another attempt on her virtue, this time, 'in the form of a man'. She confounds him again: 'She caught him by the head and threw him to the ground, and set her right foot on his neck saying, Be still thou fiend under the feet of a woman … She took her foot off his head and said, Hence thou wretched fiend, and the earth opened and the fiend sank in.'

In myth and fairy tale, the metaphor of devouring often stands in for sex: ogres like Bluebeard eat their wives, we are told, even though the story itself reveals their bodies hanging whole in the secret chamber, or chopped into pieces, apparently uneaten; Beauty, like Psyche, is terrified that the Beast will eat her, as he eats other creatures. The Cocteau film *La Belle et la bête* shows the Beast's pelt and paws smoking after a fresh kill, and Belle revolted as well as terrified. In a chapbook of 1796, the author adds a helpful footnote to explain the word 'ogre': 'An Ogree [*sic*] is a Giant with long teeth and claws, with a raw head and bloody bones, [who]runs away with naughty Boys and Girls and eats them all up.'

But consumption does not end with disciplinary measures in the nursery, or with sexual contact: the woman's fears do not focus on the act itself, but on its consequences, which are also often spoken of in images of eating: the woman's body, especially pregnant, is particularly delicious to beasts, it seems. For the greedy villains of fairy tale relish babies: their appetite first aims at women, but with an ulterior motive of devouring their offspring.

This cannibal motif conveys a threefold incorporation: sexual union, by which a form of reciprocal devouring takes place; pregnancy, by which the womb encloses the growing child; and paternity, which takes over the infant after birth in one way or another. Fairytale princesses enclosed in towers are themselves metonymically swallowed up. One of Marie-Jeanne L'Héritier's tales, 'La Princesse Olymphe, ou l'Ariane de Hollande', describes how Olymphe is abandoned on an island where a monster roams who devours young women; later, it turns out he is an ordinary man in disguise who keeps his victims alive, but captive underground. Again, the threat of being eaten stands for the dread of being immured, confined. (It is interesting that the word 'confinement' is used of the late stages of pregnancy.) The motif of deliverance – Margaret's case, when she was spewed forth safely from the dragon's belly – conveys a twofold physical salvation: first, from the act of sexual congress itself (in her legend and in those of all virgin martyrs like her, she remains a virgin), and secondly, from the threatened physical trauma of childbearing. Saint Margaret, one of the most powerful intercessors before the Reformation, had a specific jurisdiction: childbirth. The dragon, by swallowing her whole and then vomiting her up safe and sound, seemed to offer a picture of the perfect delivery. In some representations of her assailant, his yawning gullet does more than hint at the association with the maternal womb (p. 258). As the patron saint of childbirth at a time when the act carried grave dangers, she gave rise to a flourishing cult: there are over two hundred churches dedicated to her in England alone.

The sphere of Margaret's influence points to an interesting undercurrent in the Bluebeard group of fairy tales, in which flows the theme of children's and mothers' deaths. Perrault's immediate source for 'La Barbe bleue' is not known, but Gilles de Rais, the Breton nobleman, Marshal of France and companion at arms of Joan of Arc, who was hanged in 1440 for satanism and the murder of hundreds of children, has been long associated with the fairytale ogre, especially in Brittany and the Vendée, where Gilles de Rais's castle of Tiffauges stood. In Saint Joan, Shaw even calls the historical character 'Bluebeard' and gives him a goatee of that tint. But although the crimes of Gilles de Rais swelled the figure of the fairytale

15 The Zodiac sign of Virgo, in a fresco depicting the month of August, with her hair tumbling down her back in golden abundance, borrows some of the attributes of Proserpina, daughter of Ceres who presides over the harvest: she offers a pomegranate of fruitfulness in one hand, while above her head, she holds a wheatsheaf, emblematic of Spica, the brightest star in an auspicious constellation that promises fertility, plenty and ripeness. (Francesco del Cossa and Ercole de' Roberti, Triumph of Ceres and Astrological Symbols, detail, Palazzo Schifanoia, Ferrara, 1469–72.)

De virginibus in communi. Antiphona.
Sacra virginitas de
o cara et angelis eius
amis odore auntes
adolescentule mundi
gloria calcauerunt. honemoa tyri

16 *The symbolic connotations of fairness overrode the historical likelihood of diverse colouring: virgin martyrs and other female saints in heaven consist only of dazzling blondes. (Spinola Hours, c. 1515.)*

17 The Virgin Mary was associated with the celestial colours of white and gold and blue, and identified with the Woman Clothed with the Sun from the Apocalypse; in the fourteenth century, the influential visions of Saint Bridget of Sweden, which inspired Botticelli's Mystic Nativity, confirmed that the Mother of God had the ideal maiden's golden hair.

18 The Whore of Babylon inherited the mirror and comb and blondeness of Venus, goddess of Love and Beauty; in the Apocalypse, her accursed kingdom is synonymous with lust and luxury, fornication and vanity. (The Angers Apocalypse, tapestry, thirteenth century.)

19 Some virgins in Christian culture retained Venus' rich promise: in this traditional cycle of the months, the sign Virgo presides over the threshing of the harvest, and the artist has used the same gold paint for her hair and the grain on the ground. (Book of Hours, Rouen, 1520–5.)

20 Though in the scroll the wild maiden laments her life, the luxuriance of flowers and fruit all around her, her unusual blue fleece, and her power over the unicorn's horn convey the magical potency of her exile in the woods. (Tapestry, Upper Rhine, 1475–1500.)

21 Bluebeard inherits the features of the satyr and his close kin, the devils, who in the Bible are called 'pilosi', the hairy ones, and sometimes appear ambiguously coloured blue. (The Last Judgement, detail, stained glass window, Fairford, England, c. 1495.)

22 Saint Dympna ran away from home because her father wanted to marry her, and hid herself in the woods in a hermit's cell, but he pursued her, and when she still refused him, he had her confessor killed, left, while he cut off her head himself. In Jan van Wavre's altarpiece of c. 1515, still in the shrine where she died, her father seizes her by her long plume of golden hair, symbolic of her inestimable worth, while the devil hovers overhead.

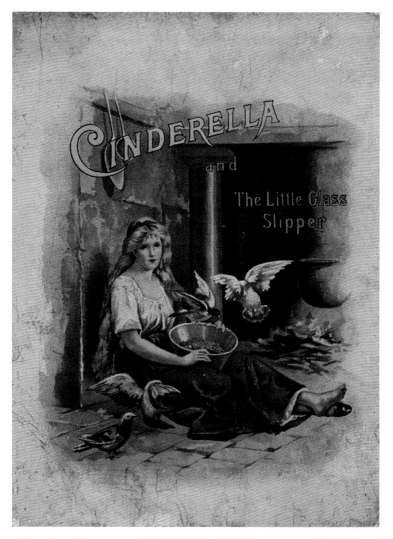

23 Fairytale heroines, like Cinderella, inherit the ancient symbolic sign of youth, purity and desirability, as in this children's illustration. (Nineteenth century.)
24 Popular imagery still draws on the ancient language of symbolism: a redhead and a brunette respectively, the ugly sisters bawl out a tawny-haired Cinderella, in the Ladybird version of Disney's 1950 film. (© The Walt Disney Company.)

"Cinderella, wash my stockings and curl my hair!" shouted one, loudly.

"Cinderella, find my fan and fetch my dancing slippers!" called the other. And all the time, Cinderella's stepmother scolded her for being so slow.

25 The white shoes trussed like a chicken on a dish were given the title Ma Gouvernante, My Nurse, Mein Kindermädchen *by the artist Meret Oppenheim, who was commemorating, in a spirit of mordant rebellion, the voice which in childhood points a girl towards love and marriage.*
26 *The dual aspect of sexuality at the core of fairy tale's concerns, here rendered as a disturbing visual oxymoron: spirals of bright hair interwined with gleaming pink pig gut. (Helen Chadwick,* Loop My Loop, *original title* Quite Contrary, *1991.)*

villain, another, earlier, Breton story offers a more thought-provoking possible original connection.

A young woman called Triphine, the daughter of Guerech, Count of Vannes, was married to Cunmar or Conomor of Brittany, surnamed 'ar Miliguet', or 'the Accursed'. In a jealous rage, he killed her, cutting off her head. But a local saint, Gildas, abbot of Rhuys in the sixth century, was miraculously able to join her head again to her body; together they then forded the stream of the Blavet to pursue Cunmar to his castle and confront him there. As they approached his castle, its walls came tumbling down. The episode was recorded in the *Vita* of Saint Gildas five hundred years after his death, by another monk of the foundation at Rhuys, and it drew on Breton legend. When Cunmar the Accursed married Triphine, he had already murdered several of her predecessors, and Triphine, his latest bride, fled from him after she was warned of her likely fate by the wives' ghosts. When she went to pray by the family tombs in the ancestral chapel, they spoke to her; there, in this foreshadowing of Bluebeard's secret chamber, they told her that Cunmar killed his wives as soon as they became pregnant. As Triphine knew that she too was expecting a child, she tried to escape, but Cunmar pursued her into a wood and killed her – and with her their unborn child.

Cunmar is a historical figure: a ruler of Brittany in the mid-sixth century who deposed the legitimate prince, became the scourge of the local clergy, and was consequently anathematized by the bishops of Brittany. In local legend, he has survived as a night wanderer, a *bisclavret*, or werewolf, while various churches are dedicated to Sainte Triphine, and to her son, Saint Trémeur, who after his mother's resurrection was safely born and given to Gildas as his godson to be brought up with him in the monastery. Some say Cunmar beheaded him too, and the seventeenth-century votive statue of mother and child in Guern, for instance, shows both saints miraculously carrying their own heads, like Roman martyrs. More vividly, the earlier, medieval frescoes in the church of St Nicholas des Eaux, also in Brittany, which were uncovered in the last century, break down the story into episodes which include Triphine's marriage to Cunmar, his handing over a small key to his castle, her opening a chamber in which seven former wives are hanging, his attempt to murder her – images which anticipate very satisfyingly the fairytale ogre, as chronicled by Perrault. On the main altar in another Breton shrine, a nineteenth-century Triphine is being seized by her hair in readiness for decapitation, an image which reproduces common children's illustrations to 'Bluebeard' (cf. Pl. 22), or the early film treatment by Georges Méliès, who showed the ogre dragging her by her hair up the spiral stairs to the top of a tower.

In this mourning portrait, Elizabeth Basse, Lady Saltonstall, lies pale in her deathbed, with her two children at the side of her husband; her successor, Mary Parker, their new stepmother, sits at her side, with her newborn in her arms. (David Des Granges, The Saltonstall Family, *English, c. 1636–7).*

As Méliès filmed using a dummy (thankfully), she bounces most grimly on the steps as her captor charges up them.

The Bluebeard figure's animus against his pregnant wives has been ascribed to the Oedipal rivalry so often dramatized in mythology: he wishes, like Oedipus' father Laius, to do away with a son before he grows up to threaten him. Or it has been attributed to jealousy: in a European ballad known over a large part of Europe (in French, '*Renaud le tueur des femmes*'), the verses follow the usual plot about the murderous husband, but explain that when he returns, after a long absence, to find his wife has had a child, he suspects her of infidelity: his rage is the unreasoning, maddened response of the man who fears cuckoldry, and believes that a child who is not his is being foisted on him. This trope gives the ballad's tale an affinity with the Accused Queen legends: the ogre's wife, innocent and faithful, is put to the test by a hard and suspicious husband. But this has also been seen from the opposite point of view: Bruno Bettelheim reversed the story's poignant message, that husbands wrongfully accuse wives of betraying them, and analysed the damn spot on the key, the spot on the egg, as the proof of the wife's roaming in her husband's absence.

But the Bluebeard figure's reaction – and his last wife's – could also reveal an experiential truth about marriages in the past, and the fairy tale, with its connections to the legend of the pregnant Triphine, may enfold a stark reality of women's lives, one which listeners and readers today might well miss, as they delve deep into the universal psychological secrets of the story. In this case, again, the seventeenth-century fairy tale can yield most interesting evidence when taken at face value: as stepmothers favoured their own children over the offspring of a previous marriage, or widowed mothers persecuted their sons' wives, as peasants starved but could advance through cunning, so, in the case of Bluebeard, widowers married many times in quick succession because wives died young, and died in childbirth, their infants with them. The fairy tale may attest to serial murderers in the past (Hincmar of Rheims in the ninth century, for instance, wrote that noblemen dealt with troublesome wives by having their throats slit), but it may also enclose a more routine cause of mortality. One of the principal causes of death before the nineteenth century was childbirth, and both child and female mortality was high. In the forbidden chamber, Bluebeard's wife had perhaps found herself face to face with the circumstances of her own future death.

The cult of Saint Triphine and her son Trémeur was not specially connected with women's fertility or childbirth, but it is associated with a devotional practice even more revealing. These are saints whose protection extends above all to children and their survival: infants were brought to their shrines when they began taking their first steps. The first steps, taken around ten months to a year old, marked, in times of high infant mortality, an improved degree of safety, a march stolen on death.

For many children did not live to walk, nor did their mothers survive their births. The wife of the English poet John Donne, for instance, died at the age of thirty-three, in 1617, soon after the stillbirth – of their twelfth child. She had borne a baby every year of their marriage. In Westminster Abbey, London, there are two monuments side by side to the wives of a certain Samuel Morland, put up by him and the dead women's parents: the stark epitaphs, which communicate a genuine, griefstricken note by their very presence, record that Carola, née Harsnett, 'bare a second son October 4/died October 10th/Anno Domini 1674/Aetatis XXIII'; and that her successor 'Ann [née Filding] died February 20th/Anno Domini 1679/80/Aetatis XIX'. Nothing is said of the children's survival. During the time in which fairy tales like Perrault's 'La Barbe bleue' were being written, childbirth did indeed present a very real danger.

Christian moral philosophy laid down that the child came first – so that it could be saved by baptism. Caesareans were performed, and no mother survived this surgery before the discovery of anaesthetic and antibiotics. The situation improved, but only very slowly. Eugen Weber gives some statistics for rural

France: in 1800 women of Lower Burgundy for instance could expect to live only an average of around twenty-five years; by mid-century, this had risen to almost forty years; by the end of the century, the average female lifespan stood at fifty-two years. Remarriage among widowers was very common indeed in France – 80 per cent in the seventeenth and eighteenth centuries, a figure which had fallen to 15 per cent in the nineteenth.

At the cheerful end of Perrault's story, Bluebeard's wife is able to dispose of his unencumbered fortune:

> Bluebeard left no heirs, so his wife took possession of all his estate. She used part of it to marry her sister Anne to a young man with whom she had been in love for a long time; she used more of it to buy commissions for her two brothers, and she used the rest to marry herself to an honest man who made her forget her sorrows as the wife of Bluebeard.

In spite of all those wives, Bluebeard had had no children. A rich man of his sort, and a widower many times over, would not have been such an oddity in Perrault's world or to generations who heard his story later, until the next century and improving rates of infant and female mortality. Perrault, a realist who clothed his witness in fancy dress, spun a tale of reassurance, in which his heroine is spared one of the most present fears of young women in the past: that marriage will be the death of her.

When Cunmar and Bluebeard figure as serial murderers, they may not have been individually responsible in the way their stories suggest to a contemporary audience. When Saint Margaret escapes first Olybrius, then the dragon, and then the fiend 'in the form of a man', and is delivered up safe and sound from the dragon, she may well inspire reassurance in her votaries' breasts as a woman who has escaped the dangers of sex, rather than escaping sex itself. Her many laudatory lives dwell on her splendid resistance to her various assailants, and sometimes qualify as 'apocryphal' the story of the dragon's belly bursting asunder to set her free. Jacobus de Voragine says so, in *The Golden Legend*, and quickly moves on to another topic, almost as if he realizes that this tale of being devoured carries suggestive implications that were better left alone. It is even possible, as one thinks oneself into the mind of a congregation listening to the story in fourteen hundred and something, to imagine that Saint Margaret represented to them a woman forced against her will by not just one man but more, who either miraculously escapes conceiving or, if she does bear a child, is spared the physical dangers and maybe even the social obloquy following rape. Certainly the look on the dragon's face, as he licks his lips looking up at Saint Margaret in the cheap woodcuts that promoted her cult in fifteenth-century Europe, leaves the onlooker in no doubt that his intentions were not merely gastronomic.

II

Fear of death in childbirth may represent one of the story's latent meanings, but it does not figure among its patent messages. Bluebeard is presented as a man of enormous wealth: his castle is filled with treasures, paintings; luxury feasting and entertainments take place be he absent or present, in a veritable potlatch of expenditure. The plot follows the heroine's transition, her passage from her native home to her new marital household, as takes place in exogamous arrangements. The castle possesses the allure and the dread of the strange, other place to which she is going. As in penny dreadfuls and Gothic romances, fairy tales dramatize the beast's castle, the place of foreboding where the heroine will be enclosed.

At the beginning of 'Bluebeard', the heroine's widowed mother, rather like a Jane Austen character, considers him a good match for one of her 'perfectly beautiful' daughters precisely because of his riches. In many Mother Goose tales, money and romance are bound up together, but of the two, money is by far the more pressing problem. Cinderella is deprived of her birthright so that her stepsisters may have larger dowries; in 'Peau d'Ane' (Donkeyskin), the king sacrifices the magic donkey that shits gold, the source of his wealth, to his illicit love for his daughter. The monetary arrangements at the conclusion of Bluebeard, after the heroine's brothers have galloped to her rescue, are also eminently hardheaded, and include remnants of a now unfamiliar kinship and inheritance system, a modified form of matrilineage which was still practised among the nobility in certain parts of Europe in the early middle ages (and is still common in some parts of the world – among the Ibo of Nigeria, for instance). It gives maternal uncles an important and continuing part to play in their sisters' affairs, in representing the family interests as well as enjoying title to the fruits of their marriages. It also places a woman at the fulcrum of continuing dynastic alliances between families which can be unbalanced for all kinds of reasons of family honour, political and economic, lying quite outside the marriage itself.

If the sanguine and practical dénouement of 'Bluebeard' is taken together with other romantic endings in Mother Goose tales, Perrault's partisanship can be seen: he was the first man to write down fairy tales, though they were women and children's literature, as he was the first to admit. But unlike some of his colleagues, Perrault was eager to espouse the woman's cause, and in his stories, however frivolous his tone, he took the part of daughters against the arranged marriages of the day, with their cynical ambitiousness for social position and wealth and their disregard for personal inclination. He also issued an open argument, by means of his tales, for the right of women to administer their own wealth.

An early English retelling gives 'Fatima' a strong motive for doing away with her monster husband: a nice lover called Selim. This story ends: 'Selim took possession of the Castle, gave the slaves their liberty, and married Fatima.' By the middle of the nineteenth century, when the story was expanded for English audiences, the same point did not have to be made, as widows could expect to inherit. In one version, Bluebeard's widow is described as a Victorian Lady Bountiful, using her late husband the ogre's goods to benefit the needy:

> Instead of the miserable hovels usually inhabited by the labouring poor, she had annually several comfortable and pleasant cottages built, and to each one she added a large plot of ground ... where there were a family of children, she added to this gift a cow and a few sheep. By this means she enabled them, by their own exertions ... always to secure a humble competence, and in a very short time, every person upon her estate was rendered happy and became her firm friend.

The legend of Bluebeard has inspired an impressive body of works over the last hundred years; something about the much married ogre catches the popular imagination and has also challenged some great artists to reinterpret him and his wives. A late Victorian writer for children, Juliana Horatia Ewing (d. 1885), the witty and reforming editor of *Aunt Judy's Magazine*, defended female independence of heart in her variation on 'Bluebeard', 'The Ogre Courting', of 1871. Managing Molly, her Finessa-like subtle heroine, tricks the dull-witted ogre, who has already eaten twenty-four wives at least at the last count ('within the memory of man'), with a series of riddling ruses that take advantage of his meanness; the final straw, for the monster, is the feather bed she insists he fills by 'plucking [the] geese in heaven' – an ancient image of snow used by the Welsh poet Taliesin in the thirteenth century. The ogre shovels snow into the mattress as fast as he can, but of course it melts away; after a night in the cold wet bed, he will do anything to get rid of this new wife with her thrifty ideas, including parting with the dowry he gave her.

British optimism shows through Mrs Ewing's robustly practical story; her comic confidence matches the expansive and prosperous confidence of the Victorian heyday, and even implies the climate that allowed a crucial measure of emancipation for women, the Married Women's Property Act of 1882, which for the first time placed the goods and dowry a wife brought to a marriage securely under her control, and allowed her to retain them after her husband's death.

By contrast, continental Europe's interpretations of 'Bluebeard' reflect the comparatively defeated mood of feminism in France after the betrayal of the Revolution and the profound *embourgeoisement* of the Second Empire. In 1899, the actress and singer Georgette Leblanc inspired her lover, the Belgian Symbolist Maurice Maeterlinck, to write a libretto based on the Perrault fairy tale. They were living in a rented château in northern France at the time, which was also to inspire the crepuscular setting of Maeterlinck's more famous dramatic fairytale poem, set to music by Debussy – *Pelléas et Mélisande*. Leblanc suggested that Maeterlinck intertwine the Bluebeard legend with the quest of Ariadne, who delivered Theseus from the monster in the labyrinth. Thus, in *Ariane et Barbe-bleue*, the wives of Bluebeard become the young Cretan maidens sacrificed to the Minotaur's lust; his most recent bride, Ariane, takes the role of her classical namesake and Theseus combined as she enters the terrifying castle, opens the door to the forbidden chamber and finds that his previous wives are all still there, enduring a living death, in torpor and darkness – and luxury – so many lulled Rapunzels, prisoners of love, like Mélisande herself, who appears as one of their number. Like the prince, Ariane wakes them to the possibility of freedom, of the world outside, of light and action and independence, and they respond, with a powerful chorus of hope. But Georgette Leblanc also proposed from the start that the subtitle of the opera be *La Délivrance inutile,* the useless rescue. In the second act, the wives, after their moment of exultation, cannot be persuaded to leave Bluebeard or his castle; they prefer the chains they know, they cling to and caress the lover with whom they are familiar.

Maeterlinck wrote the play in 1899, and gave it to the composer Paul Dukas to set to music; it was first performed in Paris in 1907, and in spite of its luscious, sparkling cascades of chromatic sound it has rarely been put on since. Dukas himself commented trenchantly on the wives' refusal:

No one wants to be rescued. Rescue is costly because it is the unknown. Men (and women) will always prefer a familiar slavery to the terrifying uncertainty of the burden of liberty. The truth is salvation is not possible; better to save one's self. Not only is it better; it's the only possible thing. The women make this very clear to poor Ariane. She didn't know; she thought the world was thirsty for freedom when in reality it only hopes for comfort.

Bluebeard himself hardly utters in the opera; passive, nearly mute, he accepts the collusion of his wives in their own idle, prosperous imprisonment. The last scene shows Bluebeard's willing captives, bedecked in shimmering silks and jewels found in his treasury; the libretto addresses a bitter reproach to those new domestic idols, those housewives happy with the booming department stores of late nineteenth-century and early twentieth-century France: the frippery represents the desolate extent of the freedom they desire.

Béla Bartók's *Duke Bluebeard's Castle* has eclipsed Maeterlinck and Dukas's interpretation in fame and frequency of performance; first staged in 1918, eleven years after *Ariane et Barbe-bleue* was produced, the libretto by Béla Balázs had been offered to one composer in 1910, and Bartók had accepted it in 1911. An extended poetic meditation on the impossibility of love between men and women, it presents Judith, the latest of Bluebeard's wives, as a questor after experience, after intensity, as a woman who has jilted a man to whom she was betrothed in order to run away with Bluebeard to his deep, secret castle. She is given the name of the biblical heroine, to invoke the assassin of Holofernes, the embodiment of lust and sin in secular as well as religious iconography. But Balázs, the librettist, was steeped in fairy tale as well as folk music, and he adds a sinister touch to the heroic moral of scripture, for his Judith is eager to go deeper into adventure, wisdom and sexual knowledge, and be annihilated with her despotic lover, rather than kill him. One by one, to ever more keyed up, swellingly sensual and iridescent music, she opens the doors to the chambers in Bluebeard's symbolic fortress and finds evils behind them, fabulous and tainted treasure, pools of tears, torture instruments, flowers with bloody petals, and finally, three living brides, immured, captives. The opera is enigmatic: the castle becomes a castle of the soul rather than a locale, a symbol of passionate interior striving, of the desperate character of sexual passion, of the doom which all passionate love must suffer. The music suggests voluptuous fulfilment and inevitable separateness simultaneously, and Judith's determination, in the face of Bluebeard's reluctance, to know more, to go further and deeper, does not stand condemned.

This Judith personifies the early twentieth-century's radical revelation of female sexuality and appetite; she can symbolize for us the new woman who desires, and expresses her desires, and Balázs and Bartók used the language of fairytale adventure to create her, for both men were committed to the folk tradition and found in the ballad singers the inspiration for contemporary works which tackled urgent issues. Bartók wrote at the time of composition: 'Women should be accorded the same liberties as men. Women ought to be free to do the same things as men, or men ought not to be free to do things women aren't supposed to do – I used to believe this to be so for the sake of equality ...' He does not go on to retract his opinion, but qualifies it as necessary because repressing women's desires constitutes a graver risk than allowing them equal expression.

The heroines of twentieth-century stories about marriage to a beast no longer reject him: they are shown welcoming the discoveries the union brings them. The opera dramatizes a ritual of an initiation which can never be fully achieved, and its ultimate import, unlike its predecessor's, stresses surrender: Judith meets the fate that the earlier heroines are spared, but she steps into the void fully aware of what she is doing.

III

Of the eight famous fairy tales in Perrault's *Contes du temps passé*, 'La Barbe bleue' contains the most deeply disturbing adult material beside 'Red Riding Hood' – for unlike Perrault's other ogres, the giant in 'Puss-in-Boots', or the wicked fairy in 'The Sleeping Beauty', Bluebeard is a Jack the Ripper, who perpetrates his evil on young women in their sexual maturity, not on children in their needs. The story can hardly be said to be a fairy tale: the only magic features the fatal key, which Perrault characterizes as *Fée*, with a capital letter, using the word as an adjective (enchanted or fey), for the only time in his work. The key, with its smear of blood which will not wipe off, betrays the errant wife to the ogre on his return: a symbol of her pollution, connected to loss of childhood innocence and of virginity, of irrepressible sexuality.

Bluebeard has entered secular mythology alongside Cinderella and Snow White. But his story possesses a characteristic with particular affinity to the present day: seriality. Whereas the violence in the heroines' lives is considered suitable for children, the ogre has metamorphosed in popular culture for adults, into the mass murderer, the kidnapper, the serial killer: a collector, as in John Fowles's novel, an obsessive, like Hannibal Lecter in *The Silence of the Lambs*. Though cruel women, human or fairy, dominate children's stories with their powers, the Bluebeard figure, as a generic type of male murderer, has gradually entered material requiring restricted ratings as well. (As patriarch, he remains at ease in the nursery.) There are several pornographic film titles which use the name

Bluebeard; more surprisingly, perhaps, the story has appealed to women writers like Margaret Atwood and Angela Carter, both of whom have produced contemporary treatments.

In an essay on the slasher movie, the scholar and critic Carol Clover first put forward the polemical view that the pursuit of the avenging female, who tracks down a murderer and finally 'slashes' him, meting out to him what he wanted to mete out to her, actually acts as a satisfying fantasy for women viewers ('enabling'). She develops her argument from looking at such films through the lens of the Icelandic sagas – she teaches Scandinavian studies – and seeks to understand twentieth-century celluloid gore in the light of bardic mayhem. Saga and fairy tale share certain features: oral transmission and the need to please the crowd. At least – they are – or were – literature to be passed on aloud and experienced in a group. The Bluebeard story can be seen as one of the slasher film's progenitors. But in the earlier versions produced by women, if not directed at them, the threatened heroine resorts to the ruse as well as the axe or her brothers' brawn to save her skin. The passage from the page (and the voice) to the moving image has profoundly affected the reception of the material; paradoxically, the visual becomes literal, imprinting the imagination and the heroine; the oral excites visualization, giving the imagination semi-free play, with hallucinatory effects, especially among children. But the dominance of imagery over word in storytelling today has pushed verbal agility into the background; even the fast-talking, wisecracking, insult-trading entertainment of 1930s thrillers like *Double Indemnity* have ceded to almost wordless narratives. Deeds of fantastic efficacy and often extravagant violence have replaced cunning and high spirits in the most popular vehicles for revenge fantasies and triumphs over adversity.

The excessive, heightened, sadistic side of fairy tales has made them even more compelling in the last decades of the century, especially among adults who value more highly than ever the imagined pristine clarity and depths of childlike fantasy.

An uneasy amalgam of different sources and the resulting non-sequiturs intensify the nastiness of the Grimms' version of 'Bluebeard', 'Fitcher's Bird', and it has rarely been retold in the single, illustrated children's format of postwar publishing of fairy tales. Recently, however, the artist Cindy Sherman illustrated it for the art publishers Rizzoli's, in New York. Sherman has specialized in an atmosphere of menace in her work and frequently picked out sex crimes as a particular area of interest. Her photography began with remarkable impersonations of *film-noir* heroines, featuring herself, alone, in black and white pretend stills. Her metamorphoses collapsed to an alarming degree any claim to irreducible or certain personal identity, as she is able to look like ... anyone. This effectively produces an eerie, baffling mood of impending danger for all: since she can occupy anybody's persona, she becomes a kind of cautionary Everywoman. But her metamorphoses do not struggle free of the grip of the assailant, as in the fairy tale, but serve to underline the crisis of subjectivity.

'Bluebeard' was a natural story for Sherman to enter, because the seriality of the dead wives also marks their anonymity, their interchangeability, the failure of stable subjectivity. Sherman followed her fake film stills with huge Cibachromes, using their unearthly, keyed-up colours to add a lurid edge to a series of new poses, some of them simulating police shots of crimes against women. In the latter, she again connected with cinematic fantasy: some of her *mises-en-scène* capture Hitchcock or De Palma visions of sexual assault and female mutilation. An unusual choice, therefore, for a children's illustrator, but one which intuits the nature of the fairytale material, especially in the Grimm Brothers' often cruel redactions.

Her collages for 'Fitcher's Bird' are only partly successful, however. Through ghoulish, fragmented, highly lit shots of wax models, using real feathers, hair, jewels and basketry, the sequence does reproduce effectively the jangling, lurid, incoherent violence of the Grimms' original, but Sherman's stock-in-trade of irony and kitsch cannot pass for the child audience, since it needs reference points – the thriller movie, the piece of forensic evidence – against which to play its own meanings. Here the art language Sherman parodies is that most commonly found in museum tableaux using waxworks, real clothes and props. Children learn this language at an early age, in theme parks where crimes are re-enacted in *tableaux vivants*, as in the Chamber of Horrors in Madame Tussaud's, London, and it speaks to them directly of actual events and real people, without irony, in a spirit of apparent admonishment and latent prurience. Sherman's photography annexes this double and dubious pleasure to make the Grimms' fairy tale real and present to the mind, uninflected by urbane irony. Needless to say, the story, in this version, misses altogether the redemptive mischief of L'Héritier's 'Finessa' or the comic high spirits of Calvino's 'Silver Nose'. Sherman's love affair with horror captures one interpretation of narrative power in this fin de siècle: hair-raising, rather than laughter, has become the motive of the teller, and damage the key motif of the tale – and anyone who escapes damage is lucky.

The seduction of difference: the Beast gazes on Beauty in Jean Cocteau's classic fairytale film. (Jean Marais and Josette Day, La Belle et la bête, *1946.)*

CHAPTER 17

Reluctant Brides: Beauty and the Beast I

I never may believe
These antic fables, nor these fairy toys.
Lovers and madmen have such seething brains,
Such shaping fantasies, that apprehend
More than cool reason ever comprehends …
And as imagination bodies forth
The forms of things unknown, the poet's pen
Turns them to shapes, and gives to aery nothing
A local habitation and a name …

A Midsummer Night's Dream, V, i

The first Beast of the West was Eros, the god of love himself. In the romance of Cupid and Psyche, Eros/Cupid makes love, unseen in the dark, to a mortal Beauty – Psyche – who rivals his own mother Venus in seductiveness; Psyche is forbidden to look at him. When she can resist no longer and breaks the prohibition, lighting a candle to look at her lover while he sleeps, he vanishes, and with him all her enchanted surroundings. But Eros, mysterious, unknown, feared, exceeds all imaginable degree of charm when Psyche sees him in the night:

> There lay the gentlest and sweetest of all wild creatures … his golden hair, washed in nectar and still scented with it, thick curls straying over white neck and flushed cheeks and falling prettily entangled on either side of his head … soft wings of purest white … the tender down fringing the feathers quivered naughtily all the time. The rest of his body was so smooth and beautiful that Venus could never have been ashamed to acknowledge him as her son.

Psyche's failure to trust, and to obey, has cost her his adorable presence and his love.

Apuleius' tale is the earliest extant forerunner of the Beauty and the Beast fairy tale in Western literature, and a founding myth of sexual difference. It includes episodes the fairy tale '*La Belle et la bête*' has made famous, from children's versions and films: the mysterious menacing lover, the jealous sisters, the enchanted castle where disembodied voices serve every wish and 'nectarous wines and appetizing dishes appeared by magic, floating up to her of their own accord'. It echoes stories of Pandora and Eve when it relies on female curiosity as the dynamic of the plot, and the overriding motive force of the female sex. Punished for her disobedience, Psyche then has to prove her love through many adventures and ordeals; pregnant by Cupid, she struggles through one test of her loyalty after another until, finally, this Beauty is reunited with her Beast and adapts him, the god of love, to the human condition of marriage, and they have a daughter, called Voluptas – Pleasure.

The role of Eros/Cupid in the second-century romance echoes the manifestation of beast bridegrooms in much more ancient stories, not only in numerous classical myths of metamorphosis, but also in Chinese and Indian tales, like 'The Girl who Married a Snake', from the *Panchatantra*. Its progeny are numerous, scattered in all the great Renaissance collections like Straparola's and Basile's and the translated *Arabian Nights*; though entertainingly heterogeneous, the tales still bear a strong family resemblance. Such a divine erotic beast as the hero of the popular fairy tale has offered writers and other artists – painters and film-makers – a figure of masculine desire, and the plot in which he moves presents a blueprint for the channelling of erotic energy – both male and female – in society at any one time. Shakespeare's *A Midsummer Night's Dream* manages both to guy this romance of enchanted love, with Titania and Bottom at the very extremes of beauty and beasthood, but at the same time to extend and deepen the reach of the fairy tale of benign metamorphosis in all its serious, spellbinding powers.

In Apuleius, which was one of Shakespeare's sources, it is Psyche who has to strive, just as it is Titania who is deluded. 'Cupid and Psyche' represents Eros biding his time, waiting for his bride to prove herself and earn him. The story is her journey, she has to expiate her error; like the knight in the fairy tale of the Sibyl's cave or the enchanted mountain, she has experienced love and lost it. Unlike that tale, however, in which the fairy wife proves a false image, an occasion of sin to be resisted, Psyche's suspicions turn out to be groundless. Her lover is no beast, but only concealed from her, and she is wrong to fear him. Her journey towards true knowledge of her hidden lover became perceived as the journey of the soul towards the concealed godhead, '*deus absconditus*', in the writings of the Neoplatonists who adopted the story as a form of secular gospel; fairy tales have carried this philosophical interpretation into domestic settings. Psyche remains in the foreground, as the protagonist who functions as the chivalrous questor. It is her activities which catalyse the plot – at first harmfully, at last triumphantly. Though she is lachrymose and given to the vapours (as are all the heroines of Greek romances), she nevertheless voyages purposefully to recover the object of her desire.

The tale consistently leaves in place the Eros figure as the goal, again, in a reversal of the more expected pattern of chivalry. In widespread contemporary popular quest narratives, it is still more common to find knights errant rather than maidens in pursuit of their loves. The Super Mario Brothers computer game gives the two heroic plumbers from Brooklyn the dominant motive of rescuing a damsel in distress in all their adventures.

Psyche's false perception, gradually modified, finally arrives at the truth: the radiant beauty of the god of love. In many ways, the inner structure of the Beauty and the Beast tale reverses the roles defined by the title: she has to learn the higher (human) wisdom of seeing past outward appearances, to grasp that monstrousness lies in the eye of the beholder, while the beast turns out to be irresistibly beautiful and the highest good. The Beauty and the Beast story is a classic fairy tale of transformation, which, when told by a woman, places the male lover, the Beast, in the position of the mysterious, threatening, possibly fatal unknown, and Beauty, the heroine, as the questor who discovers his true nature.

Apuleius' storyteller, the 'drunken and half-demented old woman' whom the author adopts as his mouthpiece in this exemplary and hopeful section of his comic romance, gives him authority in the traditionally female preserve of romantic or sexual expertise. But it also achieves, almost by accident, a crucial switch of viewpoint: the unknown is seen from Psyche's point of view. Cupid, the god of love and the personification of the masculine erotic principle, appears as a fantasy, a monster, a powerful threat. The postulated crone storyteller makes this vantage point seem logical in a way that the narrative voice of the hero Lucius or the author himself would have failed to do. Apuleius shows more storytelling wiles later: he first confirms the message of his fairy tale, telling how the abducted bride Charite escapes the horrible torments proposed by the bandits and is reunited with her lost husband, but he then undermines this happy ending, and metes out violent deaths to both bride and groom. Charite (Love/Grace) in the larger novel mirrors Psyche in the tale as a smitten heroine beset by troubles, and in her subsequent tragedy Apuleius perversely reopens the potential tragic outcome of romance in his real-life story as opposed to an old wives' tale. In this, he gainsays the normative, controlling aspect of the fairy story, which gives the male Beast the *beau rôle* and blames his female lover's folly for nearly ruining everything.

The perspective of Psyche/Charite nevertheless chimes with the female story-telling voice, and offered an opportunity to many women writers who identified themselves with romantic heroines through the medium of the scorned old gossip's advice. They too seized on Apuleius' mask to reverse the thrust of such shafts and deal with the question of opposites, embodied in the male. The beast stood for the crucial choice in a growing woman's life: to leave family (as the word implies, the familiar) for the unknown and unfamiliar. The question of exogamy, or marrying out, and its accompanying dangers lies at the heart of the romance. For boy heroes, leaving the father's house to find a princess to marry, as in so many fairy tales, like 'Puss-in-Boots' by Perrault or the Grimms' *'Die drei Federn'* (The Three Feathers), there is no anguish, only adventure, and reward. But daughters' leave-takings inspire powerful and contradictory passions, which 'Beauty and the Beast' explores.

Fairy tale as a form deals with limits, and limits often set by fear: one of its fundamental themes treats of a protagonist who sets out to discover the unknown and overcomes its terrors. 'The Tale of the Boy who Went Forth to Learn What Fear Was' (*'Märchen von einem, der auszog, das Fürchten zu lernen'*), about a hero who knows no fear, one of the Grimms' most famous fairy stories, sets out the theme in its stark simplicity: after various ordeals in which the boy plays cards with corpses, bowls skulls at skittles with skeletons for playmates, meets and subdues various hell-cats and ghouls, he at last encounters the princess, and in bed with her learns how to shudder when she tips a pail of live fish over him – perhaps a metaphor for the overwhelming power of physical passion. (In the compelling Freudian interpretation, shuddering euphemistically replaces orgasmic spasms.)

When women tell fairy stories, they also undertake this central narrative concern of the genre – they contest fear; they turn their eye on the phantasm of the male Other and recognize it, either rendering it transparent and safe, the self reflected as good, or ridding themselves of it (him) by destruction or transformation. At a fundamental level, 'Beauty and the Beast' in numerous variations forms a group of tales which work out this basic plot, moving from the terrifying encounter with Otherness, to its acceptance, or, in some versions of the story, its annihilation. In either case, the menace of the Other has been met, dealt with and exorcized by the end of the fairy tale; the negatively charged protagonist has proved golden, as in so many fairy tales where a fierce bear or loathsome toad proves a Prince Charming. The terror has been faced and chased; the light shines in the dark places.

As a female pilgrim's progress, a common rite of passage, with a heroine moving at its centre, the tale of the feared animal groom has attracted numerous women interpreters. They form a long and distinguished line which includes *ancien régime* rakes, French governesses, English bluestockings. In Victorian England, women were specially attracted to the fairy tale: Mary Lamb published a version of 'Beauty and the Beast' with her brother Charles in 1806; the fairy painter Richard Doyle illustrated his sister Adelaide's translation of around 1842 (it was not published until this century), and in 1889, *The Blue Fairy Book*, edited by the scholar and enthusiast Andrew Lang with the help of his wife Leonora Alleyne, disseminated Miss Minnie Wright's splice of two French texts, the one by Mme de Villeneuve and another by Mme de Beaumont, to create the most widely read version in English. An interesting case has been made for *Jane Eyre* as a variation on Apuleius (Rochester as blind Cupid) inspired by the Brontës' reading of the *Blackwood's Magazine* publication of the Latin tale. In film, too, women have been strongly represented, with screen-writers like Ruth Rose (*King Kong*), Caroline Thompson (*Edward Scissorhands*) and Linda Woolverton (the Disney *Beauty and the Beast*) taking different approaches to various monster bridegrooms. More recently, the artist and writer Leonora Carrington (*b*. 1917) and her younger contemporary Angela Carter have continued, in a spirit of Surrealist devilry, exploring the erotic possibilities for the heroine.

But it was in the seventeenth and eighteenth centuries that the French fairytale writers invented the pattern familiar today, and from it cut dozens of different, inventive variations. The story of Cupid and Psyche was well-known in courtly circles: *Psyché*, a spectacle with song and dance, commissioned to celebrate the peace of Aix-la-Chapelle of 1668, was performed for the king three years later; tepid stuff, it shows little of the deft hands of its creators, a remarkable trio – Molière, Corneille and Quinault. La Fontaine produced a punchier version, filled with deliciously malign shafts at the follies of the age, in *Les Amours de Psyché et de Cupidon*, a novel, which was published in 1669. Writers and friends of Mlle L'Héritier like Henriette-Julie de Murat and Marie-Catherine d'Aulnoy, contemporaries like Mlle de La Force and Mlle Bernard, struggling against prevailing Christian conceptions of women's contagious lustfulness, against the traditional blaming of Eve, adduced in women's defence certain social exactions upon them: they especially attacked the custom of marrying off daughters at very young ages (fourteen or fifteen was not uncommon) to strangers. In this regard, women of high rank suffered from total powerlessness, and there was not much change in matrimonial matters until the Revolution ushered in a new era of comparatively free choice.

When Perrault sprang to the defence of fairytale romancing, he specifically joined battle over the question of love-in-marriage, writing heatedly:

> I don't doubt at all that several people of the higher ranks find it strange that I deem it such great happiness to enjoy conjugal friendship, those who ordinarily only regard marriage as a path towards establishing themselves in society, and who believe that if you must take a wife in order to have children, you must pick a mistress in order to have pleasure.

The ancient fairy tale of Cupid and Psyche had become a secular myth, held in common, which could be used to contest or elaborate ideas about choice and eros, modern love and romance.

Beneath the literary wrangle in the capital lay a vital moral issue, about the character and purpose of marriage and the different needs of women from men, and the different experiences of women within the institution. Conjugal friendship was not an aspect of many women's lives, the testimony of fairy tale would seem to be telling us. Romance – love-in-marriage – was an elusive ideal, which the writers of the *contes* sometimes set up in defiance of destiny. As Gillian Beer has so succinctly put it: 'Revolution is one function of the romance.' When the revolutionary situation is past, readers then come to interpret the subversion it expressed in its texts in a spirit of docile nostalgia. The fairy tale of Beauty and the Beast assumed a female audience on the whole who fully expected to be given away by their fathers to men who might well strike them as monsters. The social revolution which has established both romantic and companionate marriage as the norm has irreversibly altered the reception of such romances, and ironically transformed certain women's examination of their matrimonial lot into materialistic propaganda for making a good marriage. The partial eclipse of those fairy tales which criticize marriage in favour of ones which celebrate it has arisen partly from the new, comparative freedom to choose a partner – or partners. The pact with the Beast at the beginning of the fairy tale, when Beauty's father hands over his daughter, actually narrates a common circumstance, and Beauty's wholehearted obligingness in the matter was increasingly emphasized. But the fading of fairy tales in which Beauty or her counterpart resists the arrangement her father has made on her behalf also follows from the growing control of printers, publishers, editors and writers who were themselves fathers and husbands, and may have felt threatened by the earlier redactions' forthright attacks on male tyrants. And, thirdly, the changing value of the Beast as a symbol, and the displacement of the animal as the chief site of a hostile and repressed Other, has also contributed to an important degree to the changing meanings of the tale.

The historical and social context of the printed versions alters the message and the reception of the lovers' perennial conflict and quest; remembering the changing background in which the tellers move constitutes a crucial part in understanding the sexual politics of the tale. The theory of archetypes, which is essentially ahistorical, helps to confirm gender inevitability and to imprison male and female in stock definitions. By contrast, attitudes to the Beast are always in flux, and even provide a gauge of changing evaluations of human beings themselves, of the meaning of what it is to be human, and specifically, since the Beast has been primarily identified with the male since the story's earliest forms, what it is to be a man.

II

Tales of animal bridegrooms hold out the dream that, although the heroine's father has given her into the keeping of a Beast, he will change – into a radiant young man, a perfect lover. At the start of the story, the Beast rampages in various misshapen and monstrous forms, demonic, ogreish, cannibal. His reluctant brides deal with him to different ends, sometimes by recognizing his inner qualities (so that he does not need to be changed), sometimes by effecting his disenchantment, but now and then by outwitting him, and even on occasion by doing

Joining a Madame Récamier-like Beauty for an elegant supper on his empire style furniture, a huge Beast pleads for love. (In Popular Tales of the Olden Time, *c. 1840.)*

Beauty comes flying back to the Beast's side just in time as he sprawls near death in longing for her. ('The Absence of Beauty Lamented', in Charles and Mary Lamb, (attrib.), Beauty and the Beast, c. 1811.)

The Absence of Beauty Lamented.

away with him altogether and living happily ever after with the prince of their choice.

Far harsher stories than today's rosy romances were circulating in the eighteenth century, collected in *Le Cabinet des fées*, and translated and distributed beyond France, appearing in English in the editions of Robert Samber and other printer-publishers before they fade from view in the nineteenth century, giving way to reassurances about male conversion, future love and happiness. In these tales, the Beast's savagery is no illusion, but an aspect of his nature which the heroine has to confront.

One dominant curve can be discovered in the retellings from the seventeenth century to the present day: at first, the Beast is identified with male sexuality which must be controlled or changed or domesticated through *civilité*, a code chiefly established by women, but later the Beast is perceived as a principle of nature within every human being, male and female, young and old, and the stories affirm beastliness's intrinsic goodness and necessity to holistic survival. The variations in the ways of telling 'Beauty and the Beast' offer us a text where this fundamental change of *mentalité* can be deciphered; the representations of the Beast circulating in other forms, in films and toys for instance, especially teddy bears, also illuminate one aspect of what the historian Keith Thomas in *Man and the Natural World* has termed one of the most profound changes in human sensibility in modern time: the re-evaluation of animals.

Happy endings have also come to be expected of children's stories. Red Riding

Hood's father – or a passing huntsman – now regularly springs her and her grand-mother safe and sound out of the wolf's belly. Changing ideas about children's sensitivity may be yet another reason for the fading of Beauty and the Beast sto-ries which end badly for the Beast. Notions of decorum for young women affected the selection of editors, too: the process by which the Grimms gradually made their heroines more polite, well-spoken, or even silent, from one edition to the next, while their wicked female characters become more and more vitupera-tive and articulate, was replicated in mass children's publishing of the nineteenth century, and tales of plucky or disaffected young women who baulk their suitors, defy their parents or guardians and generally offer opposition to their lot often had to wait until, in the renewed feminist mood of the 1970s and 1980s, they were reclaimed by pedagogues with other views of appropriate female conduct.

Of the women writers of fairy tales represented in *Le Cabinet des fées*, Catherine Bernard and Marie-Jeanne L'Héritier were almost the only ones who, in the years of severe state censorship and autocratic controls, managed a quiet and private life. Neither married, and both found aristocratic female patrons to support them in their writing. Their colleagues, however, had much more troubled careers.

Henriette-Julie de Castelnau, born in 1670, married to the Comte de Murat at the age of twenty-one, caused a stir when she arrived in Paris from her native Brittany and showed a preference for Breton peasant costume, thus anticipating Marie-Antoinette's peasant make-believe. But Murat was acting in a different spirit, for she was writing fiction based on her own origins, and challenging her own peers and superiors. She penned a squib about the courtesan Rhodope that clearly targeted the king's pious mistress, Mme de Maintenon, and her former husband, the poet Scarron, and in 1698 Murat was summoned as '*une femme déréglée*' by the police, and ordered into provincial exile; she managed to resist – until 1702, when her family collaborated in putting her away as mentally dis-turbed. The rumours of her *dérèglement* included, from the angle of the purified, Maintenon court, blasphemy and lesbianism; it is very difficult to assess the truth of these accusations from this distance. However, Mme de Murat continued to raise eyebrows during her exile in Loches, by wearing a red riding hood to church and announcing loudly and exuberantly that she lived for pleasure. She had to wait until the death of Louis XIV and the Regency of Philippe d'Orléans before she was released and allowed to return to Paris, but she died soon after, of chronic kidney trouble, in 1716.

Murat's misfortunes were not unusual in the climate of courtly despotism. Charlotte-Rose Caumont de La Force (1650–1724) married the son of a highly placed official, the Président Briou, without the latter's consent; the marriage was immediately broken by his family. Later, she was also dismissed from court, where she was a *dame d'honneur* or lady-in-waiting to the queen and the dauphin, after she wrote some blasphemous poems; she had to face penury, as her pension was cut off, or enter a convent. She chose the latter, and wrote fairy tales from her exile in the nunnery, publishing them in the same year as Perrault's *Mother Goose Tales* (1697).

Like Mlle de La Force, Henriette-Julie de Murat wrote volumes of tales, as well as novels, while living in detention in the country; they often convey her bitterness about love and her caustic view of society. In one, even a powerful fairy cannot hold the love of her husband after she has grown old; in another, 'Le Palais de la vengeance' (The Palace of Vengeance), Murat turns today's fairytale conventions upside down by warning that even unions born of love can turn sour. The evil enchanter Pagan had abducted the lovers and imprisoned them together in a delightful crystal palace, where they want for nothing; but after a time, the moral declares, 'Pagan made them discover the unhappy secret, / That happiness itself can become a bore.'

The three interpolated fairy stories of *Les Lutins du Château de Kernosy* (The Goblins of the Castle of Kernosy), Murat's comedy of manners, set in Brittany, reveal how such material was made up or retrieved, embroidered and reworked in leisured company in the countryside to while away long evenings. The heroines are two sisters under the chafing tutelage of their aunt, the *châtelaine* of Kernosy, who, while looking for a lover for herself, is enjoying the wealth of her two orphaned charges. The two young women are desperately confined and indeed bored until the provident arrival of two young men: the company grows gayer, and rounds of dancing, musical entertainments and games of forfeits ensue, with each member of the company completing *bouts rimés,* writing sonnets, and telling stories. A certain M. de Fatville (*fat* meaning booby) who is a *conseiller* at the local *parlement* arrives: the abusive *vicomtesse* has picked him as a suitable match for one of her nieces because, it turns out, she owes him a debt of money he is prepared to waive in return for Mlle de Saint Urbain's charms. M. de Fatville bears the brunt of the author's *précieuse* distaste for the bourgeois, the businessman, the uncouth and unlettered. For his part, he reveals his dreadful limitations in two ways: out hunting with the gallant party, he insists on taking up a gun and shoots at something moving – his prey turns out to be a black Breton milch cow. But above all, he betrays his limited nature when one of the young men begins to tell the tale of 'Peau d'ours' or 'Bearskin', and he wants to know if it is a true story.

Otherwise, he says, he is going to bed. He was assured, Murat continues, 'that he could in all certainty take himself off to bed'.

A fairy tale to the *académiciens* was a vulgar amusement of old folk and children; to a writer like Murat, appreciating its qualities was a sign of temperament, intelligence, fineness and eligibility. A man who cannot see the point of a fairy story is a man who might well mistake a milch cow for a stag and shoot her.

The tale of 'Bearskin' creates a double reflection *en abyme* of the situation in which the novel's heroines find themselves – threatened by an arranged marriage to a monster. M. de Fatville, the unwanted suitor, takes the fearsome features of the King of the Ogres, Rhinoceros, who sends his ambassador to the neighbouring kingdom and demands the hand of Noble-Epine – Hawthorn – the princess. He declares: 'That if he [the king] didn't give his daughter away, Rhinoceros himself would come at the head of a hundred million ogres to lay waste the kingdom and eat the whole royal family.' The king – grief-stricken of course – parts with Hawthorn his daughter. However, when Rhinoceros goes off to catch two or three bears for his wife's supper, the princess's selfless and resourceful servant, Corianda, sews her up into one of the bearskins lying about, and, magically, she is instantly transformed into 'the prettiest she-bear in this world'. She is eventually captured by a Prince Charming out hunting (as in an earlier Basile story, 'The She-Bear'), and after a few vicious turns of the screw, when Rhinoceros behaves like the evil stepmother of other traditional tales, all ends happily.

One aspect has faded from view in the popular recensions of this type of fairy tale today: the beauty is the beast – at least she is also changed into a beast, and the metamorphosis leads to her escape from a tyrant father as well as a tyrant husband. In a female protagonist's case, shape-shifting also shifts the conditions of confinement: this principle does not obtain for men enchanted into animal form, like the monstrous Rhinoceros himself, or the more traditional Beast of the cycle. As a she-bear, Princess Hawthorn acquires more freedom of movement than as a young woman, and more freedom of choice. In animal form, she enjoys a tender and even abandoned flirtation with her prince:

> More enchanted than ever with his she-bear, Zelindor ordered that she was to be looked after with the greatest care, and gave her a delightful rocky grotto surrounded with statues; inside there was a bed of well-tended grass where she could retire at night. He came to see her at every possible moment ... he was crazy about her.

It is a curious instance of fantasy turning out to be less fantastic than it appears that Charlotte-Rose de La Force, following the young husband from whom she had been forcibly separated, disguised herself as a bear and hid among a group of entertainers' dancing bears in order to gain entrance to the castle where he had been sequestered by his father.

III

The writer of fairy tales whose private vicissitudes reflect most dramatically of all the romantic and social tensions of the age of despotism was the prodigiously gifted, successful *femme galante*, Marie-Catherine d'Aulnoy. Among the group of women who practised the genre, D'Aulnoy is the least connected to the court of Louis XIV; she is also one of the least veiled in her allusions to despotism's frailties and caprices. None of Mlle L'Héritier's effusions on military triumphs or simpering *hommages* to the king's progeny fall from her witty, inventive pen. D'Aulnoy had put herself beyond the pale, and at the same time, it seems, secured a different source of revenue. Before she took up fairy tales, her career had been even more rackety than Henriette-Julie de Murat's. The copious and rococo tales she composed correspond to the violent upheavals in her own life, as well as responding, in a spirit of revolt, to the political conflicts and social constraints of her times.

Until the mid-nineteenth century, she featured prominently in publishers' lists, but in 1855 the impresario J. R. Planché, who translated many of the tales, and adapted others as fairy extravaganzas for the stage, baulked at her casual frankness about sex and violence, and her prevailing cynicism. In a preface he admitted he had dropped two stories, which 'could not, without considerable alteration in their details, have been rendered unobjectionable to the English reader'. For encrypted in Marie-Catherine d'Aulnoy's many variations on the Cupid and Psyche plot lie the prevailing conditions of unhappy, forced unions between incompatible mates. And when the story of her own marriage is told, the many husbands who are beasts in her stories lose their fairytale outlandishness and become metaphorical, darkly humorous reflections on the circumstances of her life.

The details of her youth are difficult to verify, as a mixture of hearsay, false memory, self-justification, writerly inventiveness and hyperbole have stirred a rich brew, but the story that survives describes how she was fifteen or sixteen when she was married to the Baron d'Aulnoy, who was thirty years older than her. He was a sidekick of the dissolute Duc de Vendôme, in whose service he had accumulated enough money to buy himself land and a title. The union was arranged by Marie-Catherine's father: she may have been abducted by arrangement from the convent where she was being educated to live with a man she had never seen, though just to complicate the picture further, her *Memoirs* in which the story appeared are probably by Henriette-Julie de Murat.

But M. d'Aulnoy did not have a monopoly on *ancien régime* raciness, and the match soon disintegrated: in 1669, when Marie-Catherine d'Aulnoy was nineteen or so, she and her mother, the Marquise de Gadagne, became involved in a personal scandal: they conspired with their lovers, or so it was alleged, to bring a charge of high treason against M. d'Aulnoy for speaking against the king. He had been overheard swearing in public against the taxes that had been imposed. In mid-seventeenth-century France, this amounted to *lèse-majesté*. Had M. le Baron d'Aulnoy been found guilty, he would have been executed.

The attempt to defame him failed, and failed catastrophically for his accusers: after three whole years in the Bastille, M. d'Aulnoy managed to convince the court of his blamelessness, and bring charges in retaliation against his wife and her mother. Both the women's alleged lovers were tortured; they confessed, and were executed. The archives of the Bastille provide reliable evidence for these accusations and counter-accusations, but the repercussions become more mysterious: the Marquise de Gadagne fled to England, and a warrant was served for Mme d'Aulnoy's arrest. She managed to escape the officers by jumping out of the window at their early-morning summons, and hiding in a church under a convenient bier. Or so one version has it. She may have then lived as an *émigrée* in Holland, Spain and England, working as a spy with her mother on behalf of France. This period of her life becomes very shadowy indeed. However, in 1685 she was allowed to return to Paris, perhaps as a reward for services rendered. Her mother was given a pension by the Spanish king and stayed on in Madrid. Mme d'Aulnoy began to receive in her house in the rue St Benoît, and her salon became one of the leading social gatherings of Paris; cultivating the polite arts, she and her friends told fairy tales and, over raspberry or gooseberry cordials and hot chocolate, dressed up to play the parts. She began to contribute significantly to literary life: the *Recueil des plus belles pièces des poètes français*, a spirited and enlightened anthology which appeared in 1692, was edited either by her or by that sceptical sympathizer with the women's party of the Moderns, Fontenelle. She also published a series of travel memoirs, giving the 'inside' story of court life in Madrid and London – significantly, not Versailles. Written with persuasive eyewitness immediacy, they enjoyed a huge success, and made D'Aulnoy money she badly needed to run her household and bring up her three fatherless daughters (not all born during her marriage). Her memoirs of court life have however been shown to be largely plagiarized and partly fabricated, so her real activities during this period remain a mystery. It is not entirely impossible that all her travels took place in the arms of the West Wind, as in her first fairy tale, 'The Isle of Happiness'. But in the memoirs, unlike the tales, she assumed a first person voice to lend authenticity to her narrative, gossiping about kings and courts like an intimate.

The make-believe in her recollections, in the tales and in the salons concealed the continuing realities of life and matrimony against which her extravagant romancing was protesting: in 1699, her friend Angélique Ticquet was beheaded in the Place de Grève after she had influenced a servant to make an attempt on her husband's life. The servant, who had shot at Councillor Ticquet and wounded him badly, was hanged. The councillor had married her, a young and orphaned heiress, without her having a say in the union; he then maltreated her and she had retaliated, allegedly abetted by Mme d'Aulnoy, who was therefore fortunate not to be found guilty of being her accomplice.

The tumult of Mme d'Aulnoy's circle reflects how difficult it was for a woman of independent spirit in the *ancien régime* to disencumber herself of a husband; and it is significant that both Mlle L'Héritier and she wrote fairy tales in which the heroine sets out alone in disguise on a quest like a man. The romancing of the salon involved contact with fancied means of illicit power – Circean powers of metamorphosis – which she craved. Here again, in a pervasive negative image of the lower-class woman, the gossip and the witch, the fairytale narrators found a sympathetic ally. But the theme to which Mme d'Aulnoy returned, almost obsessively, in a score of variations on beauties and beasts, was the animal bride and animal groom.

Rams, serpents, boars, yellow dwarves, white cats, blue birds, frogs, hinds, shape-shifters of all sorts crowd her pages: Mme d'Aulnoy seized the opportunities which the mythological theme of animal metamorphosis offered her to create a world of pretend in which happiness and love are sometimes possible for a heroine, but elusive and hard-won.

When Mme d'Aulnoy treats of beast husbands, she often offers them no quarter. In 'Le Mouton' (The Ram), the eponymous beast proves himself most delicate, during his union with the princess: subtle *bisques* and *pâtés* rain down in his gardens, he appears heaped in jewels and eats sherbet and plays shuttlecock with his courtiers like any noble prince. The Ram develops the *Lear* theme of the king who casts out the youngest and best-loved of his three daughters; the original folk tale that inspired Shakespeare ended with a reconciliation between the king and

A reluctant bride takes a pair of magic scissors to her proposed husband's diabolical beard. ('The Yellow Dwarf', after 'Phiz', Grimms' Goblins, London, 1861.)

his daughter, but Mme d'Aulnoy, unlike Shakespeare, follows and extends her triumph in hyperbolic style: the beautiful young Princesse Merveilleuse actually ascends to her father's throne by his side as his queen, and while the coronation is taking place the forsaken Ram her animal bridegroom expires of a broken heart.

The last lines of the story comment with some acerbity: 'Now we know that people of the highest rank are subject, like all others, to the blows of fortune …' The author then adds a rhymed morality, which twists the tail of the story against its audience:

> How different from our modern swains!
> Even his death may well surprise
> The lovers of the present day:
> Only a silly sheep now dies,
> Because his ewe has gone astray.

The princess sobs over his body, and 'felt she would die herself'. But unavailingly, in this case; her tears do not revive him, or transform him.

It would be crude to make a direct comparison between the stormy biographies of Mme d'Aulnoy, her mother and her friend, but nevertheless the insouciance the storyteller first shows to the Ram, then the contrast she makes with spouses of her own time cannot be overlooked: there is a bitter challenge in those final lines. The dénouement itself patently proposes – against Salic Law and the French practice – the right of daughters to inherit their patrimony rather than be handed over into another man's keeping as his childlike dependant.

'The Ram' is filled with D'Aulnoy's touches of knowing humour and deadpan heartlessness, bedecked with details of worldly frippery and dainties, and slowed down by its pleasurable reiteration of sophisticated games and pastimes; the combination achieves a slightly sinister atmosphere, the authentic recipe of frivolity, dreaminess, blitheness and sadism that we now recognize as the essential tone of fairy tale.

In another of D'Aulnoy's blithe tales of wreckage, the heroine tries to free herself from her promise to marry the Yellow Dwarf, as we have seen, but fails, and dies in the attempt; in 'Prince Marcassin' (Prince Wild Boar), the eponymous monster marries – and murders – two sisters before the third outwits him. These tales play on the Bluebeard theme; in 'Le Dauphin' (The Dolphin), the injustice takes a different direction and a haughty princess, Livorette, disdains her ugly suitor, until he changes himself into a canary and becomes her pet. Marie-Catherine d'Aulnoy's more optimistic variations on the Beast, in which she does restore him to full, innocent, erotic humanity, still illuminate the woman's lot within contemporary marriages. 'Le Serpentin vert', recently translated as 'The Great Green Worm' by A. S. Byatt, directly revises 'Cupid and Psyche' by Apuleius, but D'Aulnoy dreamed up ever more protracted and atrocious torments for her Psyche-like heroine before she allowed, in this case, a happy ending to the lovers. Interestingly, it is in this story of a fulfilled love between a Beauty and a Beast that the author also emphasizes, at numerous points, the importance of equal conversation between men and women, as proposed by the salonnières.

Her heroine is cursed at birth with 'perfect' ugliness by the wicked fairy Magotine; as a result, she is dubbed Laidronette (Little Ugly One, Hidessa) and shunned, even by her family. She withdraws from the world, and in her solitude amuses herself by writing 'several volumes of her thoughts'. (Costiveness was not a problem Mme d'Aulnoy understood.) When she returns to pay a visit to her parents, they are celebrating her beautiful sister's wedding, 'but when they saw Hidessa, everyone looked upset'. Mme d'Aulnoy catches accurately the pathos of being unlovely in the marriage economy of the time; it is regrettable that her many exquisite princesses have obscured her ill-favoured heroines in the circulation of her tales.

Back in her forest fastness, Hidessa meets the Green Serpent of the title; but his sighs are hisses, and his own looks so frightful she runs from him, until advised by a good fairy not to trust in appearances, but to discover the inner spirit of her lover. He transports her to the enchanted realm of Pagodia, where the inhabitants, the pagods, wait on her hand and foot as in Cupid's castle, and provide her with every ornament and diversion, including the most spicy conversation, plays by Corneille, and, yes, stories like 'Cupid and Psyche', 'retold in elegant words by a fashionable author'. Meanwhile her mysterious suitor remains invisible, a disembodied voice speaking amorously only at night, until she becomes bored with the constant round of pleasure in the day and longs only for his sweet words in the dark. So she agrees to marry him; in return he imposes the condition that she must not give in to curiosity, like Psyche, and look at him.

Of course she fails in the test, and sees the horrid Green Serpent with his long, bristling mane ... she faints, everything vanishes, and her ordeals begin. Forced by the evil fairy Magotine to wear tiny iron shoes, spin spiders' webs, wear a millstone and climb a mountain in order to gather water from a bottomless well in a pitcher full of holes, as well as fill a basket with four-leafed clover, she eventually – with the help of a good fairy – succeeds in these impossible tasks and is rechristened Queen Discretion for her pains. She still remains exiled, however, in a grove full of beasts. They have all been changed from their former, human, state by the fairies as a punishment: tattlers have become parrots, those who mocked their friends, monkeys, hotheads have been changed into lions and, most significant of all, a jealous lover who 'overwhelmed [his sweetheart] with unjust accusations' and 'beat her so cruelly as to leave her almost dead in the arms of her waiting-women' was at last changed into a wolf by fairies who appeared before him to stop him assaulting her again. Thus, in the pages of her own narrative, Mme d'Aulnoy opens up one set of meanings that fairytale animal metamorphosis expresses: this wolf has not been unjustly persecuted like the Great Green Worm; nor does his beastliness present a test of a true heroine's goodness and trust, as in 'Cupid and Psyche' and its direct descendants. Rather, it makes his inner nature manifest as an outward shape, like the parrot prattlers and the monkey jokers, or the sinners in Dante's *Inferno* with their congruous punishments. In the same way, the companions of Odysseus whom Circe enchants have been made to own up to their own swinishness and folly.

At last, when the three years of her solitude have elapsed, Hidessa returns to

Magotine with her cribbled pitcher duly full of water, her basket brimming with four-leafed clover, the millstone, the iron shoes. A few more vicissitudes intervene, but finally she is reunited with the Green Serpent and finds him to be a splendid prince. With heroic optimism, Mme d'Aulnoy comments, 'And whatever Magotine's powers, alas for her, what could she do against the power of Love?' Her ugly heroine's true beauty is restored, but only after the prince has committed himself to his staunch, chivalrous girl who has learned to love him and has crossed so many bridges of knives for him.

Perseverance wins Hidessa her happiness, after showing the cruelty of society towards unattractive young women, and their loneliness; Mme d'Aulnoy spiritedly fantasticates on the scale of female heroism.

D'Aulnoy's Beauty and the Beast fairy tales precede the classic tale actually entitled '*La Belle et la bête*'. Gabrielle-Suzanne Barbot Gallon, known as Mme de Villeneuve (1695–1755), included it in her novel *Les Contes marins ou la jeune Américaine*, in 1740, and it was reprinted as a discrete narrative in *Le Cabinet des fées* some fifty years later. Angela Carter has made the point that while it exhibits connections to the ancient cycle of animal bridegroom tales, it must be seen as 'a literary fairy tale of the same order of invention as the stories of Hans Christian Andersen or Oscar Wilde'. Nearly a hundred pages long, intricately plotted in a series of episodes spoken by different characters in turn, which nest one inside another (*mise-en-abyme*), this founding text of one of the most popular fairy tales of the modern world has defeated almost all readers; it has hardly ever been reprinted uncut, or unrevised. Jack Zipes, in his anthology *Beauties, Beasts and Enchantment* of 1989, provided the first full translation into English.

Villeneuve portrays the Beast as the victim of an aged and malignant fairy who laid the terrible curse on him when the handsome youth turned down her amorous advances; the story encrypts the corrupt and vicious intrigues of court life, of fortune-hunting and marriage-broking, pandering and lust in the eighteenth century, and, like so many of the first literary fairy tales, campaigns for marriages of true minds, for the rights of the heart, for the freedom of the true lovers of romance. At one point Beauty muses, 'How many girls are compelled to marry rich brutes – much more brutish than the Beast, who's only one in form and not in his feelings or his actions?' She conjures up a dream place, the Fortunate Island, where everyone, 'even the king', is allowed to marry 'according to their inclinations'. The force of this wishful thinking tends to be lost on the reader today.

The surface moral of the fairy tale offers the enchanted victim of a cruel fairy redemption from his degraded, mute, coarse animal condition: he learns to speak in the gracious cadences of 'The Land of Tenderness'; he begins to act as a human being, to express the motions of his heart and mind; in other words, to love. The condemned Other returns to Selfhood, and recovers his 'I'.

Until the most recent, twentieth-century revisions of the tale, the Beast was in fatal exile from the human, and his plight was terrible. The animals chosen for his punishment constitute a diabolical bestiary: snakes, frogs, cats, donkeys are traditional witches' familiars as well as the ingredients of their potions, their love potions at that. They are guises of the Devil: the subtle serpent from Eden, and the priapic ass of antiquity. The fairies – good and bad alike – control these metamorphoses, for the supernatural shares something in common with the animal; in early modern fairy tale, both categories converge in the realm of the monstrous.

In Mme de Villeneuve's 'Beauty and the Beast', she even devises an aetiology for their connection: according to fairy law, her principal good fairy informs her audience, a fairy must be a thousand years old before she can dispute the orders of her elders, unless – and this is where the power of the uncanny proves superior even to those who can call upon it at will – a young fairy submits to a change of shape and lives as a snake or a bear. 'We call this condition the "terrible act" because it is fraught with danger,' she explains. Surviving the animal condition, however, increases a fairy's powers, as it can a human heroine's, too.

The ambiguous position of the Beast confers mastery of magic. The surface moral of the tales offers the enchanted victims redemption from their reduced, animal condition: as in a Christian miracle play or saint's legend, the heroine vanquishes the tempter, triumphs in heaven after heroic resistance, or converts him. On awakening, he is somehow the better for his ordeal; that the Beast has learned something is often the underlying message of the tale. In Villeneuve's 'Beauty and the Beast', the Beast falls into a mortal swoon when he thinks she has abandoned him for ever; Beauty then revives him by pouring water on his face. He comes to, and his disenchantment takes place only on the morning after their wedding night; not for this scrupulous lady the erotic escapades – the pregnancy! – of Psyche before her wedding.

Villeneuve's hint at the saving waters of baptism was taken up and fully developed in the concise, popular epitome which Mme Leprince de Beaumont published in 1756 and which became one of the widely distributed sources of the famous fairy tale. There, the Beast returns to 'his proper figure' (as the 1818 English translation puts it) when Beauty pours the water from a stream on his forehead. He is released from evil to emerge a new man, fit to be loved and to give love in return, like the cleansed soul after the sacrament.

IV

Jeanne-Marie Leprince de Beaumont (1711–80) included her polished abridgement in an anthology for young people – a pioneering work of the kind – called *Le Magasin des enfants*; it is this version of the tale that has become canonical (it inspired Cocteau's classic film, for instance). Beaumont published it in London, during the fourteen-year spell she worked as a governess (a Mam'zelle) in England. She had left an unhappy marriage in France ten years before. The arranged union with M. de Beaumont, 'a dissolute libertine', had been annulled after only two years – fortunately – and in England she found a second husband, and had several children. Industrious and very high-minded, she issued a stream of pedagogical writings, often translating her own French into English for the edification of an aristocratic female pupillage under the age of eighteen. When she returned to her own country, in 1762, she produced no less busily – her bibliography numbers more than seventy volumes.

In the case of Mme de Beaumont, the figure of the élite, lettered lady of the salon merges with the proverbial storyteller of the nursery for the first time on the social plane, when she ceases to be a member of the idle nobility and becomes a working woman in a household commanded and owned by another.

Beaumont composed her stories with her pupils in mind, and sometimes invited their collaboration. The results appeared in English collections such as the *Young Ladies' Magazine or Dialogues between a Discreet Governess and Several Young Ladies of the First Rank under Her Education*, published in four volumes in 1760. Describing her teaching methods, the governess defended with the heated asperity of a Miss Jean Brodie her girls' capacity to think for themselves:

> they will tell you very gravely of a book they are reading: 'The author has taken leave of his subject; he says very weak things. His principle is false; his inferences must be so.' What is more my young ladies will prove it. We don't frame a true judgement of the capacity of children; nothing is out of their reach … Now-a-days ladies read all sorts of books, history, politics, philosophy and even such as concern religion … They should therefore be … able to discern truth from falsehood.

With such determination, it is not surprising that many of the stories are openly didactic, very far in atmosphere from D'Aulnoy's flippant perversity, or even Villeneuve's intricate romancing. Mme de Beaumont holds out rewards and punishments: she tells of suffering saints, like the put-upon skivvy Saint Zita, a

Cinderella of the early thirteenth century, and concludes with overtly Christian messages: in one story, for example, she relates how a poverty-stricken man called Perrin is rewarded when he returns a sack of gold and silver he has come across by accident; his beneficiary makes him a gift of a farm in return for his honesty. She also adduces the terrible case of Mme Angélique Ticquet, Mme d'Aulnoy's friend who attempted murder against her brutal husband. She blames her unequivocally, saying that even though she was a rich heiress, she was covetous of wealth, and thought her husband much wealthier than he was when he gave her a diamond spray brooch as a wedding present. When she discovered her error, she conceived a hatred for him, and fell for '*un cavalier fort aimable*' – one thing led to another, to the (almost) fatal pistol shot, and her beheading. 'You see, my children,' writes Mme de Beaumont, after this partial and improving account, 'the terrible extremes to which the passions may carry us!' This example from recent history, occurring so close to home, is cited in an imagined conversation, which uses fables, cautionary tales, allegory – and fairy stories – to tutor the moral sense of her girls.

It is easy to catch, in Mme de Beaumont, the worried tone of a well-meaning teacher raising her pupils to face their future obediently and decorously, to hear her pious wish that her pupils should obey their fathers and that inside the brute of a husband who might be their appointed lot, the heart of a good man might beat, given a bit of encouragement, that no extreme measures will be needed – no scissors will be used on the Yellow Dwarf. In the altered attitudes to Mme Ticquet, between D'Aulnoy's possible abetting in 1699 and Mme de Beaumont's anxious advice sixty or so years later, between D'Aulnoy's unpredictably resolved tales and Beaumont's exemplary outcomes, it becomes possible to perceive *ancien régime* raffishness on the turn, and the romantic cult of *sentimentalité* and *bonne volonté* taking hold.

Mme de Beaumont, like many before her, tackled the quandary posed by romance itself. She was well read in the English novel, and commented on Richardson and the problems his material posed for a woman concerned with other women's morals and the care of their spirit. In 1774, she wrote:

The good and honest Mr Richardson, author of *Pamela, Clarissa*, etc., has come to grief, and however much he may want to foster love of virtue, has carried into more than one heart the knowledge of vice – enlightenment that is always fateful (*lumière toujours funeste*). I could go into some great detail, and prove what I say by examples, but it would be falling into the same mistake that I reprove …

Pamela may well have inspired feelings of identification in Mme de Beaumont, for Richardson's heroine is employed like her in an ambiguous position in her pursuer's household, having fallen on hard times and been compelled to seek work as a nursemaid. A painting by Joseph Highmore, *Pamela Tells a Nursery Tale*, made shortly after the book's appearance in 1741, singled out this aspect of the heroine's duties. Mme de Beaumont even undertook the rewriting of *Clarissa*, improving Richardson's original for her pupils.

The sacramental character Mme Leprince de Beaumont gave to the moment of the Beast's redemption was therefore no accident: he is transfigured, as the civilized, pretty, moral fairy tale of this sort transfigures the teller from a witch to an angel, and brings her back within the pale. By crossing the Channel with the fairy tale, Beaumont also echoes the change from élite women's pre-revolutionary protests in France to comparative acquiescence, after the revolution in England, among *émigrées* and natives alike, and the comparable shift in the use of such stories from the social arena of the salons to the domestic interior of the home, the nursery and the schoolroom. We can see foreshadowed, already, the Victorian angel of the house, whose task it is to tame and gentle male lust and animal instinct. We also see an intelligent governess preparing her charges for this wifely duty, readying them to find the male spouse a beast at first, but, beneath the rough and uncivilized exterior, a good man. The fairy tale emerges in its modern form, as an instrument of social adaptation, spoken and circulated by women to cast themselves as civilizers in the tabooed terrain of sexuality, turning predatory men into moderate consorts. The mischief and wantonness of Psyche's troubles and discoveries, still captured by D'Aulnoy's bizarreries, fade before the moral enterprise of the Enlightenment. The stories begin to attempt to console young women beset by fears of marriage, of ogre husbands who might bring about their destruction in one way or another. And these functions – of steadying and training the young – have gradually gained ground over the critical and challenged rebelliousness of the first generation of women fairytale writers and become identified with the genre itself, establishing its pedagogical, edifying character.

Didactic intentions have influenced fairy tales increasingly strongly since the nineteenth century; the Brothers Grimm led the way, as they re-edited and reshaped successive editions of their famous *Household Tales* to improve their message. Their predecessors had been less anxious about the possible effect on children of tales of incest, adultery or murder, with the exception of Mme de Beaumont who had anticipated their anxieties. For in her lessons, we can also perceive cross-identifications, that the terror of the Beast – carnality, transgressive nature – lies in the mind of the beholder, female as well as male. The fairy tale told by women acts optatively to undo all such prejudice.

In the anonymous, characteristic version of 1818, Beauty delivers a truly Christian speech to the Beast:

'You are very obliging, (answered Beauty;) I own I am pleased with your kindness: when I consider that, your deformity scarce appears.' 'Yes, yes, (said the Beast,) my heart is good, but still I am a monster.' 'Among mankind, (says Beauty) [note 'said' changes to 'says', from the past tense to the universal present], there are many that deserve that name more than you, and I prefer you, just as you are, to those, who, under a human form, hide a treacherous, corrupt, and ungrateful heart.'

Beauty's goodness inspired some idealistic lessons; fairy tales, with their generic commitment to justice, frequently enclose a simple notion of retribution.

When men adopt this material, they often introduce special pleading on their own behalf; Cocteau's entrancing film, of 1946, for all its delicacy and dreamlike seductiveness, concentrates on awakening Beauty to consciousness of the Beast's goodness (p. 272). *He* does not have to change at all, except in outward shape; *she* has to see past his unsightliness to the gentle and loving human being trapped inside. The film presents a trial of her limits, not his. Christian Bérard's designs intensify the Beast's poignancy; he is not an animal, but a hairy anthropomorphic changeling, a Quasimodo, a pitiful Elephant Man whose male desire deserves to kindle a reciprocating love if only women would listen to the imperatives of the heart, not the eye. King Kong is one of his lineage too, as the last words of the film make plain: 'It wasn't the airplanes, it was Beauty killed the Beast.' This strand in the history of Beauty and the Beast consists of variations on the theme of the *femme fatale*, on men's anguish in the face of female indifference, on the tenderness of masculine desire and the cruelty of the female response, rather than women's vulnerability to male violence. Ironically, such interpretations make Beauty guilty of fixity, in a story that began as a narrative of a woman's passionate progress. Underlying the static serenity of Josette Day's La Belle in Cocteau's film lies the Symbolist fetishization of impassive femininity, as defined by Baudelaire, of Beauty who speaks of herself as '*un rêve de pierre*' (a dream of stone), with a granite breast on which men (poets) wound themselves and discover love '*éternel et muet ainsi que la matière*' (eternal and mute as matter). Psyche/Beauty, as woman, is material, made flesh, however cool and otherworldly her appearance; Jean

In the Aesop story, a nurse threatens a crying baby that she will hand him over to the wolves; a passing wolf rejoices to hear this, but soon meets his death when he is discovered at the door. (F. Barlow, 'The Nurse and the Wolf', Aesop's Fables, 1723.)

Marais' Eros/Beast in the film belongs to the spirit world, and his enchanted castle, with its spellbinding moving sconces and speaking furniture, emanates from the higher realm of imagination, the dimension of dream and fantasy, where poets – like Baudelaire, like Cocteau himself – are sent through the love women inspire in them.

Cocteau, as a Surrealist, was reinterpreting Symbolist doctrine of the feminine's role in creativity. Not for nothing had the *Dictionnaire abrégé du surréalisme* attributed to Baudelaire their definition of *La Femme*: 'She who casts the greatest shadow or the greatest light into our dreams.' The inflexion on 'our' here is obviously masculine. This does not prevent Cocteau's *La Belle et la bête* from spellbinding a female spectator – the film profoundly affected Angela Carter, for instance, who specially remembered the way the Beast smouldered – literally – after a kill. But its masculine sympathy does divert the story from the female subject to stress male erotic hunger for beauty as the stimulus to creativity, as the vital principle. The ravishing aestheticization of the whole film, from the flying laundry at the start to the twilit luxuries of the castle magic, extends the function of the feminine as the Beast's necessary lifeblood. And at the end, in an enigmatic twist, the disenchanted Beast turns out to have the same human face as Belle's ne'er-do-well, aspiring lover Avenant, whom she rejected kindly, but firmly (the actor Jean Marais plays both). So *La Belle et la bête* traces a promise to male lovers that they will not always be rejected, that human lovers, however profligate, can be saved, and it withdraws at the last moment any autonomy in love from Beauty herself.

For their intentionally instructive film *The Singing Ringing Tree*, a family product made in the former German Democratic Republic in 1958, the screenwriters Anne Geelhaer and Francesco Stefani (who also directed), drew on different tales in the Grimm Brothers' collection. It blended a 'Beauty and the Beast' type tale with another familiar figure: the Haughty Princess who considers herself too good for her flock of suitors. Princess High-and-Mighty's punishment is ugliness: the live action film animates the grotesque collapse of her beauty and follows her slow and painful lessons in kindness, humility and love as she cares for the magical creatures she once spurned – a giant goldfish, a golden-maned and golden-antlered horse and a flock of doves. Her pilgrim's progress eventually succeeds in freeing her mentor the prince, who himself has been changed into a bear by an evil magician. Once she has learned to love, her beauty returns.

As fairy tales begin to aim more and more exclusively at the young, their stock-in-trade becomes more didactic. Disapproval of improper romancing feeds the ambivalence towards imaginative literature for children; but, as its popularity goes on growing, the chief effect of this anxiety is to make writers attempt to turn the unsuitable into the improving, the exciting into the punitive. Lullabies that threaten babies ('Hushabye Baby on the tree top … / When the bough breaks the cradle will fall … '), nurses who warn that the wolf is at the door (left), have their counterpart in Enlightenment variations on the ancient romances, which teach the limits of a growing girl's hopes. But it was that sensible and kindhearted governess, Mme Leprince de Beaumont, in the mid-eighteenth century who pioneered the use of the fairytale form to mould the young in this way. Her vision of female love and sympathy redeeming the brute in man has made 'Beauty and the Beast' one of the best-loved fairy tales in the world, and it has not stopped inspiring dreams of experiencing love's power in little girls – and little boys.

CHAPTER 18

Go! Be a Beast: Beauty and the Beast II

Minnie loved her friend, but thought it to be a thing of horror that her friend should marry a tailor. It was almost as bad as the story of the Princess who had to marry a bear; – worse indeed, for Minnie did not at all believe that the tailor would ever turn out to be a gentleman, whereas she had been sure from the first that the bear would turn into a prince.

Anthony Trollope

For a fabulous *divertissement* given at Versailles in 1664, the king's troupes of dancers and musicians and artists and actors assembled for his entertainment and staged allegories of the seasons with the additional help of wild animals from the king's menagerie: Winter was accompanied by a bear. A skit was included in an interlude. Written by Molière, it featured a bear-fight between a certain wild man of the woods, 'Moron', who is playing with an echo when a bear comes upon him. Trying to appease the animal, Moron exclaims: ' Oh, my lord ! How delightful, how lissom your highness is! Your highness has altogether the most gallant looks and the most handsome figure in the world! Oh! what lovely fur! What beautiful looks! … Help, help!'

The beast abductor turned soft toy: a Victorian heroine enjoys life with a bear. (Richard Doyle, 'Rose Red', mid-nineteenth century.)

Charles Perrault himself may have been involved in devising the tableaux, and in producing the sumptuous feast book of engravings which commemorated the occasion. No beast in fairy tale at the time would have excited anything less than Moron's squirming terror; no courtier would have cooed and gurgled at the appearance of the bear in the manner of children today. The threat of animals was a real and frightening one in the seventeenth and eighteenth centuries; in times of scarcity and hard winters, bears and wolves came in from the wild to prey on towns and villages.

The narrators of earlier versions of 'Beauty and the Beast' frequently avoid giving precise indications of the Beast's horrible features, and generally describe his enchanted shape in the vaguest terms. D'Aulnoy is typically fanciful about her beasts; Villeneuve adds the unusual detail that Beauty's father was terrified by 'a horrible beast … It had a trunk resembling an elephant's which it placed on the merchant's neck'; as he approaches Beauty later, his scales clank. Beaumont confines herself to saying that he looked so dreadful, Beauty's father felt he was going to faint.

In the literary fairy tale of the *ancien régime*, the Beast's low, animal nature is more usually revealed by his muteness, uncouthness, inability to meet Beauty as a social and intellectual equal. In Villeneuve's version, Beauty sighs that, though he treats her well, she finds him boring because he can utter only a few words and repeats them endlessly. In these secular romances the valued arts of conversation and storytelling remain beyond him.

Authors, often keen to emphasize the unreliability of outward appearances, could hardly press the disagreeable Platonic and Christian equation of deformity of body with deformity of soul. But the illustrators needed to choose an appropriate physical form: the Beast had to be represented. The word 'monster', from the Latin *monstrare*, to show, even suggests that monstrousness is above all visible. But monstrousness is a condition in flux, subject to historical changes in attitudes. One volatile current, carrying ideas of ugliness, abnormality, abominable deformation, converges with another, carrying ideas about nature and man, and in their confluence the beastliness of the Beast diminishes.

The earliest artists concentrate on his misshapenness, repellent to Beauty. Charles Lamb's anonymous illustrator, probably recalling Circe's punitive metamorphoses of Odysseus' crew, envisaged a huge hog in one image, and a ferocious bear in another. One edition pressed the reference home, with the legend, 'Circe: "Go, be a beast!" Homer' inscribed on the back jacket.

Richard Doyle's bear dances winningly and casts doggily devoted looks at Beauty; while Walter Crane imagined a giant boar with tusks and overlapping canines.

Illustrators avoided lupine looks on the whole, because the stories stress the Beast's docile and gentlemanly behaviour, and they were often working on 'Red Riding Hood' as well. Mere animal form begins as sufficient horror in itself, but the trend soon moved towards more anthropomorphic characteristics: two-legged, upright beasts, disfigured by elephant trunks, reptiles' fangs, jowls and wattles and snouts. The less-than-human took the shape of mammals often equipped with terrific natural weaponry. In this the artists returned to Christian iconography of the Devil, multiplying phallic protuberances on face and limbs (p. 120). But they stopped short, unlike their medieval predecessors, at blazoning monstrous organs in the site of the genitals themselves.

Women illustrators – fewer in number – tend however not to stress the Beast's aggressive arsenal, or to focus on his ferocity, but incline towards characteristics of creatures traditionally classed as lower than mammals, visualizing the repellent creature as toad-like, fishy, or lizard-like. From a female point of view, the repugnant sometimes looks less-than-masculine, a clammy, flaccid manifestation more like Gollum in Tolkien's *Lord of the Rings* than the male artists' vision of a fallen angel of priapism. But both men and women do resort, frequently, to another very familiar animal in folklore and fairy tale: the bear.

The bear was the king of the beasts in early medieval lore, the strongest and heaviest of animals in the western forests, and in consequence an emblem of power in feudal heraldry; it was the totemic royal symbol of the Celtic and Germanic West and dominated, alongside the wolf, the oral literature of forest peoples. Saint Augustine had likened both the bear and the lion to the Devil, 'who is figured in these beasts, because the bear's strength is in its paw and the lion's in its mouth'. To the earliest audiences of fairy tales' ancestors, the medieval romances, the bear figures as the totem of the wild man, the dweller in the untamed forest, all natural appetite and ferocity. A much-translated work like *Valentine and Orson*, which survives in a fourteenth-century English translation

For its fierceness and its strength, the bear used to symbolize Rage – sometimes with martial grandeur, but sometimes with more pejorative overtones. (Claude Paradin, Devises héroïques, 1557.)

*Orson, a wild man of the woods in medieval romance, was brought up by a she-bear, who imbued him with her spirit; she was killed by his twin brother Valentine, ABOVE, and he turned on him in revenge. (*Valentine and Orson*, c. 1835.)*

from an earlier French original, dramatizes the contest and reconciliation between twin brothers, one of whom is raised as a prince in the city, the other suckled by a she-bear and brought up wild in the forest (above). Emblematic of the strength as well as the savagery of nature, the bear child Orson is captured by his lost brother Valentine during a hunt, and submits as he must to civilization: baptism, table manners and crusading feats of arms. Interestingly, the frontispiece to Perrault's translation of Gabriel Faerno's animal fables, of 1699, shows a story-teller wearing a bear mask, emblematic of her role as the interpreter of ancient, wild – that is unadulterated – folk wisdom.

The bear was called 'the beast who walks like a man' and thought to resemble human beings not only because the animal sometimes walks upright, but because bears are omnivorous, loving honey as well as meat. The *berserkr*, or ferocious Norse warriors may have been so called from the bearskins they wore, and they wrought such havoc they made 'berserk' a term for uncontrolled violence. Tales of women ravished by bears continued into the present century, possibly

Bears were baited in pits as well as paraded for entertainment in mock tournaments, such as one Perrault helped design. (Israel Silvestre and François Chauveau, Paris, 1670.)

contributing to the identification of the fairytale Beast with bears above all.

But anger, rather than lust, dominates the animal's meanings in the fifteenth and sixteenth centuries: it accompanied the vice of Wrath and proclaimed warlikeness (p. 300); its ready anger in real life made it a rewarding victim, of course, in the right conditions for human safety: the bear pit. Queen Elizabeth I watched a troop of mastiffs savage thirteen bears in one day: 'it was a sport very pleasant to see the bear ... shake his ears twice or thrice with the blood, and the slaver about his physiognomy was a matter of goodly relief', wrote one of her courtiers.

Bears were mocked too, and made to dance in chains, as at the king's pageants (left); the lumbering, half-wit imitation of human agility made the bear a figure of fun, part of the jester's crew, and hence an appropriate member of fairy lore's cast of semi-comic characters designed for low, secular, hintingly erotic entertainment.

So, by the seventeenth century, the animal had fallen far below his early medieval stature as King of the Beasts. And it shared something else with donkeys: from the point of view of the human, it was an intermediate beast, not exactly docile, but nevertheless biddable; a performing bear was neither a wild beast nor a domestic pet; it could be made to serve its owner's wishes – up to a point.

For reasons both symbolic and empirical, bears survive as beasts of prey in many fairy tales; 'Goldilocks', for instance, echoes the lesson given by the wolf to Red Riding Hood, and warns little girls not to wander in the woods where they might encounter frightening beasts. The spectre of being devoured, which was raised in the mind of Psyche by her sisters, and recurs in the Bluebeard legend, returns to communicate the bear's menace. Bestiality, cannibalism and eroticism are bound up together. 'Who's been lying in my bed?' cry out the bears. In 1876, Walter Crane published an unsparing version of 'Goldilocks' (right), in which the adult bears appear, almost for the last time, as irrecuperably savage and vindictive and angry. Like the ogres in the Bluebeard type story, they plan to eat the little girl: 'The mother bear saying, "For supper she shall be, and I will skin her".'

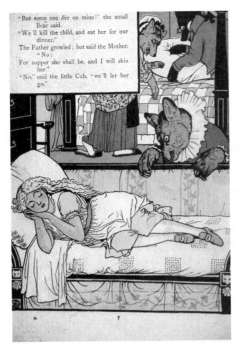

"But some one *lies* on mine!" the small Bear said.
"We'll kill the child, and eat her for our dinner,"
The Father growled; but said the Mother,
"No;
For supper she shall be, and I will skin her."
"No," said the little Cub, "we'll let her go."

Not so cuddly: Goldilocks is sleeping in his bed and his mother threatens to have her for supper. (Walter Crane's New Toy Book: The Three Bears, *London, 1873.)*

But a countervailing tendency, to find the bear a playmate, was growing throughout the nineteenth century. In the traditional Nordic tale 'East o' the Sun and West o' the Moon', a white bear comes to a poor man's cottage and asks for his daughter's hand; the threat adds a frisson to his courtship. In the folklore of many indigenous tribes in North America, the bridegroom bear similarly claims a human partner, and fears (dreams?) of such abductions still haunt tourists in Alaska today. In the Grimms' '*Schneeweisschen und Rosenrot*' (Snow White and Rose Red), the bear is a black variety. These widely distributed fairy stories possibly influenced the identity of the beast in other tales, where the species is not described; moreover, 'Beauty and the Beast' was a popular theme for the stage, and a bear costume is an easy one for an actor to wear convincingly. One Victorian drama, written specially for children to perform, specifies that the beast should 'look as rough and as much like a monster as possible. A covering for the head might be made of shaggy fur, and he should have coarse brown woollen gloves'. In the illustrations, he looks just like a great big teddy bear.

With the disappearance of bears from the wilderness, they began to be shown at the zoo; they were fed with buns in London by the public eager to see them performing. The animal began to lose its reputation for savagery, and the original, experiential menace of the fairytale conflict weakened. With the transformation of

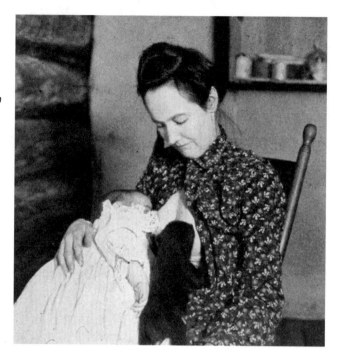

Orson was raised by a bear, and wolf or goat mothers stand behind many a hero, but the nursing of animal cubs by a human mother cuts across the animal–human divide in a different way. (William Lyman Underwood, Wild Brother, *1921.)*

perception, the story's impact changes, and the animal enchantment of the prince no longer appears to be such a curse. This shift in sensibility begins to happen around the turn of the last century; the affinity of the bear to the human becomes more marked, his monstrousness dissolves, he becomes less worthy of mockery: the gap begins to close. Richard Doyle drew the Grimms' heroine dandling the dear little bear in her lap in the forest – a scene unimaginable to a medieval mind (p. 298).

In 1921, a remarkable volume called *Wild Brother* was published by a photographer, William Lyman Underwood. What would have been a tale of terror, of bestiality, sinfulness against God and nature and provoked moral outrage at almost any time before then, becomes a high-minded parable of harmony in creation. *Wild Brother* tells the story of a foundling bear cub, Bruno, and how he was brought back by a huntsman who had killed his mother, who then raised the cub in his family as his child. He called his own baby, born at the same time, Ursula (little bear), and his wife nursed both of them at her breast. The photograph of her nursing the baby bear and the little girl at the same time is inscribed: 'Mr Underwood took this picture of Ursula and Bruno and me with my consent, and I am glad to have him use it in this book. Bruno's Foster Mother '(above). The cub then grew up to be a most enchanting character, the star of several delightful photographs, and eventually, when he became too large to handle, was turned loose.

The collapse of boundaries between the animal and the human is not altogether complete in this story, because the book itself – and the permission the foster mother was asked to give – attests to the shock which I, for one, certainly felt. Despite fairy tales' and folklore's intermingling of creatures, the talking and helpful animal familiars, despite continuing advances in ecology and changing attitudes to animal rights and human domination, it is startling and feels uncomfortable, even prurient, to look at a woman feeding a bear cub, as if she and he belonged to a common species.

The tale of *Wild Brother*, existing in the world of actual events, still has the power to inspire a sharp frisson, seventy years later, even though the symbolism of everyday life contains a wealth of animal imagery in which beasts are thought of as human, and at the same time favourably compared to the human. Again, animals are good to think with, as Lévi-Strauss famously commented. And in this regard, no bears are better to think with than the teddy bear.

The American president Teddy Roosevelt was a keen hunter, especially of grizzly bears, the symbol of native America. He wrote essays about his sportsmanship, which were collected in several volumes, with titles like *The Wilderness Hunter* (1893) and *Outdoor Pastimes of an American Hunter* (1905). His struggle against his own physical sickliness carried a wider political message: 'No nation facing the unhealthy softening and relaxation of fibre,' he wrote, 'which tend to accompany civilisation, can afford to neglect anything that will develop hardihood, resolution, and the scorn of discomfort and danger.' One of the ways he demonstrated his own fibre of vigorous hardness and masculinity was on the hunting trip, especially big-game hunting. And there was – then – no fiercer or bigger game in America than the grizzly bear, no creature more manly for a man to hunt. One such expedition, in 1902, took the president to the politically sensitive Southern state of Mississippi, where he had no luck finding bear to shoot. At length, a mangy black specimen was captured, and tied up by its captors; Roosevelt was fetched and offered the bear to kill. He refused, in high indignation, as it was against his vaunted rules of sportsmanship to kill a creature in cold blood. The incident was reported, and the cartoonist in the *Washington Post*, Clifford Berryman, used it to comment on Roosevelt's attitude to the colour bar, calling his cartoon 'Drawing the Line in Mississippi' and showing the president covering his eyes as a policeman holds a bear in collar and chain.

The future founder of the Ideal Toy Company, Morris Michtom, used the incident to christen the novelty he was producing that Christmas: 'Teddy's bear' was marketed. It was not considered as manly to kill female animals even before regulations forbade it, and it is possible that this was one of the reasons Roosevelt scorned the victim that had been brought to him. Hunters preferred their animal to be male, even of species in which the females were just as ferocious and powerful, as among the big cats, and indeed, the bears. In the midst of massacring animals, anthropomorphism is never far away: the beast as victim holds up a mirror to human values. It is interesting that Teddy Roosevelt's thirst to contend with great beasts in the American wilderness produced the most domesticated of toys, the cuddly bear; but the contradiction is not as deep as it first appears. The president saw himself as 'the apostle of the strenuous life'. He was questing in the American wilderness for virtue, he brought it back as dead beasts, and inspired the toy that symbolically returns the wilds to the nursery. At the turn of the century, he was performing a ritual sacrifice, and as the leader of the country was taking on a priest-like role in so doing; fortunately, with the change in sensibility, we prefer today to perform the sacrifice symbolically, through images, and fetish objects, soft toys.

The success of the teddy bear defies belief: in 1907, soon after the German manufacturer Steiff started producing teddy bears in Europe too, they sold nearly a million. Many famous characters in children's literature since have been teddy bears: Rupert Bear, Winnie-the-Pooh, Paddington, Sooty, and others. Their popularity is not confined to children: the English poet John Betjeman wrote poems to the bear of his childhood, Archibald; Evelyn Waugh immortalized Aloysius, Sebastian Flyte's bear in *Brideshead Revisited*. Since then, manufacturers have created Mummy bears in aprons and Daddy bears in jeans. There has even been a machine-gun-toting Rambear. Thirty-five thousand collectors of teddy bears compete for treasures in America alone; early versions sell for thousands of pounds in the salerooms. A Steiff example from the 1920s – Richard Steiff is also credited with the toy's invention – fetched £550,000 in 1989.

Just as the rise of the teddy bear matches the decline of real bears in the wild, so soft toys today have taken the shape of rare wild species. Some of these are not very furry in their natural state: stuffed killer whales, cheetahs, gorillas, snails, spiders and snakes – and of course dinosaurs – are made in the most invitingly deep-pile plush. They act as a kind of totem, associating the human being with the animal's imagined capacities and value. Anthropomorphism traduces the creatures themselves; their loveableness sentimentally exaggerated, just as, formerly, belief in their viciousness crowded out empirical observation. Bear-baiting, once upon a time; now British Rail offers an Away Break reduction to families with a documentary photograph of a brown bear with its arm around its mate. The distinction between humans and beasts is yearningly cancelled: soft toys wear clothes and perform human tasks, even going deep-sea diving. By giving a toy in the shape of a wild animal, the giver encourages the goodness of the wild in human nature, male and female. For mankind is still the issue; Keith Thomas comments, '[Such] fantasies ... enshrine the values by which society as a whole cannot afford to live.'

The transitional object was defined by D. W. Winnicott in the 1950s as something chosen by a child to give comfort, kept for a year or more since infancy, usually soft, and irreplaceable except when the child chooses to abandon or exchange it. Children themselves pick on blankets and rags and old nappies and odd bits of cloth that disintegrate; it is the parents and other adults who offer teddy bears and other animals, for the view has gained very wide currency that we have to put our animal side behind us as we grow up, and that children are lucky to be close to it. Though Walt Disney never originated a bear character, his squashy, irrepressible gallery of furry beasts, who are, like Mickey Mouse, much larger than life, continue the Aesopian tradition of speaking through animals of human dreams.

Tapping the power of the animal no longer seems charged with danger, let alone evil, but rather a necessary part of healing. Art of different media widely accepts the fall of man, from namer and master of animals to a mere hopeful candidate for inclusion as one of their number.

II

The attraction of the wild, and of the wild brother in twentieth-century culture, cannot be overestimated; as the century advances, in the cascade of deliberate revisions of the tale, Beauty stands in need of the Beast, rather than vice versa, and the Beast's beastliness is good, even adorable. Or at least, this has become the drift of the story. She has not mistaken a human lover for a monster, like Psyche, or failed to see a good man beneath the surface, like Belle; on the contrary, the Beast's beastliness will teach her something. Her need of him may be reprehensible, a moral flaw, a part of her carnal and materialist nature; or, it can represent her understanding of love, her redemption. He no longer stands outside her, the threat of male sexuality in bodily form, or of male authority with all its fearful amorality and social legitimacy, as in D'Aulnoy's stories, but he holds up a mirror to the force of nature within her, which she is invited to accept and allow to grow. In one sense the Beast has returned to define Beauty in the early medieval

In a fantastic scene of metamorphosis, inspired by Angela Carter's mix of gothic and baroque in her fairy tales, the wedding guests in Neil Jordan's film, The Company of Wolves, 1984, sprout lupine hair and claws and grow fangs and jaws as they reveal their inner animal natures.

feminine character of seductive concupiscence; only now, the stigma has been lifted. The Beast as a beast has become the object of desire.

Part of Angela Carter's boldness – which made her unpopular in some quarters of the feminist movement in the 1970s – was that she dared to look at women's waywardness, and especially at their attraction to the Beast in the very midst of repulsion. The early novel *The Magic Toyshop,* already tells the story of a beast's defeat: the puppet master makes a monstrous swan automaton to assault his niece in play-acting. But she rejects him, refuses the part in his puppet show, and eventually escapes, with the whole family, from his designs. *The Bloody Chamber* followed two years after a dry and adept translation she made of Perrault, and offers her answer to Perrault's vision of better things. Angela Carter returned to the theme of Beauty and the Beast again and again, turning it inside out and upside down; in a spirit of mischief, she was seizing the chance to mawl governessy moralizers. Rather like the heroines of the Grimms' animal bridegroom tale, 'Snow White and Rose Red', her Beauties choose to play with the Beast precisely because his animal nature excites them and gives their desires licence:

They tugged his hair with their hands, put their feet on his back and rolled him about, or they took a hazel switch and beat him, and when he growled, they laughed. But the bear took it all in good part, only when they were too rough he called out, 'Leave me alive, children. Snow White, Rose Red, will you beat your wooer dead?'

Deliberately flouting conventional ladylike aspirations (the love of the prince), with which, since the nineteenth century, fairy tales had been identified, Carter places her protagonists in the shoes of Red Riding Hood, of Beauty, of Snow White, of Bluebeard's bride. 'The Courtship of Mr. Lyon', 'The Tiger's Bride', 'The Werewolf', 'The Company of Wolves' lift the covers from the body of carnal knowledge usually more modestly draped in fairy tales. For 'The Company of Wolves', she re-imagined familiar tales in a spiny, springing prose which borrows elements from Symbolism and pornography, Gothic romance, street slang and Parnassian preciousness all at once, to conjure young girls' sexual hunger and the lure of the wild. The wolf stirs desire here far more profoundly than would the pattern of princes:

> Carnivore incarnate, only immaculate flesh appeases him.
> She will lay his fearful head on her lap and she will pick out the lice from his pelt and perhaps she will put the lice into her mouth and eat them, as he will bid her, as she would do in a savage marriage ceremony.
> The blizzard will die down …
> See! sweet and sound she sleeps in granny's bed, between the paws of the tender wolf.

As the English critic Lorna Sage writes:

> [Carter] produced her own haunting, mocking – sometimes tender – variations on some of the classic motifs of the genre … in retelling these tales she was deliberately drawing them out of their set shapes, out of the separate space of 'children's stories' or 'folk art' and into the world of change. It was yet another assault on Myth … done caressingly and seductively. The monsters and the princesses lose their places in the old script, and cross forbidden boundary lines.

But Carter could also be love's votary in more traditional fashion. Another of the tales, almost an ekphrasis of the Cocteau film, describes the Beast's rescue:

> 'I'm dying, Beauty,' he said in a cracked whisper of his former purr. 'Since you left me, I have been sick …'
> She flung herself upon him, so that the iron bedstead groaned, and covered his poor paws with her kisses.

'Don't die, Beast! If you'll have me, I'll never leave you.'

When her lips touched the meat-hook claws, they drew back into their pads and she saw how he had always kept his fists clenched but, painfully, tentatively, at last began to stretch his fingers. Her tears fell on his face like snow and, under their soft transformation, the bones showed through the pelt, the flesh through the wide, tawny brow …

The narrator's voice can be urgent, addressing the reader in the first person: 'My father lost me to the Beast at cards' is the opening line of 'The Tiger's Bride'; this story ends with the heroine's own transformation, under the Beast's caresses, into a furry, naked creature like him.

'East o' the Sun and West o' the Moon' was invoked by Carter as 'one of the most lyrically beautiful and mysterious of all Northern European fairy tales'. It closely reworks the Cupid and Psyche material, and in it a White Bear taking the role of Eros abducts the heroine, asking as he does so, 'Are you afraid?' She says, 'No,' and climbs eagerly on to his back to go forth into a new life with him. Carter also noted the hypocritical evasions of so many modern versions of 'Beauty and the Beast', commenting caustically that the tale had been increasingly employed 'to house-train the id'.

A contemporary artist who also shows Surrealist affinities, Paula Rego, has been inspired by seemingly innocuous English nursery rhymes to plumb darker sides to women's fantasy life than is openly admitted. She too manages to stir some of the same depths when she illustrates 'Baa baa black sheep', for instance, with an image of a little girl provocatively accepting the embrace of a giant ram as she waves to the little boy in the lane (right).

Beauty's attraction to the Beast before his regeneration inspires fantasies about abduction in pulp fiction, and echoes pornography's conjuration of sadism and rape. The territory is thickly sown with land mines; both Angela Carter's and Paula Rego's work excites contradictory and powerful feelings in their audience, because, while openly challenging conventional misogyny in the very act of speaking and making images, they also refuse the wholesome or pretty picture of female gender (nurturing, caring) and deal plainly with erotic dominance as a source of pleasure for men – and for women.

In 1982, the poet Ted Hughes dramatized 'Beauty and the Beast' for television. His script developed the fantasy, implicit in the classical myth of Cupid and Psyche, that Beauty's passionate desiring summons the Beast to her side, and that, after she has lost him, her yearning for him brings about their reunion. The

Hughes version, though it was made for children, does not scant the heroine's erotic fantasy as the dynamic of the story. It begins with the father crazed with worry that every night his beloved daughter the princess is visited by a monstrous and unnameable terror which takes possession of her; invisible, with a huge voice, this phenomenon occupies her dreams and her bed. Doctors are put to watch by her side, and they too are overcome with horror at what they feel, though they see nothing – one specialist's hair turns white overnight. Then a wandering musician with a performing bear comes to the palace at the king's wish, to entertain the melancholy and even mad princess – and the bear charms her. She dances with the beast, and the king her father rejoices that the bear seems to have lifted the mad darkness that was oppressing her. But then, as they are dancing, the bear seizes her in his arms and carries her off.

When, after a long search, the hunting party tracks them down, the princess begs them not to hurt her bear. They wound him, and she weeps – and then, as in other versions, her tears, the proof of her love, fall on his pelt and he stands up, transfigured.

Childish things are not always so childish: Paula Rego taps the mysteries concealed in the innocuous sounding light verse of the nonsense rhyme. (Nursery Rhymes, *London, 1989.*)

Ted Hughes's intuition that Beauty is stirred by love for the Beast, even when he terrorizes her in the night, reappeared in a more definite form in the popular 1987 CBS series for television, which was also shown in Britain, in which the Beast never casts off his hybrid form. A roaring, rampaging half-lion, half-human creature, he reigns over the subway system of New York as a defender of women and beggars, an urban Robin Hood, who was born from an immaculate virgin and the seed of two fathers, the double lord of the underworld, one a good magus, the other a wicked wizard. Beauty in this case works as an investigator in the District Attorney's office, but communicates secretly with her saviour Beast; their love is passionate, chivalrous and ... illicit. He is 'the monster of her dreams' and she likes him just as he is.

The disenchantments of the Beast take many forms, not all of them benign; women have remained consistently intrigued. As Karel Čapek has commented: 'The same fiction of evil which quickens events in fairy stories also permeates our real lives.' It would be easy to dismiss these visions of the Beast's desirability as male self-flattery, and female collusion with subjection, or, even more serious, as risky invitations to roughness and even rape. But to do so misses the genuine attempt of the contemporary versions of the fairy tale, in certain metamorphoses of its own, to face up to the complicated character of the female erotic impulse. From the post-Utopian vantage point of the 1990s, we cannot rejoice unequivocally in the sexual liberation Surrealism and its aftermath offered women: the experiences of the last decades have given former flower children pause. But what threatens women consumers – and makers – of fairy tale above all is the identification of the Beast with some exclusively male positive area of energy and expression.

The journey the story has itself taken ultimately means that the Beast no longer needs to be disenchanted. Rather, Beauty has to learn to love the beast in him, in order to know the beast in herself. Beauty and the Beast stories are even gaining in popularity over 'Cinderella' as a site for psychological explorations along these lines, and for pedagogical recuperation. Current interpretations focus on the Beast as a sign of authentic, fully realized sexuality, which women must learn to accept if they are to become normal adult heterosexuals. Bettelheim argues:

Eventually there comes a time when we must learn what we have not known before – or, to put it psychoanalytically, to undo the repression of sex. What we had experienced as dangerous, loathsome, something to be shunned, must change its appearance so that it is experienced as truly beautiful.

Belle had to learn to be a loving wife in the eighteenth century; in the late twentieth, she has to learn to be game in bed. But the Bettelheimian argument takes the exuberance and the energy from female erotic voices, and effects one last transformation of the Beast, by turning him into a mistaken illusion in unawakened female eyes. In this, the psychoanalyst works his way back, in more solemn vein, to the Hellenistic romance, in which Psyche was at fault for fearing her lover was an ogre and not trusting him in bed.

III

The cuddliness of the teddy bear, the appeal of domesticated sexuality, also informs the present trend towards celebrating the male. In Tim Burton's film *Edward Scissorhands* (1990), the outcast hero does harm, entirely inadvertently: like Frankenstein's monster, he has been made by a mad scientist but left half finished, with cutlery for hands. As a metonymy of maleness and its fumbling connection to the world of others, the scissorhands capture eloquently the idea of the redeemed male beast in current circulation. By the 1990s, the perception of the social outcast, the exile from humankind in the form of a beast, had undergone such a sea-change that any return to full human shape might have degraded rather than redeemed the hero, limited his nobility rather than restored it.

In the same year, the Disney film animation, *Beauty and the Beast*, one of the biggest box-office draws of all time, ran the risk of dramatic collapse when the Beast changed into the prince. No child in my experience preferred the sparkling candy-coloured human who emerged from the enchanted monster; the Beast had won them. Linda Woolverton and the team who collaborated on the film had clearly steeped themselves in the tale's history, on and off screen; prolonged and intense production meetings, turning over every last detail of representation and narrative, can almost be heard over the insouciant soundtrack. This fairytale film is more vividly aware of contemporary sexual politics than any made before; it consciously picked out a strand in the tale's history and deliberately developed it for an audience of mothers who grew up with Betty Friedan and Gloria Steinem, who had daughters who listened to Madonna and Sinead O'Connor. Linda Woolverton's screenplay put forward a heroine of spirit who finds romance on her own terms. Beneath this prima facie storyline, the interpretation contained many subtexts, both knotty and challenging, about changing concepts of paternal authority and rights, about permitted expressions of male desire, and prevailing notions in the quarrel about nature/nurture. Above all, the film placed before the 1990s audience Hollywood's cunning domestication of feminism itself.

Like an American buffalo, or a cartoon Picasso Minotaur, the Disney Beast, created by the animator Glen Keane, learns with Belle how to be a new man. (Beauty and the Beast, directed by Gary Trousdale and Kirk Wise, 1991, © The Walt Disney Company.)

Knowing as the film is, it could not avoid the trap that modern retellings set: the Beast steals the show. While the Disney version ostensibly tells the story of the feisty, strong-willed heroine, and carries the audience along on the wave of her dash, her impatient ambitions, her bravery, her self-awareness, and her integrity, the principal burden of the film's message concerns maleness, its various faces and masks, and, in the spirit of romance, it offers hope of regeneration from within the unregenerate male. The graphic intensity given to the two protagonists betrays the weight of interest: Beauty is saucer-eyed, dainty, slender, and wears a variation on the pseudo-medieval dresses of both Cinderella and Snow White, which, as in *Cinderella*, turn into *ancien régime* crinolines-cum-New Look débutante gowns for the scene of awakening love when she dances with the Beast. Her passage from repugnance to attraction also follows a movement from village hall to castle gate, in the conventional upwardly mobile style of the twentieth-century fairy tale. The animators have introduced certain emancipated touches: she is dark-haired, a book worm and walks with a swing. The script even contains a fashionable bow in the direction of self-reflexiveness, for Belle likes reading fairy tales more than any other kind of book, and consequently recognizes, when she finds herself in the Beast's castle, the type of story she is caught in.

But next to the Beast, this Belle is a lacklustre creature. He held the animators' full attention: the pneumatic signature style of Disney animation suited the Beast's character as male desire incarnate. He embodies the Eros figure as phallic toy. The Beast swells, he towers, he inflates, he tumesces. Everything about him is big, and apt to grow bigger: his castle looms, its furnishings dwarfed by its Valhalla-like dimensions. His voice thunders, his anger roars to fill the cavernous spaces of his kingdom. We are shown him enraged, crowding the screen, edge to edge, like a face in a comic strip; when he holds Belle he looks as if he could snap her between his teeth like a chicken wing. His body too appears to be constantly burgeoning; poised on narrow hooves and skimpy legs, the Disney Beast sometimes lollops like a big cat, but more often stands erect, rising to an engorged torso, with an enormous, craggy, bull-like head compacted into massive shoulders, maned and shaggy all over, bristling with fangs and horns and claws that almost seem belittled by the creature's overall bulk.

The Beast's sexual equipment was always part of his charm – hidden or otherwise (it is of course scattered by synecdoche all over his body in the Disney cartoon). When Titania fell in love with Bottom the weaver, the associations of the ass were not lost on the audience. But the comic – and its concomitant, the pathetic – have almost entirely slipped away from this contemporary representation of virility.

Whereas Bottom, even in his name, was a figure of fun, and the Golden Ass, his classical progenitor, a ruefully absurd icon of (male) humanity, the contemporary vision of the Beast tends to the tragic. The new Disney Beast's nearest ancestor is the Minotaur, the hybrid offspring of Pasiphae and the bull, and an ancient nightmare of perverted lust, and it is significant that Picasso adopted the Minotaur as his alter ego, as the embodiment of his priapism, in the vigour of youth as well as the impotence of old age. But the real animal which the Disney Beast most resembles is the American buffalo, and this tightens the Beast's connections to current perceptions of natural good – for the American buffalo, like the grizzly, represents the lost innocence of the plains before man came to plunder. So the celluloid Beast's beastliness thrusts in two contradictory directions; though he is condemned for his 'animal' rages, he also epitomizes the primordial virtues of the wild (left).

The Beast's longstanding identity with masculine appetite nevertheless works for him rather than against him, and interacts with prevailing ideas of healthy male sexuality. The enterprise of the earlier fairytale writers, to try to define their own desires by making up stories about beasts who either denied them or fulfilled

The story without frills: 'Beauty and the Beast' from a nursery retelling, c. 1880.

BEAUTY AND THE BEAST.

This shows the wonderful transformation. There lies the poor Beast, nothing but an ugly old Bear.

Then of a sudden in his place there kneels a handsome young Prince at Beauty's feet, and, as the story says, they lived happily ever afterwards.

them, has been rather lost to sight. The vindication of the Beast has become the chief objective; the true lovableness of the good Beast the main theme. The Disney cartoon has double-knotted the lesson in contemporary ecological and sexual politics, by introducing a second beast, another suitor for Belle's love, the human hunk Gaston. Gaston is a killer – of animals – and remains one; he is a lyncher, who preys on social outcasts (suspected lunatics and marginals), he wants to breed (he promises Belle six or seven children), and he is capable of deep treachery in pursuit of his own interests. The film wastes no sympathy on Gaston – though his conceit inspires some of its cleverest and funniest lyrics.

The penalty for Gaston's brutishness is death: he falls off a high crag from the Beast's castle. In the film, he takes the part of the real beast, the Calvinist unredeemed damned beast: socially deviant in his supremacist assumptions, unsound on ecology in both directions, abusing the natural (the forest) and culture (the library). What is above all significant about this caricature is that he is a man in a man's shape, Clark Kent as played by Christopher Reeve. The Disney version is pitiless towards Gaston; self-styled heart throbs who fancy themselves Supermen are now the renegades, and wild men in touch with nature and the beast within the exemplars.

He is moreover one of the rustics whom the sophisticated Belle despises in her opening song ('I want much more than they've got planned'), an anthem for the Me-generation; this Disney, like its predecessors, does not question the assumption that the Beast's princeliness must be material and financial. His credit card, with his social status, is no doubt bigger than Gaston's, too.

In *Edward Scissorhands*, the heroine also acts quickly, with gallantry and courage, to save this outcast from a mob; but he is fatally hampered by his hybrid form, halfway between the automaton and the creaturely; his weapon hands encumber him with man-made technology and cut him off from the desirable aspects of the human, which derive from what is perceived as natural, as animal. The further the cinematic outcast lies from the machine, the more likely his redemption; the Beast as cyborg, as in the *Terminator* movies, represents the apocalyptic culmination of human ingenuity and its diabolical perversion. Whereas, to a medieval spectator, the Devil was represented as close to the animal order in his hooved hairiness, and a bloodless and fleshless angel in gleaming armour approximated the divine artefact, the register of value has been turned topsy-turvy since the eighteenth century and the wild man has come into his own as an ideal. The evolution of the Beast in fairy tale and his portraits in film illustrate this profound shift in cultural values as well as sexual expectations.

The most significant plot change to the traditional story in the Disney film concerns the role of Beauty's father, and it continues the film's trend towards granting Beauty freedom of movement and responsibility for the rescue of the Beast and for his restoration to fundamental inner goodness. The traditional fairy tale often includes the tragic motif that, in return for his life, the father promises the Beast the first thing to greet him when he returns home; as in the story of Jephthah in the Bible (Jg. 11: 12), his daughter, his youngest and most dear, rushes to the gate to meet him, and the father has to sacrifice her. In the eighteenth-century French fairy story, which focussed on the evils of matrimonial customs, the father hands over Belle to the Beast in exactly the same kind of legal and financial transaction as an arranged marriage, and she learns to accept it. Bruno Bettelheim takes a governessy line on the matter: Beauty, learning to relinquish her Oedipal attachment to her father, should be grateful to her father for giving her away and making the discovery of sexuality possible.

Linda Woolverton's script sensibly sets such patriarchal analysis aside, and instead provides subplots to explain away the father's part in Beauty's predicament, as well as supplying Beauty herself with all the wilfulness and determination to make her mistress of her own fate. The Disney studio, sensitive to the rise of children's rights, has replaced the father with the daughter as the enterprising authority figure in the family. The struggle with patriarchal plans underlies, as we shall see, the plots of many other familiar tales.

In popular versions, 'Beauty and the Beast' offers a lesson in female yielding and its satisfactions. The Beast stirs desire, Beauty responds from some deep inner need which he awakens. (There are echoes here of 'Sleeping Beauty' too.) The Beast, formerly the stigmatizing envelope of the fallen male, has become a badge of the salvation he offers; Beauty used to grapple with the material and emotional difficulties of matrimony for young women; now she tends to personify female erotic pleasures in matching and mastering a man who is dark and hairy, rough and wild, and, in the psychotherapist Robert Bly's phrase, in touch with the Inner Warrior in himself.

In her encounter with the Beast, the female protagonist meets her match, in more ways than one. If she defeats him, or even kills him, if she outwits him, banishes or forsakes him, or accepts him and loves him, she arrives at some knowledge she did not possess; his existence and the challenge he offers is necessary before she can grasp it. The ancient tale of 'Cupid and Psyche' told of their love; apart from the child Pleasure whom Psyche bore, their other descendants – the tales in the Beauty and the Beast group – number among the most eloquent testaments to women's struggles, against arranged marriage, and towards a definition of the place of sexuality in love. The enchantments and disenchantments of the Beast have been a rich resource in stories women have made up, among themselves, to help, to teach, to warn.

CHAPTER 19

The Runaway Girls: Donkeyskin I

The pagan father ...
Began to think about his daughter night and day.
His fears were so great
That he decided to have a tower built,
A tower more beautiful than any ever seen.

Gautier de Coinci

The law forbidding sex between mother and son, father and daughter, brother and sister, holds universally in human society; it is sometimes extended to include cousins and god-siblings within its interdiction, but it always remains a founding binary opposition on which the structural foundations of society are laid. Because storytellers finger the heathen and the apostate, separate the saved from the damned, the well-behaved from the badly behaved, the transgressor from the insider, the tales that a 'Sibyl-nurse' traditionally passes on pinpoint differences between good and evil in matters of faith and doctrine and custom. In setting riddles which clarify such matters, the Queen of Sheba, for example, not

After her father's proposal of marriage, the daughter takes flight in disguise. Catherine Deneuve as Peau d'Ane in The Magic Donkey, *directed by Jacques Demy, 1971.*

only foreshadows the figure of the storyteller herself, but also embodies the function of the tale itself, as the arbiter of family relations and social order, conveying and instructing the audience, especially the young audience, in what is licit and illicit, what will earn praise and reward, and what will forfeit it. It was to fulfil this function that so many of her riddles circulating in fifteenth-century Europe focussed on the rules of exogamy and the incest taboo. Myths and folklore wrestle with defining and conveying its importance: the mother–son prohibition underlies the story of Oedipus, a founding myth both in its Sophoclean, tragic form and in its potent Freudian afterlife. Incest between father and daughter has not dominated Western mythology or mythological analysis to the same degree; but it makes a strong showing in fairy tale.

Giambattista Basile included in the *Pentamerone* the first modern variation on one of the most familiar fairy tales in Europe. His story is called '*L'Orsa*' (The She-Bear): 'There was once a King of Roccaspra,' it begins, 'who had for his wife the very mother of beauty, but he lost her early, for in the gallop of life she fell from the horse of health and broke her life ...'

The couple have a daughter, called Preziosa, Precious. On her deathbed, her mother demands on the pain of horrible curses that her husband should never marry again, unless he finds 'another woman as beautiful as I have been'.

He swears; she dies; he rails with grief and weeps rivers of tears. But, as Basile says – and in Naples cynicism was an essential of survival – 'the ache of the widower is like the ache in the funny-bone, sharp, but brief'. So he soon begins looking around him for a new wife to replace his beloved, and give him an heir – a son. He holds a contest, has candidates summoned from the four quarters; but none will do. Then the thought strikes him, 'Why should I seek [high and low] when Preziosa, my daughter, is made in the same form as her mother? I have this lovely face by me at home, and yet I go to the ends of the earth to find another like it?'

He puts the matter to the girl, but she reproaches him bitterly. He explodes: 'Make up your mind to tie the marriage knot this very night; for otherwise your ear will be the biggest bit left of you!' When Preziosa hears this, she goes to her room in desperation and an old woman, a servant who 'used to bring her mercury' for her toilette, appears and comforts her. She also gives Preziosa practical advice, handing her a little stick and telling her to put it in her mouth when her father 'wants to play the part of a stallion, though there's more of the ass in him'. She promises her, 'You will then immediately become a bear, and can run away ...'

The wedding feast takes place that night; the bride is summoned to her father's bed. There she does as the old woman had told her, and escapes from her terrified father in the shape of a bear. As she wanders in the forest in this disguise, a prince out hunting spots her, and captures her. One day, when passing the den in the palace gardens where the bear has been confined, he sees a young woman combing her golden hair. Preziosa the she-bear has taken the stick out of her mouth and become a girl again, thinking no one was looking. He falls in love with the mysterious stranger and, finally, after many vicissitudes, discovers that she and the bear are one and the same, and marries her. The prince's mother, on hearing Preziosa's story, extols her as a good, virtuous girl. Basile concludes, optimistically, 'Thus Preziosa was the sounding rod to the balance of human judgement, which declares that "To those who do good, good always comes."'

Some of the elements in this happy and reassuring story are very recognizable: the disguised princess whose virtue and beauty are at last acknowledged and properly rewarded by union with a prince, after an older woman has helped her escape her troubles, relates Basile's 'L'Orsa' to the Cinderella cycle of folk tales. But the story differs in obvious ways from the classic fairy tale, the version told by Charles Perrault. There, of course, Cinderella is not wronged by her *father*, but by her stepmother and her daughters, Cinderella's stepsisters. The more familiar story enfolds within it, not like a worm in the bud, but like the hollow in the core of an agate pebble, the motif of incestuous desire.

The she-bear variant, which itself appears in hundreds of metamorphoses in Western texts and imagery, deals with tensions that arise from possessiveness, rivalry, ownership, procreation and usurpation, in the triangle composed of mother, father and daughter, and its historical changes themselves reflect the way different moments have dealt with this central question. The wronged daughter in the folk tale known as 'Unlawful Love' embodies many of fairy tale's crucial functions, including speaking of the unspeakable and negotiating a rite of passage through story. She also takes on herself the character of an enchanted animal, and, as a she-beast, she carries very different meanings from her male counterparts.

Perrault spun a tale of the she-bear type, and it was one of the first fairy tales he wrote. 'Peau d'Ane' (Donkeyskin) was written in verse, a kind of jaunty doggerel, and was published in pamphlet form in 1694, three years before the famous group of fairy tales in Contes du temps passé. It remains the least reproduced fairy tale from Perrault's much-loved and much reproduced oeuvre; it was not included in his collection until 1781, when a much less sprightly prose version made its first appearance, a paraphrase by another, anonymous hand which inflates the ornament at the same time as flattening the wit (this is still the usual version to be reprinted).

In his preface to the story, this *académicien*, scholar, courtier and defender of the Modern school of French literature against the Ancients' emulators, confided to his readers that there were times when *'le grave et le sérieux'* (serious, weighty matters) were not as valuable as *'agréables sornettes'* (pleasant trifles): he was wrapping himself in jocularity as in a magic cloak. With his nonsense-rhyme style poem, Perrault was tackling a stock fairy tale – a *conte de Peau d'âne* – about a father who wants to marry his daughter. But he braided this material with another, durable folk motif: a magic animal whose excrement is made of gold (below). Among the bestiary available from his sources – fish, geese, cows all produce magic fortunes in fairy tales – Perrault chose a donkey.

The donkey that drops golden dung, like the goose that lays the golden eggs, is a familiar dream in folk tales, which Perrault adapted for 'Donkeyskin'.(Amsterdam, sixteenth century.)

Perrault may have lighted upon the reference to the father as ass in 'The She-Bear', and his immediate source for the tale of the ass that shits gold may have been another of Basile's tales from Naples. (No critic or scholar has been able to decide whether Perrault had a copy of Basile.) However, the donkey served his purposes. Throughout his career, Perrault's work had alternated between the overweeningly pompous and the jest: he could apostrophize the timbre of his beloved's voice, and write sonnets on her being afflicted with a cold, but when he was a young man he had also composed a mock version of Aeneas' descent into the underworld, as in Book VI of the *Aeneid*, and in 1653 had written *Les Murs de Troye*, an absurdist essay on the origins of burlesque as a form. By introducing the magic donkey into the story of the unlawful love of a father, Perrault mocked, in the style of the Milesian tale, the atmosphere of enchantment.

'Once upon a time there was a king, the greatest king there ever was on earth,' begins Perrault's *'Peau d'Ane'*, already slyly teasing fairy tale's love of hyperbole. This king has everything kings have, but in addition he keeps in the royal stables a donkey which every day provides a fortune in gold dung. But the king does suffer

The moment of epiphany: when her finger fits the ring she had cunningly slipped into the only cake the sick prince could eat, the skivvy in her filthy ass hide is recognized to be the radiant girl for whom the prince is languishing. ('Peau d'Ane' (Donkeyskin), Le Cabinet des fées, *Paris, 1785–9.)*

one of fate's blows: his beautiful and charming wife falls ill, and on her deathbed she asks him to swear that he will only marry again a woman who is more beautiful than she. He does so gladly. Time passes, and he searches high and low. Only one woman meets the conditions of his vow: his daughter. But she is reluctant, and seeks out her godmother, a marvellously powerful fairy, who does her best for the distressed young girl. Three times, on her godmother's advice, the daughter asks her father for an impossible gift: a dress the colour of Heaven, another the colour of the Moon, a third the colour of the Sun. Each time, in his unfailing potency, the father produces it, until, at last, the fairy advises the princess to demand something the kingly father surely cannot part with: the hide of the magic donkey, the source of his wealth.

Of course, the king does not refuse his daughter: to her utter dismay, he goes ahead and kills the donkey, and offers her the skin as his clinching wedding gift. She has no alternative: she must marry her father, or flee. Her godmother advises flight, in disguise, so she wraps herself in the stinking pelt, dirties her face and hands till she looks like the lowest slattern.

She wanders, meets with abuse and insult, and eventually takes a job as a skivvy in the laundry and sty of a neighbouring prince's castle. She is known only by her nickname, '*Peau d'Ane*', until one day, when she thinks nobody is looking, she tries on one of her magic dresses in secret in her pigsty, and is glimpsed through a chink by the prince. One thing leads to another, and after various ordeals Donkeyskin is recognized to be a true princess (p. 323), and she marries her prince. Her father comes to the wedding, purified of his *odieuse flamme* (his odious passion), and Perrault concludes first that virtue will be rewarded, and second, in his throwaway *mondain* manner, that bread and water are quite sufficient to a young person's needs – as long as she has some pretty clothes.

Donkeyskin's disguise confers on her the particular long-suffering character of the jennet, or she-ass, described in medieval bestiary lore, the popular *Physiologus*, as putting up with work and 'almost unlimited neglect'. But, interestingly, Perrault specifies that the enchanted, gold-producing animal is a jackass. Perrault often identifies the transitional stage of his main character with a reverse sex name: as Marc Soriano has pointed out, Cendrillon, for instance, ends with a common masculine form – *on*, rather than our Cinderella; by contrast, Noël du Fail, in his *Propos rustiques* of 1547, mentions the tale '*Cuir d'Asnette*' (Little Donkey Leather) as one of the repertory of stories told at the *veillées*, the evening gatherings of rural France; *Asnette* is the feminine diminutive.

Perrault picked the ass for effect; he was well acquainted with the vast Aesopian folklore about the jackass as fall guy in the market economy of the fabulist's harsh world. In 1699, Perrault was to translate into French verse the sixteenth-century Latin anthology of Gabriel Faerno, who had drawn on Phaedrus as well as Aesop, and included nearly a dozen of the famous harsh tales in which the donkey loses to the fox or the lion. In one, particularly bitter vignette, the pack-ass in question has open saddle sores to which a crow fastens itself and pecks savagely, and will not be shaken off by the poor howling, kicking animal. A muleteer, passing by, witnesses the scene and laughs wholeheartedly at the donkey's antics; a wolf, observing, envies the crow which provokes only merriment whereas he, the wolf, is always reproached when he shows his nature.

Her disguise degrades his heroine utterly: Perrault writes that the donkey was

La beste en un mot la plus laide
Qu'on puisse voir après le loup.

[In a word, after the wolf quite the ugliest animal one might ever see.]

And her predicament invites the ridicule of all around her:

> *On la mit dans un coin au fond de la cuisine*
> *Où les Valets, insolente vermine,*
> *Ne faisaient que la tirailler,*
> *La contredire et la railler;*
> *Ils ne savaient quelle pièce lui faire,*
> *La harcelant à tout propos;*
> *Elle était la butte ordinaire*
> *De tous leurs quolibets et de tous leurs bons mots.*

[She was put in a corner at the back of the kitchen where the valets, that insolent vermin, did nothing but plague her and cross her and mock her; they could never decide what trick to play on her next, harassing her at every turn; she was the usual butt of all their witticisms and clever jibes.]

But her day will come, whereas for the ass of fable there is usually no hope, aside from canonization in the Christian fellowship of paragons. The fairytale princess wears a skin of shame, but the pathetic degradation of her condition contains a kind of Christian grace of humility, forbearance and lack of vanity, like the fool who wears asses' ears because he knows himself to be a fool. Like the fables, which by ironic and invisible subtexts take the part of the ass, the fairy tale often feels for the least of all – A. A. Milne's Eeyore stands in direct line of descent from this classically pathetic figure of fun.

The absurd priapism of the jackass is not altogether obscured in the fairy tale, however, but underlies Perrault's choice of beast. For in this early fairy tale, he marks the daughter with her father's sin: the sign of the donkey conveys his lust. She becomes a beast, after her father has behaved like one. In 'Beauty and the Beast', the father and the Beast bridegroom collude to dispose of the heroine's desires; in the 'Donkeyskin' cycle, her rebellion means she chooses between father and lover, and they do not conspire.

Significantly, Perrault published '*Peau d'Ane*' with '*Grisélidis*', a sister parable of female degradation and forbearance rewarded, which Perrault also treated with flippant irreverence. Both tales belong to two immense groups of traditional stories: Patient Griselda is another type of Accused Queen, related to the historical stories of medieval heroines and saints like Geneviève de Brabant, Godelive of Bruges, Elizabeth of Hungary. To the wider circles of this group of tales also belongs the seminal story of the False Bride, of which 'Berthe aus grant pié' is only one variation. 'Donkeyskin' also sits in another great tangled web of stories spun in the middle ages around the figure of the loving daughter whose father loves her 'unlawfully' in return and who is then abused or rejected by him.

The late-antique romance of *Apollonius of Tyre* circulated in many different editions from the tenth century onwards, as well as being told again and again, in poems, plays and hagiography. John Gower's *Confessio amantis* of around 1390, a thesaurus almost as plundered as Ovid's *Metamorphoses*, contains a version which, for instance, inspired Shakespeare's incestuous pair at the beginning of *Pericles* – King Antiochus and his nameless daughter. Chaucer based his 'Man of Lawe's Tale' about Constance on the story, though he disinfected it of the initial overtures of incest. The *Vita* of Dympna, a virgin martyr who became the patron saint of the insane in the fifteenth century, could have inspired Perrault, as he was interested in hagiography. According to Marian Cox, the folklorist who at the turn of the century collected 345 variants of 'Cinderella', a sermon of 1501 given in Strasbourg referred to a story called '*Peau d'Ane*'; Noël du Fail mentions the tale '*Cuir d'Asnette*', as we have seen, in 1547; Straparola's collection of 1550 includes the tale of Doralice, daughter of the Prince of Salerno, who escapes from her father shut up in a wooden wardrobe and cast adrift on the sea, only to meet with horrendous misadventures and horrors at his hands in England, until she is at last spared and vindicated. Bonaventure des Périers, writing in the 1570s, gave a different spin to the story, but called it 'Of a Young Girl named Donkeyskin and how she got married with the help of little ants'. The reference to the ants returns us to Apuleius as an early origin, for in the tale of Cupid and Psyche, Venus sets Psyche the impossible task of separating grains of millet and wheat and is furious when she accomplishes it overnight – with the help of ants. The chapbooks of the *Bibliothèque bleue* included, from 1641 onwards, numerous issues of '*Le roman de la belle Helaine*', yet another variation on the tale, in an abbreviated form. In the British Isles, the fugitive's favoured disguise is more often a coat of rushes or a catskin, and her story is told in forms other than prose narrative, including chapbooks and ballads.

It is not impossible, however, that Perrault knew the story from hearing it himself; Pierre de La Porte wrote in his *Mémoires* that Louis XIV's nurses had lulled him to sleep with '*contes de Peau d'Ane*', one of Molière's child characters offers to tell it to her father, and La Fontaine, who never wrote a version but in many ways hovers as the inspiration of Perrault's tongue-in-cheek moralizing, implies that he had heard it as a child:

Si Peau d'Ane *m'était conté*
J'y prendrais un plaisir extrême.

[It would give me the utmost pleasure / If 'Donkeyskin' were told to me.]

In 1812, the Grimm Brothers published the oral version they had collected, from Dortchen Wild, '*Allerleirauh*' (All-Fur), in which the heroine escapes from her father in a coat made of the skins of all the creatures in the world. This is a magical dress, which hides her successfully until she finds a king she can love. 'All-Fur' may represent a storyteller's ingenious and trenchant solution to the confusing discrepancies about bears and donkeys and other fauna whose fur and form the heroine takes.

The extreme peculiarity of the tale and its breaching of taboo made it appeal to the Surrealists. It was mentioned in the First Manifesto of the movement, in 1924, when André Breton lamented that children are weaned from the *merveilleux* (the wonder) of fairy tales like '*Peau d'Ane*', and then writes: 'There are tales to be written for grownups, tales which are still almost blue.' 'Donkeyskin' is indeed almost blue, and has been considered on the whole suitable for adults only.

II

A 'childish intellectual puzzle', as Edmund Leach has written, lies at the heart of myth: how is it that incest forbids relations within families, yet at the beginning there were only Adam and Eve who were flesh of their flesh? Leach comments:

> Every human society has rules of incest and exogamy. Though the rules vary, they always carry the implication that for any particular male individual all women are divided by at least one binary distinction, there are women of our kind with whom sex relations would be incestuous, and there are women of the other kind, with whom sex relations are allowed. But here again we are immediately led into paradox. How was it in the beginning? If our first parents were persons of two kinds, what was the other kind? But if they were both of our kind, then their relations must have been incestuous, and we are all born in sin.

The nub is that mating with your own kind is considered the lesser evil to mating outside your kind, however that is defined: pure ancestry corresponds to pure minds and hearts in the Judaeo-Christian perspective. The beast must turn into a man, the enchanted cat into a princess, because permitted sexual relations must take place between members of the same species who are not close kin; the drawing up of definitions of interdicted degrees constitutes, in Lévi-Strauss's striking formula, the 'first writing' of society. This writing produces some of the first and hence oldest stories as well as the stories of human origin in myth, from Christian to Aborigine.

In Genesis 19, Lot's seduction follows upon an enigmatic sequence of events that take place in Sodom itself: two angels enter the city and meet Lot who is sitting by the gate; he begs them to be his guests, and they decline, but he presses them to come home with him and at least have a meal, which they do. Before bedtime, the men of the town, young and old, surround the house and call to Lot to send out his guests 'so that we may abuse them' (Gen. 19: 5). Commentators have always taken this to mean that the Sodomites wished to violate the two angels in the manner of their name. Lot, in order to spare his guests according to the law of hospitality, offers his rowdy visitors his virgin daughters instead, 'to treat as it pleases you' (Gen. 19: 8).

The biblical narrative is disjointed and fragmentary, but it seems that this offer enrages the crowd, who berate Lot for a 'foreigner' and beat at his door to break it down. The angels blind the attackers, who then 'never found the doorway', and they recommend to Lot that he leave, with his daughters and their future husbands, as Yahweh is angry and they, his angels, are to destroy this place.

At dawn, the angels take Lot by the hand and lead him out of Sodom with his wife and his daughters. (The future sons-in-law do not believe in the danger – in spite of the angels' manifest power to blind – and remain behind.) Yahweh rains fire and brimstone on the cities of Sodom and Gomorrah, and Lot's wife looks back on the destruction, though the angels have forbidden it, and, in consequence, she is turned into a pillar of salt. Lot then looks out over the cities of the plain and 'lo, the smoke of the country went up as the smoke of a furnace' (Gen. 19: 28). Later, after Lot has been living with his daughters in a cave, the elder confides her worries to the younger: 'Our father is old, and there is not a man in the earth to come in unto us … Come, let us make our father drink wine, and we will lie with him, that we may preserve seed of our father.' On the first night, the elder daughter conceives Moab, father of the Moabite tribe; on the second night, the younger does likewise, and she becomes the mother of the Ammonites. The progeny – enemy tribes of Israel – remain equivocal, though the daughters' act is not proscribed as such in Genesis.

The biblical narrative moves through a series of flouted prohibitions: the

Lot's daughters ply their (willing) father with wine as they prepare to seduce him for the benefit of the human race. (Hendrik Goltzius, Lot and His Daughters, *1616.)*

Sodomites demand a breach of hospitality when they ask Lot to hand over his guests; though Lot holds firm to his obligations as a host, he panders his own virgin daughters in exchange; his wife disobeys the angels' command; he himself is violated in turn in his drunken sleep. Severe penalties follow almost all these transgressions: blindness for the Sodomites, followed by incineration, death for the unbelieving sons-in-law who stayed behind in Sodom, metamorphosis for Lot's wife who, it is implied, regretted their leaving their home and its annihilation. The only sin that is not blasted is the incest: the nameless daughters succeed in their avowed intention to perpetuate the human race.

None of these relations conjugate according to the prevailing rules of sexual conduct. In the small space of the narrative, no one even achieves congress at all,

until Lot and his daughters lie together. Structurally, the various elements function in the baffling manner of a riddle, in which nothing makes sense until the
solution is found. Clues in riddles also occupy two areas of meaning, simultaneously, patent and latent, and the answer changes the way the question reads
and uncovers the hidden metaphorical meaning. A riddle contains negative terms
that turn into positives as soon as they are decoded: riddling means to defy logic
in peculiar couplings of like and like. In family relations, incest becomes an
analogous activity.

The family of Lot mirrors the condition of the riddle, and so can become itself
material for riddling, because the members in the group occupy two distinct sites
of meaning: Lot is father and spouse, in the same way as in a riddle a distaff is a
distaff, but the unspeakable other thing as well. Mutually exclusive terms become
one in the verbal game. It is a form which abolishes linguistic logic, just as incest
cancels kinship law.

The most celebrated myth of incest begins with a riddle, which Oedipus
solves: the Sphinx's rather simplistic question, 'What goes on four feet in the
morning, two feet at noon and three feet in the evening?' Oedipus' ability to give
the correct answer, A Man, does not save him from becoming himself a term in a
riddle, a son who is a husband too. It is interesting to set the father–daughter
incest of Lot's family in Genesis beside the Oedipus myth: Oedipus is a parricide;
Lot's wife necessarily dies before her daughters sleep with their father; plague
devastates Thebes on account of the sinner in its midst, as the oracle informs the
Thebans; the biblical cities of the plain are destroyed by God's anger against their
unnatural vices; the son, Oedipus, is accounted responsible for his desire for his
mother and the myth presents her as the passive partner; the daughters actively
seduce their father in full consciousness while he – in the texts at least – lies lost
to the world.

Even more significantly, the Oedipal tragedy begins with an episode that is not
usually cited, because it does not figure in the Sophocles trilogy. It is, however,
referred to by Plato: Oedipus' father Laius, before Oedipus was born, fell in love
with Chrysippus, the young son of his host Pelops, and abducted him. The boy
committed suicide out of shame, and his father cursed his seducer Laius that
he should either die childless, or be killed by his own son. Hera, as goddess of
marriage, heard the father's grief, and sent the Sphinx in retaliation to prey on
Thebes, Laius' kingdom. Plato refers to this, in the *Laws*, when the Athenian,
talking to two non-Athenians, mentions 'that law which held good before the
days of Laius, declaring that it is right to refrain from indulging in the same

kind of intercourse with men and boys as with women'.

The Oedipus story, in one of its variations, thus gives an aetiological myth for homosexuality: like the story of Lot and his daughters, the consequences of sodomy are destruction on the one hand, incest on the other. The structures are not identical, of course, even enantiomorphically – in mirror reversal – for the daughters do not kill their mother; she brings death on herself by her own disobedience, her inability to let go, her hankering, which is a form of desire and of curiosity, the vices of Eve. Yahweh is a judge, he metes out revenge on sinners, according to a punitive moral code, unlike the Greek gods who oversee Oedipus' tragic destiny from the moment of his birth, speak through the oracle of his double crime and predestine him to the full atrociousness of his fate, regardless of his ignorance and his innocence. Incest in Lot's story is open-eyed on the part of the daughters, but blind in Oedipus' (and Jocasta's, in Sophocles, at least); in the Bible, it is rewarded by healthy progeny and the participants apparently survive unscathed. Both stories, however, convey the premise that desire for the prohibited parent will flourish when unchecked, either through ignorance, as in Oedipus' case, or through a lack of decorum, an instinct for species survival, a conscious flouting of taboo, as in Lot's daughters' case.

The folktale material continues the traditional association of incest and riddling. The dying queen's demand that her husband should never marry anyone who is not her like in beauty and goodness itself constitutes a riddle: this Other he can marry must be her like. The only figure who can collapse this contradiction is the forbidden daughter, the solution which cannot be proposed. Shakespeare literally dramatizes the ineffability of this correct answer, when he opens *Pericles* with the riddle of the incestuous king, Antiochus. On pain of death, anyone who wants to marry his daughter must answer this enigma she puts to them:

> I am no viper, yet I feed
> On mother's flesh which did me breed.
> I sought a husband, in which labour
> I found that kindness in a father.
> He's father, son, and husband mild;
> I mother, wife, and yet his child:
> How they may be, and yet in two,
> As you will live, resolve it you.

Pericles the suitor sees the answer, that the daughter who speaks lives with her father the king as his wife. He flees the court in horror, before Antiochus can seize him to kill him like his predecessors for the princess's hand.

In *Pericles*, the father–daughter incest also takes place in full cognizance of the guilty pair; and the daughter again is represented as consenting, even keen. But the sacrilege of their union, which opens the romance, inaugurates a story in which the proper love of a father and daughter – of Apollonius and Tarsia in the medieval romance; in Shakespeare, of Pericles and Marina – can unfold; it is as if the tale first sets out the worst case, then makes reparation by overstitching the rents and wounds on the social body it has disclosed. Riddles again play a crucial part in establishing structural relationships between the characters; in the romance, when the long-lost daughter and her father at last meet again by chance, they remain strangers to each other until Tarsia begins setting him riddles. These are ostensibly intended to rouse the bereft and wandering king from suicidal despair, but they are organized in a sequence which cryptically relates his own story to himself, or at least stirs memories of its stages, and this access of memory ultimately unleashes the moment of peripeteia, the happy mutual recognition between them. Unknotting the puzzles she poses guides them both to solving the secrets of their own identity and kinship. Shakespeare does not close his plot with the riddles, but he does arm his orphaned daughter with verbal wit which actually succeeds in protecting her against all comers in the brothel where she is placed. The language of the imagination, in *Pericles* as well, acts as the guardian of real bodies, and cerebral logic, encrypted in enigmas, deflects improper conjunctions in the world of sexual relations.

The earliest manuscripts extant of *Apollonius of Tyre* date from the ninth century, but it was circulating before that in written as well as recited forms. Its vanishing from the collective body of European story constitutes one of the most glaring examples of thinning in our culture. Meanwhile, another celebrated incestuous trope – Roman Charity – with similar, long roots into ancient folklore, has survived more vigorously from the version of Valerius Maximus into the iconography of the seventeenth century of much favoured Northern artists. This prurient anecdote develops a narrative of virtuous incest which also titillated: a father who has been condemned to death by starvation is saved when his daughter visits him and feeds him at her breast through the bars of his prison. In the Italian folk tradition, this story acquired a riddling element, too: the daughter challenges the king who has condemned her father to answer the puzzle she sets him. Like the Queen of Sheba, she puts a hard question to him, on condition that if he cannot reply, he will free a prisoner of her choice. She asks:

Oggi è l'annu mi fu patri
Ed aguannu mi fu figghiu
E figghiu chi nutricu
e maritu di me' matri.

[A year ago he was my father, and for a year he has been my son, and the son whom I am nursing is the husband of my mother.]

This king's wisdom does not suffice, and her father is set free.

The American critic Lynda Boose has perceptively commented:

The daughter's struggle with her father is one of separation, not displacement. Its psychological dynamics thus locate the conflict inside inner family space. Father–daughter stories are full of literal houses, castles, or gardens in which fathers such as Danaë's or Rapunzel's ... lock up their daughters in the futile attempt to prevent some rival male from stealing them. The motif also occurs through riddles of enclosure ... which enclose the daughter in the father's verbal labyrinth and lure her suitors to compete with and lose to the preemptive paternal bond.

Several of the fairy tales by L'Héritier, Murat, D'Aulnoy and others of their generation include these metaphors of patriarchal control: Lackadaisy and Loquatia come to grief with the wicked Richcraft in spite of their father's best efforts in 'The Subtle Princess'; the orphaned princess Starlight is imprisoned by her guardians, but manages to be reunited with her beloved Izmir after he has found her by solving a riddle.

The prevalence of these plots suggests that it is frequently and even generally supposed that desire between father and daughter is stirred as it were by nature if the ban on incest is lifted or somehow effaced, intentionally or not. In post-Reformation paintings of Lot and his daughters, both Catholic and Protestant – the subject does not figure at all frequently before the sixteenth century – the unspecified lapse of time between the destruction of the cities of the plain and the daughters' seduction of their father merges into the selfsame moment; their lascivious attentions unfold against an infernal backdrop of fire and brimstone and represent the daughters like wantons in a brothel with a client past his prime. More popular in the Netherlands and Germany than in Italy, the theme inspires appetitious meditations on the wiles of women while pretending to warn against the calamities of war: it offers a perfect excuse for pleasurable puritanical reproofs. In the two versions Lucas van Leyden painted, the burning town, the foundered vessels in the bay, the bivouac where Lot besports himself, the drinking jars and brazier are realistically rendered in contemporary early sixteenth-century detail: the daughters resemble camp followers and the image warns against the penalties of vice. Hendrik Goltzius, in 1616, stresses with histrionic sensuality the guilt of the women (p. 329): he includes an emblematic vixen appearing from behind a tree with a suitably crafty look as Lot succumbs, fully awake, to the lusciously rendered flesh of his offspring.

What these paintings reveal is that, in Christian family structure, exogamy, or marrying outside the clan, is functioning as a far more forceful imperative in early modern Europe than keeping the bloodlines pure and the family impregnable as in biblical Judaic family culture. The exemplary parable of Lot and his daughters, as they survive while 'foreigners' are blasted, as they mate against inclination for the good of their family, begins to preach an entirely different lesson: against incest. And fairy tales, adapting different materials which also tell of transgressive family unions, encode a story of cultural and social change in this respect as well as contributing profoundly to its establishment as the norm.

First in the middle ages, and then in the literature of the *ruelles* in the seventeenth century, the emphasis in incest tales shifts from the daughter's responsibility to the father's, the point of view revolves to consider her actions, her motives and her rights in a most interesting proto-feminist way. Genesis 19 portrays the daughters of Lot doing their duty by patrilineage and sustaining their father's line by bearing his children; medieval and later incest stories by contrast strike a new note. They uphold the daughter, by dramatizing, often violently, her refusal to become a term in the riddle, to consent to be knotted into the skein of the paternal family, to be held prisoner in the verbal labyrinth. These stories mark awareness that a young woman may step out from paternal control and be praised for it. Such texts become important documents of social history, incorporating prevailing prejudice and morality and opening fundamental questions about them.

CHAPTER 20

The Silence of the Fathers: Donkeyskin II

I besought him to remember his promise, which was, never to force me against my will, to marry any. Will (said he) why your will ought to be no other than obedience, and in that, you should be rather wilfull in obeying, than question what I appoint ... if you like not as I like, and wed where I will you, you shall never from me receive least favour, but be accompted a stranger and a lost childe ... Who is this fine man hath wonne your idle fancy? Who hath made your duty voide? Whose faire tongue hath brought you to the foulnesse of disobedience? Speake, and speake truely, that I may discerne what choice you can make, to refuse my fatherly authoritie over you.

Mary Wroth

S aint Dympna is a seventh-century princess, the daughter of a king of Brittany, Britain, or Ireland, and of a beautiful mother who inevitably dies. A splendid polychrome sculptured altarpiece in the Northern Flemish high Gothic style, finished by Jan van Wavre in 1515, and still preserved on the high altar in the church

Saint Dympna, like a virgin martyr, holds the instruments of her passion: the sword with which her father beheaded her and crouching in chains at her feet, the hobgoblin devil who inspired his perverted passion. (Cult statue, Geel, fifteenth century.)

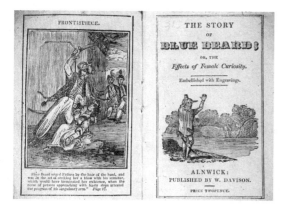

Bluebeard in turban, brandishing a scimitar finds 'his sanguinary arm' halted by the arrival of his wife Fatima's brothers in the nick of time. (Alnwick, early nineteenth century.)

of St Dympna in Geel, Belgian Flanders, illustrates the sequence of the saint's misadventures and subsequent glory (Pl. 22); her life is a fairy tale, except in the matter of the ending, yet her cult has been kept fervently in this part of Catholic Europe since the fourteenth century at least, spreading from there through Belgium, Holland and Westphalia.

The official *Vita*, or Life, of the saint was written in Cambrai, Flanders, around 1237–48; it tells how Dympna was secretly baptized a Christian, and dedicated herself to her heavenly spouse. But soon, as is only to be expected in such a story, her lovely mother dies, having extracted the usual riddling promise from the king never to remarry unless his bride comes up to the standards of beauty and goodness that she has set in her own person. The king is griefstricken, but his courtiers – evil counsellors, inspired by the Devil – plead with him to remarry for the sake of the kingdom. He refuses, until he notices that his daughter resembles her lost mother in every way. This remarkable likeness inspires, as is traditional in the narrative cycle, the 'unlawful passion' in her father, and he declares his desire to marry her. Dympna then consults her confessor, Gerebernus, who advises flight. He is a saintly and very old man – in case there should be any misunderstanding of an ulterior motive. With the help of the court fool and his wife, they disguise themselves as travelling minstrels, since 'under the guise of jongleurs, they could set out more secretly'. They embark, and eventually, owing to God's providence, they cross the Irish Sea and the Channel safely and drift ashore in Belgium, near Antwerp. There Dympna makes her way deep into the forest, and, on the outskirts of the village of Geel, with her companions, clears a space and builds a hut of trees and branches, in order to embrace the sweet solitude of the hermit's life.

But in her absence, her father's passion does not abate. He sends after her, and his spies track her down when an innkeeper remarks that the coins they are using are the same as she was given earlier by a young woman and her party – an interesting piece of material and circumstantial evidence in the fanciful tale. Once she has been traced, the king her father arrives in pursuit, and repeats his demand. She

An unbeliever who insists on denying the faith, Dympna's father sometimes appears as a Turk, like Bluebeard, as he prepares to kill her; in the background, one of his men despatches her confessor. (B. Janssens, Geel, 1935.)

refuses, and he orders his men to kill her, together with her priest. They obey, in the case of Gerebernus; but they cannot bear to touch Dympna. So her father beheads her himself.

Dympna does not metamorphose into animal shape, or put on filthy animal hides to escape her father's demands, but she does choose to be exiled from society as she knew it, to be disguised as a lower – and consequently more mobile – member of court society, a jongleur in the company of a fool, whose cap of bells often sported asses' ears (pp. 140, 352). Her forest hut symbolizes this voluntary outcast state and corresponds to the fairytale heroines' various disguises, all of them natural in different ways: the rashin coatie of Scotland, the wooden cloak of some Italian sources, the bear, the ass, the many-furred creature of the Grimms' version.

But of course in one prima facie aspect, the hagiographical story alters the folk source: animal disguise, animal metamorphosis, controlled until the moment has come to make the act of self-revelation, form the prelude to a *mariage d'amour* in the folk tales, as collected by Basile and Perrault; in the related life of Dympna, the only wedding takes place after torture and martyrdom with the Son of Heaven as bridegroom.

The author Peter of Cambrai, known in Flemish as Petrus van Kamerijk, was a canon regular of the church of St Aubert in that town. He expressly declares in his preamble that he is basing the story on vernacular sources: '*olim vulgari idiomate scripta*'. This Life was given a critical edition in 1680. Saint Dympna's *Vita* was retold by the Jesuit Pedro Ribadeneyra in his *Flos sanctorum*, first published in Madrid in 1624, then translated and reissued no fewer than six times in French, including an edition in 1686 in the widely distributed *Compagnie des Libraires*, which is where Perrault could have come across it. Before Perrault wrote his burlesque fairy tale, the related perils and ordeals of Saint Dympna were thus being related in a story which enjoyed a wide circulation in different languages and was directed at audiences of different social registers and occupations, from the tavern to the parish church. This migration, from the vernacular to Latin and back again, itself casts doubt on glib distinctions between high and low culture, and warns against notions about Latin's chronological priority. The scholars were working up folk materials to add gravitas; they were annexing highly flavoured legend to make it serve pious ends. The fairy tales do not represent degraded remnants of a lost high epic. The court jester who helps and accompanies Dympna, and who suggests she runs away disguised as one of his kind, presents a most interesting, unusual, and revealing clue: he figures in the story as an eye witness, the storyteller who was there when the great deeds, fair and foul, were done, and who survived to relate them afterwards in songs and stories. He appears, with his lute, sitting in the boat with Dympna, in one of the carved panels of the polyptych altarpiece in Geel, and again, in a painting, helping to build her forest hut on the shrine: he represents a hyphen in the tale between the sacred exemplum and the fairytale romance. When Dympna chooses his occupation for her escape, she is in effect concealing herself in a riddle, the image of an artist skilled in just such word puzzles.

Both the polyptych by Jan van Wavre and the shrine unfold the saint's dramatic story with mannered delicacy and luxuriousness, belying the macabre and violent incidents portrayed and the unworldly moral of her life. In the panel depicting her father's proposal of marriage, Dympna appears with the lofty shaved brow, wimple and diapered full high-waisted dress of courtly fashion in the late fifteenth century, while her aberrant father turns as slim a waist and as trim a hosen leg as any delectable hero of chivalric legend. Similarly, the two episodes which occupy the focal point of the entire construction strike a secular note: the king is shown discovering from a mounted spy the whereabouts of his runaway child, while above, the artist evokes the fugitives' rustic existence in their hiding place –

an odd emphasis in a hagiographical narrative, drawing the viewers' attention away from the edifying aspects of the tale to its secular character, its turbulent plot, its tricksters and its villain, in the manner of the minstrel lay rather than the sermon.

The cult objects associated with the town of Geel redress the balance, borrowing motifs from routine iconography of virgin martyrs. A fifteenth-century statue in the church, for instance, shows Saint Dympna with a sword in her hand, with a monster chained at her feet (p. 335). Dympna thus carries the weapon that won her the crown of martyrdom, and holds captive the sin of her father – incarnate in devilish form. Beast in body, goat-horned, with long canines and a tail, he represents the demon who took possession of her father, and bears a close resemblance to other furry creatures of the wilds, personifying satyriasis and other sexual evils. As a conqueror of sin, in its particular aspect of concupiscence, Dympna has many counterparts: Saint Margaret, who overcame the fiend, Saint Catherine of Alexandria, who withstood the lechery of the emperor Maxentius and tramples his beastliness under her righteous feet in many a medieval statue and illumination.

Saints are sometimes given certain areas of supervision for skittish reasons: Saint Barbara became the patron of barbers, with porcupine quills, combs and brushes for her emblems, through a pun on her name; Saint Blaise was deemed to cure sore throats because he freed a wolf from a ticklish fishbone. But in Dympna's case, she became the patron saint of the insane.

This leap, from the father–daughter incest tale to the care of the mentally ill, arises from a profound medieval perception of the affinity between mental distress and incestuous transgression. Not based on a poor pun like Barbara's sphere of interest, not quite related to her life by direct cause-and-effect, Dympna's patronage of madness reveals imaginative associations at work in the minds of her votaries. On account of the mad, diabolical lust of her father, who wanted his daughter and then killed her, Dympna was allotted the care of 'demoniacs', as the mentally ill are called in her *Vita*. Incest in her tale does not belong in a tribal chronicle about appropriate partners for carrying on the line. Nor does it inscribe a philosophy of fate and divine justice. It tells of a private fantasy of omnipotence which does harm; the passage of the story about an incestuous father into a healing cult represents a vital moment in the history of attitudes to such passions. Migrating from folklore into religious cult, the story of the fugitive daughter gained a material reality which also cancelled any residue of jocularity and fancy from the fairy tale. This is a case of fairy tale passing over into hagiography and thence into belief with effects on the lives of real people and the developments of history. Dympna is still venerated; she is popular in Ireland, for instance, as well as among the Irish Catholic community in the United States, and a special prayer, for use by those distressed in mind, invokes her protection.

The bodies of Dympna and Gerebernus were allegedly unearthed in Geel some time in the thirteenth century; her relics remained miraculously rooted to the spot where the church dedicated to her name was founded. Building began around 1450. Gerebernus' relics on the other hand were stolen and taken to Xanten on the Rhine, where they are still kept. Stone fragments of their sarcophagi are preserved in Geel, as well as Dympna's bones, which are enshrined in the wooden funerary monument, raised on stone columns and painted with scenes of her life, which stands behind the altar. Her relics brought about numerous cures in a specialized area – of epileptics, schizophrenics and other mentally sick pilgrims, who were brought to the shrine. Jan van Wavre's altarpiece of 1515 also represents the procession during which Dympna's relics were displayed, and the miracles and acts of mercy attendant upon it.

The Gospel reading for her feast day (15 May) is taken from Matthew 25, on the Seven Acts of Mercy, because her cult was socially concerned from the start. In the fifteenth century, a *Sieckkammer*, or sickroom, was incorporated in the church itself, in a chamber on the south side, which can still be seen. But as numbers swelled, a hospital grew up to house the patients, and Augustinian canonesses of St Norbert nursed the sick, and were painted at their task in 1639 by an anonymous artist (p. 341). They are shown operating on the stone, trepanning skulls and otherwise relieving – or attempting to relieve – mental distress. One large surviving *ex voto* depicts a patient, one Peter van Put, who in the eighteenth century was miraculously cured, the grateful inscription relates, of his deaf and dumb condition. In effect, the town of Geel was operating as an open asylum for the mentally ill; it still practises home care for the sick who are registered at the hospital, but lodged with families in the town. Though Catholic clergy and nuns help with the patients, the hospital was taken over by the state in 1850 after abuses were discovered (however shining the intentions of the shrine, the 'mad' were being exploited as free labour, and many were seriously neglected). The Augustinian canonesses moved away to a small building trimmed to their present needs.

By far the most famous patient at Geel was a certain Henri K., who fell in love with a parrot because it had been given to him by the woman he loved and could say her name. As his wits turned, his obsession deepened, and he came to believe he had become a parrot himself; he roosted in a tree and could only agree to come

A hospital for pilgrims looking for cure, or at least solace for their mental problems, grew up next to St Dympna's church. Here, nuns are caring for patients by bleeding and trepanning and other measures. (Flemish School, The Hospice at Geel, 1639.)

down when a parrot cage was produced. He was then sent to the Maison de Santé in Geel; Flaubert read the account of his capture in the paper, and drew on it for 'Un Cœur simple' about Félicité and her parrot, whom she sees at the end in a kind of ecstasy, transfigured into Christ her beloved.

Child abuse could be placed under Dympna's patronage too. The Epistle reading for her Mass comes from the First Letter of John, the one that repeatedly invokes his listeners as 'God's children'; Dympna acts as a symbol of child innocence, and of the sinlessness of the simple-minded. Her cult gives us an interesting insight into compassion and understanding in the medieval past. Incest connected with madness; the Devil was at work exciting the impulses of fantasy, and the victims could suffer death. Derangement could be a contagion, like temptation; it affected both perpetrator and victim. Her cult, whatever its deficiencies in practice, admits that such an 'unlawful passion' happens, has consequences for all around it, that it cannot be quarantined and causes acute distress; that the object of the passion cannot but be involved in its madness, however much s/he pulls away. The factor of relationship is recognized by implication in the imagined power of Dympna's intercession; her story acknowledges the harm done and constitutes an early attempt – weak, inadequate, wishful – to repair it.

II

Perrault dedicated 'Peau d'Ane', his fairy tale about a runaway daughter, to the Marquise de Lambert, one of the noblewomen in whose house in the rue Colbert were regularly gathered philosophically-minded men and women, to discuss just such issues as the obligations of love and the freedom to choose a partner. She herself was to write advice manuals to her children, and Perrault judged that his jaunty squib at the expense of an overweening father would coincide with the interests of the marquise and so please her.

The 'Peau d'Ane' fairy tale dramatizes the subjection of daughters to their fathers' authority, and under the pretence of flippancy Perrault delivers a harsh critique of current abuses in the area of matrimony. His story even bears traces of the earlier, medieval clerical campaign to preserve the dignity of marriage through love. The Church paradoxically gave its fervent support to men and women's autonomy in desire – principally because virginity usually conflicted with dynastic interests, but also because they struggled against expedient annulments and remarriages. Besides the *Vita* of Saint Dympna, there were dozens of supposedly edifying stories about young women who resist their family's plans for them. Without firsthand knowledge of these materials, it would be hard to credit the ferocity of Christianity's opposition to the biological family's claims, the intensity of the otherworldliness hagiography proposes. When cults today point to the Bible in support of their 'kidnapping' of young adepts, they act within a fully attested, mainstream Christian tradition which envisaged a life dedicated to Christ in violent conflict with familial and social interests. The daughters who disobey in the name of faith include Saint Christina, whose Life was written in verse by the Benedictine Gautier de Coinci around 1218. Gautier could be charming, as in his *Miracles de Nostre Dame*, but Saint Christina stimulated the sadistic side of his imagination and he describes her prolonged torments at the hands of her father, who 'felt a deep love for his daughter, /And could not spend a day without kissing her eyes and her face'. He builds a tower to enclose her (to hide her, to encipher her), but when she persists in her sacred vow of virginity, he begins a series of public tortures, which culminates in throwing her out to sea with a millstone round her neck. It turns light as a feather, and she survives, only to face another round of persecutions, at the hands of the Roman emperor's representative. Her breasts are cut off, she is bitten by serpents, burned on a pyre, and finally has her tongue torn out. She throws the mangled piece at her torturer; and it pierces him in the eye. A symmetry is here implied, between her subversive tongue and his transgressive eye, and she has the last word, of course,

Daughters defy family arrangements in the name of Christ in many legends of the virgin martyrs: Saint Barbara is another who provokes murderous rage by her recalcitrance. (Peter Paul Rubens, Saint Barbara Fleeing from Her Father, 1620.*)*

as the tale is hers, and hers the body, which in death becomes even more richly wonder-working.

Gautier's *Life of Saint Christina* includes another remarkable scene, when her mother intercedes, frantically – and touchingly – pleading on her breasts which nourished her daughter that she should not be so obdurate. Mothers rarely make any kind of appearance in these father–daughter stories, except in the opening deathbed scene, and Christina's highminded rejection of maternal love brings home powerfully the force of her story's ascetic message.

The legend of Saint Barbara also illustrates the social significance of fairytale sources as resistance to patriarchal tyranny and to marriage. In 1405, in *The Book of the City of Ladies*, Christine de Pizan gave this account of Saint Barbara:

Because of her beauty, her father had her shut up in a tower ... [He] sought a noble marriage for her, but she refused all offers for a long time. Finally she declared herself a Christian and dedicated her virginity to God. For this reason her father tried to kill her, but she was able to escape and flee. And when her father pursued her to put her to death, he finally found her, and brought her before the prefect, who ordered her to be executed with excruciating tortures ...

After appalling cruelties, which Barbara resists with miraculous strength, her father, as in the case of Dympna, beheads her himself.

Besides being the patron of barbers, Saint Barbara also has care of thunder and lightning, and of artillery and cannon, because as he was returning home from his crime her father was struck down by a thunderbolt, and reduced to ashes.

Christine de Pizan mentions that Barbara's father wanted a *noble* marriage, that the prefect ordered the torture because she had disobeyed her father. Unlike the legend of Dympna, which focusses on incest, Barbara's concentrates on authority; Barbara's refusal makes a bid for autonomy. The folk tales in which a daughter resists her father and is then punished may contain memories of actual bodily violation. But the narrative is often presented in such a way that the independent integrity of the victim as the inheritor of the family wealth becomes the issue, not her chastity. The stories focus on the daughter revolting against her father, and develop a plot to justify her action; the rebel is presented as a virtuous heroine rather than an unfilial child. In order to achieve this, the father's act must be seen to be an outrage precisely because daughters were decreed to obey their fathers by the fourth commandment. To be vindicated, the disobedient daughter must be wronged. The father's transgression against the universally held taboo against incest furnishes a sufficiently shocking pretext, as does, in a medieval context, his attempt to force a pagan husband on a Christian girl.

An episode which took place during the Wars of the Roses in England gives precious historical evidence that, when such pressure was put upon young marriageable women by men in authority over them, stratagems were adopted that, echoing the motifs of the fairy tales, help us to read the experiences in which they originate. When Richard, Duke of Gloucester, the future Richard III, showed a desire to marry Lady Anne Nevill, daughter of the Earl of Warwick and the heiress to a great estate, his brother the Duke of Clarence tried to prevent the match. Clarence was married to Anne's elder sister and he feared – rightly as it turned out – that Richard had designs on her portion of the fortune as well. 'Such being the case,' wrote the chronicler in 1471,

> he caused the damsel to be concealed, in order that it might not be known by his brother where she was ... Still however the craftiness of the Duke of Gloucester [Richard] so far prevailed that he discovered the young lady in the City of London disguised in the habit of a cookmaid; upon which he had her removed to the sanctuary of Saint Martin's ...

Here, in Lady Anne, Richard III's queen, we find a real-life girl of the fifteenth century, flying from an abhorred union by being disguised as a servant. The chronicler talks of her as a pawn in the hands of great men; but it is possible that she was a willing accomplice. Her reasons may have been different from her father's; Warwick wanted to control the family wealth, not to pass it on to a son-in-law whom he could not command.

Perrault makes this fundamental point when Donkeyskin kills her father's source of wealth – the magic donkey – and refuses to marry him at the same time. When she runs away, she literally takes her father's fortune with her.

Such coincidences between concealed heiresses and fairytale princesses support the argument that such tales as Beauty's and Donkeyskin's and Cinderella's are women's stories; they can be seen to reflect women's predicaments and stratagems from their point of view. The dissemination of fairy tales and the virtual disappearance of the gory martyrdoms of saints like Dympna from any widely circulating Catholic literature has coincided with a softening and sweetening of the character of the Beast whom the heroine flees, as in the case of the much more popular fairy tale 'Beauty and the Beast', as we saw. 'Donkeyskin' has proved the least-known of Perrault's tales; the Catholic stories for many complex reasons are no longer related with the intense admiration that Christine de Pizan – who was no credulous masochist – brought to their retelling. The ferocious father, the lustful suitor, have been transformed or made to disappear; the Cinderella stories we are familiar with now portray the father as virtuous and dead, or weak and henpecked, as we shall see, and she radiates feelings of dutiful and tender loyalty towards him.

Neither 'L'Orsa' nor 'Peau d'Ane' portrays the heroine's plight as deserved, and both tales rejoice in her escape from her father. However, at the end of Perrault's tale he is handsomely forgiven rather than pilloried. The Frenchman's romantic assertion of the goodness of choice and love in marriage conforms to the principles the women in his literary circle were struggling to establish.

Their efforts coincided with the wide distribution of a semi-erotic, semi-scientific manual by Nicolas Venette, called Tableau de l'amour conjugal, published in French in Amsterdam in 1686, and in English as The Mysteries of Conjugal Love Revealed in 1703. This volume of practical advice gained immense popularity very quickly; it was a pioneering work, partly because Venette did not concern himself at all with vice or vice's penalties like venereal disease, did not linger on prohibitions against incest, but concentrated on the naturalness of the sexual urge, the healthiest ways to assuage it and find happiness, and throughout accepts, without reproof, women's desires as equally forceful as men's. In the opinion of Roy Porter, the historian of medicine, Venette's book constitutes a watershed, because he was able to acknowledge for the first time 'the empire of love' over the human being, and to articulate the need to translate the chaos of passion into the social order of matrimony in order to achieve sexual gratification for both man and woman. 'Conjugal caresses are the ties of love in matrimony,' he wrote, 'they make up the essence thereof.' This was published around the same time as the first romantic fairy tales about princesses finding true love with the prince of their liking.

The filial action of Lot's daughters, when they conceive by their father in order to perpetuate the species, becomes superannuated under the new covenant that a fairy tale like 'Peau d'Ane' proclaims. In a cluster of stories – hagiography and fairy tale – there recurs a figure of a wronged daughter, a young woman in flight from the unwelcome desire of a man, who is her own father or otherwise a man in power, an emperor, a prefect, a tyrant. The tenor of the stories never questions the status of the plot as truth: it is a characteristic of the fairy story or wonder tale that the material is presented as matter of fact, however fanciful. Do the fantasy trans- formations, the saints' miracles, the wild swerves and unlikely incidents, the alter- nation of secrets and disclosures register at the same pitch of veracity as the incest motif? Basile's asides about human nature being the way it is often return his wild fabulations to a circumstantial setting of recognizable behaviour; in comparison, Perrault's blitheness tends to subsume everything into a gay nonsense rhyme: the magic donkey, the wicked lust, the fantastic palace, the happy ending. His final verses declare:

> Le conte de Peau d'Ane est difficile à croire,
> Mais tant que dans le Monde on aura des Enfants
> Des Mères et des Mères-grands
> On en gardera la mémoire.

[The tale of Donkeyskin is hard to believe, but as long as there are children, mothers and grandmothers in the world the memory of it will not die.]

But even Perrault does not quite level all the story's elements to the same plateau of implausibility; his last words, that mothers and grandmothers will continue to tell the tale of Donkeyskin, imply that there is something of absorb- ing consequence to tell.

III

'Grandmothers, mothers and children' could accept an incestuous father placed centre stage in full view, till the eighteenth century. But then he begins to stir anxiety in the disseminators of fairy tales, and this anxiety leads to tinkering, and eventuall, to evasions and suppression.

In the prose version attributed to Perrault, but which appears only in 1781, the father comes under the evil influence of a 'Druid', who persuades him that it would be 'an act of piety' to marry his daughter. Perrault makes a passing mention of a *casuiste*, which the paraphraser seized on to absolve the father of some responsibility. Later, when the father comes to the wedding, this author has him safely married off to a 'very beautiful widowed queen' with whom, moreover, we are told there is no likelihood of offspring. The story of a father's unlawful love begins to fade from collections of fairy stories as well as from narratives dealing with actual experience. At the same time, stories of fathers' excessive control of their daughters are also softened. The Cinderella story itself contains at its heart an unexplained mystery about her father's role in her sufferings. Why does Cinderella's father do nothing about her predicament? His part remains unspoken – neither complicity nor protest: a lost piece of the puzzle. In retellings of the fairy tale today, from pantomime and books, he either features as dead, so the women are wreaking havoc in the absence of male authority; or he too is suffering, yet another of the wicked women's victims: the dear old duffer Baron Hardup or Baron Stoneybroke of the English Victorian stage, who is much too nice to stand up to the horrid schemers he has taken under his roof. George Cruikshank even puts him in prison as a result of his wife's gambling debts.

But as recently as Jacopo Ferretti's libretto of 1816 for Rossini's *La Cenerentola*, Cinderella's poltroon of a stepfather, Don Magnifico, dreams, in a broad hint at the story's progenitors, that he is a most tremendous ass, '*un bellissimo somaro, un somaro, ma solenne*' (a beautiful ass, an ass, but dignified). This exuberantly comic opening aria again homes in on the lubricious associations of the donkey, and retains the social critique of Perrault against tyranny. Earlier 'Cinderella' variations also connect to the 'Donkeyskin' cycle – the daughter is too beautiful, she must be punished, she is dirty, she must be cast out. The most dainty and urbane retelling, Perrault's 'Cendrillon', recalls the sexual plot of the related tales of wronged girls when, as we saw, he gives his heroine's nickname as Cucendron (Cinder-bottom), and adds that the kinder of her sisters softened it to spare her.

Wicked fathers gradually drop from view in the fairytale tradition. The Grimm Brothers for instance collected a variation on '*Peau d'Ane*' in their gruesome tale

'The Maiden Without Hands'. (It had been dramatized in Philippe de Beaumanoir's verse novel *La Manékine*, in the thirteenth century, and resumed, with a smitten brother in place of the unlawful father, by Basile in the *Pentamerone*.) In both these tales, the heroine – Joie – finds the day of her incestuous wedding approaching. In acute distress, she goes to the palace kitchen, and sees there a great carving knife: 'With a single stroke of this knife, you could have severed a swan's spine, even if it had been of an extraordinary size.' Joie seizes the knife, puts her left hand on the window sill, and cuts it off. It falls into the moat, where a fish swallows it. (Later, it will be miraculously restored to her by the same fish, served up on another kitchen table, in another place, under another knife.) Here maiming takes the place of the travesty in other tales – with a savage accent on the role of hands in sexuality.

The Grimms' version of 'The Maiden Without Hands' describes the young girl mutilating herself in order to escape the claims of the Devil. The father acts like a villain and a coward, and offers his daughter to the Devil in order to save his own skin; he also willingly cuts off her hands himself when the Devil asks him to. But she weeps on the stumps so that they are too clean for the Devil to touch, and he has to give up the bride he desired. Only horribly disfigured in this way can she become inviolable and so resist on her own account, uncoerced by her father, just like her predecessor Donkeyskin. John Ellis has analysed the different editions of *Die Kinder- und Hausmärchen* to show how in their treatment of 'The Maiden Without Hands' the Grimms erased the motive of the father's unlawful love from their source, because they simply could not bear it; they were too squeamish for the motive, though not for the mutilating itself.

Similarly, the Grimms' telling of '*Aschenputtel*' includes unexplained pursuit and cruelty on the part of her father, who, using 'an axe and a pickaxe' together, hews to pieces the dovecote in which the prince tells him she has taken refuge; similarly, he cuts down her hiding place in a pear tree the second night. This Cinderella hides from both prince and father, though why the latter should pursue her so savagely has been scrambled and fallen out of the tale. Such silences help the stories to reverberate, however, as the father's crazed conduct sends shivers through the listener or the reader.

From romance to Romanticism, a well-known shift of interest takes place: the interior motions of characters in fictions become salient. With a motif like incest, a romance like *La Manékine* simply takes the father's passion for granted; the narrative focus holds the pattern of events in view, the swift shuttle figuring forth motifs in a rich peripatetic and picaresque weave, the structure of social disorder and the ensuing restoration of due order. Passions leading to adultery or murder or incest are dealt with often with compassionate intensity – as in the scene when Apollonius finds his daughter again – but the texts do not question and probe motive or seek to justify the developments on grounds of plausible and consistent character. This is obvious, but it is worth restating it here because it bears profoundly on the disappearance – the comparative disappearance or partially successful repression – of the 'Peau d'Ane' fairy tale and the whole cycle of the Apollonius romance from our culture. When interest in psychological realism is at work in the mind of the receiver of traditional folklore, the proposed marriage of a father to his daughter becomes too hard to accept. But it is only too hard to accept precisely because it belongs to a different order of reality/fantasy from the donkeyskin disguise or the gold excrement or the other magical motifs: because it is not impossible, because it could actually happen, and is known to have done so. It is when fairy tales coincide with experience that they begin to suffer from censoring, rather than the other way around. They are not altered – or even dropped – by editors and collectors to shear them of implausibilities and foolish notions, but this pretext is invoked to justify changes which constitute responses to profound, known threats. Dympna's situation, Peau d'Ane's predicament are at one and the same time ridiculous, unsuitable extremes of invention which will give children ideas, and at the same time veracious and adult, and children are no longer to be exposed to such knowledge.

The history of Freud's momentous change of mind about the status of paternal incest echoes, in thought-provoking ways, the gaps in transmission of the Donkeyskin fairy tale. In 1895, in his study of the 'hysteric' Aurelia, Freud purposively changed her molester from her father to her uncle for reasons of discretion. She was one of four cases in his *Studies on Hysteria*, but she was different from her three counterparts: Freud could write about her, 'it was a lovely case for me', because he was able to heal the young woman's trouble (solve her riddle) in the course of a single conversation in August 1893. Aurelia Kronich, whom Freud called 'Katharina', was the daughter of a servant at a mountain inn in an Alpine valley where Freud stayed in the summers, and he fell into conversation with her, according to his account, when she told him she was suffering from nervous attacks. Prompted by Freud that she might have seen or heard something that 'embarrassed' her, she described how she had come upon her cousin Barbara in her father's room, with her father lying on her. She had fallen ill after this, vomiting for three days on end. Further prompted by Freud, Aurelia then recalled that her father had acted in a similar way with her four years before.

After these admissions, Aurelia's face changed; 'her eyes were bright, she was lightened and exalted'. Aurelia's story – and her lightening after unburdening herself – became a crucial vertix where Freud's newly developing theory of sexual trauma, memory, hysteria and talk therapy converged. In a letter, he described how 'in the girl's anxiety was a consequence of the horror by which a virginal mind is overcome when it is confronted for the first time by sexuality' – the very passage which the Donkeyskin fairy tale negotiates.

The singleminded emphasis on the sexual encounter in Freud's account does however ignore the disruption of the Kronich family life after Aurelia told her mother, the guilt that the daughter felt at her part in the marriage's breakdown, her fear that her father might take his revenge on her for the disclosure, as well as the possible anger of the mother both on behalf of and possibly against her daughter – all reactions which arise in other documented cases of incest. Nor did Freud give a full explanation of his evasion in 1924 when he admitted in a footnote that he had changed the abusive father into a molesting uncle. He made other alterations, as Peter Swales has discovered through patient research. Moreover, in the years between 1895 and 1924 he was developing the Oedipal theory and was eventually to concede the ground of his 'seduction theory' and decide that, in some cases, his patients' accounts of paternal incest might be fantasies in their minds, stirred by their Oedipal desires, because memories and fantasies in the unconscious could not be disentangled. The later development of his thinking led him to propose that memories of incest tended to be rooted in forbidden, repressed desires. Nevertheless, he did not retract his account of Aurelia's real abuse, nor throw suspicion on her truthfulness. She remains a contradictory figure in his case histories: an actual incestuous child. She offers a telling reminder of the connective tissue that binds personal experience with fantasy narratives.

In between, Freud had also written his personal – and moving – meditation on *The Theme of Three Caskets*, which conveys, using the fairytale marriage test found in *The Merchant of Venice*, his own choice of the lead casket, the least and youngest daughter, and his yearning for her, only to find that she heralds his own death. Freud's denial, in psychoanalytic terms, of the father's incest in the case of Katharina/Aurelia, speaks volumes about the sensitivity of the issue for him.

The distortions that Freud's interpretation of incestuous testimony have introduced cannot begin to be straightened out here. But it is not squaring the circle to say that the 'Donkeyskin' type of story yields a common insight into minds and experiences of young women growing up, and into erotic fantasies on both sides, the father's and the daughter's, conscious as well as unconscious. And that, at the same time as reflecting Oedipal desires, the fairy tale expresses fears of actual incest and actual violation, and that the disquiet it still can produce arises from its closeness to what the Chinese call speaking bitterness.

Perrault, from a circle of campaigning women, argued for the new ideal of companionate marriage and filial autonomy; the fairy tale has since mutated again, with female tellers – of fact as well as fancy – discomfiting male hearers to varying degrees by stirring uneasy identifications and distressed denials.

The history of transmission through literary texts shows intermittently more embarrassment than the oral tradition (though this has been recorded in literary media, too, and is never pure). Nevertheless, Chaucer, who knew the plot from Gower, preferred, as noted earlier, to keep the incest motif out of sight in 'The Man of Lawe's Tale'; Shakespeare challenged it with the alternative version in *Pericles*, and transformed it into tyranny in *Lear*, both of them preceding the pedagogical anxiety of the nineteenth and twentieth centuries over any open admission of the theme.

The oral evidence, in which I include cinema and television, evinces less reluctance. Jacques Demy made a film of *Peau d'Ane* in 1971 (*The Magic Donkey*), which retains the father–daughter plot without apology (p. 319). Whimsical, pretty, and all the more unsettlingly amusing for its sugared almond appearance, it catches the perversely skittish spirit of Perrault's original verses, while its sequences of bizarre, dreamlike enchantments pay homage to Jean Cocteau's brand of cinematic poetics – the lover-father sits on a stuffed white cat for a throne, the slattern who puts Donkeyskin to work spits toads and serpents when she speaks. Catherine Deneuve's sculptured angel face turns Donkeyskin herself into a fairy-tale vision to rival Josette Day's ethereal Belle in the Cocteau film, and Delphine Seyrig as Donkeyskin's godmother, the Lilac Fairy, brings a certain elegant and worldly irony to her counsels. Jacques Demy himself first presented fairy tales in a puppet theatre he had as a child – and he heard them from his grandmother.

The Storyteller, a recent series of television films produced by Jim Henson and written by Anthony Minghella, also included a vividly realized variation on the tale, called *Sapsorrow*. Interestingly, the series framed each tale within a traditional storytelling scene – the actor John Hurt as an old man with his talking dog (live animation by Henson); the device enabled the film-makers to interpolate moral comments on the material they were showing, in order to muffle the shock of such a demand from a father. These however are rare contemporary versions that remain faithful to fairy tale's power to speak of the unspeakable through its dreamlike distancing of the story with fantastic strokes of magic, articulate beasts, and fantastic settings. The Italian children's edition of '*Pelle d'asina*' – an illustrated booklet with accompanying tape – is characteristically toothless: it merely opens with an offer of marriage from a horrible man who is much too old for the heroine.

Not all storytellers suffer from the scruples – or the anxiety – shown by the Grimm Brothers over the tale of 'The Maiden Without Hands' or Freud in the case of 'Katharina'. They do not rub at the tracing in the dust to obscure what it shows, but hold fast to the matter-of-fact tone of the fairy tale; the voice of the narrator is issuing to the circle of listeners a familiar warning, and a reassuring prohibition, as they use the tales to inscribe the laws of kinship in the minds of their audience. Perhaps the very presence of the narrator guarantees the possibility of survival: this person, who speaks of these things, has not been silenced. The American novelist Lynne Tillman, in 'The Trouble with Beauty', created a bitter tale: her heroine retreats into autism after her father, having used her sexually, hands her over to his friend, the Beast. In this Tillman follows the fairy tale's rite of passage, through disfigurement and degradation, but in her case Beauty does not achieve revolt or reconciliation.

A much heartier Italian version, still told today, called '*Maria di legno*' (Wooden Maria), begins with the familiar device that the daughter must take her dead mother's place; her nursemaid helps her to set various conditions, but the king manages to meet them, and announces, 'There's no more time to lose, my daughter. In one week we will get married.'

But the nurse makes Maria 'a wooden outfit which covered her from head to toe', and in this coffin she casts herself into the sea to escape. She floats away. Later, in the country she reaches, she finds work as a goose girl; later still, she sets a prince riddles. He falls madly in love … The final riddle, the one he manages at last to solve, opens the box in which Maria is enclosed and he finds her – 'the beautiful stranger' – inside combing her locks. This tale itself floated to shore in Rome at the beginning of this century, was discovered and transformed and shaped later by Italo Calvino and proves to have preserved safe and sound inside its resilient structure many magical elements from a very old story about unlawful love, which touches on experience in different but profound ways.

Saint Dympna disguised herself as a jongleur, or jester, to make her escape. Stories and songs offer hiding places for troubles, and 'La Sote' (The She-Fool) is danced off by the reaper last of all. (Paris, 1508.)

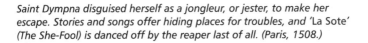

The Language of Hair: Donkeyskin III

What joy it is to see hair of a beautiful colour caught in the full rays of the sun, or shining with a milder lustre and constantly varying its shade as the light shifts. Golden at one moment, at the next honey-coloured; or black as a raven's wing, but suddenly taking on the pale blueish tints of a dove's neck-feathers ... oh, when hair is bunched up in a thick luxurious mass on a woman's head or, better still, allowed to flow rippling down her neck in profuse curls! ... unable to restrain myself a moment longer, I now planted [there] a long passionate kiss.

Apuleius

Whereas male beasts are cursed by some malignant force, the heroines of fairy tales are willingly bound by a spell; they frequently agree with alacrity to the change of outward form, in order to run away from the sexual advances of a father or other would-be seducer. Their metamorphosis changes their problematic fleshly envelope, which has inspired such undesirable desire, until a

A medieval nymph, in all other respects a candidate for the angels' ranks, reveals her kinship with animality in the down that covers her baby's body as well as her own. (Martin Schongauer, Wild Woman, *Augsburg, late fifteenth century.)*

chosen, more suitable, more lovable lover can appear who will answer the riddle, undo the animal spell, disclose their identity and their beauty and release them to speak again. In Estremadura, in Spain, in the twentieth century, the fugitive girl of the fairy tale hides herself in a cloak of pelican skins, which the anthropologist James Taggart, who collected these versions, perceptively – and poignantly – connects to the prevalence of goitres among women in the area. Only a true lover will be able to see past the disfigurement to the real beauty of the person beneath the outer, pelican skin.

As the male beast in Beauty and the Beast stories suffers from his condition, so do his enchanted and disguised female counterparts. But the meanings and value of beastliness drift differently when young women are at issue, and, surprisingly perhaps, they can often be combed out of the tales through the language of hair and hairiness, of pelt, fur and hide.

Mme d'Aulnoy, in 'La Chatte blanche' (The White Cat), portrays a heroine's animal metamorphosis as an evil enchantment laid upon her by a wicked and jealous witch; as a cat princess, she is still entrancing, still irresistible. The prince, in order to win her, has to prove his mettle and obey her utterly, even to the point of cutting off her head to release her from her animal form. By contrast, in 'L'Oiseau bleu' (The Blue Bird), the fairy tale made famous by the Ballets Russes, her heroine Florine dirties her face and body in order to struggle on her own account for her lover's disenchantment; as Mie-Souillon (Dear-Slattern) she abases herself to work the magic to restore him to human shape. The bodily transformations of fairytale heroines take them across thresholds which could not otherwise be crossed, as in the case of Princess Hawthorn, in 'Bearskin', the tale attributed to Murat; in this form, covered in her paradoxical cloak of invisibility, she can pass from her wretched state of marriage to Rhinoceros to another, happier life of relative freedom. This phenomenon of metamorphosis as liberty saturates the imagery of the tales and the language in which they are conveyed; the animal disguise of the heroine equips her to enter a new territory of choice and speech; the apparent degradation works for her, not against her. Being a beast – a she-bear – can be preferable as a temporary measure to the constrictions of a woman's shape. Animal form marks a threshold she passes over, before she can take control of her own identity.

The wronged daughter of fairy tale takes creaturely shape and keeps company with creatures, because, in the midst of repudiating a crime she finds abhorrent, and which excites her bitter reproaches and confusion, she changes into a beast-like form that simultaneously seals her connection with nature and splits her off from the society in which such an offence as marriage with her father was proposed and urged. The change of appearance casts the heroine out of family, out of the fold, and even out of society. The action in such fairy tales looks forward to the young woman's future; the father's unlawful demand opens the daughter's eyes to the choice ahead, now that she is no longer a child but a nubile woman. The particular animal forms or degradation she accepts, the insults she bears, as she is reviled in her sluttish condition as stinking and filthy, anticipate the pollution of virginity's loss. The stories express the difficulties experienced by young women entering a sexual life in a social context where the pattern of sinful woman is Eve, who had carnal knowledge and was fatal to humanity, and the pattern of goodness is Mary, the Virgin.

The appetites of Voluptas, or Lust, are shared by goats, one of the devil's beasts; sometimes she rides on a live goat, but here she drapes herself in its hide. (Freiburg Cathedral, thirteenth century.)

As an outcast, spurning the sexual demand made upon her, her disguises – donkey, cat, or bear – reproduce the traditional iconography of the very passion she is fleeing. Animal hairiness, tails and beards identify the phallic satyrs of Greek myth, embodiments of lust; they lent their features, their donkey-like and goatish parts, to conventional Christian representations of the Devil, as in the sculpted scene showing the Devil tempting a woman in the thirteenth-century allegory of Luxuria (Lust) at Chartres Cathedral. At Freiburg Cathedral, the thirteenth-century figure of Lust or Voluptas (p. 355) is shown with the 'Prince of this World', a smiling, courtly tempter, who conceals toads and vipers behind his back; she is leaning towards him, glad of his attention, with only a goat's hide draping her nakedness, its horns, head and hooves still attached and dangling.

The chosen animals of female fairytale metamorphosis – the hearth cat of '*La Gatta Cenerentola*' (The Cinderella Cat), the donkey of '*Peau d'Ane*', and the bear of '*L'Orsa*' and 'Bearskin', who offer the wronged daughter her means of escape – were animals to which were ascribed a particular predilection for pleasure, in perceptions current before the fairy tales were printed. They are all three thought to possess carnal knowledge: hearth cats were witches' familiars, of course. They also frequented the Garden of Eden, curling up at the foot of the Tree of Good and Evil and intimating the night secrets and sensual pleasures that Adam and Eve will discover when they eat the apple. Dürer's famous engraving of *The Fall* includes a large sleepy cat, as does a woodcut illustration of the Bible in 1504 by his pupil Hans Baldung Grien. Cornelisz Cornelisz. van Haarlem, in 1592, painted the scene of the Fall, and showed just between Adam and Eve the naughty hugs of a monkey and a cat, both shamelessly amorous creatures, inviting and welcoming caresses and cuddles.

The she-bear does not belong in a witch's crew, but the animal is also associated with Eve and the Fall. In Baldung's *Creation of Woman* of 1502, for instance, the bear appears as one of four creatures: on Eve's side the bear and the fox, on

This morbid parody of a reclining Venus personifies the vice of Lust: emaciated with her excesses, naked except for her abundant and unruly hair, she is attended by a rabbit, a harlot's familiar on account of its mating proclivities. (Pisanello, Luxuria, fifteenth century.)

'A brazen sensual woman [who] infests the street and plies her trade,/ Inviting every amorous blade/ To come and practice fornication', the personification of Sensual Pleasure wears the ass's ears of folly. (Master of the Bergmann Shop, in Sebastian Brant, The Ship of Fools, *1498.)*

Adam's the stag and the hare, suggesting the pride and instinct of the male, the cunning – foxiness – of the woman, and her connection with pleasure, with trickery, with play. According to Aelian, 'bears ... do not copulate by mounting; the female lies on the ground ...' The *Physiologus*, again, repeats this distinguishing characteristic of the bear. Baldung, with his sexual obsessiveness, may have been hinting at the immediate consequence of Eve's coming into the world, or even making a Reformation point that part of the helpmeet's task was to give sexual pleasure to Adam.

In images circulating during the period when the first explicit references to the story 'Donkeyskin' are made, the metaphor of animal nature recurs to characterize social outcasts, practising vice. In Sebastian Brant's satire *The Ship of Fools* of 1498, for instance, the woodcut illustrating Sensual Pleasure shows a prostitute working the street: she is wearing a cloak made of an ass-hide and herding an odd flock, which includes a goat and a ram, animals which often make a significant showing in scenes of saints' temptations (above). Illustrated retellings of '*Peau d'Ane'*, following Perrault's description of his heroine as a swineherd, uncannily echo this symbolic iconography of the middle ages, though it is unlikely the artists had the model of personified Lust consciously in mind.

At a time when tales were circulating about young girls disguised as animals in order to escape desires they found repugnant, the figure of the fugitive girl in animal disguise stood not for the rejection of sexuality but the condition of it. The wronged and runaway daughters wear the pelts of beasts, coats of rushes, and other 'natural' disguises because they have been violated, by their father's assault or by another's, and it has contaminated them, exiled them. Although they have suffered wrong in all innocence in the fairy tales, they accept the taint and enact it on their own persons. Shame and guilt do not prompt different reactions, and in this the victims behave exactly like penitents. Coats of skins covered the nakedness of Adam and Eve after they had eaten of the fruit of knowledge and marked their fallen condition; saints who have forsaken the world or repented pleasure-loving life assume wild clothing: John the Baptist in the wilderness is covered only in a camel's hide, the anchorite Saint Onufrius appears girdled in a loincloth of leaves, while the holy whores Mary Magdalen and Mary of Egypt strip themselves of the finery which gave them worldly status and wander naked out into the wilderness, where by divine providence their hair grows miraculously long to cover them. These figures of repentance accept their sinfulness, by performing it over and over in gesture and dress.

Modestly veiled in hair, Mary Magdalen or Mary of Egypt can receive communion from a priest without giving offence, as in many sequences which tell the story of their expiation in the desert. The nakedness of the penitents signifies their conversion: they have recognized the folly of the world, and shed all former vanities and trifles. Donatello's famous statue of Mary Magdalen, in the Baptistery in Florence, could easily be mistaken for Saint John the Baptist, the voice crying in the wilderness, so thickly carved are the tresses of her hair; Tilman Riemenschneider's Mary Magdalen, a compellingly virtuoso limewood carving of 1490–92, shows the saint suspended in ecstasy among seraphim. Their bodies are covered in tightly overlapping feathers, hers in curly lamb's fleece all over (right). In Cesare Ripa's *Iconologia*, the figure of Compunctio (Shame) is given a symbolic tunic woven of rushes.

The motif of bestial hairiness characterizes the Devil himself: conventionally he has a furry face (that blue beard) (Pl. 21), as well as goatish, donkey-like parts – horns, tail, hooves. Saint Jerome translated the demons of Isaiah as *pilosi*, the hairy ones, in the Vulgate version of the Old Testament (Isa. 13: 22). Hairiness indicates

Fur and fleece, scales and feathers: angels sheathed in plumage bear aloft the penitent Magdalen in ecstasy. After she repented of her worldliness and stripped herself of all her finery, her hair grew miraculously to protect her modesty. (Tilman Riemenschneider, Saint Mary Magdalen, *limewood, 1490–2.)*

animal nature: it is the distinctive sign of the wilderness and its inhabitants, and bears the freight of Judaeo-Christian ambivalence about the place of instinct and nature, fertility and sexuality. Martin Schongauer, the Augsburg goldsmith and artist, responsible for some of the most exquisite devotional images of the fifteenth century, also engraved, some time before his death in 1491, a Wild Woman sitting with her baby at her breast (p. 353). A maiden with a sweet, wistful demeanour, long fair wavy hair, she is also covered in a coat of fur all over. Jacopo de' Barbari's *Satyr Family* of *c*.1503–4 shows the mother with furry thighs, giving suck to her baby while her priapic husband serenades her. In spite of his cultivated entertainment, he still appears with cloven feet, shaggy nether parts, goat's horns and erect penis: all traditional signs of the appearance of the Devil and of the Devil's offspring, the Vices. In Mantegna's painting of almost the same date, 1502, the complex allegory *The Vices Expelled from the Garden of the Virtues*, the evil followers of Venus also appear hairy and hooved, including their babes in arms, one of whom has a plumed penis.

The Elizabethans had a proverb, 'Bush natural, more hair than wit', which associated abundant locks with the primitive and the inferior, hence the sexual, the beastly. In *The Comedy of Errors*, two wags banter:

ANTIPHOLUS OF SYRACUSE: Why is Time such a niggard of hair, being (as it is), so plentiful an excrement?
DROMIO OF SYRACUSE: Because it is a blessing that he bestows on beasts: and what he hath scanted [men] in hair, he hath given them in wit.

The maxim was credited beyond England, and specifically related to women, whose imagined carnality naturally invited the connection; a pair of young women, the predecessors of many a children's book fairytale heroine in their

In the case of the virgin martyr Uncumber, or Liberada, or Kummernis, she was spared an unwanted marriage when she grew a beard, but she was crucified for her rebellion. (Saint Kummernis, Bavaria, seventeenth century.)

medieval grace and charm, as well as their tumbling tresses, were engraved in Augsburg in 1475–1500 and captioned, 'Long-haired but Short-witted Maidens'. Hair constantly reminds us of the closeness of the dumb animal in us, and we reveal our changing sympathies and values in the way we treat the relation, now relishing the animal in the human, now sternly denying it.

In one parallel story to Dympna's and Barbara's and Christina's martyrdoms, the legend of Saint Wilgefortis, or Uncumber, hairiness in the wrong place returns as a motif, to mark the sinful flesh and its claims, which she in her firmness of purpose and with the help of her chosen lover, Christ, insists on denying.

According to the popular medieval narrative, which spread through Europe in the thirteenth century, the saint was one of seven twins born to an overbearing father, a king of Portugal and yet another dedicated heathen, who wanted her to marry another non-Christian like himself.

But, like Dympna, Uncumber has been secretly converted to Christianity and pledged herself to a life of virginity in the love of Christ. When she realizes that she is going to have to submit to her father's authority and marry the Saracen he has chosen for her, she prays for help, and immediately God sends her a covering of hair all over her body, including her face, in answer to her pleas. When the future bridegroom suitor sees the 'bearded virgin' he is being offered, he declines. Uncumber's father, in a rage at her insubordination, has his daughter crucified (left); on the cross, this female martyr invokes Heaven to remember 'the passion that encumbrance all women'. For this reason, Uncumber, who is also venerated as Livrade, Liberata, Liberada and other names all suggesting freedom, became a specially powerful holy agony aunt, the patron saint of unwilling brides and unhappy wives all over Europe until the Reformation – there is still a statue of Saint Uncumber in the Henry VII chapel of Westminster Abbey, at which the faithful used to offer oats. Thomas More commented scornfully on this cult practice:

> Whereof I cannot perceive the reason, but if it be because she should provide a horse for an evil husband to ride to the devil upon, for that is the thing that she is sought for, as they say. Insomuch that women … reckon that for a peck of oats she will not fail to uncumber them of their husbands.

The hairiness round the saint's mouth, with its reminiscence of the nether female 'mouth' and its aureole of hair, makes another hint, like the asshide and the catskin, at the lustfulness inside woman that has to be faced and dealt with. (The odd stigma may also reflect the physiological symptom of *lanugo*, or body hair, which can be caused by refusing to eat and the cessation of menses, as in anorexia.)

Many commentators, Bruno Bettelheim among them, have accepted the tradition that the glass slipper in Perrault's 'Cinderella' was originally made of *vair*, fur or ermine, and that his innovatory masterstroke – as indeed it is – arose from misunderstanding what he heard. Be that as it may – the tradition of Cinderella stories stipulates many kinds of shoes in many kinds of material. But Cinderella's element, in the wake of Perrault's reading, has become glass, and the logic of the symbolism, whether he chose it or happened upon it, is perfect. When the story became one of the chief ornaments of the pedagogue's bookshelf, the hairy animal was shed, sent into exile, put behind her, and beauty, distilled and purified, brought forth. When Cinderella puts off her rags, everything about her sparkles. In illustrations to stories, in films, on stage, the ballroom glitters, the floor is even made of mirror, its ceiling hung with crystal chandeliers. Her perfections find themselves materialized in the immaterial dazzlement of light. The glass slipper works to dematerialize the troubling aspects of her nature, her natural fleshiness, her hairy vitality, and so to give a sign of her new, socialized value. The slipper becomes the glass in which a princess sees her worth brightly mirrored. As the beast is to the blonde, so the webbed foot or ass's hoof of the storyteller is to Cinderella's glass slipper. This is the conversion classic fairy tales bring about, and the lesson they teach.

But what is applauded and who sets the terms of the recognition and acceptance are always in question, and a closer look at the meanings of blondeness can help turn the key to the answers.

II

Mme d'Aulnoy opens 'La Belle aux cheveux d'or' with a joyful echo of Apuleius' intense eroticism:

> Once upon a time there lived the daughter of a king, who was so beautiful that there was nothing quite so beautiful on earth; and because she was so beautiful, she was called Beauty with the Golden Hair, for her hair was finer than gold, and marvellously wondrously blonde, all curly, and fell to her feet. She was always covered by her wavy hair, and clothes embroidered with diamonds and pearls, so that you could not look on her without loving her.

The story develops into a classic, tender romance, about a poor, generous hero, who wins the love of the princess by his courage and trueheartedness. At the beginning, a great king wants to marry this Beauty, but she does not want to be married at all, and she refuses his suit as well as all his presents, accepting only a few English dressmakers' pins – then considered a great luxury. The hero, a courtier, called Avenant (Comely), is sent as messenger to persuade her, and she sets him three impossible tasks – which, naturally, he accomplishes, with the help of animals whose lives he has saved in the course of his questing: a carp, who brings him a ring the princess has lost from the bottom of the sea; a crow, who helps him behead an ogre; and an owl who leads him through a dark, impenetrable grotto to find the water of eternal youth and beauty she has demanded. In the end, after a few of the usual setbacks and travails, the two lovers are united, and Beauty sets a crown of gold on Avenant's head and makes him king at her side.

Beauty with the Golden Hair is only one of the teeming population of blonde fairytale heroines. The etymology of the word 'blond(e)' is not known for certain, though it appears related to *blandus*, Latin for charming (as survives in 'blandishment'), with later influence from Medieval Latin *blundus* and Old German *blund*, both meaning yellow. It enters French in the twelfth century, and is later used with affectionate diminutives for the young – and boys more than girls – as in *blondin*, *blondinet*. It appears in Chaucer as 'blounde', but then fades from view in English until the seventeenth century, when it was almost exclusively applied in the feminine, 'blonde'; it still suggested sweetness, charm, youthfulness; only in the 1930s and 1940s, under the influence of Hollywood, did the word emerge as a noun, and acquire its hot, vampish overtones, based in the jaunty ironical reversals of meaning cultivated by popular media this century.

The adjective's double resonance – in French, Italian, German, Spanish – of beauty and light colouring corresponds to the English usage of 'fair' since the middle ages: the Old English meaning of beautiful, or pleasing, developed by the thirteenth century into 'free from imperfections or blemish' and by the sixteenth carried explicit connotations of 'a light hue; clear in colour'. A 'fair' used to be a noun meaning a beauty, and indeed *La Belle aux cheveux d'or* was translated in the eighteenth century as 'The Fair with the Golden Hair', thus revealing the association of fairies with fair ones. As we saw in Chapter Two, the root may be the same for the words 'fay' and 'fair', the Middle English *'feyen'*, and Anglo-Saxon *'fegan'*, which can mean to bind. Hair's power can bind, as in spells and fate – and desire.

Blondeness and beauty have provided a conceptual rhyme in visual and literary imagery ever since the goddess of Love's tresses were described as *xanthe*, golden, by Homer. The siren-like Whore of Babylon in the thirteenth-century Angers tapestry of the Apocalypse, for instance, looks at herself in Venus' mirror and combs out her long fair tresses (Pl. 18); Botticelli's Aphrodite rising from the sea wears nothing but her blonde hair; the planet Venus, in the sumptuous manuscript illuminations of a fifteenth-century treatise on astronomy, the *De sphaera* of the D'Este family, wears flowing golden hair down her back. Homer was not able to show the same enterprise in his epithets as shampoo and hair dye makers today, who have invented grades of blondeness from ash to honey to strawberry, and his translators overdetermined the text, rendering the same word *xanthos* as redhaired when it applies to Menelaus, a king, and golden-haired when used of a goddess or a beauty (Aphrodite, Helen). In Virgil, Dido's hair is described as *flavae*, golden, but then, so are olive leaves. The vocabulary of colour in Greek and Latin does not register the range of sense perceptions; modern languages since continue to strain to denote nuance and shade as perceived by the eye and the brain. But, as Umberto Eco has pointed out, the perception of colour itself changes according to the surrounding culture and its needs: a sword can be *fulva* as jasper because the poet sees the red of blood it may spill. Some of the most precise and richest lexicons of colour developed among horse breeders and traders in order to describe their bloodstock: in Italy and Spain there were thirteen horse colours in use in the early middle ages, and in Byzantium eleven; more recently the Khirgiz of the Steppes use thirty different terms, while in central Russia sixty are in circulation.

Storytellers may have intended a shade or tint of blonde hair but it is unlikely; the colour fulfils a symbolic function, not a practical or descriptive purpose as in horse trading – though, as we shall see later, there is an element of horse trading in fairy tales, too. For fairness was a guarantee of quality. It was the imaginary opposite of 'foul', it connoted all that was pure, good, clean. Blondeness is less a descriptive term about hair pigmentation than a blazon in code, a piece of a value system that it is urgent to confront and analyse because its implications, in moral and social terms, are so dire and are still so unthinkingly embedded in the most ordinary, popular materials of the imagination. The Nazis' Aryan fantasies were partly rooted in this ancient, enduring colour code which cast gods as golden boys and girls and outsiders as swarthy. A puppet film, made in 1935, two years after Hitler came to power, by the German Paul Dihe, told the familiar Grimm story about the boy who wanted to learn how to shudder; it followed his daredevilry as he sleeps under the gibbet, enters the spooky castle, defeats the demons and wins the princess. What looks like an ordinary children's film about winning through turns out to be horrific when Hitler's own relish for the cruelty of fairy tales is borne in mind. This short film tells a story that was favoured in the education of the Hitler Youth, because it inculcated fearlessness, imperviousness, manly violence; the Boy hero is tow-haired, his assailants hook-nosed, swarthy, hairy, dark, old. In the Grimms' text, these monsters are great black cats and dogs, so the change to grotesque humans is significant, if not deliberate.

Fairy tale and romance have carried this system of values in their bloodstream since Hellenistic times: in 'Cupid and Psyche', Venus sends Psyche down to the underworld to fetch her some of Persephone's beauty cream; Psyche, afflicted as we have seen with all the conventional feminine faults, cannot resist opening the casket, whereupon a deep Stygian cloud rises out of the box and wraps her in sleep; in some interpretations this episode befouls her, turning her black – this functions, in the tale, as a sign of her lost beauty. In another of the Greek romances to influence the development of fairy tale, Heliodorus' *Aethiopica*, the plot turns on a lost daughter, the child who was born fair-skinned to her royal

Ethiopian parents after her mother during her conception contemplated a painting of the classical, blonde Andromeda. Much is made of the improbability of her belonging to them, until her unique birthmark is recognized and the right cradle tokens brought forth. This romance was translated into English in 1587 and was popular, so its values were circulated, however lamentably they may strike us today. In the fairy tale 'Starlight', where the heroine is magically changed into a Moor when a similar Stygian gloom descends, she fears that her beloved Izmir will no longer love her in this shape. But, as fairy tales also try and oppose prevailing prejudice, she is mistaken. Her prince finds her fascinating and lovable, and is disturbed only that he is being unfaithful to his true love in so doing.

Golden hair tumbles through the stories in impossible quantities. The Grimms' Rapunzel lowers her long fair hair out of the high tower as a rope for her guardian witch to climb; Mélisande, in Maeterlinck and Debussy's eerie opera, hangs it out of her window for Pelléas to wind around himself in ecstasy. The typical Cinderella of children's literature has inherited, as the mark of her perfect loveliness, this characteristic of Venus. A musical version of around 1889 by Francis Davies, set in Merrie England, invokes Cinderella's appearance:

A maiden meek, and young, and fair;
Her eyes were blue as flowers o' lint,
Her cheeks the roses' bonniest tint,
And streamed in golden waves her hair.

Cinderella's hairstyle changes according to the fashion of the day – though her hair colour never does, or hardly ever. In 1966, a popular picture book imagined Cinders with the long fringe and bouffant height of Brigitte Bardot's hairstyle.

Among the heroines of fairy tale only Snow White is dark, because her story specifically opens with her mother's wish, when she pricks her finger, looking out at the snow: 'Would that I had a child as white as snow, as red as blood, and as black as the wood of the window-frame.' In some, more lyrical variations, she wishes for hair 'the colour of a raven's wing'. Recently, illustrators and animators have drawn back from the obligatory blondeness of the heroine (the Disney Belle in the recent *Beauty and the Beast*, discussed in Chapter Eighteen, is dark), but their attempts lever feebly against the long weight of the tradition. 'If you desire to marry again after my death,' says the mother in the Grimms' 'All-Fur', 'I'd like you to take someone who is as beautiful as I am, and who has golden hair like mine.' Goldilocks, whose name indicates her blondeness, began as an old woman, as we saw, turned into 'Silver Locks', and then settled down in the conventional fairytale heroic pattern. The legacy of the heroine is passed on in the coin of blonde hair; to generations of listeners and readers, it has naturally enciphered female beauty – inner as well as outer. In 1993, the actress Jane Asher designed a range of birthday cakes for children – the Sleeping Beauty lies on one, in a pink bed diapered with rose briars, her golden hair carefully piped to fall over the turned-down sheets.

Disney's Cinders too is blonde, her ugly sisters red-haired and dark respectively, while the wicked stepmother is raven-haired, or black as a crow. In their symbolism, Walt Disney and his artists were merely following tradition (Pl. 24). Judas was conventionally portrayed with a red beard; the word 'ruffian' in English and in Italian comes from the same root as 'rufous', meaning red-haired. In Tiepolo's painting of the combat between Vice and Virtue, the goddess in the pure ether above has blonde hair; her enemy Vice below is a dark redhead; the polarity reproduces the conflict the same painter dramatized in *Time Defacing Beauty*, in which old Father Time carries off the goddess Venus – their enmity dialectically conveyed by lightness and darkness, which translates into the visual terms of fair-skinned golden-haired whiteness and hirsute, dark-haired swarthiness. The colour yellow, following red and orange in the spectrum, is freighted like them in Christian symbolism with the hot hues' ambiguities, and it is telling that hair is almost never described as yellow in English or French or Italian or German; the category of blondeness demarcates the fair-haired human from the perilous and even devilish associations of yellow, carried for instance in the generic name for thrillers in Italy (*gialli*). (There are exceptions: W. B. Yeats's poem says, 'Only God, my dear, could love you for yourself alone / And not your yellow hair.' The 'yellow' here adds, however, to the acerbity of his tone.)

Blondeness belongs within the richly layered symbolism of lightness rather than yellowness; Christian metaphysics of light contributed to a change in the associations of the Latin term *fulvus* – under the influence of ecstatic medieval conjurations of light, the embrace of gold sheds its classical kin of reds and yellows and cleaves closer to white; more distinct terms for both red and yellow begin to develop. This in turn tightens the identification of blondeness with heavenly effulgence, and heightens its value. It appears to reflect solar radiance, the totality of the spectrum, the flooding wholeness of light which Dante finds grows more and more dazzling as he rises in Paradise. In the twelfth century, liturgical spectacles relied on gold to dazzle the faithful: on the feast of Corpus Christi, the Body of the Saviour, in the form of a host (itself a solar disc), was emblazoned in

monstrances shooting rays, carried in procession and then set up in a gold tabernacle. This psychology of excess and ostentation inspired the reaction of the
Cistercians, and their great thinker, Bernard of Clairvaux, who sought to retreat
into architectural severity and more modest rituals. Even he however recognized
the power of dazzlement and allowed crusaders to wear gold or silver armour
'when they enter battle, so that the sun may shine upon them and scatter the
forces of the enemy with terror'. The symbolism remained untarnished by
Cistercian strictures, carried on in verbal imagery. For Saint Bonaventure in the
thirteenth century, *color* or *splendor* was one aspect of light's threefold character
(the others being *lux*, light as origin, and *lumen*, light travelling through space);
though light was a substance, it could pass through glass, while *color* conveyed the
light reflected by terrestrial bodies it struck, whose beauty was thereby made
manifest. 'Light was thus the principle of all beauty,' writes Umberto Eco, 'not
only because it is delightful to the senses, but also because it is through light that
all the variations in colour and luminosity, both in heaven and on earth, come into
being.' The chronicler and man of letters Olivier de La Marche (*d.* 1502) mar-
velled at the beauty of sunlight playing in fair hair. Max Lüthi, the scholar of folklore, adduces this effect of blonde hair as a vital aspect of beauty's function in fairy
tales: its capacity to awaken the senses also helps illuminate the truth – the accused
queen's innocence, the draggletailed skivvy's goodness.

Meteors were called comets after the Latin *comes*, hair, because watchers of the
skies perceived golden flowing hair in the tail. After Berenice, Queen of Egypt in
the third century BC, cut off a lock of her hair and offered it to Venus so that her
husband should return safe from battle, it disappeared from the temple; whereupon the court astrologer discovered it in the sky, where it had been placed as a
reward. He called the new constellation Comes Berenices, the hair of Berenice.

Although blondeness's most enduring associations are with beauty, with love
and nubility, with erotic attraction, with value and fertility, its luminosity made it
also the traditional colour of virgins' hair. After the fifteenth century, the Virgin
Mary herself, particularly under her apocalyptic aspect as the 'Woman clothed
with the sun', is frequently depicted as a blonde, and not only in Northern countries, but in France and Italy as well, as for example in the *Spinola Hours* of around
1515 (Pl. 16). The visions of Saint Bridget of Sweden, who saw Mary as a woman
of her own Northern climate, influenced representations of the Virgin after the
fourteenth century (Pl. 17), but she was already described as blonde in the
eleventh century. In a poem on Christ's passion, for instance, the Virgin's lament
is introduced by a description that recalls the mourners of classical sarcophagi:

Now his mother, wan with lament, approaching,
her golden hair awry, strikes heaven with these words:
O holy shoot of heaven, my only child …

Even Black Madonnas have golden hair, as in the cult statue of Montserrat in Spain, where the Byzantine original has been gilded under her wimple. The virgin saints and martyrs are represented blonde: Catherine, Agnes, Barbara. In her reliquary in Syracuse in Sicily, Saint Lucy, who tore out her eyes when a lover admired them and sent them to him saying her chosen, heavenly bridegroom had no need of eyes of the flesh, has hair cast in the metal gold while the rest of her is silver. The company of virgins in heaven, in the *Spinola Hours*, consists only of blondes, unless their hair is veiled. Blondeness is an index of the virgins' youth as well as innocence, for many children are fair in infancy and grow darker with age. The company of male saints, on the facing page of the prayer book, are allowed different hair colours, on head and chin, in their segregated section of heaven.

The tradition enfolds femininity, and its conventional link with youth and beauty, as well as with privacy, modesty and an interior life in both senses – indoor pursuits and affective experience. For blonde hair implies pale skin, which in turn entails lack of exposure, again on a doubled level, either to the rays of the sun in outdoor work, or to the gaze of others. On Greek pots, for instance, the flesh tones of women are painted lighter than men's – sometimes the goddesses will be rendered entirely white next to a god who keeps the burned earth colour of the vase itself. Cleopatra's legendary baths of asses' milk were intended to whiten her skin; the first recipe in Gianbattista Della Porta's 'How to Adorn Women, and make them Beautiful', one of the sections in his compendium *Natural Magick*, proposes several complex recipes (honey, cummin, cabbage stalks amongst other ingredients) for bleaching hair and whitening the complexion.

The symbolic pressure bears down with a certain force: Joan of Arc's hair colour for instance is not known, although for a long time it was thought that the single dark strand under a seal on one of her extant letters might have been from her head. But her haircut is famous: it was 'cut round in the fashion of a boy', as her accusers repeatedly charged her during her trial. The pressure of received ideas lies so powerfully on the imagination that illustrators of Joan's story ignored the primary and well-disseminated historical evidence. In a manuscript illumination from the mid-fifteenth century, the Maid of France has not cut her hair, but wears it long, loosely coiled on her neck, and fair. In a printed strip version of her life, an *image d'Epinal* from 1894, printed for mass distribution to celebrate her new status as the Venerable Joan, she appears, in the last frame, at the stake. The phrase *image d'Epinal* has come to mean *cliché* in French – and in this image, quite properly, the *cliché* Joan of Arc has long wavy fair hair, like a medieval virgin martyr. The quality of the engraving means we cannot see the colour; though some stray tangerine colour around the incised lines suggests fair hair rather than dark. At the turn of the century, the French artist Maurice Boutet de Monvel created one of the most influential – and splendid – picture books for children, about Joan of Arc. He commented on his representation of the heroine: '[She] had such a tender breast, so much pity – I find in her so much of womanly grace in contrast with her decision in the hour of action – that I can see her only blonde. Side by side with the brutal soldier she appeared feeble and delicate.' Joan, in her sanctity and goodness, can only be blonde.

Likewise, Lady Jane Grey, who was queen for ten days in 1553, was writing to Mary Queen of Scots that her hair had fallen out in prison; at her execution, she was nearly bald. Her story follows a martyr's pattern: harshly treated at home, then married to a man against her will to promote the interests of the male members of his family and her own, she was finally killed. Concomitantly, in the refashioning of her story, she grows the long blonde hair of the ideal heroine – as in the nineteenth-century *pompier* Paul Delaroche's maudlin icon of her beheading, now in London. The imagination works history to its grain; fairy tales could hardly be spared its improving drift. Even Snow White undergoes a change: in a garden of the village of Sauzet in the Quercy, France, a set of gnomes has been repainted by their owner, and Snow White's raven hair turned blonde.

BLONDA AND FAIRY CAPRICE

Once upon a time there was a little girl who had beautiful blond hair which touched the ground.

They called her pretty Blonda; but Blonda had more whims and fancies than she had hairs on her head.

One day a beautiful lady visited her and said : " I am the fairy Caprice. I will lend thee my wand but only on these conditions "

" Whenever thou shalt satisfy one of thy fancies, I will take one of thy beautiful hairs for I am bald and obliged to wear a wig "

Blonda takes the wand and transforms her little cottage to a large palace full of servants.

She wears satin and velvet dresses and fills her hair with pearls and diamonds. She eats nothing but the most delicate morsels.

She has so many fancies that after two years she cannot go out , without her veil, for she has not one hair left.

At last she grows unhappy and tired of her amusements, and calling the fairy Caprice asks for happiness.

" Thou shalt be happy ", says the fairy, " when thou shalt have won back thy pretty hair ". At this Blonda is greatly puzzled.

Whenever she does a good deed or assists the poor she notices that a hair appears on her head.

She then destroys her magnificent palace.

And giving to the poor all that she does not need, goes back to live in her little cottage.

She takes care of her brothers and sisters, and assists her mother in housekeeping.

She then regains her lost beauty and one day, when she takes off her cap, she sees that her hair is as heavy and long as it had been before.

Pretty Blonda marries a nice boy and is happier than the wealthiest of brides.

She teaches her children that contentment and not caprice is wisdom, and that one should never wish for anything that can not be obtained through honesty.

Punished with baldness, Blonda learns to forgo caprices and is rewarded by the return of her thick, long, golden hair. (Image d'Epinal, France, reprinted Kansas City, c. 1900.)

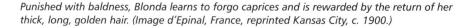

From the Beast to the Blonde: The Language of Hair II

Crack the glass of her virginity; and make the rest malleable.

Pericles, IV, vi

Something momentous would have taken place, it would be clear – that there had been a revolution – if a presenter on Iran television pulled the kerchief from her head and showed her hair to us, or if one of the mullahs, by the same token, unravelled his turban, shaved his beard, and appeared in a silvery brush top, *à la* Clinton. Joan of Arc died for cutting her hair like a boy's, among other things. The charges of witchcraft were dropped as they could not be proven, but her heretical cross-dressing and close-cropping were there for all to see, and she refused to renounce them. Frida Kahlo in her paintings presents her irreducible identity through protean selves, adorned as well as despoiled: when her husband Diego Rivera left her, she cropped her hair, put on his suit, tie, spread her legs in a sitting posture, and made a self-portrait with the clippings strewn around her, looking uncannily snaky. As in an inscription on a Catholic ex-voto, giving thanks for a miracle cure, or a wish granted, she impersonated his voice with bitter irony, writing over a musical stave as if to a popular song: 'Look, if I loved you, it was for your hair. Now that you are bald, I don't love you any more.'

The language of the self would be stripped of one of its richest resources without hair: and like language, or the faculty of laughter, or the use of tools, the dressing of hair in itself constitutes a mark of the human. In the quest for identity, both personal and in its larger relation to society, hair can help. The body reveals to us through hair the passage of time and the fluctuating claims of gender; strangers offer us a conspicuous glossary of clues in the way they do the hair on their head, for in societies all over the world, callings are declared through hairy signs: the monk's tonsure, the ringlets of the Hassidic scholar, the GI's crewcut, the sansculotte's freeflowing mane, the flowerchild's tangled curls, the veil.

Hairstyles continually perform a drama about the beastly and the human selves present within each individual, and mark off degrees of identification and repudiation in a form of animal mimicry. Our capillary arts borrow and build on the physiology of hair, which we humans share with other creatures of fur and fleece. The affective behaviour of our pelt inspires dramatic variations: the stiff spikes of punk styles imitate the bristling of aggression, and reproduce literally the hair-raising thrills of terror, both given and received: these are hackles, raised in emphasis. Peroxide blondes, like Marilyn Monroe in her winsome dumb babyish act, recall the fluffy down of some children's heads, or baby chicks, or ducklings. The conflict between this pretence at innocence and knowing sexiness creates the special effect of the Hollywood blonde, the woman in the picture, the motive in the plot. Madonna provokes one of her perverse frissons by simultaneously mimicking the blonde bombshells of Hollywood in all their rampant, in your face sexuality, and at the same time singing from the position of a little girl, who is still only on the verge of womanhood, with the pale golden hair of childhood in glaring contradiction to the emphasized thighs, breasts, crotch.

Blonde hair shares with gold certain mythopoeic properties: gold does not tarnish, it can be beaten and hammered, annealed and spun and still will not diminish or fade; its brightness survives time, burial, and the forces of decay, as does hair, more than any other part or residue of the flesh. It is hair's imperviousness as a natural substance that yields the deeper symbolic meanings and warrants the high place hair plays in the motif repertory of fairy tales and other legends. For although it is one of the most sensitive registers of temperature, and a single human strand is used in museum hygrometers in order to measure humidity for the purposes of conservation, hair does not register pain, except at the roots. It can be cut and curled, sizzled with hot tongs, steeped in chemicals and dyes without apparent suffering, and will go on growing, even abundantly in some cases, and is not even stopped by death. This phenomenon, noted in the case of great heroes like Charlemagne (d. 814) and Saint Olav, King of Norway (d. 1030), stimulated the cult that grew up round their tombs.

Such quasi-magical properties make it a symbol of invulnerability, and have helped to nourish the rich mythology of hair as power, as in the stories of Samson, and also, as we have seen, in 'Bluebeard' to a lesser degree. Above all, its imperishability must count as the intrinsic and material quality of hair that most inspires its symbolic meanings. Hair is organic, but less subject to corruption than all our organs; like a fossil, like a shell, it lasts. (We know the colouring of some pharaohs, of their queens and – even – their slaves.) In spite of its fragility, lightness, even insubstantiality, hair is the part of our flesh nearest in kind to a carapace. Its mythic power, its centrality to body language, and its multiplicity of meanings, derive from this dual character: on the one hand, hair is both the sign of the animal in the human, and all that means in terms of our tradition of associating the beast with the bestial, nature and the natural with the inferior and reprehensible aspects of humanity; on the other hand, hair is also the least fleshly production of the flesh. In its suspended corruptibility, it seems to transcend the mortal condition, to be in full possession of the principle of vitality itself.

As such, hair is central to magic; clippings have long been effective in curses and love charms alike. In Britain, the Devil could be kept at bay by offerings of pubic hair, because he has no power to straighten it. In some fairy tales, plucking hairs from the Devil's head gives power over him. Hair partakes of the body and transmits that body's special powers: Dindraine, in Malory's *Le Morte d'Arthur*, has vowed herself to a life of chastity. Only she can weave a girdle strong enough for Galahad to use to wear the sword of Solomon: from her hair she makes a belt for his blade. Together in chastity, both their sexual energies converted into an invincible holy syzygy.

Like a fetish, hair can be used to represent loss: it has been used the world over in rituals of fertility and of mourning. The Greeks cut locks or tufts to throw them on the funeral pyre; hair relics of Charles I after his beheading were set in rings by the disconsolate, and among the Trobriand islanders, a widow in full mourning wears a necklace of balls woven from her husband's hair, while her own head is shaven and braided into a gorget. Knotted in bracelets and lockets, it also pledges indissoluble love: La Fontaine mentions a gage of a bracelet of hair, the Victorians set their dear ones' hair into lockets and rings and exchanged them as tokens of eternal plighting, and as recently as in the Western *The Outlaw Josey Wales*, Clint Eastwood's girl, the loving young daughter of pilgrims from Kansas, gives him a watchchain she has woven from her hair to bind him to her – it is indeed fay, and proves effective. These ornaments possess the power of the uncanny: neither dead nor alive, they make the beholder's flesh creep, like the human remains incorporated into sorcerers' wands, or the straggling locks still adhering to the shrunken heads of the Jivaro Indians' enemies.

The variety of profane, ritual uses to which hair has been put possibly helped ban it from the catalogue of Christian relics. For although every kind of remnant of the Virgin, Jesus and the saints was venerated, the colour of Mary's or Jesus' hair has not been demonstrated by firsthand evidence.

Characteristically, though, the hair in Victorian tokens and memento moris was braided or coiled or otherwise set to rights. In hairdressing, whether on the scalp or off it, dishevelment is always at issue, and the magic of hair seems more closely directed, controlled and contained when the hair is groomed than when it is unkempt (wild). Liberty characteristically wears her hair loose, Order pins it up. In Mendocino, in northern California, an anonymous sculptor carved from a redwood trunk a remarkable work of folk art, representing a variation on the theme of Death and the Maiden. Father Time does not seize the modest young woman to rape her or otherwise snatch her away, in the style of Hans Baldung Grien or Holbein, but instead stands calmly behind her, braiding her hair, like a good father sending his young daughter off to school. Here, hair stands for the flow of life, and plaiting it stands for the delimitations imposed on the human course by the hand of time.

Maidenhair can symbolize maidenhead – and its loss too, and the flux of sexual energy that this releases, as we know from fairy tales, like Persinette/Rapunzel who pulls her lover up her hair into her tower (right). There is a German proverb, 'A woman's hair pulls stronger than a bell rope', or, 'A woman's hair is stronger than a hempen rope', and in the story, in the punning manner of dreams, Rapunzel enacts this belief literally. Similar cascades of golden hair dominate illustrations of fairy tales from the late nineteenth century onwards, tumbling in unselfconscious, golden superabundance from the heads of hundreds of exemplary Victorian heroines. One of the inspirations of the Dada movement's name was a hair cologne from Zurich, which showed on the label a young girl with a luxuriant mane of golden waves that stirs in the breeze as she holds up a bottle of the magic stuff called Dada; it guarantees just such crowning glory – to men as well as to women, no doubt (right).

II

The astrological sign Virgo also appears blonde; as the symbol for August to September, she is connected with the season of harvesting in the Mediterranean, where the first representations of her as a young woman occur. Comparative iconography can help to decipher the obsessive persistence of this sign of value; by comparing the traditional virgin martyr and the fairytale heroine with the sign Virgo, some clues emerge to develop the meaning of this dominant motif in the representation of valuable feminine gender.

Artists frequently create a correspondence between the maiden's hair and the corn she carries, emblematic of the chief star in the constellation, Spica (Wheatear). In a manuscript of the influential Arabic astronomical treatise by Abu Masar, finished before 1403, the plaited shape of the wheatear echoes the braids

Rapunzel is enclosed in a high tower, but she lets down her hair – literally – to find a way out and a new life; in Zurich, the Dadaists's name picked up a local echo of the fin-de-siècle adoration of hair. (H. J. Ford, in Andrew Lang, The Red Fairy Book, London, 1890 LEFT; ABOVE Dada, hair lotion advertisement, Zurich, c. 1917.)

In a manual on the care of horses, the star sign of the Virgin can be seen in the centre, ruling over the belly, or site of the womb. (Bonifacio di Calabria, Libro de la Menescalcia, *Venice, 1400–15.)*

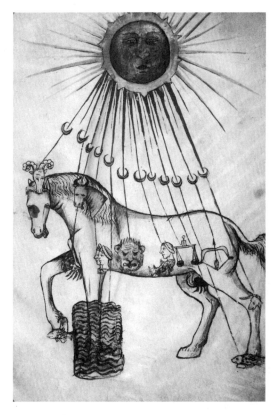

around her head; in a later, richly gilded illumination from a northern French book of hours of the early sixteenth century, the same gold pigment has been used for the wheat on the threshing floor as for the hair and aureole of Virgo behind them – the artist's brush moved from one to the other without hesitation in applying the precious paint to those three different elements in the image (Pl. 19). The abundance and ripeness of her hair promises fertility: she is Virgo in the pagan sense of nubile, eligible, and young ('*almah*, as the girls were called in the harem of King Solomon in the Bible), rather than immaculate and impregnably celibate, like the virgin goddess Athena. The sun, source of light, has ripened the gold of her body into goodness. At the Palazzo Schifanoia in Ferrara, the sign Virgo may have been assimilated to Proserpina, goddess of spring, in the human- ist circle of the court of the d'Este, and again, her tumbling golden hair flickers with vitality like the unruly wheatsheaf in her hand (Pl. 15).

In astrological microcosmic schemae, Scorpio rules over the genitals; Libra over the lower abdomen, and intestinal functions; and Virgo over the upper abdominal region, where the organs of gestation were believed to lie. The early medieval treatise on the zodiac shows the star signs linked to the areas of the body which they influence. Virgo is attached, almost by an umbilical cord, to the figure's navel, the last vestige of the mother on every human body. Even a fifteenth-century manuscript on the care of horses shows the signs arranged in their spheres of influence on a horse's body: the sequence from genitals to womb runs Scorpio, Libra, Virgo (left). The famous astrological microcosmic man of *Les Très Riches Heures du Duc de Berry,* painted at the beginning of the fifteenth century, disposes the signs in similar fashion, with Virgo emblazoned in the centre of his body. The male gender of the youth himself can distract us from the connection clearly made by the sign between parturition and virginity. The Limbourg Brothers' Virgo, as shown in the miniature in the margin, could be a female virgin martyr, with her long blonde hair, and her palm fronds of glory.

The sight of uncovered hair at this period and later in Western Europe signifies innocence on the one hand, youth and its promise. Eligibility follows closely from these qualities in a woman: the blonde maiden promises herself. The Dance of Death in Simon Vostre's Book of Hours, defines the departed women's station in life by their demeanour and their dress, but above all by the styling and concealment of their hair, as noted in Chapter Three. Only the bride – *la espouse* – at the top, who wears a garland of flowers, *la fille pucelle*, or virgin girl, and *la jeune fille*, the young girl, at the bottom of the ladder of life, have their heads uncovered and their hair loose (right).

Typologically, the maidenhair of Virgo and young unmarried girls corresponds to vegetation. Hair is to the body as flowers and other growth are to the earth. In a peculiar group of fairy tales, hair and good fortune are dramatically connected in a magic way, as we saw. George Peele's *The Old Wives' Tale*, with its cantrip rhymes, dramatizes the harvest of golden sheaves and precious jewels that fall from the hair of the three heads in the well. Mme de Villeneuve, in one of her fairy stories, described how the bad sister grew stinking weeds and rushes on her head ever after her refusal to do as the heads asked. Italo Calvino collected a variation on the story in which the sister who was kind to an old woman finds that, whenever she combs her own hair, roses and

Maidenhair is loose and long and promises plenty: 'La fille pucelle' (The virgin girl) shows her state in the fashion and abundance of her hair.(Paris, 1508.)

jasmine pour down one side, pearls and rubies down the other. 'You shall be beautiful,' says the old woman. 'Your hair shall be golden …' She returns home rich, with a star on her forehead. The wicked sister rushes off to seek a similar fortune, but treats the old woman roughly; she grows a donkeytail on her forehead, and whenever she cuts it it grows longer.

The reward matches the favour asked: when it is a drink of water, the visitor from the other world grants a boon to the mouth of her or his benefactor, or a curse, the diamonds and toads. When the kindness consists of combing and grooming, as the peasants performed on one another at Montaillou, and as we see in Dutch seventeenth-century paintings of mothers delousing their children's hair, the benefit falls from the same place.

In stories like 'Three Heads in a Well', hair's connotation with luxuriance and fertility becomes material wealth, literal gold and jewels and riches. Fertility used to be considered a treasure of great price, valuable to society as its future prosperity, valuable to the family too. Blondeness, a particular manifestation of hair, with its much noticed sensuous association with wholesome sunshine, with the light rather than the dark, evoked untarnishable and enduring gold; all hair promised growth, golden hair promised riches. The fairytale heroine's riches, her goodness and her fertility, her foison, are symbolized by her hair.

In both Basile and Perrault, the moment of epiphany occurs when she abandons her animal disguise and is seen combing her hair. Basile specifies her *trezze d'oro*, her golden tresses. In Perrault, Donkeyskin has been summoned by the prince. The court is ready to scoff at the mere sight of her, but then she appears: the ladies of the court are instead roused to joyful marvelling by

> … *ses aimables cheveux blonds*
> *Mêlés de diamants dont la vive lumière*
> *En faisait autant de rayons …*

[Her lovely blonde hair intermingled with diamonds, whose lively light turned it into a sunburst of rays.]

Perrault uses the adjective *'blond'* in only one other place in the same tale, embedded in a similar vision of dazzling light: when he is describing the magic donkey. In an exact reflection of the sight of Donkeyskin shooting rays of light from the gems mingled in with her golden hair, he describes the magic donkey's stall each morning:

il ne faisait jamais d'ordure
mais bien beaux Ecus au soleil
Et Louis de toute manière,
qu'on allait recueillir sur la blonde litière
Tous les matins à son reveil.

[He never made manure, but only very beautiful golden Sun coins and Louis of all kinds, which were gathered from his blond litter every morning when he awoke.]

In the engraving illustrating the appearance of the restored Peau d'Ane in *Le Cabinet des fées*, her breasts are bare, her hair loose, to emphasize her unsullied promise of plenty.

Perrault's version discloses the value of the heroine: her status as the repository and security of her father's wealth. Her golden hair reveals to the prince that she is not the beast – the she-bear – or the slatternly donkey everyone knows and despises; she becomes available to him as a bride, she sheds her animal lowness to become his equal. When she marries him, she consigns her worth to his care: as we saw in Chapter Twenty, she takes her father's fortune with her, in the form of the asshide that used to excrete his fortune every morning, and she makes it over to the prince she marries. Ideas of eligibility and female fertility and women's worth are once more entangled together. Her blonde hair becomes the symbol of her status as treasure, safely transferred from the control of one paternal household to another, marital home. Perrault was taking the side of his friends, the *précieuses* who wanted control of their own fortunes, legacies, dowries. But the story reads differently in a context where that issue is no longer pressing. The literary fairy tale reinterpreted Christian ascetic teaching about young women's rights to withhold their fertility, and reformulated the chivalrous ideal of emotional and erotic fulfilment with a partner of their choice. The old battles now look like materialist ambition and romantic naivety; the passing years have blunted the radicalism of Perrault and his friends among the women writers who were attempting to redraw the map of tenderness to give themselves a stake in it, materially as well as emotionally.

In the case of the virgin martyrs, their choice of bridegroom also sets a seal of approval on their conduct: they have kept their treasure safe for another reaper. Virginity literally cannot scatter paternal wealth, but locks it up. The iconography of the sign Virgo also enfolds this social, and earthly, meaning: for Virgo presides over the threshing of the corn, the process that gathers up the useful part of the harvest, as can be seen in any number of illuminations, like the Book of Hours painted by the Master of Guillebert de Metz in Flanders around 1450–60. This particular aspect of virginity, nuanced towards production, positioned with regard for the harvester rather than the tiller, lies concealed within the immediate erotic appeal of the virgin's bridal blondeness. In another, French manuscript, of 1480–85, the imagery remains constant; however, here the Zodiac sign of Virgo stands, like a saint, with the bound sheaves on either side of her. They are standing to dry in the fields before being threshed. Like the corn that will feed human beings, she promises fruit, nourishment and wealth. Her purity guarantees that the riches will not be scattered.

The bridal connotations of blonde hair persist, and in surprising places. Bakers tend to offer wedding cakes with exclusively fair brides to this day – in Los Angeles, for instance, where the population is mainly dark, a leading catalogue of wholesale cake ornaments offered, in 1988, page after page after page of blondes. In this the wedding confectioners were conforming to an ancient canon of beauty and the conventions of bridal iconography, which has carried into fairy tale. Only one page, called 'Ethnic', represented the brides and grooms as dark-haired and dark-skinned.

The banishment from the contemporary Angeleno wedding cake of the dark-haired bride corresponds to certain historical forgettings we also find in folklore and hagiography – disjunctions between experience and symbol, the breeding ground of ignorance and bigotry. In Joan of Arc's familiar story, several attested historical features – her rebellion against her parents, her attempted suicide and, as we have seen, her short boy's hair – are usually omitted, and she is presented instead as an exemplary female saint, devout daughter, unshaken believer; in this, her historiography corresponds to the loss of certain topoi in the 'Donkeyskin' cycle of folk tales, like the father's incestuous desire. When such stories are aimed at a reading rather than a listening public, and angled at children especially, they no longer seem suitable material, and undergo alteration in order to edify and instruct and elevate. Historical circumstances, Joan's dark colouring, Lady Jane Grey's griefstricken baldness, are lost in the retellings.

Two current fairy tales offer eloquent illustration of the changes in the genre. Goldilocks, as we saw in Chapter Ten, begins life in print as an old woman: the antic behaviour of the old is reproved and the young audience trained that decorum and caste must be observed. However, the child called 'Silver-Hair' and eventually Goldilocks enters the tale and takes the old woman's place to drive home without question the specific lesson against curiosity in little girls. To deserve her name, this blonde beauty should be good. Similarly, the cautionary tale of 'Blonda', another *image d'Epinal* from the turn of the century, reprinted as an American strip cartoon in the 1900s, illustrates the moral enterprise of the fairy tale, conveyed again through the symbol of a potentially good (blonde) child (p. 370). Set in a medieval countryside, with a shift to a sixteenth-century palace, 'Blonda' draws on the illusory authenticity of a fictive past; and by creating a heroine who belongs to fairy tale and to pious literature, the story is intended to provide a lesson for its contemporary youthful audience.

Blonda's fairy godmother, whose name is Caprice, grants the beautiful young girl every wish, but warns her that for each one she will lose a hair of her head. Blonda is wicked, and asks only for riches and vanities, luxuries and follies, till she hasn't a single hair left. Then she repents, and begins to do good. Her hair grows back, one strand at a time. She works hard at home, at household tasks. The medieval cauldron, a must in the life of a Cinderella, makes its appearance with Blonda scouring it. At last, she regains her lost glory; one day, when she takes off her cap, she sees that her hair has grown as heavy and long and blonde as it was before. So she marries a nice boy and grows up in wisdom and kindness with her children around her: a naughty beauty who has learned into whose keeping she should consign her golden hair.

The literary fairy tale mixed hagiography with romance to pioneer a new heroine, a proto-romantic champion of the truth of the imagination and the holiness of the heart's affections. But this kind of tale, which D'Aulnoy and L'Héritier perfected in the late seventeenth century, no longer issued any kind of challenge to the established code of femininity in the nineteenth-century nursery. By forgetting that fairy tales interact with social circumstances, we miss seeing how the copybook blonde princess becomes instead a stick with which to beat young women, as in 'Blonda'. The conventions of fairy tale, including the shining beauty and goodness of the heroine, become clichés, used by moralists to enforce discipline (and appearance) on growing girls. Good behaviour earns a reward: beauty, sex appeal, the very desirability the stories used to dramatize as so painful and problematic. In Blonda's baldness, we find the *derogatory* equivalent of Cinderella's rags, Donkeyskin's hide, the she-bear's animal metamorphosis, Rashin Coatie's coat of grass. Blonda regains her loveliness only by giving up Caprice. In this nineteenth-century version of a type of ancient story, the heroine is crowned with the outward sign of her return to obedience, the garland of her newfound conformity: the blonde hair of the goddess of love.

III

Blondeness as a trophy has been worn with knowing mockery, since the 1920s, while the hairiness of the Beast has exercised greater and greater appeal, not only as the alluring opposite (as in Chapter Eighteen) but as the alter ego of the female subject. The Surrealist writer and painter Leonora Carrington (*b.* 1917) returns again and again to the theme in her perverse and comic fairy tales of the late 1930s and early 1940s; her contemporary, the artist Meret Oppenheim, was also possessed by hairy motifs in fairy tales from the German tradition to make her own feline assaults on convention.

Carrington was writing her tales chiefly between the ages of seventeen and twenty from the midst of a circle of writers and artists in France centred on André Breton and Max Ernst, and she responded to their Surrealist dreams of young women – *femmes enfants* – as the innocent, and therefore pure, mediums of erotic power. She voices the movement's dream of sexual freedom for men and women, intertwining the macabre English nursery-rhyme tradition with avant-garde transgressiveness in a sequence of replies – retorts – both written and painted, which challenge the male Surrealist idea of women's place.

Max Ernst's collage novels of the 1920s and early 1930s folded together the matter-of-fact tone of the German fairy tale with the florid style of penny catechisms and other improving literature. In *La Femme 100 Têtes* (The Hundred Headed Woman) of 1929, he gleefully adopts the Lustucru emblem that the best woman is all body, no head, and consequently tongueless; in *Une Petite Fille rêve d'entrer au Carmel* (A Little Girl Dreams of Taking the Veil) a year later, he took the motif of a nun's sacrifice of her hair, and made clever mischief of its erotic undertones: the pope calls to little Marie-Madeleine, 'Baldness lies in wait for you, my child!' The Holy Father needs her hair, he beseeches her, for his own sumptuous, yet invisible, adornment. She protests, she begs him not to touch her hair, but he insists: 'Dearly beloved child, heaven is covetous of your hair.' One of the most resolved formal images of the novel then follows, showing the hair of the heroine sailing away, '*majestueusement*'. Throughout the work, Ernst plays on the analogies of hair with water, with flux, with turmoil and erotic outpouring. When, later, the lost hair addresses the little girl, he uses the phrases of the wolf from 'Red Riding Hood', embodying the threat – the delicious, pleasurable threat – of being engulfed. The artist was also mocking, with brilliant economy, the preceding generation's obsession with female hair, with tentacular, suffocating, prehensile locks of the *femmes fatales* of Gustav Klimt, or Aubrey Beardsley, or Edvard Munch.

The third of these profane fables in pictures, *Une Semaine de bonté* (A Week of

Surrealism satirized at the same time as relishing the lurid fantasies of popular illustrated narrative. Leonora Carrington RIGHT with a mermaid at St Martin d'Ardèche, c. 1937–8, explored animal metaphors in her writing and art, identifying strongly with a range of hybrid beasts; LEFT Max Ernst, 'Le Lion de Belfort', in A Week of Kindness, *1934, where he dramatized erotic dreams.*

Kindness), followed in 1934, three years before Leonora Carrington and Ernst met. It adopts with glee penny-dreadful commonplaces of women mauled, ravaged and possessed by various winged and monstrous hybrid beasts, finding in misogynist excess a potent weapon against bourgeois decorum (above). Ernst drew on steel engravings from lurid serials and stuck them together with cut-out scientific illustrations in imitation of the savage couplings and violence of the Victorian serial.

Carrington's tales respond in kind, but take the monstrous figures for her own purposes, and conjure equally fierce, hostile matings of her feral heroines and their lovers. In 'As they rode along the edge … ', the heroine, Virginia Fur, lives in a forest and travels at the head of a procession of a hundred cats, riding on a wheel. She has a huge mane and 'enormous hands with dirty nails', and 'one couldn't really be altogether sure that she was a human being. Her smell alone threw doubt on it – a mixture of spices and game, the stables, fur and grasses.' Virginia makes love tempestuously with Igname, a boar, after he has presented himself to her in apparel worthy of a wooer: 'a wig of squirrels' tails and fruit hung around Igname's ears, pierced for the occasion by two little pikes he had found dead on the lakeshore. His hoofs were dyed red by the blood of a rabbit ... He hid his russet buttocks (he did not want to show all his beauty at one go).'

In this world of the imaginary the conventional hierarchy of values is turned upside down in a spirit of rebellion: the animal (hairy) world is seen as wild, sensual and free and is valued higher than the world of civilized, indoor humanity. Unbridled sexuality itself becomes a mark of liberty – setting aside the consequences for the women themselves.

Significantly, the Carrington heroine's beast friends and partners are not always male: in the most famous of her macabre, witty tales, 'The Débutante', the Beast is a she-hyena, with whom the heroine makes friends at the zoo. Something of an alter ego, the hyena goes to the heroine's coming-out ball in her stead after eating her maid in order to borrow her face (the only bit left of her) and take her clothes. The Beast within is a good beast, but he isn't only male; he can live within Beauty too. In a self-portrait, painted around the same time, she shows herself with a tousled mane of black hair, attended by two animal familiars – a hyena leaking milk from her swollen dugs, and a white horse leaping out of the window of her room behind her. The wildness and freedom of horses made them the creatures she identified with most closely, but she also returned to their bridling, taming, and even killing: her novel *Little Francis* describes how the heroine, abandoned by her lover, metamorphoses into a young horse – a colt – whose head is cut off in a solemn public ritual; Carrington also painted herself as a horse.

Leonora Carrington's stories throw important light on the development of the beast symbol in the literature of women, for women. Generally speaking, her beast represents the inner dynamic of desire, creativity, self-expression inside her heroines' spirits, which is so often crushed by conventional forces. In 'The Oval Lady', a story later dramatized for the stage as well as interpreted on canvas, Lucretia's father rages against her love of Tartarus, a rocking horse that comes alive, and eventually storms up to her nursery and strangles him. This force within, in the manner of post-Freudian optimism, is erotic in character: in the wake of early utopian revolutionaries, the Surrealists believed that the liberation of sexual energy would lead to wider freedom and fulfilment.

Meret Oppenheim was born in 1913 in Berlin, the daughter of a doctor who practised in Zurich and attended sessions at the Jung Institute in nearby Kusnach. He influenced his daughter to record her inner fantasies, waking and sleeping, in journals – a habit she kept most of her life; her grandmother wrote and illustrated a folk tale which is a children's classic in Switzerland. Thus Meret Oppenheim was raised in the German folklore tradition on the one hand and in the Jungian field of dream symbolism and archetype on the other; later, in Paris, she became part of the Surrealist circle and friends with Carrington and Ernst, amongst others. Her work reveals a richly imaginative use of the fabulous, continually questioning the relation of humanity and nature, of the cultivated and the wild, the tame and the savage, the tranquil and the violent. Some of her quick, nervous drawings of the 1930s also introduce herself in the persona of a child spectator, who confronts the horrific without flinching, as in a tiny, disturbing *esquisse*, *One Person Watching Another Dying*.

In 1935 she began consciously identifying with the protagonist of the story 'Genoveva'. Geneviève or Genoveva is the virtuous queen of a jealous king, who casts her out and orders a huntsman to kill her. He takes pity on her, and she lives on in the forest, in the wilds, and there bears the king a child, whom she calls Schmerzereich (Kingdom of Pain). At length, the king discovers her again, while out hunting one day, recognizes her true worth and takes her, and his son and heir, back again. Meret Oppenheim made a series of works inspired by the story, including a laconic poem, which opens, 'At Last! Freedom!' In it she describes how, after the birth of the baby, Genoveva swaddles him in her hair, since in her forest state that is all she has to clothe herself and her child.

Meret Oppenheim's *Le Déjeuner en fourrure* (The Fur Luncheon) of 1937 has become, rightly, one of the most celebrated objects of the Surrealist movement. The teacup and saucer and spoon of Chinese antelope hide wittily combine erotic innuendo, the outrageous and bristling inversions dear to Surrealist humour, and a deadpan comment on polite society's manners. It makes visible, with quite remarkable economy, the problematic presence of the wild in the civilized, the place of the animal in society, and the containment and ordering of female sexuality. It was not her first work to draw on the power of animal hair to unsettle and invite and amuse: her *Project for Sandals* of the preceding year consisted of a high-heeled shoe with a furry foot and toes; she also designed a pair of gloves, a highly comic, tingling, slightly sinister evocation of a bear or werewolf's paws, like the costume of Native American shamans. These fashion accessories, conceived in high spirits, act as a reminder, in a spirit of mischievous fairytale humour, of the Beast within.

But Oppenheim even surpassed her own achievement with the fur pieces in her most brilliantly achieved challenge to the conventions of fairy tale: *Ma Gouvernante, My Nurse, Mein Kindermädchen* of 1936 (Pl. 25). It too, like the *Fur Luncheon*, makes a tight visual pun on the twin themes of sex and food, but it also suggests another theme, through the connections of its title with its materials. For the sculpture shows a pair of white high-heeled shoes trussed on a dish, like a chicken, with butcher's frills on the heels. The shoes were purloined – to her fury – from Max Ernst's wife, Marie-Berthe Aurenche, and it is not impossible that Oppenheim was burying a protest at the thraldom Ernst exercised over his women. But the title directs the viewer in another direction. *Ma Gouvernante, My Nurse, Mein Kindermädchen* invokes the voices of the different women – governesses and nannies – who had told Meret stories when she was a little girl, maybe in three languages. These stories pointed to the future that lay in store for her: they prepared her to be a young woman, they introduced her to the idea of being handed over to the Beast, to that Other and his appetite. Hence the combination of the title with the bridal white shoes, which trussed and dished up offer another image of the female body apt to be consumed. Oppenheim was creating the piece in a spirit of revolt against the bourgeois expectations of her class and her time, and she saw in the white wedding a metaphor of virgin flesh surrendered, as in the dénouement of fairy tales in which the heroine escapes one kind of sexual ordeal for another, finds her way out of the woods into the kitchen and the bedroom. But she also rang a consummately witty change on the bridal hope chest with its warning images, using the recurrent fairytale image of the shoe.

Oppenheim was playing knowingly on this metonymy, substituting shoes for carnal knowledge. She was recognizing, with a certain mordancy, that the matched footwear leads to the true bride's recognition and thence to her wedding. The imagery of an ill-fitting shoe for an unhappy union has a long history: the Wife of Bath, admitting she took merciless revenge on her philandering fourth husband, says, 'in earth I was his purgatory ... he sat full oft and sung, / When that his shoe full bitterly him wrung'. Bruno Bettelheim analysed the symbolic substitutions in 'Cinderella', reading menstruation in the bleeding toes, the bleeding heels of the ugly sisters, and virginal prepubertal purity in the glass slipper. But the symbolism of footwear has also taken its place in the social language of ritual: in Judaism, for instance, when a man dies childless, and his widow does not wish to marry her husband's brother, and vice versa, thus going against the prescription of Levirate marriage, he may 'undo her shoe', that is, take off rather than put one on, in order to dissolve the bond and be free to marry elsewhere.

In *Ma Gouvernante*, Oppenheim, through the symbolism of a pair of shoes, proposed an acerbic gloss on the preconditions the fairytale bride has to fulfil; she began to reverse the terms of value, to reject the groomed beauty (the golden blonde) for the dishevelled beast she recognized and affirmed inside herself.

CHAPTER 23

The Silence of the Daughters: The Little Mermaid

I was in one hour an ashen crone
A fair-faced man, a fresh girl,
Floated on foam, flew with birds,
Under the wave dived, dead among fish,
And walked upon land a living soul.

Old English riddle

Geoffrey of Monmouth, in his *History of the Kings of Britain*, written around 1136, tells a familiar folk tale, known as 'Love Like Salt': an old and widowed king calls his three daughters to him and asks them how much they love him. The two older girls protest their undying love; they will love him till China and Africa meet, they will prize him as riches above pearls, above rubies, they will be true till the stars fall down, till salmon jump in the street. But the youngest, when it is her turn to speak, merely says she loves her father as meat loves salt. He feels himself slighted by this answer. It is an enigma, and he does not yet love

'The Wonder of Wonders': 'a Mermaid, that was seen and spoke with, on the Black Rock nigh Liverpool, by John Robinson, Mariner, who was tossed on the Ocean for six Days and Nights.' (Chapbook, eighteenth century.)

wisely enough to divine its meaning; his daughter is testing him with her wisdom, she is acting like a riddling figure of cryptic truth, a kind of Zen master who sets a *koan* and waits three-score years for the slow-witted acolyte to catch up and grasp it.

The daughter will not say anything more, she will not explain her mysterious simile, and the purblind king lets fly at her, casting her from him, disowning her altogether. He does not understand that the great passions can lock the tongue, that some thoughts lie too deep for words. Then, many years later, when he has himself been beggared by his elder children's treachery, and is wandering, alone, he chances upon a wedding feast; he goes in and sits down at the table. The bride notices him, and recognizes her father; he does not see that it is the daughter he lost. She gives an order to the servants: to serve all the food without salt. It arrives, and the guests taste it and push it aside; one by one they put down their cutlery and refuse to eat, crying out in disgust that the meat has no flavour. Then the old king realizes the meaning of his daughter's image of long ago, and he begins to cry.

The folk tale has a happy ending, unlike the tragedy of *King Lear*, which opens with the famous scene when Lear asks Cordelia how much she loves him. Her sisters have been effusive, but Cordelia, his youngest and most dear, does not answer her father's question. Lear presses her; he orders her to declare her love and allegiance to him:

> 'Now, our joy,
>
> Although our last and least ...
>
> Speak.'

And she answers, 'Nothing, my lord.'
He echoes, 'Nothing?'
And she repeats herself, again saying, 'Nothing.'
Lear retorts, 'Nothing will come of nothing.'
Some actors speak this as raillery, disbelieving, almost chaffing; other Lears rage already.

When Cordelia does begin to speak, she cannot talk of her love for her father before she has placed herself in relation to utterance itself:

> Unhappy that I am, I cannot heave my heart
> Into my mouth: I love your Majesty
> According to my bond; nor more nor less.

Lear urges her again, and she continues:

> Why have my sisters husbands, if they say
> They love you all? Happily, when I shall wed,
> That lord whose hands must take my plight shall carry
> Half my love with him, half my care and duty.
> Sure I shall never marry like my sisters,
> To love my father all.

With this eloquently measured dose of filial love, Cordelia refuses the empty show put on by her sisters, and the external trappings of loyalty Lear mistakes for truth; but she also formulates, with steady wisdom, the law of exogamy which qualifies the relationship of father and daughter and puts a term to its duration. But Lear does not accept it; he explodes, strips Cordelia of her birthright, banishes her, and forswears her. Later in the tragedy, amid all the fooling, the snatches of song, the babble of madness both real and feigned, and all the word-spill around Lear's disintegration, the figure of silent Cordelia haunts the king's memory, a figure of staunchness, love and truth.

Lear was produced the same year as *Pericles* (1608), and the troubling question of incestuous love and loss hangs over both plays. Cordelia's refusal to defend her speech is shocking, enigmatic, and the audience fears for her. But when Lear sentences her, he says, 'Let truth be thy dower ...', acknowledging, for all the irony of his bequest, that in her taciturnity she has retained a special lien on truthfulness. He too knows the ambiguities of silence – its latent virtue. As Shakespeare expresses it: 'The silence often of pure innocence / Persuades, when speaking fails.' Cordelia indeed shines out of Shakespeare's heroines as a pattern of womanly, and heroic, grace and devotion, of trueness of heart and unflinching goodness. Lear is reconciled to her, and at the end, when he finds her hanged, he keens over her body, saying,

> Her voice was ever soft,
> Gentle, and low, an excellent thing in woman.

The epitaph to Cordelia's perfections returns to the issue of her speech: what had been dumb insolence turns out to have been model honesty as well as modesty. Cordelia stands at the opposite pole of the garrulous old woman, the gossip; but simultaneously she represents the tale itself, operating according to the first convention of wonder, that it never offers an explanation, a rationale for the events and passions it recounts.

In *The Theme of Three Caskets* of 1912, Freud commented on the relationship between Cordelia and Cinderella:

> Cordelia makes herself unrecognizable, inconspicuous like lead (the lowest of metals), she remains dumb, she loves and is silent. Cinderella hides so that she cannot be found. We may perhaps be allowed to equate concealment and dumbness ...

Freud goes on to identify Cordelia/Cinderella with the Goddess of Death, herself disguised in the form of the goddess of love and beauty, and he concludes the short paper movingly with the words:

> It is in vain that an old man yearns for the love of woman as he had it first from his mother; the third of the Fates alone, the silent Goddess of Death, will take him into her arms.

We do not have to follow Freud that far in his identification with the figures of great and tragic old men, Lear and Oedipus, and perceive Anna Freud, his devoted daughter, in the role of his Cordelia and Antigone; we do not have to accept that Love and Beauty personified by a young girl shield the Goddess of Death, mortality itself; if we return to the cycle of stories from the point of view of the female protagonist, we can interpret the death of which Freud speaks metaphorically, and take it as the closure of a certain period in her life, her death to the past of her childhood. The child can protest that she loves her father all; but the wise young woman who has become aware of her eligibility and stands on the threshold of marriage knows that her bond to her father has limits; that husbands or lovers will take a measure of the love that in innocence she might have once given to her father.

In wordlessness lies sincerity; as a mute subject, Cordelia speaks from the heart, as even her name suggests. Words are lies – Hamlet, too, curses their fraudulence; he hears speech as 'promise-crammed' and knows it to be insubstantial as air; imagery is a counterfeit fabric deployed to deceive. This paradox of language torments Shakespeare's protagonists; it has long been a Neoplatonist conundrum, a snag in the fabric of literature itself, and one that continues to halt the hand of contemporary poets. Derek Walcott, for instance, yearns for 'a wide page without metaphors', a space of truth blank like the sea, in the very midst of a book-length poem, *Omeros*, itself of necessity a tissue of metaphors.

Shakespeare folded into the single figure of Cordelia in the opening scene several paragons of folklore who prove their virtue by their silence. This type of paragon in popular narrative seems to have begun as a boy, but since the middle ages, and in fairy tale and folklore today, the type is almost always a woman: sacrificial dumbness does not appear to be any longer as praiseworthy in a man or boy, and indeed the proverbial dummling of folklore, the simpleton, is not dumb, in the English sense of mute.

Unlike *King Lear*, the folk tale 'Love Like Salt' ends happily, with the survival of the reconciled father and his daughter. The motif of absence works both ways in this folk tale: the heroine does not trick out her sentiments with false words, but lacking salt, the ingredient that denotes integrity ('the salt of the earth'), aboriginal and unadulterated authenticity, love can have no flavour. Silence is not entirely absence, but another kind of presence; the trace of salt tastes not of itself, but enhances the life of another organism, of other matter. Cordelia's lack of words generates truth, as will be borne out in the course of the tragedy, in a way that outpourings like Goneril's and Regan's mask it. But is it that ideal area of truthfulness, the page beyond metaphors? Or does even silence, and in particular the silence of Cordelia and her sisters in muteness, whirr and hum? Do history and morals and values and prejudices interrupt the silence – 'interrupt' hardly being the *mot juste* – do they rather make up the silence? Is there something scrawled even on the page beyond metaphors, something ringing in the blankness of the heroine's true speech?

Cordelia protests her innocence before she leaves the stage; in this Shakespeare dramatizes her more realistically, less emblematically than her counterparts in folklore with whom he was familiar: the accused queens like Constance from Chaucer's 'Man of Lawe's Tale' or Patient Griselda, who bear with the false accusations and vicious punishments of their lords and masters uncomplainingly. Part of Donkeyskin's plight after her father's assault becomes silence: in her disfigurement, she never speaks again, in her own defence or to any other purpose, except to herself, in private. Before her transmutation and flight, she enunciated her horror of the proposed marriage, she made her three wishes for the magic dresses, and finally, demanded the donkeyskin itself. Once she has put it on, she becomes mute, and in her muteness, her fate recalls many other fairytale heroines who were defended by the stories told about them while they were scorned and degraded within them. The heroine who suffers wrongs in silence and is eventually triumphantly vindicated appears in two of the Grimm Brothers' tales, '*Die Zwölf Brüder*' (The Twelve Brothers), and '*Die Sechs Schwäne*' (The Six Swans); she figures in Hans Christian Andersen's version of the same tale, 'The Wild Swans', and in numerous later retellings from all over Europe and further afield.

In this fairy tale a girl child is born, and all her brothers – there are usually several of them – are immediately cursed: they either die or are turned into birds (right). When their sister discovers the horror her birth has brought about, she agrees to all manner of ordeals to restore them to life in human shape. The evil genius of the story, usually a wicked witch or other wardress, sets her sadistic tasks – spinning nettles with her bare hands to make them shirts and similar tortures – but one of the conditions of her brothers' redemption is always silence. She must not weep or laugh or speak until she has finished the appointed labour or her brothers will remain swans or ducks or dead or whatever for ever. At this point in the story, her beauty attracts a roaming king or prince who marries her in spite of her silence; the story then merges with the cycle of Cinderellas and Accused Queens, and the heroine becomes the victim of her mother-in-law, or other evil stepmother figure, who switches her newborn babies for whelps or worse monsters and brands her as a witch. The story often ends at the stake, with the heroine, still silent, spinning or knitting the last of the shirts for her brothers as the flames leap up, or the executioner prepares to toss her into the boiling oil, and the sound of wingbeats breaks over the scene, the brothers descend to save their sister, she throws her completed shirts over them – and they turn back into men. In the nick of time. She regains her voice, and, laughing and weeping, proclaims her innocence. Only one brother retains the wing of a bird, for she did not complete the last sleeve of the last shirt in time.

This rapid recension merges several different versions, but by and large this was the story which, when I was a child, was one of my favourites. Sometimes the woman at the centre of the story is the transformed men's mother, not their sister, and sometimes she does not escape the vindictiveness of the evil female nemesis; the latter usually receives great emphasis. But it still seemed to me to tell a story of female heroism, generosity, staunchness; I had no brothers, but I fantasized, at night, as I waited to go to sleep, that I had, perhaps even as many tall and handsome youths as the girl in the story, and that I would do something magnificent for them that would make them realize I was one of them, as it were, their equal in courage and determination and grace. Sewing was a skill my mother possessed – as did the nuns who taught the more nimble pupils at my school invisible mending – so it was easy to identify with the descriptions of the heroine's fingers as she spun the nettles or the thistles or the flax, whatever cruel stuff the witch insisted she used to weave for her brothers' shirts. Women's capacity for love and action tragically exceeded the permitted boundaries of their lives – this self-immolatory heroism was one of the few chivalrous enterprises open to them.

'The Twelve Brothers', in the Grimms' *Kinder-und Hausmärchen,* was taken down by them from the sisters Julia and Charlotte Ramus, friends in Kassel; the tale of 'The Six Swans', which resembles 'The Twelve Brothers' in many ways, was passed on to the Grimms by Dortchen Wild. Many of the tales the brothers collected were transcribed in the Low German of the vernacular. Such a dialect – now almost died out – belongs intrinsically to precise locales and domestic milieux; it is a language of private life, of women and children – and of men, too, in their homes – of people when they are living and working together in the

'Hardly had she plucked the flowers when her brothers were turned into twelve ravens ...'
The youngest child, the little sister, who causes such disaster to fall on her brothers, proves her love through a vow of silence. (H. J. Ford, 'The Twelve Brothers', in Andrew Lang, The Red Fairy Book, *London, 1890.)*

economic unit of the family. Though the Grimms – Wilhelm especially – selected, edited, combined and buffed the published tales, it is not farfetched still to catch from the stories the female voices of one generation raised to instruct the next, stressing different qualities for boys and girls.

The proper housewife from the propaganda prints of the Reformation who wears a padlock on her lips still hovers in the tales as the model heroine. But the ideal was not restricted to German fairytale circles. Mme de Beaumont had earlier included in one of her collections for young people a story about a wife ('*de basse condition*' – of the lower orders) who was continually beaten by her husband. She goes to find help from a neighbour, reputed locally to be a wise woman, maybe even a witch. The old woman listens, and gives her a remedy: a jug of water, which she puts on the table and makes three turns around, and then sprinkles with salt. When her husband comes home, she must take a swallow, keep the water in her mouth. 'As long as you've got it in your mouth,' she says, 'I promise you that your husband will not beat you.' At the end of eight days, when she has not been beaten and the jug is empty, the wife goes back to the witch, for she is now convinced that she has marvellous powers, and the old woman tells her that the water was just plain water, and that all she need do, if her husband comes home drunk and raging, is not to heap reproaches on him, but to keep quiet, as if she had water in her mouth. 'And you will see, his anger will pass.' The story ends with the reform of the husband: the implication being that her bitter tongue had spurred him on in his bad habits.

Ruth Bottigheimer, in her study of the Grimms' fairy tales, *Bad Girls and Bold Boys*, has analysed the speech patterns of female heroines and villains, and found that, as the editing progressed, virtue spoke up less and less, while villainy became more loquacious, with the witches and wicked stepmothers far surpassing other women in articulacy. The equation of silence with virtue, of forbearance with femininity, does not only hold up an entrancing ideal of loving self-abnegation, harmony and wisdom; as transmitted in fairy tales told to children, the ideal also meets certain particular socio-cultural requirements of family equilibrium in the climate of early nineteenth-century Germany which persist as desiderata. It is a paradox frequently encountered in any account of women's education that the very women who pass on the legacy are transgressing against the burden of its lessons as they do so; that they are flouting, in the act of speaking and teaching, the strictures against female authority they impart: women narrators, extolling the magic silence of the heroic sister in 'The Twelve Brothers', are speaking themselves, breaking the silence, telling a story.

The cruel dealings of masters and mistresses in the tales possibly encrypt known procedures of authority at different stages in history; the bleeding fingers of the heroine at her endless task would not jar for instance on the ears of an audience of textile workers in the Huguenot community of Hesse, of which Kassel was the capital. Similarly, the patience and perseverance of the heroine under the injunction to silence acquires a different patina when one thinks oneself into the circumstances in which disadvantaged workers were struggling for their livelihood. Silence could be a stratagem of survival for women; men in fairy tales are often cheeky and cunning and high-spirited (women are too, sometimes), but keeping your head well down – 'layin' low and sayin' nuffin' as the English motto goes – has been an immemorial survival technique of the groundlings – of the powerless. As the Irish graffito puts it: 'Whatever you say, say nothing.' The silence of the heroine presents as heroic a common, defeatist response which the audience listening to such a tale would perhaps recognize as one of the few paths open to them. With the essential heroic optimism of fairy tale as a genre, the story snatches victory from the jaws of defeat, eloquent vindication from the sentence of silence, triumph from the degradation of voicelessness.

Mutiny can be conveyed in silence: the military crime of dumb insolence. The journey fairy tales and other stories have taken, from confidential gossipings around women's beds or in their work rooms to the open circulation of the printed book, has in itself breached the secrecy of some of the contents. The private injunctions, the *sotto voce* warnings, the intimate exchange of experience have been brought into full public view. In one sense, and one sense only, the mutism of fairytale heroines indeed forms a defensive strategy. 'A proverb,' wrote Walter Benjamin, '… is a ruin which stands on the site of an old story and in which a moral twines about a happening like ivy around a wall.' Discretion as the better part of valour stands on the ruins of tales about the powerless paradoxically grasping that speechlessness can be their only strong line of defence. When he is not jesting, the Fool puts his finger to his lips.

But this very speechlessness can also intersect with the desires of the more powerful; the desirability of silence, or at least reticence, and of women's silence in particular, lies enmeshed in a web of other ideal criteria held up for the sex, as was discussed earlier. It is even possible that an additional, buried reason for the vanishing mothers of fairy tale is that perfection in a woman entails exemplary silence and self-effacement – to the point of actually disappearing out of the text.

The more loquacious a (female) character in popular culture, the more likely she is to be up to no good. Curiosity was a characteristic Plutarch lambasted in the

Moralia, immediately following his diatribe against Garrulity; he recommended the example of Pythagoras, who had taken a vow of silence for five years. These ancient moral and philosophical arguments have had a hard time dying. Sometimes, a contemporary story will reverse received values, with conscious irony, as in the fine film, based on the life of Anja Rosmus, significantly called *The Nasty Girl*, about a schoolchild in post-war Germany who will not be quiet until she has found out what went on in her calm and perfect home town Passau during the Nazi period. This bad girl, like Red Riding Hood, like Goldilocks, is impelled by curiosity to enter forbidden territory; but her trespass is not reproved by the narrative, though it was fiercely opposed – and she was punished – by characters in the story who wanted to keep silent and wanted her to follow their example. In refusing, she flouted deep strictures on female behaviour.

II

The beautiful and virtuous sister saves her brothers by her toil and sacrifice; the Little Mermaid, in the famous fairy tale by Hans Christian Andersen, saves her beloved prince from death by drowning, and then, yearning to acquire an immortal soul like a human and win his love as one of his own kind, maybe even his equal, she exchanges her siren's voice for human form. In 'The Twelve Brothers' and its analogous tales, the offering of silence redeems another – or several others – from the zoomorphic enchantment which binds them, as in tales of Beauty and the Beast. In 'The Little Mermaid', the diabolical bargain requires that the heroine lose her tongue for ever in return for human shape and life on earth. Andersen elaborated his disturbing story in 1836–7, from varied strands of oral and written tales in Eastern as well as Western tradition, about undines and selkies, nixies, Loreleis and Mélusines, in which the fairy creature appears on earth and stays with a mortal as his bride only on certain conditions. The story of 'Julnar the Sea-born' in *The Arabian Nights* opens with the motif of the mysterious silent bride who comes from the sea; La Motte Fouqué's earlier German fairy story 'Undine' (1811) – in which a man loses his heart to a mermaid – also partly inspired Maurice Maeterlinck's poetic drama *Pelléas and Mélisande* to which Debussy wrote the music in his opera, begun in 1893. A few years later, Jaroslav Kvapil wrote the libretto for Dvořák's powerful, lyrical opera *Rusalka* (1901), which also tragically unfolds the cost of silence: the selkie, *Rusalka*, loses the love of her prince to the human princess who can speak (and sing). When he becomes bored with her, and rejects her, the conditions of the bargain she made begin inexorably to work: she becomes outcast from both earth and water, and can survive

'She came now to a big, slimy clearing in the forest, where big, fat water-snakes romped about and showed their nasty, whitish-yellow bellies ... There sat the sea-witch and let a toad eat out of her mouth, just the way humans let a little canary eat sugar.' (J. Leech, in Hans Christian Andersen, 'The Little Mermaid', London, 1846.)

only if she kills her beloved. She refuses; when he comes to find her again, he insists on a kiss, which deals him his death wound. Rusalka's beauty is fatal, in the tradition of opera; Mélisande, her predecessor in the Debussy, is found by water and will not speak of her enigmatic origin or past, and throughout her mysterious short life she is connected with wells, pools and watery depths around the gloomy moated castle of her husband Golaud. Both continue to refract legends of the siren's fatal attraction through the prism of Symbolist and decadent worship of Woman. But like one of her story's sources, the medieval legend of Mélusine, the Little Mermaid is a fairy queen, an enchantress who lives in a magical elsewhere (in her case under the sea, in the Sibyl's or Venus's case inside the mountain) whence she beckons to her lovers to enter her paradise.

Andersen's powerful, morbid tale helped establish his fame – in 1913, the city of Copenhagen commissioned the bronze statue that has become the Danish national monument. But his telling it specifically for children changes its character, intensifying its moral preachiness about feminine love and duty, self-sacrifice and expiation. The very first illustration done, by J. Leech, for the English translation of 1846, showed the mermaid's visit to the Sea Witch (above). Andersen relates the episode with the affectless, matter-of-fact tone that has come to seem a hallmark of the children's fairy tale. The Little Mermaid has asked the Sea Witch to help her:

> 'But then you must pay me too!' said the witch, 'and it is no small price I ask. You have the loveliest voice of all down here at the bottom of the sea, and you think you will be able to enchant him with it all right, but your voice is just what you have to give me … Come, stick out your little tongue so that I can cut if off for my payment, and then you shall have my powerful potion!'

Sister to Philomel, and to Lavinia from *Titus Andronicus*, and to other raped and mutilated figures of myth and tragedy, the silenced mermaid of Hans Andersen instantly became an approved and much-loved nursery character. In the Andersen version, her transformation into a human girl brings her explicit pain: the witch tells her: 'your tail will part and shrink into what humans call nice legs but it will hurt just as if a sharp sword were passing through you … every step you take will be like treading on a knife sharp enough to cause your blood to flow'. When she dallies with the prince later, her new feet bleed; some of his attendants notice, but he does not, and she does not complain, of course, not even in sign language. At the end, the mermaid's sisters cut off their magically beautiful hair to give to the Sea Witch in return for a sword which, when used to kill the prince, will restore the Little Mermaid to her original form and to safety in the sea once again. But she refuses to turn against him, and instead throws herself, her heart breaking, into the 'deadly cold sea foam' and dissolves into air.

Andersen's story brings quick tears, but not in any pleasurable way, as it seems to gloat on the morbid outcome. The story's chilling message is that cutting out your tongue is still not enough. To be saved, more is required: self-obliteration, dissolution. Unlike Philomel, who metamorphoses into a nightingale, so that out of dumbness may come forth strength and sweetness, the Little Mermaid sacrifices her song to no avail – except for the story which keeps faith with her memory. Her siren song condenses all inherited belief in women's sexual powers; the Little Mermaid surrenders them when she becomes bifurcated and bleeds, as if, once the innocence of childhood has passed, that very sexuality turns against its possessor and makes the young woman herself a victim. David Pountney's imaginative, intense production of *Rusalka* for the English National Opera (1983) insisted on this underlying story with piercing contrasts of dazzling white and blood-red in the costumes and décor. Neither in *Rusalka* nor in Andersen can reconciliation be achieved, contrary to the characteristic upbeat conclusion of the fairy tale. The mermaid's seductiveness remains under interdiction; the only redemption death through self-sacrifice.

Homer calls the sirens' song 'liquid' and says that anyone who listens to them will be lost, so Circe gives Odysseus practical advice, and he makes his men stop up their ears with wax so that they cannot hear them. He has himself tied to the mast, and when he signals, frowning, that he wants to be unbound so that he can join the sirens, his deaf men cannot hear his pleas and go on rowing. The end the sirens bring is not identified as fatal pleasure in Homer, though in Christian Europe the passage has been read with these (sexual) overtones. The content of the song is knowledge, the threefold wisdom possessed by beings who are not subject to time: knowledge of the past, of the present, and of the future. Cicero stressed this, introducing the sirens into his argument that the human mind naturally thirsts after knowledge. 'It was the passion for learning,' he strives to persuade his audience, 'that kept men rooted to sirens' rocky shores.' He then went on to give a free verse translation of the Homeric episode into Latin. From their flowery meadow by the sea the sirens sing to Odysseus: 'We have foreknowledge of all that is going to happen on this fruitful earth.' It is for this the hero struggles to join them, not for their personal charms. Yet, however promising that sounds, it means that they can give warning of disaster, too, and their meadow is strewn with the mouldering remains of their prey. Cicero, in the transmission of sirens' mythology, failed to prevail over the more popular, Christian folklore portraying them as *femmes fatales*.

The names of the sirens in different traditions are often connected to speech in some way – this is the era before writing was common practice. Aglaophonos (Lovely Voice), Ligeia (Shrill), Molpe (Music), Thelxepeia (Spellbinding Words), Thelxiope (Enchanting Face), implying lullabies and scoldings and confidences and persuasion, a taxonomy of oral rhetoric which must indeed have drawn the hero of the *Odyssey*, himself no slouch at wordsmithery. And, as voices, Homer's irresistible sirens are bird-bodied, as are enchanted musicians of one kind or another the world over since, until sonic devices could record the conversations of dolphin, birdsong was nature's only voiced chorus. But they live by the sea and lure sailors; they are amphibious, and have birds' claws as well as wings, and women's faces with two feathers for a diadem on their brows. Hybrid between worlds in more ways than one, they ceaselessly seek connection, turning their faces and their calls outwards, to bring others to them. Like the enchantress who lures knights into her grotto, they beckon. Some say they have 'hungry', even 'starving' faces as they wait for their prey, but this may have passed from folklore

Sirens as songbirds tempt Odysseus, tied to the mast: 'Draw near,' they sang, 'illustrious Odysseus ... No seaman ever sailed in his black ship past this spot without listening to the sweet tones that flow from our lips, and none that listened has not been delighted and gone on a wiser man.' (Attic red-figured jar, Vulci, c. 480 BC.)

about Harpies. They can no longer fly, however, because the Muses stole their pinions for their own crowns. But this must be a later legend, as on a famous Greek pot in the British Museum the sirens appear plummeting and swimming around Odysseus' galley, like ospreys after fish (above). Sometimes they stand like court musicians called in to sing and play at a nobleman's banquet.

Ovid tells the story that the sirens in their former incarnation were Persephone's friends, so distressed when she was abducted that they prayed to be given wings to search for her over the seas, and were granted their wish by the gods, finding golden plumage growing all over their bodies except their faces. In the form of bird-women, they are often confused with the Harpies, through their bird-like hybridity and their association, on funerary monuments, with the rituals of death. But this is a mistake. The sirens carried mortals to the underworld, the place where all is indeed known, though by then nothing can be done about it, and knowledge has become futile, even bitter. Surviving vessels and carvings show enigmatically smiling women with stiff braided hair bearing the souls of the dead in their feathered arms in the form of small human beings; they sometimes carry the corpse on their backs, where it can seem an Icarus bound to a flying machine, giant classical hang-glider, or they clasp the tiny bodies tenderly to their plump pigeon breasts, and row with their wings upwards. In one embrace, the siren appears to be steadying the inertly dangling legs of the dead mortal (a woman, too) with her bird claws. There is no suggestion in such artefacts that this classical order of angels seize the dead like prey, in the way of the filthy, vindictive, greedy and foul monsters of the storm in the *Iliad*, whose name, Harpy, means snatcher. Such sculptures of the sirens' role suggest that death is but a sleep, and the deceased pillow themselves languidly on their aerial psychopomps in their voyage to the beyond – Hypnos, in Homer, brother of Thanatos, and winged, too, like the sirens. Later sarcophagi from Magna Graecia from the third century BC show the souls of the dead similarly clinging to the sirens who are ferrying them across the river dividing the earth from the Isles of the Blessed – the journey to the other side is no flight, but a watery passage.

But the sirens above all possess 'utmost music', these web-footed, hybrid women were mouthpieces for others' stories. The dead pleaded with the sirens, their companions on the other side, to sing for them:

> My gravestones, and sirens, and you, pain-bringing urn
> that holds the paltry ashes which belong to Hades,
> Give greeting to those who pass beside my mound,
> Whether they are native or of another city …
> Tell them, I went into the tomb a bride …

So said the verses written by Erinna in memory of Baucis in the late fourth century BC: a poem which imagines the farewell of a girl who died young. Speaking in her voice, the poem invokes the keepers of her memory: the funerary monuments themselves and their allies in this task, the mythic birds who can negotiate the passage between the land of the living and the land of the dead. That passage is enduring knowledge, the memory of storytelling. In the poem, the sirens, as vocal muses of death, replicate the medium of the epitaph and the poem itself. The sirens are to speak for the dead girl, and this is of course what Erinna the poet is herself doing. The Muses robbed the sirens of their wing tips in the later legend because they are sister spirits, both of them voices caught by the ear and internalized by the poet who has heard them.

The Greeks were ambivalent about the sirens' song because they both feared and valued 'things that come into the mind'. As Ruth Padel writes:

Innards can be damaged by what comes in through sight and hearing, wounded by emotion. But 'what comes in' also stimulates, and gives innards skill and power. The innards' vulnerability is precious, and makes them a source of power and knowledge. 'What comes in' moves them.

Passion and poetry: bane and boon. The anxiety about word-music and its lure – the fear of seductive speech – changes character and temper down the centuries, but the sirens' reputation does not improve. Their connection with carnal danger, with moral breakdown, with potent fictions, with bewitchment, deepens, and, under the influence of the rich Northern mythology about undines and selkies, mermaids and sea-nymphs, they shed their relation to wisdom and retained only their oneness with sex and death – though knowledge of these is a form of wisdom. 'You who are living think about it now,' warns one from the wall of a house in Saint Rémy. 'Is your end going to be heaven, or hell without end?'

The middle ages still remembered the sirens' bird-likeness: the *Hortus deliciarum* follows the imagery on Greek vases when it depicts Odysseus' boat attacked by birds like sea eagles. In Christian interpretations, the encounter became an allegory of the soul's struggle with vice – a Psychomachia.

In 1819, the French inventor Cagniard de la Tour called an instrument which emitted sweet high sounds at a measurable frequency a *sirène*, and his invention was adapted half a century later to ships' foghorns and mineworkings. The name 'siren' stuck and passed into usage for machines which warn by giving voice to the presence of danger. The usage follows the implications of the classical story of the sirens' fatefulness, but reverses it: in Homer, the sirens lure hapless sailors on to the rocks with their song, whereas the sirens of the modern world call out in order to save ships, miners, passing cars and pedestrians from peril. The baying of police cars, the wail of air-raid warnings, the lowing of buoys, the frenzied tolling of fire engines, the screech of the vehicles winking and lapping at the scene of an accident do not make liquid music in quite the way Odysseus heard. But they do signal the dangers of an ordinary life: 'Sirens … tell them, I went into the tomb a bride … .'

III

The Homeric fantasy that the siren brings death finds echoes in Andersen's morbid reversal at the end of 'The Little Mermaid' when the heroine dies; to defeat death by sexual surrender, he himself deals death to the principle of desire. The marvellous kindles appetites – to know, to live, to experience – but that very principle of wonder, which drives the story, is crushed by its outcome. The recent film of the fairy tale, produced by the Walt Disney Corporation, has entered the ranks – alongside other Disney classics like *Snow White* and, now, *Beauty and the Beast* – of the most popular films ever made for children. The writer-directors John Musker and Ron Clements adapted the story to suit present sensibilities – giving the story a last-minute happy ending, above all. The issue of female desire dominates the film, and may account for its tremendous popularity among little girls: the verb 'want' falls from the lips of Ariel, the Little Mermaid, more often than any other – until her tongue is cut out.

The Sea Witch, much the most successful creation of the film in graphic terms, expresses the shadow side of this desiring, rampant lust; an undulating, obese octopus, with a raddled bar-queen face out of Toulouse-Lautrec and torso and tentacles sheathed in black velvet, she is a cartoon Queen of the Night, avid and unrestrained, what the English poet Ted Hughes might call 'a uterus on the loose'. Marine forms, like octopus and polyps, have prompted fantasies of female genitalia, as we saw in the case of the double-tailed siren on the Otranto pavement. Freud made explicit the association with Medusa's tentacular hair (*Méduse* is French for jellyfish), as the poet Paul Valéry made clear in a magnificent and ferocious passage of prose-poetry written in the 1930s. Inspired by seeing a film of jellyfish, Valéry conjures a pneumatic, invertebrate, fluid world (not unlike the plastic ideal of the Disney studio):

Point de solides, non plus, dans leurs corps de cristal élastique, point d'os, point d'articulations, de liaisons invariables, de segments que l'on puisse compter …

Jamais danseuse humaine, femme échauffée, ivre de mouvement, du poison de ses forces excédées, de la présence ardente de regards chargés de désir, n'exprima l'offrande impérieuse du sexe, l'appel mimique du besoin de prostitution, comme cette grande Méduse, qui, par saccades ondulatoires de son flot de jupes festonnées, qu'elle trousse et retrousse avec une étrange et impudique insistance, se transforme en songe d'Eros; et tout à coup, rejetant tous ses falbalas vibratiles, ses robes de lèvres découpées, se renverse et s'expose, furieusement ouverte.

[No solids, either, in their bodies of crystalline elastic, no bones, no joints, or unchanging attachments, or segments which can be counted …

No human dancer, no woman overheated and drunken with motion, with the toxic charge of her overextended energies, with the burning proximity of looks loaded with desire, ever conveyed so imperiously the offering of her sex, that beckoning pantomine of compulsive prostitution, as this great jellyfish who, by undulating shakes of her train of ruffled skirts, which she tosses up and tosses up again with strange and shameless insistence, transforms herself into a dream of Eros and suddenly, throwing aside all her vibrating petticoats, her dress of cut-out lips, turns herself upside down and exposes herself, terribly open.]

In the Andersen tale, the Sea Witch, an ancient bawd in direct line of Charite's or Juliet's nurse, bequeaths mature human sexuality on the young mermaid (dividing her legs) in return for her voice. In the Disney cartoon, she then imprisons the siren's lovely voice in a shell around her neck, and uses it to enthral the prince and usurp the Little Mermaid's place as his bride. It is voice, in the last analysis, that is more powerful than beauty – or even goodness. Only when the shell shatters and the Little Mermaid's voice is spirited back into her throat does she prevail and win – in this version – human shape and the love of the prince.

The sugary, luscious graphics of the animation, especially where the heroine is concerned, spoil the humour and high spirits of the Disney film as a whole, but the altered structure of the tale, doubtless produced after hours of script discussion and audience research, offers an illuminating angle of vision on current attitudes to gender. The seductiveness of women's tongues still seems a paramount issue in the exercise of their sexuality; directing its force, containing its magic, is still very much to the point. Female eloquence, the siren's song, is not presented as fatal any longer, unless it rises in the wrong place and is aimed at the wrong target. Romance constitutes the ultimate redemption, and romantic love, personified by the prince, the justification of desire. The Little Mermaid, in the film, defies her father the God of the Sea to follow the dictates of her heart; like Cordelia, this modern paragon of the animated film speaks of her bond – but whereas Cordelia halved her love and duty between her father and her husband, the modern mermaid, like Madonna in the song 'Pappa, don't preach', teaches her father to listen to her desire: to love her man. This is the contemporary audience desire encapsulated; the message the circle of listeners wanted to hear. Like Belle, the Disney Little Mermaid Ariel is a fairytale heroine of our time. She now comes as a kind of Sindy doll, with various costumes: calypso ruffles as well as the more regulation shiny aqua sheath. She has red hair down to well below her fishtail; this compelling fetish of today's toybox can be groomed and dressed – comb and mirror are provided.

Beyond this mermaid's call of love, however, rings of silence keep spreading out, whirring. The muteness of fairytale protagonists exists in relation to the circumstances in which they are told; there is always a meaning, a lesson. Sometimes the narrative contradicts tales of heroic mutism, or tragic self-immolation in dumbness, and they break the silence. In the tale of Sir Gawain's marriage to the Loathly Lady, the most inspiring medieval Beauty and the Beast story, in which the sexes are reversed, the woman who has been bound by a spell cannot speak the truth of her state, and must wait for a true knight to release her – as Gawain does when he marries her and learns her secret, that she must be a loathly monster either by day or by night. She puts a riddle to him – she is another princess trapped in a riddle – and he answers it correctly, and breaks the spell, finding in his arms the most beautiful creature that there ever was. What she asks is the same question a baffled Freud would put, later: 'What is it women really want?' The knight says: 'Sovereignty'.

Contemporary women writers have been attracted by the figure of the silent heroine who has not been enchanted, or taken a vow of silence, but just does not know how to speak or to laugh or to cry. Angela Carter picked up the ancient motif in *The Magic Toyshop*, in which the lovely Aunt Margaret, wife of the maleficent toyshop owner, is choked by a silver collar her husband has fastened round her neck; the plot obeys the fairytale function of dispelling silence, of releasing the laughter of hope and pleasure. When the puppet master's powers are broken, Aunt Margaret is able to take off the silver choker and speak and sing again. In Jane Campion's recent film *The Piano*, her romantic heroine Ada is mute; she is also unresponsive, taut with restrictions and unexpressed anger; the film contains multi-layered references to fairy tales, and this must be a consciously adopted motif. 'Bluebeard' is much quoted in the course of the story, and Ada's husband even chops off one of her fingers, mutilating her in jealous rage like so many frustrated and desiring patriarchs in the traditional tales.

The film's grandiloquent first scene shows Ada sheltering on a stormy beach under a makeshift tent made of her elaborate boned and beribboned stays and petticoats. Beside her, and her small daughter, the piano stands on the beach, a weighty symbol of her inner voice. She tells us, 'The strange thing is I don't think myself silent, that is, because of my piano.' From this extraordinary and atmospheric start, Campion establishes her twin motifs of repression and rebellion: Ada resists and overcomes her constricted fate by her refusal to acquiesce, symbolized by her muteness. It makes no difference to her prospective husband that she cannot speak. She tells us he has written to her that God loves dumb creatures, so why not he! He has mistaken her for the Good Wife of Lustucru's smithy, who cannot answer back. Her dumbness, even while marking out her singularity, represents her strangulated, muted, diminished state. Ada communicates through the music she makes; but the piano also embodies, like the underwear, the encumbrances of Victorian femininity. This is the voice Ada is allowed – a parlour skill (and parlour comes from *parler*, to speak). In the film's dream-like climax, she slips her foot into the noose of the rope attached to the piano, as it is being shipped, and is dragged overboard and underwater and nearly drowned: she nearly hugs her prison cell to her, as it were, but finds the energy to release herself at the very last moment. In the happy ending she is living with her lover, and tells us, 'I am learning to speak.'

The elemental union between the mute heroine and the watery wastes which first give birth to her, as it were, when she appears on the pounded beach, and which almost reclaim her, places *The Piano* – consciously or unconsciously on Campion's part – within the body of mermaid legends to which both Mélisande and the Little Mermaid belong. The siren embodies, in her fascination, the configuration of voice, fate and eros; in classical myth she threatens loss of identity to her victims, and in the fairy tales she is herself erased when she wants to leap out of her in-between-ness and become a full human being. Mélisande dies in childbirth, the Little Mermaid dissolves into spume. But in *The Piano*, she survives, she begins to speak, falteringly ('my sounds are so bad'), and though some critics have baulked at this rampantly romantic resolution, it follows in the tradition of revolt some women interpreters have shown to the prescriptions on virtue in fairy tales, and their advocacy of the virtue of silence.

It is not possible to pinpoint the moment or the place when and where the fish-tailed mermaid becomes conflated with the bird-bodied siren of Greek myth, but the fusion was made possible by both creatures' command of voice, by their siren song. In the Angers tapestry, from the thirteenth century, an emblematic enchantress like the Whore of Babylon has been given Aphrodite's traditional comb and mirror (Pl. 18) – these pass swiftly to the mermaid as emblems of her irresistible form. The long hair which the mermaid combs out has been bequeathed to her by Venus, too, who traditionally rises from the sea and wrings out her long hair. But the mermaid's hair also represents the toils in which she ensnares her prey, as well as the flowing abundance of her appetites, and it bears an interesting, complex relation both to voice and to water.

The morphological echo between waves, between the motion of water and of hair, between the varieties of wave, of comber, of rill and curl, was famously explored by Leonardo in his notebook drawings; but the aural affinity between the element of water and the flow of a song, between the sea and music (sound-waves), determines the character of the siren in nineteenth- and twentieth-century fairy tales. The imagination's response to the coupled figure hair/voice stirs memories of water, and, with water, of bliss of erotic engulfment, oceanic floating: Debussy's music soars to raptures when Pelléas wraps himself in Mélisande's tumbling tresses, which she has let down from the window of her bedroom. Invoking her *'chevelure'*, he strokes it and kisses it to a passionate sere-nade: a climactic moment in the turn of the century's love affair with swirling eddies of women's hair. This commingling of the lovers' bodies, mediated through Mélisande's hair, is seen by the jealous Golaud and leads to tragedy for them all.

But the coupled image of voice and water also connects with another face of bliss, which may also have its being outside history, in the memory of the haven of the womb, and in the first sounds of the mother's voice, that acoustic mirror. Fairy tales attempt to restore its resonance; they pretend to a world of nursery cer-tainties. But they also often record that voice's obliteration, and never more so than in the tales of silenced mermaids. The anxiety about word-music and its lure – the fear of erasure by the sirens' spell – changes character and temper down the centuries, but the stories, in the midst of celebrating their heroines and mourning their tragic fates, also often mete out punishment to them for their enchantments. The situation of engulfment and loss is reversed, and the sirens, who threaten entanglement and erasure, are themselves done away with. In Andersen's 'The Little Mermaid', her sisters want to save her, and they cut off their hair and give it to the Sea Witch, begging for their sister's restoration in exchange; they plead for her voice with their hair:

> Out of the sea rose her sisters, but the wind could no longer play with their long beautiful hair, for their heads had been shorn.
> 'We have given our hair to the sea-witch, so that she would help you and you would not have to die this night ... Our grandmother mourns; she, too, has no hair; hers has fallen out from grief ...'

But the Sea Witch determines that the Little Mermaid must plunge a knife into the heart of the prince in order to be turned back into a mermaid, and she refuses. Here, hair stands for life itself, and a surrogate for voice, with its connections to seduction and to love. In *The Piano*, too, Ada's muteness is all of a piece with her scraped-back hair. The body's mythopoeic potency does not generate a set of immutable symbols, embedded in an unchanging structure of the imagination. The changes to the siren's voice alter the meanings she conveys; the social context of the story in which she figures, eloquent or silent, modifies the message. But natural symbols, as Mary Douglas has analysed, form a structure of relationships within which changes are rung in endless permutations. The body offers as it were an alphabet, or an eight-note scale, and the patterns of arrangement, though almost infinite, cluster in recognizable groups and figures, like chords, like certain syntagms in language. Fairy tales are of course only one form of narrative that has tackled the all-absorbing issue of sexual attraction, but they have constantly cast and recast the question of the love spell, and looked again and again at the beloved, and how she survives – her silencing, among other trials.

Holding a pomegranate in one hand, and pipes in the other, a bird Siren in the shape of a vial for precious oils, gives support to the shade of a man on his last journey: will her song keep his memory? (Bronze, Southern Italy, 450–400 BC.)

Conclusion

'Odysseus,' said Alcinous, 'we are far from regarding
you as one of those impostors and humbugs whom this dark world
brings forth in such profusion to spin their lying yarns
which nobody can test ...'

Homer

The tea is poured, the stitching put down.
The child grows still, sensing something of importance.
The woman settles and begins her story.

Believe it, what we lost is here in this room
on this veiled evening ...

Eavan Boland

Like a standup comedian, the tale must sense the aspirations and prejudices, the fears and hunger of its audience; like seaside pier palm-readers, fairystory-tellers know that a tale, if it is to enthral, must move the listeners to pleasure, laughter or tears; if they fail in this, nobody will want to hear their stories any more. The genre's need of an audience forces the teller to enter that audience's economy of beliefs; the memory of its oral origin makes fairy tale long to please. The sultan is always there, half asleep, but quite awake enough to rouse himself and remember that death sentence he threatened. In the kingdom of fiction, the tension between speaking out and staying silent never eases.

The voice of the traditional storyteller, negotiating the audience's inclination, may well entrench bigotry, if that is what is expected: how thrilling is the wicked queen; she loves her face in the looking-glass; let her dance in red-hot shoes. The contrary directions of the genre, towards acquiescence on the one hand and rebellion on the other, are all of a piece with its fabulism, intrinsic to its role of moral arbitration and soothsaying. Because the teller struggles to locate and find an audience who will receive the stories' message with favour, children emerge as hearers, established in printed literature as the special audience by the mid-eighteenth century: they are still, in the lucrative market of mass entertainment that draws on fairytale material. Children are not likely to be committed to a certain way of thought; they can be moulded, and the stories they hear will then become the ones they expect. They do not present the same problem as the adult circle, at the *veillée* or in the preview film theatre, who might shuffle or heckle or boo.

Fairy tales often engage with issues of light and darkness - the plots represent struggles to distinguish enemies from friends, the normal from the monstrous, and the slant they take is by no means always enlightened. The tales often demonize others in order to proclaim the side of the teller good, right, powerful - and beautiful. Fairy tale's simple, even simplistic dualism can be and has been annexed to ugly ends: the Romantic revival of folk literature in Germany unwittingly heralded the Nazi claim that 'their' fairy tales were racially Aryan homegrown products; in former Yugoslavia, the different factions are using folklore as one more weapon in their civil strife, raising heroes from the past, singing old ballads as battle cries, performing folk dances to a cacophony of competing regional music. Folk tales powerfully shape national memory; their poetic versions intersect with history, and in the contemporary embattled quest for indigenous identity, underestimating their sway over values and attitudes can be as dangerous as ignoring changing historical realities.

But vernacular culture is multiple, many-throated and remarkably robust in its resistance to state propaganda, and less brutal nationalist passions than those raging today have also drawn inspiration from folk culture in all media, as in opera (Prokofiev's *The Love for Three Oranges*, Puccini's *La Wally*), in ballet (Tchaikovsky's *Nutcracker Suite*, and original Ballets Russes productions – Stravinsky's *Firebird* and *Petrouchka*); in film (Walerian Borowczyk's *Blanche*, 1971, drew on the novel *Mazeppa* by the great Polish Romantic nationalist Juliusz Slowacki); in poetry Wordsworth and Coleridge's *Lyrical Ballads* looked to traditional people's songs, in the midst of heralding a revolutionary age; even a fiction as ironically poised and cosmopolitan as Milan Kundera's *The Book of Laughter and Forgetting* contains committed passages about local Moravian music, rituals and stories, while his first novel, *The Joke*, bears a relation to Middle European *Schwankmärchen*, or jesting tales, about foxes outfoxed – then foxed again. The very territory of popular, anonymous storytelling has proved an arena of resistance to tyranny, as well as a site of reconciliation and reversal for ostracized and condemned figures. Storytelling can act to face the objects of derision or fear and sometimes – not always - inspire tolerance and even fellow-feeling; it can realign allegiances and remap terrors. Storytellers can also break through the limits of permitted thought to challenge conventions; fairy tales, I have argued in this book, offer a way of putting questions, of testing the structure as well as guaranteeing its safety, of thinking up alternatives as well as living daily reality in an examined way. The Irish poet Eavan Boland has defined this first principle of an imaginative life: 'Only a subversive grasp on the private reality, it seemed to me, could guarantee the proper tension with the public one.'

For what is applauded and who sets the terms of the recognition and acceptance are always in question. Nor are the measure and weight of those terms assigned fixed values; unlike the statutory yards and metres kept safe in government vaults, they can and do change. Creating and contributing to the inhabited culture is not just a matter of individual creative genius, the exceptional masterwork. We, the audience, you, the reader, are part of the story's future as well, its patterns are rising under the pressure of your palms, our fingers, too.

While fairy tales have shored up traditional aspirations (for fame and fortune, above all), they can also act as fifth columnists, burrowing from within, in the very act of circulating the lessons of the status quo. And because utopian ambitions beat strongly in the heart of fairy tale, many writers have hidden and hide under its guileless and apparently childish façade, have wrapped its cloak of un reality around them; adopting its traditional formal simplicities they have attempted to challenge received ideas and raise questions into the minds of their audience: protest and fairy tale have long been associated. In conditions of censorship – in Paris under Louis XIV as well as Prague before 1989 – fantasies can lead the censor a merry dance. The writings of the French *précieuses* and their disciples like Marie-Jeanne L'Héritier and Marie-Catherine d'Aulnoy campaigned for women's emancipation; nineteenth- and early twentieth-century writers of both sexes also struggled to shape an egalitarian, communal, anti-materialist ethic, as Ruskin did with 'The King of the Golden River', George MacDonald in his *Princess* books and Frank L. Baum with *The Wizard of Oz* and its sequels. Karel Čapek wrote against the rise of Fascism in the 1930s, shoring up the qualities of tolerance and mercy in his tender, comic, blithe shaggy-dog fairy tales, poking fun at greed and folly, bureaucrats and bullies. The Czech poet Miroslav Holub has described what pleasure it gave writers to trick the Communist system by encoding their dissidence in bafflingly innocuous images, of Cinderella and other irreproachable figures. Today, writers for children (and sometimes for adults, too) who draw on fairytale motifs and characters, like Terry Jones, Joan Aiken, Jane Yolen, Tove Jansson, Terry Pratchett, are conjuring up dream worlds as personally idealistic, as politically and socially contentious, and often as spiritedly wary and iconoclastic, as their more apparently sophisticated precursors, Erasmus, Voltaire, and Swift.

But the case of *The Satanic Verses* throws into sharp relief the contradictory forces that tug at wonder tales as a genre: Salman Rushdie is a writer whose fiction is rooted in ancient fables and the mythic tradition, who has drawn on *The Arabian Nights*, on the *Ramayana* – and the Koran. The wonder tale that everyone knows, the common heritage of narrative, is there to be reshaped for each generation by the teller, but its potential is so rich that many seek to control it in their interests: it is a central ironical paradox of his case that his enemies, as they desire to destroy him admit that they recognize and fear the power of the teller to recast an old story and direct the way it is heard.

Different listeners, different readers will pull the storyteller towards affirming their point of view: a different audience, a different message. Every work is 'a link in the chain of speech communion', and is made by source, narrator, receiver acting in conjunction. The fairy tale becomes the arena where beliefs struggle for ascendancy. But who has the sultan's ultimate power to determine the tale's outcome? Does it belong to Scheherazade? Or to her listeners, who determine her fate (her story) by the depth of their enthralment? If we are to let the story be told, we, too, have to deal with the sultans, and show the utmost courage, as Rushdie has done.

The story itself becomes the weapon of the weaponless. The struggles of women, for example, are not resolved by combat, on the whole (one or two Amazon heroines excepted), as the contests of men may be in heroic epic; when they need to undo error or redeem wrongdoing or defend the innocent, they raise their voices, if only in a conspiratorial whisper – hence the suspicion of women's talk that haunts the whole history of the old wives' tale. Women's arts within fairy tales are very marked, and most of them are verbal: riddling, casting spells, conjuring, understanding the tongues of animals, turning words into deeds according to the elementary laws of magic, sometimes to comic effect. Whereas saints, knights, and fairytale heroes assault the beast with weapons – Perseus and the sea monster, Theseus and the Minotaur, St George and the Dragon, Jack the Giantkiller, Tom Thumb and the ogre – women in fairy tale align themselves with the Odyssean party of wily speechmakers, and with the Orphic mode of entrancement. In this they simply extend the practice of storytellers themselves.

But the uses of enchantment in the contemporary world of the leisure industry, of competing theme parks and a commercialized culture of play, culminate in a sugar-candy replica of the Sleeping Beauty's castle, and an opening ceremony (at

EuroDisney) in which everyone pretended to be asleep until the prince kissed the princess. Tocqueville was indeed prescient when he wrote (if we take his 'poetry' as culture in general):

> We have also seen, among democratic nations, that the sources of poetry are grand, but not abundant. They are soon exhausted: and poets, not finding the elements of the ideal in what is real and true, abandon them entirely and create monsters. I do not fear that the poetry of democratic nations will prove insipid, or that it will fly too near the ground; I rather apprehend that it will be forever losing itself in the clouds, and that it will range at least to purely imaginary regions. I fear that the productions of democratic poets may often be surcharged with immense and incoherent imagery, with exaggerated descriptions and strange creations; and that the fantastic beings of their brain may sometimes make us regret reality.

Tocqueville contrasts, in the conventional way, fantasy and reality: but a deeper understanding of the workings of fantasy within reality (partly due to the ability of film to render the imaginary for real) has developed since, and with it a need to analyse the forms this interweaving takes. After the 1939–45 war, psychoanalytic approval of fairy tales as highly therapeutic and educational – a view crystallized by Bruno Bettelheim's study – undoubtedly helped this return to respectability, and thence to the realization of illusory fairylands. But psychoanalysis has hardly been alone in contributing to revived interest in fairy tales. Italo Calvino, for example, began by writing, as a young communist, a realist novel about the partisans, *Il Sentiero dei nidi di ragno* (The Path to the Nests of Spiders), which appeared in 1947. The cultural politics of the nineteenth and early twentieth centuries had assumed that representing the interests of the people as well as communicating with them required a naturalistic, documentary mode – a print off life to demonstrate the heroism and the injustice of the common folk. But then Calvino became interested in folklore, and after he published his resonant collection *Fiabe Italiane*, the fruit of years of scavenging and collating and editing fairy tales from all over Italy, Calvino himself became a fabulist – he gave himself to a literature of dreaming rather than representation, and began to see the writer as a shaman who takes flight to another world. In his last series of lectures, he wrote:

> I am accustomed to consider literature a search for knowledge. In order to move onto existential ground, I have to think of literature as extended to

anthropology and ethnology and mythology. Faced with the precarious existence of tribal life – drought, sickness, evil influences – the shaman responded by ridding his body of weight and flying to another world, another level of perception, where he could find the strength to change the face of reality.

Through fairy tales he had heard, he said, the voices of the people, he had discovered the knowledge of another way of being, the fruits of struggle and hope. Crucially, he had also discovered common ground on which the agnostic and literate mandarin like himself stood beside the unlettered worker. It is a very important discovery: that fairy tale and fantasy can unite societies, across barriers of all kinds.

Storytelling can act as a social binding agent – like the egg yolk which, mixed up with the different coloured powders, produces colours of a painting. A story like 'Rashin Coatie', collected in Scotland in the last century, relates to similar tales of wronged orphan girls all over the world, but it has particular Scottish resonances and emphases – this Cinderella meets her prince at the kirk, not the palace. Of course there are fairy tales unique to a single place, which have not been passed on. But there are few really compelling ones that do not turn out to be wearing seven-league boots. The possibility of holding a storehouse of narrative in common could act to enhance our reciprocal relations, to communicate across spaces and barricades of national self-interest and pride. We share more than we perhaps admit or know, and have done so for a very long time: early in the fifteenth century, when Richard, Earl of Warwick, made a pilgrimage to the Holy Land, an emir asked him if he were descended from Guy of Warwick, that celebrated hero of Arthurian romance, whom he had read about 'in bokes of their langage'. The late twentieth century has been seeing a radical reappraisal of such universally known tales – the Grimm Brothers proclaimed their fairy stories the pure uncontaminated national products of the *Volk* or German people, but we now know that many of their tales had been travelling through the world for centuries before the Grimms took them down.

The balance between popular taste and democratic representation poses one of the most urgent questions facing all the narrative arts, performance and broadcasting as well as literature, for adults and children alike, but it seems a simple admission of defeat to weep and gnash one's teeth at the thought of EuroDisney (a 'cultural Chernobyl', grieved the French philosopher Alain Finkielkraut); it is simply unthinking and lazy to denounce all the works of Disney and his legacy. Theme parks and popular entertainment quarry the tradition of fairy tale – from

Snow White and the Seven Dwarfs (one of the largest grossing films ever, and still earning) to the recent *Hook* and *Aladdin*; they rely not only on the characters and stories, but on the idea that adults enjoy being children again, that a public can include different generations and classes, who will lose themselves in the make-believe in a different way, united by the pleasures of enchantment. Fairy tales are indeed still criticized – and with reason – for the easy lies, the crass materialism, the false hopes they hold out, but in the last decade of the century, in conditions of radical change on the one hand, and stagnation on the other, with ever increasing fragmentation and widening polarities, with national borders disappearing in some places and returning with a bloody vengeance in others, as a millenarian feeling of ecological catastrophe gathers momentum, and the need to belong grows ever more rampant as it becomes more frustrated, there has been a strongly marked shift towards fantasy as a mode of understanding, as an ingredient in survival, as a lever against the worst aspects of the status quo and the direction it is taking.

Many characteristics of fairy tale as a tradition have contributed to this change: first, the stories' fallaciousness, the very quality that inspired scorn, makes them potential conduits of another way of seeing the world, of telling an alternative story. The mythical hope they conjure actually builds a mythology in which utopian desires find their place. Fairy tales often attack received ideas: monsters turn out to be handsome young princes, beggars princesses, ugly old women powerful and benevolent fairies (especially if you are nice to them and give them something to eat and do their laundry without a fuss). Fairy tales often champion lost causes, runts of the litter, the slow-witted and the malformed. An analogy would be the maxim of the Czech dissidents before the Velvet revolution: Live as if the freedoms you desire were yours already. Only by refusing the constraints that are imposed can they be broken – this is also true of imagining another life, making a new world.

Fairy tales feel out the rules: the forbidden door opens on to *terra nova* where different rules may apply. Curiosity, so closely linked to speech, runs live electricity through many of the stories, and though the questor (Psyche, Bluebeard's wife, Goldilocks) is often punished for not abiding by the rules, the story also runs against its own grain by rewarding her just the same. Since the first medieval romances, with their fairies and monsters, the unreal settings and impossible situations have made possible the exploration of sexual experience and sexual fantasy. One of the chief tropes by which approaches to this forbidden territory are negotiated is animal metamorphosis: confronting or defining the outlawed and

The body of the schoolteacher Lisa (played by Alice Kriege) is carried into an inner chamber to be enshrined in Institute Benjamenta, *a film by the Quay Brothers inspired by* Snow White *and other writings of Robert Walser.*

alien literally affects the figures in the stories; the beastly or less than human becomes an index of alienation, and often of one's own otherness; the story relates the possibility of acceptance, an end to the ache of longing to belong.

The domain of fantasy where fairy tales grow has a long, heterodox pedigree, and there has been in history a prolonged struggle between different social groups to control the storyteller. The genre's fortunes have entered a new phase: a certain view of fairy tales is being naturalized by companies like Disney, and then domesticated by publishers like Ladybird Books, who have now struck a deal with Disney so that all the illustrations are based on the films' graphics and storyline. The voices whom L'Héritier and Calvino and Schwartz-Bart heard, for instance, risk being lost in the noise of these loud standard numbers, with certain prejudices and values deeply instilled. This is one of the prima facie problems of corporate reach in the global village: in the same way as hedgerows are shedding variety of species, flora and fauna, the imagination of children reared on Ladybird fairy tales will be saturated with the Disney version, graphic and verbal.

This process of loss has to be resisted: as individual women's voices have become absorbed into the corporate body of male-dominated decision-makers, the misogyny present in many fairy stories – the wicked stepmothers, bad fairies, ogresses, spoiled princesses, ugly sisters and so forth – has lost its connections to the particular web of tensions in which women were enmeshed and come to look dangerously like the way things are. The historical context of the stories has been sheared away, and figures like the wicked stepmother have grown into archetypes of the human psyche, hallowed, inevitable symbols, while figures like the Beast bridegroom have been granted ever more positive status. Generally speaking, the body of story has passed out of the mouth of the quiltmaker from Palermo, on to the lips of film-makers – Steven Spielberg – or psychoanalysts – Bruno Bettelheim – or therapists – Robert Bly. The danger of women has become more and more part of the story, and correspondingly, the danger of men has receded: Cinderella's and Snow White's wicked stepmothers teach children to face life's little difficulties, it is argued, but films about a Bluebeard or a child murderer, as in 'Tom Thumb', are rated Adults Only.

There are grounds for profound pessimism about the narrative possibilities that remain. Yet fairy tale provides motifs in common, a sign language and an image store which can be interpreted and re-interpreted, as many contemporary artists and writers are now doing, from Robert Coover's fictional reworking of 'Pinocchio', to Salman Rushdie's *Haroun and the Sea of Stories*, an amalgam of *Sinbad* with *The Wizard of Oz* as well as his own personal trials; to Jeanette Winterson's experimental novels. Among artists, Paula Rego has continued to explore conflicts and tenderness within families and between the sexes using the shared terms of nonsense verses, and new fairy tales like *Peter Pan*; the Quay Brothers, with *The Comb* (1991) and *Institute Benjamenta* (1994), inspired by Robert Walser's *Snow White* and other writings, and Joanna Woodward, in *Princess Brooch and the Sinful Clasp* (1981), have used a mixture of live action and animation to dramatize psychological discovery and erotic adventure in a true fairytale spirit of 'insatiable curtiosity'.

The idea of awakening, sometimes erotic but not exclusively, goes to the heart of fairy tale's function. But Sleeping Beauty's angle of vision, when she opens her eyes, is different from the point of view of the prince. Of course Italo Calvino, Angela Carter, and the new executives of The Disney Corporation did not imagine a similar world or indeed see it in a similar way – but they would agree that the uses of enchantment are extremely powerful, and that what is expressed and what is denied, what is discovered and what is rejected, form a picture of the possible world to which Sleeping Beauty, say, will be waking up.

Who tells the story, who recasts the characters and changes the tone becomes very important: no story is ever the same as its source or model, the chemistry of narrator and audience changes it. Karel Čapek puts it valiantly:

> Every narration is a creative and superlatively free story-creating activity … I cannot conceal my satisfaction that the word *'epos'* [epic] in its origin means, and in truth is, the spoken word.

Angela Carter puts the same thought more modestly:

> Ours is a highly individualized culture, with a great faith in the work of art as a unique one-off, and the artist as an original, a godlike and inspired creator of unique one-offs. But fairy tales are not like that, nor are their makers. Who first invented meatballs? In what country? Is there a definitive recipe for potato soup? Think in terms of the domestic arts. 'This is how I make potato soup.'

Both Čapek and Carter have written 'marvellous tales' of their own which defy rules of sexual and social conduct in a spirit aglow with mischief. Čapek's simple honest peasant comes into a fortune, but does not get to marry the princess and become a king because he loses it all through a hole in his pocket.

The French thinker Félix Guattari, in a powerful historical essay, has asked some fundamental questions about the direction in which the century and its achievements in technology are taking us; he calls for a new vitality in the relations between individuals and the language of the culture they inhabit: 'Unconscious figures of power and knowledge are not universals. They are tied to reference myths profoundly anchored in the psyche, but they can still swing around toward liberatory paths / voices.' He too sketches the possibility of a utopia, dreaming of 'transforming this planet – a living hell for over three quarters of its population – into a universe of creative enchantments'.

The store of fairy tales, that blue chamber where stories lie waiting to be rediscovered, holds out the promise of just those creative enchantments, not only for its own characters caught in its own plotlines; it offers magical metamorphoses to the one who opens the door, who passes on what was found there, and to those who hear what the storyteller brings. The faculty of wonder, like curiosity, can make things happen; it is time for wishful thinking to have its due.

Abbreviations

Notes

Bibliography

Index

List of Plates and Picture Credits

ABBREVIATIONS

A   Lucius Apuleius, *The Transformations of Lucius, otherwise known as The Golden Ass*, tr. Robert Graves (Harmondsworth [1950] 1988)

ACA   Christine Megan Armstrong, *The Moralizing Prints of Cornelis Anthonisz.* (Princeton, 1990)

AHA   Aristotle, *Historia animalium*, tr. A. L. Peck, 2 vols (London, 1965, 1979)

APT   *Apollonius of Tyre: Medieval and Renaissance Themes and Variations*, ed. Elizabeth Archibald (Cambridge, 1991)

AT   Antti Aarne and Stith Thompson, *The Types of the Folk Tale: A Classification and Bibliography* (Helsinki, 1964)

B   Giambattista Basile, *Il Pentamerone*, tr. B. Croce, ed. N. M. Penzer (2 vols, Bari [1932] 1982)

BB   Jeanne-Marie Leprince de Beaumont, *Beauty and the Beast* (Glasgow, 1818)

BN   Bibliothèque Nationale, Paris

C-Eng   *Italian Folk Tales*, selected and retold by Italo Calvino, tr. George Martin (Harmondsworth, 1982)

C-It   Italo Calvino, *Fiabe Italiane* (2 vols, Turin, 1956)

CAG   Angela Carter, *American Ghosts and Old World Wonders* (London, 1993)

CBC   — , *The Bloody Chamber* (London, 1979)

CPB   F. J. Child, *English and Scottish Popular Ballads* (5 vols, London, 1882–98)

CBK   John Ashton (ed.), *Chap-Books of the Eighteenth Century* (London, 1882, repr. 1992)

CF-I   *Le Cabinet des fées* (41 vols, Amsterdam and Paris, 1785–9)

CF-II   *Le Cabinet des fées*, ed. Elisabeth Lemirre (3 vols, Arles, 1988)

DA   *The Fairy Tales of Madame d'Aulnoy*, tr. Annie Macdonnell and Miss Lee, intro. Anne Thackeray Ritchie (London, 1892)

EQ   *Les Evangiles des quenouilles*, ed. and tr. Jacques Lacarrière (Paris, 1987)

FSE   *The Standard Edition of the Complete Psychological Works of Sigmund Freud*, ed. James Strachey with Anna Freud (24 vols, London, 1953–74)

G   *The Complete Grimm's Fairy Tales*, tr. anon., commentary by Joseph Campbell (London, 1975)

GL   Jacobus de Voragine, *The Golden Legend, or Lives of the Saints*, tr. William Caxton [1483] (7 vols, London, 1900)

GZ   *The Complete Tales of the Brothers Grimm*, tr. and ed. Jack Zipes (New York, 1992)

HCA   Hans Christian Andersen, *The Complete Fairy Tales and Stories of Hans Andersen*, tr. Erik Haugaard (London, 1975)

JAF   *Journal of American Folklore*

JFH   *Journal of Family History*

JWCI   *Journal of the Warburg and Courtauld Institutes*

LCL   Loeb Classical Library

LHBI   Marie-Jeanne L'Héritier de Villandon, *Bigarrures Ingénieuses, ou Recueil de diverses pièces galantes en prose et en vers* (Paris, 1696)

LHCD   — , *Les Caprices du destin, ou Recueil d'histoires singulières et amusantes arrivées de nos jours* (Paris, 1718)

LHTT   — , *La Tour ténébreuse et Les jours lumineux. Conte Anglois, accompagné d'Historiettes, et tirez d'une ancienne Chronique composée par Richard, Coeur de Lion* (Paris, 1705)

LPB   Marie-Jeanne Leprince de Beaumont, *Le Magasin des enfants, ou Dialogues entre une sage gouvernante et plusieurs des ses élèves de la première distinction* (London, 1757)

LRB   *London Review of Books*

M   Henriette-Julie de Castelnau, Comtesse de Murat, *Les Lutins du Château de Kernosy* in *Voyages imaginaires, songes, visions, et romans cabalistiques*, vol. 35 (Amsterdam and Paris, 1789), 153–423

MCF   — , *Les Contes des fées* [also called *Les Nouveaux contes des fées*] (Paris, 1698)

MHS   — , *Histoires Sublimes et allégoriques* (Paris, 1699)

MC   *Merveilles et Contes* Marvels & Tales (Boulder, Colorado, 1987)

MGM   *Mother Goose's Melodies*, ed. E. F. Bleiler, facsimile edn (Monroe and Francis: Boston 1833; New York, 1970)

NOEV   *The New Oxford Book of English Verse 1250–1950*, ed. Helen Gardner (Oxford, 1972)

NYRB   *The New York Review of Books*

OM   *The Metamorphoses of Ovid*, tr. Mary M. Innes (Harmondsworth, 1973)

OCFT   Iona and Peter Opie, *The Classic Fairy Tales* (Oxford, 1974)

ONC   — , *A Nursery Companion* (Oxford, 1980)

ONR   — , *The Oxford Dictionary of Nursery Rhymes* (Oxford, 1977)

P   Charles Perrault, *Contes*, ed. G. Rouger (Paris, 1967)

PAC   *The Fairy Tales of Charles Perrault*, tr. Angela Carter (New York, 1977)

S   Giovan Francesco Straparola, *Le piacevoli notti*, ed. Giuseppe Rua (2 vols, Bari, 1927)

SC   Madame de Sévigné, *Correspondance*, ed. Roger Duchêne (3 vols, Paris, 1972)

TLS   *Times Literary Supplement*

VFT-I   *The Virago Book of Fairy Tales*, ed. Angela Carter (London, 1990)

VFT-II   *The Second Virago Book of Fairy Tales*, ed. Angela Carter (London, 1992)

WT   *Wonder Tales: Six Stories of Enchantment*, ed. Marina Warner (London, 1994)

ZBB   *Beauties, Beasts and Enchantment: Classic French Fairy Tales*, ed. and tr. Jack Zipes (New York, 1989)

ZSE   *Spells of Enchantment: The Wondrous Fairy Tales of Western Culture*, ed. and tr. Jack Zipes (New York, 1991)

ZVFT   *Victorian Fairy Tales: The Revolt of the Fairies and Elves*, ed. Jack Zipes (London, 1987)

NOTES

INTRODUCTION

xi   **even sultans**: Jan Knappert, *Myths and Legends of the Swahili* (London, 1970), 132; *VFT*-I, 215.

xii   '... **image of desire**': Beer, 79.

xii   **Baronne d'Aulnoy**: D'Aulnoy's publication history is very complicated; I consulted a varied group of editions, including *The Diverting Works of the Countess d'Anois: (I) Memoirs, (II) All Her Spanish Novels and Histories, (III) Her Letters, (IV) Tales of the Fairies in 3 parts compleat* (London, 1707); *Les Contes de fées par Mme. d*** (3 vols, Amsterdam, 1708); *History of the Tales of the Fairies* (London, 1708); *Les Illustres fées – Contes galans* (Amsterdam, 1710); *Le Gentilhomme bourgeois* (Paris, 1710–15); *Le Nouveau Gentilhomme bourgeois, ou les fées à la mode* (Paris, 1711); *Les Nouveaux contes de fées* (Paris, 1719); *A Collection of Novels and Tales Written by that celebrated Wit of France, the Countess D'Anois* (3 vols, London, 1721-2); *Mother Bunch's Fairy Tales* (London, 1790). See for a full bibliography of her Englished works, Palmer (1975).

xii   '**La Reine fantasque**': *CF*-I, XXVI; tr. Jack Zipes, ZSE, 160–71.

xii   '**Voyages imaginaires**': 36 vols (Amsterdam and Paris, 1788).

xiii   '... **willingly become children again**': 'Lettre à La Motte' (22 Nov. 1714), quoted Delaporte, 33.

xiv   '... **silly and idle imaginations**': Anon., *A History of Genesis*, 1690, quoted Gillian Avery, *Child's Eye: A History of Children's Books Through Three Centuries* (Oxford, 1989), 4.

xiv   **love of fantasy and excitement**: Jean-Jacques Rousseau, *Emile, ou de l'éducation*, in *Oeuvres complètes* (Paris, 1969), 287ff.

xiv   '... **trash of preliterate peoples ...**': John Updike, *Hugging the Shore* (New York, 1988), 661-2.

xiv   **girl's ultimate goal**: See Marcia K. Lieberman, '"Some Day My Prince Will Come": Female Acculturation through the Fairy Tale', in Zipes (1986); Karen E. Rowe, 'Feminism and Fairy Tales', ibid., 207-24; Kay Stone, 'Things Walt Disney Never Told Us', *Women and Folklore*, ed. Claire R. Farrer (Austin and London, 1975); Colette Dowling, *The Cinderella Complex: Women's Hidden Fear of Independence* (New York, 1981); Madonna Kolbenschlag, *Kiss Sleeping Beauty Goodbye: Break the Spell of Feminine Myths and Models* (New York, 1979); see Kay Stone, 'Feminist Approaches to the Interpretation of Fairy Tales', in Bottigheimer (1986), 229-36, for an overview of the changes.

xiv   '**it really seems to pay**': *The Children's Musical Cinderella* (London, 1879).

xiv   **the term 'wonder tale'**: Propp (1968).

xvi   **donkeytail sprouting**: '*L'acqua del cestello*', C-It, I, 409–11; C-Eng, 353–5.

xvi   **anything can happen**: Wonder 'has no opposite and is the first of the passions'. Descartes, *Philosophical Works*, tr. E. Haldane and G. R. T. Ross (2 vols, Cambridge, 1911), I, 363, quoted by Stephen Greenblatt in *Marvelous Possessions: The Wonder of the New World* (Chicago, 1991), 20; see also, Marina Warner, Intro., *WT*, 3-17.

xvi   **Wallace Stevens believed**: See Helen Vendler, 'Posthumous Work and Beautiful Subjects', *New Yorker*, 12 Nov. 1990, 124–33.

xvi   **do not ... enter unnegotiated areas**: See Tsvetan Todorov, *The Fantastic: A Structural Approach to a Literary Genre*, tr. Richard Howard (Ithaca, 1975) on ambiguity and the uncanny.

xvi   '... **even if it won't last**': Angela Carter, Intro., *VFT*-I, XVIII.

xvii   **Panchatantra (The Five Books)**: tr. Franklin Edgerton (London, 1965).

xvii   **a volume by Bidpai**: Bidpai, *Livre de Lumières, ou la Conduite des roys, composé par le sage Pilpay, indien, traduit en français par David Sahid d'Ispahan (et Gilbert Gaulmin)*

(Paris, 1644); see *CF*-I, XVII–XVIII.

xvii   **fairy story in the Caribbean**: See Spufford, 13–24, on communications in the seventeenth century; Velay-Vallantin, *Fille en Garçon*, for a fascinating collection of different versions.

xviii   **leave [no] trace in medieval narrative**: Michael Reeve, 'Are there such things as folk-tales?' delivered in British, Academy conversazione, 20 Nov. 1992, kindly lent to MW.

xviii   **surviving manuscript is recovered**: Henriette-Julie de Murat, 'Starlight', tr. Terence Cave, *WT*, 149-87.

xviii   **recognition to their audiences**: See Dollerup *et al.* for an excellent analysis of this polymorphousness of meaning in relation to the context of the telling.

xix   '**selfish word-string**': Irwin, 234-5.

xx   **plea of extenuating circumstances**: See Davis, *passim*.

PART ONE

1   '... **a little better**': A, 96.

1   '... **beguile them**': Pindar, *Olympian* 1, lines 42–4, adapted from Maurice Bowra (tr.), *The Odes* (Harmondsworth, 1969), 65, with the kind help of Peter Dronke.

CHAPTER ONE: IN THE CAVE OF THE ENCHANTRESS

3   '**The devil in disguise**': Anon., tr. J. W. Thomas, in *Richard Wagner, Tannhäuser: Opera Guide 39*, ed. Nicholas John (London, 1988), 58–9.

3   **their total destruction**: Parke, 136–43; 190–215.

3   **contenders for this title**: Among them, Hermes, and Palamedes, hated by Odysseus who was jealous of his wisdom. See Graves, I, 182–5; Calasso, 351–4.

3   **The 'Grotta della Sibilla'**: I consulted the edition of 1521 in the British Library and used the versions edited by Werner Söderhjelm, 101–67 and by F. Desonay, La Sale (1930), 1-53; also La Sale (1963), 125-68, and F. Desonay, 'Le Fonti italiane della leggenda di Tannhäuser', in La Sale (1963), 17–58; Gaston Paris, 'Le Paradis de la Reine Sibylle', *Légendes du Moyen-âge* (Paris, 1903), 67ff; J. Neve, *Antoine de La Sale, sa vie, et ses oeuvres* (Paris, 1903); Luigi Paolucci, *La Sibilla Appeninica* (Florence, 1967); Giuseppe Santarelli, *Le Leggende dei Monti Sibillini* (Montefortino, 1988), 19–38; Romano Cordella and Paolo Lollini, *Castelluccio di Norcia Il Tetto dell' Umbria* (Castelluccio, 1988), 205–15; Domenico Falzetti, *Alla Ricerca della Dea d'amore nella Grotta della Sibilla di Norcia* (Milan, 1991).

4   '... **courtesy in her beyond measure ...**': Desonay (1963), 21.

4   '... **seemed to be made of ivory ...**': ibid.

4   **God would ... and took flesh**': F. Neri, 'Le tradizioni italiane della Sibilla', *Studi Medievali 4* (1912–13), 213–30.

5   '**salad one puts many good herbs**': Antoine de La Sale, *La Salade* (Paris, 1521); Söderhjelm, 101.

6   '**chatter of the common people**': La Sale (1930), 17; The lake was also called Il Lago di Pilato (and still is). La Sale tells the legend of Pilate's death by drowning, after he had been tied at his own request to a cart drawn by buffaloes and dragged from Rome to the mountains – his punishment for his part in Christ's death.

7   '... **afeared of any mortal fear ...**': Söderhjelm, 112.

7   **The writer in La Sale ... his own**: One was Hans Van Bamberg, and his squire Thomin de Pons. See La Sale (1963), 156–7, for facsimiles.

7   '... **peacock which seemed very far away**': La Sale (1930), 15; Söderjhelm, 114.

7   **Mélusine**: Jean d'Arras, *Le Roman de Mélusine* [1387], retold in F. Nodot, *Histoire de Mélusine* (Paris, 1697 – the same date as Perrault's *Contes*), 1–271; id., ed. Edmund Lecesne (Arras, 1888); see also Harf-Lancner, 85–113; also Jean Markale, *Mélusine* (Paris, 1993) for a study

of the legend.

7   **Lamia**: 'The Phairie or Lamia', Topsell, 1, 352–5; Rowland (1973), 115–6: see also Warner *Monsters*, 5–6.

8   **'... snakes and serpents all together'**: La Sale (1930), 28–9; Söderhjelm, 121.

8   **'... though love is hell'**: Clive Bell, *The Legend of Monte della Sibilla or Le Paradis de la Reine Sibille* (London, 1923).

9   **'... welcome and feast you in very great joy'**: La Sale, *Salade*, 168. La Sale believed in literature for therapy and pleasure: some years later, in 1457, he gathered together another album of tales and fables to cheer up Catherine de Neufville, Dame de Fresne, after her first child had died. See *Le Réconfort de Madame de Fresne*, ed. Ian Hill (Exeter, 1979).

9   **all pagan devilry to an end**: La Sale (1930), 51; Söderhjelm, 133–4.

9   **Venus herself**: In a letter to his brother in 1431, he mentions how he described the cave to a Saxon astronomer who wanted to brush up his skills and had heard that a certain Monte di Venere – the mountain of Venus – was the right place to do it. Pius II linked this with the Sibyl's grotto near Norcia, where the astronomer could talk to devils and polish his necromancy. Paris, 93; Cordella and Lollini, op. cit., 206ff.

9   **oral, learned and popular**: Leandro Alberti, *Descrittione de tutta Italia* (Bologna, 1550), 248, quoted Santarelli, 130. See also Paris, 95.

9   **enchanted sleep in the cave**: Ginzburg, 108.

9   **'... devil in disguise!'**: 'The Tannhäuser Ballad', tr. J. W. Thomas, in *Richard Wagner, Tannhäuser*, op. cit., 58.

9   **torments about love and lust**: See Stewart Spencer, 'Tannhäusere, Danheuser and Tannhäuser', ibid., 17–24.

10   **'... voice I shall be known'**: OM, XIV, 314–15.

10   **moaning that ... wanted was to die**: Petronius, *The Satyricon*, tr. J. P. Sullivan (Harmondsworth, 1977), 67.

11   **'... I have not lost my sovereignty'**: Pausanias, I, 436.

11   **buried, even secret matters**: Since writing this prologue, I have come across Mary Shelley's Introduction to *The Last Man*, her utopian novel of 1826, in which she describes a visit – with Shelley – to the Sibyl's cave at Cumae, and how they found there drifting leaves on which messages were traced. She was able to decipher these 'scattered ... divine intuitions which the Cumaean damsel obtained from heaven'. Sandra M. Gilbert and Susan Gubar, *The Madwoman in the Attic: The Woman Writer in the Nineteenth Century Literary Imagination* (New Haven, 1979, 1984), 93–104, develop the image of this cave and women's imaginations, culture, and muffled memory.

CHAPTER TWO: THE OLD WIVES' TALE

12   **'Men Talk'**: Liz Lochhead, *True Confessions and New Clichés* (Edinburgh, 1985), 134–5.

13   **'... cockell bread'**: Peele, lines 599–602; see also OCFT, 'The Three Heads in the Well' and 'The King of Colchester's Daughters', 156–61; cf. 'Bushy Bride', Lang (1890), 322–8; C-It, 1, 409–11; C-Eng, 353–5.

13   **'... without his weapon ...'**: Peele, ibid., lines 596–7.

13   **'... a goulden tree'**: ibid., lines 735–42.

13   **double entendres ... local superstitions**: See Edmund Colledge and J. C. Marler, 'Céphalologie', in *Traditio* 37 (1981), 411–26, for a fascinating discussion of the speaking head in classical and medieval lore; see also Anne Ross, 'Severed Heads in Wells: An Aspect of the Well Cult', *Scottish Studies* 6, 1962, 31–49.

13   **William Stevenson**: *Gammer Gurton's Nedle* [sic] in *Representative British Comedies from the beginning to Shakespeare*, I, ed. Charles Mills Gayley (London and New York, 1903).

14   **'... heap of old wives' tales'**: Quoted in Charles Deulin, ed., *Les Contes de ma Mère l'Oye avant Perrault* (Paris, 1879), 12.

14   **reference to the genre**: Plato, *Gorgias*, ed. E. R. Dodds (Oxford, 1959), 527a4; Plato also called them *tithon mythoi*, old wetnurses' tales, a phrase which translates into the German *Ammenmärchen* in the eighteenth century. See Rainer Wehse, 'Past and Present Folkloristic Narrator Research', in Bottigheimer (1986), 245–58.

14   **distract them from their grief**: Plutarch, *Theseus*, XXIII, in *Plutarch's Lives*, tr. Bernadette Perrin (London, 1914), 50–1; Graves, I, 98e, 337.

14   **The Golden Ass ... second century AD**: See 'Cupid and Psyche', in *The Golden Ass*, tr. William Aldington (1566), ed. S. Gaselee (London, 1915). See also Thomas Hägg, *The Novel in Antiquity* (Oxford, 1983), 177–90; Swahn, *passim*; Perry, 236–42.

14   **'fairy tale or two ... little better'**: A, 96.

14   **'Milesian' ... later retellings**: Perry, 90–1

15   **'... spindle, as the present ... to the past'**: 'Fatum autem dicunt esse quicquid dii fantur, quidquid Iuppiter fatur. A fando igitur fatum dicunt, id est a loquendo ... Tria autem fata fingunt in colo et fuso digitisque filum ex lana torquentibus, propter tria tempora: praeteritum, quod in fuso iam netum atque involutum est; praesens, quod inter digitos neentis traicitur; futurum, in lana quae colo implicata est, et quod adhuc per digitos neentis ad fusum tamquam praesens ad praeteritum traiciendum est.' Isidore of Seville, *Eymologiarum Sive Originum Libri*, VIII, XI, ed. W. M. Lindsay (2 vols, Oxford, 1911) 90–2; quoted (an unedited, slightly corrupt version) Jacob Grimm, *Dictionary of Teutonic Mythology*, tr. J. S. Stallybrass (London, 1883–8), I, 405ff. I am very grateful indeed for Peter Dronke's guidance here, and help with the Latin.

16   **response to a desire, a need**: See 'fair', 'fay', and 'fang' in *The Century Dictionary and Cyclopedia*, 12 vols (New York, 1911), III, 2119–2120, 2137, 2160. I am grateful to Lori Repetti for help with this research.

16   **female ... storyteller**: See Karen Rowe, 'To Spin a Yarn: The Female Voice in Folklore and Fairy Tale', in Bottigheimer (1986), 53–74, for an article which examines this theme in an inspiring way. Wehse, op. cit., covers the research which has been done in this area, principally in Russia and Finland.

16   **adapted cited female sources**: C-Eng, XVIII, XXII–XXIV; Hartland is one of the few to remark earlier on the importance of this aspect, 8–11.

16   **'... memory so never forgot them'**: C-Eng, XXIII.

17   **folk material in her head:** Andrew Porter, 'Stone and Fire', *New Yorker*, 16 March 1992.

17   **'... tale within a circle of listeners'**: Karel Čapek, 'Towards a Theory of Fairytale', in Čapek (1951), 59–60.

17   **intimate or domestic milieux**: See Dollerup et al., on circumstances of transmission.

18   **'princess grew up ... beautiful than the day'**: To Mme de Grignan *SC*, II, 516. *Mitonner* also means, according to Furetière, to caress, to pamper.

18   **governesses as his true predecessors**. 'une fiction toute pure et un conte de vieille ...' *P*, 4.

18   **'... we should pay them attention'**: 'Ces fables milésiennes sont si puériles, que c'est leur faire assez l'honneur de leur opposer nos contes de Peau d'âne et de ma Mère l'oye, ou si pleines de saletés comme l'asne d'or de Lucien ou d'Apulée ... qu'elles ne méritent pas qu'on y fasse attention.' Charles Perrault, *Parallèles des anciens et des modernes en ce qui regarde les sciences et les arts*, II, 126, quoted Jacques Marx, 'Perrault et le sommeil de la raison', *Cahiers internationaux du symbolisme*, 40–1 (1980), 83–90.

18   **'... death of us for the last year or so ...'**: 'Ils

ont rempli le monde de tant de Recueils, de tant de petites Historiettes; et enfin de ces ramas de Contes de Fées, qui nous assassinent depuis un an ou deux.' Pierre, Abbé de Villiers, *Entretiens sur les Contes de Fées et sur quelques autres ouvrages du Temps. Pour servir de préservatif contre le mauvais gout* (Paris, 1699), 69.

19   '... **to entertain children**': 'Contes à dormir debout, que les Nourrices ont inventés pour amuser les enfants.' Ibid, 74.

19   '... **ignorant folk and women**': 'le partage des ignorans et des femmes', ibid, 77.

19   '... **extreme pleasure in them – as does every child**': 'Cent et cent fois ma gouvernante/ Au lieu de Fables d'animaux,/ M'a raconté les traits moraux/ De cette Histoire surprenante ... /Oui, ces Contes frappent beaucoup/ Plus que ne font les faits et d'un singe et du loup/ J'y prenais un plaisir extrême,/ Tous les enfants font de même ...', LH*BI*, 169ff.

19   '... **trifles and mere old wives' tales**': Christopher Marlowe, *Doctor Faustus* (1590), v, 133.

20   **sisters passed on forty-one of the tales**: *GZ*, Notes, 728–43.

20   **area of Westphalia**: ibid., *GZ*, XXIV, 728–43.

20   **Leonora Alleyne**: There is no entry in the British Library catalogue under her name, a symptom perhaps of the disappearance of women's work in this field.

21   '... **dies, a whole library disappears**': Héliane and Roger Tousmon, 'Interview with Simone Schwarz-Bart: Sur les pas de Fanotte', *Textes, Etudes, et documents*, 2 (Paris, 1896), v, 215, quoted Ronnie Scharfman, 'Significantly Other' in *Significant Others*, ed. Whitney Chadwick and Isabelle de Courtivron (London, 1993), 215.

21   '**Donkeyskin' and 'Cinderella**': du Fail, 35–7; Edward Shorter, 'The "Veillée" and the Great Transformation', in Beauroy *et al.*, quotes Abel Hugo, *La France pittoresque* (Paris, 1835), I, 238, scorning the *veillées* as excuse to gossip, 127–40; Vaultier, 111ff.

22   **bottling and pickling**: Roche-Mazon (1935), 5.

22   '... **community of listeners disappears ...**': Benjamin, 91.

22   '... **milieu of craftsmen**': ibid., 101.

23   '... **into the storyteller's night**': 'The Storyteller Poems: "1 The Storyteller"', Liz Lochhead, *Dreaming Frankenstein* (Edinburgh, 1984), 70.

24   '... **or to meet her about the house**': Henriette-Lucy, Marquise de la Tour du Pin, née Dillon, *Memoirs of Madame de la Tour du Pin*, tr. and ed. Félice Harcourt (New York, 1971), 22; quoted Darrow, 44.

24   **nurse and her nurse's family**: Louise-Marie-Victoire de Chastenay, *Mémoires de Madame de Chastenay* (2 vols, Paris, 1896), I, 16–17, 29–30, quoted Darrow, 44.

25   '... **righteous man encounters himself**': Benjamin, 108–9.

25   **Lawrence's famous dictum**: It continues: 'The proper function of a critic is to save the tale from the artist who created it.' So my enterprise here runs counter to Lawrence's definition of the critic's function as well as to his epigram about the tale. *Studies in Classic American Literature* (1924), ch.1.

CHAPTER THREE: WORD OF MOUTH

27   '... **those lips together**': Olga Sedakova, 'Old Women', in *The Silk of Time*, tr. Catriona Kelly (Keele, 1994), 30–1.

27   **make them into properly docile wives**: J. Avalon, 'Lustucru, médecin céphalique', *Pro Medico*, 1933, X, 141–7; E. Fournier, *Variétés historiques: Description du tableau de Lustucru* (Paris, 1855); Champfleury, *Histoire de l'imagerie populaire* (Paris, 1869), 248–55; Jones (1990), 70–1; Mistler *et al.*, 33.

29   **henpecked husbands, a hero among men**: Avalon, op. cit., 146, lists seven separate contemporary works – all facetiously titled and plainly misogynist in tone.

29   **Silent Woman was an accepted ideal**: See Jones, 'Silence', *Garland Encyclopaedia*; Coates, 31–3; cf. 'Youth's Warning-Piece, or, the tragical History of George Barnwell who was undone by a strumpet', which quotes Proverbs 5:2–3 under a woodcut of the 'strumpet' Sarah Millwood who did the deed, in *CBK*, 431.

29   '... **not equally the glory of man**': Aristotle, *Politics*, 1.13 [1260a20], quoted Maclean (1980), 54.

30   **provoked much nodding of pious heads**: See Maclean (1980), 16–17.

30   **Church Fathers and classical authorities had set in**: Rudolf M. Bell, *Holy Anorexia* (Chicago, 1985), 149–79; Mathilde van Dijk, 'Speaking Saints, Silent Nuns: Speech and Gender in a Fifteenth Century Life of Saint Catherine of Alexandria', *Beyond Limits: Boundaries in Feminist Semiotics and Literary Theory*, ed. Liesbeth Brouwer, Petra Broomans and Riet Paasman (Groningen, 1990), 38–48.

31   '**Misogyny ... doing something to, women**': Bloch, 4.

31   '**our symbol is a representation of it**': I am most grateful to John Pretty, the founder of Miller's Damsel at Lower Calbourne mill on the Isle of Wight, for information about the mill's history. Correspondence, 1993, 6 May 1994.

31   '... **And spake right meekly**': *The Book of the Knight of the Tower*, tr. William Caxton, ed. M. Y. Offord (London, 1971), 62–70. I have modernized the spelling.

32   '... **shall speak thereof to your lord**': ibid., 63.

32   '... **I say to you roundly**': *ACA*, fig.129, 129–33.

32   **brazenly parodies holy pictures**: ibid., fig.29.

32   **sluggards (Sinte Luyaert; Sainte Fainéante)**: 'Bonne Sainte Fainéante, Protectrice des Paresseuses', *Image d'Epinal*, 1825, in Mistler *et al.*: Her special prayer beseeches: 'O you who possess the kingdom free from care, grant us, through our little caprices and devices, the happiness of living and doing nothing. Amen.'

32   **prattlers (Sainte Babille)**: Choirstall, Church of St Maurille, Ponts-de-Cé, C16th, illus. Gaignebet and Lajoux, 34.

32   '... **never has anything good to say ...**': Rijksprentenkabinet, Rijksmuseum, Amsterdam. Reproduced in *Kunst voor de beeldenstorm*, ed. J. P. Piledt Kok (The Hague, 1986), 278–9; tr. *ACA*, ibid., 64–76.

33   **sex's propensity to foment riot**: Rudolf Dekker, 'Women in Revolt: Popular Protest and its social basis in Holland in the seventeenth and eighteenth centuries', *Theory and Society* 16 (1987), 337–62. This account of the Dutch aspects also contains an excellent and full bibliography on the theme; see for example, Max Gluckman, 'Gossip and Scandal', *Man*, NS, IV:3 (June 1963), 307–16; Robert Paine, 'What is gossip about? An alternative hypothesis', *Man*, NS, II:2 (June 1967), 278–85; Ralph L. Rosnow and Gary Alan Fine, *Rumor and Gossip* (New York, 1976).

33   **among Catholics and Protestants alike**: Lynch, 25.

33   **honours for her skills**: British Library edition, (Venice, 1621).

34   **influence, not only the household**: Dekker, op. cit., 337–62, for informal, female lines of communication in Holland.

35   '... **canalize its catalytic effect**': Paine, op. cit., 283.

35   **His men are depicted at prayer**: *Der Ritter von Turn* (Augsburg, 1498), facsimile edn Munich, 1970; E.-J. Grillot de Givry, *Le Musée des sorciers, mages et alchimistes* (Paris, 1929), 139, fig.113; *The Book of the Knight of the Tower*, op. cit., 49–50.

35   **intrigue and secret liaisons**: See Alison G. Stewart, *The First 'Peasant Festivals': Eleven Woodcuts Produced in Reformation Nuremberg by Bartel and Sebald Beham and Erard Schon c.1524–35*. Ph.D. Thesis, Columbia University, New

York, 1986. I am grateful to Alison Stewart of the Photograph Archive at the Getty Center for the History of Art and the Humanities for showing me her chapter on B. Beham's woodcut 'The Spinning Room'.

36   **gossip, from another place**: *Les présentes heures à l'usaige de Rouan* [de Simon Vostre] (Paris, 1508), 126–37.

36   **women's gossiping and consultation**: *Les Evangiles des quenouilles*, ed. P. Jannet (Paris, 1815); see also Jeay and Roy; Jeay (1982, 1984).

37   **the lash of his tongue**: Olivier Maillard, *Oeuvres françaises: Sermons et Poesies*, ed. Arthur de la Borderie (Nantes, 1877), 95–6, describes his Sermon X, made sometime before 1470.

37   '… **delicate, round and white** …': The riddles were illustrated with engravings in the Venice edition of 1599. See Giorgio Cusatelli and Italo Sordi, *Da Edipo alle nostre nonne* (Milan, 1975), 90–1; also *Enigmata sive emblemata*, (Leiden, 1624), facsimile edn intro. Jochen Becker, tr. Gary Schwartz, *Incogniti scriptoris nova poemata* (Soest, 1972).

37   **crone inflamed with lust**: *EQ*, 55.

37   **scandalous appetites of women**: Mariët Westermann pointed this gesture out to me: it had been painted over and only emerged in the recent restoration of the picture. See her forthcoming essay on Steen.

38   **misery and shame**: Christine de Pizan, *The Book of the Duke of True Lovers*, tr. with intro. Thelma S. Fenster, with lyric poetry tr. Nadia Margolis (New York, 1991), XX–XXIV, 67–76.

38   **City of Ladies of 1405**: Christine de Pizan, *The Treasure of the City of Ladies, or The Book of the Three Virtues*, tr. Sarah Lawson (Harmondsworth, 1985), 98–105.

38   '… **end is not considered very wise**': *The Debate of Two Lovers*, quoted Thelma S. Fenster, intro., op. cit., XXVI.

39   **guilty of blasphemy and defamation**: Jones, (1990); Antonia Fraser, f.p.101.

39   **swore, but women who could conjure**: Fraser, op. cit., 114.

39   **swearing and vituperation to retaliate**: See Christina Larner, *The Enemies of God: The Witchhunt in Scotland* (London, 1981); Alan Macfarlane, 'Witchcraft in Tudor and Stuart Essex', in *Witchcraft: Confessions and Accusations*, ed. Mary Douglas (London, 1970), 81–99.

39   '**Le Caquet des femmes**': By François Bac, reproduced in Gustave Kahn, *La Femme dans la caricature française* (Paris, 1912), f.p.406

39   '**And leave off Tittle Tattle**': My thanks to Roger Malbert, who showed me this print from the British Museum, which is included in the exhibition he organized and selected for the South Bank Centre, 'Folly and Vice', 1989–90.

42   **Jests, alongside Les Evangiles des quenouilles**: See *Les Caquets de l'accouchée: Recueil général*, Nouvelle edition, M.M.D.L. and Edouard Fournier (Paris, *c*.1815).

42   **so much he would regain his health**: *Recueil général des caquets de l'accouchée, Ou discours facécieux Le tout discouru par Dames, Damoiselles, Bourgeoises, et autres* (Paris, 1623), 3.

42   **Church, the law, and science**: Elisabetta Rasy, *La Lingua della nutrice* [The Nurse's Tongue] (Rome, 1978), 66–7.

42   **padlock through her lips**: At weddings in Korea today, a brace of ducks is given to the bridal couple as a lucky charm, like old shoes and rice in Europe. The duck has her beak tied, the drake's is free: an augury of a happy marriage the *médecin céphalique*'s customers would have laughed at with pleasure. On the night, it is still the custom to stage a charivari – the groom's friends erupt into the bedroom and assault him; if the wife cries out or does anything to intervene to stop her husband's friends, the marriage is deemed to be doomed as she will be wielding the upper hand. I was told this by a member of the audience at a reading I gave in Dunedin, New Zealand, in November 1992. My thanks to my anonymous informant.

43   **shuts them up in a trunk**: Seen in exhibition 'L'enfance et l'image au XIXe siècle', Musée d'Orsay, Paris, 1988.

43   **Mill of Old Wives … print**: cf., for instance, *Le Moulin Merveilleux*, printed at Epinal, 1833–40; I am grateful to Dr Birté Carlé for her translation of the verses.

44   **with an evil tongue**: e.g. 'A grosse Hagge; and Lozell, thou art worthy to be hang'd, that wilt not stay her tongue.' *The Winter's Tale* II.iii.108. See Mary Daly, *Gyn/Ecology: The metaethics of Radical Feminism* (London, 1984), 14–17, for an attempted rehabilitation of the Hag and the proclamation of a new age: Hagocracy.

45   '… **webbed like a swan's**': René d'Anjou, *Le Livre du cuer d'amours espris*, ed. Susan Wharton (Paris, 1980), 36; see also *King René's Book of Love (Le Cueur d'amours espris)*, ed. F. Unterkircher (New York, 1980), fo. 9.

45   **good judge, the almsgiver**: Warner (1985).

47   **working under their control**: Lotte van de Pol, 'The Image and Reality of Prostitution in the Dutch Republic', paper given at the Royal Academy, London, in 1985, and kindly lent to me by the author. She combines evidence from the city archives with another precious source, *The Whoredom of Amsterdam*, a highly popular description of prostitution published in Dutch in 1681 and translated into German and Italian. See also Lotte van de Pol, 'Beeld en werkelijkheid van de prostitutie in de seventiende eeuw', in Gert Hekma and Herman Roodenburg (eds), *Soete minne en helsche boosheit: Seksuele voorstellingen in Nederland, 1300–1850* (Nijmegen, 1988), 109–44.

47   **special abuse**: See Horace, *Epode* 8, tr. Amy Richlin, in *The Garden of Priapus: Sexuality and Aggression in Roman Humor* (Yale, 1983), 109–10.

47   **De Vetula, for instance, inveigh**: *The Pseudo-Ovidian De Vetula*, ed. D. M. Robathan (Amsterdam, 1968).

47   **mane of hissing snakes**: See 'De Nicht', Cesare Ripa, *Iconologia* (Amsterdam, 1644).

48   **lizard footmen … and the pumpkin coach**: See for instance *The Cabinet of Amusement and Instruction*, published by J. Harris (London, 1819). The artist is probably Robert Branston. *ONC*, 40–3, 123–4.

48   **images of their victims**: Vaultier, 39–44.

48   **Christian principles of humility**: I am very grateful to Julian Barnes for giving me this information, in 'Montaigne's Tower', unpublished.

48   **stood in blood relationship**: Lynch, 16; Shell, *Elizabeth's Glass*, 8–73.

49   **innovations of a startling kind**: See 'The structure of dwellings as an indicator of social structure', Elias (1983), 41–55 for the social context.

50   '**salon' itself … had died out**: See *Les Salons littéraires au XVIIe siècle* (Catalogue), Paris, 1968; DeJean (1981), 301; id. (1991), 20–2.

50   **wastelands of betrayal**: It appeared in her novel, *Clélie* (10 vols, Paris, 1654–60), 7, 284; see ed. René Godenne, *Histoire de la nouvelle française aux XVIIe et XVIIIe siècles* (Geneva, 1970); G. Mongrédien, *Mlle de Scudéry et son salon* (Paris, 1946), 91–3, 221–2; DeJean (1991), 55–7; Paul Zumthor, 'La Carte de Tendre et les précieux', *Trivium*, VI (1948), 263–73; E. H. Wilkins, 'Vellutello's Map of Vaucluse and the Carte de Tendre', *Modern Philology* (1931–2), 275–80.

50   **the spoken word**: L. Belmont, 'Documents inédits sur la société et la littérature précieuses: extraits de la Chronique du Samedi publiés d'après le régistre original de Péllisson (1652–1657)', *Revue d'histoire littéraire de la France*, ix (Paris, 1902), 646–73; Marc Fumaroli, 'L'art de la conversation', in *Les Lieux de mémoire*, ed. Pierre Nora, III (Paris, 1993), 2; Erica Harth, *Cartesian Women: Versions and Subversions of Rational Discourse in the Old Regime* (Cornell, 1993).

50   '... **ordinarily best to consult women**': Vaugelas, *Remarques sur la langue française* [1646/7] (Paris, 1880), 503, quoted DeJean (1989), 301.

CHAPTER FOUR: GAME OLD BIRDS

51   '... **state of sleepy bliss**': Tadeusz Konwicki, *Bohin Manor*, tr. Richard Lourie (London, 1992), 169.
51   '... **creatures just like us**': *EQ*, 120–1. Henry Watson (tr.), *The Gospels of Distaves* (London, *c.*1510), gives the stork masculine gender so misses that the bird is the wife in disguise. Stith Thompson, in his *Motif-Index of Folk Literatures* (6 vols, Bloomington, 1955–8), includes reference to a tale about a man who winters in Egypt in the shape of a stork (B775) but does not mention the legends of Mother Stork.
51   **Dame Put-down Over-the-top**: Henry Watson has Dame Abreye the Swollen for her name, but my thanks to Dr Malcolm Jones for his help glossing this name more interestingly. With reference to the folklore about storks in this chapter, I am deeply indebted throughout to the information and insights of Malcolm Jones, Mariët Westermann and John Dickson.
52   '... **in the habit of doing**': 'comme ils avaient l'habitude de le faire', *EQ*, 121.
52   **'facétie joyeuse' (a merry jest)**: *EQ*, 122.
52   **entertain and amuse children**: 'Conte', *Le Grand Dictionnaire de l'Académie Française* (Paris, 1696).
52   **distaff to a stork**: Malcolm Jones, Letters to MW, 1 Nov. 1993 and 9 Nov. 1993. I am entirely indebted to him for this piece of recondite knowledge, as Martin Le Franc's *Estrif de Fortune et Vertu* (BN, f.Fr., 1151, 1152), where the phrase *conte de la quelongne* occurs, is not published.
53   '... **there is no semblance of reason**': 'Oye', *Le Grand Dictionnaire*.
53   '... **tales of the stork, as people say**': Quoted in Jeay (1982), 177.
54   **Isles of the Blessed ... human form**: Celorio, 32, quoting Aelian.
54   **Perrault's Contes du temps passé**: The frontispiece was considered 'the soul of a book' in the seventeenth century. See Alastair Fowler, 'The art of storing a mind', a review of Mary Carruthers, *The Book of Memory: A study of memory in medieval culture*, *TLS*, 28 Dec. – 3 Jan. 1991, 1391.
55   **It all ends happily, of course**: Rivière de Fresny, *Les Fées, ou Les Contes de ma mère l'Oye, Comédie en un acte Mise au théâtre par Messieurs du F.*★★★ *et B.*★★★ *et représentée pour la première fois par les comédiens Italiens du Roi dans leur hôtel de Bourgogne, Mars 2 1697*. In *Le Théâtre Italien de Gherardi ou le recueil général* (Paris, 1741), VI, 625–47.
55   **Hecuba's tales ... 'Donkeyskin'**: Cyrano de Bergerac, quoted Storer (1928) 12; Scarron, *Le Virgile travesti*, II (Paris, 1648), quoted P, 53; Delaporte, 43.
55   **'But of the duck of Montfort ... resembles her'**: Letter to Mademoiselle, 30 Oct. 1656, *SC* 1, 40–2, quoted P, xxi–xxii, Delaporte, 33. This is only one version of the story. See Isabelle Grange, 'Metamorphoses chrétiennes des femmes–cygnes: Du folklore à la hagiographe', *Ethnologie française*, XIII (1983) 2, 139–50, 139–40.
56   '... **more fools than wise**': See *Poems on the Underground*, ed. Gerard Benson, Judith Chernaik, Cicely Herbert (London, 1993).
56   '... **many words; many geese, many turds**': Coates, 31; cf. 'Deux femmes font un plaid, trois un grand caquet, quatre un marché complet.' Cesare Lombroso, *La femme criminelle et la prostituée* (Paris, 1896), 183, quoted Bloch, 16.
56   **laid more than a hundred**: La Fontaine, 'Les Femmes et le secret', *Oeuvres complètes*, ed. Marty-Laveaux (Paris, 1858), I, 223–4.
56   **tall tales she passes on**: Compare such Gallic saws on women's chatter as: 'La poule ne doit point chanter

devant le coq', from Molière's *Les Femmes savantes*, V.iii; or the earlier lines from Jean de Meung's *Roman de la Rose*: 'C'est chose qui moult me deplait/ Quand poule parle et coq se taist.'
56   **Sibyl of Cumae**: The Crane Bag of Irish legend similarly tells a story about the origin of writing. Made of the skin of Aaife, the metamorphosed sea-goddess, it contains the treasures of Manannan, God of the Sea – including a strip of whaleskin and the King of Scotland's shears – which encrypted the letters of the alphabet. Robert Graves, *The Crane Bag and Other Disputed Subjects* (London, 1969), 1–8.
57   '**crane with his trumpe**': John Skelton, 'Philip Sparrow', *NOEV*, 28.
57   **alarm on the Capitol**: See Rogers, lix–lx.
57   **Boeotia of the sixth century BC**: Terracotta figurine, C6th Boeotia, Louvre, Paris, illustrated in Anne Baring and Jules Cashford, *The Myth of the Goddess* (London, 1991), 357.
57   **begged and received between lovers**: 'La petite oie; enfin ce qu'on appelle/ En bon français les préludes d'amour.', La Fontaine, 'L'Oraison de saint Julien', 628–36, lines 357–1.
57   **Goosebottom, from Paris, in 1292**: Letter to MW, 16 June 1993. Malcolm Jones compares this name with a certain Aalis Hochecul, from Arras, in 1222, which he interprets as 'Wigglebottom'.
57   **convent girls, ripe for picking**: *Dictionnaire des expressions et locutions figurées*, ed. Alain Rey and Sophie Chantreau (Paris, 1979), 655–6.
57   **goslings' down**: François Rabelais, *Gargantua*, Ch.13.
57   **skilled homemaker too**: Ad de Vries, *Dictionary of Symbols and Imagery* (Amsterdam and London, 1974), 221ff.
57   **or a foul, on humans**: Delaporte, 38–9.
58   **birds and tall tales together**: cf. the discovery of 'Pterodactylus anas', a fossil with a ten-foot wing span, which was discovered by French tunnellers, still alive, or so the *Illustrated London News* reported on 9 February 1856. The bird cried out before expiring. The Victorian reader would have chuckled at the pun: anas = duck = canard = hoax. Paul Sieveking and Val Stevenson, *Fortean Times: The Journal of Strange Phenomena*, 24 Jan. 1993.
58   '... **first storks who ... experienced it themselves**': A, 553.
58   **storytelling stork ... fairy tales**: W. Davison, publishing *The History of Blue Beard: Or, the Effects of Female Curiosity* (Alnwick, n.d.), in a series of Juvenile Books, included a stork in flight holding a baby among the vignettes on the cover.
58   **Antigone ... is changed into a stork**: *AHA*, 1x, 14,1; Plutarch, *De Solertia Animalium*, 4; *OM*, 6, 93ff.
58   **bird symbolizes filial piety**: See for instance Thomas Palmer, 'Two Hundred Pooseys' Sloane MS 3794, ed. John Manning (New York, 1988), no.49, 53. Palmer, the earliest English emblem book, took its inspiration from continental works by Valeriano and Alciatus. See also Rowland (1978), 161–3. Patricia Diane Olson, from Winnipeg, Canada, communicates a legend that the stork plucked out its feathers to soften the Christ child's manger at Bethlehem, *FLS News*, 19 June 1994, 19.
58   '... **putteth out superfluities**': 'De Ciconia', *On the Properties of Things: John Trevisa's translation of Bartholomaeus Anglicus, De Proprietatibus Rerum. A Critical Text*, ed. M. C. Seymour (3 vols, Oxford, 1975), II, 619–2. John Dickson, letter to MW, 5 July 1993.
59   **benevolent picking of crocodiles' teeth**: See Herodotus, *The Histories*, tr. Aubrey de Selincourt, rev. A. R. Burn (Harmondsworth, 1983) II, 68.
59   '... **use of the clyster**': Polidoro Virgilio, *De gli inventori delle cose*, tr. Francesco Baldelli (Florence, 1592) bk 1, 60; Latin version, *De Inventione Rerum*, (Basle, 1546), 70. See also Rowland, op. cit., 84–5, for other defilements

attributed to the ibis, though not the invention of the clyster.

59   **Sainte Materne**: Gaignebet and Lajoux, 55.

60   **size of the clyster itself**: Mariët Westermann tells me of 'an elaborate comic song, in a songbook of 1658, about a young woman consumed with sexual desire who pays an old female matchmaker to fetch her a doctor.' He administers 'a good clystering'. She also points out that another Dutch painting, in Leipzig, of the 'love remedy' was also attributed to Jan Steen, but it is now lost. Letter to MW, 6 May 1993.

60   '... **entrera doucement**': Part of a series of prints illustrating Trades, quoted Donald Posner, 'Watteau's Reclining Nude and the "Remedy" Theme', *Art Bulletin,* LIV, no.4, Dec. 1972, 387. The word *seringue* has been derived from *cigogne* by the Catalan writer J. Amades, but this etymology seems strained. It does however set up echoes with the pairing *cigogne/quelongne* alluded to in ch.4, and the overtones of the distaff's shape do relate it to the beak/clyster motif. See Marlen Albert-Llorca, *L'Ordre des choses: Les récits d'origine des animaux et des plantes en Europe* (Paris, 1991). John Dickson, letter to MW, 5 July 1993.

60   '... **I know how this should be done**': Simon Schama, 'Wives and Wantons: Versions of Womanhood in 17th century Dutch Art', *Oxford Art Journal,* III:1, April 1980, 5–13. Schama gives the print the explicit title, 'The Abortion'. Mariët Westermann kindly translated the verses.

60   **bed with a syringe**: Now in the John Paul Getty Museum, Malibu, the drawing appears to be a study for the tender and exquisite small nude of a reclining woman in the Norton Simon Museum – the maid was either left out of the painting, or cut out later. See Posner, op. cit., 383–9.

61   **bodily functions of various unmentionable kinds**: See Fraser, 67, for 'uterine douches of castor oil, camphor and rue' to inhibit conception. In the last century and this, glass and pewter syringes as well as whirling sprays have been used as douches. Liquid ammonia, mixed with milk, or white wine, was sometimes injected in this way to stimulate menstruation. I am most grateful to W. A. Jackson for his information and bibliographical help on this topic. Letter to MW, 27 May 1994. See also Naomi Pfeffer, *The Stork and the Syringe* (Oxford, 1993).

62   **long, curved, beak mask**: Historical Museum, Amsterdam.

62   **shape of a stork's beak**: From the collection of Javier Lentini, *In Vitro de les mitologia de la fertilitat als limits de la ciencia* (Catalogue), ed. Viçenc Altaio and Anna Veiga, Joan Miró Foundation, Barcelona April–June 1992, 168.

62   **lore that the stork brings babies**: See Funk and Wagnall's *Standard Dictionary of Folklore, Mythology and Legend,* ed. Maria Leach (San Francisco, 1984), 10a–b, 1083a.

62   '**made some little ones**': *EQ*, 120.

62   **body of his dying mother**: *Histoire Universelle,* BN, f.Fr. 64, Flemish, C15th. See L. F. Flutre, 'La naissance de César', *Aesculape*, Oct. 1934, 245ff; Renate Blumenfeld-Kosinski, *Not of a Woman Born: Representations of Caesarean Birth in Medieval and Renaissance Culture* (Ithaca, 1990).

62   **children, especially in urban settings**: Michael Simon, 'Der Storch als Kinderbringer', in *Rheinisch-westfälische Zeitschrift für Volkskunder,* eds Martha Bringemeier, H. L. Cox, Gunter Wiegelmann, Matthias Zender, Band xxxiv/xxxv (Bonn and Munster, 1989–90), 25–39. I am very grateful to Gerard Rooijackers for bringing this article to my attention.

63   '... **far more pleasantly ... their lives**': HCA op. cit, 155.

63   **On greetings cards**: The folklore still circulates widely in Europe: I bought a greetings card in Turkey in 1992, showing a large red heart wrapped in a snowy white napkin carried in a stork's beak – an illustration which interestingly conflated Valentine's Day and newborn imagery. Copyright, Ya-Pa Ltd.

63   **stick and stock**: John Dickson, letter, 5 July 1993, quotes W. B. Lockwood, *The Oxford Book of British Bird Names* (Oxford, 1984): 'In older German dialect, Storch could have the secondary meaning of penis ...'

63   **bird who delivers babies**: Grimm, *Teutonic Mythology,* II, 672–3.

63   ... **lutje Swester**: cf. 'Klapperstorch, du Luder/ brink mich en klenen Bruder.' In Ernst and Luise Gattiker, *Die Vogel im Volksglauben* (Weisbaden, 1989).

64   **D'Aulnoy and Perrault in Amsterdam**: 'Des Harlequins Kindbetterin-Schmaus', in Simon, op. cit., 34.

64   **greet a new arrival**: Letter to MW, 6 July 1993. I am most grateful to John Heath-Stubbs.

64   **clapperatie**: As in the comment made by Bishop Antonio de Guevara's letters of advice, tr. Cornelis van Beresteyn (Delft, 1583): ' 't Gene men in de mannen noemt soete gratie, hout men inden vrouwen voor clapperatie' [that which in men is called sweet grace, in women is considered babbling]'. Mariët Westermann, letter to MW, 19 July 1993. See also Bartholomaeus Anglicus, *De Rerum Proprietatibus* (Frankfurt [1601] 1964), 528–9.

65   **bird-bodied ... classical tradition**: See ch.23.

CHAPTER FIVE: NO HIDEOUS HUM

67   '... **riot in the cave**': Virgil, *Aeneid* VI, tr. W. F. Jackson Knight (Harmondsworth, 1969), 148.

67   '... **with her voice**': McGinn, 8; for Sibylline lore see Zielinksi, *La Sibylle: Trois essais sur la religion antique et le Christianisme* (Paris, 1924); J. Haffen, *Contribution à l'étude de la Sibylle médiévale* (Besançon–Paris, 1984); Peter Dronke, 'Hermes and the Sibyls: Continuations and Creations', in Dronke (1992), 219–44; Britnell, 'Reputation of Sibyls', kindly lent to MW. See also Britnell (1989).

67   '... **named Sibyl by the Libyans**': Pausanias, 435.

67   '... **was to come true**': Pausanias, 436.

67   '... **immortal nymph ...**': ibid., 435–6.

68   **earlier flight**: For a scholarly survey of the oracles and the history of their publication and editions, see Nikiprowetzky, esp. 281–7; McGinn, 9–11.

68   **his book The Divine Institutions**: Lactantius was following a list drawn up by Varro; see 219–44, 223–6.

68   '... **a fish of the sea**': *Oracula Sibyllina,* bk 1, 356–8, ed. C. Alexandre (2 vols, Paris, 1841–56) quoted Robin Lane-Fox, *Pagans & Christians* (London, 1986), 647–54; McGinn, 12–7.

68   '... **time's utmost limit**': Dronke (1992), 227.

69   '... **purposes for us**': Lane-Fox, op. cit., 648.

69   **a new beginning**: Virgil, Eclogue IV, 4–8. The verses announce: 'The last era of the Cumaean prophecy has come,/ the great sequence of ages is born anew;/ now the Virgin returns, the golden age returns,/ now the firstborn is sent down from high heaven.' tr. Henry Rushton Fairclough, in *Works,* eds T. E. Page and W. H. D. Rowse (2 vols, LCL, 1916–18).

69   **above the Sibyl and the emperor**: e.g. Maestro Veneziano, 'Vision of Augustus and the ruins of the Temple of Peace', *c.*1400, Stoccarda, repr. Salvatore Settis, ed., *Memoria dell'antico nell'arte italiana* (Turin, 1986), III, f.p.412; see Emile Male, *L'Art religieux de fin du moyen-âge,* (Paris, 1931), 280ff.

69   **translated ... ten years later**: McGinn, 12–9; Britnell, *Reputation of Sibyls.*

69   **Latin and Greek**: McGinn, 24.

70   '... **citizen of the city of God**': Augustine, *City of God,* 18, 23; he also cited her Hymn, see Dronke (1992), 9–13.

70   '**and the Sibyl testify**': Thomas of Celano, 'Dies irae', *The Penguin Book of Latin Verse,* ed. Frederick Brittain (Harmondsworth, 1962), 239–42.

70   **pavement of Siena Cathedral**: See Dronke (1992), 220–2.

71   **in praise of women**: e.g. *Le Mistère du viel testament,* ed. J. De Rothschild, VI (Paris, 1891); Symphorien

Champier, (Paris 1515); see D. P. Walker, *The Ancient Theology* (London, 1972), ch.3; Britnell, *Reputation of Sibyls*.

71   '... those God knows': *Prophetica Sibyllae Magae*, in Dronke (1992), 233, where he attributes it to a seventh-century Spanish origin.

71   mysteries of redemption: For a detailed, comprehensive and learned survey, see Carlo de Clercq, 'Contribution à l'iconographie des Sibylles – I', *Jaarboek*, 1979, Koninklijk Museum voor Schone Kunsten-Antwerpen, 7–60; II, ibid., 1980, 7–35; id., 'Les Sibylles dans les livres des XVe et XVIe siècles en Allemagne et en France', *Gutenberg Jahrbuch 1979*, 98–119; 'Quelques séries italiennes de Sibylles', *Bulletin de l'Institut Historique Belge de Rome*, Fascicules xlviii–xlix, 1978–9, 105–27; id., 'Quelques séries de Sibylles hors d'Italie', ibid., li, 1981, 87–116; see also, Emile Mâle, *Quomodo Sibyllas: Recentiores artifices repraesentaverint* (Paris, 1899); M. Hélin, 'Un texte inédit sur l'iconographie des Sibylles', *Revue belge de philologie et d'histoire* 15 (1936), 349–66.

72   Filippo Barbieri: *Opusculum de Vaticiniis Sibillarum* (Oppenheim, c.1514).

73   '... as Heraclitus wrote ...': De Clercq, 'Quelques séries italiennes'; Hélin, op. cit., 365.

73   pictures before the reader's eyes: *Oracula Sibyllina* (*Weissagungen der zwölf Sibyllen*), eds P. Heitz and W. L. Schreiber (Strasburg, 1903).

73   beam on high: Lactantius had not mentioned this Sibyl specifically prophesying the death of Jesus Christ. His Hellespontine sibyl uttered an open oracle: 'O Felix fructus ligno quo pendet alto.' But Sozomen, *Historia Ecclesiatica*, II:1, connected this prophecy to the Crucifixion, and French artists in the fifteenth century inaugurated this interpretation in the iconography. See Mâle, op. cit., 69.

73   halt and wrinkled: In the pavement of the Duomo at Siena, for instance, even the Erythraean Sibyl, though her head is covered in the style of a married woman, has not achieved a great age, while the Hellespontine defies the sources' specifications, and in Neroccio's chiselled evocation, appears with free-flowing hair like a sister of Botticelli's Flora.

74   others had believed: Britnell, *Reputation of Sibyls*.

75   '... from the prophetic cell': 'Nativity Ode', lines 173–80; see C. A. Patrides, 'That great and indisputable miracle: The Cessation of the Oracles', in Patrides, 105–23.

75   Ralegh ... their sanctuaries: *The History of the World*, I, vi, 8, quoted Patrides, op. cit., 107.

75   '... thenceforth held their peace': 'E. K.' Commentary on 'The Shepheardes Calender: May', line 54, ibid.

76   'White Ladies, Ladies, Goodwomen ...': Pierre de Lancre, *Tableau de l'inconstance des mauvais anges et démons ou il est amplement traité des sorciers et de la sorcellerie*, intro. Nicole Jacques-Chaquin (Paris, 1982), 89.

76   give her love charms: To Mme de Grignan, 30 Jan. 1680, *SC*, 2, 819–24.

77   '... to be more orthodox': Bernard de Fontenelle, *L'Histoire des oracles* (1686), ed. Louis Maigron (Paris, 1908), f–g.

77   several incensed pages: Servatius Gallaeus, *Dissertationes de Sibyllis, earumque oraculis* (Amsterdam, 1688), 182–4.

78   version of Van Dale: Fontenelle, op. cit., 10.

79   '... By Fortune seem'd design'd': *Queen Mab: containing A Select Collection of Only the Best, most Instructive and Entertaining Tales of the Fairies. Written by the Countess D'Aulnoi, Adorned with Curious Cuts. To which are added A Fairy Tale, in the ancient English style, by Dr Parnell. And Queen Mab's Song* (London, 1782), 365. (Opie Collection, Bodleian Library, Oxford.)

79   old wives' tales: *CBK*, 84–7.

CHAPTER SIX: SAINT ANNE, DEAR NAN

81   Infant Mary: Verses by Arias Montanus (Antwerp, 1571), added to images in sequence of engravings, *Vita Deiparae Virginis Mariae*, see p.87.

81   from the Holy Land: Another legend, which connects the cult of Saint Anne in the East more tightly to its development in the Roman church, described how Saint Helena had restored Saint Anne's tomb in Jerusalem, when she was discovering and enshrining the holy places, and had kept the body there, but sent the head to Apt. Charland (1898), I, 211–14; Louis Réau, III, 1, 90–6.

82   all over the Christian world: One finger was given to the Convent of the Visitation, rue St Antoine, in Paris, another to the Praemonstratensians in the same city; yet more fragments were presented to the church of St Eustache and the Confraternity of the Goldsmiths. Charland (1898), 226.

82   pardon pilgrimages ... in the province: At Sainte Anne d'Auray and Sainte Anne-la-Palud – 'Mort ou vivant, à Sainte Anne une fois doit aller tout Breton', the popular motto goes.

83   did not initiate it: See H. M. Bannister, 'The Introduction of the Cultus of St Anne into the West', *The English Historical Review*, XVIII (Jan. 1903), 107–12, for the cult's origins.

83   Speculum humanae salvationis and the Biblia pauperum: See *Biblia Pauperum Nach dem Original in der Lyceumbibliothek zu Constanz*, ed. Pfarrer Laib and Decan Schwartz (Zurich, 1867), pls. II, XXII; *Miroure of Mannes Salvationne: The Roxburghe Club edition of a fifteenth century English version in rhyming couplets*, (London, 1888); J. Lutz and P. Perdrizet, *Speculum Humanae Salvationis: Traduction inédite de Jean Miélot (1448)* (2 vols, Mulhouse, 1907); *Biblia Pauperum: A Facsimile Edition*, ed. Avril Henry (Ithaca, 1987).

83   prodigious offspring: Gerhard Schmidt, *Die Annenbibeln des XIV Jahrhunderts* (Graz–Köln, 1959), pl. 18; H.-F. Neumuller, ed., *Speculum Humanae Salvationis: Volkstandije Facsimile–Ausgabe des Codex Cremifanensis 243 (Kreuzmunster)* (Graz, 1972), fo. 15v/16r, fo. 55r; Adrian Wilson and Joyce Lancaster Wilson, *A Medieval Mirror: Speculum Humanae Salvationis 1324–1500* (Berkeley, 1984).

88   the birth of the incomparable Mary: Ton Brandenbarg, 'St Anne and her Family', in *Saints & She-Devils: Images of women in the 15th and 16th centuries*, ed. Lène Drense-Coenders (London, 1987), 101–27.

88   spiritual daughter: BN, MS Lat., 9474, fo. 3. Victor Leroquais, *Les Livres d'Heures ms. de la BN*, I (Paris 1927), pl. CXV.

88   sitting on her lap: See Brandenbarg (1987), op. cit., for accounts of Pieter Dorland, *Historia perpulchra de Anna sanctissima* (Antwerp, 1490) and Jan van Denemarken, *Die Historie, die ghetiden ende exemplen vander heyligher vrouwen Sint Annen* (Amsterdam, 1496); Ton Brandenbarg, *Heilig Familieleven* (Nijmegen, 1990).

88   benefits of her instruction: Brandenbarg op. cit. (1990), 40.

90   pictures in support: *Images de confrérie, Paris et Ile-de-France* (Catalogue), ed. José Lothe and Agnès Virole (Paris, 1992), 168–177, exhibition 18 Dec. 1991 to 7 Mar. 1992, Bibliothèque historique de la Ville de Paris.

90   desire for education: See Rapley, *passim*.

90   lessons in literacy: *The Education of the Virgin*, Frick Collection, New York.

90   collections of stories: Jean-Claude Schmitt, *La Raison des gestes dans l'occident médiéval* (Paris, 1990), 52–3, 258.

92   '... gentle granny': Brandenbarg op. cit. (1990), English abstract.

92   bathed by some helpers: See for example, Pedro Berruguete's painting at the end of C15th, *Pinacoteca*, Montserrat Monastery, Catalonia.

92   Zurbarán's magnificent version: Norton Simon Museum, Pasadena.

92   **young women bring her food and drink**: For other examples see P. Noury, 'L'alimentation des accouchées dans l'art', *Bulletin de la Société Médico-historique* (1909–10), 76–82.

92   **stork-shaped instruments**: See Hans van Kulmbach [1476–1522], *The Birth of the Virgin*, Sammlung Lippman, Berlin, reproduced in Volker Lehmann, *Die Geburt in der Kunst* (Braunschweig, 1978).

92   **placed on the Index for excessive enthusiasm**: Charland (1898), 286.

93   **loving teacher of the young**: e.g. Joseph Parrocel's drawings, 'Les Enfans viennent à lui' engraved for *La Bible de Paris*; Nicolaes Maes's painting, *Christ Blessing Children*, in the National Gallery, London, belongs in this wave of seventeenth-century homely piety.

93   **'... tender name that little children use'**: Jean-Joseph Surin, *Correspondance*, ed. Michel de Certeau (Bruges, 1966), letter 206 (1658–9), 696–7, quoted Loskoutoff, 62.

94   **rule by women**: Abbé Fénelon, *Oeuvres*, ed. Aimé Martin, II *Recueil de Fables composées pour l'éducation de Mgr. Le Duc de Bourgogne (1689–)* (Paris, 1870), 512ff; Loskoutoff, 154–5.

95   **while one rocks the crib**: *Vita Deiparae Virginis Mariae* (see 81 (i) above).

CHAPTER SEVEN: THE MAGIC OF THE CROSS
97   **'... girt me with gold and silver'**: 'The Dream of the Rood', *The Earliest English Poems*, tr. Michael Alexander (Harmondsworth, 1966), 109.

98   **Ethiopian Christian Church**: E. A. Wallis Budge (ed. and tr.), *The Queen of Sheba and her Only Son Menyelek*, I (Oxford, 1892).

98   **Legends of the Queen of Sheba**: Chastel, I, 61–122; also Beyer; Daum; Pritchard; St John Philby.

98   **Sibyl called Sabbe**: Pausanias, 437.

98   **name was Sibylla**: Georges Monachos, *Chronique*, quoted by J. Haffen, *Contribution à l'Etude de la Sibylle Médiévale: Etude et édition du ms, BN f.Fr. 25 407 fol. 160v–172v: Le Livre de Sibile* (Paris, 1984), 37.

98   **'... events to be recognized'**: Copy in the Warburg Institute; original in the Berlin Stadtsbibliothek.

98   **heathen and Jew**: e.g: *Sibyllenbuch* (Frankfurt, 1531); *Weissagungen der zwölf Sibyllen* (Frankfurt, 1534); *Zwölf Sibyllen Weissagungen* (Frankfurt, 1565), of which several copies are extant. The queen is sometimes given the name Nicaula. Josephus, *Antiquitates Judaicae*. Viii, vi, i, refers to the Queen by this name. See Introduction in Daum, 20. See also F. Neri, 'Le tradizioni italiane della Sibilla', *Studi Medievali 4* (1912–13), 213–30.

98   **aetiology ... cross**: Mariane Overgaard gives the clearest account I have read of the composite tale's history, xxi–xxxvi; see also E. C. Quinn, *The Quest of Seth for the Oil of Life* (Chicago, 1962); Gertrude Schiller, *The Iconography of Christian Art*, tr. Janet Seligman (London, 1971), II, 12–4.

99   **omnivorous mind**: Petrus Comestor, ed. J. J. Migne, *Patrologia Latina*, 198, col.40; Johannes Beleth, writing before 1165, also passed on the material. See Jean Beleth, *Rationale Divinorum Officiorum*, ch.151; Migne, op. cit., 202, col.152.

99   **Thomas Malory**: Malory's source was a late C13th epic called *Cursor Mundi*; he tells how it was Eve who planted the very branch on which the forbidden apple grew. His story then interweaves Arthurian motifs on to the warp of the Solomon legend. Sir Thomas Malory, *Le Morte d'Arthur*, ed. Sir John Rhys (2 vols, London, 1967), II, chs.5–7, 242–7. David Freeman's dramatization and production, *Morte d'Arthur*, July 1990, at The Lyric, Hammersmith and St Paul's Church, managed to give a clear account of this tangled episode.

99   **dead father**: *GL*, III, 125–36, v, 169–76.

99   **allow Christian pilgrims to enter**: Felix Faber, *Evagatorum in Terrae Sanctae Arabiae et Egypti peregrinationem*,

tr. Aubrey Stewart (2 vols, London, 1897), I, 429.

100   **'... defaced and cease'**: *GL*, III, 170.

100   **'... whatsoever sickness he was sick of'**: *GL*, ibid.

100   **'... depths of the cistern'**: Faber, op. cit., 456.

100   **'... the cross of our Lord'**: *GL*, III, 170.

100   **Jacobus' narrative scheme**: For Piero della Francesca see Lionello Venturi, *Piero della Francesca*, tr. James Emmons (Geneva, 1954), 52–92; Michael Podro, 'Piero della Francesca's Legend of the True Cross' (Newcastle, 1974); Stephen Bann, *The True Vine* (Cambridge, 1989), 225ff.; Marilyn Aronberg Lavin, *Piero della Francesca* (London, 1992).

103   **dread and fascination**: See Elizabeth McGrath, 'The Black Andromeda', *JWCI*, LV, 1992.

103   **Moorish Queen of Sheba**: See Jean Devisse, ed., *The Image of the Black in Western Art*, II *From the Early Christian Era to the 'Age of Discovery'* (Cambridge, Mass., 1979), part 1, 132–3.

104   **behind the Queen**: *The Hours of Catherine of Cleves*, ed. and intro. John Plummer (London, 1966), pls. 79–87

104   **her flowing golden hair**: ibid., part 2, 37–8.

105   **most important saints**: Wallis Budge, op. cit., viii–xii; Marcel Griaule, 'Légende illustrée de la Reine de Saba', *Documents*, 2, 1 (1930), 9–16 reproduces a painted Ethiopian narrative variation on the legend.

106   **Egypt and Ethiopia**: Josephus, op. cit., VIII, vi, i.

106   **'... many kinds of perfume'**: Herodotus, *The Histories*, tr. Aubrey de Selincourt, rev. A. R. Burn (Harmondsworth, 1983), III, 106–12, 248–9.

106   **myth of the Orient**: In the writing of the last *fin de siècle*, the Queen of Sheba's name instantly connects with seduction (Yeats wrote: 'Sang Solomon to Sheba,/ And kissed her dusky face'; Flaubert's Saint Antoine is tormented in the desert by the myriad coloured delights when she tempts him); see also Gérard de Nerval, 'Histoire de Soliman et de la Reine du Matin', in *Voyage en Orient* (Paris, 1851).

106   **The Queen of Sheba ... the apostle Philip**: Gérard Cames, *Allégories et symboles dans l'Hortus Deliciarum* (Leiden, 1971), 53, pl. XXXIX.

107   **two compositions**: Lavin, op. cit., 78.

108   **Church of the (converted) Jews**: Cames, op. cit., 52–3.

108   **Hans Holbein**: *Solomon and the Queen of Sheba*, Royal Collection, Windsor Castle. Justifications of colonial enterprise in C16th and C17th also adopted Solomon as a forerunner. See Kate Chedgzoy, 'Moralizing the colonial body: discourses of difference in early modern writing', paper kindly lent by the author (to be published in Liverpool, *Studies in Language and Discourse*).

109   **wise dancing girl**: Edward Said, *Orientalism* (Harmondsworth, 1991), 186; see also Marina Warner, 'In and Out of the Fold' in *Out of the Garden: Women Writers on the Bible*, eds. Christina Büchmann and Celina Spiegel (New York, 1994).

CHAPTER EIGHT: THE GLASS PAVING AND THE SECRET FOOT
111   **John Donne**: 'Tell me where all past years are,/ Or who cleft the Devil's foot ...', 'Song', *NOEV*, 184.

111   **Sheba ... in the Koran**: 'The Ant', *The Koran*, tr. N. J. Dawood (Harmondsworth, 1972), 82–4; St John Philby, 43–52.

111   **beetle for her lunch**: J. C. Mardrus, *The Queen of Sheba Translated into French from his own Arabic text* (London, 1918); tr. E. Powys Mathers (London, 1924), 63.

111   **'... Lord of the creation'**: *Koran*, ibid., 84.

112   **suffers from hairy legs**: The extant sources of the Arabic story include Al-Tabari [*b*.838], *Annals*; Abu Mansur al-Tha'labi [*b*.1038] and Izz al-Din Ibn al-Athir [*b*.1160], see St John Philby, 43–9.

112   **lime and arsenic**: After this some versions continue, 'He smeared her with it and washed her and her hair fell off. Then he had intercourse with her right away.' *The Alphabet of Ben Sira*, tr. and ed. Norman M. Bronznick, in *Fiction (Rabbinic Fantasy)*, VII, nos. 1, 2 (New York, 1983), 99–135.

113   **stork or an ostrich**: Chiara Settis Frugoni, 'Per una Lettura del mosaico pavimentale della Cattedrale di Otranto'(Rome, 1968), *Bullettino dell'Istituto storico Italiano per il Medio Evo e Archivio Muratoriano*, 80, 213ff.; Carl Arnold Willemsen, *L'Enigma di Otranto: Il mosaico pavimentale del presbitero Pantaleone nella Cattedrale* (Otranto, 1980).

113   **'… longed-for sight of the female member'**: 'Fetishism' (1927), FSE, XXI, 152–7.

113   **'feet' here stand for sexual organs**: My thanks to Scott Mandelbrote for pointing this out to me. I have quoted the Jerusalem Bible because the Authorized Version, reiterating the euphemism, treats the seraphim as male angels. See Rooth, 104–5, on shoes' symbolism.

114   **neither a siren song**: John Skelton noted, 'He [the ostrich] cannot well fly/ Nor sing tunably …', 'Philip Sparrow', *NOEV*, 29.

114   **have cloven feet**: Linnaeus calls the bird '*Struthio camelus*' for this reason; Rowland (1978), 55.

114   **'… which are crested and fly'**: St Jerome, Letter 21: 13, 4, quoted Paul Antin, 'Les Sirènes et Ulysse dans l'oeuvre de S. Jérome', *Revue des études Latines, xxxix* (1961), 232–41.

114   **'… bestial forms of angels or demons …'**: ibid., 233.

115   **'… the songs of poets'**: St Jerome, Letter 21: 13, 4, quoted Antin, op. cit., 238.

115   **'… difficult to keep one's modesty'**: St Jerome, Letter 117: 6, 4, quoted Antin, op. cit., 235.

115   **The Queen of Sheba … had webbed feet**: Honorius Augustodunensis, 'Saba quoque Ethiopissa et regina quoque et Sibilla habens pedes anserinos'. See W. Hertz, 23–4, Overgaard, XXV.

115   **a drawing from 1739 survives**: Dom Urbain Plancher, *Histoire générale et particulière de Bourgogne* (Dijon, 1739), reproduced in Isabelle Grange, 'Métamorphoses chrétiennes des femmes-cygnes: Du folklore à l'hagiographie', *Ethnologie française xiii* (1983), 2, 139–47, 143.

117   **'… Sibilla was filled with joy'**: 'Sibyllen Weissagung', ed. I. Neske, *Göppinger Arbeiten zur Germanistik* 438 (Göppingen, 1985). Peter Dronke directed me to this poem; without his help I would never have read it. He also generously translated the relevant verses for me.

117   **many interpreters**: See also O. Schade, 'Sibillen Boich', in O. Schade, *Geistliche Gedichte des XIV, und XV Jahrhunderts vom Niederrhein* (Hanover, 1854), 293–332, for two prints of 1513 and 1515 from Cologne which reprise the story and the message.

118   **hellfire for those who do not**: *Sibillen Weissagen* (Ulm, 1492), Berliner Stadtsbibliothek. See *Drucke von Johann Schaffler* (Ulm, 1498), iii, pl. 106;

118   **recognizing the bridge**: Faber, op. cit., 522.

119   **playwright Terence**: Heinrich Steinhovel, translator of Aesop and Boccaccio is said to be portrayed as Terence, and Hans Neithard, the humanist mayor, as Cicero. Wolfgang Lipp, *Guide to Ulm Cathedral* (Ulm, 1991), 20; see also Reinhard Wortmann, *Das Ulmer münster* (Stuttgart, 1972).

119   **Jorg Syrlin strategically placed**: See Reinhard Workmann, *Das Ulmer münster* (Stuttgart, 1972), and Wilhelm Vöge, *Jorg Syrlin der Altere und Seine bildwerke*, (2 vols, Berlin, 1950).

120   **Boec van der Houte**: *Historia Sanctae Crucis* or *Boec van den Houte* (Kuilenburg, 1483); *The Legendary History of the Cross*, ed. and pub. John Ashton (London, 1887), intro. Sabine Baring-Gould.

120   **Thomas Malory rather than The Golden Legend**: See ch.7.

120   **torture of the Sibyl**: In the 1887 facsimile, the beautiful young Sibyl tied to a stake and beaten by the miscreant unbelievers has an ordinary shaped foot – so imagine my delight then when I went to the King's Library in The Hague to see an original copy, printed by John Veldenaer in 1483, and found there, her foot is visibly splayed, long and webbed. Ashton commissioned M. J. Ph. Berjeau to make the facsimile woodcuts, and he must have misunderstood this distorted shape in the original (in the verses attached, her goosefoot is not mentioned).

121   **'… hands or the feet'**: *A Marvellous History of Mary of Nimmegen*, tr. Harry Moragan Ayres (The Hague and London, 1923), 12.

121   **listing to the left**: F. Saxl, 'A Spiritual Encyclopaedia of the Later Middle Ages', *JWCI*, V (1942), 82–134. See for instance the woodcuts to Ulrich Molitor, *De Laniis et Phitonicis Mulieribus* (Basel, 1495).

121   **'lust scatters all that it possesses'**: *Mitologiarum libri tres*, ed. R. Helm (Leipzig, 1898), II.viii, 48–9. I am most grateful to Nick Havely for this citation.

121   **'… cats' paws or horses' hooves'**: Ginzburg, 122.

122   **girls to seduce victims**: Graves, I, 189–90.

122   **witch of the title**: *Games and Songs of American Children*, ed. William Wells Newell and Carl Withers (New York, 1963), 215–21.

123   **defects as splay feet**: See John Gross, *Shylock: Four Hundred Years in the Life of a Legend* (London, 1992), 297–8.

123   **from her rump**: F. Saxl, 'Illustrated Pamphlets of the Reformation', *Lectures* (London, 1957), I, 255–66, pls. 179a, c.

123   **'… Then womans shape would beleeve to bee …'**: Edmund Spenser, *The Faerie Queene*, ed. J. W. Hales (2 vols, London, 1966), Canto II, XLI, i, 41.

123   **'… yet never living creature saw'**: ibid., Canto VIII, XLVIII, i, 115.

124   **women's vulvae speak**: Irwin, 239, perceptively places Diderot in the tradition of the wonder tale.

124   **did not complete it**: Storer, 144.

125   **Adenet le Roi**: Adenes li Rois, *Li Roumans de Berte aus Grans Pies*, ed. A. Scheler (Brussels, 1874); Berlioz, *et al.*, 165–72. See also Gaston Paris, *Histoire poétique de Charlemagne* (Paris, 1865), and id., 'La Légende de Pepin "Le Bref"', in *Mélanges Julien Havet* (Paris, 1895).

126   **'… dame de son courant'**: 'Berta da li pè grandi' in *'Le Geste Francor' di Venezia*, ed. Aldo Rosellini (Brescia, 1986), lines 1301–2.

126   **La Reine Pédauque**: No images have survived, unfortunately. But Rabelais reported seeing one in Toulouse, and sculptures from St Pierre in Nevers and at Nesles-la-Reposte and St Pourçain in Burgundy were described and drawn by different sources. See Emile Mâle, *L'Art religieux du 12e siècle en France* (Paris, 1940), 394ff.

126   **Flor and Blancheflor … star-crossed love**: See Charles Méla, *Blanchefleur et le saint homme ou la semblance des reliques: Etude comparée de littérature medievale* (Paris, 1979); the medieval romance was translated, as a book for children: *The Sweet and Touching Tale of Fleur and Blanchefleur*, tr. Mrs Leighton, illus. Eleanor Fortescue Brickdale (London, 1922).

126   **'daughter of the King of Hungary'**: Schlauch, 62–78, 132–4; Godefroy of Viterbo, *Speculum Regum*, towards the end of the C12th, wrote an early version; Alexandre Eckhardt, *De Sicambria à sans-souci: Histoires et légendes franco-hongroises* (Paris, 1943), 96–100.

126   **'powerful athlete of Christ'**: See *Les Belles Heures du Duc de Berry*, intro. James J. Rorrimer, notes Margaret B. Freeman (London, 1959), fo. 174, where the Limbourg Brothers have depicted the Suffrage of Saint Charlemagne.

127   **defamed or otherwise wronged wife**: Schlauch, *passim*, esp. 54–6, 62–78, 120–3; AT 403, 450, 706. Vincent of Beauvais included in the *Speculum Historiale* a pious

version, in which the victim is rescued by the Virgin Mary; the story was not often represented, but it was painted on the walls of Eton College Chapel (mostly now covered over) and was sculpted in the C15th in Norwich Cathedral. See M. R. James, *The Sculptured Bosses in the Roof of the Bauchun Chapel of Our Lady of Pity in Norwich Cathedral* (Norwich, 1908).

128   '... **a mark of her higher nature**': Grimm, I, 279ff.

128   **woman who works a spinning wheel**: See Joseph Needham, *Science and Civilisation in China*, 5, part 9 (Cambridge, 1988), 163–9. The earliest images in the West appear in the windows of Chartres, *c.*1240–5; Leonardo drew one of the most advanced ideas of his time for combined spindle, bobbin, and flyer, *c.*1490 in the *Codex Atlanticus*.

CHAPTER NINE: ON RIDDLES, ASSES AND THE WISDOM OF FOOLS

130   '**Kneeling shows the female sex**': Ostoia, 73ff., gives the fullest and most inspiring account of these legends and their expressions.

130   **beliefs about Solomon's wizardry**: Innocent III had *Le Livre de Salomon* burned in 1359, for instance, though a first edition – magically – appears in Rome in 1629, Grillot de Givry, E.-J., *Le Musée des sorciers, mages et alchimistes* (Paris, 1980), 86ff.

132   **forty-two similar posers**: J. Archer Taylor, 'Riddles dealing with Family Relationships', *JAF* 51 (1938), 25–37, 27.

132   **Exeter Book of riddles**: W. S. Mackie, *The Exeter Book* (Oxford, 1934).

132   '... **the others are opened**': From Yachya Ben Suleiman, 'The Yemen Midrash (Hachephez): Commentary on the Pentateuch' (*c.*1430), British Library, Oriental MS, 2351, 2380–82. See S. Schechter, 'The Riddles of Solomon in Rabbinic Literature', *Folklore 1* (1890), 349–58; Daum, 36–8; Ostoia, 85.

132   **fast horses and other pleasures**: J. B. Pritchard (ed.), *Ancient Near Eastern Texts Relating to the Old Testament* (Princeton, 1974), 72–3.

133   **as well as storytelling**: Calderon de la Barca dramatized a riddle contest in *La Sibila de Oriente y Gran Reina de Saba*. Ostoia, 91.

133   '... **Roman pikemen and the dwarf**': *Verklaringe van verscheyden kunst-rijcke wercken en hare bewinginghe, door oorlogie-werck ghedreven* [Explanation of different art works and their movements, moved by clockwork ...], (Amsterdam, 1648). Ostoia, 82, alludes to the attraction, and I am very grateful indeed to Dimphena Groffen for finding the guide book and translating the passage for me.

133   **non-Christian trickery**: Servatii Gallaeus, *Dissertationes de Sibyllis, earumque oraculis* (Amsterdam, 1688), 199–200.

133   **impossible tasks ... of folk narrative**: Bengt Holbek, 'Hans Christian Andersen's Use of Folktales', in *The Telling of Stories: Approaches to a Traditional Craft* (Odense, 1990), 165–82, 174.

134   '**Serpentin vert**': Marie-Catherine d'Aulnoy, 'The Great Green Worm', tr. A. S. Byatt, *WT*, 189–229.

134   **poor peasant's clever daughter**: See Jones (1989); id., 'Marcolf and the Bum in the Oven'; Michael Camille, *Image on the Edge: The Margins of Medieval Art* (London, 1993), 26–7, pl. 15, showing the early C14th Ormesby Psalter's image of the solution. See also, 'The Wise Little Girl', in *VFT-I*, 28–30 .

135   '**He flew away in a blazing flame**': In *The Unco Knicht's Wowing*, *CPB*, I, 4–5; cf. Judith Weir's libretto for her opera *The Vanishing Bridegroom*, part III, Scottish Opera, 1990, printed in Royal Opera House programme, n.p.

135   '**Profound, profound**': Colin Radford, 'Wittgenstein and "Fairy Tales"', in *MC*, II,2 (Dec. 1988), 106–10.

135   **gives the right solutions**: Puccini's librettists were Giuseppe Adami and Renato Simoni, and their immediate source was Carlo Gozzi's play of 1761; one of the earliest extant literary versions is 'The Story of Prince Calaf', early C13th, Persian. See Irwin, 101; also Mike Ashman,'From Peking to Milan', in programme of *Turandot*, Royal Opera House, Covent Garden, 1993.

135   **her sex is put to the proof**: AT, 514; '*Marmoisan, ou l'Innocente tromperie*', *LHBI*, 3–66; see Caroline Trost, '*Belle-Belle ou le Chevalier Fortuné*: A Liberated Woman in a Tale by Mme d'Aulnoy', *MC*, v,1 (May 1991), 57–67.

135   **spoofs this basic convention of romance**: 'Histoire de la Marquise-Marquis de Banneville', *Le Mercure galant*, Feb. 1695; see Ranjit Bolt (tr.), 'The Counterfeit Marquise', *WT*, 123–47.

136   '**churning tub**' ... **beginning of the century**: *Icogniti scriptoris nova poemata enigmata, sive emblemata amatoria* (Leiden, 1624), intro. Jochen Becker (Soest, 1972), n.p. Thanks to Mariët Westermann for drawing this edition to my attention.

136   **alone at her spinning**: ibid., 26, 70–1.

136   '**It is a candle**': *New Riddles* (Derby, *c.*1790), Osborne Collection, Toronto.

136   **which told riddles**: *A Book of Riddles* was among the ten favourite chapbooks in the seventeenth century, see Watt, 270–1; e.g. *Food for the Mind: or, a new Riddle Book* (E. Newbery: London, 1778).

136   '... **in this riddle book**': *The Riddle Book; or, Fireside Amusements* (Derby, n.d), Osborne Collection, Toronto.

137   **commendable prophets**: Daum, 57.

139   **precious to God in consequence**: See L. Charbonneau-Lassay, *La Mystérieuse emblématique de Jésus-Christ* (Milan, 1940), 224–233.

140   **add their voices to the chorus**: Dronke (1992), 228; Karl Young, *The Drama of the Medieval Church* (Oxford, 1933), 2, 126–31.

141   '... **like someone crazed**': Young, op. cit., 145.

141   **with a drawn sword**: ibid., 152; see also William Hone, *Ancient Mysteries Described: especially the English Miracle Plays including ... the Festivals of Fools and Asses...* (London, *c.*1825), 160–6. My thanks to Peter Hay for bringing this entertaining miscellany to my notice.

142   **then provides the solutions**: op. cit. *The Riddle Book; or, Fireside Amusements*.

143   **classicists are still reviewing**: See Lucian of Samosata, ed. M. D. Macleod (London, 1967), *Lucius, or the Ass*, intro., 47–51; Perry, 211–82.

143   **formation of fairy tale**: Perry, ibid.; Hägg, 182–6; Reardon, 44–5.

144   '**no vice of which I am less guilty**': Lucien, *Histoire véritable*, tr. Perrot d'Ablancourt [1654] (Arles, 1988).

144   '... **a reed for a mast**': ibid., 27.

145   **that most famous of fairy plays**: See Jan Kott, *The Bottom Translation: Marlowe and Shakespeare and the Carnival Tradition*, tr. Daniela Miedzyrzecka and Lillian Vallee (Evanston, 1987), 29–68.

146   '... **ass his master's crib**': *Les Pensées chrétiennes de Charles Perrault: Papers on French seventeenth century literature*, ed. Jacques Barchilon and Catherine Velay-Vallantin (Paris, Seattle, Tübingen, 1987), 75–80.

146   '... **I should cry out indeed!**': 'Li Response du Bestiare', in Richard de Fournival, *Li Bestiare d'amours/Il bestiario d'amore*, ed. Francesco Zambon (Parma, 1987), 96, lines 20–5.

CHAPTER TEN: SWEET TALK, PLEASANT LAUGHTER

147   '**Aye, by-and-by**': *ONR*, 433–4. *MGM* has 'a blanket' instead of 'a basket', and other small variations.

148   **no further resistance**: *OM*, XIV, 621–769, pp.328–32.

148   **The theme enters art**: e.g. Paulus Morelsee

[*d*.1638], *Vertumnus and Pomona*, Boymans van Beuningen Museum, Rotterdam; Hugo von Hofmannsthal, in the libretto of *Die Frau ohne Schatten* (1919), borrows this stock character of the Nurse who speaks as a tempter.

148 **the voice of an old woman**: A, 96.

149 **place and power of laughter**: See Mihail Bakhtin, *Rabelais and His World*, tr. Helene Iswolsky (Bloomington, 1984), 82ff.; Propp, 'Ritual Laughter in Folklore', in Propp (1984), 124–46.

149 **titter out of her**: B, I, 3–12.

150 **prince of Camporotondo's true bride**: ibid., II, 533–5. 12.

150 **Baubô's similar antics**: See Propp, op. cit. (1984), 129 for related tales, including a remarkable Eskimo parallel in which the exposed woman is a ravenous goddess called Erdlaverissok (the disemboweller).

150 **youth with the flute**: 'Von der Königstochter die nie lachen wollte' in *Kroatische Volksmarche*, ed. Maja Bosovic-Stulli, tr. Antoinette Baker, quoted Baker, '"A Time to Laugh" A Study of Laughter: Its Psychology, and its Role in Analysis' (Dipl. Thesis, Jung Institute, Zurich, 1980), 81–2; the Grimms collected a cleaner version of this story, 'The Golden Goose', for their 1812 anthology, GZ, 256–9.

151 '**... unkindness of the real circumstances**': 'Humour', FSE, XXI, 161–6.

151 **potential for disruption and change**: Cixous and Clément, 32–4.

151 **made her smile again, even laugh**: Apollodorus, *The Library*, tr. J. G. Frazer (Harvard and London, 1921), bk 1, v, 36–7; see also C. G. Jung and C.Kerenyi, *Essays on a Science of Mythology: The Myth of the Divine Child and the Mysteries of Eleusis*, tr. R. F. C. Hull (Princeton, 1969), 130–1.

151 '**... from out the glancing cup**': Clement of Alexandria, *Exhortation to the Greeks*, ch.II, 17, ed. and tr. G. W. Butterworth (London and Cambridge, 1960), 40–3; *Orphicum Fragmenta*, ed. Otto Kern (Berlin, 1963), 128; Jung and Kerenyi, 244.

153 '**... jesting with made up stories**': Phaedrus, Prologue to bk III. *Babrius and Phaedrus*, ed. and tr. B. E. Perry (Harvard and London, 1965), 245–55.

153 '**Only equals may laugh**': Alexander Herzen, *On Art* (Moscow, 1954), 223, quoted Bakhtin, op. cit., 92.

154 '**... And make you laugh your Fill**': *A Whetstone for Dull Wits or a Poesy of New and Ingenious Riddles*, title page, CBK, 295.

154 **Fool's ... physical sides of the part**: e.g. cross-dressed in *King Lear*, dir. Max Stafford-Clark, Royal Court, 1992.

154 **nursery rhymes, pantomime plots**: e.g. *MGM*; Mother Goose, *Mother Goose's Melody: or, Sonnets for the Cradle* (London, *c*.1780); *Histories of Past Times: Told by Mother Goose with Morals*, Englished by G. M. Gent (Salisbury, 1802); *Fairy Tales of past times from Mother Goose* (Edinburgh, 1805, Glasgow, 1814); *The History of the Celebrated Nanny Goose and the History of the Prince Renardo and the Lady Goosiana* [1813] (Toronto, 1973); *Old Mother Goose* (Routledge 3d. Toy Book: London, n.d.); Kate Greenaway, *Mother Goose, or the Old Nursery Rhymes* (London, 1881); *Familiar Selections from the Rhymes of Mother Goose*, with new pictures by Chester Loomis (London, 1888), 154; *Mother Goose's Nursery Rhymes and Fairy Tales* (London, 1892); *Grandpapa Easy, Mother Goose and the Golden Eggs* (London, n.d.); J. Barchilon and H. Pettit (eds), *The Authentic Mother Goose Tales and Nursery Rhymes* (Denver, 1960). See Humphrey Carpenter, 'Mother Goose', in *Oxford Companion to Children's Literature* (Oxford, 1986), 362ff.; Marina Warner, 'Speaking with Double Tongue: Mother Goose and the Old Wives' Tale', in *The Myths of the English*, ed. Roy Porter (Cambridge, 1992), 33–67.

155 '**... book of Suffolk names**': *MGM*, 4.

155 **Newbery's Mother Goose's Melody**: It was reprinted in the US in 1794; see *MGM*.

155 **Sarah Martin in 1805**: 'The Comic Adventures of Old Mother Hubbard and her Dog', in ONC, 5–8, 28–31.

156 '**And yet the old woman could never be quiet**': *Denslow's Mother Goose, being the old familiar rhymes and jingles of Mother Goose* (London and Edinburgh, 1902), 155.

156 '**... bimble bamble bumble**': *Willy Pogány's Mother Goose* (New York, 1928), n. p.

157 **pranks ... intended to be funny**: Eleanor Mure, *The Story of the Three Bears* [1831] (Toronto, 1967).

157 '**... St Paul's churchyard steeple**': ibid.

157 '**... set about helping herself**': Robert Southey, 'The Story of the Three Bears', in *The Doctor, etc.* iv, (London, 1837), 320–1.

157 '**... the Three Bears never saw anything more of her**': ibid., 326.

157 **often been taken for witches**: See Christina Larner, *Enemies of God: The Witch-Hunt in Scotland* (London, 1981); Alan McFarlane, 'Witchcraft in Tudor and Stuart Essex', in Mary Douglas (ed.), *Witchcraft Confessions and Accusations* (London, 1970), 81–99.

158 **crease of her Bible**: e.g., Saint Anne in *A Geertgen tot Sint Jans* [The Holy Kinship] (1485), Rijksmuseum, Amsterdam. See Robert Maitron, 'Des Lunettes et des Hommes ou la satire des mal-voyants au XVIe siècle' *Annales: Economies-Sociétés-Civilisations* 30 (1975), 375–93).

158 **ancient and mannish hag**: Ryoji Tsurumi, 'The Development of Mother Goose in Britain in the Nineteenth Century', *Folklore*, 101:1 (1990), 28–35; David Mayer III, *Harlequin in his Element: The English Pantomime* (London, 1949), 25.

160 '**... present as well as future happiness**': 'Advice to her Young Readers', i.e. *Tales of Past Times by Old Mother Goose with Morals* (London and York, 1798), 93–4.

CHAPTER ELEVEN: IN THE KINGDOM OF FICTION

161 '**... better to tell a plain truth?**': *The Complete Letters of Lady Mary Wortley Montagu*, ed. Robert Halsband (Oxford, 1965), I, 293.

161 '**The Isle of Happiness', of 1690**: Marie-Catherine d'Aulnoy, 'L'Ile de la Félicité', in *Histoire d'Hypolite, Comte de Duglas* (Paris, 1690; repr. Robert: 1984); 'The Island of Happiness', in ZBB (New York, 1989), 299–308.

163 '**... people of good breeding**': *Les Contes de fées par Mme. d***, III (Paris, 1710), 108–9.

163 '**denying him ... use of speech**': La Fontaine, 'La vie d'Esope le Phrygien', *Oeuvres complètes*, 12.

163 **a very fine wit**: ibid.

165 '**... liberty to say what they think**': *Les Fables de Pilpay Philosophe Indien ou La Conduite des Rois* (Paris, 1697), n.p.

165 **Tales of the Fairies appeared**: Palmer (1974), 237–53.

166 '**like a monkey a chestnut**': D'Aulnoy, 'La Belle aux cheveux d'or', in *CF-II*, I , 268.

166 **baby eagles and other nestlings**: D'Aulnoy, 'La Chatte Blanche', *CF-II*, 26; idem, tr., John Ashbery, 'The White Cat', *WT*, 27.

166 '**... the Countess Danois**': D'Aulnoy, *Collection* (1721–2).

166 **accordingly modified**: e.g. *Mother Bunch's Fairy Tales. Published for the Amusement of all those Little Masters and Misses, who By Duty to their Parents, and Obedience to their Superiors, Aim at Becoming Great Lords and Ladies* (E. Newbery: London, 1790).

167 '**That on thee I may cast an eye**': D'Aulnoy (1708), 38.

167 '**... notre siècle est fertile ...**': D'Aulnoy, 'L'oiseau bleu', ibid., 154; *CF-II*, 138; Anne Thackeray Ritchie's translation (1892) dropped the morals altogether.

167 '**And Wedlock throw her Chains aside ...**': D'Aulnoy, *Collection* (1721–2).

168 **position of protest**: See DeJean (1981), DeJean

(1991), 142ff.; Marina Warner, intro., *WT*, 3–17.
168   **Catherine of Siena and Héloïse**: Aegidio
Menagio, *Historia Mulierum Philosopharum* (Amsterdam,
1692).
168   **because she was a woman**: Storer, 63.
169   **'... horror of vice inspires in them'**: Fénelon,
De l'Education des filles, ed. Charles Defodon (Paris, 1902),
71–2; quoted Gibson, 19.
169   **touching hymn of praise**: Charles Perrault,
Oeuvres posthumes (Paris, 1706), 358ff.
169   **of comparatively recent date**: See *Lettre de M.*
Mignot de Bussy de L'Académie de Villefranche à M. de Vertron de
l'Académie Royale d'Arles au sujet de la préférence que doit avoir la
langue française sur la Latine, que M. de C. soutient être la plus
belle (Villefranche, 1687), for a good example of the kind of
passionate and pedantic intervention the debate inspired.
169   **bastard child of the vulgar crowd**: See Villiers,
passim; Paul Bonnefon, 'Les dernières années de Charles
Perrault', *Revue d'histoire littéraire de la France* (1906), 606–57.
169   **Frenchmen like Racine and Poussin**: See
Perrault, *Hommes Illustres*, I (Paris, 1696); II (Paris, 1700).
170   **milk here can be taken to mean language**: See
Louis Marin, 'La voix d'un conte: entre La Fontaine et
Perrault, sa récriture', in *Littératures populaires: Du dit à l'écrit*,
Critique Paris (1980), vol.36, no.394, 333–42; Hélène Cixous
on 'white ink', *Sorties*, in Cixous and Clément, 94, inspired
the idea of this connection.
170   **'... ordinarily best to consult women'**: DeJean
(1981), 301.
170   **either sisters or cousins**: see Hallays, 293–4.
However the writer is almost always referred to as
Perrault's niece. See also Storer, 42–60; DeJean (1991), 212.
170   **eulogy after her friend's death**: Marie-Jeanne
L'Héritier, *L'Apothéose de Mlle de Scudéry* (Paris, 1702).
170   **attend the chariot of Clio**: ibid., 25.
170   **Muses as the tenth**: LH*BI*, 326–7.
171   **Perrault's Mother Goose ... but also hers**: See
Storer, 44ff.; Delarue.
171   **'... held my spirit enthralled'**: Charles Perrault,
Griselidis Nouvelle avec le conte de Peau d'Asne des celuy des
Souhaits ridicules (Paris, 1694) n.p.
171   **'... hollow of her hand'**: Jeanne Roche-Mazon,
'Les Fées de Perrault et la Véridique Mère l'Oye', *Revue*
Hebdomadaire (17 Dec. 1932), 158.
173   **troubadours and storytellers of Provence**:
LH*TT*, 236ff.
173   **'The Subtle Princess'**: LH*BI*, 169ff.; tr. Gilbert
Adair, *WT*, 65–97.
173   **... and as one speaks**: LH*BI*, 169.
173   **'... troubadours invented'**: ibid., 171.
174   **aficionados the manuscript itself**: M, 153–263;
'Starlight', tr. Terence Cave, *WT*, 149–87; Dronke (1994),
76–81, 136–7, 143.
174   **'... keep them under wraps'**: LH*BI*, repr. in
Perrault, *Contes*, ed. Giraud (Paris, 1865), 296.
175   **'... ancient, foolish stories'**: Marie-Jeanne
L'Héritier, '*Ricdin-Ricdon*', LH*TT*; *CF*-I, XII, 126.
175   **... King Richard who is speaking, but me'**:
CF-I, XII, 24.
176   **salon name ... was Télésille**: Claude-Charles
Guyonnet de Vertron, *La Nouvelle Pandore, ou Les femmes*
illustres du siècle de Louis le Grand, 2 vols (Paris, 1698) (II)
'Illustres sçavantes modernes'.
176   **led them into battle**: Pausanias, 1 , 178–9.
176   **at traditional men's ordeals**: For D'Aulnoy and
Murat's treatments of cross-dressed heroines, see '*Le*
Sauvage', M-I, 1–65; *DA*, '*Belle-belle*', 377–409; Sylvie
Cromer, '"*Le Sauvage*" – Histoire Sublime et allégorique de
Madame de Murat', *MC*, I,1 (May 1987), 2–19; Caroline T.
Trost, 'A Liberated Woman in a Tale by Mme d'Aulnoy',
MC, v,1 (May 1991), 57–67; Velay-Vallantin, *La Fille en*
garçon, 61–132.
176   **family's collection of tales**: LH*BI*, 3.

176   **travesty uncovered – to rejoicing all round**:
The story of the Amazon princess was adapted from a
slightly older writer, the Comte de Prechac, whose book,
L'Héroïne mousquetaire, related the true exploits of Christine
de Meirak, who fought disguised in the French army in
1675–6. See Rudolf Dekker and Lotte van de Pol,
'Republican Heroines: Cross-dressing women in the
French Revolutionary Armies', *History of European Ideas*, x,
no.3 353–63, n.23 for full details of the translations of
Prechac's tale.
177   **Quietlife Island**: M, 352–7; 'Starlight', tr. Terence
Cave, *WT*, 173–17.
178   **sleep in the armchair**: LH*BI*, 362; *CF*-I, XII, 206.

CHAPTER TWELVE: GRANNY BONNETS, WOLVES' COVER

181   **meets a wolf**: '*Le Petit chaperon rouge*', P, 113–15;
PAC, 23–8; see Zipes (1983, 1994); Dundes (1989).
181   **slip the knot and get away**: Paul Delarue, 'The
Story of Grandmother' (*c*.1885), in Dundes, op. cit., 13–20;
and Dundes, 'Interpreting "Little Red Riding Hood"
Psychoanalytically', ibid., 192–236; Zipes, op. cit., 20–3.
182   **child's aggressive ... mother's breast**: Géza
Róheim, 'Fairy Tale and Dream: "Little Red Riding Hood"',
in Dundes, op. cit., 159–67.
182   **compound of old woman and child**: I read
Lewis C. Seifert's excellent article 'Tales of Difference:
Infantilization and the Recuperation of Class and Gender
in seventeenth century "*Contes de fées*"', in Hilgar, 179–92,
after writing this chapter: he makes many similar
observations, but is more jaundiced in his view of the class
tensions; see also Louis Marin, 'Les enjeux d'un
frontispice', *L'Esprit créateur*, vol.XXVII, no.3 (Fall 1987)
49–57.
182   **regenerated by the granddaughter**: Werner von
Bülow, quoted Dundes, op. cit., 239.
183   **'... dangerous beasts of all'**: PAC, 28.
183   **'... tough, though lovely and white'**: P, 105;
PAC 69.
184   **'The Enchantments ... gentleness'**: Perrault
turned this particular tale more concisely and more
memorably in his collection as '*Les Fées*', sometimes known
as 'The Fairy', and by folklorists as 'Diamonds and Toads'.
But specialists – Paul Delarue notably – have examined the
manuscript evidence and convincingly shown that Perrault
must have had the story from Mlle L'Héritier, and adapted
it. The Grimm Brothers collected a variation of it in their
'Three Little Men in a Wood' (no.13). The plot does not
turn as narrowly on the question of proper language as in
the earlier French versions, but more on proper conduct.
See *G*, 78–83.
184   **'Diamonds and Toads'**: LH*BI*, 119ff.; cf. '*Les*
Fées', P, 147–50; PAC, 75–80; AT, 480: 'The Kind and
Unkind Girls'.
185   **beast in a single tirade**: LH*BI*, 147.
185   **ingredients of the witches' broth**: Perrault
tidied up the plausibility and the dynamics of the story,
introducing a single fairy in a single test of the protagonists:
both girls meet her disguised as a beggarwoman at the well,
and react in their own way. But both narrators despatch
Alix to the same coldblooded end.
186   **'... lightning flashes ... Pericles'**: LH*BI*, 164–5.
186   **·genre was so closely identified**: Fumaroli,
153–86.
186   **tale-telling associated with Mother Goose**:
Sanjay Sircar, 'The Victorian Auntly Narrative Voice and
Mrs Molesworth's *Cuckoo Clock*', *Children's Literature*, XVII,
1–24.
187   **'... all the rest ... just beggarwomen'**: *MHS*,
preface.
188   **'... child must be an ironic child'**: Novalis,
Notes on the Fairytale, 3, 280–1, kindly translated by David
Constantine for MW.

190   'acoustic mirror': Silverman, 72–100.
191   the von Haxthausen family: Jack Zipes, 'Once there were two brothers named Grimm', in GZ, XVII–XXXI, 728–43.
192   against the male authorities in the household: Annette von Droste-Hülshoff, Ledwina, in Bitter Healing: German Writers 1700–1830, ed. Jeannine Blackwell and Susanne Zantop (Lincoln and London, 1990), 480–526, esp. 482–3.
192   'Among people who follow the old ways ...': Joseph Campbell, 'The Work of the Brothers Grimm', G, 833.
192   '... return of a better day': ibid., 836.
193   '... wholly unconscious of its simplicity': Laurence Housman (ed.), Gammer Grethel's Fairy Tales (London, n.d.).
194   dawn breaks ... victim go: e.g. 'Funderogel', ('Foundling'), GZ, no.51, 189–92; 'Keep your secrets', Tales Told in Togoland, ed. A. W. Cardinall (Oxford, 1931); VFT-I, 64–5.
194   The Passion of New Eve: See Suleiman (1990), 136–40.
196   '... centred on the arsehole': 'In Pantoland', C4G, 98–109; see also programme notes by Billy Leeston, 'A Dame', London Palladium, April 1991.
197   what the Panto Dame – intended: See Adam Phillips, 'Cross-Dressing' in Flirting (London, 1994), 122–30.
197   instrinsically ironic: Suleiman (1990), 163–4; see also Marina Warner, 'Bottle Blonde; Double Drag', in Lorna Sage (ed.), The Flesh and the Mirror (London, forthcoming) for a fuller discussion of Carter's comedy.

PART TWO
199   Like glitter ascended into fire: Wallace Stevens, 'The Sail of Ulysses', Opus Posthumous (London, 1990), 126–31.

CHAPTER THIRTEEN: ABSENT MOTHERS
201   'What happened to the mother ...': Ruth Padel, 'Reading Snow White to my Daughter in Greek, thinking of the Stepdaughter I never see', in Summer Snow (London, 1990), 56–7.
202   The earliest extant version of 'Cinderella': Waley, 226–38, quoting Tuan Ch'eng-shih, Miscellany of Forgotten Lore. The teller was born in the South of China, and was called Li shih-yuan; see also R. D. Jameson, 'Cinderella in China'; Dundes (1988), 71–97; Philip, 17–20.
203   Perrault's 'Cendrillon': 'Cendrillon, ou la petite pantoufle de verre', P, 157–65; PAC 83–96.
203   'Turn and peep ... waits for you': 'Cinderella' (no.21), G, 127; GZ, 86–92.
203   Egypt to make her his wife: Aelian, Varia Historia (Leiden, 1701).
203   explored by Bruno Bettelheim: Bettelheim, 266–72.
204   '... petals of a daisy': Anon., Cinderella (London, 1963), Renier Collection.
204   fairy godmother familiar today: Cox, 16, 37, 127–8, 189, 354–5; Propp (1968), 79–83; Dundes (1988), passim; Joseph Jacobs, 'Cinderella in Britain', Folklore, IV, 3 (Sept. 1893), 269–841: Philip, passim.
205   meet her young prince there: Jacobs (1894), 150–5; Lang, (1910); reprinted Kevin Crossley-Holland, (ed.), Folk-Tales of the British Isles (London, 1985), 355–61; Philip, 60–2, cf. 'Burenushka, the Little Red Cow', 'The Poor Girl and her Cow', 'Rushycoat and the King's Son', and others in Philip, op. cit.; see also Jane Yolen, The Moon Ribbon and Other Tales (New York, 1976) for a beautiful modern retelling.
205   daughter's ultimate escape from pain: Brewer, 25–30.
205   'Now everything is all right': Angela Carter, 'Ashputtle or The Mother's Ghost', C4G, 110–20.
206   '... from the sceptre to the spit': B, I, 62.
206   '... love her as her own child': Aunt Mavor's Picture Books for Little Readers (London, c.1889).
206   '... she had no one who loved her': Anon., Cinderella (Palette Publications: c.1965), Renier Collection.
207   wearing sackcloth and ashes: Dan. ix: 3.
207   a daughter who continues to grieve: Bettelheim, 255.
207   stories were drastically purged: Kay Stone, 'Things Walt Disney Never Told Us' in Women and Folklore, ed. Claire R. Farrer (Austin and London, 1975), 42–50.
207   vicious power of the evil stepmother: See Tatar (1992).
208   Holbek ... Bottigheimer: Holbek, 618; Bottigheimer (1994); Herranen, 105–15 compares two oral accounts in Swedish of the same tale, told by two blind storytellers, one a man, one a woman; both follow the Grimm text closely, with interesting differences: among other things, the woman imagines the scene in practical detail (the daughter is sweeping dust so she can cook). See Tharu and Lalita, 1–37, for a brilliant survey on approaches to reading women's writings.
208   control of their dowries and labour: Reimar Schefold, 'The meaningful transformation: The anthropological field of study, the analysis of myths and the gender perspective' in Variant Views: Five lectures from the perspective of the 'Leiden Tradition' in Cultural Anthropology, ed. Henri J. M. Claessen (Leiden, 1989), 94–131.
209   storytelling in Estremadura: Taggart, passim.
210   '... falsely against my kind': Olga Broumas, 'Cinderella', in Beginning with O (New Haven and London, 1977); Mieder, 85–6.
210   '... favourite daughter died': 'Tattercoats', Jacobs (1894), 61–5.
211   pivot of the violent plot: Bottigheimer (1987), 180–2; this is a fundamental study of the Grimms, to which I am deeply indebted.
211   more beautiful than her: 'Nourie Hadig', 100 Armenian Tales, ed. Susie Hoogasian-Villa (Detroit, 1966), 84; VFT-I, 192–9.
211   Christian and social values: Bottigheimer (1987); also id., 'Marienkind (KHM 3): A Computer-Based Study of Editorial Change and Stylistic Development within Grimms' Tales from 1808 to 1864', in ARV-Scandinavian Yearbook of Folklore, 46 (1990), 7–31.
211   mother into a wicked stepmother: Bottigheimer, op.cit, 81, 181–2; in one nasty case, however, 'The Stepmother', they omitted the tale altogether from the second edition. GZ, 739.
212   '... good relation to Mother': Bettelheim, 68–9.
213   embedded in stories as eternal truths: e.g., Cnut's widow, Emma, schemed after his death in 1035 to advance her son with Cnut against his elder half-brother, Harold Harefoot, and even against her own two older sons by her first marriage to the earlier English king, Aethelred the Unready. Stafford, 4–5.
213   wife and started another family: Klapisch-Zuber (1985), 120–1.
213   seventeenth and eighteenth centuries: Weber, 93–113.
214   decorated with pictures ... 'Cinderella': E. H. Gombrich, 'Apollonio di Giovanni: A Florentine Cassone Workshop Seen Through the Eyes of a Humanist Poet', JWCI, XVIII, nos.1–2 (1955), 16–34; B. Fredericksen, The Cassone Paintings of Francesco di Giorgio (Malibu, 1969); E. Callman, Apollonio di Giovanni (Oxford, 1974); Marina Warner, 'Pronubi legni: I cassoni nuziali di Francesco di Giorgio', FMR 10/1990, 41–72 .
214   '... I am an orphan': 'The Market of the Dead', Dahomean Narrative, ed. Melville and Frances S. Herskovits (Evanston, 1958), 290; VFT-I, 168–9.

215   **the narrator identifies with her too:** cf. Suleiman, 13–63 where the author points out that for Melanie Klein as well as Freud 'psychoanalytic theory invariably places the artist, man or woman, in the position of the child. Just as motherhood is ultimately the child's drama, so is artistic creation.'; ibid., 17, She turns this perspective around and discusses the creative mother instead who looks at her child.

215   **reversals in the protagonist's life:** Nikos Papastergiadis, 'John Berger: The act of approaching', *Third Text*, 19 (Summer 1992), 94.

215   **the evil-tongued sister:** LH*BI*,147.

CHAPTER FOURTEEN: WICKED STEPMOTHERS

218   '**This is the world …':** Louise Glück, 'Gretel in Darkness', *House of Marshland* (New York, 1975); Mieder, 68.

219   **mother's best friend:** Gabrielle-Suzanne de Villeneuve, 'La Belle et la Bête', *CF-I* , 26; 'Beauty and the Beast', *ZBB*, 173–5 .

220   **eventual sexual fulfilment:** Bettelheim, 234–6.

220   **whose daughter she has become:** See Darrow, 46–7.

220   **fourteenth century, Perceforest:** Jacques Barchilon and Ester Zago (eds and trs into modern French), '"La Belle au bois dormant" à travers l'aventure de Troylus et Zellandine dans le roman de *Perceforest*', *MC*, II,1 (May 1988), 37–46; *MC*, II,2 (Dec. 1988), 111–19; *MC*, III,2 (Dec. 1989), 240–6; Susan McNeill Cox (tr.), 'The complete tale of Troylus and Zellandine from the *Perceforest* novel: an English translation', *MC*, IV,1 (May 1990), 119–39. See also P. L. Travers, *About The Sleeping Beauty* (New York, 1975), for interesting translations and comment.

220   **known to Basile:** My thanks to Roger Cardinal, who helped me with his notes comparing the different versions. Letter to MW, 6 Feb. 1990.

220   **In Basile, the saviour hero:** 'Sole, Luna e Talia', B, II, 498–503.

220   **awake and flourishing:** See Ester Zago, 'Unwanted pregnancies: Kleist's "*Die Marquise von O …*" and the Sleeping Beauty tradition', *MC*, IV,2 (Dec. 1990), 186–95. Eric Rohmer's 1976 film of Kleist's short story develops the connections with the fairy tale through its dreamlike imagery.

221   **In Perrault's version of 'The Sleeping Beauty':** '*La Belle au Bois Dormant*'; P, 97–107; PAC, 57–71; *ZBB*, 40–6 (slightly adapted). See Marin (1980), 141–55 for an inspired reading of Perrault's cannibal theme.

222   '**Little Briar Rose':** GZ, 186–9.

222   **The macabre excesses of Basile and Perrault:** Robert Samber's chapbook translation of 1796 keeps the full tale, as do other C18th editions (I am grateful to Dr Ella Westland for sharing her research with me); the ogress mother-in-law disappears for instance from *The Sleeping Beauty in the Wood* (Tabart & Co.: London, at the Juvenile School Library, 1804); Richard Doyle and J. R. Planché, *An Old Fairy Tale Told Anew in Pictures and Verse* (London, 1865); Walter Crane, *The Sleeping Beauty* (*Walter Crane's Toy Books*) (London, 1873–6).

222   **Persinette:** Charlotte-Rose Caumont de La Force, *Les Contes des Contes* (Paris, 1697) 42–57; 'Parslinette', *ZSE*, 115–21; see Carolyn Vellenga, 'Rapunzel's desire: A Reading of Mlle de la Force', *MC*, VI,1 (May 1992), 59–73.

223   **Rusticula's legal incapacity:** Janet L. Nelson, 'Commentary on the Papers of J. Verdon, S. F. Wemple and M. Parisse', *Frauen in Spätantike und Frühmittelalter* (Freien Univ. Berlin, February 18–21 1987), ed. Werner Affeldt and Ursula Vorwerk (Sigmaringen, 1990), 325–32.

223   '**… on that side shall I lose':** Shakespeare, *King John*, III.i.326–35.

223   **women's domestic turbulence:** cf. Folk songs from India, sung in the lamenting voice of incomers against mothers- as well as sisters-in-law, Tharu and Lalita, 126–42.

224   '**… nearly shook her head off':** A, 125.

224   **lively step-dance in time to it:** A, 133.

224   **Francesco di Giorgio … goddess's presence:** *c.*1475–80, Villa I Tatti. See n.214 (1) for references.

225   **Like 'pardon tales':** Davis, *passim.*

226   **her monstrous litter:** S, I, 176–88.

226   **wickedness to the Devil himself:** Herranen, 110–13.

226   **testicles which have made her so unfeminine:** '*La dame escouillée*', quoted by Tom Shippey, 'Women beware midwives', *LRB*, 10 May 1990, 19.

227   **fifteenth-century Florence:** Klapisch-Zuber (1985), 117–31.

228   **lesion in the social body:** In Australia, among the Dyirbalyan of North Queensland (formerly called Tully River Blacks) this relation is so taboo that daughters-in-law used to speak a different language of respect, with an entirely different vocabulary, to their mothers-in-law, and vice versa. It has fallen into disuse since 1930. See Robert M. W. Dixon, *The Dyirbal Language of North Queensland* (Cambridge, 1972), 32–4.

228   **board, was granted and observed:** Stone, 60.

228   **dowry which was … survival outside:** Klapisch-Zuber (1985), 122.

228   **flouted their legal obligations:** Susan Staves, *Married Women's Separate Property in England 1660–1833* (Cambridge, Mass., 1990), 27–55, 196–230. She comments: 'One cannot help suspecting that the rights of women have been especially vulnerable to the sort of "legal accidents" that lie behind the maxim *communis error facit ius* (common error makes law)', ibid., 40; Norman F. Cantor, 'The law of dower', letter, *TLS*, 25 Jan. 1991.

228   **Dower Act of 1833:** Andrew Lewis, *TLS*, Feb. 15 1991: 'Widows became dependent for their provision on the arrangements made as part of the family settlements agreed by their male relatives rather than enjoying what had been theirs as of right at common law.'

228   **widowed women much greater independence:** Wayne Ph. te Brake, Rudolf M. Dekker, Lotte C. van de Pol, 'Women and Political Culture in the Dutch Revolutions', in *Women and Politics in the Age of the Democratic Revolution*, ed. Harriet B. Applewhite and Darlen G. Levy (Michigan, 1990), 109–46, 124–5.

228   **condition of old people:** In 1776, for instance, in France only 7.20% of the populaton were 60 and over; in 1973, this figure had grown to 18.1%. In 1776 42.8% were 19 and under; in 1973, this proportion had fallen to 32.5%.

229   **parents living with them was 9.8 years:** Troyansky, 137–54.

229   **keys to the household … business:** Michelle Perrot, 'Roles and Characters', in Perrot, 178.

229   **fireside, both in France and England:** ibid., 179.

229   **unattached and ageing was vulnerable:** Troyansky, 155–62.

230   '**… home nor protection dies':** Quoted in Perrot, op. cit., 253.

230   **ratio remained. . . years later:** ibid. 255.

230   **feast days to these needy women:** Another tablet in the same church records a similar legacy of £36 in 1780, for 3d. loaves – the price of bread was to rise.

230   '**… I don't like having useless people about':** *The Three Sisters*, Act III, in Anton Chekhov, *Plays*, tr. Elisaveta Fen (Harmondsworth, 1959), 296.

231   '**… thirty or more children':** '*La Mère Cigogne*', in *Contes de fées*, (Imagerie Pellerin, Epinal [n.d.], repr. 1984), 28.

231   '**… changed instantly into windmills':** ibid., 28.

231   '**… to watch thy bed':** 'My Mother', Walter Crane's *New Toy Book* (London, 1873).

231   **She refuses to help Hawthorn ….:** '*Peau d'ours*' M, 252; 'Bearskin', *WT*, 101.

232   '... **extend to the qualities of the heart**': Murat, 'Le Prince des Feuilles' CF-II, II, 58.
232   **Magotine's perverted desires:** D'Aulnoy, 'Serpentin vert', CF-II, I, 229–59; 'The Great Green Worm', WT, 189–229.
232   **Formidable, Danamo, Mordicante:** Henriette-Julie de Murat, 'L'Heureuse peine', MCF, 160–232; 'Le parfait amour', CF-I, I, 201–48; 'Jeune et Belle', CF-I, I, 306–43.
233   '**The Fairies' Tyranny Destroyed**': Louise d'Auneuil, 'La Tyrannie des fées detruite', CF-I, V, 183–262; ibid., ed. Alice Colanis (Paris, 1990), 24–183.
233   **young person's advancement ... is required:** 'But however great may be your God-given store, it will never help you to get on in the world unless you have either a godfather or a godmother ... for a patron.' PAC, 96.
233   **no blood relation:** Lynch, 278–9; Shell, Elizabeth's Glass, 8–15.
233   **face in their looking glass:** M, 153ff.
234   '... **the most ... delightful aspects of ours**': D'Aulnoy, Nouveaux contes des fées par Madame d*** (Amsterdam, 1708), dedication page.
234   **turn them into intertwined palm trees:** 'Le Nain jaune', CF-II, I, 295; ZBB, 423.
234   '... **to neglect them, as they have neglected me**': D'Aulnoy, ibid.
234   **compelled her to give up her child:** Gabrielle-Suzanne de Villeneuve, 'La Belle et la bête', CF-I, 26; 'Beauty and the Beast', ZBB 184–99.
235   **the relations of wetnurses ... godparents:** LHTT, 'Ricdin-Ricdon', CF-I, 12, 25–79, 83–126; ZSE 48–90; 'La Robe de sincérité', CF-I, 12, 132–278.
235   **Mère Arnault:** Jacqueline-Marie-Angélique de Sainte-Madeleine [d.1661]. Her conversations and lectures, very influential in Jansenist circles, were widely published after her death; she and her sister Jeanne-Catherine-Agnès de Saint-Paul [d.1671] are portrayed in a magnificent painting by Pierre de Champagne in the Louvre.
235   **another servant, the sorrel nag:** Jonathan Swift, Gulliver's Travels, part 2, ch.2, part 4, ch.3; Duffy, 214.
236   **nurse as the fairy godmother:** She was either Monica Zajic, who would have been around forty years old, or Resi Wittek. The Complete Letters of Sigmund Freud to Wilhelm Fliess 1887–1904, ed. J. M. Masson (Cambridge, 1984), 268, quoted Lisa Appignanesi and John Forrester, Freud's Women (London, 1992), 16–17.
236   '... **and unable to do anything**': Freud to Fliess, 269.
236   **maquerelle in colloquial speech:** cf. the mères of the compagnons who still take part in the Tour de France and meet their chosen champions at different stations on the route.
236   '... **elderly woman of the lower class**': At English boarding schools for boys, for instance, the woman looking after the house in which they lived was traditionally known as Mother (surname), or in some schools, as the 'Dame'.
236   **Old Dame Trot:** 'The Comic Adventures of Old Dame Trot and Her Cat', ONC, 40–3, 123–4.
236   **afterlife as a pantomime dame:** Harlequin and Mother Shipton, or, Riquet with the Tuft, Covent Garden, Dec. 1826, 1827.
236   **biological mother in the nuclear family:** I am grateful to Ludmilla Jordanova for drawing my attention to this historical development in the meanings of the word 'mother'.
237   **Nannies use bogeymen:** Lucy Lane Clifford [b.1853] produced a memorable example of a mother resorting to a similar stratagem in her story of 1882 'The New Mother': when two children are suborned by a bad fairy, they begin to misbehave so destructively that their mother despairs and threatens them with a replacement. And so it turns out. The children heard 'through the thin wooden door the new mother move a little, and then say to

herself – "'I must break open the door with my tail.'" She has a wooden tail which drags, and glass eyes which shoot blinding light, and the children run away, exiled from home for ever. As Clifford wrote to support herself and her two daughters after being widowed young, it's not difficult to read the story as a tired woman's threat to unruly children: Lurie, 120–39.
237   '... **And would not stop crying**': 'The Woman who Married Her Son's Wife', in A Kayak Full of Ghosts, ed. Lawrence Millman (California, 1987), 127; told by Gustav Broberg Kulusak, East Greenland; VFT-I, 170.
238   '... **cannot be exactly delineated from each other**': Propp, (1968), 79.
239   **Thesmophoria rituals:** See Froma I. Zeitlin, 'Travesties of Gender and Genre in Aristophanes' Thesmophoriazousae', in Helene Foley, Reflections on Women in Antiquity (London, 1981), 169–217.
239   **sister Lotte or himself:** Taylor and Rebel, 347–78, 354; GZ, 729.
239   '**Aschenputtel**': GZ, 86–92.

CHAPTER FIFTEEN: DEMON LOVERS
241   '**The eight one you shall be**': 'Ballad of May Colven', CPB, I, 56.
241   **the heroine's sister Anne:** It is possible that Bluebeard's wife's cry to her sister echoes the medieval tradition of Dido's deathbed lament, in which she repeatedly addresses 'Anna, soror', See 'Dido's Lament', Dronke (1992), 431ff.
242   **climaxes with a multiple wedding:** Warner, 'The Uses of Enchantment', 16.
242   '. . . **vigorous, active, quick men**': Augustine, Enarrationes in Psalmos, CXXXII, 7, quoted Giles Constable, intro. to Burchard of Bellevaux, Apologia de Barbis', ed. R. B. C. Huygens, in Apologiae Duae (Corpus Christianorum Continuatio Medievalis LXII, Turnholt, 1985), 60.
242   '... **lusts like stinking goats**': Orderic Vitalis, Hist. ecc. VIII, 10, quoted ibid., 96.
242   **pages of Regency romances:** See Marina Warner, 'Shearings', in Ann Hamilton, ed. Lynne Cooke (New York, 1994).
242   **calling Bluebeard a 'Barbe-hairy-un':** F. W. N. Bayley, Bluebeard With Illustrations Numerous and Humorous (London, c.1844).
242   **foreign name, like Abomélique:** A New History of Bluebeard written by Gaffer Black Beard. For the Amusement of Little Lack Beard, and his Pretty Sisters (New Haven, 1806).
242   **takes place near Baghdad:** The Arthur Rackham Fairy Book (London, 1933), 143.
243   **blue blood:** see Claude Brémond, 'La barbe et le sang bleus', in Une Nouvelle civilisation? Hommage à Georges Friedmann (Paris, 1973), 255–366.
243   '... **within and without the organism**': William Gass, On Being Blue: A Philosophical Inquiry (Manchester, 1979), 33.
243   **Red Riding Hood should have:** Zipes (1933), 1–88.
243   **lucky not to be skinned:** Walter Crane, The Three Bears (Routledge's New 6d. Toy Books, no. 105: London, n.d.); id., Routledge's Shilling Toy Books, no. 22.
244   '... **such a very blue beard**': P, 123.
244   '**Whatever the colour ... master**': P, 129.
244   **endangers her life:** Walter Crane's Picture Book Bluebeard (London, c.1875).
244   **Eve who ate of the forbidden fruit:** Bluebeard: or, Fatal Curiosity (London, n.d.); The History of Bluebeard; or, the Effects of Female Curiosity (Alnwick, n.d); The History of Bluebeard; or, the Fatal Effects of Curiosity (London, n.d., early C19th).
244   **uses the forbidden key:** 'Our Lady's Child', no.3, G, 23–9; 'The Virgin Mary's Child' GZ, 8–12.
244   **Beardsley's obscene marginalia:** Crowquill was

the nom de plume of Alfred Henry Forrester. F. W. N. Bayley, op. cit.

246 '... cut their throats with knives': ibid.

246 'hanging up to dry': Bayley, 23.

246 '... improper and forbidden curiosity': *The History of Bluebeard; or, the Fatal Effects of Curiosity.*

246 '... the true ape of God': Pierre de Lancre, *Tableau de l'inconstance des mauvais anges et démons* (Paris, 1982), 179.

246 '... imitation is imperfect': ibid., 179.

246 helps to assuage it: Bettelheim, 299–303; see Tatar (1987), 156–78, for a trenchant critique of his and other 'taming' views.

247 Bluestocking Ella: Sabilla Novello, 'The History of Bluebeard's Six Wives', *Mendacious Chronicles* (London, 1875).

247 run with lemonade: Cruikshank (1853).

247 The Marian miracle play: *A Marvellous History of Mary of Nimmegen*, tr. Harry Morgan Ayres, intro. Adriaan J. Barnouw (The Hague and London, 1923). It has been attributed to Flemish poet Anna Bijns [1493–1575].

248 power, in the Faustian tradition: He promises her: 'If to mermaids your love were dress'd/ I would teach you in all their parts/ Music, rhetoric, all the seven arts .../ No woman on earth in learning shall speed/ As ye shall do.' ibid., 14–15; see also De Bruyn, 3–11.

248 '... a merry art': *Mary of Nimmegen*, 17; the magic gifts she has won by forfeiting her soul are verbal, for the Devil's cunning is closely allied to fluency of speech and the arts of persuasion. In her later hymn to rhetoric itself, Mary claims that it is a gift of the Holy Ghost's bestowing – a heavy irony since she has achieved her own powers through the devil, ibid., 36–8.

248 '... heavenly glory above': ibid., 78.

248 as he had planned to kill her: 'Lady Isabel and the Elf-Knight', CPB, I, 22–62; see also 'The Ballad of Anna Molnar', taken down in Transylvania in 1872, tr. Peter Sherwood and Keith Bosley, in *The Stage Works of Béla Bartók*, ed. Nicholas John (London, 1991), 23: 'Then Annie Miller she looked up/ she peeped into the tree:/ Six pretty maids were hanging there./ A seventh he'll make me!'

249 drowned, like all her predecessors: 'Heer Halewijn', *Balladenboek*, ed. Tjaard de Haan (Amsterdam, 1979), 15–18, 21–4, 263–4 – Jet Bakels brought these parallel ballads to my attention. See also Marie Ramondt, 'Heer Halewijn en Blauwbaard', in *Miscellanea J. Gessler*, II (Deurne, 1948), 1030–43. I am grateful to Jan Herwaarden for this article.

249 Perrault ... wrote saints' lives: Charles Perrault, *Le Triomphe de Sainte Geneviève* (Paris, 1694); cf. *Saint Paulin, evesque de Nole* (Paris, 1686).

249 printing blocks were drawn: See *Perrault's Tales*, ed. Barchilon, for reproductions of fairytale vignettes as well as title-page sketch, attrib. Perrault to 'Hymnes de Santeuil' (1690) with images of saints.

249 L'Héritier's 'The Subtle Princess': LH*BI*, 170ff; CF-I, I, 78–117; this is the same volume as Perrault, to whom the story is attributed.

249 Gilbert Adair's recent translation: WT, 65–97.

249 '... shoes unutterably fatiguing': ibid., 66.

250 '... give her time to meditate': ibid., 83.

251 '... barrel down the mountain': ibid., 87.

251 '... eaten that evening': ibid., 95.

251 gentlemen of their choosing: P, 128; PAC, 128.

251 '... wholly indecipherable hand': WT, 89–90.

251 'Sapia Liccarda': B, I, 275–81.

252 'The Bold Decision': Marie-Jeanne L'Héritier, 'Le Jugement téméraire', *Les Caprices du Destin* (Paris, 1718).

252 and marry her: ibid.,

252 'The Yellow Dwarf': CF-II, 275–95; DA, 232–48; OCFT, 68–80.

253 'Ricky with the Tuft': Catherine Bernard, *Inès de Cordoue, nouvelle espagnole*. For Bernard's bibliography, see

DeJean (1991), 203; Storer, 61–75.

254 '... lovers become husbands anyway': Catherine Bernard, 'Riquet à la Houppe', ZBB, 81–6.

255 '... every word ... is wise': P, 173–81; 'Ricky with the Tuft', PAC, 99–110.

255 'Fitcher's Bird': GZ, 167–71, 730–1.

255 web-footed bird: GZ, 730–1.

256 'Silver Nose': '*Il naso d'argento*', C-It, I, 31–5; C-Eng, 26–30.

256 '... to be dashing': C-Eng, xxvi.

CHAPTER SIXTEEN: THE OGRE'S APPETITE

259 '... woman far gone in pregnancy': A, 110–1.

259 '... Christ reserveth my soul': GL, II, 615–19.

259 '... the fiend sank in': ibid.

259 '... and eats them all up': *The Sleeping Beauty in the Wood* (London, 1796): I owe this reference to the research of Ella Westland.

260 relish babies: cf. 'Le petit Poucet', P, 187–98; 'Hop O' My Thumb', PAC 113–29, in which Tom Thumb tricks the ogre into eating his own children.

260 alive, but captive underground: LHCD, 96–176, 'La Princesse Olymphe' contains a tale within a tale, of the captivity of another, Irish, maiden, Hermaingarde, both are the ogre's victims; Storer (1972), 49.

260 maternal womb: I am grateful to Jacqueline Rose for sending me a postcard with Raphael's painting from the Kunsthistorisches Museum in Vienna.

260 over two hundred churches: Farmer, 260–1.

260 castle of Tiffauges stood: See Pierre Saintyves, 'L'origine de Barbe-Bleue', *Revue de l'Histoire des religions*, lxxxiii (1921), 1–31; Ernest-Alfred Vizetelly, *Bluebeard: An Account of Comorre the Accursed and Gilles de Rais* (London, 1902); Harriet H. Mowshowitz, *Gilles de Rais and the Bluebeard Legend in France*, surveys the conflation of the historical and the fairy tale figure in the ballad tradition. *Michigan Academician*, vi, no.1 (1973), 83–92.

261 'ar Miliguet', or 'the Accursed': Sources for the story include Alain Bouchard, *Grandes Chroniques* (Nantes, 1531); Albert Le Grand de Kerigouval, *La Vie, Gestes, Mort et miracles des saints de la Bretagne-Armorique* [1636], (Rennes, 1901), 18–21; G. A. Lobineau, *Histoire de Bretagne* (1707); E. A. Vizetelly, op. cit.; F. Duine, *Memento des sources hagiographiques de l'histoire de Bretagne* (Rennes, 1917); Réau, III, 3, 1286.

261 medieval frescoes ... in Brittany: C13th or C14th; see *Bulletin Archéologique de l'association Bretonne*, 1850, II, 133; Velay-Vallantin, *L'Histoire des contes*, 85–7.

262 grows up to threaten him: see Mulvey, 'The Oedipus Myth: Beyond the Riddles of the Sphinx', in Mulvey, 177–201, for a brilliant analysis of the famous story from the point of view of the father's fears, not the son's.

262 'Renaud le tueur des femmes': Velay-Vallantin, ibid., 51–62.

262 roaming in her husband's absence: Bettelheim, 302.

263 having their throats slit: Mentioned, sceptically, by Janet L. Nelson, 'The problematic in the private', *Social History*, 15:3, 355–64.

263 their twelfth child: See Christopher Ricks 'Donne After Love', p.57, in Elaine Scarry (ed.), *Literature and the Body: Essays on Populations and Persons, Selected Papers from the English Institute 1986* NS 12 (Baltimore and London, 1988).

263 a very real danger: In ducal families in the years 1650–99, the average number of children was six. This was to fall sharply, in this social group, over the next fifty years, to two per family, and then again, in the next fifty to less than two. Darrow, table 1, 59.

263 anaesthetic and antibiotics: See Renate Blumenfeld-Kosinski, *Not of woman born: Representations of Caesarean Birth in Medieval and Renaissance Culture* (Cornell, 1990).

264   **Remarriage among widowers**: Weber, 112.

264   **'… sorrows as the wife of Bluebeard'**: PAC, 40.

265   **woodcuts that promoted her cult**: See for instance *Fifteenth Century Woodcuts and Metalcuts From the National Gallery of Art*, ed. Richard S. Field (Washington, n.d.) no.195, from a series printed in Augsburg, 1480–90.

265   **beast's castle … be enclosed**: See for instance 'Castles', in *Terrible Tales and Racy Romances* (Catalogue LXXXVIII, Jarndyce, London, 1992).

265   **love for his daughter**: See chs 19 and 20.

265   **lying quite outside the marriage itself**: cf. the treacherous attack on Shechem (Gen. 34: 6–31), when after he has married Dinah, Jacob's sister, he and his tribe are wiped out by the Israelites; also the similar, bloody outcome of the brother's arrival at Hildeburgh's marriage in *Beowulf*, when the Danes murder Finn the Bridegroom and take the bride back to 'her people' (lines 1076–78). Linda E. Boose, 'The Father's House and Daughter in it', in Boose and Flowers, 27, 61–2.

266   **'… liberty, and married Fatima'**: *A New History of Bluebeard* (New Haven, 1806).

266   **'… became her firm friend'**: *The History of Blue Beard; or, The Fatal Effects of Curiosity* (London, n.d.), 34.

266   **thrifty ideas … he gave her**: Juliana Horatia Ewing, 'The Ogre Courting', *ZVFT*, 127–133.

267   **after her husband's death**: Ruth Bernard Yeazell, 'A Favourite of the Laws', review of Susan Staves et al., *Married Women's Separate Property in England, 1660–1833, LRB*, 13 June 1991, 18–20.

267   **Maurice Maeterlinck … libretto**: See Hugh MacDonald, 'Dukas's *Ariane and Bluebeard*', in programme for *Ariane and Bluebeard*, Opera North, 1990, 11–16.

267   **rarely been put on since**: It was produced at Covent Garden in 1937.

268   **'… only hopes for comfort'**: MacDonald, op. cit., 14.

268   **Bluebeard to his deep, secret castle**: See Béla Balázs, *Duke Bluebeard's Castle*, libretto, in *The Stage Works of Béla Bartók*, ed. Nicholas John (London, 1991), 45–60.

269   **graver risk … equal expression**: ibid., 8–9.

269   **void … she is doing**: See Paul Banks, 'Images of the Self: *Duke Bluebeard's Castle*' ibid., 7–12.

269   **film titles which use the name Bluebeard**: See note p.416.

270   **Carter … contemporary treatments**: CBC; Margaret Atwood, *Bluebeard's Egg and Other Stories* (London, 1988).

270   **avenging female … 'enabling'**: Carol Clover, *Men, Women and Chain Saws: Gender in the Modern Horror Film* (Princeton and London, 1992); cf. Linda Williams, *Power, Pleasure and the Frenzy of the Visible* (London, 1990); *Dirty Looks: Women, Pornography and Power*, eds. Pamela Church Gibson and Roma Gibson (London, 1944).

270   **triumphs over adversity**: See Ward Parkes, *Verbal Dueling in Heroic Narrative: The Homeric and Old English Traditions* (Princeton, 1990), on the importance of 'flyting', 21–2; Jones, 'Trickster' (1994).

270   **Sherman … menace**: *Fitcher's Bird*, photography by Cindy Sherman (New York, 1992).

CHAPTER SEVENTEEN: RELUCTANT BRIDES

273   **'… acknowledge him as her son'**: A, 113.

274   **myth of sexual difference**: Jack Zipes, 'The Origins of the Fairy Tale, or How Script Was Used to Tame the Beast in Us', Zipes, 1994; Hägg, 182–6; Kott, 36–40.

274   **'…floating … own accord'**: A, 102.

274   **Panchatantra**: AT, 425A; see Bottigheimer, 'Cupid and Psyche v. Beauty and the Beast: The Milesian and the Modern' in *MC*, III,1 (May 1989), 4–14.

274   **strong family resemblance**: cf. the bawdy tale, 'Asinarius', of around 1200, in Berlioz et al., 211–26; S, V, 1, a beautiful fairy nearly dies laughing at the ugliness of a wild man, but he saves her life and she disenchants him; B,

Il Serpente, i, 173–82.

274   **form of secular gospel**: See Edgar Wind, *Pagan Mysteries of the Renaissance* (Harmondsworth, 1967), 58–9, 146–7, 175–6.

275   **discovers his true nature**: In some less well-known tales, the Psyche–Beauty figure is a boy, who is captured by a mysterious enchantress. cf. *The Story of Lionbruno* (Venice, 1476), ed. and tr. Beatrice Corrigan (Toronto, 1976).

275   **deaths to both bride and groom**: A, 134–47, 155–62.

276   **'The Tale of the Boy who Went Forth to Learn What Fear Was'**: GZ, 12–20.

276   **replaces orgasmic spasms**: Bettelheim, 280–2; cf. joyous, updated retelling, by Peter Redgrove 'The One Who Set Out to Study Fear', in id. (London, 1989), 3–19.

277   **Mary Lamb published**: 'Beauty and the Beast: or, a Rough Outside with a Gentle Heart' (London, 1811), has been attributed to Mary and Charles Lamb, and appeared at William Godwin's instigation; OCFT, 137–50.

277   **it was not … this century**: *Beauty and the Beast: A Manuscript by Richard Doyle* (New York, 1973); his sister's name could have been Adèle.

277   **widely read version in English**: See Hearne, 49.

277   **publication of the Latin tale**: Elizabeth Imlay, *Charlotte Brontë and the Mysteries of Love: Myth and Allegory in Jane Eyre* (London, 1989).

277   **Molière, Corneille and Quinault**: Molière (and Corneille), *Psyché*, in *Oeuvres complètes* (Paris, 1825), iii, 185–249.

277   **Les Amours de Psyché … 1669**: La Fontaine, *Oeuvres Complètes*, ed. Charles Lahure (Paris, 1858), i, 568–682.

277   **custom of marrying off daughters**: Darrow, 41–63. Table 1, 59, gives average age of women in ducal families in France at the time of their first marriage: 1650–99 as 20, 1700–49 as 19.4, and 1750–99 as 18.3, with their husbands around five to three years older.

278   **'… a mistress … to have pleasure'**: Perrault, *Oeuvres posthumes* (Paris, n.d.), 358–93.

278   **'… function of the romance'**: Beer, 13.

280   **necessity to holistic survival**: Zipes in Avery and Briggs, 119–34.

280   **re-evaluation of animals**: Thomas, 13–16, and *passim*.

281   **process by which the Grimms …**: Bottigheimer (1987), 51–70.

281   appropriate female conduct: e.g. Jay Williams's, *The Practical Princess and other liberating fairy tales* (1978), Ethel Johnston Phelps's *The Maid of the North* (1981); James Riordan's *The Woman in the Moon* (1984); Redgrove, op. cit.

281   **aristocratic female patrons … their writing**: Madeleine de Scudéry and the Duchesse d'Orléans took care of L'Héritier; Bernard lived under the patronage of the Chancelière de Pontchartrain, see Storer, 61–75, ZBB, 81.

281   **Henriette-Julie de Castelnau**: See Storer, 140–59; DeJean (1991), 142–5; ZBB, 111–12; Cromer, 2–19; WT, 7–9, 236–7.

281   **truth of these accusations**: DeJean (1991), 142–5 where she discusses *Mémoires de Madame la Comtesse de M****** as an account of Murat's struggles. tr. into English Countess of Dunois [sic] (London, 1694).

281   **Charlotte-Rose Caumont de La Force**: Storer, 109–28; DeJean (1991), 210; ZBB, 101–2; see also '"L'enchanteur" Un Conte de Mlle de La Force' ed. J. Barchilon, *MC*, II,1 (May 1988), 47–60.

282   **volumes of tales**: DeJean (1991), 214 for Murat's bibliography.

282   **after she has grown old**: *'Jeune et Belle'*, CF-I, I, 308.

282   **'… happiness … become a bore'**: MCF, 64.

282   **while away long evenings**: M, 151–423.

282   **Breton milch cow**: ibid., 233.

283   '... **off to bed**': ibid., 248.
283   **marriage to a monster**: This story, and the one which follows, '*Etoilette*' or 'Starlight', do not appear in the novel's first edition of 1710, but are introduced without further attribution in the reprint of 1756; however, internal evidence points strongly to the stories being by Mlle de Lubert [*c.*1710 – *c.*1779]. See intro., *WT*, 236–7. 'Bearskin', tr. Terence Cave, ibid., 99–121.
283   **Basile story, 'The She-Bear'**: '*L'Orsa*', B, I, 183–92.
283   **shape-shifting ... conditions**: See intro., *WT*, 5.
283   '... **crazy about her**': M, 260–1; *WT*, 107.
284   **sequestered by his father**: Barchilon, 75.
284   **Marie-Catherine d'Aulnoy**: Storer, 18–41; DeJean (1991), 183ff., and bibliography, 202ff.; *ZBB*, 257–9; Palmer (1974, 1975).
284   '... **unobjectionable to the English reader**': J. R. Planché (ed. and tr.), *Fairy Tales by the Countess d'Aulnoy* (London, n.d.), intro., xi–xii.
285   **her Memoirs ... Murat**: Palmer (1975), 239; Ros Ballaster, *Seductive Forms: Women's Amatory Fiction from 1684 to 1740* (Oxford, 1992), 59–60, 124–6; *WT*, 9–11.
285   **confessed, and were executed**: The deponents who were executed were Charles de Bonenfant, Sieur de Lamoizière, and J.-A. de Crux, Marquis de Courboyer; two others who took part in the conspiracy were set free. F. Ravaisson-Molion, *Archives de la Bastille* (Paris, 1866), VII, 335–7; see also 'D'Aulnoy', *Dictionnaire de Biographie française*, ed. J. Balteau, M. Barroux, M. Prévost (Paris, 1941), vol.4, 592–3; Foulché-Delbosc, iv–vi; Roche-Mazon (1930), gives a detailed study of the case.
285   **Recueil des plus belles pièces**: See DeJean (1991), 183.
285   '**inside' story ... Versailles**: *Mémoires de la cour d'Espagne* (1679–81), *Mémoires de la cour de France* (1692) and *Mémoires de la cour d'Angleterre* (1695).
286   **real activities ... remain a mystery**: Obituary of Madame d'Aulnoy, *Le Mercure galant*, 1705, 244–9. See Foulché-Delbosc, intro., viiff. *passim*, for a spirited demolition of D'Aulnoy's claims to historical veracity; also R. Foulché-Delbosc, 'Madame d'Aulnoy et l'Espagne', *Revue hispanique*, 67 (1926), 1–151.
286   **being her accomplice**: Intro., *DA*, xii–xiii.
287   '... **ewe has gone astray**': *CF*-I, IV, 295–355; 'The Ram', *ZBB*, 399; cf. '*Le Mouton*', *Nouveaux Contes* (1708); 'The Royal Ram', D'Aulnoy (1721–2); 'Miranda and the Royal Ram', *Mother Bunch's Fairy Tales* (1790).
288   '**Prince Marcassin**': *CF*-I, III, 185ff; *DA*, 481–508.
288   **happy ending to the lovers**: *CF*-II, 229–59; *WT*, 189–229.
289   **ill-favoured heroines ... her tales**: *WT*, 193.
289   **assaulting her again**: ibid., 221.
290   '... **against the power of Love**': ibid., 227.
290   '**La Belle et la bête**': *CF*-I, XXVI, 29–214.
290   '... **Andersen or Oscar Wilde**': Angela Carter, 'Beauty and the Beast by Betsy Hearne', *Folklore*, I (1991), 123–4.
290   **translation into English**: 'The Story of Beauty and the Beast', *ZBB*, 130–202; Louise Page adapted Villeneuve for a Christmas *Beauty and the Beast*, Liverpool Playhouse and Old Vic, 1985, but the complications rather swamped the drama. See Hearne for a clear plot outline, 22–3.
290   '... **Beast ... not in his ... actions**': *ZBB*, 159.
290   '**according to their inclinations**': ibid., 185.
291   **increases a fairy's powers**: ibid., 193.
291   **water on his face**: ibid., 165.
291   '**his proper figure**': *BB*, fig.7.
292   **Le Magasin des enfants**: LPB; *ZBB*, 203–13; see Clancy, 195–204 for the background to Beaumont's pioneering educational activities.
292   **Cocteau's classic film**: See Jean Cocteau, *La Belle et la Bête: Journal d'un film* (Paris, 1947).

292   **had several children**: *ZBB*, 203.
292   '... **truth from falsehood**': *The Young Ladies' Magazine or Dialogues between a Discreet Governess and Several Young Ladies of the First Rank under Her Education* (4 vols) in 2 (London, 1760), 1, xxi–xxii, quoted Hearne, 17.
293   **return for his honesty**: Leprince de Beaumont, *Le Trésor des familles chrétiennes* (Lille, 1827), 315–23, 347–52.
293   '... **passions may carry us!**': LPB, *Magasin*, 108–12.
294   '... **same mistake that I reprove**': Rita Goldberg, *Sex and Enlightenment: Women in Richardson and Diderot* (Cambridge, 1984), 3. I am very grateful to Tom Keymer for drawing my attention to this reference.
294   **the heroine's duties**: Fitzwilliam Museum, Cambridge, OCFT, frontispiece.
294   **rewriting of Clarissa**: Jeanne-Marie Leprince de Beaumont, *The New Clarissa – A True History* (London, 1768).
294   **nursery and the schoolroom**: Darrow, 41–63.
295   '... **corrupt, and ungrateful heart**': *BB*, 28–31.
295   '... **Beauty killed the Beast**': Edgar Wallace, *King Kong* (New York, 1933); see also Warner, *Monsters*, 60–2 .
296   **Baudelaire**: 'la femme est l'être qui projette le plus grande ombre ou la plus grande lumière dans nos rêves. La femme est fatalement suggestive; elle vit d'une autre vie que la sienne propre; elle vit spirituellement dans les imaginations qu'elle hante et qu'elle féconde.' [André Breton] *Dictionnaire abrégé du surréalisme* (Paris, 1938), q.v. 'Femme', 11. Interestingly, the quotation cannot be found in Baudelaire: my thanks to Dawn Ades for advice.
297   **love from Beauty herself**: See Sylvia Bryant, 'Re-Constructing Oedipus Through "Beauty and the Beast"', in Zipes (1994).
297   **The Singing Ringing Tree**: Rosemary Creeser, 'Cocteau for Kids: Rediscovering *The Singing Ringing Tree*', in Petrie, 111–24; Terry Staples, 'Doing Them Good', ibid., 125–39.

CHAPTER EIGHTEEN: GO! BE A BEAST
298   '... **would turn into a prince**': *Lady Anna*, ed. Stephen Orgel (Oxford, 1990), 506; Rudolf Dekker brought this passage to my attention – my gratitude to this Trollopian enthusiast.
298   '... **looks! ... Help, help!**': Charles Perrault (attrib.), *Les Plaisirs de l'Isle enchantée, ou les fêtes et divertissement du Roy à Versailles, le 7 mail 1664, pour plusieurs jours* (Paris, 1664); another sumptuous feast book, also attributed to Perrault features bears from the royal menagerie, led by Moors to symbolize America, one of the Four Quarters of the globe. C. Perrault (attrib.), *Festiva ad Capita* (Paris, 1670), see p.302.
299   **prey on towns and villages**: See *D'Ours en ours*, ed. Francis Petter (Catalogue), Museum national d'histoire naturelle, Jardin des Plantes (Paris, 1988), 5–21; Yi-Fu Tuan, *Dominance and Affection: The Making of Pets* (New Haven and London, 1984), 69–87.
299   '... **on the merchant's neck**': *ZBB*, 136, 143.
299   **going to faint**: ibid., 206.
299   **repeats them endlessly**: ibid., 154.
299   **monstrousness ... visible**: See Warner, *Monsters*, 19.
299   **beastliness ... diminishes**: See Shell, *Children of the Earth*, 148–75, for a most interesting survey of the human–animal relationship.
299   **claws in another**: Lamb (attrib.), op. cit.; OCFT, 144.
299   '**Go! be a beast.' Homer**: Lamb, ibid., Osborne Collection, Toronto.
299   **casts devoted looks**: *Beauty and the Beast, a Manuscript by Richard Doyle* (Pierpont Morgan Library, New York, 1973).
299   **overlapping canines**: Walter Crane, *Beauty and the Beast* (London, 1874).

300   **terrific natural weaponry**: See Hearne, 33–56, and *passim*, for a richly illustrated survey of illustrators.
300   **iconography of the Devil**: See Pallottino (1991).
300   **a female point of view:** e.g. illustrations by Eleanor Vere Boyle (*Beauty and the Beast*, 1875), Hearne, pl. 3, Margaret Tarrant (*Fairy Tales*, 1920), ibid., pl. 6.
300   **literature of forest peoples**: Topsell, 1, 28–34; Pastoureau (1986), 163–6; P. Sébillot, *Le folklore de France: Le Faune.* (Paris, 1984), 72–73; Gaignebet and Lajoux, 79–87; cf. A. I. Hallowell, 'Bear Ceremonialism in the northern hemisphere', *The American Anthropologist*, 28 (1926), 51–202.
300   **'... lion's in its mouth'**: Sermon clxxix, quoted Herbert Friedmann, *A Bestiary for Saint Jerome: Animal Symbolism in European Religious Art* (Washington DC, 1980), 196.
301   **brought up wild in the forest**: *Valentine and Orson*, tr. Henry Watson, ed. Arthur Dickson (Oxford, 1937); cf. *Valentine and Orson.* Morris's Cabinet of Amusement and Institution (London, 1822); *Valentine and Orson*, Aunt Primrose's Library No. 8 (London, 1860); see Warner, *Monsters*, 49–52.
301   **unadulterated – folk wisdom**: I. Mariette, Charles Perrault, *Traduction des Fables de Faerne* (Paris, 1699), reproduced in Loskoutoff, fig.XIX.
302   **bears above all**: Rowland (1973), 31–2.
302   **proclaimed warlikeness**: Claude Paradin, *Devises Heroiques* (1557), ed. Alison Saunders (Aldershot, 1989), 300; Cesare Ripa, *Iconologia*, engravings by Giovanni Zaratino Castellini (Venice, 1669), gives the personification of Malvagita (Wickedness), a bear as emblem, 385–7.
302   **'... goodly relief'**: Thomas, 147.
302   **hintingly erotic entertainment**: *D'Ours en ours*, op. cit., 28–77.
302   **encounter frightening beasts**: Eleanor Mure, *The Story of the Three Bears* [1831] (Toronto, 1967); Robert Southey, *The Doctor*, iv (London, 1837); G. N., *The Story of the Three Bears* (1837) all featured a naughty old woman as the protagonist, who comes to grief at the end; Joseph Cundall, *A Treasury of Pleasure Books for Young Children* (London, 1850), changed the old woman to a little girl, 'Silver-Hair', who he claimed was more traditional. Walter Crane (1876) and Leslie Brooke (1904) published versions with 'Silver-Locks' and 'Goldenlocks'. Tolstoy translated it into Russian in 1874–5. The name Goldielocks seems to have been established first by Flora Annie Steel, in *English Fairy Tales* (1918), illustrated by Arthur Rackham. Southey has often been credited with original authorship, but it was circulating orally before the C19th, and was collected for instance in a version called 'Scrapefoot' featuring a vixen (a cunning little vixen) in the title role (Jacobs, 1894). See the excellent anon. notes to the MS facsimile of Mure, op. cit., Osborne and Lillian H. Smith Collections, Toronto, n.p. See also Ober, v–xxiii.
302   **'... I shall skin her'**: Crane, *Goldenlocks* (London, 1876).
303   **frisson to his courtship**: Peter Christen Asbjornsen and Jorgen Moe, *Popular Tales from the Norse*, tr. George Webb Darsent (Edinburgh, 1903), 22; *VFT-I*, 122–32.
303   **black variety**: GZ, 516–21.
303   **great big teddy bear**: Miss Julia Corner and Alfred Crowquill, *Little Plays for Little People: Beauty and the Beast* (London, 1854).
304   **dandling the dear little bear**: 'Rose-Red', *Richard Doyle and His Family* (Catalogue), Victoria and Albert Museum, London, 1983–4, fig.155, see p.298.
304   **'... Bruno's Foster Mother'**: William Lyman Underwood, *Wild Brother* (Boston, 1921), f.p. 18.
305   **common species**: The reverse – a human child suckled by a bear, or other animal – is of course very frequent, however, in the myths of heroes, especially founders: Zeus, Romulus and Remus: see Shell, *Children of the Earth*, 267; Warner, *Monsters*, 52–4.

305   **'... discomfort and danger'**: From *Outdoor Pastimes*, quoted *American Bears: Selections from the Writings of Theodore Roosevelt*, ed. and intro. Paul Schullery (Boulder, 1983), 15; cf. James-Oliver Curwood, *The Grisly King* (1885), which inspired Jean-Jacques Annaud's film *L'Ours* (1988); see also 'The thrill of the chase', in Ritvo, 243–88.
305   **attitude to the colour bar**: Schullery, op. cit., 10–11.
306   **Paddington, Sooty, and others**: See Karen Hewitt and Louise Roomet, *Educational Toys in America: 1800 to the Present* (Burlington, 1979). Ophelia, who is one of the few female bear characters, works as a shop-girl in Paris, and travels to Japan, for instance. Anne Conover Heller and Michele Duckson Clise, *Ophelia's World* (New York, c.1985).
306   **£550,000 in 1989**: *Evening Standard*, 19 Sept. 1989; see also Pauline Cockrill, *The Ultimate Teddy Bear Book* (London, 1991).
307   **arm around its mate**: AwayBreak, *Happy Returns from Network SouthEast*, British Rail leaflet, January–May 1992. The habitat of the last brown bears in Europe, in the Pyrenees, was recently threatened by a new road which would have bisected their foraging grounds; but the campaign to save them was fierce and successful, in spite of the road's supporters, who argued that it would bring needed employment to the region.
307   **'... afford to live'**: Thomas, 301.
307   **abandon or exchange it**: D. W. Winnicott, 'Transitional objects and the transitional phenomena: a study of the first not–me possession', *International Journal of Psychoanalysis*, xxxiv (1952), 88–97.
307   **through animals of human dreams**: Marc Holthof, 'To the realm of fables: the animal fables from Mesopotamia to Disney', in Bart Verschaffel and Mark Verminck (eds), *Zoology: On (Post) Modern Animals* (Dublin and Antwerp, 1993), 37–53.
308   **'... beat your wooer dead'**: 'Snow White and Rose Red' (no.161), G, 666; GZ, 516–22.
309   **'... the tender wolf'**: 'The Company of Wolves', *CBC*, 118.
309   **'... forbidden boundary lines'**: Lorna Sage, 'Angela Carter', *Writers and their Work* (British Council: London, 1994).
310   **'... the wide, tawny brow'**: 'The Courtship of Mr Lyon', *CBC*, 50–1.
310   **furry, naked creature like him**: ibid., 51–67.
310   **'... most lyrically beautiful ...'**: *VFT-I*, 238.
310   **'to house–train the id'**: Angela Carter, 'Beauty and the Beast by Betsy Hearne', *Folklore* (1991), i, 123–4.
310   **embrace of a giant ram**: Paula Rego, *Nursery Rhymes* (Catalogue), London, 1989, 23.
310   **yearning for him ... reunion**: *Beauty and the Beast*, directed by John Woods.
312   **'the monster of her dreams'**: Harry F. Waters, 'The Monster of her dreams', *Newsweek*, 28 Dec. 1987, 58.
312   **'... our real lives'**: Čapek (1990).
313   **'... as truly beautiful'**: Bettelheim, 303–9.
315   **American buffalo**: I am grateful to Dr John Beebe for his thoughts on the buffalo and other symbolic aspects of the film, in a letter to MW, 8 June 1993.
317   **'... than they've got planned'**: I am very grateful to Katrina Forrester for deciphering the words for me.
318   **in touch with the Inner Warrior**: See Robert Bly, *Iron John: A Book About Men* (Shaftesbury, 1990), in which Bly builds an interpretation of the Grimms' fairy tale, 'Iron Hans' (no.136), G, 612–20, GZ, 482–8, into a new myth of male regeneration: the rusty and shaggy devil–figure in the original story is perceived as a wise mentor who initiates the golden–headed hero into full, independent masculinity. This is a 'Beauty and the Beast' in which the Beauty is a boy. Marina Warner, 'A male order catalogue of errors', *Independent on Sunday*, 22 Sept. 1991, 26; Jack Zipes, 'Spreading Myths about Fairy Tales: a

Critical Commentary on Robert Bly's *Iron John'*, Zipes (1994), kindly lent by the author.

CHAPTER NINETEEN: THE RUNAWAY GIRLS

319   **Gautier de Coinci**: 'The Life of Saint Christina', Cazelles, 138–50, lines 171–5.

319   **foundations of society are laid**: Claude Lévi-Strauss, *The Elementary Structures of Kinship*, tr. James Harle Bell, John Richard and Rodney Needham (ed.) (London, 1968), 8–11, 29–51, 481–97; Shell, *Children* (1993), 148–53; id. *Elizabeth's Glass*, 8–15; Rosemary Dinnage, 'All in the family', *NYRB*, 4 Dec. 1986, 39–40.

320   **exogamy and the incest taboo**: J. Archer Taylor, 'Riddles dealing with family relationships', *JAF*, 51 (1938), 25–37; see also ch.9.

320   '**The she–Bear**': B, I, 183–92; tr. Burton, 170–7.

321   **Cinderella's stepsisters**: B, I, 60–7; AT 510A.

321   **The she–Bear variant**: AT 510B.

321   '**Peau d'Ane**' **was written in verse**: *Grisélidis, nouvelle, avec le conte de Peau d'Ane et celui des Souhaits Ridicules* (Paris, 1694); P, 52–75.

321   **usual version ... reprinted**: e.g. Charles Perrault, *Contes de ma Mère l'Oye*, ed. André Coeuroy (Paris, 1948), 99–113. *CF*–I, I, prints both verse and prose versions.

322   '**pleasant trifles**': P, 57.

322   **chose a donkey**: Calvino, two hundred years later, would confess in the preface to his collection of folk tales that he had become so obsessed with his quest for versions, that at one time he 'would have given all of Proust in exchange for a new variant of the "gold–dung donkey"'. C-Eng, xvii.

322   **a copy of Basile**: Soriano, 113ff.

322   **burlesque as a form**: Tydaeus, the coachman is seen in Hades: 'Qui, tenant l'ombre d'une brosse,/ Nettoyoit l'ombre d'un carosse.' [Holding the shade of a broom, He was cleaning the shade of a carriage.] Quoted in Charles Perrault, *Mémoires de ma vie*, ed. Paul Bonnefon (Paris, 1909), 23.

324   '**almost unlimited neglect**': *Physiologus*, 82.

324   **than our Cinderella**: Soriano, 446–7.

324   **gatherings of rural France**: P, 53.

324   **donkey loses to ... the lion**: 'The Ass, the Crow and the Wolf', in Charles Perrault, *Fables in English and French. Translated from Original Latin of Gabriel Faerno* (London, 1741), 145–7; Perrault had also written verses for the fountains at Versailles, representing Aesop's fables; see *Le Labyrinthe de Versailles*, Paris, 1677.

324   '**... ugliest animal one might ever see**': P, 68.

325   **and clever jibes**: ibid., 66.

325   **they do not conspire**: Shell, *Children of the Earth*, 153ff., argues, in a most original chapter, that the beast metamorphosis is necessitated by the rules against incest: only by becoming herself one who is not-of-the-human family, or, in the case of Beauty and the Beast finding a partner who is not-human, can the heroine fulfil the fundamental law of exogamy.

326   **Berthe ... one variation**: See ch.8.

326   **abused or rejected by him**: AT 510B.

326   **poems, plays and hagiography**: Elizabeth Archibald, intro, *APT*, 3–106; see also *The Book of Apollonius*, tr. into Eng. verse Raymond L. Grismer and Elizabeth Atkins (Minneapolis, 1936); I am also very grateful to Alan Deyermond for drawing my attention to his edition of the Spanish versions, *Apollonius of Tyre: Two Fifteenth Century Spanish Prose Romances 'Hystoria de Apolonio' and 'Confisyon del Amante': Apolonyo de Tyro* (Exeter, 1973), and the splendid contemporary (*c*.1488) woodcuts illustrating the first of these texts.

326   **overtures of incest**: Schlauch, 56–9; V. A. Kolve, *Chaucer and the Imagery of Narrative: The First Five Canterbury Tales* (Stanford and London, 1984), 297–358. This Tale is depicted in the 33 bosses in the vaulting of the Bauchon Chapel, Norwich Cathedral, carved *c*.1475.

326   **interested in hagiography**: Perrault wrote a long verse life of Saint Paulinus of Nola, *Saint Paulin de Nole* (Paris, 1686), for instance; and a paeon dedicated to Sainte Geneviève in the same year as '*Peau d'Ane*', *Le Triomphe de Ste Geneviève* (Paris, 1694).

326   **the tale Cuir 'd'Asnette'**: Cox, 206–7.

326   **spared and vindicated**: S, I, 40–9.

326   '**... help of little ants**': *Nouvelles récréations et joyeux devis*, 129; P, 55.

326   '**... belle Helaine' ... abbreviated form**: P, 54.

326   **chapbooks and ballads**: Jacobs (1894), 240–1.

326   **tell it to her father**: Molière, *Le Malade imaginaire*, II, 8.

327   '**... were told to me**': La Fontaine, *Fables*, VIII, 4; P, 53–4.

327   '**Allerleirauh' (All-Fur)**: GZ, 259–63.

327   '**... tales which are still almost blue**': André Breton, *Les Manifestes du surréalisme* (Paris, 1946), 31.

327   '**... all born in sin**': Leach, 10–11.

330   **son who is a husband too**: Sophocles, *Oedipus Tyrannos*, in *The Thebans*. tr. Timberlake Wertenbaker (London, 1992); Graves, II, 10.

330   **episode ... not usually cited**: *The Interpretation of Dreams*, FSE, IV, 261–2, in this famous retelling does not mention the reason for the curse on Laius.

330   **and abducted him**: Apollodorus, *The Library*, III, v.5., tr. J. G. Frazer (Cambridge and London, 1921) i, 338–9; see Mulvey, 191–200.

331   '**... boys as with women**': Plato, *The Laws*, VIII, C, tr. R. G. Bury (Cambridge and London, 1926), ii, 150–1; see Jasper Griffin, review of Jay Winkler, *The Constraints of Desire*, *NYRB*, 29 Mar. 1990.

331   **as in Lot's daughters' case**: Myrrha was changed into a myrrh tree as a punishment for seducing her father, and Adonis, the child of their union, was delivered from her trunk, to grow into the beautiful youth whom Venus loved, *OM*, X, 233–9. Roberto Calasso, in *The Marriage of Cadmus and Harmony*, tr. Tim Parks (London, 1993), tells the story of two more incestuous daughters, Pallene (29–30) and Hippodameia (177–80).

331   **the solution which cannot be proposed**: On this point, I am very grateful to John Forrester, who wrote in a letter: 'Question addressed to a mother, "What will you admit to being exactly like you but yet more beautiful?"' Put it another way, a more Freudian way: what woman does every woman want both to be more beautiful than her, and less beautiful than her? (My) daughter (says the mother), (his) daughter (says the wife).' Letter to MW, 30 June 1993.

331   '**... resolve it you**': Shakespeare, *Pericles*, I.i.

332   **their own identity and kinship**: *APT*, 42–4, 162–9; see also Archibald, intro., *APT*, 24–6, ; Dronke (1994), 72–5.

332   **Roman Charity**: Valerius Maximus, '*De pietate in parentes*' in *Tracta et dicta memorabilia* (Strasburg, 1470), 5:4.

332   **bars of his prison**: John Walsh, 'Amnon and Tamar: Paulus Morelsee as a History Painter', Getty seminar, 15 May 1991, kindly lent by the author.

333   '**... husband of my mother**': Giorgio Cusatelli and Italo Sordi, *Da Edipo alle nostre nonne: Breve stori dell'enigmatisca* (Milan, 1975), 26.

333   '**... preemptive paternal bond**': Lynda E. Boose, 'The Father's House and the Daughter in it: the Structures of Western Culture's Daughter–Father relationship', in Boose and Flowers, 33.

333   **by solving a riddle**: Henriette–Julie de Murat (attrib.), 'Starlight', tr. Terence Cave, in *WT*, 149–87.

334   **warns against the penalties of vice**: One version is in the Louvre, Paris, the other in the Boymans van Beuningen, Rotterdam.

334   **flesh of his offspring**: Rijksmuseum, Amsterdam, p.329.

CHAPTER TWENTY: THE SILENCE OF THE FATHERS

335   '… **authoritie over you**': Mary Wroth, *The Countesse of Montgomerie's Urania* (London, 1621), 207, quoted Krontiris, 127.

336   '… **set out more secretly**': The device also occurs in *Le Roman de Silence*, in which the heroine, Silence, is brought up as a boy in order not to forfeit her father's fortune, and later escapes her destiny by staining her face with nettle juice and disguising herself as a *jongleur*. See *Le Roman de Silence, A Thirteenth Century Arthurian Verse Romance*, Heldris de Cornualle, ed. Lewis Thorpe (Cambridge, 1972). It is also known in history: before the battle of Brunanburh in 937, a Danish warrior smuggled himself into the enemy camp as a minstrel and played to King Athelstan; John de Montfort escaped from Philip VI's hostility in 1341, also in the disguise of a *jongleur*. See J. S. P. Matlock, *The Legendary History of Britain* , 346–7.

338   '**olim vulgari idomate scripta**': The principal source for Saint Dympna's story can be found in the *Acta Sanctorum* (15 May): 'De SS Dympna Virgine et Gereberno Sacerdote' (Antwerp, 1680), 15 May, III, 477–97, (repr. Brussels, 1968). The *Vita* is preserved in a single C15th MS. See also the critical edn of Bollandist Godefridus Henschenius, 1680, and the redaction of C. de Smet, *Acta SS*, 1789. Jan L. van Craywinckel, in the mid C17th, published another, short *Vita*, in Flemish, which continued to be reissued in the next century: *Een lelie onder de doornen, de h. maghet Dympna* (Antwerp, 1652). Many accounts of miracles were also published, in a register kept from 1604–54. A record of pilgrims and petitioners, a *Liber Innocentium*, was kept from 1687–1797, then resumed in the mid C19th for a short period.

340   **invokes her protection**: I am grateful to Marguerite MacCurtain for giving me a copy of this prayer.

340   **Gerebernus' relics**: The church in Xanten was another foundation of the Norbertian canons, whose principal possession, the great Abbey of Saint Michael in Antwerp, seems to lie at the heart of missionary operations to establish new holy places in Flanders and Germany.

340   **seriously neglected**: W. P. Letchworth, *The Insane in Foreign Countries* (New York, 1889), 239–78.

340   **a certain Henri K.**: See Julian Barnes, *Flaubert's Parrot* (London, 1984), 58.

342   **so please her**: Anne–Thérèse, Marquise de Lambert, *Avis à ma fille, Avis d'une mere à son fils, Oeuvres morales* (Paris, 1824); 'A Letter from the Marchioness de Lambert to her Son', *A Compendious Way of Teaching Ancient and Modern Languages*, ed. J. T. Philipps (London, 1728); P, 293; Burke (1993), 129–31.

342   '… **her eyes and her face**': Gautier de Coinci, in Cazelles, 139, lines 134–6.

342   **pierces … the eye**: ibid., 149.

343   **not be so obdurate**: ibid., 145–6.

343   '… **with excruciating tortures**': Pizan, 232–3.

345   '… **sanctuary of Saint Martin's**': *The Croyland Chronicle* ('Historiae Croylandensis Continuatio'), *Rerum Anglicarum Scriptores Veterum*, ed. W. Fulmar, lines 557ff.; see also Charles Ross, *Richard III* (London, 1981), 28, n.20; Michael Jones, 'Richard III and the Stanleys', in *Richard III and the North*, ed. R. Horrox (Hull, 1986). I am deeply in Michael Jones's debt for referring me to this episode of English history.

346   '… **the essence thereof**': Roy Porter, 'Love, Sex and Medicine: Nicolas Venette and his *Tableau de l'amour conjugal*', in *Erotica and the Enlightenment*, ed. Peter Wagner (Frankfurt,1991), 90–122, 109.

346   '… **will not die**': P, 75.

347   **evil influence of a 'Druid'**: Perrault, *Contes de ma Mère l'Oye*, ed. André Coeuroy (Paris, 1948), 99–113, 102.

347   **absolve … responsibility**: P, 60–1.

347   **no likelihood of offspring**: Perrault, ed. Coeuroy, 113.

347   **the English Victorian stage**: e.g. H. J. Byron,

Cinderella or the Lover, the Lackey and the little Glass Slipper (London, 1861).

347   **wife's gambling debts**: Cruikshank (1853).

348   '**Maiden Without Hands**': GZ, 118–23; '*La Fille aux mains coupées*', in Velay-Vallantin (1992), 95–134; Tatar, (1992), iv.

348   **smitten brother**: '*La bella delle mani mozze*', B, I, 251–63.

348   '… **extraordinary size**': Philippe de Beaumanoir, *La Manékine; Roman du XIIIe siècle*, tr. Christiane Marchello–Nizia (Paris, 1980), 46–7.

348   **not for the mutilating itself**: Ellis, 78; see also Tatar (1992), iv.

348   **cuts down … pear tree**: 'Cinderella' (no.121), G, 121–8, GZ, 86–92.

348   **fallen out of the tale**: See Ben Rubenstein, 'The meaning of the Cinderella Story in the Development of a Little Girl', in Dundes (1988), 219–28.

349   **Aurelia then recalled … years before**: Peter Swales, 'Freud, Katharina, and the First "Wild Analysis"', in *Freud: Appraisals and Reappraisals, Contributions to Freud Studies*, I, ed. Paul E. Stepansky (Hillsdale, 1988), 78–164, gives a remarkably detailed account of the case, and I am grateful to the author for sending me the offprint; see also Lisa Appignanesi and John Forrester, *Freud's Women* (London, 1992), 104–8.

350   **Donkeyskin fairy tale negotiates**: Correspondence between Breuer and Freud, 1893–95, 127, quoted Swales, op. cit., 121.

350   **documented cases of incest**: ibid., 116–20.

350   **could not be disentangled**: Otto Rank is likely to have contributed to Freud's shift from an experiential to a symbolic interpretation of incest confessions.See *The Incest Theme in Literature and Legend* [1912], tr. Gregory C. Richter (Baltimore, 1992). See also J. M. Masson, *The Assault on Truth: Freud's Suppression of the Seduction Theory* (New York, 1984).

350   **the issue for him**: John Forrester argues that Freud was very matter-of-fact about incest, did not react to it with horror, and 'took it very much in his stride – a day to day occurrence, certainly for him in his practice, but also – and this should not be forgotten, in the conventional mores of Jews just out of the ghettos: he did himself marry his sister's sister–in–law …' Letter to MW, 30 June 1993.

351   **from his grandmother**: Agnes Varda directed *Jacquot de Nantes*, a biographical tribute to her husband, in 1991, in which his productions of 'Cinderella' and other fairy tales are dramatized.

352   **a bitter tale**: Lynne Tillman, 'The Trouble with Beauty', in *Absence Makes the Heart* (London, 1990), 85–90.

352   **combing her locks**: '*Maria di legno*', C–It, I, 437–41; C-Eng, 378–82.

CHAPTER TWENTY-ONE: THE LANGUAGE OF HAIR I

353   '… **long passionate kiss**': A, 45–6.

353   **father or other would–be seducer**: OCFT, 121.

354   **outer, pelican skin**: Taggart, 94–5.

354   **release her from her animal form**: CF-II, WT, 39–40.

354   **magic to restore him to human shape**: CF-I, 132. Agathe Moitessier translates Mie-Souillon as Darling-Dirty Face, in 'Three Fairy Tales by Madame d'Aulnoy', tr. with commentary (unpublished thesis, Bard College, 1982). I am grateful to the author for letting me read the typescript.

354   **life of relative freedom**: WT, 103–7;

355   **satyrs … of lust**: Lynn Frier Kaufmann, *The Noble Savage: Satyrs and Satyr Families in Renaissance Art* (Philadelphia, 1979).

356   **attached and dangling**: See Wolf Hart, *Die Skulpturen des Freiburger Munster* (Freiburg, 1981).

356   **caresses and cuddles**: Rijksmuseum, Amsterdam.

357   '… **lies on the ground**': AHA, 338–9.

357   **Sensual Pleasure**: woodcut by the Master of the Bergmann Shop, in Sebastian Brant, *The Ship of Fools*, [1944] tr. Edwin H. Zeydel (New York, 1962), 178.
358   **anchorite Saint Onufrius**: Williams, part II, 81–5.
358   **long to cover them**: ibid., 107–10; Velay-Vallantin (1992), 303–35.
358   **symbolic tunic woven of rushes**: Cesare Ripa, *Iconologia* (Amsterdam, 1644), 422.
359   **a plumed penis**: In the Louvre, Paris.
360   '**... Short–witted Maidens**': in Hugo von Trimberg, *Der Renner*, (Austria, *c.*1475–1500), repr. *Mediaeval and Renaissance Manuscripts: Major Acquisitions of the Pierpont Morgan Library 1924–1974* (New York, 1974), fig.50.
361   '**... passion that encumbrance all women**': J. Gessler, *La Vierge barbue* (Brussels and Paris, 1938); G. Schurer and J. M. Ritz, *Sankt Kummeris und Volto Santo* (Düsseldorf, 1934).
361   '**... uncumber them of their husbands**': Farmer, 404.
361   **lustfulness inside woman ... dealt with**: In Memling's painting in Bruges, golden wisps are discreetly visible on her chin; but in numerous anonymous cult crosses and statues from Germany, this Saint is more heavily bearded than Jesus. See the exceptionally rich collection of votive images, made by Dr Rudolf Kriss, in the Bayerisches Nationalmuseum, Munich.
361   **... as in anorexia**: J. Hubert Lacey, 'Anorexia Nervosa and a bearded female saint', *British Medical Journal*, vol.285, 18–25 Dec. 1982.
362   '**... without loving her**': '*La Belle aux cheveux d'or*', *CF-II*, I, 261–74; 'The Fair with Golden Hair', was used by J. R. Planché in his translation (London, n.d.), 22–34.
363   '**... clear in colour**': C. T. Onions (ed.), *The Oxford Dictionary of English Etymology* (Oxford 1969), 342.
363   **fate – and desire**: See 'fair', 'fay', and 'fang' in *The Century Dictionary and Cyclopedia*, 12 vols, III (New York, 1911), 2119–20, 2137, 2160. I am grateful to Lori Repetti for help with this research.
364   **blood it may spill**: Umberto Eco, 'How Culture Conditions the Colours We See', in *On Signs*, ed. M. Blonsky (Baltimore, 1985), 171; on the symbolism of colour, see also Linda Woodbridge, 'Black and White and Red All Over: The Sonnet Mistress Amongst the Ndembu', *Renaissance Quarterly*, XL, 2 (Summer 1987), 247–7. Gage is the most recent, definitive study on colour symbolism and use.
364   **sixty are in circulation**: Gage, 79.
364   **a puppet film, made in 1935**: Warner, 'Uses of Enchantment', in Petrie, 18–20; I am grateful to Kathleen Davies for her information about Nazi uses of fairy tales.
364   **sign of her lost beauty**: 'Cupid and Psyche', 130–1; La Fontaine, *Les Amours de Psyché et de Cupidon* (1669), *Oeuvres complètes* (1858), I, 568–682, 670.
365   **lamentably they may strike us today**: cf *Heliodorus, Aethiopica (An Aethiopian Romance)*, tr. Thomas Underdowne (1587), rev. F. A. Wright (London and New York, 1928). See McGrath, 'Black Andromeda' *JWCI*, LV, 1992; Jack D'Amico, *The Moor in English Renaissance Drama* (Tampa, 1991).
365   **unfaithful to his true love in so doing**: Murat, 'Starlight', tr. Cave, *WT*, 185–6.
365   '**...golden waves her hair**': Francis Davies, *A Musical Cinderella*, music arr. B. Hobson Carroll (London, *c.*1885), Renier Collection.
365   '**... the window-frame**': 'Little Snow–White' no.53, *G*, 249; *GZ*, 196–204.
365   '**... golden hair like mine**': 'All–Fur' no.65, *GZ*, 259.
366   **with a red beard**: Ruth Mellinkoff, 'Judas's Red Hair and the Jews', *Journal of Jewish Art*, IX, 1982, 31–46.
366   **Vice below is a dark redhead**: Norton Simon

Museum of Art, Los Angeles.
366   **Tiepolo's Time Defacing Beauty**: in the National Gallery, London.
366   **hot hues' ambiguities**: On yellow, as the colour of folly, buffoonery, madness, disorder, see Pastoureau (1986), 23–34; Mellinkoff, I, 48ff. for representations of Synagoga, Judas, the impenitent thief in yellow clothing.
367   **more modest rituals**: I am grateful to Conrad Rudolph for this perception.
367   '**... scatter ... enemy with terror**': Bernard of Clairvaux, *De Consideratione*, bk 2:10. Again, my thanks to Conrad Rudolph for this reference.
367   '**... come into being**': Umberto Eco, 'The Aesthetics of Light', in *Art and Beauty in the Middle Ages*, tr. Hugh Bredin (New Haven, 1986), 50.
367   **hair in the tail**: Michel Tournier explores in *Gaspard, Melchior et Balthazar* (Paris, 1980) the symbolism of blackness and whiteness from the point of view of the black king, Gaspard, who has bought a blonde concubine. Michel Tournier, *The Four Wise Men*, tr. Ralph Manheim (New York, 1982), 25–6.
368   '**... my only child**': 'Illius adveniens planctu iam livida mater/ Et flavas disiecta comas his ethera pulsat:/ O celi sacra stirps, o proles unica ...', Eupolemius, *Messias*; quoted Peter Dronke, 'Laments of the Maries', Dronke (1992), 483.
368   **colour of the vase itself**: Jean-Thierry Maertens, *Ritanalyses*, I (Paris, 1987), 35–7. I am very grateful to Henri Colomer for this reference and for his help over many aspects of colour symbolism.
368   **whitening the complexion**: [John Baptist Porta], *Natural Magick in XX Bookes* (London, 1658), 233–4.
368   '**... the fashion of a boy**': See Marina Warner, *Joan of Arc, The Image of Female Heroism* (London, 1981), 143.
368   **coiled on her neck, and fair**: *Vigiles de Charles VII* (1484), BN MS, Fr. 5054.
369   '**... appeared feeble and delicate**': Boutet de Monvel, 'The National Hero of France', *The Country Magazine*, liii, 17, 119–30.
369   **Delaroche's maudlin icon**: Guildhall Art Gallery, Corporation of London.

CHAPTER TWENTY-TWO: THE LANGUAGE OF HAIR II

371   '**bald, I don't love you any more**': 'Mira que si te quise, fué por el pelo, Ahora que estás pelona, ya no te quiero.' Frida Kahlo, *Self-portrait with Cropped Hair*, 1940, Museum of Modern Art, New York. See Hayden Herrera, *Frida: A Biography of Frida Kahlo* (New York, 1983), 285–6.
371   **hair can help**: See Edmund Leach, 'Magical Hair', in *Journal Royal Anthropological Institute,* 88 (1958), 147–63; C. R. Hallpike, 'Social Hair', *Man,* NS, 4, 2 (1969), 256–64; Ann Charles and Roer De Anfrasio, *The History of Hair* (New York, 1970); Wendy Cooper, 'Hair', *Sex, Society, Symbolism* (New York, 1972); Brook Adams and David R. McFadden, *Hair, Cooper–Hewitt Museum*, 1980; *Hair Raising* (Catalogue), Whitworth Art Gallery, Manchester, 13 Mar. – 9 May 1987; Marina Warner, 'Bush Natural', *Parkett*, 27, 1991, 6–17.
371   **the monk's tonsure**: See Louis Trichet, *La Tonsure Vie et mort d'un pratique ecclesiastique* (Paris, 1990)
371   **flowerchild's tangled curls, the veil**: e.g. The flavour of the Protestant tradition is captured by the tract: Thomas Wall, *Spiritual Armour to defend the head from the superfluity of naughtiness; Being a loving and Christian tender, humbly offered to the pious and serious consideration of the ministers of the Gospel and to all others it may concern: wherein is proved that it is unlawful for women to cut their hair polled or shorn and men to wear the same to cover their heads: together with how men and women ought according to the written law of God and nature to wear their hair* (London, 1688).
372   **museum hygrometers**: I am grateful to Jacqueline Burckhardt for her help in this area.
372   **cult ... round their tombs**: P. I. Robert, *Les Saints*

rois du moyen-âge en occident, 6–13e siècles (Brussels, 1984), 67. Patricia Morison kindly informed me of these cults.

372   **stories of Samson …**: Dale Alexander, *How I Stopped Growing Bald and Started Growing Hair* (New York, 1969), is only one of many books to address the anxiety some men feel about this issue.

373   **power to straighten it**: I am indebted to Jacqueline Simpson for this superstition, reported in Nancy Arrowsmith and George Moorse, *A Field Guide to the Little People* (London, 1978).

373   **gives power over him**: 'The Devil with the Three Golden Hairs', no.29, *G*, 151–8; *GZ*, 109–16.

373   **braided into a gorget**: Bronislaw Malinowski, *The Sexual Life of Savages* (London, 1931), f.p. 131.

373   **fay, and proves effective**: La Fontaine, *'Joconde'*, *Oeuvres Complètes* (1991), 561; Pamela A. Miller, 'Hair Jewelry as Fetish', in *Objects of Special Devotion. Fetishes and Fetishism in Popular Culture*, ed. Ray B. Browne (Bowling Green, 1982).

373   **Mary's or Jesus' hair**: Patricia Morison has passed on to me this story, about the English hermit Saint Godric [*d.*1170]: 'An abbot came to converse with him; his monk–companion noticed a hair about to descend from the holy man's beard, and asked if he could pluck it. Godric agreed but self–consciously said he must look after it. The monk used it, steeped in water, when he was ill some time later – and recovered.' *Liber de vita et miraculis S. Godrici, heremitai de Finchale,* Surtees Society 19 (1847), 126, p.263. Some hair and beard relics appear in Christian lists before the Reformation, e.g. St Peter's, in the Old English relic list of Exeter, *c.*1010. See Marina Warner, 'Shearings', in *Ann Hamilton* (New York, 1994) for discussion of hair as a different kind of human leaving from relics. I am very grateful to Patricia Morison for help in this area.

374   **men as well as to women**: *Dada Haarwasser*, Bergmann & Co. Zurich, reproduced *Dames in dada*, eds. Carolien van der Schoot, Marleen Swenne (Amsterdam, 1989), 24.

374   **also appears blonde:** For the iconography of Virgo, I consulted: A Barzon, *I cieli e la loro influenza* (Padua, 1924); H. Bober, 'The Zodiacal Miniature of *Les Très Riches Heures* of the Duke of Berry – Its sources and meanings', *JWCI*, XI, 1948, 1–34; Albumasar, *De magnis coniunctionibus* (Augsburg, 1489); id., *De revolutionibus nativitatum*, ed. D. Pingree (Leipzig, 1968); F. Saxl, 'Macrocosm and Microcosm in Medieval Pictures', *Lectures* (London, 1957), I, 58–72; Eric Burrows, *Virgo in Christian Documents* (London, 1941); Lucio Grosseto, 'La decorazione pittorica del Salone', in *Il Palazzo della Ragione*, ed. Carlo Guido Mor *et al.* (Venice, 1963); Luigi Aurigemma, *Il segno zodiacale dello Scorpione nelle tradizioni occidentali dall'antichità greco-latina al rinascimento* (Turin, 1976); Samek Ludovici, *Il 'De sphaera' estense e l'iconografia astrologica* (Milan, n.d.); Gioia Mori, 'Arte e astrologia', *Arte*, Dossier no.10, Feb. 1987. I am most grateful to Amy Morris for her research assistance with this topic.

374   **Spica (Wheatear):** Aratus, *Phaenomena* (*c.*276–274 BC): 'Beneath both feet of Bootes, mark the Maiden, who in her hands bears the gleaming Ear of Corn.' *LCL*, 214–15.

376   **wheatsheaf in her hand:** Paolo d'Ancona, *I mesi di Schifanoia in Ferrara* (Milan, 1954), 69–72.

377   **heads uncovered and their hair loose**: *Les présentes heures à l'usaige de Rouan* [de Simon Vostre] (Paris, 1508), 126–37.

377   **refusal to do as the heads asked**: Villeneuve, *Les Contes marins ou La Jeune Américaine* (Paris, 1740).

378   **it grows longer**: Variations on 'Diamonds and Toads' (see ch.11); *'L'acqua nel cestello'*, C-It, I, 409–11; C-Eng, 353–5.

378   **performed on one another at Montaillou:** Emmanuel Le Roy Ladurie, *Montaillou: Cathars and Catholics in a French Village*, tr. Barbara Bray (Harmondsworth, 1980),

141–2.

378   **delousing their children's hair**: Pieter De Hooch, 'A Mother's Duties', Wallace Collection.

378   **golden hair promised riches**: On meanings of gold, see Grahame Clark, *Symbols of Excellence: Precious metals as expressions of status* (Cambridge, 1986), 50–8.

378   **' … a sunburst of rays …'**: *P*, 73.

379   **' … when he awoke'**: ibid., 58–9.

382   **mediums of erotic power**: See Whitney Chadwick, *Women Artists and the Surrealist Movement* (London,1985), 66ff.; Marina Warner, intro., Carrington (1989); id., 'The Art of Playing Make–Believe', *Leonora Carrington* (Catalogue), Serpentine Gallery, London, 1991; Suleiman (1990), 26–32, 144–6, 169–79; id., 'Artists in Love (And Out): Leonora Carrington and Max Ernst', Suleiman (1994), 89–121.

382   **'Baldness lies … my child'**: Max Ernst, *A Little Girl Dreams of Taking the Veil*, tr. Dorothea Tanning [1930] (New York, 1982).

384   **' … all his beauty at one go'**: 'As they rode along the edge', Carrington, *Seventh Horse*, 3–15.

384   **and take her clothes**: 'The Débutante', in Carrington, *The House of Fear*, 44–8.

384   **white horse … room behind her**: *Leonora Carrington* (Catalogue), cover; Chadwick, op. cit., 77.

384   **painted herself as a horse**: Warner, intro.; Chadwick, op. cit., 78–81; Carrington, *The House of Fear*, 6–12; Suleiman (1994), 89–121.

384   **strangles him**: Carrington, *House of Fear*, 37–43.

384   **Meret Oppenheim was born …**: Bice Curiger, *Meret Oppenheim: Defiance in the Face of Freedom* (Catalogue) Zurich, New York, London, 1989; 'Collaboration Meret Oppenheim', *Parkett* no.4, 1985, 20–49, including Jacqueline Burckhardt, 'The Semantics of Antics', ibid., 23–9. I am very grateful to Bice Curiger and Jacqueline Burckhardt for their help throughout my research.

384   **children's classic in Switzerland**: Lisa Wenger, *Joggeli söll ga Birli schüttle!* [1908] (Muri bei Bern, 1988).

385   **clothe herself and her child**: Meret Oppenheim, 'Endlich! Die Freiheit!', in *Husch, husch, der schönste Vokal entleert sich. Gedichte, Zeichnungen* (Frankfurt, 1984), 15.

386   **' … full bitterly him wrung'**: 'The Wife of Bath's Prologue', Chaucer, 289; Malcolm Jones also draws attention to Saint Jerome, who cites Plutarch's story about a Roman sage, who, 'divorcing his wife, said that only the wearer of an ill–fitting shoe knos where it pinched.' Letter to MW, 24 June 1994.

386   **free to marry elsewhere**: Rachel Biale, *Women and Jewish Law* (New York, 1984), 113–15.

CHAPTER TWENTY-THREE: THE SILENCE OF THE DAUGHTERS

387   **' … upon land a living soul'**: Answer: 'Siren', see Michael Alexander, *Old English Riddles From the Exeter Book* (London, 1980).

388   **he begins to cry**: AT 923 (Love like salt). See Alan Dundes, '"To love my father all": A psychoanalytic study of the Folktale Source of King Lear', in Dundes (1982), 229–44; also Ann Pasternak Slater, *Shakespeare the Director* (Brighton and New Jersey, 1982), 121–36.

389   **loss hangs over both plays**: Shakespeare recast his own will, to favour Susannah, his elder daughter, over her sister Judith. See S. Schoenbaum, *Shakespeare's Lives* (Oxford, 1991), 20–2.

389   **honesty as well as modesty**: See Lisa Jardine, *Still Harping on Daughters: Women and Drama in the Age of Shakespeare* (London, 1983), 108–10.

390   **' … concealment and dumbness'**: 'The Theme of the Three Caskets', FSE, XII, 291–301, 294.

390   **' … into her arms'**: ibid., 301.

391   **tissue of metaphors**: Derek Walcott, *Omeros* (London, 1991), 296.

391   **English sense of mute**: cf. *Secundus the Silent*,

Irwin, 75–6; see Johannes de Alta Silva, *Dolopathos, or The King and the Seven Wise Men*, tr. Brady B. Gilleland (Binghamton , 1981) for a C12th romance in which a youth, accused by a wicked stepmother of attempted rape, does not speak in his own defence.

392   **Europe and further afield**: *GZ*, no.9, 35–9; no.49, 182–5; a third story, 'The Seven Ravens' (no.25), *GZ*, 99–101 is also related to this group, but does not include the motif of the heroine's silence; HCA, 117–31; 'The Twelve Wild Ducks', *VFT*-II, 3–9; see Taylor and Rebel for a most interesting analysis of the relations between these tales and the conscription of young men during C19th.

392   **female nemesis ... great emphasis**: The C12th *Dolopathos* op. cit. ends with 'Virgil' issuing a tirade which climaxes: 'Woman is a great evil.' 71–7.

393   **chivalrous enterprises open to them**: I wrote a version of the story in *The Lost Father* (London, 1988) and gave it to the fantasy of my protagonist, Rosa, who is growing up in provincial Southern Italy in the early part of the century. Though Rosa casts herself as the chivalrous questor, who defies all for love – in this case, not of a brother, but a lover – she represents the channelling of women's vitality that these ancient and exemplary stories tend to hold out for approval; she expresses, on my behalf, the distressing limits on women's capacity for energy and passion encoded within the most beckoning and inspiring material.

394   **'... husband will not beat you'**: LPB, 122–4.

394   **'And you will see, his anger will pass'**: ibid.

394   **other women in articulacy**: Bottigheimer (1987), 177–87; see also, 'Silenced Women in the Grimms' Tales: The "Fit" between fairy tales and society in their historical context', in Bottigheimer (1986), 115–32.

395   **'... say nothing'**: Julia O'Faolain, 'Interview with Myself', *LRB*, 23 June 1994, 26–7.

395   **the secrecy of some of the contents**: See Mary H. Nooter, Preface and 'The Impact of the Unseen', in *Secrecy: African Art that Conceals and Reveals* (New York and Munich, 1993), 18–21, 235–40 on the power of discretion.

395   **'... ivy around a wall'**: Walter Benjamin, 'The Storyteller', in Benjamin, 108, 395.

395   **finger to his lips**: cf. Quentin Massys, *Allegory of Folly*, Metropolitan Museum, New York, *c.*1510–20; E. Tietze-Conrrat, *Dwarfs and Jesters in Art*, (London, 1957).

395   **criteria held up for the sex**: chs 2 and 3.

395   **actually disappearing out of the text**: Bottigheimer (1987), 53.

396   **silence for five years**: Plutarch, *De Curiositate (Moralia III), La Curiosità*, ed. Emidio Pettine (Salerno, 1977), 43.

396   **moral and philosophical arguments**: I am very grateful to Laura Mulvey, for lending me her paper on 'Godard's *Hail Mary*' (not then published), in which she develops a powerful insight into the importance of female curiosity as a leverage against the reification of women and their bodies. See 'Marie/Eve: Continuity and Discontinuity in J. L. Godard's Iconography of Women', in M. Locke and C. Warren (eds) *"Hail Mary": Women and the Sacred in Film*, (Carbondale, 1993).

396   **Passau during the Nazi period**: Directed by Michel Verhoeven, 1989.

396   **strictures on female behaviour**: See Warner, 'Through a Child's Eyes' and 'Women against Women in the Old Wives' Tale', in Petrie, 57–8, 67–8; also, Ian Buruma, *The Wages of Guilt* (London, 1994), 267–74, about the twists and turns Rosmus' tale has taken since.

396   **siren's voice for human form**: 'The Little Mermaid' first appeared in *Tales Told for Children*, iii, 1837, and in English in *Bentley's Miscellany* (London, 1846); HCA, 57–76.

396   **bride on certain conditions**: cf. Jean d'Arras, *Mélusine*, ed. Edmund Lecesne (Arras, 1888); V. Bruhier,

Caprices d'imagination (1740) *Lettre III, Sur les Sirènes, Tritons, Néréides, et autres Poissons rares, qui se trouvent dans la mer*; Friedrich de La Motte-Fouqué, *Undine and Other Stories*, tr. Edmund Gosse (Oxford, 1932); Jean Markale, *Mélusine* (Paris, 1993); also A. S. Byatt's magical treatment of the themes in *Possession* (London, 1990).

396   **bride who comes from the sea**: *The Arabian Nights*, tr. Richard Burton, adapt. and tr. Jack Zipes (New York, 1991), 223–63.

396   **speak (and sing)**: First produced in March, 1901 in Prague. Libretto by Jaroslav Kvapil. See Karel Brusak, 'A lyrical fairy-tale' (prog.), *Rusalka*, English National Opera, London, 1983.

397   **worship of Woman**: See Catherine Clément, *Opera or the Undoing of Women*, tr. Betsy Wing (London, 1989), 111–15.

397   **Danish national monument**: The sculptor was Edvard Eriksen [1876–1959].

398   **'... have my powerful potion'**: HCA, 48.

398   **Titus Andronicus**: See Pasternak Slater, op. cit., 123–4.

398   **'... cause your blood to flow'**: HCA, 48–9.

398   **red in the costumes and décor**: Des. Stefanos Lazaridis.

399   **go on rowing**: Homer, *The Odyssey*, XII, tr. E. V. Rieu (Harmondsworth [1942], 1982), 193–4.

399   **present, and of the future**: See Padel, 65.

399   **'... sirens' rocky shores'**: Cicero, *De Finibus*, V, xviii–xix, *LCB*, 448–51. I am very grateful to Nick Havely for bringing this passage to my notice.

399   **Thelxiope (Enchanting Face)**: Graves, II, 361.

399   **nature's only voiced chorus**: The presence of feathers on musical angels' bodies as well as their wings points to their affinity with birds; Sri Lankan ivory plaques from the C17th and C18th, for instance, represent heavenly musicians as bird-bodied. British Museum 1943.7–12.2,4.

400   **folklore about Harpies**: Graves, I, 128; II, 230

400   **play at a nobleman's banquet**: An imposing, life size terracotta group of two sirens on either side of a seated man, from Apulia, Magna Graecia, fifth century BC, is in the John Paul Getty Museum, Malibu.

400   **golden plumage ... their faces**: *OM*, V, 551–63.

401   **Harpy, means snatcher**: The pomegranate – emblem of Persephone, goddess of the underworld – appears in the relief carvings on the so-called Harpy Tomb from Xanthos in Turkey (erected 480–470 BC) offered by seated figures who may be making their goodbyes in this manner to the dead. They are much more likely to be sirens, instead, the accompanying angels of the dead in classical mythology, and the tomb's traditional name mistaken. F. N. Pryce, *British Museum Catalogue of Sculpture*, i, part 1, 1928 B286–318, 122ff.

401   **flight, but a watery passage**: Pierre Courcelle, 'Quelques symboles funéraires du Néo-Platonisme Latin. Le Vol de Dédale – Ulysse et les sirènes', *Revue des Etudes anciennes*, XLVI (1944), 65–93.

401   **possess 'utmost music'**: Padel, 65.

401   **'... into the tomb a bride'**: Peter Dronke, 'The Lament of Jephtha's daughter', in Dronke (1992), 345ff.

402   **... 'What comes in' moves them**: Padel, 65.

402   **hell without end**: I am most grateful to Nicholas John for noticing this siren.

402   **Psychomachia**: See The *Hortus Deliciarum* of Herrad of Hohenburg (Landsberg) ed. Rosalie Green, Michael Evans, Christine Bischoff, Michael Curschmann, 2 vols (London, 1979); also Courcelle, op. cit., 82.

402   **the presence of danger**: George Steiner, in a lecture on Sirens, 9 Nov. 1991, in Cambridge, first drew my attention to the word's growth in meaning.

403   **'uterus on the loose'**: Ted Hughes, *Shakespeare and the Goddess of Complete Being* (London, 1993), 11.

404   **'... exposes herself, terribly open'**: Paul Valéry, *Degas. Danse. Dessin*. (Paris, 1938), 30–1. My deepest thanks

to Terence Cave for tremendous help (and inspiration) with this difficult translation.

405   **The knight says: 'Sovereignty'**: 'The Marriage of Sir Gawain and Dame Ragnell' (East Midlands, C15th) in D. B. Sands (ed.), *Middle English Verse Romances* (London, 1966). The Wife of Bath tells a variation on this tale. See Chaucer, 303–10; Warner, *Monsters*, 14–6.

405   **laughter of hope and pleasure**: Angela Carter, *The Magic Toyshop* (London, 1967).

405   '**… because of my piano**': Jane Campion, *The Piano* (London 1993), 9.

405   '**… so why not he!**': ibid., 9.

406   '**I am learning to speak**': Campion, ibid., 122.

406   **rampantly romantic resolution**: Sarah Kerr, 'Jane Campion's *The Piano*', *NYRB*, 3 Feb. 1994; Letter from Martha Nussbaum, *NYRB*, 7 April 1994

408   **a structure of relationships**: Douglas (1973), 189–201.

CONCLUSION

409   '**… which nobody can test**': Homer, *Odyssey*, XI, 181.

409   '**on this veiled evening**': Eavan Boland, 'What we lost', in *Outside History* (Manchester, 1990).

410   **heckle or boo**: Robert Altman's *The Player* (1992) brilliantly satirized Hollywood's accommodations to audience desires.

410   **competing regional music**: See Dubravka Ugrešić, *Have a Nice Day* (London, 1994).

410   **resistance to state propaganda**: Serbian songs, traditionally sung by women, are well capable of flyting the bloody pretensions of the heroes building their nation states. See e.g. 'The Best Place for the Village', in Vuk Stefanović Karadžić [1787–1864], *Red Knight: Serbian Women's Songs*, ed. and tr. Daniel Weissnort and Tomislav Longinovic (London, 1992), 26–7.

410   **revolutionary age**: See Ted Hughes, 'Myths, Metres, Rhythms', in *Winter Pollen* (London, 1994), 330–4.

411   '**… tension with the public one**': Eavan Boland, 'In a Time of Violence', *Poetry Book Society Bulletin* (Spring 1994), no.160, 2.

411   **Oz books**: See Salman Rushdie, *The Wizard of Oz* (London, 1993), for an astute analysis of the film's ideological changes to Baum's original series of novels, beginning with *The Wonderful Wizard of Oz* (1900).

411   **bureaucrats and bullies**: See Capek (1990).

411   **irreproachable figures**: Personal communication to MW, Annual Conference of the Welsh Academy, Cardiff, 1991.

412   '**… chain of speech communion**': Mihail Bakhtin,'The Problem of Speech Genres', *Speech Genres and Other Late Essays*, tr. Vern W. McGhee, ed. Caryl Emerson and Michael Holquist (Austin, 1986), 60–102, quoted in ZVFT, 100.

412   **as Rushdie has done**: See Salman Rushdie, *Haroun and the Sea of Stories* (London 1990), which reveals the crisis of the storyteller today: Rushdie's protagonist Rashid has lost his powers through grief at the elopement of his wife, and his son Haroun, like a questing hero, defies the forces of silence, led by the sinister Khattam Shud (whose name means All Is Silence), to recover his father's tongue. With magnanimity of spirit and an effervescent energy, the novella transparently allegorizes the situation of Rushdie himself, whom the Ayatollah and his supporters have attempted to silence when they objected to the story he told in *The Satanic Verses* and the way that he told it.

413   '**… make us regret reality**': Alexis de Tocqueville, *De la Démocratie en Amérique*, ed. A. Gain (2 vols, Paris, 1951), vol.2, 110.

413   **flight to another world**: See Calvino (1988), esp. 'La Tradizione popolare nelle fiabe' (1973), 109–28; I am very grateful to Lorna Sage for her insights into Calvino's writing.

413   '**… change the face of reality**: Calvino (1992), 27.

414   **descended from Guy of Warwick**: *Pageant of the Birth, Life and Death of Richard Beauchamp Earl of Warwick K. G. 1381–1439*, 36–40. *Guy of Warwick* was still included, alongside *King Arthur, 100 Merry Tales* and *Robin Hood*, among the ten favourite chapbook titles of the seventeenth century in England. Watt, 270–1. I am most grateful to Martin Lowry for communicating this information. The scarf of St Cunera, on exhibition in Museum Het Catherijneconvent, Utrecht, gives another example of cross-fertilization between East and West, romance and real life, hagiography and fairy tale: silk embroidered with silver, it is Byzantine work from Syria, made in the sixth century, and the label says it was used to strangle St Cunera by a wicked queen who was jealous of her beauty and goodness. St Cunera, according to her legend, was the only one of St Ursula's 11,000 virgins to survive the massacre at Cologne by the Huns (in the seventh century). See Marina Warner, 'Les trois coffrets européens', *Lettre Internationale*, no.31, Winter 1991–2, 3–4; id., 'The Three Caskets of Europe', *PN Review* 82, 18:2, 15–7.

417   **Adults Only**: e.g. *Bluebeard*, directed by Edward Dmytryk, with Richard Burton in the title role, and publicity declaring: 'Bluebeard had *a way* with the world's most beautiful, most seductive, most glamorous women … he did *away* with them … Raquel Welch … suffocated … Virna Lisi … guillotined … Karin Schubert … shot …' Press release, Cinerama UK, 1972.

418   '**… the spoken word**': Čapek (1951), 63.

417   '**how I make potato soup**': Angela Carter, intro, *VFT*-I, x.

417   **a hole in his pocket**: 'The Tramp's Tale' in Čapek (1990), 145–63.

418   '**… liberatory paths/voices**': Guattari, 35.

418   '**… universe of creative enchantments**': ibid., 31.

BIBLIOGRAPHY

Details of works frequently quoted can be found above in the list of abbreviations; the following titles fill out the references in the notes and offer a guide to background reading.

TELLERS AND TALES

Antoninus Liberalis, *The Metamorphoses*, ed. and tr. Francis Celorio (London, 1992).

Aulnoy, Marie-Catherine Le Jumel de Barneville, Baronne de, *Les Contes de fées, ou Les Fées à la mode* [1696], ed. M. F.-A. de Lescure (Paris, 1881).

— , *La Cour et la ville de Madrid vers la fin du XVIIe siècle,* including *Relation du voyage d'Espagne* and *Mémoires de la Cour d'Espagne*, ed. B. Carey (Paris 1874–6).

— , *A Collection of Novels and Tales Written by that celebrated Wit of France the Countess D'Anois* (3 vols, London, 1721–2).

The Authentic Mother Goose Fairy Tales and Nursery Rhymes, ed. Jacques Barchilon and Henry Pettit (Denver, 1960).

Basile, Giambattista, *The Pentamerone, or The Story of Stories, Fun for the Little Ones*, tr. J. E. Taylor (London, 1847).

— , *The Pentameron*, tr. Richard Burton (2 vols, London, 1893).

Berlioz, Jacques, Claude Brémond and Catherine Velay-Vallantin, eds, *Formes médiévales du conte merveilleux* (Paris, 1989).

Briggs, Katharine, *A Dictionary of British Folk-Tales in the English Language, incorporating the F. J. Norton Collection* (2 vols, London, 1970).

Calasso, Roberto, *The Marriage of Cadmus and Harmony*, tr. Tim Parks (London, 1988).

Čapek, Karel, *Nine Fairy Tales and One More Thrown in for Good Measure*, tr. Dagmar Herrmann (Evanston, 1990).

Carrington, Leonora, *La Débutante: Contes et pièces* (Paris, 1978).

— , *The House of Fear: Notes from Down Below*, tr. Kathrine Talbot and Marina Warner (London, 1989).

— , *The Seventh Horse and Other Tales*, tr. Kathrine Talbot and Anthony Kerrigen (London, 1989).

Carter, Angela, *The Magic Toyshop* (London, 1967).

— , *The Passion of New Eve* (London, 1977).

— , *Wise Children* (London, 1991).

Cazelles, Brigitte, ed. and tr., *The Lady as Saint: A Collection of French Hagiographic Romances of the Thirteenth Century* (Philadelphia, 1991).

Celorio, Francis, see Antoninus Liberalis

Chaucer, Geoffrey, *The Canterbury Tales*, tr. Nevill Coghill (Harmondsworth, 1960).

Cruikshank, George, *Cinderella and the Glass Slipper* (London, 1853).

— , *The Fairy Library* (London, 1853–64).

Fénelon, L'Abbé, 'Recueil de Fables composées pour l'éducation de Monseigneur le Duc de Bourgogne' (1689) in *Oeuvres*, II, ed. Aimé Martin (Paris, 1870).

Graves, Robert, *The Greek Myths* (2 vols, Harmondsworth, 1955/60).

The Hours of Catherine of Cleves, ed. John Plummer (London, 1966).

Jacobs, Joseph, *English Fairy Tales* (London [1890] 1968).

— , *More English Fairy Tales* (London [1894] 1968).

La Fontaine, Jean de, *Oeuvres complètes, (I) Fables, contes et nouvelles*, ed. Jean-Pierre Collinet (Paris, 1991).

La Force, Charlotte-Rose Caumont de [1697], *Les Fées Les Contes des Contes* (Amsterdam, 1708).

— , *Les Jeux d'esprit, ou La Promenade de la Princesse de Conti* (Paris, 1862).

Lang, Andrew, ed. and tr., *Perrault's Popular Tales* (London, 1888); *The Blue Fairy Book* (London, 1889); *The Red Fairy Book* (London, 1890); *The Green Fairy Book* (London, 1892); *The Yellow Fairy Book* (London, 1894); *The Pink Fairy Book* (London, 1897).

La Sale, Antoine de, *Le Paradis de la reine Sibylle,* ed., Fernand Desonay (Paris, 1930).

La Sale, Antoine de, *Il Paradiso della Regina Sibilla* (Norcia, 1963).

Leprince de Beaumont, Jeanne-Marie, Mme, *Contes de fées, tirés du Magasin des Enfants* (Paris, 1883).

— , *Instructions for Young Ladies* (4 vols, London, 1764).

— , *Moral Tales* (2 vols, London, 1775).

— , *Le Trésor des familles chrétiennes* (Paris, 1827).

L'Héritier de Villandon, Marie-Jeanne, Mlle, attrib., *L'Erudition enjouée, ou Nouvelles scavantes satiriques et galantes* (Paris, 1703).

Lurie, Alison, ed., *The Oxford Book of Fairy Tales* (Oxford, 1993).

Martines, Lauro, *An Italian Renaissance Sextet: Six Tales in Historical Context*, tr. Murtha Baca (Berkeley, 1994).

Mieder, Wolfgang, ed., *Disenchantments: An Anthology of Modern Fairy Tale Poetry* (Hanover and London, 1985).

Molitor, Ulrich, *De Laniis et Phitonicis Mulieribus* (Ulm, 1490).

Murat, Henriette-Julie de Castelnau, Comtesse de, *Mémoires de la Comtesse de M*** avant sa retraite* (Paris [1698] 1753).

— , *Voyage de Campagne* (Paris, 1700).

Mure, Eleanor, *The Story of the Three Bears* [1831] (Toronto, 1967).

Parthenius, *De amatoriis affectionibus*, in Thomas Gale, *Historiae poeticae scriptores antiqui,* II (Paris and London, 1675).

Pausanias, *Guide to Greece, (I) Central Greece*, tr. Peter Levi (Harmondsworth, 1984).

Peele, George, *The Old Wives' Tale*, ed. F. B. Gummere, in *Representative British Comedies from the beginning to Shakespeare*, I, ed. Charles Mills Gayley (London and New York, 1903).

Perrault, Charles, *Histories or Tales of Olden Times*, tr. Robert Samber (London, 1737).

— , *Les Hommes illustres qui ont paru en France pendant ce siècle. Avec leurs portraits au naturel* (Paris, 1696).

— , *Mémoires de ma vie* [Claude Perrault, *Voyage à Bordeaux*] ed. Paul Bonnefon [1669] (Paris, 1909).

— , *Oeuvres posthumes, avec l'apologie des femmes* (Paris, 1706).

— , *Parallèles des anciens et des modernes* (Paris, 1688).

— , *Recueil de pièces curieuses et nouvelles* (Paris, 1694).

Contes de Perrault: Facsimile of the original editions of 1695–97, with a preface, ed. Jacques Barchilon (Geneva, 1980).

Perrault's Tales of Mother Goose: The Dedication Manuscript of 1695, facsimile, intro. and ed. Jacques Barchilon (2 vols, New York, 1956).

Philip, Neil, ed., *The Cinderella Story: The Origins and Variations of the Story Known as 'Cinderella'* (Harmondsworth, 1989).

[Physiologus] The Book of Beasts: Being a translation from a Latin Bestiary of the Twelfth Century, tr. and ed. T. H. White (London, 1954).

Pitré, Giuseppe, *Fiabe, novelle e racconti popolari siciliani* (4 vols, Palermo, 1982).

Pizan, Christine de, *The Book of the City of Ladies*, tr. Earl Jeffrey Richards (New York, 1882).

Ritchie, Anne Thackeray, *Bluebeard's Keys and Other Stories* (London, 1874).

Robert, Raymonde, ed., *Contes parodiques et licencieux du 18e siècle* (Nancy, 1987).

— , *Il Etait une fois* (Nancy, 1984).

Tales from the Thousand and One Nights, tr. N. J. Dawood (Harmondsworth, 1973).

Zipes, Jack, ed., *Don't Bet on the Prince: Contemporary Feminist Fairy Tales in North America and England* (New York and London, 1986).

BACKGROUND

Abel, Elizabeth, ed., *Writing and Sexual Difference* (Brighton, 1982).

Avery, Gillian and Julia Briggs, eds, *Children and Their Books: A Celebration of the Work of Iona and Peter Opie* (Oxford, 1989).

Baader, Renate, *Dames de Lettres: Autorinnen des preziosen, hocharistokratischen und 'modernen' Salons (1649–1698): Mlle de Scudéry – Mlle de Montpensier – Mme d'Aulnoy* (Stuttgart, 1986).

Banner, Lois, *In Full Flower: Aging Women, Power and Sexuality; A History* (New York, 1992).

Barchilon, Jacques, *Le Conte merveilleux français de 1690 à 1790, cent ans de féerie et de poésie ignorées de l'histoire littéraire* (Paris and Geneva, 1975).

Beauroy, Jacques, Marc Bertrand and Edward T. Gargan, eds, *The Wolf and the Lamb: Popular Culture in France from the Old Régime to the Twentieth Century* (Saratoga, 1977).

Beer, Gillian, *The Romance* (London, 1970).

Benjamin, Walter, 'The Storyteller: Reflections on the Work of Nicolai Leskov', in *Illuminations*, tr. Harry Zohn (London, 1969).

Bettelheim, Bruno, *The Uses of Enchantment: The Power and Importance of Fairy Tales* (Harmondsworth, 1978).

Beyer, Rolf, *Die Königin von Saba: Engel und Dämon der Mythos einer Frau* (Bergisch Gladbach, 1987).

Bloch, Howard R., *Medieval Misogyny and the Invention of Western Romantic Love* (Chicago, 1991).

Bonnefon, Paul, 'Les dernières années de Charles Perrault', in *Revue d'histoire littéraire de la France,* 1906, 606–57.

Boose, Lynda E. and Betty S. Flowers, eds, *Daughters and Fathers* (Baltimore, 1989).

Booth, Wayne, *The Rhetoric of Fiction* (Chicago, 1983).

Boswell, John, *The Kindness of Strangers: The Abandonment of Children in Western Europe from Late Antiquity to the Renaissance* (London, 1988).

Bottigheimer, Ruth B., ed., *Fairy Tales and Society: Illusion, Allusion, and Paradigm* (Philadelphia, 1986).

— , *Grimms' Bad Girls and Bold Boys: The Social and Moral Vision of the Tales* (New Haven, 1987).

— , 'Luckless, Witless, and Filthy-Footed: A Socio-Cultural Study and Publishing History Analysis of "The Lazy Boy"', in *JAF* 106:421 (1994), 259–84.

Brewer, Derek, *Symbolic Stories: Traditional Narrative of the Family Drama in English Literature* (Cambridge, 1980).

— , 'The Interpretation of Fairy Tales: Implications for Literature, History and Anthropology', *British Studies Distinguished Lecture* (Austin, 1992).

Briggs, Katharine, *The Anatomy of Puck: An Examination of Fairy Beliefs among Shakespeare's Contemporaries and Successors* (London, 1959).

Britnell, Jennifer, 'Revelation to the Pagans: the Sibyls in Sixteenth-Century France', in *Durham French Colloquies*, 2 (Durham University Press, 1989), 21–35.

— , 'The Reputation of the Sibyls in Renaissance France', paper delivered at the Institute of Romance Studies, University of London, March 1994.

Brooks, Peter, *Reading for the Plot: Design and Intention in Narrative* (New York, 1984).

Burke, Peter, *The Art of Conversation* (Cambridge, 1993).

— , *The Fabrication of Louis XIV* (London and Newhaven, 1992).

— , *Popular Culture in Early Modern Europe* (London, 1978).

— , and Roy Porter, *The Social History of Language* (Cambridge, 1987).

Calvino, Italo, *Sulla fiaba*, ed. Mario Lavagetto (Turin, 1988).

— , *Six Memos for the Next Millenium*, tr. Patrick Creagh (London, 1992).

Čapek, Karel, *In Praise of Newspapers and other essays on the margin of literature*, tr. M. and R. Weatherall (London, 1951).

Cardigos Brennan, Isabel, 'In and Out of Enchantment: Blood Symbolism and Gender in Portuguese Fairytales', Ph.D. Dissertation, King's College, London, 1993.

Cave, Terence. *Recognitions. A Study in Poetics* (Oxford,

1988).

Charland, P.-V., *Les Trois Légendes de Madame Saincte Anne* (3 vols, Montreal, 1898).

— , *Madame Saincte Anne et son culte au moyen-âge* (2 vols, Paris, 1911/13).

Charrière, G., 'Du social au sacré dans les contes de Perrault', in *Revue des histoires des religions*, 197:2 (1980), 159–89.

Chastel, André, 'La Légende de la reine de Saba', *Fables, Formes, Figures* (Paris, 1978).

Cixous, Hélène and Catherine Clément, *The Newly Born Woman*, tr. Betsy Wing (Manchester, 1986).

Clancy, Patricia, 'A French writer and educator in England: Mme Leprince de Beaumont', *Studies on Voltaire and the Eighteenth Century*, 201 (1982), 195–208.

Coates, Jennifer, *Women, Men and Language: A sociolinguistic account of sex differences in language* (London, 1986).

Cox, Marian Roalfe, *Cinderella: Three Hundred and Forty-Five Variants of Cinderella, Catskin, and Cap o' Rushes* (London, 1893).

Crary, Jonathan and Sanford Kwinter, eds, *Incorporations: Zone 6* (New York, 1992).

Cromer, Sylvie, ' "Le Sauvage" Histoire Sublime et allégorique de Madame de Murat', in *Merveilles et Contes*, 1:1 (May 1987), 2–19.

Darnton, Robert, *The Great Cat Massacre and Other Episodes in French Cultural History* (London, 1984).

Darrow, Margaret H., 'French Noblewomen and the New Domesticity 1750–1850', in *Feminist Studies*, 5:1 (Spring 1979), 41–65.

Daum, Werner, ed., *Die Königin von Saba: Kunst Legende und Archaeologie zwischen Morgenland und Abendland* (Stuttgart and Zurich, 1988).

Davis, Natalie Zemon, *Fiction in the Archives: Pardon Tales and their Tellers in Sixteenth-Century France* (Stanford, 1987).

De Bruyn, Lucy, *Women and the Devil in Sixteenth Century Literature* (Tisbury, 1979).

Dégh, Linda, 'Grimm's *Household Tales* and its Place in the Household: The Social Relevance of a Controversial Classic', in Metzger and Mommsen, op. cit., 21–53.

— , 'The Magic Tale and its Magic', ibid., 54–74.

DeJean, Joan, *Tender Geographies: Women and the Origin of the Novel in France* (New York, 1991).

— , 'Salons, Preciosity, and Women's Influence', in Hollier, Denis, ed., *A New History of French Literature* (Harvard, 1981), 297–303.

Delaporte, Victor, *Du Merveilleux dans la littérature française sous le règne de Louis XIV* (Paris, 1891).

Delarue, Paul, 'Les Contes merveilleux de Perrault: Faits et rapprochements nouveaux', in *Arts et traditions populaires* (1 Jan.–Mar. 1954), 1-22; (3 Jul.–Nov. 1954), 250–74.

— , and Marie-Louise Ténèze, *Le Conte populaire français: Catalogue raisonné des versions de France et des pays de langue française d'outre-mer; Canada, Louisiane, îlots français des Etats-unis, Antilles françaises, Haiti, Ile Maurice, La Réunion*, II (Paris, 1964).

Deulin, Charles, *Les Contes de ma Mère l'Oye avant Perrault* (Paris, 1879).

Devlie, Judith, *The Superstitious Mind: French Peasants and the Supernatural in the Nineteenth Century* (New Haven and London, 1987).

Dollerup, Cay, and Bengt Holbek, Iven Reventlow, Garsten Rosenberg Hansen, 'The Ontological Status, the Formative Elements, the "Filters" and Existences of Folktales' in *Fabula* 25, 241–65.

Dorfman, Ariel and Armand Mattelart, *How to Read Donald Duck: Imperialist Ideology in the Disney Comic* (New York [1971] 1975).

Douglas, Mary, *Implicit Meanings: Essays in Anthropology* (London, 1975).

— , *Natural Symbols: Explorations in Cosmology* (Harmondsworth, 1973).

Dronke, Peter, *Intellectuals and Poets in Medieval Europe*

(Rome, 1992).

—, *Verse with Prose from Petronius to Dante: The Art and Scope of the Mixed Form* (Harvard and London, 1994).

Duchartre, Pierre-Louis and René Saulnier, *L'Imagerie Parisienne (L'Imagerie de la rue Saint-Jacques)* (Paris, 1944).

Duffy, Maureen, *The Erotic World of Faery* (London [1972] 1980).

Dundes, Alan, ed., *Cinderella: A Casebook* (Wisconsin [1982] 1988).

—, *Little Red Riding Hood: A Casebook* (Wisconsin, 1989).

Elias, Norbert, *The Court Society*, tr. E. Jephcott (Oxford, 1983).

—, *Power and Civility*, tr. E. Jephcott (New York, 1982).

Ellis, John, *One Fairy Story Too Many: The Brothers Grimm and their Tales* (Chicago and London, 1983).

Fail, Noël du, *Propos rustiques,* ed. Louis-Raymond Lefèvre (Paris, 1928).

Fairchilds, Cissie C., *Domestic Enemies: Servants and their Masters in Old Régime France* (Baltimore, 1984).

Farmer, David Hugh, *The Oxford Dictionary of Saints* (Oxford, 1977).

Forbes, Irving, P. M. C., *Metamorphosis in Greek Myths* (Oxford, 1990).

Foulché-Delbosc, R., intro., Marie-Catherine d'Aulnoy, *Travels into Spain* (London, 1930).

Franz, Marie-Louise von, *Problems of the Feminine in Fairy Tales* (Dallas, 1988).

—, *The Interpretation of Fairy Tales* (Dallas [1970] 1987).

—, *A Psychological Interpretation of the Golden Ass of Apuleius* (Dallas, 1980).

Fraser, Antonia, *The Weaker Vessel: Woman's Lot in Seventeenth-Century England* (London, 1984).

Fumaroli, Marc, 'Les enchantements de l'éloquence: Les Fées de Charles Perrault, ou De la littérature', in *Le Statut de la Littérature, Mélanges offerts à Paul Bénichou*, ed. Marc Fumaroli (Geneva, 1982).

Gage, John, *Colour and Culture Practice and Meaning from Antiquity to Abstraction* (London, 1993).

Gaignebet, Claude, and Dominique Lajoux, *Art profane et religion populaire au moyen âge* (Paris, 1985).

Gatto Trocchi, Cecilia, *La Fiaba italiana: Ipotesi di ricerca in magia semiotica* (Rome, 1972).

Gibson, Wendy, *Women in Seventeenth-Century France* (London, 1989).

Gilligan, Carol, *In a Different Voice* (Cambridge, Mass., 1982).

Ginzburg, Carlo, *Ecstasies: Deciphering the Witches' Sabbath*, tr. Raymond Rosenthal (London, 1990).

Goody, Jack, *Family and Inheritance: Rural Society in Western Europe 1200-1800* (Cambridge, 1976).

Gottlieb, Gerald, *Early Children's Books and Their Illustrators* (New York, 1975).

Grimm, Jacob, *Teutonic Mythology*, tr. J. S. Stallybrass (London, 1883–8).

Guattari, Félix, 'Régimes, Pathways, Subjects', tr. Brian Massumi, in Crary and Kwinter, op. cit., 16–37.

Gumuchian et Cie, *Les Livres de l'enfance* [Catalogue XIII, 2 vols, Paris, 1985]; *A Catalogue of 15th to 19th Century Nursery Books* (London, 1985).

Haase-Dubosc, Danielle and Eliane Viennot, *Femmes et pouvoirs sous l'ancien régime* (Paris, 1991).

Hägg, Thomas, *The Novel in Antiquity* (Oxford, 1983).

Haight, Elizabeth Hazelton, *Apuleius and his Influence* (New York, 1963).

Hallays, André, *Les Perrault* (Paris, 1926).

Harf-Lancner, Laurence, *Les Fées au moyen-âge: Morgane et Mélusine, La naissance des fées* (Paris, 1984).

Hartland, E. S., *The Science of Fairy Tales: An Inquiry into Fairy Mythology* (London, 1891).

Harvey-Darton, F. J., *Children's Books in England: Five Centuries of Social Life*, rev. edn Brian Alderson (London, 1982).

Hearne, Betsy, *Beauty and the Beast: Visions and Revisions of an Old Tale* (Chicago, 1989).

Heiserman, Arthur, *The Novel before the Novel: Essays and Discussions about the Beginnings of Prose Fiction in the West* (Chicago and London, 1977).

Herlihy, David, *Medieval Households* (Cambridge, 1985).

—, and Christiane Klapisch-Zuber, *Tuscans and their Families: A Study of the Florentine Catasto of 1427* (New Haven and London, 1985).

Herranen, Gun, ' "The Maiden without Hands" (AT 706)', in *D'un Conte à l'autre: La variabilité dans la littérature orale*, ed. Veronika Gorog-Karady (Paris, 1987), 105–15.

Hilgar, Marie-France, ed., *Théorie dramatique. Théophile de Viau. Les Contes de fées. Actes du xxiie colloque de la North American Society for Seventeenth Century French Literature*, University of Las Vegas, 1-3 Mar. 1990, 17: 60 (Paris-Seattle-Tübingen, 1991).

Holbek, Bengt, *Interpretation of Fairy Tales: Danish Folklore in a European Perspective* (Helsinki, 1987).

Irwin, Robert, *The Arabian Nights: A Companion* (London, 1994).

Jacobs, Joseph, 'Cinderella in Britain', in *Folklore* 4 (1893), 269–84.

Jeay, Madeleine, 'La popularité des *Evangiles des Quenouilles*; un paradoxe révélateur', in *Renaissance and Reformation* 18 (1982), 166–82.

—, 'Lectures de la derision dans les *Evangiles des Quenouilles*', in *Florilegium* 6 (1984), 159–76.

— and Bruno Roy, 'L'émergence du folklore dans la littérature du XVe siècle', in *Eighteenth Century Studies* 2 (1979), 95–117.

Jones, Malcolm, 'The Fool', 'Green Man', 'Silence', 'Trickster', 'Wild Man', in *Garland Encyclopaedia of Medieval Folklore* (New York, 1994).

—, 'Marcolf the Trickster in Late Medieval Art and Literature or: The Mystery of the Bum in the Oven', in *Spoken in Jest*, ed. Gillian Bennett (Sheffield, 1991), 139-74.

—, 'Folklore Motifs in Late Medieval Art I: Proverbial Follies and Impossibilities', in *Folklore* 100, ii (1989), 201–17.

—, 'Folklore Motifs in Late Medieval Art II: Sexist Satire and Popular Punishments', in *Folklore* 101, i (1990), 69–87.

—, 'Folklore Motifs in Late Medieval Art III: Erotic Animals', in *Folklore* 102: ii (1991), 192–219.

—, 'Sex and Sexuality in Late Medieval and Early Modern Art', in *Privatisierung der Triebe. Sexualität in der frühen Neuzeit*, ed. Daniela Erlach, Markus Reisenleitner, Karl Vocelka (2 vols, Frankfurt, 1994), 187–304.

Kaplan, Cora, *Sea Changes: Essays on Culture and Feminism* (London, 1986).

Keightley, Thomas, *The Fairy Mythology: Illustrative of the Romance and Superstition of Various Countries* (London, 1850).

Klapisch-Zuber, Christiane, *Women, Family, and Ritual in Renaissance Italy*, tr. Lydia G. Cochrane (Chicago, 1985).

—, ed., *A History of Women in the West Vol II: Silences of the Middle Ages* (Cambridge, Mass., and London, 1992).

Kott, Jan, *The Bottom Translation: Marlowe and Shakespeare and the Carnival Tradition*, tr. Daniela Miedzyrzecka and Lillian Vallee (Evanston, 1987).

Krontiris, Tina, *Oppositional Voices: Women as Writers and Translators of Literature in the English Renaissance* (London, 1992).

Kurth, Betty, 'The Riddles of the Queen of Sheba in Swiss and Alsatian Tapestries', *The Connoisseur* 106 (1940–1), 234–7, 266.

Leach, Edmund, *Genesis as Myth, and other essays* (London, 1969).

Le Roy Ladurie, Emmanuel, *Love, Death and Money in the Pays d'Oc*, tr. Alan Sheridan (New York, 1982).

Loskoutoff, Yvan, *La Sainte et la fée: Dévotion à l'enfant Jesus et la mode des contes merveilleux à la fin du règne de Louis XIV*

(Geneva, 1987).

Lougee, Carolyn, *Le Paradis des femmes: Women, Salons and Social Stratification in 17th Century France* (Princeton, 1976).

Lüthi, Max, *The Fairytale as Art Form and Portrait of Man*, tr. Jon Erickson (Bloomington, 1984).

— , *Once Upon a Time: On the Nature of Fairy Tales*, tr. Lee Chadeayne and Paul Gottwald (Bloomington, 1976).

Lynch, Joseph, *Godparents and Kinship in Early Medieval Europe* (Princeton, 1986).

Lyons, Heather, 'Some Second Thoughts on Sexism in Fairy Tales' in Elizabeth Gugeon and Peter Walden, eds, *Literature and Learning* (London, 1978).

McGinn, Bernard, ' "Teste David cum Sibylla": the Significance of the Sibylline Tradition in the Middle Ages', in *Women of the Medieval World*, ed. Julius Kirshner and Suzanne F. Wemple (Oxford, 1985), 7-35.

McGlathery, James M., *Fairy Tale Romance: The Grimms, Basile, and Perrault* (Urbana, 1991).

Maclean, Ian, *The Renaissance Notion of Woman: A study in the fortunes of scholasticism and medical science in European intellectual life* (Cambridge, 1980).

— , *Woman Triumphant: Feminism in French Literature 1610-1652* (Oxford, 1977).

Magne, Bernard, 'Le Chocolat et l'ambroisie: le statut de la mythologie dans les contes de fées', *Cahiers de la littérature du XVIe siècle* (Toulouse, 1979), 2 (1980), 95-146.

Marin, Louis, *La Parole mangée et autres essais théologico-politiques* (Paris, 1986).

— , 'La voix d'un conte: entre La Fontaine et Perrault, sa récriture', *Littératures* (1980), 36, 394, 333-42.

Mechoulan, Eric J., 'De la mémoire à la culture: la fabrication des contes de fées à la fin du XVIIe siècle', in 'Les lieux de mémoire et la fabrique de l'oeuvre', *Biblio* 17, *Papers on Seventeenth Century Literature* (Paris, Seattle, Tübingen, 1993) 91–102.

Mellinkoff, Ruth, *Outcasts: Signs of Otherness in Northern European Art in the Late Medieval Ages* (2 vols, Berkeley, 1994).

Metzger, M. and Katharina Mommsen, eds, *Fairy Tales as Ways of Knowing: Essays on Märchen in Psychology, Society and Literature* (Berne, 1981).

Mieder, Wolfgang, 'Modern Anglo-American variants of "The Frog Prince" (AT 440)', *New York Folklore* 6 (1980), 111-35.

Mistler, Jean, François Blaudez and André Jacquemin, *Epinal et l'imagerie populaire* (Paris, 1961).

Mulvey, Laura, *Visual and Other Pleasures* (London, 1989).

Mylne, Vivien, *The Eighteenth Century Novel in France* (Manchester, 1965).

Neumann, Erich, *Amor and Psyché: The Psychic Development of the Feminine. A Commentary on the Tale by Apuleius*, tr. Ralph Manheim (New York, 1956).

Nikiprowetzky, V., *La Troisième sibylle, Etudes juives* IX (Paris and The Hague, 1970).

Ober, Warren U., *The Story of the Three Bears: The Evolution of an International Classic* (New York, 1981).

Ong, Walter, *Orality and Literacy: The Technologizing of the Word* (London, 1982).

Ostoia, Vera K., 'Two Riddles of the Queen of Sheba', *Bulletin of the Metropolitan Museum of Art*, 6 (1972), 73-96.

Overgaard, Mariane, ed., *The History of the Cross-Tree down to Christ's Passion: Icelandic Legend Versions* (Copenhagen, 1968).

Padel, Ruth, *In and Out of the Mind: Greek Images of the Tragic Self* (Princeton, 1992).

Pallottino, Paola, 'Alle radici dell'iconografia del fiaba: Note sulle prime illustrazioni dei Contes', *MC*, V:2 (Dec. 1991), 289-320.

— , 'Beauty's Beast', *MC*, III:1 (May 1989), 57-74.

Palmer, Melvin D., 'Madame d'Aulnoy in England', *Comparative Literature*, 27 (1975), 237-53.

Palmer, Nancy and Melvin, 'English Editions of French contes de fées attributed to Mme. D'Aulnoy', *Studies in Bibliography*, 27 (1974), 227-32.

Pardailhé-Galabrun, Annik, *La Naissance de l'intime: 3000 foyers parisiens XVIIe- XVIIIe siècles* (Paris, 1988).

Paris, Gaston, 'Le Paradis de la Reine Sibille', in *Légendes du Moyen-âge* (Paris, 1903).

Parke, H. W., *Sibyls and Sibylline Prophecy in Classical Antiquity*, ed. B. C. McGing (London and New York, 1988).

Pastoureau, Michel, *Traité d'héraldique* (Paris, 1979).

— , *Figures et couleurs: étude sur la symbolique et la sensibilité médiévales* (Paris, 1986).

Patrides, C. A., *Premises and Motifs in Renaissance Thought and Literature* (Princeton, 1982).

Perrot, Michelle, ed., *The History of Private Life, (IV) From the Fires of Revolution to the Great War*, tr. Arthur Goldhammer (Cambridge, Mass., and London, 1990).

Perry, B. E., *The Ancient Romances: A Literary-Historical Account of Their Origins* (Berkeley and Los Angeles, 1967).

Petrie, Duncan, ed., *Cinema and the Realms of Enchantment* (London, 1993).

Picard, Roger, *Les Salons littéraires et la société française 1610-1789* (New York, 1943).

Pozzi, Victoria Smith, 'Straparola's "Le Piacevoli notti": Narrative Technique and Ideology', Ph.D. Thesis, University of California, 1981.

Pritchard, J. B., ed., *Ancient Near Eastern Texts Relating to the Old Testament* (Princeton, 1974).

Propp, Vladimir, *Morphology of the Folktale*, tr. L. Scott, intro. Svatava Pirkova-Jakobson; rev. edn Louis A. Wagner, intro. Alan Dundes (Austin, 1968).

— , *Theory and History of the Folktale*, tr. Ariadna Y. and Richard P. Martin *et al.*, ed. Anatoly Liberman (Manchester, 1984).

Rapley, Elizabeth, *The Dévotes: Women and Church in Seventeenth Century France* (Montreal, 1993).

Ravaisson-Molion, F., *Archives de la Bastille* VII (Paris, 1866), 335-7.

Reardon, B. P., *The Form of Greek Romance* (Princeton, 1991).

Réau, Louis, *L'Iconographie de l'Art chrétien* (3 vols, Paris, 1958).

Ritvo, Harriet, *The Animal Estate: The English and Other Creatures in the Victorian Age* (Harvard, 1987).

Robert, Raymonde, *Le Conte de fées littéraire en France de la fin du XVIIe à la fin du XVIIIe* (Nancy, 1981).

Roche-Mazon, Jeanne, *Autour des contes de fées* (Paris, 1935).

— , *En Marge de 'L'Oiseau bleu': Cahiers de la Quinzaine* XVII, Ser.19 (Paris, 1930).

Rodari, Gianni, *Grammatica della fantasia: Introduzione all'arte di inventare storie* (Turin, 1973).

Rogers, Benjamin Bickley, ed., *The Birds of Aristophanes* (London, 1906).

Rooth, Anna Birgitta, *The Cinderella Cycle* (Lund, 1951).

Rose, Jacqueline, *The Case of Peter Pan Or the Impossibility of Children's Fiction* (rev. edn, London, 1992).

Rossi, Angelina, 'Le sibille nelle arti figurative italiane', *L'Arte*, XVIII (1915), 209-21, 272-85, 427-58.

Rowe Townsend, John, *Written for Children: An Outline of English Language Children's Literature* (London, 1990).

Rowland, Beryl, *Animals with Human Faces: A Guide to Animal Symbolism* (Knoxville, 1973).

— , *Birds with Human Souls: A Guide to Bird Symbolism* (Knoxville, 1978).

St John Philby, H., *The Queen of Sheba* (London, 1981).

Saintyves, P., *Les Contes de Perrault et les récits parallèles, leurs origines (coutumes primitives et liturgies populaires)* (Paris, 1923).

Santarelli, Giuseppe, *Le Leggende dei Monti Sibillini* (Montefortino, 1988).

Schectman, Jacqueline, *The Stepmother in Fairy Tales: Bereavement and the Feminine Shadow* (Boston, 1993).

Schiebinger, Londa, *The Mind has No Sex? Women in the*

Origins of Modern Science (Harvard, 1989).

Schlauch, Margaret, *Chaucer's Constance and Accused Queens* (New York, 1927).

Shell, Marc, *Children of the Earth: Literature, Politics and Nationhood* (New York and Oxford, 1993).

— , *Elizabeth's Glass With 'The Glass of the Sinful Soul' [1544] by Elizabeth I and 'Conclusion' by John Bale* (Lincoln, 1993).

Shorter, Edward, *The Making of the Modern Family* (New York, 1975).

Showalter, Elaine, *A Literature of Their Own* (London, 1984).

Silverman, Kaja, *The Acoustic Mirror: Female Voice in Psychoanalysis and Cinema* (Indiana, 1988).

Söderhjelm, Werner, 'Antoine de La Sale et la légende de Tannhäuser', *Mémoires de la Société Néo-philologique*, 2 (1897), 101-67.

Soriano, Marc, *Les Contes de Perrault: Culture savante et traditions populaires* (Paris [1968] 1977).

Spierenburg, Pieter, *The Broken Spell: A Cultural and Anthropological History of Preindustrial Europe* (New Brunswick, 1991).

Spufford, Margaret, 'The Pedlar, the Historian and the Folklorist: Seventeenth Century Communications', *Folklore*, 105 (1994), 13–24.

Stafford, Pauline, *Queens, Concubines, and Dowagers: The Queen's Wife in the Early Middle Ages* (London, 1983).

Stone, Lawrence, *The Family, Sex and Marriage in England 1500-1800* (London, 1977).

Storer, Mary Elizabeth, *Un Épisode littéraire de la fin du XVIIe siècle: La Mode des contes de fées (1685-1700)* [1928] (Geneva, 1972).

Suleiman, Susan Rubin, *Risking Who One Is: Encounters with Contemporary Art and Literature* (Camb. Mass., 1994).

— , *Subversive Intent: Gender, Politics and the Avant-Garde* (Harvard, 1990).

Sutton, Dana F., *The Greek Satyr Play* (Meisenheim, 1980).

Swahn, Jan-Öjvind, *The Tale of Cupid and Psyche (AT 425 and 428)* (Lund, 1955).

Taggart, James M., *Enchanted Maidens: Gender Relations in Spanish Folktales of Courtship and Marriage* (Princeton and Oxford, 1990).

Tatar, Maria, *The Hard Facts of Fairy Tales* (Princeton, 1987).

— , *Off with their Heads! Fairy Tales and the Culture of Childhood* (Princeton, 1992).

— , 'Folkloristic Phantasies: Grimms' Fairy Tales and Freud's "Family Romance" ' in Metzger and Mommsen, op. cit., 75-98.

Taylor, Peter and Hermann Rebel, 'Hessian Peasant Women, Their Families, and the Draft: A Social-Historical Interpretation of Four Tales from the Grimm Collection', *JFH* (Winter 1981), 347-78.

Tharu, Susie and Lalita, K., eds., intro., *Women Writing in India 600 BC to the Present, (I) 600 BC to the Early 20th Century* (New York, 1991), 1-37.

Thelander, Dorothy R., 'Mother Goose and Her Goslings: The France of Louis XIV seen through the Fairy Tale', *Journal of Modern History*, 54 (Sept. 1982), 467-96.

Thomas, Keith, *Man and the Natural World: Changing Attitudes in England 1500-1800* (Harmondsworth, 1984).

Tolkien, J. R., 'On Fairy Stories', in *Tree and Leaf* (London, 1964).

Topsell, Edward, *The Historie of Four-Footed Beasts and Serpents and Insects*, ed. Willy Ley [1658] (3 vols, London, 1967).

Troyansky, David G., *Old Age in the Old Régime: Image and Experience in Eighteenth Century France* (Ithaca and London, 1989).

Tucker, Nicholas, *The Child and the Book: A Psychological and Literary Exploration* (Cambridge, 1981).

Vaultier, Roger, *Le Folklore pendant la guerre de cent ans d'après Les Lettres de Permission du Trésor des Chartes* (Paris, 1965).

Velay-Vallantin, Catherine, *L'Histoire des contes* (Paris, 1992).

— , *La Fille en Garçon* (Carcassonne, 1992).

— , 'Tales as a Mirror: Perrault in the *Bibliothèque bleue*', in *The Culture of Print*, ed. Roger Chartier, tr. Lydia Cochrane (Cambridge, 1989), 92-135.

Verdi, Laura, *Il Regno incantato: Il contesto sociale e culturale della fiaba in Europa* (Padua, 1980).

Verschaffel, Bart and Mark Verminck, eds, *Wordlessness* (Dublin and Antwerp, 1993).

Villiers, Pierre, Abbé de, *Entretiens sur les contes de fées et sur quelques autres ouvrages du temps. Pour servir de préservatif contre le mauvais goût* (Paris, 1699).

Walckenaer, C. A., *Lettres sur les contes de fées attribués à Perrault, et sur l'origine de la féerie* (Paris, 1826).

Waley, Arthur, 'The Chinese Cinderella Story', *Folklore*, 58 (1947), 226-38.

Wallis Budge, J. A., *The Queen of Sheba and her Only Son Menyelek* (London, 1932).

Warner, Marina, *L'Atalante* (London, 1993).

— , *Managing Monsters: Six Myths of Our Time. The 1994 Reith Lectures* (London, 1994).

— , *Monuments and Maidens: The Allegory of the Female Form* (London, 1985).

— , 'The Uses of Enchantment' and other seminars, in Petrie, op.cit.

Watt, Tessa, *Cheap Print and Popular Piety 1550–1640* (Cambridge, 1991)

Weber, Eugen, 'Fairies and Hard Facts: The Reality of Folktales', *Journal of the History of Ideas*, XLIII:1 (Jan. – Mar. 1981), 93-113.

Westland, Ella, 'Cinderella in the Classroom: Children's Responses to Gender Roles in Fairy-tales', *Gender and Education*, 5, 3 (1993), 237-49.

Weyer, Johann, *Witches, Devils and Doctors in the Renaissance*, ed. George Mora *et al.*, tr. John Shea [Tr. Johann Weyer, *De Praestigiis Daemonum* (1563)] (Binghamton, 1991).

Whalley, Irene and Tessa Chester, *A History of Children's Book Illustration* (London, 1988).

Whalley, June, 'The Cinderella Story 1724-1919', *Signal*, May 1972, 49-62.

Williams, Charles Allyn, *Oriental Affinities of the Legend of the Hairy Anchorite: The Theme of the Hairy Solitary in its early forms with reference to 'Die Lügend von Sanct Johanne Chrysostomo' (Reprinted by Luther, 1537) and to other European variants* (Urbana, 1927).

Yates, Paula, *Blondes: A History from their Earliest Roots* (London, 1983).

Zielinski, T., *La Sibylle: Essais sur la religion antique et le christianisme* (Paris, 1924).

Zimmer, Heinrich, *The King and the Corpse*, ed. Joseph Campbell (Princeton, 1948).

Zipes, Jack, *Breaking the Magic Spell: Radical Theories of Folk and Fairy Tales* (London, 1979).

— , *Fairy Tales and the Art of Subversion: The Classical Genre for Children and the Process of Civilisation* (New York, 1983).

— , *Fairy Tale as Myth, Myth as Fairy Tale* (Lexington, 1994).

— , *The Trials and Tribulations of Red Riding Hood: Versions of the Tale in a Socio-historical Context* (London [1983], rev. 1993).

LIST OF PLATES

Plates appear between pages 164–165, and between pages 260–261.

1 *Cinderella* by Arthur Rackham, from *The Arthur Rackham Fairy Book*,1933. **2** *The Birth of the Virgin* by Domenico Ghirlandaio, Church of Santa Maria Novella, Florence (Bridgeman Art Library, London; K & B News Foto, Florence). **3** *Celebrating the Birth* by Jan Steen, 1664 (Bridgeman Art Library, London; Wallace Collection, London). **4** The Cumaean Sibyl by Michelangelo, Sistine Chapel ceiling, Rome (Scala Istituto Fotografia, Florence). **5** *The Procuress* by Dirck van Baburen (Courtesy, Museum of Fine Arts, Boston). **6** The Queen of Sheba watched by King Solomon, from *The Assembly of Lovers* by Sultan Husayn Mirza, 1552 (Bodleian Library, Oxford, MS Ouseley Add. 24 f. 127). **7** The Queen of Sheba from Conrad Kyeser's *Bellifortis*, c.1405 (Niedersächsische Staats– und Universitätsbibliothek, Göttingen). **8** The Queen of Sheba in Piero della Francesca's fresco cycle of *The Legend of the True Cross*, Church of San Francesco, Arezzo (Scala Istituto Fotografia, Florence). **9** The Queen of Sheba by Pantaleone, in a mosaic pavement, Otranto Cathedral, Southern Italy. **10** Mermaid by Pantaleone: mosaic pavement, Otranto Cathedral. **11** *Vertumnus and Pomona* by Jan van Kessel (Bridgeman Art Library, London; Johnny van Haeften Gallery, London). **12** *A Winter Night's Tale* by Daniel Maclise, c.1867 (Manchester City Art Galleries). **13** There was an old woman' . . .', from *Mother Goose* by W.W.Denslow, 1902 (Victoria & Albert Museum, London). **14** Old woman with padlocked lips: postcard, c.1985, Chapala, Mexico. **15** The Zodiac Sign of Virgo: detail from *Triumph of Ceres and Astrological Symbols* by Francesco del Cossa and Ercole de' Roberti, Palazzo Schifanoia, Ferrara (Scala Istituto Fotografia, Florence). **16** Female saints in heaven by Gerard Horenbout, from *The Spinola Book of Hours*, c.1515, Flemish (Collection of the J. Paul Getty Museum, Malibu, California). **17** *The Mystic Nativity* by Sandro Botticelli, detail (Bridgeman Art Library, London; National Gallery, London). **18** *The Whore of Babylon* from *The Angers Apocalypse* tapestry (Musée d'Angers de la Tapisserie, Angers; Photographie Giraudon, Paris). **19** Threshing the harvest under the sign of Virgo, from a *Book of Hours*, Rouen, c.1520–25 (Collection of the J. Paul Getty. Museum, Malibu, California). **20** A wild maiden with a unicorn: tapestry, Upper Rhine, 1475–1500 (Historisches Museum, Basel). **21** A blue-bearded devil: detail from *The Last Judgement*, stained glass window, c.1495, Fairford, England (Photograph © Sonia Halliday and Laura Lushington). **22** Saint Dympna in Jan van Wavre's sculptured altarpiece, c.1515, Church of Saint Dympna, Geel, Belgium. **23** A nineteenth-century Cinderella, with doves, from a Grimm Brothers' book cover (Renier Collection, Victoria & Albert Museum, London). **24** Cinderella and her sisters, from the Ladybird Books version of Disney's 1950 film (© Walt Disney Productions. The Walt Disney Company Ltd; Ladybird Books, Loughborough). **25** *Ma Gouvernante, My Nurse, Mein Kindermädchen* by Meret Oppenheim, 1936 (© Meret Oppenheim; Statens Konstmuseer, Stockholm). **26** *Loop My Loop* (originally titled *Quite Contrary*) by Helen Chadwick, 1991 (© Helen Chadwick).

PICTURE CREDITS

Black and white illustrations are published by kind permission of the following: Atlas van Stolk, Rotterdam 22; Basilica di S. Francesco, Arezzo 101; Bayerisches Nationalmuseum, Munich 359, 360; Bodleian Library, Oxford x, 60, 120; Bridgeman Art Library, London (Agnew & Sons) 109; British Film Institute, London 241, 272, 308, 319; British Museum, London 40/41, 51 (left), 400; Brüder Grimm Museum, Kassel 189 (top), 191; Bulloz, Paris 89, 164 (Musée de Troyes); © Leonora Carrington 383; Ceskoslovenska Akademie Ved. Prague 118 (left); Davis Museum & Cultural Center, Wellesley College, Mass. (Museum purchase 1953.8) 140; The Walt Disney Company Ltd 225, 314; Dulwich Picture Gallery, London 343; Fitzwilliam Museum, Cambridge 46; © Jill Furmanowsky 416; J. Paul Getty Museum, Malibu CA 139, 408; © Tara Heinemann 195; © Sophie Herxheimer 449; © David Hockney 227; Institüt fur Realienkunde, Krems (Austria) 122; Kunsthaus, Zurich 375 (right); Kunsthistorisches Museum, Vienna 258; Mander and Mitchenson Theatre Collection, London 147; Mansell Collection, London xiii, 80; Metropolitan Museum of Art, Cloisters Collection, New York 131; National Gallery, London, 84; National Museum of Denmark, Copenhagen 61 (right); National Library, Vienna 45; Osborne Collection of Early Children's Books, Toronto Public Library xi; Pierpont Morgan Library, New York 64, 376, 110; © Paula Rego (photo Marlborough Graphics Ltd) 311; Rijksmuseum, Amsterdam 66, 87 (top and bottom), 93 329; Royal Photographic Society, Bath 20; Statens Museum for Kunst, Copenhagen 159; Scala Istituto, Florence 2, 85 (Uffizi), 104/5; Tate Gallery, London 200, 262; Madame Tussaud's, London 211; Warburg Institute, London 218; Witt Library, Courtauld Institute of Art 172. Other illustrations: author's collection.